# The World Since 1945

# The World Since 1945

6TH EDITION

# THE WORLD
# SINCE 1945

## A History of
## International Relations

WAYNE C. MCWILLIAMS
HARRY PIOTROWSKI

LYNNE
RIENNER
PUBLISHERS

BOULDER
LONDON

Published in the United States of America in 2005 by
Lynne Rienner Publishers, Inc.
1800 30th Street, Boulder, Colorado 80301
www.rienner.com

and in the United Kingdom by
Lynne Rienner Publishers, Inc.
3 Henrietta Street, Covent Garden, London WC2E 8LU

**Library of Congress Cataloging-in-Publication Data**
McWilliams, Wayne C.
The world since 1945 : a history of international relations /
    Wayne C. McWilliams, Harry Piotrowski.— 6th ed.
      Includes bibliographical references and index.
      ISBN 1-58826-347-9 (pbk. : alk. paper)
      1. World politics—1945–1989. 2. World politics—1989–
3. Military history, Modern—20th century. 4. Developing countries.
I. Piotrowski, Harry.  II. Title.
D840.M363   2005
327'.09'045—dc22                                   2005000400

**British Cataloguing in Publication Data**
A Cataloguing in Publication record for this book
is available from the British Library.


Printed and bound in the United States of America

        The paper used in this publication meets the requirements
 ∞      of the American National Standard for Permanence of
        Paper for Printed Library Materials Z39.48-1992.

   5  4  3  2  1

*In Memoriam*

*Bill Sladek*
*1938–1993*

*friend and colleague*

# ■ Contents

# ■ Illustrations

## ■ MAPS

## ■ PHOTOGRAPHS

# ■ Introduction

A survey of current world conditions and a reading of the recent past reveal that the world is neither a fair nor a friendly place. Insurrections and wars abound, and more than half the world's inhabitants live in misery and hunger while others live in comfort and luxury. In this age of modern science and technology, of space exploration and heart transplants, how does one account for the absence of peace and the prevalence of poverty in a world of plenty? What are the roots of the perilous condition of human affairs? Today's students, young and old, must ask and seek to answer these questions. This book, a history of the world since 1945, was undertaken in order to assist them in that endeavor.

Tribal hostility and war between nations have been common throughout history, but in modern times, and especially in the twentieth century with the development of modern military technology, war has become increasingly deadly. World War II brought death and destruction on an unprecedented scale, and it ended with the use of a powerful new weapon of mass destruction, the atomic bomb. From the ruins of that war came a cry, expressed even by military leaders, that there must never be another such war. Yet, even as the ashes of World War II were still smoldering, friction developed among its victors, and they—the United States and Britain on one side and the Soviet Union on the other—became locked in a new power struggle that threatened the very peace they had sacrificed so much to attain. The postwar friction between them rapidly hardened into a political Cold War that soon turned into a military confrontation between East and West marked by mutual mistrust, suspicion, and hostility. After World War II the Cold War continued for more than forty-five years as the major determinant of international affairs. The two superpowers, the United States and the Soviet Union, aggressively sought to establish and maintain blocs of allies, thus dividing the world into two hostile camps. And since each

1

claimed to be the champion of a superior system, one capitalist and the other Communist, the world became the arena of an ideological conflict that endured for nearly half a century.

Meanwhile, both superpowers began rearming, and a relentless arms race was soon under way. Each claimed that security—both national and global—lay in military strength, but that the other's armaments threatened world peace. Thus they justified the building of massive arsenals containing thousands of nuclear weapons far more powerful than the ones used against Japan in 1945. Their arsenals have long since been large enough to destroy each other many times over and possibly extinguish human life on this planet, and yet year after year they continued piling up more weapons, spending at a rate of millions of dollars per day. When they decided to scale back their nuclear arsenals, they found out that the genie was already out of the bottle, that even poor Third World nations had the capability to build and launch them.

The military standoff between the nuclear powers brought about a precarious truce between them, but the rest of the world was not free of war. On the contrary, there have been more than one hundred wars since World War II, and many of these lesser wars, though contained geographically and limited to conventional weapons, carried the potential of igniting a larger conflagration. Indeed, the combatants were all too often clients of the major powers and were armed by them.

Equally dangerous to the safety and well-being of humanity was the growing gulf between the world's rich and poor, between the industrially advanced nations of the North and the underdeveloped nations of the South. In the South, often referred to as the Third World, one finds the world's lowest standards of living, lowest economic growth rates, lowest levels of education, lowest rates of life expectancy, and the highest population growth rates and infant mortality rates. Thus, millions of the inhabitants of the Third World are dreadfully impoverished, malnourished, disease-ridden, and unable to live productively and in dignity. Governments of Third World nations struggled, usually ineptly, to lift their countries from such impoverishment, and while some have made marginal progress, many others were merely marking time or slipping even further behind. Many of these countries contracted enormous foreign debts they were unable to pay, and their indebtedness threatened the financial stability of the wealthier nations of the North. Economic failure made the Third World more volatile politically and more vulnerable to intervention and militarization by the superpowers. Nearly every war fought since World War II was fought in Third World countries, and all were fought with weapons supplied by industrialized nations.

This is the world into which the youth of today were born. Their chances of resolving the immense problems they have inherited, of reducing the nuclear threat, and of alleviating the misery of the majority of mankind, thus making this world a safer and more civilized place, depend to a great extent on what they know of the causes of these problems. The clear-eyed vision needed to come to terms with these difficult problems and to progress toward a resolution of them must be based on an understanding of the past. To remain ignorant of that past is to compound the chances of either perpetuating the current problems or committing grievous and possibly irretrievable errors.

It was for the purpose of combating such ignorance and supplanting it with a knowledge of world affairs that we undertook the writing of this text. Our aim is to provide our readers with an evenhanded, yet critical, explanation of the political history of this troubled world and to expose them to more than one viewpoint. We seek to advance our readers' knowledge of the recent past and to develop a better understanding of the difficult issues and dangerous conditions in the world today. Above all, we hope to instill an appreciation of the need for greater objectivity and for careful, critical thinking about political issues. It is, therefore, our hope that this text will serve as a primer for responsible global citizenship.

It should be emphasized that we are primarily dealing with political history in this text, except in certain chapters where economic themes are particularly relevant. We do not address social or cultural dimensions of recent world history, as interesting or important as they may be. We also wish to point out that a text with a scope as broad as the world cannot help but be selective. Obviously, not every political development around the globe is discussed within these pages. We have attempted to provide a balanced coverage of global history, rather than a Western world or U.S.-centered approach. Thus, a substantial portion of the text is devoted to Asia, Africa, and Latin America.

The study of the recent past is no substitute for studying the longer haul of human history. Obviously, World War II had antecedents, the knowledge of which deepens our understanding of that momentous event, its consequences, and the course of events in the postwar period. Nonetheless, because World War II represents a historic watershed, one of the landmarks in history, it is not inappropriate that it be taken as a starting point for the study of recent world history. And because the postwar period was distinctly a new era with many new features—the advent of nuclear warfare, the development of high-speed aviation, the emergence of two superpowers, and the end of European colonialism, to name just a few—it makes sense to treat it as a distinct historical period. To be sure, for certain topics treated in this text, such as the Arab-Israeli conflict or the revolution in China, it will be necessary to trace historical roots further back in time, but our focus remains on the postwar period.

## ■ SEVEN MAJOR CONSEQUENCES OF WORLD WAR II

The enormous consequences of World War II gave shape to the postwar world, and they are treated as major themes in this text. We have identified the following as the most important of those consequences:

1. *The end of the European age.* Europe ceased to be the center of international power. At war's end, Europe was in shambles; its nations were prostrate, its cities in ruins, its people exhausted, and its economies shattered. The total defeat and destruction of Germany created a power vacuum in central Europe, and since nature and politics both abhor a vacuum, the victors inevitably filled it.

2. *The rise of the United States to superpower status.* Having played a decisive role in the global war and emerging from it militarily and economically supreme among the nations of the world, the United States shed for good its earlier isolationism and assumed a leadership role in the international arena.

3. *The expansion of the Soviet Union and its rise to superpower status.* Despite its severe war damage and its dire economic condition, the Soviet Union was determined to extend its power, especially in Eastern Europe, and play a major role in world affairs.

4. *The emergence of the Cold War.* Contention, mistrust, and hostility between the two emerging superpowers, the United States and the Soviet Union, developed quickly and produced an ongoing, global, bipolar power struggle.

5. *The beginning of the nuclear age.* The use of the atomic bomb by the United States and the world's failure to achieve international control of atomic energy resulted inevitably in the ever-growing nuclear arms race.

6. *The rise of nationalism and independence movements in Asia and Africa.* Although the roots of nationalism may be traced back to prewar times, it was not until the postwar period that nationalist movements became strong enough to challenge the colonial order in Asia and Africa. The struggle for independence was stimulated by the defeat of Japan and the weakening of the European colonial powers, and, in a remarkably short span of time, many Asian and African states won their independence.

7. *A renewed effort to secure lasting peace through international organization.* The United Nations was created in the hope that it might help preserve the global peace and security that the old League of Nations had failed to maintain.

Most of these interrelated themes are discussed in Part 1, "The Origins of the Cold War." In it we examine the global state of affairs at the end of World War II, and analyze the origins of the Cold War and its development in both Europe and Asia. In Part 2, "Nationalism and the End of Colonialism," the sixth theme is taken up. In this part, we also trace the development of Arab and Israeli nationalism and the course of the Middle East conflict. Part 3, "The Shifting Sands of Global Power," focuses mainly on the 1960s. In it we examine the changing configuration of the Cold War, the strains within the Eastern and Western blocs, the Sino-Soviet split, and the resulting emergence of multipolarity, which replaced the bipolar confrontation of the earlier Cold War period. This section also includes coverage of the Vietnam War and its consequences.

Part 4, "The Third World," takes us back to Asia and Africa to trace their postindependence progress—or lack thereof—and to Latin America as well to examine its similar problems. In addition to investigating the political and economic patterns on the three Third World continents, we also devote sections to such topics as the problem of the Third World's debt, the issue of apartheid in South Africa, the economic progress of certain Asian nations, and the revolution in the Philippines.

Part 5, "The End of the Postwar Era," treats the major global developments and issues since the 1980s. We have selected for special attention the rise of Japan and the European Community as new economic superpowers, and such late Cold War issues as the rise of Solidarity in Poland, the Soviet invasion of Afghanistan, and the nuclear arms race, potentially the most dangerous challenge to modern man. We also analyze the momentous changes in the Soviet Union and Eastern Europe since the end of the 1980s, changes that signal the end of the postwar era. We conclude the book with a discussion of the rise of militant Islam, as manifested in the Iranian revolution and in the Arab world.

We urge our readers to join with us in a quest for a fuller, more objective understanding of the world of turmoil in which we live. And we would remind them that history, especially recent political history, is not merely the compilation of dead facts; it is alive with controversy and conflicting ideas. We challenge our readers to confront these controversies, to weigh the conflicting ideas and viewpoints, and to formulate their own opinions.

# PART 1

# THE ORIGINS OF THE COLD WAR

In light of the enormous impact of the Cold War since World War II—the immeasurable human energies it has exhausted, the gargantuan amounts of wealth it consumed, the shifting of national priorities it demanded, the attention it diverted from other concerns, the civil liberties it has impinged on and the intellectual freedom it constrained, the anguish and fears it caused so many people, the threat it posed to the earth's inhabitants, and the enormous loss of life in the proxy wars (Korea, Vietnam, Afghanistan, etc.)—it becomes necessary to inquire into its origins.

By its very nature, the Cold War was for many years so divisive a subject that it was all but impossible to study it with detachment and objectivity. So strong were the feelings and so total the commitment of each side to its cause, and so contemptuous and mistrusting was each of the other side, that each had its own self-serving version of the history of the Cold War.

The United States and the Soviet Union each perpetuated a series of Cold War myths that sustained them over the years. The people of the United States generally felt (1) that the Soviet Union broke its postwar promises regarding Eastern Europe and was therefore responsible for starting the Cold War; (2) that its aggressive action in Eastern Europe was a manifestation of the determination of the Soviet Union to capture the entire world for Communism; (3) that so-called international Communism was a monolithic (that is, singular) movement centered in and controlled by the Soviet Union; (4) that Communism was enslavement and was never accepted by any people without coercion; and (5) that the great victory of the United States in World War II, as well as its immense prosperity and strength, attested to the superiority of its values and its system—that, in short, the United States represented humanity's best hope.

The Soviets argued (1) that the United States and the Western allies purposely let the Soviet Union bleed in World War II, and furthermore lacked gratitude for the role that it played in the defeat of Hitler, as well

7

as for the losses it suffered in that cause; (2) that the United States was committed to the annihilation of Communism in general and to the over-throw of the Communist government of the Soviet Union in particular; (3) that the laws of history were on its side, meaning that capitalism was in decline and Communism was the wave of the future; (4) that the U.S. political system was not really democratic but was controlled by Wall Street, or at any rate by a small clique of leading corporate interests; and (5) that capitalist nations were necessarily imperialistic and thus responsible for the colonization across the globe, and that the leading capitalist nation, the United States, was the most imperialistic of them all.[1]

As unquestioned assumptions, these myths became a mental strait-jacket. They provided only a narrow channel for foreign policy initiatives by either country. When notions such as these were imbedded in the thinking of the two adversaries, it became all but impossible for the two countries to end the Cold War and equally impossible to analyze objectively the history of the conflict.

The myths came into play throughout the Cold War, and especially in its earliest phase even before the defeat of Nazi Germany—when the Allied leaders met at Yalta in February 1945. For this reason, in the opening chapter of this book, we examine the wartime relationship between the United States and the Soviet Union, and their respective strengths at the end of the war. We also analyze the U.S. decision to use the atomic bomb against Japan and the impact it had on U.S.-Soviet relations. In Chapter 2, we turn to the Yalta Conference and examine its bearing on the beginning of the Cold War. We then trace the hardening of Cold War positions over critical issues in Europe in the four years following the end of World War II. By 1947, when the U.S. policy of "containment" of Communism was in place, the Cold War myths were firmly entrenched on both sides.

The Cold War quickly became global, and in fact it was in Asia where it became most inflamed in the first decade after the war. In Chapter 3, we pursue the Cold War in Asia by treating the Allied Occupation of defeated Japan, the civil war in China, and the Korean War—all Cold War issues. The Allied Occupation of defeated Japan was thoroughly dominated by the United States over the feeble objections of the Soviets, and eventually the United States succeeded in converting Japan into an ally in the global Cold War. The Chinese revolution, which brought the Communists to power in 1949, was fought entirely by indigenous forces, but the stakes were great for the two superpowers. The United States responded to the Communist victory in China with still firmer resolve to stem the advance of Communism in Asia. Less than a year later, that resolve was tested in Korea where Cold War tensions grew most intense and finally ignited in the Korean War. The armed conflict between East and West was contained within one Asian country, but it threatened to explode into the dreaded World War III.

After the standoff in Korea, Cold War tensions oscillated during the remainder of the 1950s. During this period, covered in Chapter 4, new leaders—Dwight Eisenhower in the United States and Nikita Khrushchev in the Soviet Union—exhibited a new flexibility, which made possible some reduction in tensions and the solution of a few of the Cold War issues. But the embrace of the Cold War myths remained undiminished during this period as manifested by sporadic crises and the substantial growth in the nuclear arsenals of both countries. The two superpowers came to the brink of nuclear war in 1962 over the deployment of Soviet nuclear missiles in Cuba. The Cuban missile crisis was the most dangerous of the many confrontations between East and West.

## ■ NOTE

1. These myths are an adaptation of a similar set of Cold War myths presented in Ralph B. Levering, *The Cold War, 1945–1972* (Arlington Heights, Ill.: Harlan Davidson, 1982), pp. 8–9.

As early as March 1964, William Fulbright, the chairman of the Senate Foreign Relations Committee, speaking before a nearly empty Senate chamber, challenged some of these and other Cold War myths. He questioned whether Communist China's "implacable hostility" to the West was "permanent," whether Fidel Castro posed "a grave danger to the United States," and whether there was something "morally sacred" about the U.S. possession of the Panama Canal, which it had seized in 1903. *New York Times,* March 29, 1964, p. E1.

# 1

# The End of World War II and the Dawn of the Nuclear Age

World War II was a cataclysmic event. It was by far the most deadly and destructive war in human history. The war raged on for almost six years in Europe, beginning with Nazi Germany's attack on Poland in September 1939, and ending with the surrender of Germany to the Allied Powers led by the United States, the Soviet Union, and Great Britain on May 9, 1945. The war lasted even longer in Asia, where it began with the Japanese invasion of China in July 1937, and ended with Japan's capitulation to the Allies on August 14, 1945. World War II represented a new dimension in warfare: total war. It was total in the sense that all of the great powers and most of the nations of the world were engaged in it, and in that it involved or affected the entire population of nations, not just the men and women in uniform. Because a nation's military might rested ultimately on its industrial capacity, the civilian work force had to contribute to the war effort; moreover, entire populations, especially urban dwellers, became targets and victims of new and more deadly modern weapons.

Another major dimension of World War II that was of immense importance in ending the war and shaping the postwar world was the introduction of atomic weapons. There are many difficult questions to ponder concerning the U.S. use of the atomic bomb against Japan at the end of World War II, one of the most important and most controversial issues in modern history. But the fundamental question remains: Was it necessary or justifiable to use the bomb? It is also important to consider what bearing the emerging Cold War had on the U.S. decision to drop the bomb on Japan, and what bearing its use had on subsequent U.S.-Soviet relations.

After the war, it was the victorious nations—mainly the United States and the Soviet Union—that took the lead in shaping the postwar world. In order to better understand their respective postwar policies, one must consider the impact World War II had on these two nations, which emerged as "superpowers" and as major adversaries in the ensuing Cold War.

The "Grand Alliance" fashioned by the United States, the Soviet Union, and Great Britain during the war hardly lasted beyond it. But before the alliance began to crumble and give way to Cold War hostility, leading political representatives of these and other nations endeavored to create a new international structure for the maintenance of global peace through collective security—the United Nations. Although the founding of the United Nations was attended by great hope, it was from the beginning severely limited in its capacity to attain its objective of world peace.

## ■ HISTORY'S MOST DESTRUCTIVE WAR

The carnage of World War II was so great as to be beyond comprehension. Most of Europe and East Asia were in ruins. Vast stretches of both continents were destroyed twice, first when they were conquered and again when they were liberated. Germany and Japan stood in ruins. It is impossible to know the complete toll in human lives lost in this war, but some estimates run higher than 70 million people. The nation that suffered the greatest loss of life was the Soviet Union. It lost an incredible 27 million people in the war, a figure that represents at least half of the total European war fatalities. Poland lost 5.8 million people, about 15 percent of its population. Germany lost 4.5 million people, and Yugoslavia, 1.5 million. Six other European nations—France, Italy, Romania, Hungary, Czechoslovakia, and Britain—each lost more than a half million people. In Asia, perhaps as many as 20 million Chinese and 2.3 million Japanese died in the war, and there were large numbers of casualties in various Asian countries from India in the south to Korea in the northeast. In some European countries and in Japan, there was hardly a family that had not lost at least one member in the war.[1]

Over one-half of those who died in World War II were civilians. Never before had warfare taken such a heavy toll of noncombatants. (In World War I only about one-twentieth of the dead were civilians.) An estimated 12 million civilians were killed as a direct result of military action, mainly bombing, and millions more died of starvation or epidemics in Europe and Asia, although we have no way of knowing exactly how many. An estimated 12 million people—Jews, Slavs, gypsies, the disabled, conscientious objectors, and political opponents (notably Communists)—were systematically exterminated as a result of the policy of Adolf Hitler, the dictator of Nazi Germany. This unspeakable act of barbarism, known as the Holocaust, was aimed primarily at exterminating the Jewish people; it resulted in the reduction of the Jewish population in Europe from 9.2 million to 3.8 million. All mankind was indelibly scarred by this most heinous of crimes committed by the Nazi rulership against the Jewish people.

The main cause for the huge toll of civilian lives was no doubt the development of air power—bigger and faster airplanes with longer range and greater carrying capacity. Indiscriminate bombing of the enemy's cities, populated by noncombatants, became common practice during the war. It began with Hitler's effort to bomb Britain into submission early in the war with a relentless bombing of British cities.[2] Later in the war, British and U.S. bombers retaliated with a massive bombardment of Germany. One Anglo-U.S. bombing raid on the German city of Dresden, in February 1945 (when Germany was all but defeated), killed some 135,000 people, mainly civilians. The Japanese, who also used air power, suffered the destruction of virtually all of their cities by the saturation bombing carried out by U.S. bombers. And the war ended with the use by the United States of a dreadful new weapon of mass destruction, the atomic bomb, which wrought the horrible devastation of Hiroshima and Nagasaki in August 1945. In total war fought with these methods and weapons, there was no place to hide. In the end, the nations that fought in the name of democracy in order to put an end to militarism resorted to the barbaric methods of their enemies. If unrestrained warfare had come to mean sustained, indiscriminate bombing of noncombatants with weapons of mass destruction, what hope was there for mankind should total war ever again occur?

The suffering and sorrow, the anguish and desperation of the survivors of the war lingered long after the last bombs had fallen and the victory celebrations had ended. Never in history had so much of the human race been so uprooted. In Europe alone there were between 20 and 30 million homeless refugees. Many of these displaced persons were people who fled their homelands to escape political persecution and to seek a greater measure of security and freedom elsewhere. Some were fleeing bombed-out cities and others were fleeing the advancing Soviet Red Army. Still others included those who had been forcibly moved to Germany during the war to work in its fields and factories. And then there were those, such as the several million ethnic Germans who had lived in Eastern Europe, whose homelands were transferred to the victors. (Former German territories, which became parts of Poland, Czechoslovakia, and the Soviet Union, remained for decades among the unresolved issues of the Cold War.) For these millions of homeless people, the struggle for survival was especially difficult, and we have no way of knowing how many of them did not survive.

There was also a large refugee problem in Asia, where the Japanese had forced population transfers during the war and where some 6 million Japanese—half of them military personnel—were scattered all over Asia at war's end. After the war, the United States transported most of these Japanese back to safety in Japan and returned Koreans, Chinese, and others to their homelands. However, in Manchuria, which was temporarily occupied by the Soviet Union after the war, several hundred thousand Japanese were never repatriated. They succumbed either to the severity of the Manchurian winter without adequate food, shelter, or clothing or to the brutality of Soviet labor camps in Siberia. Elsewhere in Asia, particularly in China,

there were large population movements as millions of people, who had earlier fled from the Japanese invaders, returned to reclaim their lands and
homes. In China, cities such as Beijing (Peking) and Shanghai were swollen
with weary, desperate people for whom there was no livelihood and insufficient food and other staples. In these places people were plagued by disease,
poverty, the black market, inflation, and corruption, all of which ran rampant
in China during and well after the war.

The inferno of World War II left many cities gutted and vacant. Dresden, Hamburg, and Berlin in Germany and Tokyo, Yokohama, Hiroshima,
and Nagasaki in Japan were virtually flattened, and many other cities in
these and other countries were in large part turned to rubble. Some were
entirely vacated and devoid of life for a while after the war, and most lost
a substantial portion of their people. For example, the huge and once
crowded city of Tokyo, which lay mostly in ruins, saw its population dwin-
dle to only a third of its prewar size. In these once bustling cities, survivors
scrounged in the debris in hopes of salvaging anything that might help them
in their struggle for survival. At war's end homeless people moved into
those few buildings that still stood—an office building, a railroad station,
a school—and lived sometimes three or four families to a room, while others threw up shanties and shacks made of scraps of debris. Decades later
one could still find here and there in many of these cities rubble left over
from the war.

The physical destruction wrought by the war, estimated at over $2 tril-
lion, continued to cause economic and social disruption in the lives of survivors long afterwards. Not only were cities and towns destroyed but so too
were industrial plants and transportation facilities. The destruction of factories, farmlands, and livestock and of railroads, bridges, and port facilities made it extremely difficult to feed and supply the needy populations in
the war-torn nations of Europe and Asia. Thus, acute shortages of food and
scarcity of other life essentials continued well after the fighting was over.
In these dire circumstances, many became desperate and demoralized, and
some sought to insure their survival or to profit from others' misfortune by
resorting to hoarding goods and selling them on the black market. These
were grim times in which greed, vengeance, and other base instincts of
humanity found expression.

The widespread desolation and despair in Europe bred cynicism and
disillusionment, which in turn gave rise to a political shift to the left.
Shaken and bewildered by the nightmarish devastation all about them,
many Europeans lost confidence in the old political order and turned to
other more radical political doctrines and movements. Many embraced
Marxism as a natural alternative to the discredited fascism and as an ideology that offered hope for the future. The renewed popularity of the left was
reflected primarily in postwar electoral victories of the moderate left, such
as the Labour Party in Great Britain and the Socialist Party in Austria. But

the Communists, too, were able to make strong showings in elections, particularly in France and Italy. In Asia the political swing to the left could be seen in China, Indochina, and to a lesser extent in Japan. Alarmed by this resurgence of the left, U.S. leaders soon came to the view that massive aid was necessary to bring about a speedy economic recovery and thereby eliminate the poverty that was seen as the breeding ground for the spread of Communism.

During the war the United Nations Relief and Rehabilitation Administration (UNRRA) was created to rehabilitate war-torn areas after liberation. Economic aid from this agency as well as from the United States directly not only provided relief for the destitute peoples of Europe and Asia, but also provided much needed credit that made possible the beginnings of economic recovery. By the fall of 1946, many of the transportation facilities and factories in Western Europe had been rapidly repaired, and industrial production began to climb slowly toward prewar levels. But the harsh winter of 1946–1947 brought new economic setbacks with a depletion of food supplies, raw materials, and financial reserves. Economic stagnation and attendant deprivation therefore continued for masses of people throughout Europe, especially in Germany, which had suffered the greatest physical destruction in the war, and in Great Britain, one of the victors. A similar situation prevailed in the war-ravaged nations of Asia, especially China and Japan.

When we consider all the death, destruction, suffering, and social dislocation that it caused for so many people, we realize that World War II was much more than a series of heroic military campaigns, and more than a set of war games to be played and replayed by nostalgic war buffs. It was human anguish and agony on a scale unprecedented in the history of mankind. And nowhere were the scars any deeper than on the two Japanese cities, Hiroshima and Nagasaki.

## ■ THE ATOMIC BOMBING OF JAPAN

On August 6, 1945, the United States dropped an atomic bomb on Hiroshima, and three days later it used another one on Nagasaki. In each instance a large city was obliterated and tens of thousands of its inhabitants were either instantly incinerated, or left to succumb to radiation sickness weeks, months, or even years later. According to Japanese estimates, about 140,000 people were killed in Hiroshima by the atomic bomb strike, and about 70,000 in Nagasaki.[3] Thus, World War II ended and the nuclear age began with the use of this new weapon of unprecedented destructive power, a weapon that one scientist later called "a magnificent product of pure physics."[4]

The people of the United States and their wartime president, Franklin Roosevelt, were determined to bring about the earliest possible defeat of

Japan. The costly war in the Pacific had been raging for almost three and a half years by the time Germany surrendered in May 1945. President Roosevelt, who had commissioned the building of the atomic bomb, was prepared to use it against Japan once it was ready, but he died in April 1945. The decision to employ the revolutionary new weapon fell to the new president, Harry S. Truman, who had not even been informed of its existence before he took office. In consultation with the secretary of war, Henry Stimson, Truman set up an advisory group known as the Interim Committee, which was to deliberate on the matter of introducing the new weapon into warfare. Ultimately, the Interim Committee recommended that the atomic bomb be used against Japan as soon as possible, and without prior warning, on a dual target (meaning a military or war plant site surrounded by workers' homes, that is, a Japanese city).[5] The rationale for this strategy for the use of the bomb was to enhance its shock value. The atomic bomb was successfully tested in a remote New Mexico desert on July 16, just as Truman was meeting British prime minister Winston Churchill and Soviet leader Joseph Stalin at Potsdam, Germany. Nine days later, on July 25, Truman, elated by the news of the test, approved the military orders for its use. The following day he issued the Potsdam Proclamation, which spelled out terms for Japan's surrender and warned of "prompt and utter destruction" for noncompliance, but made

Hiroshima, Japan, August 1945. Located near ground zero, this building with its "A-Bomb Dome" has been preserved as a peace monument. *(National Archives)*

no specific reference to the new weapon. The proclamation was rejected by the Japanese government, and thus the orders for the first atomic bomb strike were carried out as planned.

The Japanese government dismissed the proclamation, for it was silent on the most important question, a guarantee by the victors that Japan would be allowed to retain the most sacred of Japanese institutions, the emperor. The U.S. intelligence community, which from the very beginning of the war had been able to decode Japanese diplomatic cables, had become well aware that the Potsdam Proclamation had a "magnetic effect" on the emperor, Prime Minister Suzuki, and the army. Some Japanese officials thought that Article 10 of the Potsdam Proclamation implied the retention of the emperor and thus could be used as the basis of a Japanese surrender; others wanted a clarification. The Potsdam Proclamation, far from triggering an expression of Japanese intransigence, had the earmarks of the terms of surrender of the armed forces of the empire of Japan. Only one question remained: Would the U.S. government clarify Article 10 and accept a Japanese surrender before or after atomic weapons were used?[6]

Many people have since questioned the use of the atomic bomb, and opinions differ sharply. The orthodox view, presented by U.S. officials after the event and generally shared by the U.S. public, is that, by cutting short the war and sparing the casualties that would have occurred in the planned invasion of Japan, the atomic bomb actually saved many lives, Japanese as well as U.S. This explanation concludes that, although use of the bomb was regrettable, it was nonetheless necessary. Japan's diehard military leaders were determined to fight to the bitter end, as they had in the Pacific islands, and they were prepared to fight even more fanatically on their own soil to prevent defeat. Thus, in order to bring about the earliest possible surrender of Japan and an end to the long and costly war,[7] the United States was compelled to use the revolutionary, powerful new weapon its scientists and engineers had secretly produced.

However, this interpretation, basically a justification of the atomic bombing of Japan, neglects many important historical facts. First, Japan was all but defeated. Its home islands were defenseless against the sustained naval and air bombardment they were undergoing, its navy and merchant marine were sunk, its armies were weakened and undersupplied, and it was already being strangled by a U.S. naval blockade. U.S. leaders, who had underestimated the Japanese at the beginning of the war, were now overestimating Japan's remaining strength. Although the diehard determination of its military leaders kept Japan from surrendering, the nation's capacity to wage war had been virtually eliminated.

Second, before the United States had tested the atomic bomb in mid-July, the Japanese were already attempting to begin negotiations to end the war through Soviet mediation. (Direct communication between Tokyo and Washington was not possible because of the state of war between the two countries, but Japan was not at war with the Soviet Union.) The U.S. government was fully aware of these efforts and of the sense of urgency voiced by the Japanese in their communications to Moscow. U.S. decisionmakers chose to ignore these diplomatic overtures, which they dismissed as unreliable and possibly a trick. The major obstacle to Japan's effort to achieve a diplomatic settlement to the war was the U.S. insistence upon unconditional surrender. (Unconditional surrender calls for the enemy's acceptance of complete submission to the will of the victor, as opposed to a negotiated settlement to end the war.) This was entirely unacceptable to the Japanese, who wanted at least a guarantee of the safety of their sacred imperial institution—which is to say, they insisted on the retention of their emperor, Hirohito, in whose name the imperial forces had fought the war. The U.S. government steadfastly refused to offer any such exception to the unconditional surrender policy. The Potsdam Proclamation, the final Allied ultimatum, issued on July 26, 1945, did not offer Japan any guarantees regarding the emperor, and thus the Japanese did not accept it as a basis for surrender. This condition was the only one the Japanese insisted upon, and eventually it was granted by the United States, *after* the nuclear destruction of Hiroshima and Nagasaki. On August 11, the Japanese government agreed to surrender provided that it "does not comprise any demand which prejudices the prerogatives of His Majesty as a sovereign ruler."[8] This was a condition the United States finally accepted in its reply when it demanded the unconditional surrender of the Japanese forces. If this condition had been granted beforehand, the Japanese may well have surrendered and the atomic bombs would then have been unnecessary to attain that objective.

Third, the Japanese might have been spared the horrendous fate of Hiroshima and Nagasaki had the U.S. government provided them with an explicit warning about the nature of the new weapon and possibly an actual demonstration of an atomic blast as well. If Tokyo had still refused to accept the surrender terms after such a warning or demonstration, the use of the atomic weapons might have been morally justifiable. The Japanese were given no warning of the atomic bombing outside of the vague threat in the Potsdam Proclamation of "prompt and utter destruction." The Interim Committee ruled out the idea of providing Japan with either a warning or a demonstration of the bomb in favor of its direct use on a Japanese city in order to shock the Japanese into surrender. It was also argued that a demonstration would be risky because of the possibility of the bomb's failing to work, thus causing the United States to lose credibility and the Japanese military leaders to gain confidence.

Fourth, an unquestioned assumption of most of those who defend the use of the two atomic bombs is that it produced the desired results: Japan quickly surrendered. But questions do arise. Did the atomic bombings actually cause the Japanese to surrender? And was the second bomb necessary to bring it about? (It should be pointed out that there was no separate set

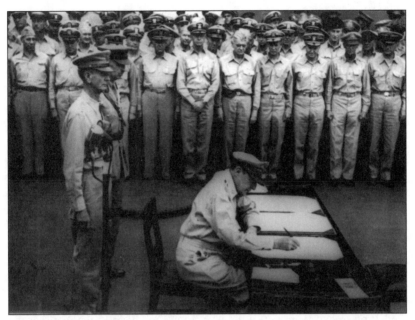

General Douglas MacArthur on the deck of the USS *Missouri* signing the Japanese surrender documents. *(National Archives)*

The formal Japanese surrender ceremony, September 3, 1945, on board the USS *Missouri*. *(National Archives)*

of orders to drop a second atomic bomb on Japan. Instead, the plan was to use a "one-two punch" using both bombs in rapid succession, and, if necessary, a third, which was to be ready within ten days, so as to maximize the new weapon's shock value and force Japan to capitulate as rapidly as possible.)

Those who specifically protest the bombing of Nagasaki as unnecessary, and therefore immoral, assume that the bombing of Hiroshima was sufficient to cause Japan's surrender, or that Japan should have been given more time to assess what had hit Hiroshima. One may indeed question whether the interval of three days was long enough for the Japanese military leaders to assess the significance of the new force that had destroyed one of their cities. But a more fundamental question is whether the atomic bombings—the first or both—actually caused Japan's surrender. Japanese newspapers, the testimony of Japanese leaders, and U.S. intercepts of Japanese diplomatic cables provide reason to believe that the Soviet entry into the war against Japan on August 8 was as much a cause for Japan's surrender as the dropping of the two atomic bombs. The Soviet Union was the only major nation in the world not at war with Japan, and the Japanese leaders were still desperately hoping for Soviet neutrality or possible Soviet mediation to bail them out of the war. They took heart in the fact that the Soviet Union had not signed the Potsdam Proclamation or signified support for it, even though Stalin was meeting with Truman and Churchill when it was issued. But with the Soviet attack the last shred of hope was gone, and Japan could no longer avoid admitting defeat. As for the effect of the atomic bombings on Japanese leaders, Japan's inner cabinet was divided three-to-three for and against accepting the Potsdam Proclamation before the bombing of Hiroshima, and it remained so afterward. And it remained equally divided after the Soviet entry into the war and the bombing of Nagasaki, until finally the emperor himself broke the deadlock in favor of ending the war.

What were the thoughts of the U.S. leaders about the role of the Soviet Union in bringing about Japan's defeat? Clearly, at the Yalta Conference in February 1945, President Roosevelt and his military advisers strongly desired the early entry of the Soviet Union into the war against Japan, and he was willing to concede much to Stalin to attain this. But five months later, after the atomic bomb was successfully tested, leading figures in the Truman administration were not so sure they wanted the Soviet Union to enter the war against Japan. Nor did they want the Soviets to know anything about the atomic bomb. In fact, both Roosevelt and Truman pointedly refused to inform Moscow about the development of the new weapon and the plans to use it against Japan, despite the advice of some of the leading atomic scientists to do so in order to prevent a nuclear arms race after the war.

This last point raises intriguing and important questions about the connection between the U.S. use of the bomb and its policies toward the Soviet

Nagasaki before. *(National Archives)*

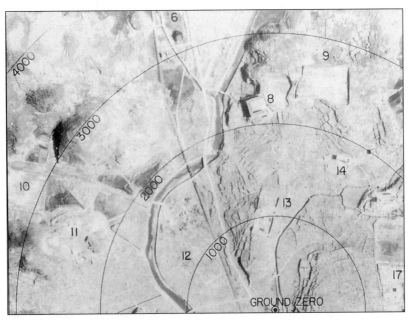

Nagasaki after. *(National Archives)*

Union at the end of the war. One historical interpretation asserts that the United States used the atomic bomb on defeated Japan not so much as the last attack of World War II, but as the first attack in the Cold War. In other words, the bomb was used in order to coerce the Soviet Union into behaving itself in Europe, Asia, and elsewhere. This interpretation would explain the hurried use of the bomb before the Soviet Union had entered the war against Japan and nearly three months prior to the planned invasion of Japan by U.S. forces. And it would explain Truman's refusal to inform Stalin officially about the new weapon before (or even after) its use against Japan. In this way, it is argued that the United States sought to maintain its nuclear monopoly (shared with Britain) and to use it as a means to curb Soviet expansion. This has been referred to as nuclear diplomacy.

Although this interpretation by revisionist historians is based on rather substantial evidence and logic, it remains speculative, and those who hold the orthodox view, of course, reject it and offer counterarguments. They emphasize the fanaticism and intransigence of the Japanese military leaders, who even resorted to suicidal kamikaze airplane attacks on U.S. ships. And they argue that the atomic bomb was needed to subdue an irrational enemy who seemed determined to fight suicidally to the bitter end. Therefore, they conclude, it was solely for military purposes that President Truman decided to use the atomic bomb. They also argue that President Truman, as commander in chief, had the responsibility to use the military power at his command to produce the earliest possible defeat of Japan, and that, if he had not used the atomic bomb and more U.S. military personnel had died in the continuing war, he would surely have been condemned as being politically and morally liable for their deaths.

Those who hold this view also point out that Truman could hardly have decided against use of the atomic bomb. As a new occupant of the White House following the popular Roosevelt, Truman inherited Roosevelt's cabinet, his policies, and specifically his resolve to treat the new weapon as a legitimate one of war. General Leslie Groves, head of the Manhattan Project (the code name of the secret program to build the atomic bomb), certainly assumed and fully expected that it would be used as soon as it became operational. The military planning for its use was well under way. There was, among the scientists and military personnel involved in the project, a rising anticipation of the successful deployment of the weapon they had brought into being after four years of herculean effort. Truman, who had only learned about the new weapon when he took office in April, could hardly have stemmed the momentum. The military leaders, and General Groves in particular, seemed especially determined to deploy the new weapon in order to know its destructive force. They had decided upon a set of Japanese cities as targets and had ordered that these cities be spared from conventional bombing so that they would remain unspoiled targets for the new weapon.

# ■ THE POLITICAL FALLOUT

Historians are also in disagreement over the impact of the atomic bomb on the Cold War. Did the Truman administration actually attempt to employ nuclear diplomacy after the war? If it did, it is safe to say that it did not work. The nuclear threat, implicit in the exclusive Anglo-U.S. possession of the atomic bomb, did not seem to produce any significant change in Soviet behavior and policies anywhere. But it did, no doubt, affect attitudes on both sides that contributed to Cold War mistrust. U.S. possession of the bomb caused its leaders to be more demanding and less flexible in dealing with the Soviet Union, and the U.S. possession and use of the bomb surely caused the Soviet leaders, in turn, to increase their suspicions of the West.

It is fairly certain that the secretive manner of the United States in building and then using the atomic bomb made a postwar nuclear arms race likely, if not inevitable. Truman's secretary of state, James Byrnes, who also served on the Interim Committee, contended that it would take the Soviet Union at least ten years to develop an atomic bomb and that in the interval the United States could take advantage of its "master card" in dealing with the Soviet Union. However, leading U.S. nuclear scientists, including Robert Oppenheimer, predicted that the Soviet Union could build the bomb within four years.[9] Several of the Manhattan Project scientists attempted to warn the Truman administration that the atomic monopoly could not be maintained for long and that a nuclear arms race would surely follow and threaten the peace of the world if the U.S. government did not share information about this revolutionary new weapon of mass destruction with its wartime ally, the Soviet Union, and did not attempt to bring it under international control. This advice, given both before and after the Hiroshima and Nagasaki bombings, went unheeded, and the result was exactly what the scientists had predicted. Indeed, Oppenheimer's prediction that the Soviets would have their own atomic weapons in four years was right on target.

The U.S. government did, however, after months of careful study of the complicated issues involved, offer a proposal for international control of atomic power. This proposal, the Baruch Plan, presented to a committee within the United Nations in June 1946, was unacceptable to the Soviet Union because, among other reasons, it permitted the United States to retain its nuclear arsenal indefinitely, while restricting Soviet efforts to develop one. The Soviets countered by proposing the immediate destruction of all existing nuclear weapons and the signing of a treaty outlawing any future production or use of them. The United States, understandably unwilling to scuttle its atomic monopoly, flatly rejected this. Talks continued for the next three years at the United Nations, but they proved fruitless. In the meantime, the Soviet Union's frantic effort to build an atomic bomb did bear fruit as early as the U.S. atomic scientists had predicted—July 1949. The nuclear arms race was joined.

## ☐   The United States and the Soviet Union at War's End

The two nations that emerged from the war as the most powerful shapers of the postwar world, the two new superpowers, the United States and the Soviet Union, had very different wartime experiences. No nation suffered as many casualties as the Soviet Union, and no major nation in the war suffered as few as the United States.

In June 1941, the German army of more than 2 million soldiers invaded the Soviet Union. Immense areas of the Soviet Union were devastated by the ensuing war, leaving some 1,700 cities and 70,000 villages in ruins and some 70 percent of its industries and 60 percent of its transportation facilities destroyed. During the war, the Germans took several million Soviet prisoners, many of whom did not survive their ordeal, and several million others were forcibly conscripted to labor in German factories and on farms during the war. The horrors of the German invasion and occupation policies and the siege of Soviet cities aroused the patriotism of both the Russian and non-Russian peoples of the Soviet Union who fought heroically to defend the nation in what is still called the Great Patriotic War. Ultimately, these people endured, and the Soviet Red Army drove the shattered German armies off their land and across Eastern Europe back to Germany where they were finally defeated. But the cost in lives was enormous: an estimated 7.5 million military deaths and twice—possibly three times—as many civilian lives. Any discussion of postwar policies of the Soviet Union and its relations with the United States must begin with a recognition of the incredible losses it suffered in its war against Nazi Germany and its insistence that there be no repetition of this history.[10]

In contrast, the United States emerged from the war virtually unscathed. Except for the Japanese attack on Pearl Harbor at the outset of the war, it had not been invaded or bombed and there had been no bloody battle lines across its terrain. In comparison with the huge Soviet death toll, the number of U.S. soldiers killed in the war—approximately 330,000—was small. For every U.S. death resulting from the war there were 85 to 90 Soviet deaths. The Soviet Union lost more people in the siege of Leningrad or in the battle of Stalingrad than the United States did in the entire war.

In comparison to the immense physical destruction sustained by the Soviet Union, the United States suffered very little damage. On the contrary, the U.S. economy experienced a great wartime boom, which brought it out of the Great Depression. While the Soviet Union's industrial output fell by 40 percent during the war years, that of the United States more than doubled. And while the Soviet Union sorely needed economic rehabilitation to recover from the ravages of war, the United States possessed unparalleled economic power. Indeed, no nation has ever achieved such economic supremacy as that achieved by the United States at the end of World War II. In a war-ravaged world where every other industrial nation had suffered extensive damage and declining production, the U.S. economy, with its wartime growth, towered over all others like a colossus. What is more, the United States had the capacity to greatly extend its huge lead. It possessed in great abundance every resource necessary for sustained industrial growth in the postwar era: large, undamaged industrial plants, skilled labor, technology, raw materials, a sophisticated transport system, and, last but not least, a huge supply of capital for investment.

The United States emerged from the war with another important although intangible asset: a greatly inflated national ego. The nation was brimming with renewed confidence and optimism. The pessimism spawned by the Great Depression was a thing of the past. The U.S. people saw their victory in war as proof of the superiority of their way of life. With their nation standing tall at the pinnacle of power in the war-torn world, the people exhibited what has been called an "illusion of American omnipotence."[11] Bolstered by this new confidence and sense of supremacy, the United States now displayed a new determination to play the role of a great power and to exercise its leadership in shaping the postwar world.

## ☐ The Quest for Collective Security

The task of establishing a new world order after the defeat of Germany and Japan fell, of course, to the victors, especially the most powerful among them, the United States, the Soviet Union, and to a lesser degree, Great Britain. During the war, the leaders of these countries—the "Big Three," Franklin Roosevelt, Joseph Stalin, and Winston Churchill—met not only to coordinate war plans but also to lay plans for the postwar settlement. These men, especially Roosevelt, were confident that the harmony and trust developed during the war would endure and that through personal diplomacy they could settle the enormous problems of the postwar world, such as the future of Germany, Eastern Europe, Japan, and the rest of Asia. However, before the war ended, two of the three were no longer in power: Roosevelt died in April 1945, and Churchill was defeated in the British election of July of that year. But it was already apparent before Roosevelt's death that the wartime alliance would not outlast the war. In retrospect, it is clear that the Big Three had little more in common than a common enemy, and once Nazi Germany was defeated, their conflicting interests came to the fore.

The wartime solidarity attained by the personal diplomacy of the Big Three could not be counted on to guide the postwar world to safety and security, and would not in any case endure beyond the war; however, they did endeavor, albeit cautiously, to erect a new international structure of peace. While sharp differences arose among the Big Three over a number of issues as the war was coming to an end, they were in general agreement on the concept of maintaining peace through collective security. President Roosevelt was most ardent in advocating the creation of a new international

settle or moderate international disputes in such places as Iran, India, Malaya, and the Middle East, when and where the interests of both the United States and the Soviet Union were either minimal or not in conflict. However, the veto power that both superpowers had insisted on and the Cold War contention between them rendered the Security Council all but powerless to keep the peace in the postwar era.

## ■ RECOMMENDED READINGS

### ☐ World War II

Calvocoressi, Peter, and Guy Wint. *Total War: Causes and Courses of the Second World War.* New York: Pantheon Books, 1972.
A comprehensive account of the war both in Europe and Asia.

Dower, John W. *War Without Mercy: Race and Power in the Pacific War.* New York: Pantheon, 1986.
A frank analysis of the racial nature of the war.

Hart, B. H. Liddell. *History of the Second World War.* New York: Putnam, 1971.
One of the most highly regarded single-volume studies of World War II.

Saburo, Ienaga. *The Pacific War: World War Two and the Japanese, 1931–1945.* New York: Pantheon Books, 1978.
A strong indictment of Japanese militarism.

Toland, John. *The Rising Sun.* New York: Random House, 1971.
One of the best books on Japan's war.

Werth, Alexander. *Russia at War, 1941–1945.* New York: Dutton, 1964.
Excellent on the Soviet Union's wartime experience, by a British war correspondent, a native of Leningrad.

Wright, Gordon. *The Ordeal of Total War.* New York: Harper and Row, 1968.
A classic study of the war.

### ☐ The Atomic Bomb

Alperovitz, Gar. *Atomic Diplomacy: Hiroshima and Potsdam.* New York: Simon and Schuster, 1965.
The foremost revisionist interpretation of the atomic bomb decision.

———. *The Decision to Use the Atomic Bomb.* New York: Knopf, 1995.
A comprehensive and thoroughly argued analysis.

Bernstein, Barton J., ed. *The Atomic Bomb: The Critical Issues.* Boston: Little, Brown, 1976.
An excellent anthology, which provides excerpts from the writings of some of those involved in the atomic bomb project and by various other writers.

Committee for the Compilation of Materials on Damage Caused by the Atomic Bombs in Hiroshima and Nagasaki. *Hiroshima and Nagasaki: The Physical, Medical and Social Effects of the Atomic Bombs.* New York: Basic Books, 1981.
The definitive study on the subject.

Feis, Herbert. *The Atomic Bomb and the End of World War II.* Princeton: Princeton University Press, 1966; originally published as *Japan Subdued,* 1961.
A standard work that focuses on both the military and diplomatic aspects of the atomic bomb decision.

Herken, Gregg F. *The Winning Weapon: The Atomic Bomb in the Cold War,
1945–1950.* New York: Knopf, 1981.
   A discussion of the role of the atomic bomb in immediate postwar diplomacy.
Hersey, John. *Hiroshima.* New York: Bantam Books, 1959.
   A classic on the death and destruction caused by the first atomic bomb attack.
Rhodes, Richard. *The Making of the Atomic Bomb.* New York: Simon and Schuster,
1986.
Sherwin, Martin J. *A World Destroyed: The Atomic Bomb and the Grand Alliance.*
New York: Knopf, 1975.
   Among the best studies of the politics and diplomacy involved in the decision
to drop the atomic bomb on Japan.

## ■ NOTES

1. The magnitude of the slaughter was such that no exact figures are possible.
For a breakdown of the figures, particularly in Asia, see John W. Dower, *War Without Mercy: Race and Power in the Pacific War* (New York: Pantheon, 1986), pp.
295–301.

2. Aerial bombardment actually began before World War II. Its effectiveness
was demonstrated by the German bombing of Spanish cities in the Spanish civil war
and the Japanese bombing of Chinese cities in Manchuria. In World War II, Britain
carried out bombing raids on Berlin before Germany began its bombardment of
Britain, but the latter represents the first sustained, large-scale bombing attack on
the cities of another country.

3. U.S. estimates of the death toll from the atomic bombings are 70,000 in
Hiroshima and 40,000 in Nagasaki. The discrepancy in the fatality figures apparently results partly from different methods of calculation and partly from differing
intentions of those doing the counting.

4. Dr. Yoshio Nishina, "The Atomic Bomb," Report for the United States
Strategic Bombing Survey (Washington, D.C.: National Archives), p. 1, Record
Group 243, Box 56.

5. "Notes of the Interim Committee," Record Group 77, Manhattan Engineering District Papers, Modern Military Branch, National Archives (Washington, D.C.:
National Archives, May 31, 1945), pp. 9–10.

6. Pacific Strategic Intelligence Section, intelligence summary of August 7,
1945, "Russo Japanese Relations (28 July 6 August 1945)," National Archives,
Record Group 457, SRH-088, pp. 3, 7–8, 16. For the Japanese attempts to surren-
der, beginning on July 13, 1945, see "Magic Diplomatic Extracts, July 1945," MIS,
War Department, prepared for the attention of General George C. Marshall,
National Archives, Record Group 457, SRH-040, pp. 1–78.

7. One commonly finds the figure of 1 million as the estimate of Allied (mainly
U.S.) soldiers who would have been killed in the invasion of Japan if the atomic
bomb had not been used, but this figure seems grossly exaggerated. It is more than
three times the total number of U.S. military deaths resulting from World War II—
both in Europe and in the Pacific in four years of warfare. The 1 million figure was
used by Secretary of War Stimson after the war in an article intended to justify the
use of the atomic bomb on Japan. In point of fact, at a meeting of top U.S. military
officials to discuss the planned invasion of Japan on June 18, 1945, General George
C. Marshall, the army chief of staff, expressed the view that it was impossible to
give an estimate of the casualties in such an invasion, but he said that in the first
month they would probably not exceed those suffered in the invasion of Luzon—

31,000. See Herbert Feis, *The Atomic Bomb and the End of World War II* (Princeton: Princeton University Press, 1966), pp. 8–9.

8. Harry S. Truman, *Memoirs, I, 1945: Year of Decisions* (New York: Signet, [orig. 1955] 1965), p. 471.

9. "Notes of the Interim Committee," May 31, 1945, pp. 10–12; Gregg Herken, *The Winning Weapon: The Atomic Bomb in the Cold War, 1945–1950* (New York: Random House, 1981), pp. 109–113. Byrnes was apparently less influenced by the views of the scientists than he was by General Groves, who speculated that it would take the Soviet Union from ten to twenty years to produce an atomic bomb.

10. It is estimated that there were about as many Soviet deaths in the Battle of Stalingrad alone as the United States suffered in the entire war (330,000), and it is estimated that over 1 million died in the siege of Leningrad.

11. Sir Denis Brogan, cited in Louis Halle, *The Cold War as History* (New York: Harper and Row, 1967), p. 25.

12. The secretary general was appointed by the General Assembly on the recommendation of the Security Council. In effect, this meant finding a neutral candidate from a neutral country acceptable to the two sides in the Cold War. The first secretary general was Trygve Lie of Norway (1946–1953), who was followed by Dag Hammarskjöld of Sweden (1953–1961), U Thant of Burma (1961–1971), Kurt Waldheim of Austria (1972–1981), Javier Pérez de Cuéllar of Peru (1982–1991), Boutros Boutros-Ghali of Egypt (1992–1996), and Kofi Annan of Ghana (1997–   ).

# 2

## The Cold War Institutionalized

At the end of 1944, it became clear that it was only a matter of time until the Allies would defeat Nazi Germany. It also became evident that the reason for the wartime alliance—always a marriage of convenience—was coming to an end. Postwar considerations were beginning to play an ever increasing role in the relations between the Allies. Throughout the war, the Allies had made it clear repeatedly that they fought for specific aims and not merely for the high-sounding principles of liberty and democracy. In 1945, the moment thus came to consider the postwar world, to present one's claims. For these reasons the Allied heads of state—Franklin Roosevelt of the United States, Joseph Stalin of the Soviet Union, and Winston Churchill of Great Britain—met in February 1945 in the Soviet resort of Yalta on the Crimean Peninsula in the Black Sea. It was here that the Big Three attempted to sort out four central issues.

### ■ THE YALTA CONFERENCE

The main topic at Yalta was the status of postwar Eastern Europe, and mainly that of Poland, which had been—and still was at the time of the conference—an ally in the war against Germany. It had been on behalf of the government of Poland that Great Britain and France had declared war on Germany in 1939. This action by the Western powers had transformed the German-Polish war into a European conflict, which then spilled over into the Atlantic, the Mediterranean, and North Africa, and with the Japanese attack on Pearl Harbor in December 1941, into Asia and the Pacific. In short, the governments of France and Great Britain had taken the momentous decision to go to war—and thus risk the welfare and the independence of their own nations, not to mention their people's lives and fortunes—to prevent the German conquest of a nation in Eastern Europe.

31

The Big Three. Soviet marshal Joseph Stalin, U.S. president Franklin D. Roosevelt, and British prime minister Winston Churchill at the Tehran conference in November 1943. *(National Archives)*

As the war drew to a conclusion and the Germans were expelled from Poland, the fate of that nation became the overriding political concern of the Allies. To complicate matters for the West, the government of Poland, virulently anti-Russian and anti-Communist, had fled Warsaw in the wake of the German invasion and had taken up residence in London, waiting to return to power at the end of the war. The Poles in London now insisted that the West had an obligation to facilitate their return to Warsaw as the legitimate government of Poland. The Western leaders, Churchill and Roosevelt, wanted to oblige, but it was the Red Army of the Soviet Union that was in the process of occupying Poland. It became increasingly clear that Stalin, not Roosevelt or Churchill, held the trump cards.

The second issue at Yalta was one of prime importance for the U.S. armed forces, which at that time were still engaged in a bitter war with Japan that promised to continue perhaps into 1946. Japanese resistance was as fierce as ever. The sustained bombing of Japanese cities was under way, but the Battle of Okinawa (where the United States first set foot on Japanese soil) had not yet taken place. For the U.S. Joint Chiefs of Staff, therefore, Yalta was primarily a war conference with the aim of bringing the seasoned Red Army into the war against Japan in the Pacific.

The third question was the formation of the United Nations to replace the old League of Nations, a casualty of World War II. Roosevelt sought an organizational structure for the United Nations acceptable to Churchill and Stalin, as well as to the U.S. people back home. Roosevelt firmly believed that there could be no effective international organization without U.S. and Soviet participation.

Finally, there was the question of what to do with the German state, whose defeat was imminent. The Allies, after all, would soon be in control of the devastated land of the once-powerful Germany, whose uncertain future was in their hands.

## ☐ The Polish Question

The first question, the status of Poland, proved to be the thorniest. It came up in seven of the eight plenary (full, formal) sessions. Roosevelt and Churchill argued that Poland, an ally, must be free to choose its own government. Specifically, they sought the return of the prewar government of Poland, which had gone into exile in London during the war and was anxious to return to power in Poland.

But there was a problem. This "London government" consisted of Poles who did not hide their strong anti-Russian and anti-Communist sentiments, the result of age-old struggles between the Russians and Poles. Their animosity toward the Communist government in Moscow was so great that on the eve of the war with Germany they had refused even to consider an alliance with the Soviet Union. Stalin then made his famous deal in 1939 with Hitler whereby the two agreed to a Non-Aggression Pact,[1] by which Stalin hoped to sit out the war. As part of the bargain, Hitler offered Stalin the eastern portion of Poland, a large piece of territory that the victorious Poles had seized from a devastated Soviet state in 1921. The Polish conquest of what the Soviets considered part of their empire and the Soviets' reconquest of these lands with Hitler's complicity were but two events in the long and bloody relationship between these two peoples. In 1941, Hitler used Poland as a springboard to invade the Soviet Union and at the end of the war the Soviets returned to Poland with a powerful army once more.

Stalin understood only too well the nationalistic and bitterly anti-Russian attitudes of the Poles, particularly that of the prewar government, which had sworn eternal hostility to his government. As the Soviet soldiers moved into Poland they became targets of the Polish resistance, which took time out from fighting the Germans to deal with the invader from the east. Stalin had no difficulty understanding the nationalistic and religious divisions in Eastern Europe. He himself, an ethnic Georgian, was after all a product of the volatile ethnic mix of the old tsarist empire. He knew, as he told his Western allies at Yalta, that the Poles would be "quarrelsome."[2]

Hitler's invasion of the Soviet Union cost the Soviet Union an estimated 27 million lives. At Yalta, Stalin was determined to prevent the reestablishment of a hostile Poland along his western border. Stalin had no intentions, therefore, of permitting the London Poles to take power in Warsaw. This was a major concern Stalin repeatedly conveyed to his allies, Roosevelt and Churchill, who grudgingly accepted in principle the reality that Eastern Europe in general, and Poland in particular, had already become part and parcel of the Soviet Union's sphere of influence. To this end, even before Yalta, Stalin had created his own Polish government, with its seat in the eastern Polish city of Lublin, which consisted primarily of Communists and socialists.

Roosevelt and Churchill faced a dilemma. World War II had been fought for the noble ideals of democracy and self-determination. But in postwar Poland there would be neither. Britain, moreover, still had a treaty obligation with the London Poles.[3] Yet Stalin held the trump card: the Red Army controlled Poland.

The long disputation on the Polish question pitted the demands of Roosevelt and Churchill for self-determination against Stalin's insistence on a government answerable to Moscow. Specifically, it came down to an argument over the composition of a provisional (interim) government, with Stalin arguing for recognition of the Lublin regime as the provisional government and Roosevelt and Churchill insisting that Poland's provisional government include as many "democratic" politicians as Communist. Finally, the two sides arrived at an ambiguous agreement that papered over their broad differences. The agreement stated that the Polish government was to be "reorganized on a broader democratic basis with the inclusion of democratic leaders from Poland itself and Poles abroad."[4] It went on to say that this reorganized government was to be provisional and was to hold elections on the basis of which a permanent government would be established later. The ambiguity of the agreement allowed both sides to interpret it as they saw fit.

After the conference, Roosevelt and Churchill chose to accentuate Stalin's concession to allow "free elections" so as to claim that they had won a victory for the London Poles and for democracy at Yalta. Stalin, however, had no intention of allowing "democratic" politicians—that is, the Western-oriented and anti-Soviet London Poles—into the provisional government or of permitting them to run for office later. In any case, his definition of free elections was so narrow that the supposed promise of free elections became meaningless. When elections were finally held, the slate of candidates was restricted to "safe" political figures who posed no threat to the Soviet domination of Poland.

Stalin apparently was under the impression that the Western powers had essentially yielded at Yalta to the Soviet Union's presence in Poland and that their complaints were largely cosmetic and for domestic consumption. He thus considered the question resolved. But in Britain, and in particular the

United States, the Soviet Union's control of Poland never sat easily. After all, Stalin, in effect, violated his promise of free elections, his control of Poland was in direct conflict with the Western war aims, such as freedom and democracy, and the Red Army in Poland pushed Stalin's political and military influence toward the center of Europe.

From these events came the following arguments, which Roosevelt's Republican critics often made: (1) Roosevelt had yielded Poland (as well as the rest of Eastern Europe) to Stalin; and (2) Stalin had broken his promise at Yalta to hold free elections, and this act of infidelity precipitated the Cold War. The Democrats, stung by these charges, replied that Roosevelt had not ceded Eastern Europe to the Soviets. Geography and the fortunes of war, they contended, had been responsible for putting the Red Army into Eastern Europe, not appeasement on the part of Roosevelt or of his successor, Harry Truman, who became president upon Roosevelt's death on April 12, 1945.

## ☐ The Ghost of Munich

At this juncture the two major allies in World War II became locked into positions that were the result of their peculiar readings of the lessons of history—particularly, the "lessons of Munich." This refers to the event that many politicians and historians have considered the single most important step leading to World War II.

In the autumn of 1938, Adolf Hitler insisted that a part of western Czechoslovakia—the Sudetenland with a population of 3 million ethnic Germans—must be transferred to Germany on the basis of the principle of national self-determination, a principle ostensibly dear to the victors of World War I, who had created the sovereign state of Czechoslovakia. Germans must live in Germany, Hitler threatened, otherwise there will be war. France had a treaty of alliance with Czechoslovakia that committed France to war in case Germany attacked that country. But the French government was psychologically and militarily incapable of honoring its treaty and sought a way out to resolve the crisis Hitler's threats had created. At this point England's prime minister, Neville Chamberlain, stepped in. The result was the Munich Conference, by which the Western powers avoided war, if only for the time being, and Hitler obtained the Sudetenland. Hitler promised that this was his last demand in Eastern Europe. Chamberlain returned to London proclaiming that he had "brought peace in our time."

Events quickly showed that Hitler had lied. In March 1939, he annexed the rest of Czechoslovakia and then pressured the Poles to yield on territorial concessions. When the Poles refused to budge, the British, and later the French, determined that the time had come to take a stand and offered the Poles a treaty of alliance. Hitler then invaded Poland, and a European war was in the making.

The lessons of Munich for the West were clear. A dictator can never be satisfied. Appeasement only whets his appetite. In the words of the U.S. secretary of the navy, James Forrestal, there were "no returns on appeasement."[5] When Stalin demanded his own sphere of influence in Eastern Europe after the war, the West quickly brought up the lessons of Munich and concluded that Western acceptance of the Soviet Union's position would inevitably bring further Soviet expansion and war. Western leaders, therefore, proved to be psychologically incapable of accepting the Soviet Union's presence in Eastern Europe: there could be no business-as-usual division of the spoils of victory.

The Soviets had their own reading of these same events. To them, Munich meant the first decisive move by the capitalist West against the Soviet Union. The leaders in the Kremlin always believed that they, and not the West or Poland, were Hitler's main target. Throughout the latter half of the 1930s, the Soviet Union had repeatedly called for an alliance with the West against Germany, but the pleas had always fallen on suspicious ears. Instead, the West's deal with Hitler at Munich appeared to have deflected Hitler toward the East. In rapid order Hitler then swallowed up Czechoslovakia and a host of other East European nations, confirming the Soviet leaders' deep suspicions. By June of 1941, when Hitler launched his invasion of the Soviet Union, he was in control of all of Eastern Europe—not to mention most of the rest of Europe as well—and proceeded to turn it against the Soviet Union.

For the Soviets the lessons of Munich were obvious. Eastern Europe must not fall into the hands of hostile forces. Stalin would not tolerate the return to power of the hostile Poles in London, nor the return of the old regimes in Hungary, Romania, and Bulgaria, which had cooperated with the Nazis. No foreign power would have the opportunity to do again what Hitler had done and turn Eastern Europe against the Soviet Union. The old order of hostile states aligned with the Soviet Union's enemies must give way to a new reality that served Moscow's interests.

From the same events the two antagonists in the Cold War thus drew diametrically opposed conclusions. The Western position held that its containment of the Soviet Union and its unwillingness to legitimize the Kremlin's position in Eastern Europe kept the peace. A lack of resolve would surely have brought war. The Soviets in their turn were just as adamant in insisting that the buffer they had created in Eastern Europe kept the capitalist West at bay and preserved the security of their nation. These opposing visions of the lessons of history were at the core of the conflict between the West and the Soviet Union.

## □ Polish Borders

At Yalta, Stalin also insisted on moving Poland's borders. He demanded a return to the Soviet Union of what it had lost to the Poles in the Treaty of

**Central and Eastern Europe:**
**Territorial Changes After World War II**

Riga in 1921 (after the Poles had defeated the Red Army). At that time Lord Curzon, the British foreign secretary, had urged the stubborn Poles to accept an eastern border 125 miles to the west since that line separated more equitably the Poles from the Belorussian and Ukrainian populations of the Soviet empire. But in 1921, the victorious Poles rejected the Curzon Line and, instead, imposed their own line upon the defeated Soviets. In 1945, it became Stalin's turn to redraw the border.

To compensate the Poles for land lost on the east to the Soviet Union, Stalin moved Poland's western border about 75 miles farther west into what had been Germany, to the Oder and Western Neisse Rivers. At Yalta, Stalin sought his allies' stamp of approval for the Oder-Neisse Line but without success.

A third readjustment of Poland's border called for the division between the Soviets and the Poles of East Prussia, Germany's easternmost province. Stalin intended that East Prussia become part of the spoils of war. His reasoning was simple. The Soviet Union and Poland had suffered grief at the hands of the Germans and the peoples of both nations felt that they deserved compensation. The West reluctantly acceded to Stalin's demands.

Since 1945, the Soviets and Poles have considered the border changes at the expense of Germany as a fait accompli. Germans, however, were reluctant to accept these consequences of the war. When, after World War II, the Western powers and the Soviet Union failed to reach an agreement on the political fate of Germany, the result was the division of that nation into the U.S.-sponsored Federal Republic of Germany (commonly known as West Germany) and the Soviet creation, the Democratic Republic of Germany (or East Germany). The East German government had little choice but to accept the new German-Polish border. The West German government always insisted that it was the sole legitimate German government and that it spoke for all Germans, East and West. The original West German government of Chancellor Konrad Adenauer—the champion of German territorial integrity—bitterly opposed Soviet expansion westward and refused to accept the new, Soviet-imposed boundaries. In the late 1960s, the West German government, under the leadership of Willy Brandt, began to acknowledge that new borders existed in fact; but for more than forty years after the conclusion of the war, no West German government formally accepted the legality of the transfer of German territory. Until the reunification of Germany in 1990, it remained one of the unresolved consequences of the war.

☐  *The Japanese Issue*

The second issue at Yalta was more straightforward. The U.S. Joint Chiefs of Staff wanted the Soviet Red Army to enter the war against Japan. The

Soviets, as it turned out, needed little prodding. Stalin promised to enter the Japanese war ninety days after the end of the war in Europe. The Japanese had handed Russia a humiliating defeat in the Russo-Japanese War of 1904–1905 and took the island of Sakhalin, which had been under Russian control. In the wake of the Bolshevik Revolution of 1917 and the civil war that followed, the Japanese had invaded eastern Siberia and remained there until 1922.[6] In the 1930s, it seemed for a while as if the Soviet Union might become Japan's next target after the Japanese annexation of the northeastern Chinese region of Manchuria. In fact, in late summer 1939, the Red Army and the Japanese clashed along the Mongolian-Chinese border at Khalkin Gol. Japan's thrust southward—which ultimately brought it into conflict with the United States—and the Soviet Union's preoccupation with Nazi Germany kept the two from resuming their old rivalry. When the Soviets attacked the Japanese army in Manchuria at the very end of World War II, it marked the fourth Russo-Japanese conflict of the twentieth century. From the Soviet point of view, here was a golden opportunity to settle past scores and to regain lost territories.

## □ The UN Question

The third major topic at Yalta dealt with the organization of the United Nations. Roosevelt proposed, and Churchill and Stalin quickly accepted, the power of an absolute veto for the world's great powers, of any United Nations action they opposed. In 1919, when President Woodrow Wilson unsuccessfully proposed the U.S. entry into the League of Nations, his opponents argued that in doing so, the foreign policy of the United States would be dictated by the League. A U.S. veto would prevent such an eventuality in the new United Nations. Naturally, however, the United States could not expect to be the only nation with a veto. Roosevelt proposed that each of the "Big Five"—the United States, the Soviet Union, Great Britain, France, and China—be given the power to veto a UN action. It also meant that the United Nations could not be used against the interests of any of the big powers. The United Nations, therefore, could act only when the Big Five were in concert—and that proved to be a rare occasion. The weakness of the United Nations was thus built into its charter.

An example of what this sort of arrangement meant in practice may be seen in this exchange between Stalin and Churchill at Yalta (concerning the issue of Hong Kong, a colony Great Britain had taken from China in the nineteenth century):

Stalin:     Suppose China . . . demands Hong Kong to be returned to her?
Churchill:  I could say "no." I would have a right to say that the power of [the United Nations] could not be used against us.[7]

## ☐ The German Question

The fourth question, the immediate fate of Germany, was resolved when the Big Three decided that as a temporary expedient the territory of the Third Reich—including Austria, which Hitler had annexed in 1938—was to be divided into zones of occupation among the three participants at the Yalta Conference. Shortly, the French insisted that as an ally and a major power they, too, were entitled to an occupation zone. Stalin did not object to the inclusion of another Western, capitalist power, but he demanded that if France were to obtain a zone it must come from the holdings of the United States and Great Britain. The result was the Four-Power occupation of Germany and Austria, as well as of their respective capitals, Berlin and Vienna.

As the Big Three returned home from Yalta, they were fairly satisfied that they had gotten what they had sought. But, as events would show, Yalta had settled little. Instead, it quickly became the focal point of the Cold War. The issues under discussion at Yalta—Poland and its postwar borders, the United Nations, the Red Army's entrance into the war against Japan, and the German and Austrian questions—all became bones of contention between East and West in the months ahead.

## ■ THE POTSDAM CONFERENCE

By mid-summer 1945, with Berlin in ruins and the defeat of Japan all but a certainty, the Grand Alliance of World War II fell apart with remarkable speed. The first signs of tension had appeared upon the conclusion of the war in Europe, when both the Western powers and the Soviet Union sought to carve out spheres of influence in Eastern Europe. Whatever cooperation had existed during the war had turned into mutual suspicion. Still, the two sides were consulting with each other and they were slated to meet again in July 1945, this time for a conference in Germany at Potsdam (not far from Berlin, the bombed-out capital of Hitler's Third Reich).

The Big Three at Potsdam were Joseph Stalin, Harry Truman (who had succeeded Roosevelt in April 1945), and Winston Churchill (who later in the conference would be replaced by Britain's new premier, Clement Attlee). This meeting accomplished little. The Polish question came up at once, particularly the new border drawn at the expense of Germany, which the Western leaders reluctantly accepted. The Western leaders also grudgingly recognized the new socialist government in Poland, but they repeatedly voiced their objections to other client governments Stalin had propped up in Eastern Europe, particularly those of Romania and Bulgaria. The Soviets considered the transformation of the political picture in Eastern Europe a closed issue, comparing it to the creation of the new government in Italy under Western supervision, replacing the previous fascist government that had been an ally of Nazi Germany. The sharp exchanges at Potsdam only heightened suspicions and resolved virtually nothing.

Another source of disagreement was the issue of reparations from Germany. The Soviets insisted on $20 billion from a nation that was utterly destroyed and could not possibly pay such a huge amount. This demand would therefore mean the transfer of whatever industrial equipment Germany still possessed to the Soviet Union. Such measures would leave Germany impoverished, weak, and dependent on outside help. This scenario presented several disadvantages to the West: a helpless Germany was no physical deterrent against potential Soviet expansion westward; it might succumb to Communism; and it could become neither an exporter of the goods it produced nor an importer of U.S. goods. Moreover, the United States was already contemplating economic aid to Germany, and thus the Soviet demand meant that U.S. money and equipment would simply pass through Germany to the Soviet Union as reparations.

The Soviets insisted that at the Yalta Conference in February 1945 their allies had promised them the large sum of $20 billion. U.S. representatives replied that this figure was intended to be the basis of discussion depending upon conditions in Germany after the war. The devastation of Germany at the very end of the war, therefore, meant that the Soviets would have to settle for far less.

To Truman the solution was simple. He would exclude the Soviets from the Western zones of occupation, leaving the Soviets to find whatever reparations they could come up with in their Eastern zone. They did so by plundering the eastern part of Germany. The reparations question marked the first instance of the inability of the wartime allies to come to an agreement on how to govern Germany. It established the principle that in each zone of occupation the military commander would have free reign. As such, the occupation powers never came up with a unified policy for Germany. The main consequence of this was the long-enduring division of Germany. Within three years there was no point in pretending that a single German state existed.

The only thing on which Truman and Stalin seemed to agree at Potsdam was their position on Japan. Neither, it seems, was willing to let the Japanese off the hook. Surrender could only be unconditional. While at Potsdam, Truman was notified that the first atomic bomb had been successfully tested at Alamogordo, New Mexico. Truman knew of Japanese efforts to end the war, but with the atomic bomb he could now end the conflict on his own terms and keep the Soviet Union out of postwar Japan. Stalin, for his part, did not want a quick Japanese surrender. At Yalta he had pledged to come into the war with Japan ninety days after the war against Germany had ended, and he had every intention of doing so. It would give him the chance to settle old scores with the Japanese and to extend his influence in the Far East. Truman did not tell Stalin about the atomic bomb

President Harry S. Truman and General Dwight Eisenhower, January 1951. Two years later, the general would succeed Truman as president. *(National Archives)*

and his plans to use it against Japan. He was led to believe that Truman still wanted the Soviet Union to attack Japan. With the United States secretly planning to drop atomic bombs on Japan and Stalin secretly planning to attack its forces in Manchuria, there was apparently no way out for the Japanese.

The defeat of Japan, however, brought no improvement in East-West relations. Both sides constantly voiced their grievances and suspicions of each other. The U.S. bombing of Hiroshima and Nagasaki gave the Soviets still more reason to distrust and suspect the intentions of the United States. Each point of disagreement was magnified, each misunderstanding became a weapon; each hostile act was positive proof of the other side's evil intentions. But one could not yet speak of a full-blown, irreversible Cold War. This came in 1947, when the conflict reached a new plateau. In fact, many historians, in the Soviet Union as well as in the West, see that year as the true beginning of the Cold War. It was then that the United States declared its commitment to contain—by economic as well as military means—all manifestations of Communist expansion wherever it occurred. In the same year a Soviet delegation walked out of an economic conference that concerned itself with the rebuilding of Europe. With this act all East-West cooperation came to an end and the battle lines were clearly drawn.

## ■ THE TRUMAN DOCTRINE

"The turning point in American foreign policy," in the words of President Truman, came early in 1947 when the United States was faced with the prospect of a Communist victory in a civil war in Greece.[8] The end of World War II had not brought peace to Greece. Instead, it saw the continuation of a bitter conflict between the right and the left, one which in early 1947 promised a Communist victory. The British, who for a long time had played a significant role in Greek affairs, had supported the right (the Greek monarchy), but they were determined to end their involvement in Greece. The British, exhausted by the war, could not go on. Unceremoniously, they dumped the problem into Truman's lap: If the United States wanted a non-Communist government in Greece, it would have to see to it and it would have to go it alone. Truman, a man seldom plagued by self-doubt, quickly jumped into the breach. But he also understood that the U.S. public would be slow to back such an undertaking. At the end of World War II, the U.S. public had expected that within two years the U.S. military presence in Europe would end. Truman's involvement in Greece would extend it and postpone the U.S. disengagement from Europe indefinitely. In fact, it meant an increased, continued U.S. presence in Europe. To achieve his aim, Truman knew he would have to "scare the hell out of the American people."[9] And he succeeded admirably.

In March 1947, Truman addressed a joint session of Congress to present his case. In his oration, one of the most stirring Cold War speeches by a U.S. political leader, Truman expounded his views: the war in Greece was not a matter between Greeks; rather, it was caused by outside aggression. International Communism was on the march and the orders came from its center, Moscow. It was the duty of the United States "to support free peoples who are resisting attempted subjugation by armed minorities or by outside pressures." The United States must play the role of the champion of democracy and "orderly political processes."[10] Truman argued that there was even more at stake here than the upholding of political and moral principles. A Communist victory in Greece threatened to set off similar events in other countries, like a long chain of dominoes. "If Greece should fall under the control of an armed minority, the effect upon its neighbor, Turkey, would be immediate and serious. Confusion and disorder might well spread throughout the entire Middle East."[11] This speech, which became known as the Truman Doctrine, firmly set U.S. foreign policy on a path committed to suppressing radicalism and revolution throughout the world.

But there was no clear evidence that the guiding hand of Stalin was behind the Greek revolution. Stalin, it seems, kept his part of the bargain made with Churchill in October 1944, by which the two agreed that after the war Greece would fall into Britain's sphere of influence. Churchill later wrote that Stalin adhered to this understanding.[12] If anything, Stalin wanted the Greek revolt to "fold up . . . as quickly as possible" because he feared precisely what ultimately happened.[13] He told the Yugoslav vice president, Milovan Djilas: "What do you think? That . . . the United States, the most powerful state in the world will permit you to break their line of communications in the Mediterranean Sea? Nonsense, and we have no navy."[14] But to Truman and most of the U.S. public it was a simple matter: all revolutions in the name of Karl Marx must necessarily come out of Moscow.[15] The Republican Party, not to be left behind in the holy struggle against "godless Communism," quickly backed Truman. Thus, a national consensus was forged, one which remained intact until the divisive years of the Vietnam War.

The first application of the Truman Doctrine worked remarkably well. U.S. military and economic aid rapidly turned the tide in Greece; the Communists were defeated and the monarchy was spared. And this was achieved without sending U.S. troops into combat. There appeared to be no limits to U.S. power. This truly appeared to be, as Henry Luce, the influential publisher of *Time* and *Life* had said earlier, the "American Century."[16] Yet, at about the same time, events in China showed that there were in fact limits on the ability of the United States to affect the course of history, when the position of the U.S.-supported government there began to unravel.

# ■ THE MARSHALL PLAN

Three months after the pronouncement of the Truman Doctrine, the United States took another step to protect its interests in Europe when the Truman administration unveiled the Marshall Plan, named after General George Marshall, Truman's secretary of state, who first proposed the program. The program was intended to provide funds for the rebuilding of the heavily damaged economies of Europe. The Marshall Plan was in large part a humanitarian gesture for which many Europeans expressed their gratitude. Because of it, the United States was able to draw on a residue of goodwill for decades after the war. The Marshall Plan was also intended as a means to preserve the prosperity the war had brought to U.S. society. At the very end of the war, the United States had taken the lead in establishing an international system of "free trade" or at least relatively unrestricted trade. But international commerce demanded a strong and prosperous Europe. The United States proved to be extremely successful in shoring up the financial system of the Western, capitalist world. In this sense, the Marshall Plan became a potent political weapon in the containment of Soviet influence.[17] It well complemented the Truman Doctrine. The Marshall Plan, Truman explained, was but "the other half of the same walnut."[18]

The United States was willing to extend Marshall Plan aid to Eastern Europe, including the Soviet Union, but not without a condition. The money would have to be administered there, as in Western Europe, by the United States, not by its recipients. Several Eastern European states were receptive to the plan, particularly Czechoslovakia, which was governed by a coalition of Communist and non-Communist parties. The Soviet Union, too, at first appeared to be ready to participate in the rebuilding of Europe under the auspices of the Marshall Plan.[19] Its foreign minister, Viacheslav Molotov, came to Paris with a large entourage of economic experts to discuss the implementation of the plan. But shortly afterward, he left the conference declaring that the Marshall Plan was unacceptable to the Soviet Union since its implementation would entail the presence of U.S. officials on East European and Soviet soil and would, therefore, infringe upon his country's national sovereignty. Molotov did not say publicly that the presence of U.S. representatives in Eastern Europe would reveal the glaring weaknesses of the Soviet Union and its satellites. The Marshall Plan was a gamble Stalin apparently felt he could not afford. Stalin then pressured the governments of Poland and Czechoslovakia to reject the Marshall Plan.

Stalin went beyond merely applying pressure on Czechoslovakia. In February 1948, a Communist coup in that country ended the coalition government and brought Czechoslovakia firmly into the Soviet orbit. This act regenerated in the West the image of an aggressive, brutal, and calculating leadership in Moscow. The Communist coup in Czechoslovakia, only ten years after Hitler had taken the first steps to bring that nation under his heel, did much to underscore in the West the lessons of Munich.[20] The coup had a deep impact on public opinion in the West and it became prima facie evidence that one could not do business with the Soviets.

Stalin's rejection of Marshall Plan aid also meant that the East European countries would have to rebuild their war-torn economies with their own limited resources and without U.S. aid and Western technology. In fact, Stalin's economic recovery program for Eastern Europe was exploitative since it favored the Soviet Union. As Churchill had remarked in his speech in Fulton, Missouri, in 1946, an "Iron Curtain" had descended across Europe from Stettin on the Baltic Sea to Trieste on the Adriatic Sea.

## ■ LIMITS OF SOVIET POWER

Yet, immediately after Stalin appeared to have consolidated his position in Eastern Europe, the first crack appeared in what had been a monolithic facade. The Yugoslav Communist leadership, under the direction of Joseph Tito, broke with the Kremlin over the fundamental question of national sovereignty. Moscow insisted that the interests of a foreign Communist party must be subordinate to those of the Soviet Union, officially the center of an international movement. The Yugoslavs insisted, however, on running their own affairs as they saw fit. In the summer of 1948, the bitter quarrel

Berlin children on rubble mounds cheer the arrival of a U.S. aircraft filled with food during the airlift, 1948. *(German Information Center)*

became public. Tito refused to subordinate the interests of his state to those of Stalin and the result was the first Communist nation in Eastern Europe to assert its independence from the Soviet Union.

Stalin contended that "Titoism" (that is, a nationalist deviation from the international Communist community) was no isolated phenomenon. Other East European nations could readily fall to the same temptation. In order to forestall such an eventuality, Stalin launched a bloody purge of East European "National Communists." The purge was so thorough that until Stalin's death in March 1953, Eastern Europe remained quiet. The prevailing—and, as events later showed, incorrect—view in the West was that Titoism had proven to be an isolated incident.

In 1948, it also became evident that the division of Germany and Berlin would become permanent. All talks on German reunification had broken down, and the West began to take steps to create a separate West German state, with West Berlin, a city 110 miles inside the Soviet sector, becoming a part of West Germany. When the Soviets had agreed on the division of Berlin among the allies, Stalin had not bargained on such an eventuality. The last thing he wanted was a Western outpost inside his zone. Berlin had little military value for the West since it was trapped and outgunned by the Soviet Red Army which occupied East Germany. But it served as a valuable political, capitalist spearhead pointing into Eastern

Europe. Moreover, West Berlin was invaluable as a center of espionage operations. In June 1948, Stalin took a dangerous, calculated risk to eliminate the Western presence in that city. He closed the land routes into West Berlin in the hope of convincing the West to abandon Berlin. The West had few options. It wanted neither World War III nor the abandonment of West Berlin and its 2 million people to the Communists. The result was the "Berlin Airlift," by which the West resupplied West Berlin by transport planes flying over East Germany. During the next ten months over 270,000 flights were made, carrying an average of 4,000 tons a day to the beleaguered city. Stalin dared not attack the planes for he would not risk World War III either. Finally, in May 1949, Stalin yielded by reopening the highways linking the city once again with West Germany. Stalin had lost his gamble and there was no point in perpetuating the showdown. This crisis, which had brought both sides to the edge of war, was over if only for the time being.

Throughout the late 1940s, the U.S. assumption was that the Soviet Union was preparing for an attack on Western Europe, an assumption based largely on fear rather than on fact. The image of an expansionist, aggressive Soviet Union was the result of three conditions. First, the Red Army had pushed into the center of Europe during the war. Second, in the West, this act was regarded not so much as the logical consequence of the war but as the fulfillment of Soviet propaganda stressing the triumph of socialism throughout the world. Third, the differences of opinion between the Soviet Union and the West quickly took on the character of a military confrontation, and people began to fear the worst.

Once the specter of an inevitably expansionist Soviet state gripped the Western imagination, it became almost impossible to shake this image. This view of Soviet intentions buttressed the U.S. arguments that the Soviet Union must be contained at all cost. The "containment theory," first spelled out in 1947 in a lengthy essay by George Kennan, a State Department expert on the Soviet Union, seemed to be working reasonably well with the application of the Truman Doctrine and the Marshall Plan. But Kennan never made clear the nature of the containment of the Soviet Union he had in mind. Later, he insisted that he had meant the political, and not the military, containment of the Soviet Union. Yet, the central feature of Truman's containment policy was its military nature. In 1949, the United States created NATO, the North Atlantic Treaty Organization, an alliance that boxed in the Soviet Union along its western flank. One person's containment theory is another person's capitalist encirclement. Stalin responded by digging in.

## ■ RECOMMENDED READINGS

Andrzejewski, Jerzy. *Ashes and Diamonds.* London: Weidenfeld and Nicholson [orig. 1948], 1965.

The classic novel on life in Poland at the very end of World War II.

Clemens, Diane Shaver. *Yalta.* New York: Oxford University Press, 1970.

The best monograph on the Yalta Conference, which sees Yalta not as an ideological confrontation but an exercise in horse-trading.

de Zayas, Alfred M. *Nemesis at Potsdam: The Anglo-Americans and the Expulsion of the Germans: Background, Execution, Consequences.* 2d rev. ed. London: Routledge and Kegan Paul, 1979.

Focuses on the refugee problem after the war, a topic generally ignored in Cold War histories.

Fleming, D. F. *The Cold War and Its Origins, 1917–1960.* 2 vols. Garden City: Doubleday, 1961.

By one of the first practitioners of the revisionist school of history of the Cold War.

Halle, Louis J. *The Cold War as History.* New York: Harper and Row, 1967.

One of the few books on the Cold War that puts it into a historical perspective.

Ulam, Adam B. *The Rivals: America and Russia Since World War II.* New York: Viking, 1971.

Discusses the first phase of the East-West confrontation.

Ulam, Adam B. *Expansion and Coexistence: Soviet Foreign Policy, 1917–1973.* 2d ed. New York: Frederick A. Praeger, 1974.

A useful treatment of Soviet foreign policy.

Volkogonov, Dmitri. *Stalin: Triumph and Tragedy.* Rocklin, Calif.: Prima Publishing, 1991.

The product of Gorbachev's "new thinking" and glasnost, a critical reassessment of the reign of Stalin.

## ■ NOTES

1. Often called the Molotov-Ribbentrop Pact, after the foreign minister of Nazi Germany, Joachim Ribbentrop, and the Soviet Union's commissar for foreign affairs, Viacheslav Molotov, who worked out the details of the arrangement.

2. Winston S. Churchill, *The Second World War, VI, Triumph and Tragedy* (New York: Bantam, [orig. 1953] 1962), p. 329.

3. The treaty with the Polish government in London consisted of an obligation on the part of Britain to defend its ally only against Germany, not the Soviet Union, a point the British government stressed in April 1945, when it released a secret protocol of the 1939 treaty. With this release, Britain's legal obligation to the Polish government came to an end. But there was still the moral duty to defend a former ally against the aspirations of a totalitarian ally of convenience.

4. Quoted from "The Yalta Declaration on Poland," as found in U.S. Department of State, *Foreign Relations of the United States: The Conferences at Malta and Yalta, 1945* (Washington, D.C.: U.S. Government Printing Office, 1955), p. 938.

5. Quoted from a cabinet meeting of September 21, 1945, in Walter Millis, ed., *The Forrestal Diaries* (New York: Viking, 1951), p. 96.

6. The U.S. president, Woodrow Wilson, also sent troops into eastern Siberia at that time, ostensibly to keep an eye on the Japanese. Earlier, at the end of World War I, Wilson had sent troops into European Russia, ostensibly to protect supplies that had been sent to the Russian ally—led at the time by Tsar Nicholas II—to keep them from falling into German hands. The Soviets have always rejected this explanation and have argued that U.S. intentions were to overthrow the fledgling Communist government.

7. James F. Byrnes, *Frankly Speaking* (New York: Harper and Brothers, 1947), p. 37.

8. Harry S. Truman, *Memoirs, II, Years of Trial and Hope* (Garden City: Doubleday, 1956), p. 106.

9. The words are Senator Arthur Vandenberg's, cited in William A. Williams, *The Tragedy of American Diplomacy*, rev. ed. (New York: Delta, 1962), pp. 269–270.

10. "Text of President Truman's Speech on New Foreign Policy," *New York Times*, March 13, 1947, p. 2.

11. Ibid.

12. Churchill's report to the House of Commons, February 27, 1945, in which he stated that he "was encouraged by Stalin's behavior about Greece." *The Second World War, VI*, p. 334. In his "Iron Curtain" telegram to Truman, May 12, 1945, Churchill expressed concern about Soviet influence throughout Eastern Europe, "except Greece"; Lord Moran, *Churchill: Taken from the Diaries of Lord Moran, The Struggle for Survival, 1940–1965* (Boston: Houghton Mifflin, 1966), p. 847. Churchill to the House of Commons, January 23, 1948, on Greece: "Agreements were kept [by Stalin] when they were made." Robert Rhodes James, *Winston S. Churchill: His Complete Speeches, 1897–1963, VII, 1943–1949* (New York: Chelsea House, 1974), p. 7583.

13. Milovan Djilas, *Conversations with Stalin* (New York: Harcourt, Brace and World, 1962), pp. 181–182.

14. Ibid., p. 182.

15. After World War II, the most militant Communist head of state was Joseph Tito of Yugoslavia. It was Tito, rather than Stalin, who openly supported the Greek Communist insurgency by providing them weapons and refuge in Yugoslavia. Tito's actions were seen in the West as evidence of Stalin's involvement via a proxy; yet even Tito, once he broke with Stalin in 1948, shut his border to the Greek Communists and abandoned them.

16. Henry Luce, "American Century," in W. A. Swanberg, *Luce and His Empire* (New York: Dell, 1972), pp. 257–261.

17. The political move to the left in Western Europe after World War II had in fact largely burned itself out by 1947, at the time the Truman administration proposed the Marshall Plan. The Soviet Union's influence in Western Europe was dependent on the strength of the Communist parties. After initial strong showings, particularly in France and Italy, the Communist parties' fortunes declined. The Marshall Plan then helped to accelerate the swing to the right.

18. Quoted in Walter LaFeber, *America, Russia, and the Cold War, 1945–1984*, 5th ed. (New York: Knopf, 1985), pp. 62–63.

19. At the end of World War II, after the U.S. wartime Lend-Lease Program to the Soviet Union had come to an end, Moscow had applied for economic assistance from the United States, but nothing came of it. Lend-Lease, a massive wartime assistance program to U.S. allies, provided the Soviet Union with $11 billion in aid. Subsequent U.S. aid to the Soviet Union, however, was dependent upon proper Soviet behavior in Eastern Europe.

20. During the coup, Czechoslovakia's foreign minister, Jan Masaryk, was probably murdered under mysterious circumstances, an act generally attributed in the West to Stalin.

# 3

## The Cold War in Asia: A Change of Venue

The Cold War, which had its origins in Europe where tensions mounted between East and West over the status of Germany, Poland, and other Eastern European countries, became even more inflamed in Asia. In 1945, U.S. policy in East Asia was focused primarily on the elimination of the menace of Japanese militarism and on support of the Nationalist government of China under Jiang Jieshi (Chiang Kai-shek)[1] as the main pillar of stability in Asia. But within five short years the United States was confronted with a set of affairs very different from what Washington had envisioned just after the war.

The Nationalist regime in China was defeated by the Chinese Communists who, under the leadership of Chairman Mao Zedong (Mao Tse-tung), proclaimed the founding of the People's Republic of China on October 1, 1949. The largest nation on earth was now under Communist rule. Only nine months later the Communist forces of North Korea invaded the U.S.-supported, anti-Communist regime in South Korea, and in the Korean War, for the first time, the rivals of the Cold War, East and West, clashed in the field of battle. These two major events had a profound effect on the U.S.-led military occupation of defeated Japan, which had begun immediately after Japan's surrender. All three of these interrelated events developed in the context of the Cold War and contributed toward making Cold War tensions ever more dangerous in this area of the world. The contention between East and West, evident from the very outset of the military occupation of defeated Japan in 1945, hardened by the early 1950s.

### ■ THE ALLIED OCCUPATION OF JAPAN

The Allied Occupation of Japan, which lasted almost seven years (from September 1945 to May 1952), is unique in the annals of history, for, as the historian Edwin Reischauer says, "Never before had one advanced nation

50

attempted to reform the supposed faults of another advanced nation from within. And never did the military occupation of one world power by another prove so satisfactory to the victors and tolerable to the vanquished."[2] From the outset, the U.S. policy in Japan was benevolent and constructive, although it also had its punitive aspects as well. The Japanese, who had never in their long history been defeated and garrisoned by foreign troops, expected the worst. Not only did their fears of U.S. brutality prove unfounded, but so also did U.S. fears of continued hostility by Japanese diehards. The two nations, which had fought each other so bitterly for almost four years, made amends, and in a remarkably short time they established enduring bonds of friendship and cooperation. This was partly the result of the generous treatment by the U.S. occupation forces, and partly the result of the receptivity and goodwill of the Japanese themselves. They welcomed the opportunity to rid themselves of the scourge of militarism that had led their nation into the blind alley of defeat and destruction. And they appreciated the sight of U.S. GIs brandishing not rifles, but chocolate bars and chewing gum. Even more important for securing the active support of the Japanese was the decision by U.S. authorities to retain the emperor on the throne rather than try him as a war criminal, as many in the United States had demanded. Indeed, one important reason why the Japanese were so docile and cooperative with the U.S. occupation forces was that their emperor, whom they were in the habit of dutifully obeying, had implored them to be cooperative.

Prior to the defeat of Japan, officials in Washington were already planning a reform program to be implemented under a military occupation. The Allied Occupation of Japan was, as the name implies, supposedly an Allied affair, but it was in fact dominated by the United States, despite the desire of the Soviet Union and other nations to play a larger role in it. General Douglas MacArthur was appointed Supreme Commander of Allied Powers (SCAP), and under his authority a broad-ranging reform program was imposed on Japan. The government of Japan was not abolished and replaced by a military administration as was the case in defeated Germany; rather, the Japanese cabinet was maintained as the instrument by which the reform directives of SCAP were administered. Also, unlike the case of Germany, Japan was not divided into separate occupation zones, largely because of the insistence of the United States on denying the Soviet Union its own occupation zone in Japan.

The principal objectives of the U.S.-controlled occupation program were demilitarization and democratization. Demilitarization was attended to first and was attained promptly. Japan's army and navy were abolished, its military personnel brought home from overseas and dismissed, its war plants dismantled, and its weapons destroyed. Some 3 million Japanese soldiers were repatriated to Japan from all over Asia and the Pacific mainly by U.S. ships, as were almost as many Japanese civilians. Also, as a measure

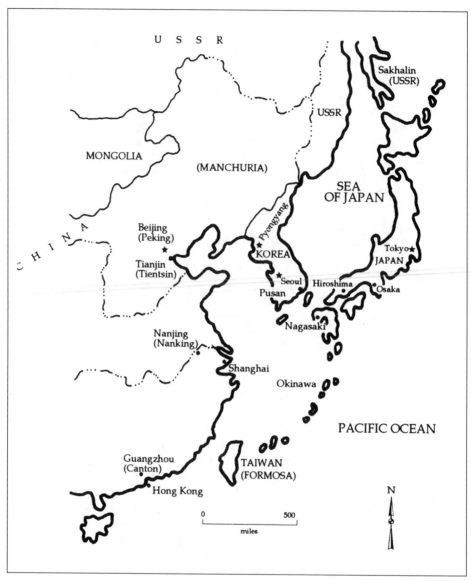

**East Asia (1945)**

to rid Japan of militarism, Japanese wartime leaders were put on trial at an international military tribunal in Tokyo. In court proceedings similar to the Nuremberg trials of Nazi war criminals, twenty-eight leading figures were accused of "planning a war of aggression" and "crimes against humanity," found guilty, and given severe sentences. Seven were sentenced to death and seventeen were sentenced to prison for life. Additionally, several thousand other Japanese military officers were tried and found guilty of a variety of wartime atrocities.

The occupation reformers also sought to rid Japan of its ultranationalist ideology, often referred to as emperor worship. On New Year's Day 1946, the emperor was called upon to make a radio speech to the nation renouncing imperial divinity. Steps were also taken to abolish "State Shinto," the aspect of the religion native to Japan that promoted the belief in the divine descent of Japan's imperial ruler. Textbooks were censored to rid them of such ideas and other content considered militaristic.

Democratization of Japan was a more complex matter and would take longer to achieve, but the first major step in that direction was taken with the writing of a new constitution for Japan in 1947. The new constitution, which was actually drafted by MacArthur's staff, provided for a fundamental political reform. It provided Japan with a parliamentary system similar to that of Britain, and consistent with Japan's own prewar political experience. The people of Japan were made sovereign (meaning, in effect, that government power ultimately rested on the consent of the governed, the people). The emperor, who had been sovereign in the old constitution, became no more than a symbol of the state, which is to say, he would no longer have any political authority. All laws were to be passed by a majority in the popularly elected House of Representatives in the Diet (Japan's parliament). The 1947 constitution also included extensive Bill of Rights provisions spelling out the civil rights of Japanese citizens in great detail. The most striking feature of the new constitution—one in keeping with the demilitarization objective—was Article Nine, which outlawed war and forbade Japan to maintain land, sea, or air forces. MacArthur himself ordered that this provision be put into the constitution, but the idea was enthusiastically endorsed by the political leaders and the common people of war-weary Japan.

As the occupation continued under the watchful eye of MacArthur, a host of other reforms were imposed upon the Japanese. The economic reforms included the dismantling of the old *zaibatsu* (the huge financial cartels that dominated Japan's prewar economy), a land reform that redistributed farmland for the benefit of poor farmers and at the expense of wealthy landowners, and a labor reform creating Japan's first genuine trade union movement. There were also far-reaching social and educational reforms, all of which were intended to make Japan a more democratic society. Generally, these various reform programs were remarkably successful, largely because they addressed real needs in Japan and because the Japanese themselves desired the reforms. Indeed, the Japanese genuinely rejected past militarism and wholeheartedly embraced the new democracy.

One of the anomalies of the occupation is that democracy was being implanted in Japan by a military command, that is, by General MacArthur and his staff. SCAP's mode of operation was military. It censored the Japanese press, disallowing free speech, and it ruled by fiat, its directives to the Japanese government not being arrived at by democratic means. Also anomalous was the character of General MacArthur as a reformer. In Japan he was aloof, arrogant, and almighty. The defeated Japanese seemed to need an august authority figure, and the imperious MacArthur seemed destined to play just such a role. Although he claimed to like the Japanese people, his manner toward them was condescending, and he often expressed contempt for their culture. In his view, the Japanese were but twelve-year-old children who must be shown the way from "feudalism" to democracy.[3] But despite MacArthur's arrogance and the military cast of the occupation, he and his staff possessed a genuine reformist zeal, and their sense of mission contributed greatly toward the successful rooting of democratic ideas and institutions in Japan.

The menace of Japanese militarism was thus eliminated and supplanted by democracy, but U.S. minds soon perceived a larger menace looming on the Eastern horizon: the spread of Communism in Asia. The Communist victory in the civil war in China in 1949, and Communist aggression in Korea in the following year, caused the U.S. government to recast its policy in Japan reflecting Cold War exigencies. Safely under U.S. control, Japan was to be prepared to play a key role in the U.S. policy of containment of Communism.

It is difficult to arrive at a final assessment of the occupation of Japan, for opinions differ greatly according to one's ideology and nationality. That the occupation program, with its various reforms, was in every instance a grand success is certainly debatable. Many Japanese historians as well as revisionist historians in the United States argue that the U.S. exercise of power in postwar Japan was excessive, that the "reverse course" policies (see p. 73) negated the democratic reforms, and that Japan was victimized by zealous U.S. anti-Communist policies. But there is little question that Japan emerged from the experience with a working democratic system of government and a more democratic society, a passionate pacifism, the beginnings of an economic recovery, and a large measure of military security. And the United States emerged with a new, potentially strong ally strategically located in a part of the world confronted with the spread of Communist revolution.

## ■ THE CIVIL WAR IN CHINA

The victory of the Chinese Communists over the Nationalist government of China in 1949 was the culmination of a long struggle between two revolutionary parties—the Communists and the Nationalists—that began back in the 1920s. After winning the first round of that struggle and coming to power in 1928, the Nationalist Party, under its domineering leader Jiang Jieshi (Chiang Kai-shek), sought to exterminate the rural-based Communist Party led by Mao Zedong. In 1935, the Communists barely escaped annihilation by embarking on the epic "Long March," a trek of over 6,000 miles, after which they secured themselves in a remote area in northwest China. When the war with Japan began in mid-1937, Mao persuaded Jiang to set aside their differences and form a united front for the purpose of defending China from the Japanese invaders. During the war against Japan (1937–1945), the Chinese Communist Party (CCP) and its army grew enormously while the Nationalist regime deteriorated badly. The Communists' success was the product of inspired leadership, effective mobilization of the peasantry for the war effort, and skillful use of guerrilla warfare tactics against the Japanese. By the end of the war the Communists controlled nineteen "liberated areas," rural regions mainly in northern China, with a combined population of about 100 million, and the size of their army had increased tenfold from about 50,000 to over half a million. In contrast, the Nationalist government and army retreated deep into the interior to Chungking during the war and failed to launch a successful counteroffensive against the Japanese. Meanwhile, wartime inflation became rampant, as did corruption within Jiang's Nationalist government and army. Growing political oppression was met by growing public discontent and declining morale. The Nationalist Army, supplied and trained by the United States, was hardly used against the Japanese, but rather was deployed to guard against the spread of Communist forces or languished in garrison duty. Thus, military morale sank as well.

When World War II ended with the U.S. defeat of Japan, civil war within China was all but a certainty as the two rivals, Nationalists and Communists, rushed to fill the vacuum created by the defeated Japanese. Both sought to expand their areas of control and particularly went after the major cities in northern China. Jiang issued orders, sanctioned by the United States, that Japanese commanders were to surrender only to Nationalist military officers rather than turn over areas under their control to the Communists. Moreover, the United States landed some 53,000 marines to take and hold several key cities in northern China until the Nationalist forces arrived.

While the United States continued to support Jiang's government as it had during the war, it wished to avert the impending civil war and thus urged Jiang Jieshi to find a peaceful solution to his conflict with the Communists. Before World War II had ended, Washington had sent a special envoy, Patrick Hurley, to China to serve as a mediator between the two sides. He was successful only in bringing the rivals Mao and Jiang to the negotiating table in August 1945, but not in finding a solution to their feud. After his efforts ended in failure, President Truman sent General George C. Marshall to China in December 1945 to mediate the dispute. Despite Marshall's initial success in getting the two sides to agree—on paper at least—to an immediate cease-fire and to a formula for mutual military demobilization and political cooperation, he too ultimately failed as the conflict escalated into a full-fledged civil war in the spring of 1946. The U.S. efforts to mediate between the CCP and Jiang's regime were destined to failure largely because Jiang refused to share power with the Communists. Essentially, Mao demanded the formation of a coalition government, followed by the mutual reduction and integration of Communist and Nationalist military forces, whereas Jiang insisted on the reduction of Communist forces and their integration into the Nationalist Army as the precondition for sharing power with the Communists. The U.S. position as mediator was weakened by its lack of neutrality, for continued U.S. military and economic aid to the Nationalists served to alienate the Communists. However, the civil war that the United States had tried so hard to prevent was not initiated by Mao, but rather by Jiang, who was convinced that the only solution to the problem was a military one and that it was obtainable.

At the outset of the Chinese civil war, the Nationalists had good reason to be confident of victory. Despite Communist gains, the Nationalist Army still had a numerical superiority of three to one over the Communist forces. The Nationalist Army was much better equipped, having received huge amounts of U.S. military aid, including artillery pieces, tanks, and trucks, as well as light arms and ammunition. Moreover, the Nationalists benefited by having the use of U.S. airplanes and troop ships for the movement of their forces. In contrast, the Communist army, reorganized as the People's

Mao Zedong (Mao Tse-tung), chairman of the Chinese Communist Party, October 1, 1950, the first anniversary of the founding of the People's Republic of China. *(National Archives)*

Liberation Army (PLA), was relatively poorly equipped and had practically no outside support. Given the Nationalist edge, it is not surprising that Jiang's armies were victorious in the early months of the war, defeating the PLA in almost every battle in northern China. But within a year of fighting the tide began to shift.

The battle for China took place mainly in Manchuria, the northeastern area of China, which had been under Japanese control since the early 1930s. It was prized by both sides for its rich resources and as the most industrialized area of China (thanks to the Japanese and to the earlier imperialist presence of Russia). Immediately after World War II, Manchuria was temporarily under the control of the Soviet Union, whose Red Army had attacked the Japanese forces there in the closing days of the war and "liberated" the area. On August 14, 1945, the Soviet Union concluded with the Nationalist government of China a treaty of friendship, which included provisions for the withdrawal of Soviet forces from Manchuria to be completed within three months after the surrender of Japan. Before the Nationalists could occupy the area with their forces, the Soviet Red Army hastily stripped Manchuria of all the Japanese military and industrial equipment it could find and shipped it—together with Japanese prisoners of war—into the Soviet Union in order to support its own economic rehabilitation. Meanwhile, Chinese Communist forces had begun entering Manchuria immediately after the surrender of Japan. A poorly equipped PLA force of about 100,000 troops was rapidly deployed in rural areas surrounding the major cities of Manchuria. Jiang was determined to maintain Nationalist military control of Manchuria, and he decided—against the advice of his U.S. military advisers—to position his best armies in that remote area, where they could be supported or reinforced only with great difficulty. Thus, when the battle for Manchuria began, Jiang's Nationalist forces held the major cities, railways, and other strategic points, while the PLA held the surrounding countryside. The Chinese Communists were not assisted by the Soviet Red Army in Manchuria (or elsewhere), but before the Soviets left Manchuria they did provide the PLA with a much-needed cache of captured Japanese weapons (mainly light arms—rifles, machine guns, light artillery, and ammunition).

In the major battles in Manchuria in late 1947 and 1948, the Chinese Communists were big winners. Not only did the Nationalist Army suffer great combat casualties, running into the hundreds of thousands, but it lost almost as many soldiers to the other side either as captives or defectors. Moreover, the PLA captured large amounts of U.S. weapons from the retreating Nationalist Army. The Communist forces, which were better disciplined and had stronger morale, used their mobility to advantage, since they were not merely trying to hold territory as were the Nationalists. In the end, it was they, not the Nationalists, who took the offensive. With their greater maneuverability they were able to control the time and place of battle and to inflict great losses on their less mobile enemy. The Nationalists, on the other hand, had spread their forces too thin to maintain defensive positions and were unable to hold open the transportation lines needed to bring up reinforcements and supplies.

After the last battle in Manchuria, the momentum in the civil war shifted to the Communists. The last major engagement of the war was fought in the fall of 1948 at Xuzhou (Hsuchow), about a hundred miles north of the Nationalist capital of Nanjing (Nanking). In this decisive battle Jiang deployed 400,000 of his best troops, equipped with tanks and heavy artillery. But after two months of fighting, in which the Nationalists lost 200,000 men, the larger and more mobile Communist army won a decisive victory. From that point it was only a matter of time before the Nationalist collapse. During the spring and summer of 1949, Jiang's forces were rapidly retreating south in disarray, and in October Jiang fled with the remainder of his army to the Chinese island of Taiwan. There the embattled Nationalist leader continued to claim that his Nationalist regime (formally titled the Republic of China) was the only legitimate government of China, and he promised to return to the mainland with his forces to drive off the "Communist bandits." In the meantime, on October 1, 1949, Mao Zedong and his victorious Communist Party proclaimed the founding of the People's Republic of China (PRC) with Beijing (Peking) as its capital.

The Chinese civil war, however, was not entirely over, but instead became a part of the global Cold War. The new Communist government in Beijing insisted it would never rest until its rival on Taiwan was completely defeated; conversely, the Nationalist government was determined never to submit to the Communists. The continued existence of "two Chinas," each intent on destroying the other and each allied to one of the superpowers, would remain the major Cold War issue and source of tension in East Asia for the next three decades.

The outcome of the Chinese civil war was the product of many factors, but direct outside intervention was not one of them. Neither of the superpowers, nor any other nation, became engaged militarily in the conflict once it began in 1946. By that time the United States had pulled its troops out of China. Nor was indirect foreign assistance a major factor in determining the outcome of the conflict. If military aid had been a major factor, the Nationalists surely should have won, for the United States provided them far more assistance, military and otherwise, during and after World War II than the Soviet Union provided the Chinese Communists. The United States had provided Nationalist China with a massive amount of military and economic aid since 1941, amounting to more than $2 billion.[4]

The postwar policy of the Soviet Union toward Nationalist China was ambivalent, as was its attitude toward the Chinese Communists. It is noteworthy that at the end of World War II Stalin signed a treaty with the Nationalist government of China and publicly recognized Jiang's rulership of China. The Soviet Red Army did little to deter the takeover of Manchuria by Jiang's Nationalist Army, and it withdrew from Manchuria not long after the date to which the two sides had agreed.[5] The Soviet Union's looting of Manchuria for "war booty" was of benefit to neither of the combatants in China and was objectionable to both. Moreover, Stalin made no real effort to support or encourage the Chinese Communists in their bid for power in China, except for turning over the cache of Japanese arms in Manchuria. On the contrary, Stalin is known to have stated in 1948, when the victory of the Chinese Communists was all but certain, that from the outset he had counseled the Chinese Communist leaders not to fight the Nationalists because their prospect for victory seemed remote. Indeed, when we take all this into account and take note of how guarded Moscow was in its dealings with the Chinese Communists after their victory, we can speculate that Stalin might have been happier with a weak Nationalist government in China rather than a new and vigorous Communist government. Jiang's regime could more readily be exploited than could a strong fraternal Communist regime.

More important as a determinant of the civil war's outcome than outside support (or the lack of it) were domestic factors: the popular support of the peasantry for the Communists, the high morale and effective military strategy of the Communist forces, the corruption of the Nationalist regime, the low morale and ineffective strategy of its army, and the inept political and military leadership of Generalissimo Jiang Jieshi. Still another factor was the deteriorating situation on the Nationalist home front, where runaway inflation, corruption, and coercive government measures combined to demoralize the Chinese population. The Communists, by contrast, enjoyed much greater popular support, especially from the peasantry (which made up about 85 percent of the population), because of its successful land redistribution programs. The Nationalists had alienated the peasantry for lack of a meaningful agrarian reform, having provided neither a program of land redistribution nor protection for tenant farmers against greedy and overbearing landowners.

The turn of events in China had immediate political repercussions in the United States. Shortly before the civil war ended, the U.S. Senate Foreign Relations Committee heard the testimony of U.S. teachers, businesspeople, journalists, and missionaries who had lived in China for years. They were unanimous in their criticism of Jiang's regime and warned that any additional aid would only fall into the hands of the Communists. The Truman administration understood this, but it nevertheless continued to provide aid. It knew that to cut off aid to its client promised to invite the inevitable political charges that Truman had abandoned a worthy ally, albeit a hopelessly corrupt one, in the struggle against international Communism. The Republicans, of course, who had been sharpening their knives for several years, did not disappoint him. No sooner had the civil war ended in

China than they were blaming the Democratic administration of President Truman for "losing China." Republican Senator Joseph McCarthy went so far as to blame the "loss of China" on Communists and Communist sympathizers within the State Department. Although McCarthy's charges proved unfounded, the Democrats were nonetheless saddled with the reputation of having lost China to Communism.

The "loss of China," as perceived by the U.S. public, and the intensified Cold War mentality it engendered within the United States, served to drive the Truman administration still further to the right in its foreign policy. Consequently, Truman became ever more vigilant to check the spread of Communism to other parts of Asia, and when, soon afterward, he was faced with Communist aggression in Korea and the prospect of "losing" Korea, it is little wonder that he responded immediately and forcefully.

## ■ THE KOREAN WAR

On June 25, 1950, only nine months after the Communist victory in China, the armed forces of Communist North Korea launched a full-scale attack on South Korea. The United States and its major allies responded swiftly and decisively to halt what they perceived to be the forceful expansion of international Communism and a blatant violation of the United Nations Charter. Korea thus became the first real battleground of the Cold War and the first major threat of an all-out war between the East and West. Even though it remained a limited war and resulted in an inconclusive stalemate, it proved to be a bitter and bloody conflict that lasted over three years, produced over 2 million fatalities, and left Korea devastated and hopelessly divided. The Korean War was a product of the Cold War and had profound effects on its continuation.

The roots of the Korean conflict go back to the last days of World War II, when the United States and the Soviet Union divided the Korean peninsula at the 38th parallel. The division, which was agreed to by U.S. and Soviet diplomats at Potsdam in July 1945, was meant to be a temporary arrangement for receiving the surrender of Japanese military forces in Korea after the war. The Soviet military occupation of northern Korea after Japan's defeat and the U.S. occupation of the southern half of Korea were to last only until a unified Korean government could be established—an objective agreed to by both parties. However, before any steps were taken to achieve that objective, Korean Communists, who had been in exile in either the Soviet Union or in northern China during the war, established in the north a Soviet-styled government and speedily carried out an extensive land reform program. Meanwhile, in the south, U.S. occupation authorities attempted to bring order to a chaotic situation. Korean nationalists opposed continued military occupation of their country and agitated for immediate independence. Rival nationalist parties, some of which were virulently anti-Communist, contended with each other in a political free-for-all.

In 1948, South Korea with Syngman Rhee as its first president, joined the "free world" under U.S. auspices. It would take another forty years, however, before democracy became established. In the meantime, force prevailed. The "April 3 Cheju Incident" is a case in point. On the island of Cheju, off the southern coast of Korea, socialist "people's committees" organized in March and April 1948 demonstrations against the U.S. presence in Korea and against the upcoming elections in the south designed to legitimize a separate government there and in effect divide the country. U.S. forces and local police fired on demonstrators, killing several. U.S. authorities then branded Cheju as "the second Moscow" and its people as Communists. A general insurrection that began on April 3 was put down, with a loss of life estimated between 14,000 (official South Korean count), 30,000 (U.S. estimates), and 80,000 according to the islanders. Another 40,000 fled to Japan. Under penalty of the National Security Law of December 1948, it became forbidden to mention the Cheju massacre for the next 45 years. Not until after a democratic government had come to power 45 years later, could it be discussed publicly. In 1998, at the 50th anniversary of the massacre President Roh Moo-hyun profusely apologized to the residents of Cheju.[6]

Political disorder in the south was further exacerbated by economic problems—namely, runaway inflation and the demand for land redistribution.

Under these circumstances, unification of the north and the south proved impossible. U.S. and Soviet diplomats had agreed in late 1945 to set up a provisional Korean government, which for five years would be under a joint U.S.-Soviet trusteeship, and a joint commission was set up in Seoul to implement this plan. However, the first session of this commission in March 1946 produced a typical Cold War scene, with the U.S. and Soviet officials hurling accusations at one another. The Soviet side accused the U.S. military command in South Korea of fostering the development of an undemocratic anti-Communist regime in the south, and the U.S. side similarly accused the Soviets of implanting an undemocratic Communist regime in the north. The Soviets insisted that no "antidemocratic" (meaning anti-Communist) Korean political party be allowed to participate in the political process, while U.S. representatives insisted on the right of all parties to participate. The Soviets also proposed the immediate withdrawal of both Soviet and U.S. occupation forces from Korea; but the United States, concerned about the Soviet advantage of having a better-organized client state in the north, insisted on a supervised free election to be carried out in both the north and the south prior to troop withdrawal.

Failing to solve the impasse in bilateral talks, the United States took the issue of a divided Korea to the United Nations in September 1947. As a result, the UN General Assembly passed a resolution calling for free elections

only since the collapse of the Soviet Union, makes it clear that Kim Il Sung did visit with Stalin in Moscow in March 1949 and again in March 1950 and in the latter meeting sought Stalin's support for an invasion of South Korea aimed at unifying Korea by force. But the Soviet dictator's response is less clear. By some accounts Stalin acknowledged Kim's plans for war and wished him success but did not offer specific instructions, much less orders for carrying out such plans. Stalin neither blocked Kim's proposed war nor gave it enthusiastic support. Stalin did advise Kim to consult first with Mao Zedong, which Kim did in Beijing in May 1950. It seems that he was there merely to inform the Chinese leader of his plans and that Mao, although skeptical, raised no objections and speculated that the United States was not likely to intervene in such a distant and small country.[9] Thus, on the evidence available to date, it is reasonable to conclude that the decision for war—specifically the strategy and timing of the attack—was made by Kim himself in Pyongyang, the North Korean capital, after he had secured at least general acquiescence from both Stalin and Mao.[10] Kim, whose nationalist convictions were as strong as his Communist ones, was convinced that his North Korean army was strong enough to gain a swift victory by waging a full-scale offensive. He also assumed that the United

United Nations Security Council session, New York, June 27, 1950, at which the resolution condemning North Korean aggression was approved in the absence of the Soviet representative, who was then boycotting the UN. *(National Archives)*

States lacked either the will or the means to come to the rescue of South Korea, but this would prove to be a serious miscalculation.

Far from ignoring or standing by idly while its former client was being overrun by a superior Communist force, the U.S. government rapidly swung into action. First, President Truman immediately ordered U.S. naval and air support from bases in nearby Japan to bolster the retreating South Korean army, and, second, he immediately took the issue of North Korean aggression to an emergency session of the United Nations Security Council. In the absence of the Soviet delegate, who was boycotting the United Nations in protest against its refusal to seat the People's Republic of China in the world body, the Security Council passed a resolution on June 25 condemning the invasion by North Korea and calling for the withdrawal of its forces from South Korea. Two days later the Security Council passed a second resolution calling for member nations of the United Nations to contribute forces for a UN "police action" to repel the aggression. It seems unlikely that the Soviet delegate to the United Nations would not have been at his seat in the Security Council—or even in New York—if Moscow had known in advance of, much less planned, the North Korean attack on the south.

By virtue of the second resolution, U.S. military involvement in Korea was authorized by the United Nations. Actually, Truman had already, the previous day, ordered U.S. ground troops (in addition to air and naval support) into action in Korea. The Soviet Union made use of this point to argue that U.S. military action in Korea was an act of aggression. Moreover, Moscow contended that the war in Korea was started by South Korea and that the deployment of UN forces in Korea was in violation of the UN Charter because neither the Soviet Union nor the People's Republic of China was present at the Security Council session to cast a vote. The Soviets protested that the UN operation in Korea was actually a mask for U.S. aggression. In point of fact, some planners within the U.S. National Security Council welcomed the outbreak of war in Korea as an opportunity for the United States to roll back Communism on the Korean peninsula.[11] Clearly, the UN engagement in Korea was largely a U.S. operation. Although some sixteen nations ultimately contributed to the UN forces in Korea, the bulk of UN troops, weapons, and matériel were from the United States; UN operations in Korea were largely financed by the U.S. government; the UN forces were placed under the command of U.S. Army General Douglas MacArthur; and the military and diplomatic planning for the war was done mainly in Washington.

The swift and resolute U.S. response to halt Communist aggression in Korea belied the Acheson statement of January 1950. It instead reflected the thinking of NSC-68. The Truman administration, which had been ready to write off Korea earlier in the year, decided that the United States must meet the Communist challenge to its containment policy. On second look, Washington determined that South Korea's defense was vital to the defense

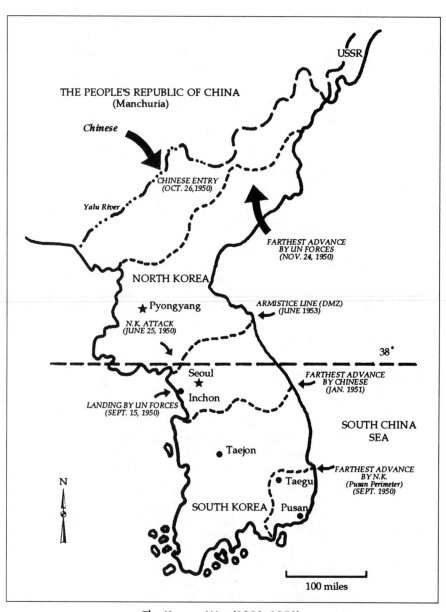

**The Korean War (1950–1953)**

of U.S. interests in Asia, especially since the prospect of a Soviet-controlled Korea would threaten the security of Japan, which had suddenly become the major U.S. ally in Asia. Moreover, President Truman saw the defense of Korea as important to the maintenance of U.S. credibility and defense commitments elsewhere in the world, and thus to the maintenance of the Western alliance. Indeed, he likened the situation in Korea in June 1950 to the Nazi aggression in the late 1930s and invoked the lesson of Munich: appeasement of an aggressor does not bring peace but only more serious aggression. Korea represented a test of U.S. will. Thus, the United States must not fail to stand up to that test.

The South Korean army, which lacked tanks, artillery, and aircraft, was no match for the heavily armed North Korean forces, and it therefore took a beating in the early weeks of the war. The first units of U.S. ground troops to come to its rescue were also undermanned and ill-equipped, but still they succeeded in holding the Pusan perimeter in the southeastern corner of Korea. Then, in September 1950, MacArthur engineered a dramatic reversal of the war with his successful landing of a large U.S./UN force at Inchon several hundred miles behind the Communist lines. Taken by surprise by this daring move, the North Korean forces then beat a hasty retreat back up the peninsula. By early October the North Koreans were driven across the 38th parallel; the U.S./UN forces had gained their objective in a spectacular fashion.

At this juncture the U.S. government had a critical decision to make: whether or not to pursue the retreating enemy across the 38th parallel. General MacArthur, riding the wings of victory, was raring to go, and so, of course, was Syngman Rhee, who hoped to eliminate the Communist regime in the north and bring the whole of Korea under his government. But the use of military force to achieve the unification of Korea had not been the original purpose of the UN engagement; the June 27th resolution called only for repelling the North Korean invasion. Moreover, U.S./UN military action in North Korea ran the risk of intervention by Communist China and possibly the Soviet Union as well in an expanded conflict. At the United Nations, the United States rejected proposals by the Soviet Union and by India aimed at achieving an overall peace in Asia, including both an armistice in Korea and the seating of the People's Republic of China in the United Nations. Instead, the United States succeeded in getting a resolution passed in the UN General Assembly that called for nationwide elections in Korea after "all appropriate steps [are] taken to ensure conditions of stability throughout Korea." The United States had opted for a UN General Assembly resolution because the Soviet Union would surely have vetoed any Security Council resolution sanctioning the use of UN forces to unify Korea. (No nation has veto power in the General Assembly.)

Tentatively, Washington then decided first to authorize the entry of the South Korean army into the north and then to give the go-ahead to

MacArthur's UN forces on the condition that they would halt their advance northward if either Chinese or Soviet forces entered the war. Nonetheless, by entering North Korea the U.S. war objective was now significantly altered; the goal was no longer limited to repelling an attack but was extended to eliminating the Communist regime in the north and militarily unifying the whole of Korea. Despite the caution manifested in Washington, General MacArthur, sensing the imminent collapse of the North Korean army, pressed on, rapidly advancing his forces toward the Yalu River, the boundary between Korea and China. In doing so he ignored the repeated warnings from Washington and those from Beijing, which threatened intervention by Chinese forces if its territory were threatened. To Beijing, the prospect of a hostile "imperialist" military presence across the border from the most industrialized area of China was intolerable.

MacArthur's aggressive pursuit of the enemy caused Washington and its allies qualms. In mid-October President Truman met with his field commander on Wake Island in the Pacific in order to urge caution against provoking the Chinese or Soviet entry into the war, but at that meeting MacArthur confidently predicted an imminent victory and assured Truman that if the Chinese dared to intervene they could get no more than 50,000 troops across the Yalu and the result would be "the greatest slaughter."[12] Back in Korea, MacArthur launched a major offensive, which, he predicted, would have the U.S. soldiers back home in time for Christmas.

With U.S. forces rapidly advancing toward the Chinese border, the Chinese did exactly as they had warned they would; they sent their armed forces into battle in Korea. Beijing insisted that these troops were "volunteers," thereby disclaiming official involvement in the war in order to ward off a possible retaliatory attack by UN forces on China itself. After an initial surprise attack on October 25, the Chinese made a strategic retreat for about a month, only to come back in much greater numbers. MacArthur's intelligence reports badly underestimated the number of Chinese troops involved and China's capacity to increase the size of its forces. Suddenly, on November 26, a vast Chinese army of over 300,000 soldiers opened a massive counteroffensive. Overwhelmed by this superior force, MacArthur's UN forces swiftly retreated southward over 250 miles to below the 38th parallel.

The Chinese intervention with a force much larger than MacArthur thought possible made it, in his words, "an entirely new war," and it also provoked a sharp dispute with President Truman over political and military policy. MacArthur, frustrated by having an imminent victory denied him and by the limitations placed on him by his superiors in Washington, favored widening the war, including using Chinese Nationalist forces from Taiwan, bombing Chinese Communist bases in Manchuria, and blockading the coast of China. The president, his military advisers, and his European allies feared that such steps might touch off World War III—possibly a nuclear war with the Soviet Union—or that the overcommitment of U.S.

forces in an expanded Korean War would leave Europe defenseless against a possible Soviet attack. MacArthur publicly criticized the policy of limited warfare that he was ordered to follow. In March 1951, he clearly exceeded his authority by issuing a public statement threatening China with destruction if it refused to heed his demand for an immediate disengagement from Korea. It was this unauthorized ultimatum that caused President Truman to dismiss the general from his command. Truman, who later stated that this was the most difficult decision he had ever made, felt it necessary to reassert presidential authority over the military and make it clear to both enemies and allies that the United States spoke with a single voice. Moreover, there was good reason to fear that continued insubordination by MacArthur, in his quest for total victory, might indeed instigate an all-out war between East and West. For his part, MacArthur minimized such prospects and argued that the West was missing an opportunity to eliminate Communism not only from Korea but from China as well.

It has been frequently alleged that it was General MacArthur's advocacy of use of the atomic bomb against the Chinese that resulted in his dismissal. Although there may be some truth to the allegation, it must be pointed out that on at least three separate occasions U.S. presidents considered the use of the bomb in the Korean War. Truman threatened use of the bomb in a press conference in November 1950, just after Chinese soldiers entered the war in large numbers, and he suggested that the decision rested with the field commander in Korea. The latter point caused so much consternation among U.S. allies and Truman's own advisers that he quickly modified his statement, saying that the final decision on the use of the bomb rested with the president. Several months later, when a new UN offensive was stymied by Chinese forces near the 38th parallel, Truman conferred with his advisers on the possibility of using the bomb. And near the end of the war, in June 1953, when armistice talks were deadlocked, the new U.S. president, Dwight Eisenhower, seriously considered using the atomic bomb to break the stalemate.

The dismissal of MacArthur on April 11, 1951, brought no change in the war. His replacement, General Matthew Ridgeway, held against a new Chinese offensive in late April, and several weeks later he was able to force the Chinese to retreat to near the 38th parallel. Soon thereafter, the war stalemated with the battle line remaining in that general vicinity. The war dragged on for two more years without a major new offensive by either side. Still, the toll of casualties mounted as patrol action on the ground continued. All the while, the United States conducted devastating bombing attacks on North Korea, destroying virtually every city as well as hydroelectric plants and irrigation dams. The toll on the civilian population of Korea of these bombing attacks was immeasurably large.

The military deadlock of the spring of 1951 brought about the beginning of peace talks. In June of that year, Moscow and Washington agreed to

General MacArthur, September 15, 1950, observing the shelling of Inchon, from the USS *Mt. McKinley. (National Archives)*

North Korean prisoners, September 11, 1950, in the town of Yongsan. *(National Archives)*

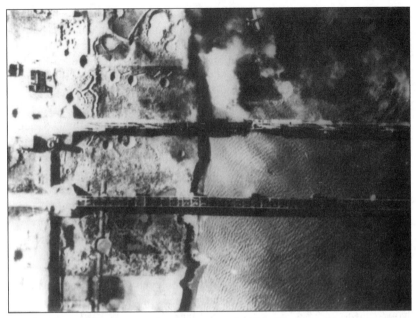

U.S. bombing of bridges, at Sinuiyu, across the Yalu River into Manchuria, November 15, 1950. (*National Archives*)

U.S. Army trucks at the 38th parallel, crossing into North Korea, October 1950, heading toward a showdown with the People's Liberation Army of Communist China. (*National Archives*)

begin negotiations for a cease-fire in Korea, and both Beijing and Pyong-yang concurred. Talks began in July and continued on-again, off-again for the next two years at Panmunjom, a town situated along the battle line. Two main questions divided the negotiators: the location of the cease-fire line and the exchange of prisoners. The Communist side insisted on returning to the 38th parallel but finally agreed to the current battle line, which gave South Korea a slight territorial advantage. On the second issue, the Communists insisted on a complete exchange of all prisoners, but the U.S. negotiators called for allowing the prisoners to decide for themselves whether they wished to be returned to their homelands. The truce talks remained deadlocked on this issue, which carried great propaganda value for the United States. In point of fact, many North Korean captives—perhaps as many as 40,000—did not wish to be repatriated, and the United States wanted to exploit this matter as much as the Communists wanted to prevent this mass defection, and thereby deny the United States a major propaganda victory.

After the emergence in 1953 of new leadership in Moscow with the death of Stalin and in Washington with the inauguration of Eisenhower, the two sides finally exhibited the flexibility necessary to break the impasse in Korea and to end the costly stalemated war. On June 8, 1953, the negotiators at Panmunjom signed an agreement that made repatriation of prisoners voluntary, but allowed each side the opportunity (under the supervision of a UN commission) to attempt to persuade their defectors to return home. However, the truce settlement was delayed because of a drastic attempt by South Korean president Syngman Rhee to sabotage it. Rhee, who desired to continue the fight to unify the country under his regime, released some 25,000 North Korean prisoners, who allegedly rejected repatriation to the north. The Chinese responded with a new offensive against South Korean units. Finally, after U.S. negotiators offered assurances to pacify and restrain Rhee, the two sides signed a truce on July 23, 1953. The fighting ended with the final battle line as the truce line, which was widened to become a two-and-a-half-mile-wide demilitarized zone (DMZ). The truce, however, did not mean the end of the war; it merely meant a halt in the fighting by the exhausted adversaries. Officially, a state of war has continued ever since, and the truce line between North and South Korea has remained the most militarized border anywhere in the world. For over fifty years it remained a potential flash point in the Cold War.

Even though the Korean War ended at about the same place it began, both its costs and its consequences were enormous. The United States lost over 35,000 men in combat (nearly 60,000 in all); South Korea, an estimated 300,000; North Korea, 52,000; and China, 900,000 (Washington estimates).[13] While its outcome represented something short of victory for either side, both could claim important achievements. The United States succeeded, with the help of its allies, in standing firm against Communist aggression. This brought greater security to Japan and it contributed to the strengthening of NATO as well. The Chinese emerged from the Korean conflict with greatly enhanced prestige, especially insofar as its now battle-hardened army had stood up to technically superior Western armies in a manner that no Chinese army ever had.

For the Koreans in both the north and the south, the war was disastrous. The war had been fought with great ferocity by Korean partisans who did not hesitate to inflict vicious punishment on their enemies—not only enemy soldiers but civilians thought to be informers or collaborators. Consequently, many atrocities were committed by both sides, and caustic bitterness would persist for years to come. In addition to the great death and destruction suffered by the Koreans, the division of their country was made permanent, and there would be no reduction of tensions and animosity between the Communist regime in the north and the anti-Communist regime in the south. The war produced millions of refugees, and when the fighting ended, several hundred thousand Korean families remained separated. The Cold War thus remained deeply entrenched in Korea.

## ■  THE UNITED STATES AND THE COLD WAR IN ASIA

The Communist victory in China represented a major setback for U.S. foreign policy. The threat to U.S. power in East Asia was made all the greater when the new Communist government of China promptly cemented its relations with the Soviet Union with a thirty-year military alliance aimed at the United States, and vehemently denounced U.S. "imperialism." The United States was then confronted by what seemed to be a global Communist movement that had suddenly doubled in size and now included the world's most populous nation. The turn of events in China meant that the United States's immediate postwar Asian policy, which had envisioned the emergence of a strong, united, democratic China to serve as the main pillar of stability in Asia, was completely shattered. Now the U.S. government fashioned a new Asian policy that called for the containment of Communism and featured Japan, the United States's former enemy, in the role of its strategic partner and base of operations.

In 1948, when it became apparent that the Chinese Communists would defeat the Nationalists in the civil war raging in China, the U.S. occupation policy in Japan took a strong turn to the right. The new policy, often called the "reverse course," called for rebuilding the former enemy, Japan, so that it would play the role of the United States's major ally in Asia, acting as a bulwark against the spread of Communism in that part of the world. Beginning in

1948, Washington, which heretofore had made no effort to assist Japan economically, now began pumping economic aid into Japan and assisting its economic recovery in other ways. The reverse course was evidenced by a relaxation of the restrictions against the zaibatsu, a new ban on general labor strikes, and the purge of leftist leaders. And with the outbreak of war in nearby Korea in 1950, the security of Japan became an urgent concern to the United States. In order to maintain domestic security within Japan, General MacArthur authorized the formation of a 75,000-person Japanese National Police Reserve, thus reversing his earlier policy for an unarmed Japan. This step was the beginning of the rearmament of Japan, and it was bitterly disappointing to many Japanese who were sincere in their conversion to pacifism.

In the midst of the intensified Cold War, the United States not only groomed Japan to become its ally, but also took the lead in framing a peace treaty with Japan in 1951 that would secure the new relationship. The treaty, which formally ended the Allied Occupation and restored full sovereignty to Japan, was crafted by the U.S. diplomat John Foster Dulles in consultation with major U.S. allies. The Communist bloc nations, which were not consulted, objected to the final terms of the treaty and they chose not to sign it. Tied to the treaty, which went into effect in May 1952, was a U.S.-Japan Mutual Security Pact, which provided that the United States would guarantee Japan's security. It also allowed U.S. military bases to remain in Japan to provide not only for Japan's security but also for the defense of U.S. interests in Asia, or, more specifically, for the containment of Communism. Moreover, the United States retained control of the Japanese island of Okinawa, on which it had built huge military installations. The reborn nation of Japan thus became a child of the Cold War, tied militarily and politically as well as economically to the apron strings of the United States.

Within Japan the Cold War was mirrored by political polarization between the right and the left. The right (the conservative political parties, which governed Japan for the next four decades) accepted the Mutual Security Pact and favored the maintenance of strong political and military ties with the United States. It recognized the threat that the war in nearby Korea represented and the advantages provided by the security arrangement with the United States. Moreover, it was fully aware of Japan's economic dependence on the United States and did not wish to jeopardize these vital economic ties. The left, comprised of the opposition (leftist) parties, affiliated labor unions, and many—probably most—of Japan's intellectuals and university students, was bitterly opposed to the Security Pact, to U.S. military forces remaining on Japanese soil, and to the rearmament of Japan. It favored instead unarmed neutrality for Japan, rather than its becoming a party to the Cold War. But since the conservative party remained in power, Japan continued to be a close partner of the United States in the international arena, and over 40,000 U.S. forces remained on U.S. military bases in Japan.

The Korean War had a great and lasting impact on the global Cold War. Beyond the fact that the two sides fought to a standstill in Korea, the war occasioned a large general military buildup by both East and West, and this meant the militarization of the Cold War. "Defense" budgets of both the United States and the Soviet Union skyrocketed during the Korean War to record peacetime levels, and they continued to grow thereafter. The military budget of the People's Republic of China also grew commensurately, and that nation remained on a war footing in the years that followed.

A less tangible, but no less important, consequence of the Korean War was the great intensification of hostility between the United States and the People's Republic of China. The possibility for accommodation between them, which still existed before they crossed swords in Korea, vanished. Both continued to accuse each other of aggression, and both increased their vigil against each other. For the PRC, the increased U.S. military presence in Asia meant a rising threat of U.S. "imperialism," and for decades to come this perceived threat remained the central point of Chinese diplomacy and security policy. For the United States, the continuing threat of "Chinese Communist aggression" required a greatly strengthened commitment to the containment of Communist China, and this became the central feature of the U.S. Asian policy for the next twenty-five years. This was reflected in the policy of making Japan the United States's major ally and base of operations in Asia, a decision to guarantee the security of South Korea and maintain U.S. forces there, a commitment to defend the Nationalist Chinese government on the island of Taiwan against an attack from the mainland, and a growing U.S. involvement in Vietnam in support of the French in their efforts to defeat a Communist-led revolutionary movement. The United States thus locked itself into a Cold War position in Asia in its endeavor to stem the spread of Communism, and its Communist adversaries in Asia strengthened their own resolve to resist U.S. intervention and "imperialism." The Cold War battle lines were thus drawn by the early 1950s, and for the next two decades, the two sides maintained their respective positions in mutual hostility.

## ■ RECOMMENDED READINGS

### □ Japan

Dower, John W. *Empire and Aftermath, Yoshida Shigeru and the Japanese Experience, 1878–1954.* Cambridge, Mass.: Harvard University Press, 1979.
An in-depth analysis of the policies of and politics between U.S. occupation authorities and the government of occupied Japan.

Kawai, Kazuo. *Japan's American Interlude.* Chicago: Chicago University Press, 1960.
A critical "inside view" of the occupation by a Japanese-American scholar who edited an English-language newspaper in Japan during the period.

Minear, Richard. *Victor's Justice: The Tokyo War Crimes Trials*. Princeton: Princeton University Press, 1971.
  Argues that the war crimes trials were unjust.
Perry, John C. *Beneath the Eagle's Wings: Americans in Occupied Japan*. New York: Dodd, Mead, 1980.
Reischauer, Edwin O. *Japan: The Story of a Nation*. 4th ed. New York: Knopf, 1988.

## ☐ China

Bianco, Lucien. *The Origins of the Chinese Revolution, 1915–1949*. Stanford: Stanford University Press, 1971.
  A lucid analysis of the Communist revolution in China stressing the strengths of the Communists and the failures of the Nationalists.
Fairbank, John K. *The United States and China*. 4th ed. Cambridge, Mass.: Harvard University Press, 1979.
Pepper, Suzanne. *Civil War in China: The Political Struggle, 1945–1949*. Berkeley: University of California Press, 1979.
Purifoy, Lewis M. *Harry Truman's China Policy: McCarthyism and the Diplomacy of Hysteria, 1947–1951*. New York: New Viewpoints, 1976.
  Strongly critical of the U.S. policy of supporting Jiang Jieshi.
Tsou, Tang. *America's Failure in China, 1941–1950*. Chicago: Chicago University Press, 1963.
  Argues that the United States had neither the means nor the will to achieve its goals in China.
Tuchman, Barbara. *Stilwell and the American Experience in China, 1911–1945*. New York: Macmillan, 1970.
  A blistering attack on Jiang Jieshi and critical of U.S. support for him.

## ☐ Korea

Cumings, Bruce. *The Origins of the Korean War: Liberation and the Emergence of Separate Regimes, 1945–1947*. Princeton: Princeton University Press, 1981.
——, ed. *Child of Conflict: The Korean American Relationship, 1943–1953*. Seattle: University of Washington Press, 1983.
  Essays by revisionist historians that refute orthodox (Western) interpretations of the origins of the Korean War.
——. *The Origins of the Korean War: II, The Roaring of the Cataract, 1947–1950*. Princeton: Princeton University Press, 1990.
  The best scholarly analysis of the background and the early stages of the Korean conflict.
Rees, David. *Korea: The Limited War*. Baltimore: Penguin, 1964.
  A military history focusing on the uniqueness of this conflict as the first U.S. limited war.
Spanier, John W. *The Truman-MacArthur Controversy and the Korean War*. New York: W. W. Norton, 1965.
Stone, I. F. *The Hidden History of the Korean War*. New York: Monthly Review Press, 1952.
  A provocative early revisionist version of the Korean War.
Whiting, Alan S. *China Crosses the Yalu: The Decision to Enter the Korean War*. New York: Macmillan, 1960.

# ■ NOTES

1. One finds in English-language materials on China two quite different spellings of Chinese names depending on when they were published. The pinyin system of romanization of Chinese names and words, the method used in the People's Republic of China, was adopted by U.S. publishers in 1979 in place of the Wade-Giles system that had been standard previously. Prior to 1979, Jiang Jieshi's name was rendered Chiang Kai-shek, and Mao Zedong's name was rendered Mao Tse-tung. In this text the pinyin system is adopted, but in most instances, the old spelling of a Chinese name will also be provided in parentheses. Also note that personal names for Chinese, Japanese, and Koreans are given in the manner native to their countries, that is, the surname or family name precedes the given name.

2. Edwin O. Reischauer, *Japan: The Story of a Nation* (New York: Knopf, 3d ed., 1981), p. 221.

3. MacArthur referred to the Japanese as twelve-year-olds in his testimony to the joint committee of the U.S. Senate on the military situation in the Far East in April 1951. Cited in Rinjiro Sodei, "Eulogy to My Dear General," in L. H. Redford, ed., *The Occupation of Japan: Impact of Legal Reform* (Norfolk, Va.: The MacArthur Memorial, 1977), p. 82.

4. After Jiang launched a full-scale civil war in mid-1946, General Marshall made it clear to him that the United States would not underwrite his war. Thereafter, Washington turned down Jiang's urgent requests for additional military aid and provided only a reduced amount of economic aid after the end of 1946.

5. Soviet withdrawal from Manchuria was completed in May 1946, four months later than called for in the initial agreement with Nationalist China, but this was partly because Jiang Jieshi actually requested the Soviets to postpone their withdrawal until the Nationalist forces were prepared to take control.

6. Chalmers Johnson, *Blowback: The Costs and Consequences of Empire* (New York: Henry Holt, 2000), pp. 98–100. U.S. authorities, too, participated in the cover-up.

7. The National Security Council duplicates much of the work of the State Department, and during the days of the Kennedy administration (1961–1963) a tendency emerged whereby presidents began to consult the NSC rather than the professionals in the State Department. The discussion in 1950 on the nature of the Soviet threat proved to be one of the first instances where the professionals in the State Department played second fiddle to the National Security Council. The State Department's experts on the Soviet Union, Charles Bohlen and George Kennan, both of whom later served as ambassadors to Moscow, challenged the argument that Stalin had a master plan of conquest. They saw the Soviet threat largely as a potential political problem in Western Europe. But they were overruled by Dean Acheson, who sided with the hard-liners on the National Security Council who argued that the United States must create order throughout the world.

8. The first to make this case was I. F. Stone, *The Hidden History of the Korean War* (New York: Monthly Review Press, 1952), pp. 1–14. Also see Bruce Cumings, "Introduction: The Course of Korean-American Relations, 1943–1953," in Bruce Cumings, ed., *Child of Conflict: The Korean American Relationship, 1943–1953* (Seattle: University of Washington Press, 1983), pp. 41–42.

9. See Sergei N. Goncharov, John W. Lewis, and Xue Litai, *Uncertain Partners: Stalin, Mao, and the Korean War* (Stanford: Stanford University Press, 1993), pp. 136–146.

10. Soviet sources show that throughout 1949, Stalin opposed a North Korean attack on the south, repeatedly telling Kim that "the 38th parallel must remain

peaceful." Stalin feared that a war would give the United States a pretext for getting involved in Korean affairs. Kim, however, continued to lobby for a green light from Stalin. It was not until April 1950 that Stalin accepted Kim's view that the war could be contained to the Korean peninsula and would not draw foreign intervention. See Natal'ia Bazhanova, "Samaia zagadochnaia voina XX stoletniia," *Novoe vremia*, 6 (February 1996), pp. 29–31.

11. Cumings, "Introduction: The Course of Korean-American Relations, 1943–1953," pp. 29–38.

12. Quoted in Richard Rovere and Arthur Schlesinger, Jr., *The General and the President* (New York: Farrar, Straus, 1951), pp. 253–262.

13. Bruce Cumings estimates that the total number of fatalities was as high as 2 million; *The Origins of the Korean War: II, The Roaring of the Cataract, 1947–1950* (Princeton: Princeton University Press, 1990).

# 4

# Confrontation and Coexistence

For centuries the nations of Europe had waged war against each other. France and Britain had been enemies in past centuries, and in modern times the strife between France and Germany has been even bloodier. Within the span of seventy-five years, they fought in three wars. Twice in the first half of the twentieth century, the nations of Europe divided into warring camps and fought each other with ever more destructive consequences. During and immediately after World War II, leading political representatives of war-ravaged Europe spoke fervently of the necessity of burying the violent past and embarking on a new future of peace and unity among Europeans.

The onset of the Cold War and the closing of the Iron Curtain by Stalin over Eastern Europe meant that Western designs for European unity would be limited to Western Europe. Indeed, the East-West division of Europe and the perceived threat posed by the Soviet Union to the security of Western European nations served to reinforce the need for greater unity among them. In order to counter the Soviet Union's hegemony in Eastern Europe, the United States and its allies began to take steps in the late 1940s to secure the integration of Western Europe. In its turn, Moscow set out to create its own unified empire in Eastern Europe. The result was a rigid political division of the continent.

## ■ WEST EUROPEAN ECONOMIC INTEGRATION

After 1945, the focal point in the East-West power struggle in Europe was Germany, which had been divided into four occupation zones. Disagreements over reparations to be extracted from Germany and other issues led to a closing off of the Russian zone in East Germany from the U.S., British, and French zones in West Germany. By early 1947, less than two years after the conclusion of the war, it became clear to Washington and Moscow that the chances for a settlement of the German question had vanished in the Cold War climate of acrimony, suspicion, and fear. The United States began to consolidate its position in Western Europe, a position centered around a North Atlantic community of nations with common economic and political systems and security interests. In essence, it meant the integration of parliamentary, capitalist nations of Western Europe, such as Great Britain, France, Italy, Belgium, the Netherlands, Luxembourg, Denmark, and Norway (but excluding the dictatorial states of Spain and Portugal), into a defensive alliance. Within a decade, West Germany, by virtue of its location, size, and economic potential, also joined this community and it was destined to play a major role in it. Thus, in the late 1940s, West Germany, like Japan in East Asia, became the first line of defense for the United States against Soviet expansion.

The creation of a separate West German state and its economic recovery were matters of high priority in U.S. foreign policy in the late 1940s. The United States, with the concurrence of Britain and France, took the lead in creating a West German parliamentary government, officially known as the Federal Republic of Germany. From the very moment of its formation in May 1949, the West German government insisted that it spoke for all of Germany, including what at the time was still the Soviet zone of occupation.[1] In rapid order, the United States integrated West Germany into a system of international trade, supplied it with generous amounts of economic aid (through the Marshall Plan), introduced a new currency, and eventually brought West Germany into the U.S.-led military alliance, NATO. Under such circumstances, West German democracy flourished, as did its economy. Indeed, West Germany was the first of the world's war-torn industrial nations to attain an economic recovery, and by the late 1950s its postwar growth was considered an economic miracle, or *Wirtschaftswunder.*

When the United States and West Germany introduced the new German mark into West Berlin, the Soviets realized that not only had the United States created a new German state, but that this state now had an outpost 110 miles inside the Soviet zone. When, during the war, the Soviets had agreed to the Allied occupation of Berlin, they did not expect a permanent Western outpost within their zone. In June 1948, the Soviets attempted to force the West to abandon Berlin by closing the overland routes into West Berlin from West Germany. The Allies responded with the Berlin Airlift, an operation involving daily flights of U.S., British, and French transport planes over East Germany delivering food and other goods to the West Berliners. For political, psychological, and practical reasons, the West was in no mood to yield.[2] When Stalin finally relented by lifting the overland blockade in May 1949, it was a tacit recognition that West Berlin would remain part of West Germany.

Once West Germany officially came into existence in 1949, its chancellor, Konrad Adenauer, doggedly pursued a policy of integrating it into the community of West European nations. He insisted that the postwar German state develop democratic, liberal institutions under the aegis of the West. In fact, there is ample evidence to suggest that Adenauer, who came from the westernmost part of Germany—the Rhineland—and whose credentials as an opponent of the Nazi regime were impeccable, did not trust the German people. He feared that left alone, they would succumb once more to the lure of political, economic, and, in particular, military power. Germans needed to be under the lengthy tutelage of the Western democracies. A West Germany under Western control suited him and many of his compatriots just fine. In fact, in March 1952, when Stalin sought talks with the West about the possibility of establishing a neutral, unified Germany, it was Adenauer who lobbied strenuously—and successfully—with his Western allies to reject Stalin's diplomatic note without even bothering to discuss it.[3] For Adenauer, the inclusion into the company of Western nations was more important than German unification. The unification of Germany had to wait, and it had to be accomplished on Western terms.

What endeared the Roman Catholic Adenauer to the Western powers was his conservatism and staunch opposition to Communism. The West German voters, not inclined to another round of social experimentation, gave their votes to Adenauer's conservative Christian Democratic Union. *Der Alte* ("the old man") Adenauer, already seventy-three years old at the time of his first election as chancellor, held that post until 1963 and put West Germany firmly onto its postwar path.

During Adenauer's tenure, West Germany experienced rapid economic recovery, established viable democratic institutions, and tried to come to grips with its recent past. It acknowledged Germany's responsibility for World War II and the Jewish holocaust and paid large sums in reparations to Jewish victims. It took steps to purge the nation of its Nazi past; the Nazi Party and its symbols were outlawed, and students were taught the causes and consequences of the rise of Nazism.

When dealing with the West, Adenauer always said the right things, but he and many Germans had a more difficult time acknowledging the consequences of German actions in the East. Not only did Adenauer insist that Poland and the Soviet Union return German lands they had seized at the end of the war, but his government refused to pay reparations to the millions of Poles, Russians, and others in Eastern Europe who had been forced to work in Nazi slave labor camps or had family members murdered. There was no opening to the East under Adenauer. Stalin had created the Iron Curtain, but politicians such as Adenauer also played a role in maintaining the partition of Europe. (For details on Adenauer's foreign policy and that of his successors with regard to Eastern Europe, see Chapter 18.)

Western European economic integration had its beginnings in the Marshall Plan, the U.S. economic aid program announced in June 1947, which was intended to rescue Europe from the economic devastation of the war.

However, insofar as the Marshall Plan was rejected by Moscow, which spoke for most of Eastern Europe, the aid and the integrative impact of the program was limited to Western Europe.

In short order, the countries of Western Europe took bold steps toward greater economic integration. In April 1951, six nations—France, West Germany, Italy, and the Benelux countries (Belgium, the Netherlands, and Luxembourg)—signed a treaty establishing the European Coal and Steel Community. This program, designed primarily by the French economist Jean Monnet and French foreign minister Robert Schuman (both of whom have been called the "father of Europe"), called for the pooling of the coal and steel resources of the member nations. It created a High Authority which, on the basis of majority vote, was empowered to make decisions regulating the production of coal and steel in the member countries. In effect, it internationalized the highly industrialized Saar and Ruhr regions of West Germany. Not only did this program eliminate a source of national contention and greatly raise production, but it was considered at the time as the platform on which to build both the economic and political integration of Europe.

So well did the integrated coal and steel program work that in a few years the same six nations decided to form a European Economic Community (EC), also known as the Common Market, to further integrate their economies. The Treaty of Rome of March 1957 brought a more comprehensive organization formally into existence. In addition to coordinating economic production, the EC established a customs union for the purpose of the lowering of tariffs among the member states and the establishment of one common tariff rate on imports from outside countries. This easing of trade restrictions greatly increased the flow of goods, which in turn stimulated production, provided jobs, and increased personal income and consumption. Western Europe began to reemerge as one of the thriving economic regions of the world. In fact, the economic growth rate of the Common Market countries surpassed that of the United States by the end of the 1950s and remained significantly higher for many years thereafter.

Great Britain did not share in the benefits of the Common Market because it initially chose not to join. Britain already enjoyed the benefits of a preferential tariff system within its own community of nations—the Commonwealth—and it could not reconcile its Commonwealth trade interests with those of its European neighbors in the Common Market. Other reasons for Britain's rejection of the Common Market included its conservative inclination to retain the old order rather than join in the creation of a new one, its reliance on its strong ties with the United States and Commonwealth friends, and its reluctance to give up a measure of its national sovereignty to a supranational body whose decisions were binding on member nations. However, after both its economy and its international status faltered in the 1950s, Britain saw fit in 1961 to apply for membership in the

Common Market, only to find that admission now was not for the mere asking. The issue of Britain's entry was hotly debated both within Britain, where the Labour Party opposed it, and in France, where President Charles de Gaulle had his own terms for British admission. After over a year of deliberation, de Gaulle, who had attempted in vain to draw Britain into a European military pact, suddenly announced in January 1963 his firm opposition to British membership in the EC. Since decisions within the Common Market required unanimity—a point de Gaulle had insisted upon—the French president's veto unilaterally kept Britain out. When Britain renewed its application to join the Common Market in 1966, de Gaulle—who was critical of Britain's close political and economic ties with the United States and with the Commonwealth nations in other parts of the world—still objected, and it was only after de Gaulle's resignation as president of France in 1969 that Britain gained entry. After lengthy negotiations, Britain finally joined the EC in January 1973 (together with Denmark and Ireland.)

From its inception, the EC was divided between the "supranationalists," who desired total integration, and the "federalists," who wished to retain for each nation essential decisionmaking power. The tug of war between these two camps remained unresolved. Moreover, since decisions on key issues were binding for all member states, certain members (most notably France and later Britain) successfully insisted on unanimity rather than by majority vote on issues such as expansion of the membership, a common currency, social legislation, and so on.

## ■ NATO: THE MILITARY INTEGRATION OF WESTERN EUROPE

In April 1949, a number of nations heeded a call on the part of the United States to create an alliance against the potential Soviet threat. Once again, the main obstacle was the force of nationalism, especially as personified by France's Charles de Gaulle. The result was the creation of NATO, the North Atlantic Treaty Organization, as a collective security system for Western Europe and North America. It was the military equivalent of the Marshall Plan, designed to extend U.S. protection to Western Europe. The ten European countries that originally joined NATO (Britain, France, Iceland, Norway, Denmark, Belgium, the Netherlands, Luxembourg, Portugal, and Italy), together with the United States and Canada, signed a treaty of mutual assistance. An attack on one was an attack on the others. (NATO remained intact even after the demise of the Soviet Union, against which it was directed. It was invoked for the first time immediately after September 11, 2001, after al Qaeda's assault on the World Trade Center in New York and the Pentagon in Washington.) NATO brought U.S. air power and nuclear weapons to bear as the primary means to prevent the Soviet Union from using its large land forces against West Germany or any of the member states. Each of the NATO nations was to contribute ground forces to a collective army under a unified command.

The first serious question facing NATO was whether to include West Germany. Its territory was covered by the initial NATO security guarantee, but it was not a treaty member; in fact, it was still under Allied military occupation until 1952 and had no armed forces of its own. As early as 1950, after the outbreak of the Korean War, U.S. officials began to encourage the rearmament of Germany and integration of its forces into NATO. But the French and other Europeans, fearing the return of German militarism, were reluctant to see the rearmament of Germany.

The fear of a reappearance of German militarism was, however, overshadowed by the fear of Soviet aggression. Moreover, German troops were badly needed to beef up the under-strength NATO ground forces. At the urging of the United States, Britain, and West Germany itself, the NATO members agreed by the end of 1954 on West Germany's entry into NATO—on the conditions that it supply twelve divisions of ground forces and that it be prohibited from the development of nuclear, bacteriological, and chemical weapons as well as warships and long-range missiles and bombers.

The Soviet Union, too, opposed the rearmament of West Germany and made an eleventh-hour attempt to block its entry into NATO. In March 1952, Stalin proposed the immediate and total evacuation of all occupation forces from Germany—East and West—the reunification of Germany, and the creation of a security pact to defend it as a neutral nation. It is idle to speculate whether such a generous proposal would have received a better reception in Western capitals had it been made earlier, but the plan was rejected out of hand as a Soviet propaganda ploy aimed merely at disrupting the Western military alliance.

In its first decade, the weak link in the NATO collective security system was France, which lacked political stability until the emergence of General Charles de Gaulle as president of the newly established Fifth French Republic in 1958. France had been unable to supply its share of ground troops to NATO because they were needed first in Indochina and later in Algeria where it was desperately trying to hold on to its colonial empire. De Gaulle, however, was intent on cutting France's losses abroad and regaining for France a dominant position in Europe. De Gaulle, France's great World War II hero and always the supreme nationalist, wished to remake Europe in his own way. His vision of a powerful Europe was not one of economic integration as suggested by the Common Market, but rather an association of strong nations. He was staunchly opposed to the notion of supranationalism, for his real objective was to elevate the role of France in a reinvigorated Europe. His determined pursuit of French domination of the new Europe was the cardinal point of what came to be called Gaullism.

French president Charles de Gaulle and visiting U.S. president John F. Kennedy, Paris, June 2, 1961. *(National Archives)*

De Gaulle's boldly assertive nationalism was also reflected in his view of the security needs of France (and Europe). Because he sought the strengthening of the posture of France within Europe and the reassertion of European power in global affairs, de Gaulle wished to put the United States at a greater distance from Europe. He felt that Europe, especially NATO, was dominated by the United States and, secondarily, by its closest ally, Great Britain. De Gaulle also questioned the commitment of the United States to the defense of Europe and, therefore, he considered NATO to be flawed. He thought while the United States might wage a nuclear war in defense of its West European allies in case of a nuclear attack by the Soviet Union, it could not be counted on to risk its own nuclear destruction to defend Western Europe from an invasion by conventional ground forces. De Gaulle rejected a U.S. offer to place nuclear weapons in France; instead, he went ahead with the development of France's own nuclear arsenal, its *force de frappe,* or "strike force." It promised to enhance France's inter-national prestige by joining the exclusive club of nuclear powers. De Gaulle also felt that, even if France's nuclear force were far smaller than that of the superpowers, it still would serve as a deterrent. In the 1960s, de Gaulle turned a deaf ear to foreign critics when he refused to join other nations in signing a series of nuclear arms control agreements and to halt France's atomic bomb testing program in the Pacific Ocean.

Charles de Gaulle persistently challenged U.S. leadership of the Western alliance as he sought to assert France's independence. In 1964, he broke ranks with the United States by extending diplomatic recognition to the People's Republic of China. Later, in 1966, de Gaulle again challenged U.S. dominance of the Western alliance when he decided to withdraw all French troops from NATO (although he did not formally withdraw France from the NATO alliance) and when he called for the withdrawal of all U.S. forces from French soil. French security, the general insisted, must remain in French hands.

De Gaulle disliked the confrontational approach taken by the United States in the Cold War, especially in the 1962 Cuban missile crisis (to be discussed later), and he did not want to be left out of diplomatic meetings between the superpowers where decisions might be made affecting the security and interests of France. He sought to counter U.S. Cold War diplomacy and its domination of the Western allies by conducting his own diplomacy with the Soviet Union and Communist China, and by strengthening France's ties with the most powerful continental West European state, West Germany.

The *entente* (understanding) between France and West Germany was achieved by the political skill of de Gaulle and West Germany's aged chancellor, Konrad Adenauer. After Adenauer accepted an invitation to meet with de Gaulle in Paris in July 1962, de Gaulle undertook a triumphant tour of West Germany two months later. This exchange of visits was followed by the signing of a Franco-German treaty aimed at strengthening their relations and thereby making it the cornerstone of Western European solidarity. This act served to check the Anglo-U.S. domination of the Western alliance, but it did not result in putting greater distance between West Germany and the United States, as de Gaulle had wished. It did, however, symbolize the marked improvement in the postwar era of the relations between these two powerful European nations with a long history of mutual hostility.

## ■ EAST EUROPEAN INTEGRATION

In Eastern Europe, Moscow had its own program of political and economic integration. What had begun in 1944–1945 as a military occupation by the Red Army shortly became a social, political, and economic revolution with Stalin's Soviet Union serving as the model. In 1949, in response to the Marshall Plan, Stalin's foreign minister, Viacheslav Molotov, introduced the Council of Mutual Economic Aid, commonly known as COMECON. Its purpose was to integrate the economies of the East European nations of Poland, Hungary, Romania, Czechoslovakia, and Bulgaria (and later Albania) with that of the Soviet Union. It was designed to aid in the postwar reconstruction of the Soviet Union and in the industrial development of Eastern Europe, which was still largely an agricultural region. It also supplemented the Kremlin's political control of Eastern Europe by giving it an economic lever.

The transformation of the East European economies took place along Soviet lines. The emphasis was on heavy and war industries, with consumer goods taking a back seat. Expropriation decrees, issued as early as September 1944 in Poland, led to the confiscation of the estates of nobles and the churches. These measures eliminated the "landlord" classes and paved the way for collectivization of agriculture.

The economic transformation of Eastern Europe was accompanied by sweeping political changes. In Bulgaria, Albania, Yugoslavia, and Romania, the monarchies were officially abolished. Moscow's East European satellites followed the Soviet example by adopting constitutions similar to Stalin's Constitution of 1936. Everywhere, parties in opposition to the new political order were declared illegal.

The dominant force in Eastern Europe since the end of World War II was the Soviet army, augmented by the forces of the new socialist regimes. In 1955, the Soviet Union, ostensibly in response to the inclusion of West Germany into NATO, created its own military alliance, the Warsaw Treaty Organization, commonly known as the Warsaw Pact. Its membership included Albania, Bulgaria, Czechoslovakia, East Germany, Hungary, Poland, Romania, and the Soviet Union. Unlike NATO, its members did not have the right to withdraw from the organization, an act the Kremlin considered the supreme political sin its satellites could commit. Albania, by virtue of its geographic position and relative lack of importance, did manage to leave the Warsaw Pact in 1968, but Hungary's flirtation with neutrality in 1956 met with an attack by the Soviet army. When Czechoslovakia in 1968 and Poland in the early 1980s moved dangerously close to a position similar to that of Hungary in 1956, the Soviet leadership made it clear that it would not tolerate the disintegration of its military alliance.

The most interesting manifestation of the force of nationalism in Eastern Europe was that of Romania, which since the mid-1960s sought to carve out a measure of independence from Moscow. Under the leadership of Nicolai Ceausescu, the Romanian Communist Party successfully maneuvered to secure a limited economic and political independence, particularly in its dealings with Western Europe. Over the years, Ceausescu circumvented his nation's role in agricultural and petrochemical production as allocated by COMECON, retained diplomatic ties with Israel after all other East European nations had broken relations with Israel after the 1967 "Six Day War," refused to participate in Warsaw Pact maneuvers, maintained diplomatic relations with the People's Republic of China at a time of ever-increasing hostility between Moscow and Beijing, gave warm receptions to visiting U.S. presidents, and sent his athletes to the 1984 Olympic Games in Los Angeles in defiance of the Soviet boycott of the games. Throughout, the Kremlin cast a wary eye on the Romanian maverick but refrained from taking drastic action. After all, there was no pressing need to discipline Ceausescu since he remained a loyal member of the Soviet Union's military alliance and, perhaps even more important, he showed absolutely no tendency toward any sort of political reform. Moscow always considered political reform in Prague and Warsaw as a greater threat to its hegemony in Eastern Europe than Ceausescu's actions, which, although an irritant, did not pose a major problem. As long as Ceausescu retained the most harshly repressive political system in Eastern Europe, the Kremlin was willing to tolerate his unorthodox behavior in certain matters.

Despite the Kremlin's insistence on maintaining its hegemony over Eastern Europe, the forces of nationalism repeatedly made it clear that Eastern Europe contained restless populations with whom the Kremlin's control did not sit easily. In the face of repeated Soviet pronouncements that considered Eastern Europe a closed issue (notably General Secretary Leonid Brezhnev's statement in 1968 that the Soviet Union's defensive borders were at the Elbe River separating East and West Germany), the region remained a potentially volatile problem.

## ■ THE FIRST ATTEMPTS AT DÉTENTE

The Korean War, one of the most dangerous moments in the Cold War, brought about the remilitarization of both the United States and the Soviet Union. Immediately upon the conclusion of World War II, the two nations had reduced their armed forces despite the shrill accusations in Washington and Moscow focusing on the evil intentions of the other. U.S. intelligence records show that a Soviet attack was not in the cards—unless an uncontrolled chain of events led to miscalculations on the part of the leaders in the Kremlin. By early 1947, U.S. forces had dwindled from a wartime strength of 12 million to fewer than 1 million soldiers under arms. Because of this reduction, Western Europe was exposed to a possible assault by the Soviet army. If that occurred, U.S. troops in Western Europe were under orders not to fight but to find the quickest way across the English Channel.

The Soviets showed no inclination to initiate World War III on the heels of the just-concluded World War II. Stalin reduced the Soviet army to its prewar level of about 3.5 million soldiers, much of the Soviet Union was in ruins and in need of rehabilitation, and there was always the U.S. trump card, the atomic bomb. Washington did not consider it likely that Stalin would direct his armed forces across the Iron Curtain; similarly, Moscow did not contemplate a U.S. attack. For the next five years the protagonists maintained their forces at a level just sufficient to repel a potential attack. In 1950, the outbreak of the Korean War proved to be the catalyst for the rapid remilitarization of both sides.

**Europe (1990)**

In the United States in April 1950, nine weeks prior to the outbreak of the war in Korea, National Security Council directive NSC-68 recommended to President Truman a drastic increase in the military budget. The prospects of attaining this were slim, for popular sentiment was against it. Yet the opportunity to implement NSC-68 came in June 1950 when, according to Secretary of State Dean Acheson, "Korea came along and saved us."[4]

In the Soviet Union a similar process took place. Stalin long ago had demanded unity and sacrifice from his people. In the late 1940s, he renewed his insistence that the socialist, Soviet fatherland must be defended at all cost. There could be no deviation from this principle. A renewed emphasis on ideological rigidity and conformity became the order of the day, and with it purges of individuals suspected of ideological nonconformity. When the war in Korea broke out, Stalin rapidly increased the size of the Red Army from 3.5 million to about 5–6 million troops, the approximate level the Soviet armed forces retained until the late 1980s. The five-year period after World War II during which both sides had reduced their armed forces and curtailed their military expenditures was at an end.

Truman's retirement from political life took place in January 1953, and Stalin's death came six weeks later. The exit of the two chief combatants in initial stages of the Cold War made it possible for the new leaders to try a different tack, for they were not locked into the old positions to the same degree their predecessors had been. (In late 1952, there had been a brief flurry of speculation that Stalin and Truman might meet for the first time since 1945. Nothing came of it, for apparently they had nothing to talk about.)

President Dwight Eisenhower and the new Soviet premier Nikita Khrushchev, who had emerged as the Soviet Union's leader by September 1953, began a dialogue that resulted in the lessening of tensions. It was in this context that the word *détente* ("relaxing the strain") first entered the vocabulary of the Cold War.[5] Eisenhower, the hero of World War II, had no need to establish his anti-Communist credentials. He had greater latitude in dealing with the Soviets than did Harry Truman or his secretary of state, Dean Acheson, whom the Republicans (notably Joseph McCarthy and Richard Nixon) had berated time and again for being "soft on Communism." There was nothing they could do to shake off the Republican charges, and in fact, McCarthy had gone far beyond charging Truman with a lack of vigilance. He went so far as to allege that Truman's State Department was filled with Communist subversives.

Khrushchev and his colleagues began to move away from the Stalinist pattern of conduct at home and abroad shortly after they buried Stalin. Khrushchev was determined to avoid a military showdown with the West and declared, by dusting off an old Leninist phrase, that "peaceful coexistence" with the West was possible. With it he rejected the thesis of the inevitability of war between the socialist and capitalist camps.

At Geneva in 1954, the great powers convened to deal with the central problems of the day. The more relaxed climate, the "Spirit of Geneva," made possible the disengagement of the occupying powers from Austria. It proved to be the first political settlement of any significance by the belligerents of the Cold War.[6] In May 1955, Austria, under four-power occupation since the end of the war, gained its independence as a neutral state. Austria became a nonaligned buffer in the heart of Europe, separating the armies of the superpowers. The Iron Curtain shifted eastward to the borders of Czechoslovakia and Hungary. Western and Soviet troops thus disengaged along a line of about two hundred miles. In return, Austria pledged its neutrality in the Cold War, a condition that suited the Austrian temperament perfectly. In particular, Austria was not to join in any alliance—particularly military or economic—with West Germany. Austria quickly became a meeting ground between East and West. Its capital, Vienna, became a neutral site for great-power meetings as well as a city with one of the largest concentrations of foreign spies in the world.

A solution similar to the Austrian settlement had earlier been envisioned for Germany. But in contrast to Austria, by 1955 two Germanies already existed. Austria's good fate was that at the end of the war it was treated not as a conquered, but a liberated nation. Also, it had a relatively small population of just over 7 million and was insignificant as an economic and military power. Yet the latter may also be said of Korea and Vietnam, while no political solution was ever found for these nations. One of the main reasons why a solution for Austria ultimately proved to be feasible was Stalin's unilateral action in April 1945. He appointed the moderate socialist Karl Renner as the new head of Austria and in this fashion Austria, unlike Germany, Korea, and Vietnam, was from the very beginning under one government, which all of the occupying powers eventually recognized. Churchill and Truman were initially unhappy with Stalin's action, not because they objected to Renner, but because he had acted unilaterally and without consulting them. Nevertheless, they grudgingly accepted Stalin's choice. Renner then proceeded to guide his nation carefully on a middle course between the superpowers. When the time came to disengage in 1955, Austria already had a neutral government ten years in existence. The German experience had been quite different. At the end of the war the Allies had spoken of creating a German government that all sides could accept, but it never happened during the Cold War.

The partial rapprochement between the United States and the Soviet Union made possible Nikita Khrushchev's visit to the United States in 1959. His itinerary took him to New York City, a farm in Iowa, Los Angeles, and the presidential retreat of Camp David in the hills of western Maryland, where he and Eisenhower conferred in private. The "Spirit of Camp David" produced recommendations for disarmament and a decision for the two men to meet again at a summit meeting in Paris in May 1960, to be followed by an Eisenhower visit to the Soviet Union.

The Austrian settlement and talks between the heads of state did not mean that the Cold War was over. Nor did it mean that a process of disengagement had begun. Détente was always tempered by a heavy residue of mistrust and a continued reliance on military might. At the high-point of détente in the 1950s, the Cassandras were always in the wings warning of dire consequences.

The Soviets spoke of peaceful coexistence—as they called détente—but the ideological struggle and the preservation of the empire continued. Nikita Khrushchev always had his critics at home, particularly the old Stalinist, Viacheslav Molotov, who remained foreign minister until Khrushchev replaced him in 1956.[7] Détente did not mean, therefore, the abandonment of one's spheres of influence. The Soviets were unwilling to cede territory they considered vital to their security. When they were challenged in Eastern Europe, they did not hesitate to act. They quickly suppressed rebellions in East Germany in 1953 and in Hungary in 1956. The empire, the Soviet bloc, remained one and indivisible.

A similar conflict between détente and Cold War aspirations was also evident in the United States. The Republican president, Eisenhower, pursued the high road of compromise and negotiations; his secretary of state, John Foster Dulles, in contrast, was an uncompromising anti-Communist. Containment of the Soviet Union, a policy pursued by his Democratic predecessors Dean Acheson and George Marshall, was not enough, for it suggested tolerance of an evil, godless system. To Dulles, the Cold War was not merely a struggle between two contending economic and political orders; it was also a clash between religion and atheism. Dulles, therefore, proposed the "rollback" of the Soviet Union's forward position and the "liberation" of lands under Communist rule. Officially, U.S. foreign policy abandoned what had been a defensive position, and took on a "new look," an offensive character.[8] But as events showed, particularly in Hungary in 1956, it is the president who ultimately determines foreign policy, and Eisenhower had no desire to start World War III by challenging the Soviets in their sphere. Despite Dulles's rhetoric, U.S. foreign policy had to settle for containment.

Dulles acted vigorously to preserve and protect the U.S. presence throughout the world. When in 1954 the Communist Viet Minh of Vietnam triumphed over the French, he moved to preserve the southern half of that country for the Western camp. When the United States felt its interests threatened in Iran in 1953 and in Guatemala in 1954, the CIA, under the guidance of Allen Dulles, John Foster's brother, quickly moved into covert action and accomplished some of its most successful coups.

In Iran, the CIA returned the shah to power when it engineered the overthrow of Premier Mohammed Mossadegh, who had sought to nationalize the nation's oil industry in order to take it out of the hands of British and U.S. companies. In Guatemala, the CIA replaced the socialist Jacobo

Arbenz, who had proposed the nationalization of lands held by U.S. corporations, with a military junta.

## ■ MOSCOW'S RESPONSE TO CONTAINMENT

In the mid-1950s, the Kremlin's foreign policy underwent a significant transformation when Khrushchev took the first steps to negate the U.S.-led system of alliances designed to contain the Soviet Union. Until that time the country had resembled a beleaguered fortress, defying what it perceived to be an aggressive West. The United States was in the process of implementing one of the provisions of NSC-68, the creation of regional alliances directed against the Soviet Union. In 1954, the United States created the Southeast Asia Treaty Organization and, in 1955, the Baghdad Pact. In conjunction with NATO and its military ties in the Far East (South Korea, Japan, and Taiwan), the United States was about to close a ring around the Soviet Union.

The Baghdad Pact was intended to be a Middle Eastern alliance, consisting largely of Arab states, led by the United States and Great Britain. Yet the only Arab state to join was Iraq; the other members were Turkey, Pakistan, and Iran. In March 1955, Egypt's Gamal Abdel Nasser created an Arab alliance, which included Syria and Saudi Arabia, to counter the West's influence in the Middle East. In this fashion, Nasser sought to establish his independence from the West. Nasser's act of defiance and his anti-Western rhetoric contributed to the rapid deterioration of relations. The United States sought to bring Nasser to heel by withdrawing its funding for the Aswan High Dam on the upper Nile. Nasser then turned to the Soviet Union to complete the dam. By that time he had already concluded an arms agreement with the Soviet Union (its first with a non-Communist state). When, in the summer of 1956, Nasser nationalized the Suez Canal, which had been in British hands since 1887,[9] the stage was set for a retaliatory strike by the West. In October 1956, France and Britain joined Israel in an attack on Egypt. The Cold War once again spilled over into the Third World.

In 1954, when Kremlin leaders began to take the first steps in arming a client beyond the Communist world,[10] this change in Soviet foreign policy did not come without intense debate in the high echelons of the Soviet Union's ruling circle. From the end of World War II until Stalin's death, the Soviet Union had conducted a relatively conservative foreign policy. To be sure, Stalin had refused to yield to the West on a number of central issues, notably Eastern Europe, but he had not challenged the West outside the confines of the Soviets' own sphere. The successful Communist insurgencies in Vietnam and China, for instance, had not been of his making. Stalin had dug into his fortress behind his massive land army. Shortly after Stalin's death, the CIA, in a special report to President Eisenhower and the National

Security Council, described Stalin as a man "ruthless and determined to spread Soviet power," who nevertheless "did not allow his ambitions to lead him to reckless courses of action in his foreign policy." The CIA warned, however, that Stalin's successors might not be as cautious.[11]

Events quickly bore out the CIA's prediction. In 1954, a bitter debate took place in the Kremlin over the nation's foreign policy. One faction, led by Prime Minister Georgi Malenkov and Foreign Minister Viacheslav Molotov, urged caution, favoring a continuation of the Stalinist pattern of defiance and rearmament. The majority in the Presidium of the Central Committee of the party,[12] led by Nikita Khrushchev, who was the first secretary of the party and thus its leader, argued for a more active foreign policy, calling for a breakout from what they called capitalist encirclement. This argument stressed that those who accept the status quo and merely stand still will suffer defeat at the hands of the capitalists. (Interestingly, this position echoed that of John Foster Dulles, who could not tolerate the mere containment of the foe. The conflict, both sides argued, must be taken to the enemy.)

Molotov and his allies warned that involvement in the Middle East was bound to fail. After all, British and U.S. navies controlled the Mediterranean Sea and were bound to stop all shipments, as the United States had intercepted a Czechoslovak arms shipment to Guatemala earlier in 1954. But Khrushchev and his faction prevailed, and the Soviet Union began early in 1955 to arm Nasser in secret, a fait accompli revealed to the world later that year.

In return for its support of Nasser, the Soviet Union obtained a client in the Middle East, and it was thus able partially to offset the effects of the Baghdad Pact.[13] For the first time the Soviet Union was able to establish a foothold in a region beyond the Communist world. The person largely responsible for this significant departure in Soviet foreign policy and who reaped handsome political dividends at home was Nikita Khrushchev. He had begun to challenge the West in what had formerly been a Western preserve. The monopoly of Western influence in the Third World would not go unchallenged. It marked the beginning of a contest for the hearts and minds of the nonaligned world. With this in mind, Khrushchev undertook in 1955 a much-publicized journey to South Asia. He visited India and on his way home stopped in Kabul, the capital city of Afghanistan, to forestall apparent U.S. designs on that country. "It was . . . clear that America was courting Afghanistan," Khrushchev charged in his memoirs. The U.S. penetration of that country had "the obvious purpose of setting up a military base."[14] In 1960, Khrushchev paid a second visit to Asia. Eisenhower, concerned with the growing Soviet influence in southern Asia, followed in 1960 in Khrushchev's footsteps when he visited India and other nonaligned nations.

In May 1960, relations between the Soviet Union and the United States took a sudden turn for the worse when a U.S. spy plane, a U-2, was shot down deep inside the Soviet Union. The Soviet Rocket Force Command had finally been able to bring down one of the high-flying U.S. spy planes, which had periodically violated Soviet air space since 1956. This event wrecked the summit between Khrushchev and Eisenhower later that month, and it canceled Eisenhower's scheduled goodwill visit to the Soviet Union. Khrushchev's vehement denunciation of Eisenhower overstepped the boundaries of both common sense and good manners.[15] Western historians have often speculated that Khrushchev had to placate the hard-liners at home who had never been happy with his rapprochement with the West.

The year 1960 was also a presidential election year in the United States. Presidential election campaigns have never been known for elevated discussions of the issues, and this was no exception. The "outs," in this case John Kennedy and his Democratic Party, accused the "ins," Richard Nixon (Eisenhower's vice-president) and the Republicans, of having fallen asleep on their watch. The Soviets had (supposedly) opened up a "missile gap" that endangered the security of the United States. The Cold War was back in full bloom.

## ■ THE CUBAN MISSILE CRISIS

The division of Europe and its integration into two distinct blocs was both the result of the Cold War and a source of the continuation of the conflict. The belligerents continued to arm for a military showdown that neither wanted. The main feature of the Cold War during the 1950s was the arms race, both conventional and nuclear. In conventional land forces, the Soviet bloc always held the lead, while the West relied primarily upon the U.S. nuclear umbrella. The U.S. nuclear monopoly, however, was short-lived. In 1949, the Soviet Union tested its first atomic weapon; in the early 1950s, it exploded its first thermonuclear bomb; and in 1955, it obtained the capability of delivering these weapons by means of intercontinental bombers. By the end of the 1950s, both Washington and Moscow had successfully tested intercontinental missiles. The stage was set for the escalation of the arms race and the dangers inherent in it.

The Cold War reached its most dangerous stage in a most unlikely place. It was over Cuba in 1962 that the first and only direct nuclear confrontation between the United States and the Soviet Union took place. The showdown came as a consequence of the Cuban revolution of the late 1950s, a revolution by which Fidel Castro took Cuba out of the U.S. orbit and gave it a new political and economic direction.

Castro's direct challenge to the existing Cuban order and its president, Fulgencio Batista, began on July 26, 1953, when he led an unsuccessful attack on the Moncada army barracks. He spent eighteen months in prison and then went to Mexico, only to return to Cuba for a second attempt in

December 1956. On May 28, 1957, Castro and his band of eighty guerrillas scored a significant psychological victory with an attack on the garrison at Uvero. For the next year and a half, Castro's forces, which never numbered more than three hundred guerrillas under arms, remained in the field as a visible challenge to the bankrupt Batista government, which at the end could count on no one to come to its defense. Because of Castro's small force and the fact that Batista's support rapidly began to crumble, the revolution never did reach the magnitude of a civil war in the proper sense of the word. Castro himself admitted that had Batista enjoyed a measure of popular support, his revolution would have been easily crushed. Instead, whatever support Batista had melted away, and in January 1959, Castro and his small band triumphantly entered Havana. Batista then fled the country. It was not that Castro had won political power, but that Batista had lost it.

Castro was by no means the first Cuban to seize power by force, but he certainly was the first to take steps to challenge the unequal relationship between the United States and his country, one that had been in existence since the days of the Spanish-American War of 1898 when the United States gained a foothold in Cuba. Castro demanded the nationalization of U.S. property in Cuba and its transfer into Cuban hands. At first Castro appeared to be willing to offer compensation to U.S. companies, but not at the high level that the U.S. businesses demanded. The result was a deadlock with severe repercussions. It was not so much the differences in opinion over the value of U.S. property as it was ideological principles that led to

Soviet leader Nikita Khrushchev and Cuban president Fidel Castro, at the United Nations, New York, November 1960. *(National Archives)*

the impasse. The United States became the champion of the right to private property of U.S. citizens in Cuba; Castro became the defender of Cuban national sovereignty.

Shortly, high-ranking U.S. officials in the Eisenhower administration became convinced that Castro was a Communist. At what point he did in fact become a Communist is difficult to say. His brother Raul had long been a Communist. Castro's conversion apparently came sometime after the revolution. The time had come to get rid of Castro. There were reasons to believe that the CIA could duplicate its successes in Iran and Guatemala.

The crisis in Iran was the consequence of a decision in April 1951 by Iran's parliament, the *majlis,* to nationalize the property of the Anglo-Iranian Oil Company (AIOC), Britain's most profitable business in the world. Not only had the AIOC taken Iran's wealth out of the country, its workers in Abadan suffered the indignities of surviving on wages of 50 cents a day, living in a shantytown (called "paper city"), and battling pollution, rats, and disease. In May, the *majlis,* under the leadership of the nationalist Mohammed Mossadegh, forced the shah, Mohammed Reza Pahlavi, to agree to the founding of the National Iranian Oil Company. Britain's prime minister, the old imperialist Winston Churchill, needed the assistance of the CIA to get rid of Mossadegh. The Truman administration, however, was unwilling to become involved in the dispute. Churchill had to wait until the Eisenhower administration with its "new look" came to power. The new secretary of state, John Foster Dulles, and his brother, Allen, the head of the CIA, were more than willing to engage in covert actions to overthrow Mossadegh, a man already demonized in the U.S. press.

Eisenhower gave the Dulles brothers the green light to initiate covert action, which the CIA saw as a cheap way to affect the course of history. The CIA spent money to foment demonstrations in the streets, paid off religious leaders, and bribed army officers. In August 1953, after the nationalists had driven the shah into exile, the CIA managed to create a volatile situation that led to the army's arrest of Mossadegh and the shah's return from Rome. Three hundred Iranians died in the violence, but on balance, CIA intervention had worked like a charm. When the leading CIA operative in Iran, Kermit Roosevelt (Theodore Roosevelt's grandson), briefed John Foster Dulles on the agency's success, Dulles "purred like a giant cat."

But that was not the end of his story. As a critic of the operation later explained, "nations . . . cannot be manipulated without a sense on the part of the aggrieved that old scores must eventually be settled." The day came in 1979, when demonstrations forced the shah into exile once more and when Iranian students took possession of the U.S. embassy in Tehran. While Dulles purred, many in the CIA understood that the United States might pay a price someday.[16] In the month after the overthrow of Mossadegh, a CIA report spoke for the first time of "blowback."[17]

In the following year, in Guatemala, the CIA moved into action once more. A revolution in 1944 had overthrown Guatemala's military dictatorship and had brought to power civilians who sought to address the country's social and economic problems. In 1950, 2.2 percent of landowners owned 70 percent of the land (of which they cultivated but one quarter) and the annual income of agricultural workers was $87. Most of the economy was in foreign—mostly U.S.—hands and, consequently, large profits went abroad. The greatest employer was the United Fruit Company with its vast land holdings, 85 percent of which consisted of excess, uncultivated land.

The nationalist Jacobo Arbenz, upon winning a democratic election, became president of Guatemala in March 1951. Arbenz and his congress— which had but a handful of Communist deputies with little influence—then proceeded to take steps to limit the power of foreign corporations, notably that of the United Fruit Company. They nationalized unused land and supported strikes against foreign businesses. In March 1954, Arbenz told his congress that this was a matter of protecting the "integrity of our national independence." John Foster Dulles raised the specter of Communism. The nationalization of land did not sit well with him or his brother Allen. They decided to act for reasons of national security, ideology, and the fact that both owned stock in the United Fruit Company and had previously provided legal services for the company. The CIA organized and outfitted disaffected elements of the Guatemalan army led by Colonel Carlos Castillo Armas who earlier, in November 1950, had sought to overthrow the civilian government, and then had fled into exile. A successful coup took place in July 1954, when Arbenz's own army would not support him.

For Washington, the crisis was over. For Guatemala, it was the first step of a descent into hell. Castillo Armas, who was assassinated in July 1957, never managed to bring order or prosperity to Guatemala. Instead, a revolutionary movement began to gain in strength. In the early 1960s, a succession of military regimes—some of them of extraordinary brutality— launched a campaign in an attempt to return the country to the "quiet days" before 1944.[18]

For more than three decades, the military killed an estimated two hundred thousand Guatemalans, most of them indigenous Mayans. Of particular viciousness was the reign of General Efrain Rios Montt, a born-again Christian who became the darling of the U.S. religious right in the early 1980s. During his seventeen-month reign, his army murdered an estimated seventy thousand rebels, mostly Mayan peasants, and razed thousands of villages. Rios Montt's scorched-earth policy, directed primarily against an ethnic group, came close to the definition of genocide. Rios Montt was arguably the worst human rights abuser in Latin American history since the arrival of the Spanish *conquistadores*. Guatemala's civil war produced more fatalities than the "dirty wars" of El Salvador, Nicaragua, Argentina, and Chile combined.

There was little reason to believe that the United States could not repeat the Iranian and Guatemalan scenarios and reestablish its economic and political position in Cuba. The first weapon Washington employed was economic; if needed, other weapons would be used later. At first, the United States closed its market to Cuba's main source of income, the export of sugar cane. The U.S. market previously had taken half of Cuba's exports and provided nearly three-quarters of its imports. As anticipated, the U.S. trade embargo had severe repercussions on the Cuban economy.

At this point events began to move rapidly. Castro refused to yield to U.S. pressure. Instead, he turned to the Soviet Union for economic, political, and military support. Also, he saw his revolution as a model for other countries in Latin America, and as such he posed a direct challenge to U.S. hegemony there. His reform program at home acquired a Marxist flavor and it resulted in the exodus of thousands of Cubans who opposed the accompanying political and economic restrictions and sweeping changes. They settled mainly in Florida, waiting to return to their native land.

In March 1960, a frustrated Eisenhower administration turned the Cuban problem over to the CIA and subsequently to the new president, John Kennedy. Cuba became Kennedy's first foreign policy adventure. In the spring of 1961, Allen Dulles assured Kennedy that Castro could be removed with little difficulty. After all, the CIA had dealt with similar problems before and had handled them successfully. Dulles then put together a plan. It called for Cuban exiles, trained and supplied by the CIA, to land on the beaches of Cuba and call upon the Cuban population to rise up against Castro. The plan was based on the assumption that the Marxist regime of Cuba had no popular support and would collapse. All that was needed was a push and the corrupt house of cards would come down.

President Kennedy decided to put the CIA plan into operation in April 1961. But something went wrong. The population did not rise against Castro, and his armed forces destroyed the force of 1,500 Cuban exiles who had landed on the beaches of the Bay of Pigs. It was all over in seventy-two hours. A vague understanding between the CIA and the Cuban exiles had led the exiles to believe that the United States would not abandon them. They expected direct U.S. military intervention in case they ran into difficulty. When Kennedy did not respond militarily to the fiasco at the Bay of Pigs, many Cubans in the United States felt betrayed. But Kennedy never had contemplated the need for such a contingency in case something went wrong. Moreover, such an action would have been in violation of international law and promised international and domestic repercussions.

Kennedy, stung by this defeat, blamed Allen Dulles for the fiasco. Castro's Cuba then became an obsession with Kennedy. Three days after the Bay of Pigs, he offered Castro a warning: "Let the record show that our restraint is not inexhaustible."[19] Kennedy's obsession, coupled with domestic politics and questions of national security, made it difficult for him to accept the presence of Castro in nearby Cuba.

The Soviet Union could do little to aid Castro. It could not readily challenge the United States in the Caribbean in an attempt to protect a client. The United States enjoyed a vast naval superiority, particularly in the Gulf of Mexico, not to mention a large advantage in delivery systems of nuclear weapons. When John Kennedy entered the White House, the United States possessed over 100 intercontinental and intermediate-range ballistic missiles, 80 submarine-launched missiles, 1,700 intercontinental bombers, 300 nuclear-armed airplanes on aircraft carriers, and 1,000 land-based fighters with nuclear weapons. In contrast, the Soviets possessed 50 intercontinental ballistic missiles, 150 intercontinental bombers, and an additional 400 intermediate-range missiles capable of reaching U.S. overseas bases.[20]

In the presidential election of 1960, Kennedy had charged that the Eisenhower administration had been responsible for a "missile gap" to the detriment of the United States. But that political myth was laid to rest shortly after Kennedy became president. In October 1961, Deputy Secretary of Defense Roswell Gilpatric announced that there was no missile gap; on the contrary, there was a gap favoring the United States. "We have a second-strike capability," Gilpatric stated, "which is at least as extensive as what the Soviets can deliver by striking first."[21]

The Soviet premier, Nikita Khrushchev, understood this all too well. His boasts of Soviet military might had only masked the reality. There seemed to be little he could do about this state of affairs. But one day in 1962, a solution came to him in a flash. He reasoned that if he could establish a Soviet nuclear presence in Cuba, he could solve several problems in one bold stroke.[22] Such a plan promised three dividends. First, Khrushchev would be able to present himself as the defender of a small and vulnerable state. Second, and more important, medium-range missiles in Cuba would essentially give the Soviet Union nuclear parity—if only symbolically—with the United States. The missile gap, which favored the United States, would be no more. Third, nuclear parity with the United States would greatly enhance the international prestige of the Soviet Union.

Khrushchev quickly decided to act. His memoirs suggest that neither he nor his advisors spent much time considering the consequences of this rash act. (He was, after all, a man of action, not of reflection.) In the past, Khrushchev had several times taken decisive yet potentially dangerous steps that, however, had brought him political rewards. Now the stakes were higher than ever before. Success promised to bring great gains, but failure promised to contribute to the early end of his political career. And in fact, two years after the Cuban missile crisis, when his party turned him out, he was accused of "hare-brained" and "wild schemes, half-baked conclusions and hasty decisions," none too subtle reminders of what had gone wrong in the Caribbean.[23]

When the CIA became aware of the construction of Soviet missile sites in Cuba, Kennedy had to act. Military and domestic political considerations demanded it. The Joint Chiefs of Staff understood that the presence of some ninety Soviet intermediate-range missiles in Cuba, while posing a formidable threat to much of the eastern part of the United States, did not change the balance of terror. Both sides were already capable of annihilating the other. But when Kennedy and his advisers met, they knew that theirs was first and foremost a domestic political problem. At the height of the crisis, Secretary of Defense Robert McNamara told National Security Advisor McGeorge Bundy: "I'll be quite frank, I don't think there is a military problem here. . . . This is a domestic, political problem. . . . We said we'd act. Well, how will we act?"[24]

One option was to launch preemptive air strikes against the missile sites, which could bring about the deaths of Soviet troops and would mean the humiliation of a great power. Such an action could touch off a nuclear war. Two of Kennedy's advisers, Air Force chief of staff General Curtis LeMay and the commander of the Strategic Air Command, Thomas Power—both of whom for over a decade had advocated a preventive nuclear war against the Kremlin—now took the opportunity to urge a nuclear resolution of the confrontation over Cuba, even to the point of launching a nuclear attack on the Soviet Union that, they agreed, should it retaliate, would be able to inflict only minimal damage on the United States. In fact, LeMay thought the Soviets would not retaliate with nuclear weapons in the face of the U.S. arsenal. During the crisis he stated that "the Russian bear has always been eager to stick his paw in Latin American waters. Now we've got him in a trap, let's take his leg off right up to his testicles. On second thought, let's take off his testicles too." Somehow, LeMay thought the bear would accept his castration without trying to reclaim his manhood.[25]

The Joint Chiefs of Staff and the CIA had a more sobering assessment. They told Kennedy that in an all-out war the Soviet nuclear arsenal was capable of destroying the United States without the Cuban missiles. This bleak assessment had a sobering impact on Kennedy and his advisers, who met around the clock in an effort to find a political solution to the crisis.

A second possibility was an invasion of Cuba, but such action was as dangerous as the first option. The destruction of Soviet forces in Cuba would leave Khrushchev with few options. He could accept a defeat, contemplate a nuclear exchange, or attack the West's isolated and vulnerable outpost in Berlin where the Soviet army had a marked advantage.

Kennedy decided on a third option, a blockade of Cuba (which he called a "quarantine" since a blockade is an act of war) that would give both sides additional time to resolve the issue. The blockade was a limited one since its purpose was only to intercept ships carrying missile components. Khrushchev, in the face of U.S. action, was prepared to back down. But he, like Kennedy, had his own political problems at home. Since he

This low-level reconnaissance photograph, taken by the United States on October 23, 1962, provided evidence that the Soviet Union was setting up missile bases in Cuba. *(U.S. Department of Defense)*

could not afford to come away from the confrontation empty-handed, Khrushchev demanded concessions. First, he insisted on the Soviet Union's right to place defensive missiles in Cuba. After all, the United States had done the same when it had placed missiles in Turkey, along the Soviet Union's southern border. At the least, therefore, the U.S. missiles should be removed from Turkey. But Kennedy refused publicly to discuss this demand. He, too, could not afford to appear to back down, despite the fact that the U.S. missiles in Turkey were obsolete and already had been sched-uled for removal. Second, Khrushchev wanted a pledge from the United States not to invade Cuba and to respect the sovereignty of that nation.

The standoff was resolved with the help of two unlikely intermediaries. Soviet journalist Alexander Feklisov (who was also a KGB agent) and U.S. journalist John Scali (who had contacts in the White House) met in a restaurant in Washington on October 26 to discuss the crisis. Feklisov pointed out that "mutual fear" drove the two superpowers: Cuba feared a U.S. invasion, and the United States feared the rockets in Cuba. A U.S. pledge not to invade Cuba would resolve the matter. Feklisov got in contact with his embassy, Scali with the White House. They met again for dinner that same day, and Scali informed Feklisov that "the highest power"— namely, John Kennedy—had accepted the deal to trade the Soviet rockets in exchange for a public pledge that the United States would not invade

Cuba.[26] For several days the standoff continued. A false move could mean disaster for everyone involved.

Eventually, Kennedy saw the absurdity of his position. He was at the verge of bombing a small nation, an act that could touch off a nuclear war, over the issue of obsolete missiles in Turkey—missiles that he had already ordered to be removed. Kennedy ignored Khrushchev's belligerent statements and instead decided to reply to a conciliatory letter from the Soviet prime minister in which Khrushchev expressed his desire to resolve the dilemma:

> We and you ought not to pull on the ends of the rope in which you have tied the knot of war, because the more the two of us pull, the tighter that knot will be tied. And a moment may come when that knot will be tied too tight that even he who tied it will not have the strength to untie it. . . . Let us not only relax the forces pulling on the ends of the rope; let us take measures to untie that knot.[27]

Robert Kennedy, the president's brother and closest adviser, met with Soviet ambassador Anatoly Dobrynin to tell him that the United States was prepared to pledge not to invade Cuba in the future and that after a sufficient interval it would remove the missiles from Turkey. But there would be no official U.S. acknowledgment of this second concession. On the next day, Dobrynin told Robert Kennedy that the Soviet missiles would be withdrawn. The crisis was over.

After the first Soviet ships were turned back by the U.S. blockade, Secretary of State Dean Rusk said: "We looked into the mouth of the cannon; the Russians flinched."[28] But it was not merely the Soviets who had flinched. The United States had reacted in a similar fashion. The Cuban missile crisis had a profound sobering effect on the nuclear powers. Both the United States and the Soviet Union realized that the constant state of confrontation had been in part responsible for the nuclear showdown. The time had come for a constructive dialogue. And, in fact, relations between the United States and the Soviet Union improved markedly shortly thereafter. The most notable, immediate achievement was the partial Nuclear Test Ban Treaty of 1963, which forbade nuclear testing in the atmosphere. It set the stage for further East-West discussions and the beginning of the détente of the late 1960s.

In the aftermath of the crisis, historians, politicians, and soldiers have sought to determine the lessons of this confrontation. A view commonly held in the United States emphasized that the crisis showed that the Soviets yielded only in the face of determination and will. According to Cold War rhetoric, force was the only thing they understood. On the surface, Khrushchev had surrendered to Kennedy's demands by removing the Soviet missiles from Cuba. But this explanation has several serious flaws. On balance, the victory did go to Kennedy. But it came at a price. Until the very end, Khrushchev always insisted on a quid pro quo—something in return—and he continued to hold out for concessions until he received them. In the meantime, his government granted Kennedy nothing. As long as the deadlock persisted, the Soviets continued to work on the Cuban missile sites and they challenged the U.S. U-2 spy planes that continued their surveillance flights. A Soviet missile—fired by Cubans at the express order of Fidel Castro—shot one down and killed its pilot, Major Rudolph Anderson. And when, during the crisis, a U.S. intelligence plane took off on a routine flight over the Soviet Union, the Soviet air force met it and chased it back.

The Cuban missile crisis was first and foremost a political test of wills. Nothing that either side did or contemplated doing would have changed the military balance of power. The crisis was political in nature, one that called for a political solution, a quid pro quo. And that is how, in fact, it was resolved, not by one side dictating a settlement to the other. It ended only after Kennedy gave assurances on the missiles in Turkey and a pledge of noninterference in Cuban affairs. As Khrushchev emphasized in his memoirs, the crisis had been settled by political compromise, and he spared no words in thanking John Kennedy for settling it in that fashion rather than going to war.[29]

The Cuban missile crisis sobered up the belligerents and ushered in a climate of cooperation and the reduction of tension. The crisis revealed the Soviet Union's relative weakness in the face of U.S. military might. This imbalance in favor of the United States was in part the result of a modest build-down on the part of the Soviets, which had begun in the late 1950s. But after Kennedy's demand for an increase in the U.S. nuclear arsenal, Kremlin leaders committed themselves to the quest for genuine—and not just symbolic—nuclear parity with the United States. The Soviet Union's rearmament program, however, had done nothing to change the balance of power by the time of the Cuban crisis of October 1962. The Soviets then vowed that the United States would never again humiliate them. The result was a renewed Soviet effort to close the gap or, at the least, to create parity between the two nuclear powers.

## ■ RECOMMENDED READINGS

### □ Western Europe

Calmann, John. *The Common Market: The Treaty of Rome Explained.* London: Blond, 1967.
    An analysis of the origins of the Common Market.
Hiscocks, Richard. *The Adenauer Era.* Philadelphia: Lippincott, 1966.
    A study of the accomplishments of the architect of West Germany.
Sampson, Anthony. *Anatomy of Europe: A Guide to the Workings, Institutions, and Character of Contemporary Western Europe.* New York: Harper and Row, 1968.
    A readable analysis of postwar Europe.
Williams, Philip, and Martin Harrison. *Politics and Society in de Gaulle's Republic.* New York: Doubleday, 1971.

A book that focuses on the politician most responsible for the political orientation of postwar France.

## ☐ The Cold War, 1953–1962

Beschloss, Michael. *The Crisis Years: Kennedy and Khrushchev, 1960–1963*. New York: HarperCollins, 1991.
Detailed and definitive account of the Cold War confrontation of the early 1960s.
———. *Mayday: Eisenhower, Khrushchev and the U-2 Affair*. New York: Harper and Row, 1986.
A detailed analysis of the U-2 incident and its impact on U.S.-Soviet relations.
Bundy, McGeorge. *Danger and Survival: Choices of the Bomb in the First Fifty Years*. New York: Random House, 1988.
By the assistant to Secretary of War Henry Stimson and national security advisor to Lyndon Johnson.
Dallin, David. *Soviet Foreign Policy After Stalin*. Philadelphia: Lippincott, 1961.
A scholarly treatment of Soviet foreign affairs during the 1950s.
Lebow, Richard Ned, and Janice Gross Stein. *We All Lost the Cold War*. Princeton: Princeton University Press, 1994.
Analyses of how three confrontations were resolved: the Cuban missile crisis, crisis management during the Yom Kippur War of 1973, and management of the nuclear deterrent.
Ra'anan, Uri. *The USSR Arms the Third World: Case Studies in Soviet Foreign Policy*. Cambridge, Mass.: M.I.T. Press, 1969.
A valuable account of the debates in the Kremlin over foreign policy.

## ☐ Cuba

Abel, Elie. *The Missile Crisis*. Philadelphia: Lippincott, 1966.
A journalist's scholarly account of the nuclear confrontation.
Kennedy, Robert F. *Thirteen Days: A Memoir of the Cuban Missile Crisis*. New York: W. W. Norton, 1969.
By the president's brother and close adviser, who presents what may be called the official U.S. view.
Kinzer, Stephen. *All the Shah's Men: An American Coup and the Roots of Middle East Terror*. Hoboken, N.J.: John Wiley and Sons, 2003.
The definitive study of how the CIA overthrew Mossadegh's elected government in Iran.
Schlesinger, Stephen, and Stephen Kinzer. *Bitter Fruit: The Untold Story of the American Coup in Guatemala*. New York: Anchor Books, 1990.
The definitive account of the CIA's coup of 1954.
Szulc, Tad. *Fidel: A Critical Portrait*. New York: Morrow, 1986.
A detailed biography that offers the thesis that Castro was already a Communist before seizing political power.
Walton, Richard J. *Cold War and Counterrevolution: The Foreign Policy of John F. Kennedy*. New York: Viking, 1972.
Contains two chapters highly critical of Kennedy's handling of the Bay of Pigs and the missile crisis.
Wyden, Peter. *Bay of Pigs: The Untold Story*. New York: Simon and Schuster, 1979.
A detailed account of the CIA's ill-fated attempt to overthrow Fidel Castro.

# ■ NOTES

1. West Germany's choice of a capital, the small provincial city of Bonn, signified its provisional and temporary status. The traditional German capital, Berlin (which was divided into East and West German sectors), was within East German territory.

2. West Berlin's main practical strategic value to the West was that it was a most important center of intelligence operations. It also became a symbol of the steadily improving Western European standard of living. West Berlin stood out in sharp economic contrast to that of East Germany, by which it was surrounded.

3. For details, see Rolf Steininger, *Eine Chance zur Wiedervereinigung? Die Stalin-Note vom 10. März 1952: Darstellung und Dokumentation auf der Grundlage unveröffentlichter britischer und amerikanischer Akten* (Bonn: Verlag Neue Gesellschaft, 1985).

4. Cited in Walter LaFeber, *America, Russia, and the Cold War: 1945–1990* (New York: McGraw-Hill, 6th ed., 1991), p. 98.

5. *Détente* is a French word meaning an unbending or relaxing; specifically, in the case of the Cold War, the relaxation of strained international relations.

6. A bold and sweeping statement, to be sure. Other agreements on trade, arms limitations, travel, and the like, must not be lightly dismissed. Yet none of them settled a major political problem. The stubborn fact that it took the two sides ten years and new leaders to agree on the Austrian solution—and on little else—is testimony to the intensity of the Cold War.

7. In 1957, Andrei Gromyko became foreign minister; he retained his post until July 1985, when Mikhail Gorbachev kicked him upstairs to take the ceremonial post of president of the Soviet Union.

8. Dulles's "rollback" and "liberation" and Eisenhower's "new look" are discussed in Stephen E. Ambrose, *Rise to Globalism: American Foreign Policy, 1938–1970* (Baltimore: Penguin, 1971), pp. 221–225.

9. The Suez Canal was owned by a joint-stock company in which British and (to a lesser extent) French money had been invested.

10. Charges in the West that Nasser was a Communist were incorrect. In fact, Nasser had outlawed the Egyptian Communist Party. The Soviet Union turned a blind eye to Nasser's actions in order not to jeopardize its new relationship with the Arab world. Similarly, when the Soviets began to sell arms to the Sukarno government of Indonesia, the powerful Indonesian Communist Party complained bitterly. The party's fears were well founded; in October 1965, the Indonesian army launched a bloodbath, killing up to half a million real and suspected Communists.

11. CIA special estimate, advance copy for National Security Council, March 10, 1953, "Probable Consequences of the Death of Stalin and the Elevation of Malenkov to Leadership in the USSR," p. 4, in Paul Kesaris, ed., *CIA Research Reports: The Soviet Union, 1946–1976* (Frederick, Md.: University Publications of America, 1982), reel II, frames 637–648.

12. The Presidium (known as the Politburo during 1966–1991) of the Central Committee of the Communist Party was the decisionmaking body, which consisted of approximately a dozen individuals. The number was not fixed; it varied frequently.

13. The Baghdad Pact, at any rate, did not last long, nor did it accomplish much. Similarly, the Soviet Union's national interests were hardly served by supplying arms to Nasser. Time and again, the actions of the superpowers had little more than symbolic value.

14. N. S. Khrushchev, *Khrushchev Remembers: The Last Testament* (Boston: Little, Brown, 1974), pp. 299–300.

15. The event had embarrassed Eisenhower, who had first lied about it and then had to acknowledge that he had approved the spying mission. It had also proved to be an embarrassment for Khrushchev, whose military and scientific establishment had launched the first earth satellite and the first intercontinental missile and yet had been unable to bring down a U.S. plane at 75,000 feet until engine trouble apparently forced it to a lower altitude.

16. Stephen Kinzer, *All the Shah's Men: An American Coup and the Roots of Middle East Terror* (Hoboken, N.J.: John Wiley and Sons, 2003), pp. 2, 5–6, 67, 161–163, 209. The citation is by William Roger Louis, p. 215.

17. Chalmers Johnson, "Abolish the CIA!" *London Review of Books,* October 21, 2004, p. 25.

18. Stephen Schlesinger and Stephen Kinzer, *Bitter Fruit: The Untold Story of the American Coup in Guatemala* (New York: Anchor Books, 1990), pp. 49–63, 76, 108, 253–254.

19. Cited in Richard J. Walton, *Cold War and Counter-Revolution: The Foreign Policy of John F. Kennedy* (Baltimore: Viking, 1972), p. 50.

20. David Horowitz, *The Free World Colossus: A Critique of American Foreign Policy in the Cold War,* rev. ed. (New York: Hill and Wang, 1971), pp. 342–345. Also, Edgar M. Bottome, *The Balance of Terror: A Guide to the Arms Race* (Boston: Beacon Press, 1971), pp. 120–121, 158–160.

21. "Gilpatric Warns U.S. Can Destroy Atom Aggressor," *New York Times,* October 22, 1961, pp. 1, 6.

22. In 1955, Khrushchev had argued for a secret arms shipment to Nasser's Egypt, and it had proven to be a bold and successful plan of action. In Cuba, he could perhaps do the same.

23. "Nezyblemaia leninskaia general'naia linia KPSS," *Pravda,* October 17, 1964, p. 1.

24. Kai Bird and Max Holland, "Dispatches," *The Nation,* April 28, 1984, p. 504.

25. After the political resolution of the crisis, LeMay publicly berated Kennedy for having "lost" the showdown. See Richard Rhodes, *Dark Sun: The Making of the Hydrogen Bomb* (New York: Simon and Schuster, 1995), pp. 571, 574–575.

26. See A. S. Feklisov, "Neizvestnoe o razviazke karibskogo krizisa," in M. V. Filimoshin, ed., *KGB otkryvaet tainy* (Moscow: Patriot, 1992), pp. 118–132.

27. Robert F. Kennedy, *Thirteen Days: A Memoir of the Cuban Missile Crisis* (New York: Norton, 1969), pp. 89–90.

28. Ibid., p. 18.

29. Khrushchev, *Khrushchev Remembers,* pp. 513–514.

# PART 2

# NATIONALISM AND THE END OF COLONIALISM

After World War II a wave of nationalism swept across Asia and Africa, and in its wake a host of new nations proclaimed independence from their European colonial masters. Within two decades about one-third of the world's population was freed from colonial rule. The scope and the speed of the dismantling of the colonial empires were unforeseen. But by 1960, it had become clear to even the more conservative rulers of the colonial powers that they could no longer resist the demands rising from the colonized peoples of Asia and Africa for independence and nationhood. None stated it better than British prime minister Harold Macmillan in his famous "Wind of Change" speech delivered at the end of a tour of Africa in January 1960:

> We have seen the awakening of national consciousness in peoples who have for centuries lived in dependence upon some other power. Fifteen years ago this movement spread through Asia. . . . Today the same thing is happening in Africa and the most striking of all the impressions I have formed since I left London a month ago is the strength of this African national consciousness. The wind of change is blowing through the continent, and whether we like it or not this growth of national consciousness is a political fact, and our national policies must take account of it.[1]

Several historical developments merged to bring about this rise of nationalism and rapid decolonization in the postwar period. First, the war itself caused strains on the European colonial powers, which caused them to lose grip on their overseas colonies. Some of them had lost their colonies during the war and found it difficult to restore control of them afterward, while others were so exhausted by the war that they came to view the maintenance of a colonial empire as a burden greater than it was worth. Another factor was the emergence of a Western-educated elite among the natives of the colonies who took seriously the lessons they had learned in the Western universities and now demanded democracy, self-government, and national sovereignty. In some cases the colonial peoples took part as allies in the war and, having contributed to the victory of freedom, they now demanded a measure of that freedom for themselves.

Still another factor with relevance to Asia, as we shall see in Chapter 5, was the role of Japan in bringing an early end to European colonialism. On the one hand, Japan lost its own colonies, and on the other hand, it had promoted and provoked in various Asian countries nationalist movements, which opposed the return of the colonial powers after the war. Britain responded with greater alacrity than did France and the Netherlands to the strength of the independence movement in Asia and took the lead in decolonization. Once it granted independence to India, long its most important colony, the grounds for maintaining its rule over lesser colonies vanished. France, however, resisted granting independence to its colonies, for it saw in the restoration of the French empire a means of compensating for its humiliating defeats in World War II. In Chapter 5, we relate the frustrations of France in Indochina, where it was met and ultimately defeated by a determined Vietnamese nationalist movement led by Ho Chi Minh.

In Africa, decolonization came later than in Asia largely because national consciousness and strong nationalist movements were slower to develop. There are several historical reasons for this, but as we explain in Chapter 6, the persistence of ethnic divisions in Africa was a major obstacle to the development of nationalism. As in Asia, the pattern of decolonization in Africa was determined, to a great extent, by the policy of the European colonial nations. In general, Britain did more to prepare its African colonies for self-rule and independence than France, Belgium, or Portugal. In fact, the abrupt departure of France and Belgium from Africa left their former colonies particularly ill prepared for either political or economic independence. France, in addition, refused to abandon Algeria, which many French citizens called home and which their government considered a province of France and not a colony. But the Muslim majority among native Algerians was determined to win independence from France, and the result was that France had on its hands another long and bitter revolutionary struggle.

Nationalism was a key ingredient in the postwar struggles in the Middle East as well. Here, two peoples, Jews and Arabs, clashed over claims to the same land on which to establish their nations. The Jews, fortified by their particular brand of nationalism—Zionism—returned to settle a land they had parted from centuries before, while the Palestinians, who had occupied this same land for centuries, were determined not to make room for the Jews who came in greater and greater numbers after World War II. Chapter 7 provides a review of the long historical background to their conflicting claims, without which their postwar feud cannot be understood. The state of Israel came into being in 1948, at the expense of the Palestinians, and ever since it has been embattled by its Arab neighbors.

The continuing struggle for national self-determination in Vietnam is treated in Chapter 9 in the following section, and the postindependence drive of the new nations of Asia and Africa for political and economic modernization is taken up in Part 4, "The Third World."

## ■ NOTE

1. James J. McBath, ed., *British Public Addresses, 1828–1960* (Boston: Houghton Mifflin, 1971), pp. 75–83.

# 5

# Decolonization in Asia

Independence movements in Asian nations had been brewing since about the beginning of the twentieth century, and by the end of World War II they had become boiling cauldrons, the contents of which the lid of colonialism could no longer contain. The demand for self-determination and national independence was sounded by ardent nationalists throughout Asia, in India and Burma, in Vietnam and Malaya, in Indonesia and the Philippines. In some cases, independence was achieved peacefully, because the imperial nation became resigned to the termination of its colonial rule, as was the case of the United States in the Philippines and Great Britain in India and Burma. In other cases, imperial powers were determined to resist the national independence movements in their colonies and ultimately granted independence only after engaging in a long and bloody struggle, as was the case of the French in Indochina and the Dutch in the East Indies.

The primary ingredient in all independence movements was nationalism. The beginnings of nationalist resistance to European colonial rule in Asia may be traced to the turn of the century. Gradually, the colonized peoples awakened to their precolonial traditions and developed a sense of national consciousness. Their quests for national independence were mixed with strong anti-imperialist and antiwhite racial sentiments. They were outraged by imperialist domination, by being treated as inferior citizens in their own native lands. They could point out to the Europeans the blatant contradiction between their own professed ideals of democracy and self-government and their denial of the same to their Asian colonies. After witnessing the destruction European nations had wrought upon one another in World War I, the Asian colonial peoples began to doubt the superiority of their colonial masters. By the end of World War II, Asian nationalist movements had become quite strong, and they were determined to fight for an end to colonial rule and for full national independence.

# ■ THE IMPACT OF WORLD WAR II

World War II, and especially the role played by Japan in the war, greatly stimulated the national independence movements in Asia. During the war, several of the imperial powers of Europe were either overrun by Nazi Germany, as were France and the Netherlands, or were fighting desperately for survival, as was Great Britain. These nations were unable to maintain their colonial regimes in Asia, or did so only with difficulty. Moreover, Japan quickly took advantage of this situation and filled the power vacuum by its own conquest of most of Southeast Asia in 1942. The Japanese claimed that they came not as enemies of the Asian peoples but as their liberators, fighting to free Asia from the chains of Western imperialism and to make Asia safe for Asians. While it is true that under Japanese rule Asian colonies merely replaced one master for another, Japan did much to generate nationalism in Southeast Asia, and strengthened the independence movements in the Philippines, Indochina, the Dutch East Indies, Malaya, and Burma. The swiftness and apparent ease with which the Japanese defeated the European forces in Asia signaled to the Vietnamese, Indonesians, Burmese, and others that their former European masters were not as powerful as they had thought.

In Indonesia the Japanese released native political prisoners from the jails and threw the Dutch colonial officials into the same cells. They banned the use of the Dutch language and promoted the use of native languages. They granted nominal independence to the Philippines and to Burma in 1943, and promised it to others. In some cases, such as in India and Burma, Japan helped arm and train national armies to fight the British. By the end of the war, when Japan was forced out, the nationalist organizations Japan had assisted stood ready to oppose the efforts by the European powers to reimpose their colonial rule. This was especially the case in Indonesia, where nationalist leaders immediately issued a declaration of independence at the time of Japan's surrender.

The United States, too, played a role in hastening the end of colonialism in Asia. During the war, U.S. leaders, especially President Roosevelt, had been outspoken in their opposition to the continuation of European colonialism in postwar Asia. The United States became the first Western nation to relinquish its colonial power there after the war. The U.S. government had long before promised independence to the Philippines, a U.S. colony since 1898, and no sooner was the war over than plans for the transfer of power were made. In 1946, with great fanfare, the Republic of the Philippines was proclaimed on an appropriate date, July 4th.

# ■ INDEPENDENCE AND THE PARTITION OF INDIA

The decolonization of British India has deeper historic roots. Resistance to British rule began back in the nineteenth century with the founding of the

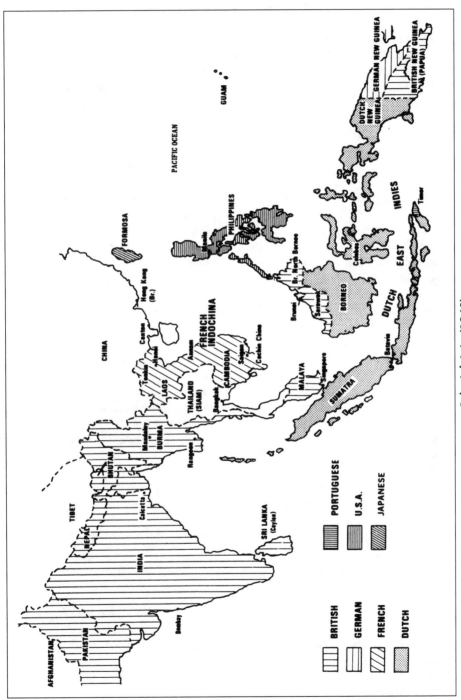

Colonial Asia (1940)

Indian National Congress (a political party usually known as Congress). Prior to World War II, the British were already committed to eventual self-government and independence for India, but the war speeded up the timetable. In May 1942, the British government sent a special envoy, Sir Stafford Cripps, to India on a mission aimed at placating the Indian nationalists (and world opinion). In what became known as the Cripps proposal, he promised India dominion status (self-government but continuing membership in the British Commonwealth) and an election for a native constituent assembly to draft an Indian constitution—*after* the war. This provoked a negative reaction from Indian nationalist leaders, notably Mohandas Gandhi and Jawaharlal Nehru, who were determined to turn Britain's disadvantage—the war emergency—into India's advantage. Their firm rejection of the Cripps proposal and their inspirational rhetoric aroused the nationalism of their fellow Indians, which found expression both in Gandhi's passive resistance to British colonial laws as well as in violent political demonstrations. Gandhi had become a unique force to be reckoned with because of his long-suffering and selfless pursuit of national independence using such nonviolent methods as organizing work stoppages and fasting until near death.[1] Flushed with the heady wine of nationalism, Congress, in August 1942, not only rejected the British offer for eventual independence but passed the Quit India Resolution, which demanded instead the immediate departure of the British from India.

The British response to the Quit India Resolution was to arrest Gandhi and Nehru. Congress followers rebelled but were suppressed in several weeks. One expatriate Indian nationalist leader, Subhas Chandra Bose, went so far as to put an army in the field (with Japanese assistance) to fight the British. Toward the end of the war, the British viceroy, the Crown's representative in India, repeatedly advised London that the demand for independence in India was so strong that it could be postponed no longer. Prime Minister Winston Churchill, the guardian of Britain's empire, had little tolerance for the Indian nationalist movement and had no intention of granting independence. His public reaction to the Quit India Resolution was:

> We intend to remain the effective rulers of India for a long and indefinite period. . . . We mean to hold our own. I have not become the King's First Minister in order to preside over the liquidation of the British Empire. . . . Here we are, and here we stand, a veritable rock of salvation in this drifting world.[2]

Churchill reduced the issue to two clear-cut alternatives: the British could either stand and rule or they could cut and run, and he never seriously considered the latter. He did, however, consider adopting a policy aimed at undermining the Indian National Congress by enlisting the support of the impoverished rural masses with a land reform program that would benefit them at the expense of wealthy landowners, who were identified with Congress.[3]

In June 1945, in anticipation of the end of the war, British authorities in India convened a conference of Indian leaders (several of whom were released from prison so that they could take part) aimed at creating an interim coalition government pending the granting of independence after the war. These talks, however, were complicated by the presence of a third party, the Muslim League. Muslims made up the largest religious minority in India, and they feared being swallowed up by the far more powerful Hindu majority. They feared becoming a helpless minority in an Indian nation in which the Hindu-Muslim population ratio was about five to one. Centuries of Hindu-Muslim antagonism could not easily be resolved, and the Muslim League, led by Mohammed Ali Jinnah, insisted on nothing less than a separate state for the Muslims. Gandhi and Nehru were staunchly opposed to such a division, and they tried to reassure Jinnah and the British that Muslim autonomy and safety would be guaranteed within the new Union of India. The British, too, wished to preserve the unity of India, but Jinnah remained adamant in his demands for a separate Muslim nation.

In London, the new prime minister, Clement Attlee, whose Labour Party had unseated Churchill's government in July 1945, agreed to the transfer of power to the Indian people as soon as possible, and at the same time to preserve the unity of India. However, these two goals were in conflict because of the Muslim insistence on a partition of India. In an effort to resolve the partition/unity issue, Attlee dispatched, in March 1946, a cabinet mission to India, where tensions were rapidly mounting. Indian nationalist aspirations for independence clashed with Muslim aspirations for nationhood. Indian nationalism was made manifest in a mutiny by Indian sailors against their British naval officers, and by the outpouring of the inspired nationalist rhetoric of Gandhi and Nehru. The Muslim leader, Jinnah, was equally articulate and passionate in his demand for the creation of a separate nation for the Muslims. The cabinet mission released its report, rejecting partition as impractical but favoring instead a formula for assuring the autonomy of Muslim provinces within a greater Indian unity. But efforts to implement this plan were forestalled by mutual mistrust and quarreling. With the outbreak of communal violence between Hindus and Muslims (and among other minorities), there was too little time to work out a peaceful solution.

The tense situation developing in India caused the British to advance the timetable for independence. A new initiative was made with the appointment of Lord Louis Mountbatten, the popular wartime hero, to the post of viceroy of India. On his arrival there in March 1947, Mountbatten announced July 1948 as the new deadline for the transfer of power from the British to the Indians. Instead of pacifying the Indians—both Hindus and Muslims—as he had intended, his announcement had the opposite effect. As violence mounted and thousands of people were killed, negotiations among the three parties intensified. Although Mountbatten at first reaffirmed the

British desire to preserve the unity of India, he could not satisfy the Muslim League with anything less than partition, and he therefore decided to settle the matter speedily on the basis of establishing two successor states to British rule. The result was a hasty agreement on the division of India to go into effect on a new, earlier date set for independence: August 15, 1947.

Thus, not one but two nations came into being: India and Pakistan, the new Muslim state. This event, known as the partition, was followed by the movement of some 15 million people from one area to the territories designated for another, mainly the flight of Muslims from various regions of India to Pakistan. A commission was set up to define the boundaries of Pakistan, one part of which was to be in the west and another part in the east, two ethnically diverse regions separated by 1,000 miles. The agreement on the partition of India did not specify the future status of the Sikhs, another religious minority, and the 560 small, independent princely states scattered throughout the Indian subcontinent. It was presumed, however, that they would look to one or the other of the two new governments for protection and thus be integrated into either India or Pakistan.

Indian prime minister Jawaharlal Nehru, addressing an audience in the United States, October 11, 1947, two months after independence was granted to India. *(National Archives)*

Mohammed Ali Jinnah, president of the Muslim League and later the first president of Pakistan, August 9, 1945. *(National Archives)*

While the partition met the nationalist aspirations of the Muslims, who were jubilant over the birth of Pakistan, it was a disappointment to both the Indian nationalists and the British, who would have preferred the preservation of a united India. But none of the three could be pleased by the terrible brutality that attended the partition. Instead of putting an end to the civil strife between Hindus and Muslims, partition led to much greater bloodletting. Hysterical mobs of Hindus, Muslims, Sikhs, and others savagely attacked one another in acts of reprisal, bitterness, and desperation. In many cities terrorism raged out of control for many days when arson, looting, beatings, murder, and rape became common occurrences. Numerous villages became battlegrounds of warring groups, and massacres were frequent along the highways clogged with poor and usually unprotected migrants. Before it was over, an estimated 1 million people lost their lives. The British, in fact, had warned the two impatient and obstinate sides of this possible result of moving too hastily on partition, but it had been to no avail. Indeed, the British laid themselves open to charges of moving with excessive haste and without adequate planning for an orderly population transfer.

## ■ THE BRITISH AND DUTCH IN SOUTHEAST ASIA

The process of decolonization in Southeast Asia varied from country to country but, in general, it was more orderly in the U.S. and British colonies (excepting, of course, the violence involved in the partition of India) than it was in the French and Dutch colonies.[4] The British granted independence to Ceylon (now known as Sri Lanka) in 1947 and to Burma (now called Myanmar) in 1948. They were prepared to transfer power to a Malayan union in 1948, but this was delayed for a decade by internal strife between the Malays, the Muslim majority, and the Chinese, who were in the minority except in the city of Singapore.[5] An unsuccessful ten-year-long Communist insurgency complicated matters further. Finally, in August 1957, after the Communist movement was suppressed and a greater degree of ethnic harmony between the Malays and the Chinese was attained, the British granted full independence to the Federation of Malaya.

Britain also relinquished control of its other colonies on the periphery of Malaya. Singapore remained a British Crown Colony until it became an independent nation in 1959. Sarawak and North Borneo, British colonies located on the northern side of the island of Borneo (the southern part belonged to the Dutch East Indies), were granted independence in 1963 and, together with Singapore, joined Malaya to form the new state of Malaysia.

In contrast to the British, the Dutch had no intention of granting independence to the Dutch East Indies, a colony comprised of eight thousand ethnically diverse islands, which the Dutch had exploited for three centuries. But Dutch intransigence was met by equally strong resistance on the part of the Indonesian nationalists. During World War II, the Japanese military rulers who controlled the Dutch colony gave their active support to an anti-Dutch, nationalist organization known as Putera. By the end of the war, this organization, under the leadership of Achem Sukarno, had developed a 120,000-troop army. When news of Japan's surrender reached Jakarta, the capital, Sukarno, who had been under intensive pressure from the more radical student element in Putera, quickly drafted a declaration of Indonesian independence. He read it on August 17, 1945, to a huge crowd that had gathered to celebrate the event. At about the same time, the British landed an occupying force to receive the Japanese surrender and to maintain order until Dutch forces could arrive.

The Dutch returned with a design to restore colonial rule, only to be confronted by a strong nationalist movement with a large, well-equipped army and by an even more hostile Communist movement. Negotiations produced a compromise in late 1946 whereby the Dutch would recognize Indonesian independence only on the islands of Java and Sumatra, on the condition that this new Indonesian republic remain within the Dutch colonial empire in a "Union of Netherlands and Indonesia." Indonesian leaders, however, rejected this plan, and when the Dutch resorted to police action to quell demonstrations in July 1947, they were met by armed resistance. Despite United Nations efforts to arrange a cease-fire and diplomatic pressures by the United States and Britain on the Dutch, the Indonesian war of independence continued for another two years, with thousands of casualties on both sides. Finally, in 1949, the Dutch conceded, and a fully independent Federation of Indonesia came into being with Sukarno as its president.

## ■ THE FRENCH IN INDOCHINA

The French, not unlike the Dutch, were also opposed to granting independence to their Asian colony in Indochina, and their efforts to reimpose colonial power there would also meet with failure.

France's colonial presence in Vietnam dates back to 1858, when its troops occupied the Mekong River Delta in the south. By 1883, when the native ruling dynasty submitted to French rule, the French extended their rule to the Red River Delta in the north. The conquest of Vietnam was then complete. But, according to the Museum of the Revolution in Hanoi, the struggle against this latest manifestation of foreign domination of Vietnam began on the very day the French had extended their dominion over all of Vietnam.[6] At first, defiance consisted of unorganized peasant uprisings, which the French quickly suppressed. At the turn of the century, French rule, like that of other colonial powers elsewhere, appeared to be secure. Vietnamese nationalists, humiliated by the French presence, found themselves incapable of challenging the colonial power. Imprisonment and the public use of the guillotine had their intended impact.

The central figure in the Vietnamese independence movement was Ho Chi Minh. Late in life he defeated the French, but as a young man he could do no more than humbly request justice for his native land. In 1919, he happened to be living in Paris, where the victors of World War I were meeting to decide the fate of the losers. U.S. president Woodrow Wilson had come to the conference as the champion of national self-determination, the one who spoke for the rights of all subjugated peoples. Ho Chi Minh submitted a petition to the U.S. delegation in the hope that Wilson would intervene on Vietnam's behalf. But the delegates had more pressing issues to consider, and the French, whose overriding concern was the punishment of Germany, were in no mood to discuss with a U.S. president (with whom relations were strained as it were) their colonial rule in a faraway land. Ho's calls for amnesty for all political prisoners, equal justice, freedom of the press, and "the sacred right of all peoples to decide their own destiny" fell on deaf ears.[7]

In the following year, Ho became one of the founders of the French Communist Party. He saw Communism as the only political movement in France that concerned itself "a great deal with the colonial question." For Ho, Communism thus became a vehicle for national liberation of his native land from French colonialists who professed the sacred principles of liberalism and democracy. Ho's identity as a Marxist and anticolonialist took him to Moscow in 1924, at a time, however, when the Kremlin began to focus on domestic problems and all but abandoned its commitment to international revolution. By the late 1920s, he made his way to China, where revolutionary ferment promised to spread to the rest of Asia. For nearly twenty years, he remained a man without a country, living in exile and waiting for a chance to return to Vietnam to challenge the French.

The opportunity came in 1941, during the early years of World War II. The French army, the world's best on paper, had collapsed in the face of the German attack in the spring of 1940. In the following year, when the Japanese swept over Southeast Asia, the French again offered little resistance. Japan had humbled one of Europe's great powers, but this proved to be little solace for the Vietnamese since they merely exchanged one master for another. The Japanese conquest of Southeast Asia, however, put into sharp focus the vulnerability of the European colonial presence in Asia, a lesson that was not lost on the Vietnamese, who at the end of the war demanded the end of French colonial rule.

In the meantime, Ho Chi Minh had returned to Vietnam in 1940 to create a native resistance movement, the Viet Minh (the League for the Independence of Vietnam), and turned against the Japanese, who now controlled Vietnam. Thus, by a strange twist of fate, Ho and the United States became allies during World War II in their common struggle against the Japanese empire. The United States recognized the usefulness of the Viet Minh, and in fact the OSS (the U.S. Office of Strategic Services, the forerunner of the CIA) provided Ho with weapons and supplies.

When the war ended in 1945, it was Ho and his men who controlled much of Vietnam. France's colonial ambitions in Southeast Asia seemed to be at an end. Toward the end of the war, President Roosevelt had urged the French to follow the U.S. example in the Philippines and grant Vietnam its independence. But the French, humiliated in World War II and insisting on the restoration of France as one of the world's great powers, refused to accept the loss of a prized colony. They sought refuge in a page out of the nineteenth century, which equated colonialism with national pride and prestige. They insisted on reasserting their authority as they had done in the past.

In the meantime, on September 2, 1945, Ho Chi Minh declared the independence of Vietnam in Hanoi. He drew on hallowed French and U.S. political documents to justify a Vietnam free from colonial rule. Ho made use of the Declaration of the Rights of Man and Citizen from the French Revolution of 1789 and the U.S. Declaration of Independence. Talks between Ho and the French came to nothing. At a minimum, the Vietnamese insisted on a genuine measure of autonomy within the context of the French empire. The French, however, refused such a solution. The French navy eventually replied with a classic example of gunboat diplomacy. In November 1946, it bombarded the Vietnamese sector of the port of Haiphong. According to French estimates, six thousand civilians died in the shelling of the city. The French then drove the Viet Minh out of Hanoi, and the first Indochina War began.

## ■ THE FIRST INDOCHINA WAR

Initially, the Viet Minh proved to be no match for the French army, which possessed superior weaponry as well as more troops. The French were able to put airplanes, tanks, trucks, and heavy artillery into battle. In a conventional head-to-head clash the French were destined to win. The Viet Minh, therefore, had no choice except to pursue the tactics of the weak against the strong: guerrilla warfare.

Guerrillas (from the Spanish meaning "little war") have little chance of defeating their more powerful enemy in a decisive battle, because they simply do not have the means to do so. They rely instead on a series of small campaigns designed to tie down the enemy army without engaging it directly. Once the enemy forces bring their superior power into play, the guerrillas break off the fight and withdraw, leaving the battlefield to the conventional forces who then plant their banners and proclaim victory. Armies fighting guerrillas can often point to an uninterrupted string of "victories," in the traditional sense of the word. The guerrillas are almost always "defeated."

Such a scenario is frequently misleading. Ché Guevara, one of the better-known practitioners of guerrilla warfare and who had fought alongside

Fidel Castro in Cuba in the 1950s, compared a guerrilla campaign to the minuet, the eighteenth-century dance. In the minuet, the dancers take several steps forward and then back.[8] The "steps back" are of central importance to the guerrillas. They cannot afford to hold their ground since they know they will be decimated; therefore, they must always retreat after going forward. They must gather their dead and wounded and their supplies, and then reorganize to fight another day. Little wonder that the conventional forces are always able to claim that they are winning the war and that it will only be a matter of time until the guerrillas suffer their "final" defeat.

The guerrillas' ultimate victory comes only after a prolonged struggle that wears down the enemy physically and psychologically. Of utmost importance for the guerrillas is the conduct of political action necessary to gain recruits for their cause. For conventional forces, the conflict is frequently of a purely military nature; in contrast, successful guerrilla movements always focus on the psychological and political nature of the conflict. The French colonel Gabriel Bonnet reduced this to a quasi-mathematical formula: "RW = G + P (revolutionary warfare is guerrilla action plus psychological-political operations)."[9]

In Vietnam, the French forces generally held the upper hand, and with it came repeated predictions of victory. But they were unable to suppress the insurrection. The Viet Minh always managed to reappear and fight again. And, thus, what was intended as a short punitive action by the French turned into a long and costly war of attrition. And because all wars have political and economic repercussions, successive French governments were beginning to feel the heat. At the outset of the war, the French public had supported the efforts to suppress an anticolonial rebellion, but as the years went by and the financial burden became increasingly heavy, public dissatisfaction grew.

In 1950, the United States became involved in the Korean War, which it considered part of a general Communist offensive in Asia across a wide front. Its view of the Viet Minh insurgency was no different. President Harry Truman became concerned with the French position in Vietnam, and he thus became the first U.S. president to involve the United States in that region when he offered the French financial aid. When the war ended in 1954, most of the French expenditures in Vietnam were being underwritten by the U.S. taxpayer.

Cold War orthodoxy in Washington insisted that revolutions tend to be fomented from the outside (a view that lies at the core of Washington's view of the Cold War). The Soviet Union, however, offered the Viet Minh no aid, and when the Chinese Communists came to power in 1949, Ho Chi Minh emphatically rejected the idea of using Chinese troops against the French although he did accept Chinese supplies, particularly artillery. Chinese-Vietnamese enmity is age-old, and Ho feared the Chinese, their Communism notwithstanding, as much as he did the French.

President Truman's Asian experts in the State Department warned him that unless the French granted the Vietnamese "true autonomous self-government," there would be "blood-shed and unrest for many years, threatening the . . . peace and stability" in the region.[10] Truman and his secretary of state Dean Acheson, however, chose to support French colonialism. They saw the anticolonial rebellion in Indochina as part of a global Communist movement, and in the process Southeast Asia was destined to become a focal point of the Cold War.

After years of fighting, the French public grew tired of the war. Predictions of victory by French generals and politicians had proven to be hollow promises. In desperation, the French military command, hoping to find a solution to the elusiveness of the Viet Minh guerrillas, sought to entice the Vietnamese to stand up and wage a conventional battle at the remote outpost of Dien Bien Phu, near the border of Laos. If the Viet Minh took the bait, it would result in a conventional showdown and they would be crushed. The French, after all, possessed superior firepower and they controlled the air and the roads leading to Dien Bien Phu.

General Vo Nguyen Giap, the military genius of the Viet Minh, decided to oblige the French, but only after he had made adequate preparations for the battle. With great difficulty he brought into combat heavy artillery, which the Viet Minh had not used previously to any great extent. To the surprise of the French, Giap managed to place the artillery on the hilltops overlooking the valley of Dien Bien Phu, and the decisive battle of the war began. The French soon realized their position was doomed and they appealed for U.S. intervention.

The new U.S. administration of Dwight Eisenhower, as Truman had done before him, weighed in on the side of colonialism. Some of Eisenhower's advisers urged a nuclear strike, but Eisenhower rejected this option because he understood that nuclear weapons are tools of destruction, not war. It made no sense to incinerate Dien Bien Phu—French and Vietnamese alike—to "save" it. Eisenhower refused to become directly involved in Vietnam, particularly after the Senate majority leader, Lyndon Baines Johnson, told him that the U.S. people would not support another war in Asia, particularly in light of the fact that the cease-fire in Korea had been signed only the previous year.[11] Eisenhower did, however, offer the French clandestine assistance at Dien Bien Phu. The CIA flew 682 airdrop missions, and two of its pilots were killed.[12]

The battle of Dien Bien Phu ("hell in a very small place," in the words of the French historian Bernard Fall) took place in the spring of 1954. In early May, the French garrison finally fell and with it some of France's finest soldiers. Two thousand of the French forces died; ten thousand were taken prisoner, and only seventy-three managed to escape.[13] The French defeat was total and the French role in Indochina was over. The French government and the public both welcomed the end.

Ho Chi Minh at Dien Bien Phu, May 1954. *(National Archives)*

By coincidence, the world's leading powers—both Communist and capitalist—were engaged at that time in discussing several issues in Geneva. The French and Vietnamese agreed, after the battle of Dien Bien Phu, to take their dispute to this forum. At the conference, however, the Vietnamese Communists received precious little support from the other Communist powers, the Soviet Union and China, both of whom were more interested in other issues. As a consequence, the talks produced a strange agreement—which none of the parties signed. The Geneva Agreement called for a Vietnam temporarily divided along the 17th parallel with a Communist government in the north and a non-Communist government in the south. This division was to last only until a nationwide election was held in July 1956. The election would give the country a single government and president and bring about the "unity and territorial integrity" of Vietnam. In the meantime, the agreement demanded the neutrality of both regions of Vietnam, north and south.[14]

The U.S. delegates at Geneva were hypnotized by the specter of a global monolithic Communism. But they need not have worried. Both the Communist Chinese and the Soviets were more interested in cutting a deal with the French than in coming to the aid of their Vietnamese comrades. It appears that it was the Chinese foreign minister, Zhou Enlai (Chou En-lai), much to the surprise of the French, who first proposed a division of Vietnam. The Viet Minh finally yielded, but they insisted on a dividing line along the 13th parallel, which would leave them with two-thirds of the country. The French wanted the 18th parallel; the Vietnamese, under Chinese and Soviet pressure, backed down and accepted the 17th parallel, which cut the country roughly in half. At the farewell banquet, Zhou hinted to the South Vietnamese delegation that he favored a permanent partition of Vietnam. This suggestion reflects China's centuries-old animosity toward Vietnam rather than solidarity among Communist nations.

The Viet Minh also yielded on the question of the timetable for the scheduled election. They wanted an election as soon as possible to cash in on their stunning defeat of the French. It was the Soviet foreign minister, Viacheslav Molotov, who asked rhetorically: "Shall we say two years?"[15] The French and the U.S. delegates quickly endorsed Molotov's proposal. It was the best deal the U.S. delegation could hope to obtain. Secretary of State John Foster Dulles was not happy with the prospect of pitting a candidate hand-picked by the United States against the popular Ho Chi Minh. He knew full well that a free election throughout all of Vietnam would bring Ho to power. Earlier in the conference, Dulles had cabled the U.S. ambassador in Paris:

> Thus since undoubtedly true that elections might eventually mean unification Vietnam under Ho Chi Minh this makes it all more important that they should be held only as long after cease-fire agreement as possible. . . . We believe important that no date should be set now.[16]

As it was, losing even half of the nation to Communism did not sit well with Dulles. The United States refused to sign the Geneva Agreement, but in a separate statement the U.S. negotiator, General W. Bedell Smith, acting on behalf of Eisenhower, pledged U.S. adherence to the agreement.

The postponement for two years of the creation of a single government for Vietnam had predictable consequences. In a development reminiscent of Korea and Germany, two separate governments came into being: a pro-Western dictatorship in the South (with its capital city of Saigon) and a Communist dictatorship in the North (with the capital in Hanoi). The United States soon began to prop up the anti-Communist government in the South, which it dubbed as "democratic," and which refused to abide by the Geneva Agreement calling for free elections. The elections were never held. Instead, the United States became increasingly tied to the unpopular and repressive regime of Ngo Dinh Diem in South Vietnam. From the very beginning, the United States provided military assistance, as well as economic aid, thus sowing the seeds for direct U.S. intervention once the very existence of the Diem regime was threatened.

For the United States, South Vietnam became the gate guarding the "free world," and the United States became "the guardian at the gate." Once that metaphor took root in popular thought, the anti-Communist regime in South Vietnam became identified with the very survival of the United

States. For psychological, geopolitical, and domestic political reasons, therefore, U.S.–South Vietnamese relations became a Gordian knot that a succession of U.S. presidents did not dare to cut. When Diem was challenged by Communist insurgency in the late 1950s, the second Indochina War began.

## ■ RECOMMENDED READINGS

### ☐ *India and Pakistan*

Brown, W. Norman. *The United States and India, Pakistan, Bangladesh.* 3d ed. Cambridge, Mass.: Harvard University Press, 1972.
A lucid treatment of Indian independence and partition and the subsequent division of Pakistan.

Hutchins, Francis G. *India's Revolution: Gandhi and the Quit India Movement.* Cambridge, Mass.: University Press, 1973.
An excellent analysis of Gandhi's role in the Indian nationalist movement.

Merriam, Allen H. *Gandhi vs. Jinnah: The Debate over the Partition of India.* Calcutta: Minerva, 1980.
Re-creates the debate between Gandhi and Jinnah over partition, with many quotations from the speeches and writings of each man.

Thorne, Christopher. *Allies of a Kind: The United States, Britain, and the War with Japan.* Oxford: Oxford University Press, 1978.
An authoritative study of Britain's wartime and immediate postwar policies regarding its colonies in Asia.

### ☐ *Vietnam*

Duiker, William J. *Ho Chi Minh.* New York: Hyperion, 2000.
Definitive biography with an emphasis not on Ho's Communism as the decisive force behind his ideology, but nationalism.

Giap, Vo Nguyen. *People's War, People's Army.* New York: Frederick A. Praeger, 1962.
Giap's assessment of the nature of wars for national liberation and the reasons for his victory at Dien Bien Phu. Introductory biographical sketch by Bernard B. Fall.

Fall, Bernard B. *Hell in a Very Small Place: The Siege of Dien Bien Phu.* Philadelphia: Lippincott, 1966.
The definitive history of the battle by a recognized French expert.

———, ed. *Ho Chi Minh on Revolution: Selected Writings, 1920–66.* New York: Praeger, 1967.
A valuable collection of primary sources.

Joint Chiefs of Staff. *The Joint Chiefs of Staff and the War in Vietnam: History of the Indochina Incident, 1940–1954.* Washington, D.C.: Joint Chiefs of Staff, 1955; declassified 1981.
The Pentagon's critical assessment of why the French lost.

Lacouture, Jean. *Ho Chi Minh: A Political Biography.* New York: Random House, 1968.
A standard biography of the Vietnamese revolutionary.

Patti, Archimedes. *Why Vietnam? Prelude to America's Albatross.* Berkeley: University of California Press, 1980.
    An account of immediate postwar Vietnam by a U.S. OSS officer who established a working relationship with Ho Chi Minh in 1945.

# ■ NOTES

1. Gandhi's career of passive resistance to the laws of Britain that he considered immoral drew upon the writings of the nineteenth-century U.S. writer Henry David Thoreau, and in turn Gandhi's philosophy influenced the U.S. civil rights leader Martin Luther King Jr.

2. As quoted in Francis G. Hutchins, *India's Revolution: Gandhi and the Quit India Movement* (Cambridge, Mass.: Harvard University Press, 1973), p. 143.

3. Churchill once expressed the view that the Indian National Congress represented hardly anybody except lawyers, moneylenders, and the "Hindu priesthood." Ibid., p. 284.

4. Southeast Asia refers to the area of Asia stretching from Burma to the Philippine Islands, and includes such countries as Thailand, Vietnam, Indonesia, and Malaysia.

5. Brunei, another British protectorate in northern Borneo, was scheduled to join its neighbors, Sarawak and North Borneo, in becoming members of the new union of Malaysia, but, prompted by Indonesia, it refused to do so at the last minute. It remained a source of contention among Britain, Malaysia, and Indonesia until it attained self-government under British tutelage in 1971. Singapore separated from Malaysia in 1965 and became a sovereign state.

6. Harrison E. Salisbury, *Behind the Lines—Hanoi: December 23, 1966–January 7, 1967* (New York: Harper and Row, 1967), pp. 52–53.

7. Jean Lacouture, *Ho Chi Minh: A Political Biography* (New York: Random House, 1968), pp. 24–25; Chalmer M. Roberts, "Archives Show Ho's Letter," *Washington Post,* September 14, 1969, p. A 25.

8. Ché Guevara, *Guerrilla Warfare* (New York: Vintage Books, 1969), p. 13.

9. Bernard B. Fall, *The Two Vietnams: A Political and Military Analysis,* 2nd rev. ed. (New York: Frederick A. Praeger, 1967), pp. 349–350. For an analysis of Bonnet's formula, see Bernard B. Fall, *Last Reflections on a War* (Garden City, N.J.: Doubleday, 1967), pp. 209–223.

10. James Bamford, *Body of Secrets: Anatomy of the Ultra-Secret National Security Agency* (New York: Doubleday, 2001), p. 286.

11. David Halberstam, *The Best and the Brightest* (New York: Random House, 1969), p. 141; also Stanley Karnow, *Vietnam: A History* (New York: Viking, 1983), p. 197.

12. Bamford, *Body of Secrets,* p. 286.

13. Bernard B. Fall, "Dienbienphu: A Battle to Remember," in Marvin E. Gettleman, ed., *Vietnam: History, Documents, and Opinions* (Greenwich, Conn.: Fawcett, 1965), p. 107.

14. The text of the Geneva Agreement may be found in several anthologies, as well as in Appendix 2 in George McTurnan Kahin and John W. Lewis, *The United States in Vietnam,* rev. ed. (New York: Delta, 1969), pp. 422–443, particularly the Final Declaration, pp. 441–443.

15. Karnow, *Vietnam,* pp. 198–204.

16. Neil Sheehan et al., *The Pentagon Papers* (New York: Bantam, 1971), p. 46. Dulles also sent a copy of the cable to the U.S. delegate at Geneva, Bedell Smith. Eisenhower wrote in his memoirs that Ho Chi Minh would have won an election with 80 percent of the vote.

# 6

# Decolonization in Africa

Africa was the last frontier of white colonialism. At the close of World War II, the European powers—Britain, France, Belgium, Portugal, and Spain—still held firmly to their colonies, which collectively encompassed virtually the entire continent. But this was soon to change with the awakening of African nationalism. In 1945, there were only three independent nations on the African continent (Ethiopia, Liberia, and South Africa), but by 1970 there were no less than fifty-two independent African nations.

By the mid-1950s, the British government recognized the inevitability of decolonization and began preparing for it rather than resisting it. By the end of that decade the French, too, had resigned themselves to the new reality, and they also willingly handed over political power to the nationalist leaders in their African colonies, except Algeria. The 1960s in Africa were full of excitement and expectation as power changed hands from the white colonial masters to new black African rulers who were flushed with nationalistic pride and eager to face the new challenges of nationhood. The transition was remarkably smooth and was achieved faster and with far less bloodshed than an earlier generation—black or white—had dreamed possible.

The decolonization process in Africa differed from region to region and colony to colony, and it is therefore difficult to generalize about it. The colonial system and the pattern of decolonization varied not only according to region but also according to the European nation involved. British colonial rule differed substantially from the French or Belgian colonial systems. There were also great differences in native populations from colony to colony, and from tribe to tribe within a colony.

The bloodiest struggle for national independence in Africa took place in Algeria, where the French made their last stand for colonial empire. The revolution in Algeria, which lasted for eight years, was an especially violent one, and it may be considered an archetype of an armed struggle for national liberation that features terrorism as a means toward a political end.

# ■ THE RISE OF NATIONALISM

The ethnic makeup of the African population had an important bearing on the decolonization process. The colonies that sought nationhood had boundaries that had been artificially created by the Europeans in the past century. The black African inhabitants of any given colony were not all of the same tribe or ethnic group, and in some cases one ethnic group was spread over more than one colony. In sub-Saharan Africa, no colony contained a majority ethnic group. The growth of nationalism required that loyalty to tribe be shifted to loyalty to nation. The timing of decolonization in the various colonies therefore depended, to a great extent, on the growth of a national consciousness and the development of a sense of political unity in the native population. This was a slow process and was still far from complete in the 1950s. The persistence of tribal loyalties not only retarded the growth of nationalism and the birth of independent nations in Africa, but it would continue to plague the new African nations once independence was granted.

Prior to World War II, European colonial rule was hardly challenged by the subject peoples of Africa. The colonial administrations seemed so secure that they needed little military force to protect them. In some cases, especially in British colonies, this was achieved by use of the protectorate system, whereby local African rulers were allowed to retain considerable autonomy and were protected by the colonial "overlords." Local rulers were made more secure by the military, political, and financial support supplied by their colonial masters. Also, the European rulers used the divide-and-rule method, whereby they restricted or blocked the development of African unity, or even tribal unity, that might threaten their colonial rule. In general, the Africans, the majority of whom were illiterate, viewed the Europeans with mixed awe and fear, and they were hesitant to attempt armed insurrection. And since political consciousness remained relatively low, there seemed little prospect of effective, organized anticolonialist action by the African blacks.

Gradually this situation changed as more Africans received an education—ironically, at the hands of the Europeans—and gained more experience in and exposure to the world of the Europeans. The very presence of Europeans in Africa fundamentally altered African society, particularly in the cities. On the one hand, the Europeans created a labor class among the blacks, whose cheap labor was exploited; and on the other hand, the Europeans created new educational and economic opportunities as well as new models for the Africans. One might say that colonialism carried within it the seeds of its own destruction, especially when the colonial powers were nations that espoused democracy and civil liberties. Some Africans, the more privileged and able among them, became well educated, urbanized, and Westernized. Thus, after several generations under colonial rule, a native elite emerged, marked by its Western education and values. It is this

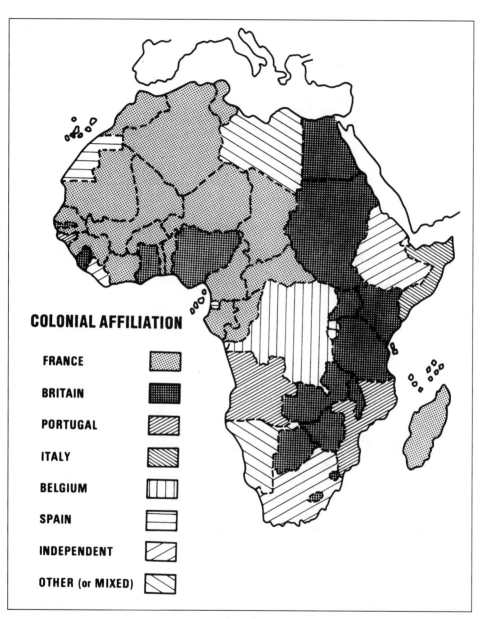

## COLONIAL AFFILIATION

FRANCE

BRITAIN

PORTUGAL

ITALY

BELGIUM

SPAIN

INDEPENDENT

OTHER (or MIXED)

Colonial Africa (1945)

class that first developed a sense of grievance and frustration, and then a political consciousness marked by a strong desire to liberate black Africans from colonial rule. It was from them that the new leaders of the independence movements emerged: leaders who educated their fellow Africans and aroused in them a political consciousness and who established bonds with nationalist leaders of other colonies to strengthen their mutual endeavor for independence. The bond among these new nationalist leaders developed into a pan-Africanist movement in which they found unity in the cause of liberating the whole of Africa from colonial rule.

Although some signs of African restiveness appeared in the prewar period, especially as African businesspeople and workers felt the effects of the Great Depression of the 1930s, it was not until World War II that nationalism and the demand for independence gained strength in Africa. Some African leaders pointed out that their people, who had been called upon to participate in that war to help defeat tyranny and defend liberty, deserved their just reward, a greater measure of that liberty. Their military experience in the war suggested a means of gaining national independence—the use of armed force. They were also stimulated by the example of colonies in other areas of the world, mainly in Asia, winning their independence from the same Europeans who ruled them. These new nations, especially Nehru's India, vigorously championed the cause of decolonization in the United Nations and other forums. The founding of the United Nations also gave heart to the African nationalists, who looked forward to the day when their new nations would join its ranks as full-fledged member nations. Initially, the two superpowers, the United States and the Soviet Union, both urged early decolonization. All these factors contributed to the growing force of nationalism in Africa in the postwar period.

As important as the growth of nationalism in Africa was in preparing the way for independence, that objective would not have been achieved so swiftly or smoothly had Britain, France, and the other colonial nations not come to the realization that it was not in their interest to perpetuate their colonial empires on that continent. Economically underdeveloped colonies were increasingly viewed as both an economic and political liability. The British were the first to come to that realization, but within the decade of the 1950s, the French and Belgians also came to the same view.

## ■ THE BRITISH DEPARTURE

The British colonial system after the war envisioned eventual independence for its colonies. In a gradual, step-by-step manner, the British permitted greater participation by the native peoples in the governing of their colonies. They established executive and legislative councils to advise the royal governors of the colonies, and began to appoint a few well-educated black Africans to these councils. Next, black political leaders were permitted to seek election to the legislative council. Once this was granted, the nationalist leaders began convening national congresses and organizing political parties, which became organs of nationalistic, anti-imperialist propaganda. They also began agitating for expanding the right to vote in the legislative council elections. The granting of universal suffrage—the right to vote—was the turning point, for it paved the way for the nationalist, proindependence parties to gain power. According to the parliamentary system that operated in British colonies, the party that won the election and gained the majority in the legislative council earned a majority of seats in the executive council. The leader of the majority party was then chosen to fill the post of chief minister. The first native Africans to achieve this position were usually charismatic figures who had long been recognized as leaders of the national independence movement. Typically, the one chosen was an able and articulate leader who had a Western education, had spent many years as a political organizer and agitator, and had spent not a few years in the jails of the British colonial administration before gaining the opportunity to lead the independence party to power. Finally, when the British authorities judged that the new native ruler could maintain order and govern responsibly, they prepared for a transfer of power to this responsible leader and his party and granted the colony self-rule and ultimately full independence.

This procedure took place first in the Gold Coast, which became the first of Britain's African sub-Saharan colonies to gain independence. In this West African colony, the able nationalist leader Kwame Nkrumah organized an effective political movement, taking advantage not only of the legal political process, but also of various forms of illegal political pressure, including "positive action"—namely, strikes and boycotts. In 1951, in the first election under universal suffrage, Nkrumah managed his party's campaign while sitting in a British prison. After his party won a large majority, the British governor had little choice but to release Nkrumah, now a national hero, and granted him a seat on the executive council. Three years later the colony, now renamed Ghana, was made self-governing under Nkrumah's leadership, and in March 1957, Nkrumah, now prime minister, was able to announce that Ghana had won its full independence.

Ghana immediately became the model for other African independence movements, and Nkrumah became the continent's most outspoken champion of liberation. In 1958, Nkrumah invited leading African politicians, representing African peoples from the entire continent, to two conferences at Accra, the capital of Ghana. These conferences (the first in April and the second in December 1958) greatly promoted the cause of pan-African unity. It was there that the Organization of African Unity was created. The delegates at the December 1958 conference unanimously endorsed Nkrumah's pronouncement that all Africans must work together for the complete liberation of all of Africa.

Kwame Nkrumah, on a visit to the United States, addresses a New York audience. *(National Archives)*

Kenyan prime minister Jomo Kenyatta, November 1964, ruler of Kenya from independence in 1963 until his death in 1980. *(National Archives)*

The demand for independence spread rapidly across Africa. The British were more responsive than were the other Europeans. They attempted to institute in their other colonies a decolonization process similar to that employed in Ghana, but the timing differed according to circumstances. For example, in Nigeria, the most heavily populated British colony, whose nationalist leaders were among the earliest and most vocal in demanding liberation, the process was delayed until 1960 by serious ethnic conflicts. And in East Africa, Kenya's independence was forestalled by other, very different problems.

Kenya, like other British colonies in Eastern and Southern Africa (but unlike those in Western Africa), was a settlers' colony, meaning it contained permanent European settlers on the land. The loss of land reduced the once independent black farmer to serving someone else. These white settlers, numbering about fifty thousand, lived in the Kenyan highlands, possessed the best lands, and discriminated against the black population. Whites, understandably, were opposed to any independence movement based on majority rule.

The largest tribe in Kenya, the Kikuyu, reacted against the domination of the white settlers, and in 1952, it launched a movement known as the "burning spear," or Mau Mau. The primary aim of the Mau Mau was to return the land to the displaced black population. The Mau Mau uprising, between 1952 and 1956, terrorized the white settlers, but it in fact directed most of its violence toward other blacks who collaborated with the British. In all, approximately one hundred Europeans lost their lives. The toll among blacks was far higher. The Mau Mau killed Christian Kenyans, estimated between 2,000 and 13,000, who had refused to take the blood oath swearing loyalty to them. British troops killed innocent civilians, resettled Kikuyus in "new villages" (detention camps), strafed villages from airplanes, and in the end acknowledged they had killed 4,686 Mau Mau out of a total of 10,527, although other estimates range as high as 50,000.[1] Eventually, the Mau Mau lost popular support and by the end of 1959, soldiers and police crushed the rebellion.

The Kikuyu and other tribes eventually formed a national party under the able leadership of Jomo Kenyatta. Kenyatta, a Western-educated member of the Kikuyu tribe, had languished in a British jail for over seven years as a political prisoner. After he was released in 1961, he led his party to electoral victories and eventually to independence in December 1963. The few remaining Mau Mau handed over their weapons to him. Kenyatta's party and the outgoing British colonial authorities worked out a political formula, embodied in a new constitution, designed to provide for majority rule and yet protect the white minority. Still, fear caused many settlers to leave. But those who remained in the country were neither victimized by Kenya's black majority nor by the new government. Under Kenyatta's enlightened rule, Kenya became one of the most politically stable of Africa's new nations—at least until the mid-1970s.

In south-central Africa there remained three British settler colonies: Nyasaland, Northern Rhodesia, and Southern Rhodesia. They were joined to form a federation in 1953, partly for economic reasons and partly as a means of retaining rule by the white minorities. However, in response to increasing pressure by the majority black populations, the British dissolved the federation and imposed on Nyasaland and Northern Rhodesia constitutions guaranteeing majority rule, thus ending white minority rule. In 1961, Nyasaland under black rule became independent Malawi, and in 1963, Northern Rhodesia became the African-ruled state of Zambia. In Southern Rhodesia, however, a white minority regime, led by Ian Smith, defied the British government and its own black majority by rejecting its British-made, majority-rule constitution and by unilaterally declaring its independence in 1965. Only after prolonged guerrilla attacks by African nationalist parties from bases in neighboring countries and sustained international pressure did Smith finally relent, accepting a plan in 1976 to allow majority rule two years afterward. Continued fighting among rival nationalist parties delayed until 1980 the creation of a black majority government in the country, now known as Zimbabwe.

# ■ THE FRENCH DEPARTURE

The French colonial system was different from the British, and this meant that the decolonization process was also different, even though the timetable was similar. The aim of French colonial policy had been the assimilation of its African colonies into the French empire and the transformation of the African natives into French citizens. The blacks were enjoined to abandon their culture in favor of the "superior" French civilization. They were taught the French language and culture, and the elite among them received their higher education at French universities. No attempt was ever made to prepare the native Africans for independence; however, because the colonies were part of the French empire, they were permitted to send elected representatives to Paris, where they held seats in the French National Assembly.

There always was a problem with the French program of assimilation in that it assumed that the population of the French African colonies wanted to become and in fact were somehow capable of becoming "French." In the case of Algeria, the assimilation of Muslim Arabs proved to be impossible, as the French settlers and the Arabs both rejected it. The Arabs and black Africans always understood that they were, first and foremost, conquered subjects. There was no point for black schoolchildren to recite the lessons written for French children in Paris: "Our ancestors the Gauls had blue eyes and blond hair." At its worst, assimilation as Paris envisioned it was racist; at its best, it was unabashedly ethnocentric. A greater French union of France and the former colonies could only have succeeded on the basis of equality and on the recognition of cultural and racial diversity.

Until the mid-1950s, none of the short-lived cabinets in postwar France responded to the African demands for self-rule. However, at this juncture, shortly after abandoning its colonial empire in Asia, France was faced with a revolutionary movement in Algeria and a growing demand for independence in its other African colonies. With the exception of Algeria, where the French refused to budge, the African colonies of France were surprised to find a new French receptiveness to change. The French no longer insisted upon assimilation; instead, they began to search for a workable alternative.

African nationalists who desired the liberation of their people still found it necessary to work within the French system. The most politically successful of the black African leaders from the French colonies was Félix Houphouët-Boigny, a medical doctor from the Ivory Coast. Shortly after World War II, he had taken the lead in forming a political party that championed the cause of the blacks. As a member of the French National Assembly, Houphouët-Boigny played a leading role in drawing up a new colonial policy that set in motion the movement for colonial self-government. The effect of this bill, which was passed by the assembly in 1956, was to permit greater autonomy for the separate French colonies, which heretofore were under one centralized colonial administration. Each colony was now to have a French prime minister and African vice-ministers, and elections for legislative assemblies under universal suffrage. Meanwhile, in the various French colonies, Houphouët-Boigny's party established branches, which began organizing for elections under the banner of nationalism.

Still, it remained the intent of France to maintain some form of indirect control over its African colonies. A plan for continued association was endorsed by President Charles de Gaulle, after he came to power in Paris in May 1958. Later that year, he offered the twelve sub-Saharan colonies the option of membership in the French Community or immediate and full independence. The former meant autonomy but continued association with France; more important, it meant continued French economic and military aid. This was the preference of all of the colonies except Guinea, which opted instead for independence. In response to Guinea's decision, France immediately pulled out all of its personnel and equipment and terminated all economic aid in hopes of forcing the maverick back into the fold. Guinea, however, stuck with its decision.

The example of Guinea, and nearby Ghana as well, inspired the nationalist leaders in the neighboring French colonies in West Africa. In 1960, after two years of agitation and negotiations, President de Gaulle, with his hands full in Algeria, abruptly granted independence to all of the remaining French colonies in sub-Saharan Africa. These new nations were relatively unprepared either politically or economically for independence, and consequently they tended to remain politically unstable and economically dependent on France for years to come.

## ■ THE FRENCH STRUGGLE IN ALGERIA

France's determination to retain control over Algeria must be viewed in the historical context of its war in Vietnam, a conflict that had drained the French people emotionally, physically, and economically. When defeat came in 1954, the French accepted the loss of Vietnam without bitter recrimination. Vietnam had become a burden to be lifted from their shoulders. There were few dissenting voices in the spring of 1954 when Prime Minister Pierre Mendès-France promised to end the war by granting the Vietnamese their independence. With the Geneva Conference of July 1954, the French colonial presence on the Asian mainland came to an inglorious end.

Yet, within five months of the Geneva settlement, the French faced once more the prospect of losing an important colony. This time it was Algeria. The French, however, having lost one colony, were in no mood to accept again a humiliation at the hands of a colonized people of a different color and religion. At stake were France's honor, its role as a great power, and its position in Africa.

The French insisted that Algeria was not a colony but an integral part of France, a province across the Mediterranean, in the same manner that Brittany, Alsace, or Lorraine were provinces. More important, Algeria was the home of 1 million French citizens who considered themselves to be living in France. Algeria is "part of the republic," Mendès-France insisted; it has "been French for a long time. Between it and the mainland, no secession is conceivable. . . . Never will France . . . yield on this fundamental principle." The minister of the interior, François Mitterand, added: "Algeria is France."[2]

France's presence in Algeria dated back to 1830 when its troops first landed there. It took the French seventeen years to complete the conquest of a people who spoke Arabic and professed the faith of Islam, a religion remarkably impervious to Christian missionaries. (For a summary of Islam, see Chapter 20.) In 1848, the first French, Roman Catholic settlers arrived. The French quest for empire here became a bitter struggle between two cultures and two religions. In 1870–1871, in the wake of France's defeat in its war with Prussia, the Arab population rose in rebellion. The uprising was put down in blood and was followed by the widespread confiscation of Muslim lands. Algeria became a land divided between the immigrant French, who had seized the best lands along the coast and who enjoyed the rights and protection of French citizenship, and the native Algerians for whom the law offered little protection. The French always justified their colonial conquest as part of their civilizing mission, yet the blessings of French democracy were meant only for Europeans in Algeria, not for the indigenous Arab and Muslim population.

In the years between the two world wars (1918–1939), the French government grappled repeatedly with the question of the status of native Algerians. Liberals, both French and Algerians, urged the integration of the Muslim Algerians into French society by granting them citizenship without first having to convert to Catholicism. To that effect, in 1936 France's premier, Leon Blum, proposed a bill granting a number of select Arabs—soldiers with distinguished records in World War I, teachers, graduates from French institutes—the privilege of French citizenship even though they continued to profess the faith of their ancestors.[3] Unrelenting opposition killed the bill—and with it the opportunity of integrating Algeria with France.

A synthesis of Algerian and French societies was a pipe dream pursued by a liberal minority. The French settlers in Algeria refused to consider it; the same may be said of most Muslims. They, too, could not envision themselves as French. As one Muslim scholar put it: "The Algerian people are not French, do not wish to be and could not be even if they did wish."[4] Children in Muslim schools were taught to recite: "Islam is my religion. Arabic is my language. Algeria is my country."[5]

World War II had been fought for the noblest of reasons: against fascism, racism, and colonialism, and for democracy and human rights. It was little wonder that at the end of the war the colonial peoples in Asia and Africa demanded the implementation of these ideals for which, moreover, many of their compatriots had died fighting in the armies of the colonial powers. Inevitably, after the war the Algerians presented the bill for their services to the French.

The first manifestation of the new Algerian attitude became apparent even before the guns fell silent in Europe. On May 1, 1945, during the May Day celebrations in Algiers, Algerian demonstrators staged an unauthorized march carrying banners denouncing French rule and demanding Algerian independence. The French attempt to halt the demonstration led to the deaths of ten Algerians and one Frenchman. The French then boasted that they had ended all disorder. But several days later, on May 8, 1945, the V-E (Victory-in-Europe) Day parade in the Algerian city of Setif turned into a riot. The French had hoisted their victorious tricolor flag. Algerian participants, however, had their own agenda. Again they came with banners calling for the independence of Algeria—and one young man defiantly carried Algeria's forbidden green-and-white flag with the red crescent. A police officer shot him to death.

This act touched off an anticolonial rebellion. The heavy-handed French response brought into combat police and troops as well as airplanes and warships to bomb and strafe villages. The British, as they did later that year in Vietnam when they secured that colony for the French upon the defeat of the Japanese, came to the assistance of the French colonial administration when they provided airplanes to carry French troops from France, Morocco, and Tunisia. When the fighting was over, the French conducted wholesale arrests—the traditional French policy after colonial outbreaks. The French killed between 1,165 (according to their official count) and 45,000 Arabs (according to Algerian estimates).[6] The OSS (the Office for Strategic Services), the U.S. wartime intelligence-gathering organization, put the number of casualties between 16,000 and 20,000, including 6,000 dead.[7] The rebellion claimed the lives of 103 Europeans. On May 13, the French staged a military parade in Constantine to impress upon the Algerians the decisive nature of their victory. The Algerians quickly found out that World War II had been a war for the liberation of the French from German occupation, not for the liberation of the French colonies from French domination.

French society was nearly unanimous in its response to Algerian defiance. Politicians of all stripes, including the Communist Party—whose official position was one of anticolonialism—strongly supported the suppression of the uprising. The French colonial authorities admitted that the violence had been in part the result of food shortages. They refused to acknowledge, however, that the rebellion had been fueled primarily by a deep-seated opposition to French colonialism.

For nine years relative stability prevailed in Algeria. When the next rebellion broke out it was not a spontaneous uprising as had been the case in 1945. This time the revolution was organized by the FLN (Front de liberation nationale), which turned to the traditional weapon of the weak—terror.[8] Terrorists have little hope to defeat an adversary whose military strength is formidable. They seek, instead, to intimidate and to keep the struggle alive in the hope of breaking the other side's will. The conflict became one of extraordinary brutality. The FLN resorted to bombing attacks against European targets; the Europeans then, logically and predictably, bombed Muslim establishments. The French army responded with its own version of terror by torturing and executing prisoners in order to uncover the FLN's organizational structure. In 1956, Parliament—with the express support of the Communist Party—granted General Jacques Massu of the Tenth Parachute Division absolute authority to do whatever was necessary. The subsequent "Battle of Algiers" ended with the destruction of the FLN's leadership. Brute force had triumphed over brute force, and within a year the uprising appeared to be over.

But the rebellion continued, nevertheless, as new leaders emerged. Algerians, such as Ferhat Abbas, who had devoted their lives to cooperation with the French, joined the rebellion. The million French settlers in Algeria demanded an increase in military protection. French military strength, initially at 50,000, rose to 400,000. In the end, between 2 and 3 million Arabs (out of a population of 9 million) were driven from their villages to become refugees, and perhaps as many as 1 million had died.

Gradually, many in France began to comprehend the unpalatable truth that Algeria would never be French. By the late 1950s, the French, who had been unified on the Algerian question in 1954, began an intense debate of the subject. The war now divided French society to the point that it threatened to touch off a civil war. One of the telling arguments against the continued French presence in Algeria was that it corrupted the soldiers who were serving in an army guilty of repeated atrocities. Many French (not unlike many of their U.S. counterparts during the war in Vietnam) became more concerned about the effect the killing, the brutality, and the torture had on their own society than their impact on the Arab victims. The costs of the continuing struggle were outweighing the benefits. The time had come to quit Algeria.

It took an exceptional political leader to take a deeply divided France out of Algeria. The colonials in Algeria continued to insist that as French citizens they had the right of military protection; the army, too, was determined to stay. By 1957, the gravest issue before France was no longer the Algerian uprising, but a sequence of "white rebellions," which threatened to topple the constitutional government of France itself. Only a politician of the stature of General Charles de Gaulle was able to accomplish the difficult task of resolving the Algerian dilemma without plunging France into civil war. De Gaulle had emerged from World War II as the sacred symbol of French resistance to Nazi Germany and had thus salvaged France's honor. In May 1958, he announced that he was ready to serve his nation once again. After he became president in June 1958, he sought at first to resolve the conflict by offering the Algerians what all previous French governments had refused. He announced the rectification of inequalities between Algerians and Europeans, which included the Algerians' right to vote. In this way, Algeria was to remain a part of France. Arab nationalists, however, rejected this solution, which might have worked before hostilities had commenced in 1954. Now nothing short of independence would do. De Gaulle's choices were now narrowed down to two. He could either crush the rebellion—or withdraw. He chose the latter. In the summer of 1960, he began talking publicly of an *"Algérie algeriénne,"* which, he declared, would have "its own government, its institutions and its laws."[9] When he took an inspection trip to Algeria in December 1960, the European residents organized a general strike to protest his policies. They demanded an *"Algérie française!"* But it was to no avail.

In July 1962, de Gaulle quit Algeria in the face of intense opposition within his own army and from the settlers in Algeria, nearly all of whom left for France and never forgave de Gaulle for his act of betrayal. Only 170,000 French residents remained when Algeria formally declared its independence in July 1962. The withdrawal marked the end of France as a colonial power.

The rebellion was led by men who had been educated by the French, many of whom had fought with distinction in the French army during World War II. Although Muslim leaders threw in their lot with the FLN, the French-educated, socialist leadership had no regard for Islam. At the time of the FLN's creation in Cairo in March 1954, Ahmed Ben Bella, one of the legendary nine founders of the FLN, profusely apologized to an Egyptian audience for his inability to address them in Arabic.[10]

These men did not seek a social revolution, although they described themselves as socialists—in line with the prevailing trend. Nearly all independence leaders after World War II—from Mao to Nehru, Ho Chi Minh, Castro, and so on—professed one form of socialism or another.

Ben Bella, who became independent Algeria's first president, was overthrown by his defense minister and then imprisoned. The revolution was over. The military then sought—successfully—to preserve one-party rule. In 1991–1992, however, under the influence of the Islamic revolution in Iran and the rise of Islamic fervor throughout the Arab world, the Islamic Salvation Front party was about to win the elections. The cancellation of the elections plunged Algeria into an extraordinarily bloody civil war during which an estimated hundred thousand people perished. The army and the Islamic militants both committed untold atrocities. Journalists were prevented—by means of press censorship and assassination—from investigating independently the army's complicity in massacres it attributed to the insurgents. The army also controlled the political candidates, settling in 1999 on Abdelaziz Bouteflika, the new front man for the military dictatorship. The generals then made new friends in 2001 as U.S. president George W. Bush welcomed Algeria as an ally in his global war on terrorism.[11]

## ■ THE BELGIAN AND PORTUGUESE DEPARTURES

The Belgian government paid even less attention than France to preparing to grant colonial independence to that huge colony in June 1960. The Belgian Congo, which had once been the private domain of King Leopold, was one of the largest and richest of the African colonies. Leopold's rapacity knew no end. His legacy was the rule of terror leading to the deaths of perhaps up to 10 million Africans over a period of twenty-five years, either killed outright or worked to death mining ore or harvesting rubber.[12]

In the twentieth century, the Belgian colonial policy was designed to allow African workers a modicum of material advancement while denying them political rights. In response to the wave of nationalism spreading over the continent, and especially to the outbreak of insurrection in the city of Leopoldville in early January 1959, the Belgian government hastily issued plans for the creation of what was meant to be a new democratic order for the Congo. The new government in Leopoldville was to be based on universal suffrage and was to guarantee the liberties of all of its people and eliminate any further racial discrimination. In January 1960, the Belgian government made the stunning announcement that in only six months it would formally transfer power to the new sovereign state of the Republic of the Congo.

However, the turbulent events that followed independence suggest that the Congo was ill-prepared for self-rule and that it had been too hastily abandoned by Belgium. The Belgians left behind but a handful of university-trained Congolese. Kwame Nkrumah charged that the Belgians' motto appeared to be "no elite, no trouble."[13] The explosion of ethnic rivalry and separatist wars was, in part, the consequence of the lack of development of a nationalism sufficient to pull its approximately two hundred tribes into a national union. Even before the Belgians exited, a rift had developed between the two most noted nationalist leaders: Patrice Lumumba, who became the country's only democratically elected prime minister and who favored a unitary state with a strong central government, and Joseph Kasavubu, who insisted upon a loose federation of autonomous regions based on tribal affiliation. No sooner had the two established rival regimes than Moise Tshombe, the separatist leader of the rich copper-mining province of Katanga, announced the secession of that province from the new republic. The result was not only a complicated, three-sided political struggle, but a tragic war that soon involved outside forces, including UN troops, the CIA, and the Soviet Union. It was an extraordinarily violent war that lasted over two years and left tens of thousands dead.

The Congolese army, weakened by the mutiny of black soldiers against their white officers and divided in loyalty between the contending leaders, Lumumba and Kasavubu, was unable to maintain order. Nor could either leader match the Katangan forces of Tshombe, whose army remained under the command of Belgian officers. Tshombe, who had the support of the Union Minière, the huge corporation that controlled the copper mines, and of the white settlers, invited Belgian reinforcements into Katanga to defend its independence. Desperate to maintain Congolese national unity, Lumumba requested military assistance from the United Nations. The UN Security Council called upon Belgium to withdraw its forces from the Congo and dispatched a peacekeeping force with instructions to prevent a civil war. The UN intervention, however, proved unsuccessful, as its member states were in disagreement about its role in the Congo.[14] Frustrated by the UN's failure to act decisively against Katanga, and still unable to defeat Katanga's Belgian-led forces, Lumumba then turned to the Soviet Union for support. This complicated the situation all the more as the Western powers sought to make use of the UN presence in the Congo as a means to check Soviet influence. Kasavubu, with the help of Colonel Joseph Mobutu and the CIA, overthrew Lumumba who was then delivered to his Katangan enemies, who murdered him. The democratic experiment was over.

The Republic of the Congo managed to survive with the province of Katanga included, but only after Kasavubu brought Tshombe and his followers into the government on their own terms. About a year later, in November 1965, both Kasavubu and Tshombe were overthrown in a military coup by their erstwhile ally Mobutu, by now a general, who then established a lasting, brutal, and dreadfully corrupt regime. Under Mobutu, the Congo (which Mobutu renamed Zaire in 1971, as part of an Africanization campaign) reverted to the status under King Leopold when Mobutu, too, treated it as his private preserve. In the process, Mobutu—as Leopold before him—became one of the richest men on earth, living in the midst of poverty and degradation.

The Katangan secessionist war and its aftermath severely damaged the credibility of African nationalists who had insisted on the readiness of Africans for self-government. It also had the effect of tarnishing the reputation of the United Nations as a neutral, peacekeeping body, and of draining its resources as well. Moreover, the conflict in the Congo proved to be a forerunner of recurrent East-West power struggles now shifting to the arena of the Third World.

Not all of Africa was liberated from colonial rule by the end of the 1960s. In the south, Portugal still stubbornly held onto its colonies, Angola and Mozambique. Portugal, a small country that had remained under the dictatorship of Dr. Oliveira Salazar from 1929 to 1969, regarded its African possessions—which together amounted to twenty times the size of Portugal itself—as "overseas provinces." Thus, they were considered an integral part of the nation and not colonies at all. Portugal savagely suppressed a nationalist insurrection in Angola in 1961, killing about fifty thousand people, and quashed a similar uprising in Mozambique in 1964. The Salazar regime ignored UN condemnation and continued its use of force to subdue guerrilla resistance. Not until the autocratic regime in Portugal was overthrown in April 1974 did that country take steps to grant independence to its African colonies. The transfer of power to an independent Angola in 1975 was accompanied by the eruption of warfare between rival nationalist parties, each of which had international supporters, and the country remained a scene of domestic turmoil and East-West contention for many years. The Portuguese, exhausted by the conflict in Angola, decided in June 1975 to grant independence to Mozambique as well.

After most of Africa was liberated by the early 1960s, the remnants of colonialism and white minority rule in South Africa (see Chapter 12) served as an impetus for pan-Africanism. Although the heads of the newly independent states persisted in their quest for black African solidarity, the goal remained elusive, partly because the concept itself remained vague and ill-defined. While all the black African leaders affirmed that the liberation of the entire African continent was their first order of business, they in fact lacked the military power and the economic leverage, either singularly or in unison, to achieve that objective. In reality, the various leaders were forced to direct their immediate attention to the difficult tasks of nation building awaiting them in their own countries. They were confronted with a host of political, economic, and military problems that came with independence. The greatest political challenge was that of creating and maintaining an effective central government whose authority was accepted and whose power was sufficient to enforce its laws throughout the entire nation.

The African nationalist leaders who had led in the struggle for independence also championed the cause of democracy, but it soon became clear that the attainment of the former did not guarantee the success of the latter. Even where genuine efforts were made to establish democratic institutions, those who had gained power by the democratic electoral process were, all too often, loath to risk their positions in another election. The principle of a loyal opposition (that is, tolerance of opposing political parties) was never firmly established. Eventually, most elected African governments gave way to dictatorships, the notable exceptions being Senegal, the Ivory Coast, Tanzania, and Botswana.

The rulers of the newly independent African nations, especially the former French colonies, also found it extremely difficult to maintain a sound economy and raise their people's standard of living—as they had earlier promised. They were soon to find that independence itself brought no magic solution to the struggle against poverty, and that they would remain far more dependent economically on their former colonial rulers than they had hoped. One unanticipated financial burden on the new governments of Africa was the ever-increasing cost of building armed forces that were deemed necessary to maintain internal security. Eventually, such armies everywhere became the major threat to the security of African rulers and their governments.

Yet, despite the numerous problems that lay ahead (see Chapter 12), the liberation of Africa stands as a momentous historical event. In retrospect, however, the tasks of nation building, economic growth, and the maintenance of democratic institutions proved to be more difficult than anyone had anticipated.

## ■ RECOMMENDED READINGS

### □ Black Africa

Anderson, David. *Histories of the Hanged: The Dirty War in Kenya and the End of Empire*. New York: W. W. Norton, 2005.
Anderson focuses on the savagery of Britains quest to defeat the Mau Mau uprising.

Cameron, James. *The African Revolution*. New York: Random House, 1961.
A stirring contemporary account of the independence movement in Africa by a British journalist.

Cartey, Wilfred, and Martin Kilson, eds. *The African Reader: Independent Africa*. New York: Random House, 1970.
A useful anthology of writings by participants in the African independence movement.

Elkins, Caroline. *Imperial Reckoning: The Untold Story of Britain's Gulag in Kenya*. New York: Henry Holt, 2005.
Like Anderson above, Elkins describes the harsh British response to the Mau Mau rebellion.

Hochschild, Adam. *King Leopold's Ghost: A Story of Greed, Terror, and Heroism in Colonial Africa*. Boston: Houghton Mifflin, 1999.
The story of unchecked colonialist exploitation, slavery, and the murder of millions.

Mazrui, Ali A. *The Africans: A Triple Heritage*. Boston: Little, Brown, 1986.
An introduction to the culture and politics of Africa by a native of Kenya whose emphasis is on the European colonial heritage; a companion volume of the BBC/WETA television series.

Mazrui, Ali A., and Michael Tidy. *Nationalism and New States in Africa*. London: Heineman Educational Books, 1984.
A survey of the decolonization process in Africa, focusing on Ghana.

Oliver, Roland, and Anthony Atmore. *Africa Since 1800*. 3d ed. New York: Cambridge University Press, 1981.
A survey focusing mainly on former British colonial regions.

## ☐ *Algeria*

Fanon, Frantz. *A Dying Colonialism.* New York: Monthly Review Press, orig. 1959; English edition, 1965.
By a native of the West Indies, a psychiatrist, whose focus is the psychological oppression and disorientation French colonialism created in Algeria.
———. *The Wretched of the Earth.* New York: Grove Press, 1963.
Fanon's most influential book on the psychological and economic impact of colonialism.
Horne, Alistair. *A Savage War of Peace: Algeria, 1954–1962.* New York: Viking Press, 1977.
Another fine explanation of a brutal anticolonial conflict.
Talbott, John. *The War Without a Name: France in Algeria, 1954–1962.* New York: Random House, 1980.
A fine history of the Algerian war.

## ■ NOTES

1. John McGhie, "British Brutality in Mau Mau Conflict," *The Guardian,* November 9, 2002.

2. Pierre Mendès-France and François Mitterand, cited in John Talbott, *The War Without a Name: France in Algeria, 1954–1962* (New York: Random House, 1980), p. 39.

3. During the first year, 21,000 Muslims were to be admitted to French citizenship. In later years the list was to increase.

4. Abdelhamid Ben Badis, one of the founders in 1931 of the Society of Reformist Ulema, in Tanya Matthews, *War in Algeria: Background for Crisis* (New York: Fordham University Press, 1961), p. 20.

5. Ibid.

6. Frantz Fanon, *A Dying Colonialism* (New York: Monthly Review Press, 1965), p. 74.

7. "Moslem Uprisings in Algeria, May 1945," Record Group 226, OSS Research and Analysis Report 3135, May 30, 1945, pp. 1–6, National Archives, Washington, D.C.

8. The distinction between terrorism and guerrilla tactics has always been blurred, particularly when the charge of terrorism became a political buzzword. Guerrilla action is a type of warfare (which frequently uses terror); terror is a form of political propaganda. The FLN in Algeria was primarily a terrorist organization. The guerrillas of the NLF in Vietnam, no stranger to the uses of terror, went into combat. (All guerrilla movements have been labeled by their opponents as terrorists, bandits, and the like.) None of the studies on contemporary terror have yet come up with a generally accepted definition of the term. Richard E. Rubenstein, *Alchemists of Revolution: Terrorism in the Modern World* (New York: Basic Books, 1987) defines it as "politically motivated violence engaged in by small groups claiming to represent the masses." That would include the FLN and the French government. To complicate matters further, no one ever admits to being a terrorist.

9. The political discussions revolved around the fate of Algeria: *Algérie française* or *Algérie algérienne.* In 1947, de Gaulle had tied the fate of Algeria to the sovereignty of France: "This means that we must never allow the fact that Algeria is our domain to be called into question in any way whatever from within or

from without." For de Gaulle's position in 1960, see Samuel B. Blumenfeld's epilogue in Michael Clark, *Algeria in Turmoil: The Rebellion, Its Causes, Its Effects, Its Future* (New York: Grosset and Dunlap, 1960), pp. 443–454.

10. Gamal Nkrumah, "Ahmed Ben Bella: Plus ça change," *Al-Ahram Weekly Online,* May 10-16, 2001.

11. "The Horrors of War Aren't Over Yet," *The Economist,* July 11, 2002.

12. Revelations of Leopold's greed and brutality prepared the way for the first great human rights crusade—augmented by the writings of Mark Twain and Joseph Conrad—of the twentieth century. See Adam Hochschild, *King Leopold's Ghost: A Story of Greed, Terror, and Heroism in Colonial Africa* (Boston: Houghton Mifflin, 1999.)

13. Kwame Nkrumah, *Class Struggle in Africa* (New York: International Publishers, 1970), p. 38.

14. Secretary-General of the United Nations Dag Hammarskjöld made great efforts to resolve conflicts among the disputants in the Congo and among member states of the United Nations disputing the Congo issue. In this effort, he made frequent trips between the UN headquarters in New York and the Congo, and on a trip to Katanga in September 1960 he died in an airplane crash.

# 7

---

# The Middle East:
# The Arab-Israeli Conflict

The Middle East did not escape the anticolonial revolts of the twentieth century. There, however, the resistance to foreign domination was first directed not against a European power but against the Ottoman Turkish Empire, which had been in control of the region for several centuries. But with the defeat of Turkey in World War I, the Middle East fell under the dominion of other outside forces, namely, Britain and France. Thus, the Arab states merely exchanged one master for another and, predictably, the anticolonial movement continued. The result was the gradual weakening of the hand of the European colonial overlords who slowly began to understand that ultimately they would have to leave. The Arab world had long been impervious to European cultural penetration, a lesson hammered home to the French during their bloody attempt to suppress the Algerian revolution. Arab nationalism and culture steeped in Islamic tradition undermined, gradually yet irrevocably, the French and British positions in the Middle East.

Yet, by a twist of fate, at the same time Arab cultural and political nationalism began to assert itself, the Middle East saw the introduction in the 1880s of another cultural and political element: the first attempts to recreate a home for Jews, to reestablish the biblical Zion in Jerusalem, in a region populated largely by Arabs. The Zionists, primarily of European background, thus launched their experiment at a time when the European presence in the world beyond Europe was under direct challenge and retreat.

## ■ THE REBIRTH OF ZIONISM

Contemporary Zionism has its origins in the rebirth of European nationalism, which soon became transformed—in Germany and elsewhere—into a virulent manifestation of racism. The late eighteenth and early nineteenth

148

centuries witnessed the revival of romantic national consciousness among Europeans who sought to define their histories, origins, and contributions to civilization. The result was an increased fragmentation of what is commonly called European civilization. The Germans, Italians, Russians, and Irish, to mention just a few, discovered their uniqueness in their ancient histories and professed cultural superiority over their neighbors. They all had this in common: they sought to find their proper places in the context of European civilization.

The Jews of Europe were another case in point. Their religion set them apart from the rest of Christian Europe and generally made it impossible for them to achieve cultural and political assimilation. Moreover, the nineteenth century was an extraordinarily race-conscious age. The relative toleration of Jews during the previous century, the Age of Reason, was no more. The legal status of Jews was beginning to deteriorate, particularly in Eastern Europe. As a consequence, a number of European Jews began to contemplate the re-creation of the ancient Jewish state in the biblical land of Zion. The result was the rebirth of Jewish nationalism.[1] It was intended to become an escape from the destructive fury of a rejuvenated anti-Semitism during the last decades of the nineteenth century.

Appropriately, the father of modern Zionism was Leon Pinsker, a Jew from Russia, a nation where anti-Semitism had become state policy. The assassination of Tsar Alexander II in 1881 was blamed on the Jews and touched off anti-Semitic pogroms (massacres). Jews made up a large percentage of the revolutionary movement, and although ethnic Russians had carried out the murder of the tsar, the assassination let loose anti-Semitic passions of unprecedented scope and intensity. It became evident to Pinsker and others that self-preservation demanded the creation of a Jewish state. In 1882, Pinsker published his pamphlet, *Auto Emancipation: An Appeal to His People by a Russian Jew.* The book was instrumental in the creation of a Zionist organization (the "Lovers of Zion") that launched the first wave of emigrants to Palestine. By the end of the 1880s, the Jewish population of Palestine was between thirty thousand and forty thousand, about 5 percent of the total population.

In 1897, an Austrian Jew, Theodor Herzl, became the best-known publicist of the Zionist cause when he organized the First World Zionist Congress and published his pamphlet, *The Jewish State.* The creation of such a Jewish state, however, faced numerous obstacles. Palestine, as well as nearly the entire Middle East, was in the hands of the Ottoman Empire, a power that sought to suppress manifestations of Jewish as well as Arab nationalism. It was little wonder that Herzl called the first Zionists "beggars ... with dreams."[2]

The nationalist movements of modern times (that is, since the end of the Middle Ages) have grown up in the main as reactions to foreign imperialism. The Napoleonic Wars gave birth to German nationalism; the Mongol invasion of Russia gave rise to Russian nationalism; American nationalism came with the struggle against the British. Modern Jewish nationalism was the product of an assault on the culture and, ultimately, the very existence of the Jews. Similarly, the resurgence of Arab nationalism came with the struggle against the Turkish Ottoman Empire. Jewish and Arab nationalism reappeared at about the same time. Arabs sought to reclaim their lands; desperate Jews sought a safe haven from the gathering fury of anti-Semitism. In the process, both sought the same piece of land.

The early Zionists were slow to grasp the fact that their struggle would ultimately be against the Arabs. Eventually, it became clear to them that the defeat of Turkey would be but the first step of a long journey. David Ben-Gurion, one of the early Zionist settlers and later Israel's first prime minister, overlooked the Arabs until 1916. It was a friend, a Palestinian Arab, who awakened him to the prospect of an Arab-Jewish conflict. The Arab expressed his concern over Ben-Gurion's incarceration when he visited the Zionist in a Turkish military prison. "As your friend, I am deeply sorry," he told Ben-Gurion, "but as an Arab I am pleased." "It came down on me like a blow," Ben-Gurion later wrote, "so there is an Arab national movement *here*."[3]

The possibility of a Jewish state came during World War I when Great Britain launched a drive against Turkey, an ally of imperial Germany. In December 1916, the British advanced from Egypt, and in the following month they entered Jerusalem. By this time, Britain and France had already decided to carve up the Middle East after Turkey's defeat. By this arrangement, the secret Sykes-Picot Agreement of May 1916, Britain was to extend its influence into Palestine, Iraq, and what shortly became Trans-Jordan, while France claimed Lebanon and Syria.

The British did not foresee the troubles ahead. While fighting the Turks, they had enlisted Arab support and had promised the Arabs nationhood after the war. These pledges had contributed to anti-Turkish rebellions in Jerusalem, Damascus, and other cities long controlled by the Turks. At the same time, however, the British government also enlisted Jewish aid and in return "viewed with favour" the creation of a "national home for the Jewish people" in Palestine. This pledge came in November 1917 in the Balfour Declaration (named after the British foreign secretary) in a one-page letter to Lord Rothschild, a representative of the Jewish community in England. The declaration also insisted, however, that "nothing shall be done which may prejudice the civil and religious rights of the existing non-Jewish communities in Palestine."[4] The declaration and its later endorsement by the League of Nations gave international sanction to what since 1881 had been a haphazard experiment to create a homeland for Jews.

The Arabs rejected the Balfour Declaration. The promises made by the British, they argued, were at best limited and conditional. A Jewish "national home" in Palestine, they insisted, did not constitute a Jewish state. Moreover,

Great Britain had no right to give away Palestine over the heads of its inhabitants, particularly at a time when Britain had not yet gained possession of Palestine. If anything, Britain earlier had promised Palestine to the Arabs in the Hussein-McMahon Letters of 1915–1916. This exchange of letters had led to the Hussein-McMahon Agreement of 1916 (between Sherif Hussein, emir of Mecca, and Sir Henry McMahon, Britain's high commissioner in Egypt), whereby the Arabs, in exchange for Britain's recognition of a united Arab state between the Mediterranean and Red Seas, joined Britain in the war against Turkey.

The best that can be said about the British policy is that the authorities in London did their best to satisfy all claimants to the lands of the Middle East that became a part of the British postwar mandate. First, to satisfy the Arabs, they granted Abdullah, the second son of Sherif Hussein, a stretch of territory east of the Jordan River. The British here transferred the easternmost portion of Palestine to what became the Emirate of Trans-Jordan, today's Kingdom of Jordan. The creation of this artificial realm constituted the first partition of Palestine. The remainder of Palestine west of the Jordan River, with its restless Arab and Jewish populations, remained under British rule.

The British soon found out, however, that one cannot serve two clients with conflicting claims. Arabs and Jews both suspected that the British were backing away from the commitments they had made. Arabs feared the British were in the process of creating a Zionist state; Jews feared the British favored the numerically superior Arabs and thus had no intention of honoring the Balfour Declaration. The British had no clear policy except to try and keep the antagonists apart. The consequence of British fence straddling was that the British were destined to come under a cross fire when they incurred the enmity of both Jews and Arabs.

After World War I, both Jews and Arabs were determined to create their own national states in Palestine. The clash between Zionists and Palestinians became a conflict fueled by passion, anger, and hatred between two movements insisting on their historic and religious rights to the same land. The Balfour Declaration had asserted the rights of two peoples whose claims and aspirations clashed. The result was that Jews and Arabs acted out a tragedy of classic proportions in which the protagonists became victims of inexorable forces over which they had but little control.

During the 1920s, Jews and Arabs were engaged in mortal combat. Each side engaged in acts of violence, which in turn led to additional violence. Particularly bloody were the riots of 1929, the first instance of large-scale bloodshed between Jews and Arabs. In Jerusalem, in a dispute over the Wailing Wall and the Dome of the Rock, 133 Jews and 116 Arabs lost their lives. In Hebron, the Jewish inhabitants, a people with an ancient linear connection to biblical times, were driven out of the city in a riot that claimed 87 Jewish lives. The British authorities sought to keep the peace

The Dome of the Rock, Jerusalem. *(Harry Piotrowski)*

The Western Wall—or Wailing Wall—in Jerusalem. *(Harry Piotrowski)*

but with limited success. Both sides felt the British had betrayed them for not fulfilling the promises made during the war. In 1939, Britain, to placate the Arabs who had risen in bloody rebellion (1936–1939), issued its controversial "white paper," or position paper. With it the British authorities sought to limit the Jewish population of Palestine to one-third and to severely curtail the transfer of land to Jews. (The Jewish population at that time was already at 30 percent, up from 10 percent in 1918.)

The new British directive came at a time when life in Nazi Germany had become unbearable for Jews. Yet no country would take them in, and Hitler later initiated his program of extermination of Jews. Militant Zionists began to suspect collusion between the British and the Nazis. The British decision, which had the effect of closing the door of a safe haven for Jews seeking to escape the inferno of Nazism in Europe, created a legacy of bitterness. After the war this bitterness led to violence between the British army and militant Jewish organizations, such as the Irgun (Irgun Zvai Leumi, or National Military Organization) headed by Menachem Begin.

The murder of 6 million European Jews at the hands of Nazi Germany during World War II, all too frequently with the collusion of peoples— Poles, Ukrainians, French, and others—who themselves had been conquered by the Germans, seared the consciousness of Jews. It underscored the necessity of a Jewish state as a matter of self-preservation, as the only place where Jews could be assured a sanctuary against the fury of anti-Semitism. Israel was created by the survivors of the holocaust, whose actions were constantly marked by the remembrance of that cataclysmic event. Years later, when Egyptian president Gamal Abdel Nasser spoke of the destruction of Israel, its citizens could not help but invoke the memory of Hitler's attempt to annihilate the Jews.

After World War II, the British decided to wash their hands of Palestine. At this point, the United Nations agreed to take its turn in trying to solve this problem. It was clear by then, however, that a single Palestinian state consisting of Arabs and Jews, as the Balfour Declaration had suggested, was an impossibility. Few Zionists or Arabs were interested in such a solution. Both saw themselves as the legitimate heirs to the land of Palestine. Moreover, too much blood had already been shed between them. In November 1947, the United Nations therefore called for the creation of separate Israeli and Arab states. Jerusalem, a holy city for both Jews and Muslims, was to have international status with free access for all worshipers. The UN decision marked the second partition of Palestine. It divided what was left after the British had initially granted the east bank of the Jordan River to the emir of Trans-Jordan.

Nearly all Arabs rejected the UN resolution. They were in no mood for such a compromise with what they considered to be a foreign presence in their land. The Arabs also harbored the suspicion that Zionism in control of only half of Zion—not to mention the fact that the very heart of Zion itself,

Jerusalem, was slated to remain a separate entity, apart from the state of Israel—would ultimately satisfy few Israelis and inevitably lead to a renewal of Zionist expansion. In 1947, however, most Jews were generally willing to accept the borders the United Nations had drawn, despite the fact that they fell far short of what the Zionist movement had originally envisioned. David Ben-Gurion, Israel's first prime minister, who once had argued that Israel's eastern border must reach the Jordan River, rejected all pressure for expansion in the hope of gaining Arab recognition of what in his youth had been but a dream—the state of Israel. The early Zionists, particularly people such as Begin whose Irgun (military organization) had as its logo a map of Israel with borders beyond the Jordan River, had a much different map of Israel in mind than the one that came into existence in 1948. The territorial confines of Israel in the wake of the 1948 war were at the heart of the conflict between Ben-Gurion and Begin.

The Arabs remained adamant in their refusal to recognize Israel's existence. At best, some were willing to accept the presence of a Jewish minority in an Arab state. More significant, many Arabs were convinced that they could prevent the establishment of the Israeli state by military means and could drive the Zionists into the sea. The UN resolution and the Arab rejection of the partition of Palestine were but the last of a series of events that made the first Arab-Israeli war inevitable.

In 1947, the Zionist dream had finally borne fruit. The state of Israel (no longer merely a homeland for Jews) had obtained international sanction. The first state to extend diplomatic recognition to Israel was the United States; the Soviet Union and several Western nations quickly followed suit. No Arab state, however, recognized Israel.[5] Arab intransigence—coupled with the threat of another holocaust a scant three years after Hitler's defeat—made it clear that Israel's right to exist would have to be defended by the sword.

## ■ THE ARAB-ISRAELI WARS

The British were slated to withdraw from Palestine in May 1948, and both sides prepared for that day. Violence between Arabs and Jews, already endemic, escalated. On April 9, 1948, Begin's Irgun killed between 116 and 254 Palestinians (depending upon whose account one credits) in the village of Deir Yassin, and three days later an Arab reprisal caused the deaths of 77 Jews. These and other acts of violence became etched into the collective memory of both peoples. Each massacre had its apologists who defended the bloodletting as a just action in a just war. In this fashion the first Arab-Israeli war began.

The 1948 war was essentially over in four weeks. A number of Arab states—Jordan, Syria, Egypt, Lebanon, and Iraq—invaded Israel, but their

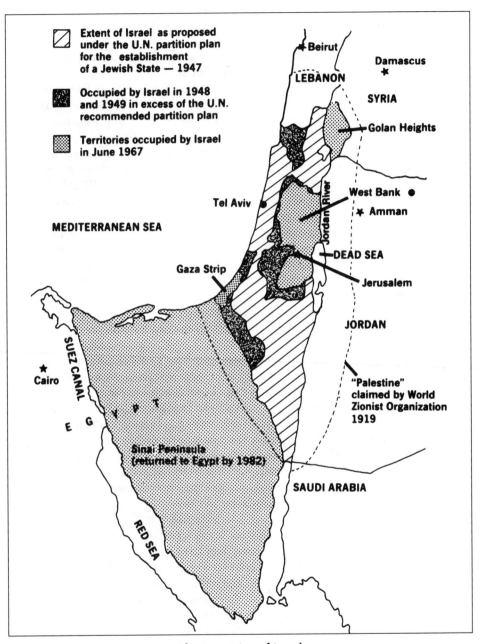

**The Expansion of Israel**

actions were uncoordinated and ineffectual. The Israeli victory resulted in the third partition of Palestine. The Israelis wound up with one-third more land than under the UN partition plan when they seized West Jerusalem, the Negev Desert, and parts of Galilee. King Abdullah of Jordan made the best of his defeat at the hands of the Israelis by annexing the West Bank and East Jerusalem. The Palestinians, defeated by Israel and betrayed by the Kingdom of Jordan, saw the dream of a state of their own vanish into thin air.

The war also led to a refugee problem that continued to plague the Middle East for decades. By the end of April 1948, even before the outbreak of the first Arab-Israeli war, Israeli forces expelled 290,000 Palestinian Arabs. The expulsions became a contributing factor of the subsequent war. During the war Israelis expelled another 300,000 Palestinians. By 1973, the number of refugees was over 1.5 million; in 2004, their number and those of their descendants stood at 4 million, many of them wards of the United Nations relief organizations. Most of the refugees fled across the Jordan River into Jordan.[6] The flight of the Palestinians determined the nature of the new state of Israel. It guaranteed that Israel would be a Zionist state dominated by a Jewish majority at the expense of what was now an Arab minority left behind. Whatever property the Arabs had abandoned, if only to seek shelter elsewhere during the war, was confiscated by Israel.[7] The displaced Palestinians settled in refugee camps in Jordan, Lebanon, and Gaza. They considered their status as temporary and looked—in vain—to the day of return to land and homes that once had belonged to them.

When the war ended, the Israelis considered the armistice lines, which gave them the additional lands, to be permanent and refused to permit the return of the refugees. To the Arabs, the new borders and the refugees were a humiliating reminder of their defeat, and they remained incapable of accepting the consequences of the war. These factors, coupled with Arab intransigence on the question of Israel's right to exist, remained at the core of the continuing deadlock in Arab-Israeli relations.

The partitions of Palestine were the result of actions taken by Great Britain, the United Nations, Israel, and Jordan with the complicity of the nations of Europe, both capitalist and Communist. From the beginning, the United States and other major Western powers had offered the Israelis diplomatic support, whereas the Soviet bloc had provided most of the weapons for the Jewish victory in the first Arab-Israeli war.

It was only a matter of time until the second war broke out. The 1948 war had been a bitter blow to the pride and national consciousness of the Arabs. The war had exposed their weaknesses and their inability to unite. Throughout the war, Israeli forces outnumbered those of the Arabs by a ratio of roughly two to one. Arabs spoke fervently of Arab unity and of fighting another war against Israel to drive the Israelis into the sea, but their rhetoric only masked their impotence and frustration.

A palace revolution in Egypt in 1952 swept aside the ineffectual King Farouk and in 1954 brought to power one of the conspirators, Gamal Abdel Nasser, who promised the regeneration of both Egypt and the rest of the Arab world. He envisioned a pan-Arab movement uniting all Arabs, and for a short time Egypt and Syria were in fact merged into one nation, the United Arab Republic. Nasser's rejuvenation of Arab pride and ethnic consciousness also called for the ouster of the Western presence—notably that of the British, French, and Israelis—which in the past had been responsible for the humiliation of the Muslim world. Another war between Israel and the Arabs seemed inevitable. Nasser, instead of coming to grips with the reality of Israel, was busy putting another Arab-Israeli war on the agenda.

As tensions in the Middle East increased, so did the arms race. Nasser turned to the Soviet Union and in September 1955 announced a historic weapons deal by which he became the recipient of Soviet MIG-15 fighter planes, bombers, and tanks. The Soviet Union, in turn, gained for the first time a client outside its Communist sphere of influence. Israel immediately renegotiated an arms agreement with France. The Middle East was now on a hair-trigger alert waiting for a crisis to unfold. The wait was not long. In July 1956, Nasser boldly seized the Suez Canal, thus eliminating British and French control and operation of that important waterway.

The British and French prepared a counterattack to retake the Suez Canal. They were joined by the Israelis who, for a number of years, had listened to Nasser's bloodcurdling rhetoric promising the destruction of their state. They now saw their chance to deal with Nasser and to halt the border raids by the Arab *fedayeen* (literally "those who sacrifice themselves"). These raids had produced an unbroken circle of violence, a series of "little wars" consisting of incursions and reprisals, which in turn led to other raids and reprisals.

In October 1956, Britain, France, and Israel signed the secret treaty of Sèvres in preparation for a second Arab-Israeli war. Israel attacked in Egypt's Sinai Desert and, with the support of French airplanes, swept all the way to the Suez Canal and the southern tip of the Sinai at Sharm-el-Sheikh. British and French naval, air, and land forces joined the battle against the outgunned Egyptians. The war lasted only a few days, from October 29 until November 2, 1956. Egypt's defeat on the battlefield—not to mention its humiliation—was complete.

When the Anglo-French forces launched an assault aimed at retaking the Suez Canal, President Eisenhower's stated opposition to more war, Soviet threats of intervention, and UN condemnations persuaded Britain, France, and Israel to halt the attack. Israel eventually agreed to withdraw from the Sinai, whereas Egypt pledged not to interfere with Israeli shipping through the Straits of Tiran, which gave Israel an outlet to the Red Sea. The United Nations negotiated the evacuation of the British and French from the canal zone, leaving Nasser in control of the canal, which remained bottled up with war-damaged ships for several years. The United Nations also agreed to patrol the border between Egypt and Israel and in this fashion helped to preserve an uneasy truce for more than ten years.

The 1956 war resolved none of the grievances held by the Israelis and Arabs. Officially, the state of war between the Arabs nations and Israel continued. Israel was still unable to obtain recognition from any Arab government, and the Arabs continued to call for the destruction of the Israeli state. Both sides had no illusions that another war was in the offing, and they took steps to prepare for it.

In spring 1967, Nasser, in an attempt to negate the consequences of the 1956 war, closed the Straits of Tiran to Israeli shipping in the face of Israeli warnings that such an action constituted a casus belli, a cause for war. Inevitably, tensions rose rapidly. Nasser then demanded that the UN forces leave Egyptian territory along the Israeli border and concluded a military pact with King Hussein of Jordan. When Iraq also joined the pact, the Israelis struck. Their preemptive attack initiated a third war, the Six Day War of June 1967.

As its name suggests, the war was over in less than a week, by which time Israel had decimated the forces of Egypt, Syria, and Jordan and in the process rearranged the map of the Middle East. Its political repercussions still haunt the region. Once again—as it had done in the 1956 war—Israel conquered the Sinai all the way to the Suez Canal. It also took from Egypt the Gaza Strip, a small stretch of land inhabited by Palestinian refugees. It turned against Syria and stormed the Golan Heights, a 20-mile-wide strategic plateau rising 600 feet above Galilee from which the Syrian army had fired repeatedly on Israeli settlements below. But most significantly, Israel also took what had been Jordanian territory west of the Jordan River and the Dead Sea—a region generally known as the West Bank (west of the Jordan River). With it, Israel came into possession of the entire city of Jerusalem. All the conquered territories—the Sinai Peninsula, the Golan Heights, the West Bank, Gaza, and East Jerusalem—became Israeli-occupied lands, and as such they became the source of still further contention between Arabs and Israelis.

In November 1967, the great powers once again sought to use the United Nations to resolve the conflict. The United States and the Soviet Union were fearful of being increasingly drawn into the Arab-Israeli wars, each backing one of the belligerents. In a rare display of U.S.-Soviet cooperation, the UN Security Council sought to resolve the crisis by passing Resolution 242, which called for an Israeli withdrawal from territories conquered in the Six Day War, accompanied by a political settlement that would include Arab recognition of Israel and a fair deal for the Palestinian refugees. After some hesitation, Egypt and Jordan accepted Resolution 242, but Syria and the militant Palestinians rejected it. The Israelis were not inclined to give up all the spoils of victory, and they, too, rejected it. In the decades to come, leaders of various political and national persuasions repeatedly reached for Resolution 242 as a potential answer to this deadly dispute. But the overwhelming strength of Israel's military in effect negated the resolution. The Israeli government had no pressing need to return to its pre-1967 borders; moreover, it never contemplated the return of East Jerusalem. And the Arabs always insisted that in Resolution 242, "the territories occupied [by Israel] in the hostilities" meant "all territories."[8] General Moshe Dayan, the architect of Israel's victory in the Six Day War, expressed the extremist conviction when he said, "I would rather have land than peace," to which King Hussein of Jordan prophetically replied, "Israel can have land or peace, but not both."[9] The resultant deadlock became but another manifestation of how in the Middle East the militants nearly always carried the day.

With the acquisition of the West Bank, Israel now came into possession of land containing 750,000 hostile Arab inhabitants. As early as 1968, a handful of Jews began to settle in the West Bank. In 1977, however, an election in Israel brought to power Menachem Begin, who had always insisted that the West Bank was not merely conquered Arab territory or a bargaining card to be played eventually in exchange for Arab recognition of

Egyptian president Anwar Sadat, U.S. president Jimmy Carter, and Israeli prime minister Menachem Begin after signing the Middle East peace treaty at Camp David, Maryland, March 27, 1979. *(AP/Wide World Photos)*

Israel's right to exist. Instead, he argued, it consisted of the biblical lands of Judea and Samaria, an integral part of Israel's religious heritage. For Begin, these lands must never be returned to the Arabs. He proceeded to treat them as a natural part of Zion, and for that reason he urged that Israelis settle in the region. Despite the objections of Arab states, the United Nations, the United States, and other nations, Begin considered the annexation of the West Bank a closed matter. His government also officially annexed the Golan Heights and considered that matter closed as well.

The problem of the West Bank was complicated by the fact that its largest city, Hebron, contains the tomb of Abraham, who is revered by both Jews and Muslims. Both groups consider Abraham God's messenger and their spiritual and physical patriarch. The Jews consider themselves the direct descendants of one of Abraham's sons, Isaac; the Arabs see themselves as children of his other son, Ishmael.

The 1967 Arab defeat had another, unexpected result. It strengthened the hand of Palestinian liberation/terrorist organizations, which now operated under the aegis of a newly established umbrella organization, the Palestine Liberation Organization (PLO), led by Yassir Arafat. It was guerrilla fighters of this organization, rather than the armies of the Arab nations generally, that since 1967 have kept the Middle East in turmoil by conducting their private wars against the Israelis. During the 1972 summer Olympic Games in Munich, for instance, Palestinian terrorists dramatized their cause before a worldwide audience by kidnapping and killing fifteen Israeli athletes. This act propelled the Palestinian question into the consciousness of the Western world. But this example of "propaganda by the deed" (to use a phrase from the Russian revolutionary movement of the nineteenth century) strengthened the hands of the extremists on both sides and continued to impede any and all efforts to resolve the conflict. It should not have been surprising, therefore, that the consequence of the inability to resolve Arab-Israeli differences was another war.

The fourth Arab-Israeli conflict, the Yom Kippur War, took place in October 1973, when Egyptian president Anwar Sadat, who had succeeded Nasser in 1970, initiated an offensive against the seemingly impregnable Israeli position across the Suez Canal. Owing to its surprise attack, Egypt enjoyed some initial successes, but Israeli forces successfully counterattacked and threatened to destroy the Egyptian army. The United Nations and the two superpowers, the United States and the Soviet Union, hastily intervened to stop the war. Neither Israel nor Egypt was to be permitted to destroy the other. Egypt was permitted to retain a foothold on the east side of the Suez Canal, and the United Nations then created a buffer zone to keep the two sides apart.

This Egyptian offensive proved to be the first time an Arab state had been able to wrest any territory from the Israelis. After suffering one humiliation after another for a quarter of a century, an Arab army had finally proven its battleworthiness. Sadat felt he could now negotiate with Israel as an equal. With encouragement from Washington, he began to take steps to recognize the existence of the state of Israel and in this fashion became the first Arab head of state to do so. In an act of supreme courage, Sadat responded to an invitation from the Israeli government and flew to Jerusalem in 1977 to address the Knesset, Israel's parliament. Israeli prime minister Begin reciprocated with his own visit to Cairo.

These remarkable diplomatic actions set the stage for a summit meeting of the two leaders together with U.S. President Jimmy Carter in September 1978 and for the Camp David Agreement signed by all three, which led directly to the Egyptian-Israeli peace treaty. The treaty ended a state of war of thirty years' duration between Egypt and Israel and brought about the diplomatic recognition of Israel by Egypt. In turn, Israel pledged to return the Sinai to Egypt and did so by April 1982. This marked the first and only instance whereby an Arab state managed on its own to regain territory lost to Israel. Sadat had achieved through negotiation what no Arab nations had achieved by war. For their efforts, the three leaders were nominated for the Nobel Peace Prize. In the end, Begin and Sadat—former terrorists turned diplomats—shared the prize; inexplicably, Jimmy Carter was excluded.

But the Camp David agreement of 1979 did not adequately address the thorny questions of Jerusalem, the West Bank, and the Palestinian refugees. Sadat showed little interest in the Palestinian issue. Begin spoke vaguely of Palestinian "autonomy" within the state of Israel. He was more interested in peace with Egypt and diplomatic recognition than in discussing the fate of the inhabitants of what he considered to be an integral part of Israel and thus an internal matter. Nor did the Camp David Agreement settle the issue of Jerusalem, Israel's capital city. Virtually all Israelis insisted on their claim to Jerusalem and that it remain one and indivisible. But the Palestinians, too, envisioned Jerusalem as the capital of their future state.

The PLO was not consulted in these negotiations. Begin refused to talk to the terrorists in the PLO. Nor was the PLO's leadership interested in joining the talks. Participation in the negotiations, after all, would have meant the de facto recognition of Israel. Inevitably, many Arabs saw Sadat as a man who had betrayed the Palestinian and Arab cause. His dealings with Israel contributed to his domestic problems. As his critics became more vocal, his regime became increasingly dictatorial and his opponents, in turn, became increasingly embittered. Radical Muslims, members of the Egyptian Islamic Jihad, assassinated Sadat in October 1981.[10]

The festering Palestinian problem continued to vex the region. In 1970, King Hussein of Jordan drove the PLO leadership from his country after it had become clear that its presence in Jordan posed a threat to his regime. Searching for a home, the PLO found a new base of operation in Lebanon, a nation already divided between a politically dominant Christian minority and the majority Muslim population, who at that time were already on the edge of civil war with a government incapable of maintaining order. Lebanon's political factions operated private armies in an unrestricted manner. It was into this volatile environment that the Palestinians introduced their own private armies. And it was from Lebanon that the PLO launched its raids into Israel.

The Israelis responded in kind. Raids and reprisals were the order of the day along the Lebanese-Israeli border. In July 1981, however, the PLO and Israel agreed on a "cessation of all armed attacks." The cease-fire over the next ten months was in part the work of the special U.S. envoy to the Middle East, Philip Habib. Both sides abided by the terms of the agreement until June 1982, when the government of Menachem Begin attempted to eliminate the Palestinian threat in Lebanon once and for all by launching an invasion into southern Lebanon.

The Israeli government's official explanation for the resumption of war against the Palestinians was to secure "Peace for Galilee" and to root out the Palestinians across the border. This rationale for the invasion had a hollow ring to it since there had been no Palestinian attacks across that border for nearly a year. The scope of the operation, the Begin government announced, would be limited. The Israeli army would go no farther than 40 kilometers (25 miles) into Lebanon. Events proved, however, that Begin, and his defense minister, Ariel Sharon, had more ambitious plans.

In December 1981, Sharon outlined the following scenario to Philip Habib. Sharon called for a strike into Lebanon in the hope of quickly resolving several problems at once. He sought to dislodge the Syrians, who had been invited several years earlier by the Lebanese government to restore order at a time when the country was beginning to disintegrate into civil war. Once invited, however, the Syrians had stayed. Sharon considered the Syrians, with whom the Israelis had been on a war footing since 1948, to be the real masters of Lebanon. Second, Sharon intended to destroy the PLO, a "time bomb" in Sharon's words, in southern Lebanon and with it to subdue the restless Palestinian population of about half a million.[11] When Habib asked of the fate of the hundred thousand Palestinians directly across the border in Lebanon, Sharon told him that "we shall hand them over to the Lebanese. . . . Fifty-thousand armed terrorists won't remain there, and the rest will be taken care of by the Lebanese." Habib protested the impending violation of a cease-fire he had worked out. Shortly afterward, President Reagan warned Prime Minister Begin against any moves into Lebanon, but to no avail.

The invasion of Lebanon did bring about the military (although not the political) defeat of the PLO and the Israeli bombardment and destruction of parts of Beirut containing Palestinian populations. The invasion also led to the massacre of an estimated 700–2,000 Palestinian civilians at the refugee camps of Sabra and Shatila. The slaughter—first with knives, then with firearms—was the handiwork of Lebanese Maronite Christian Phalangist (fascist) militia forces, with the approval and assistance of the Israeli armed forces who witnessed the massacres.[12] Israeli forces also crippled Syrian forces in Lebanon and destroyed much of the military hardware the Soviets had provided them, but the Syrians quickly recovered their losses and remained as deeply entrenched in Lebanon as ever. Israel did not withdraw completely but left some of its forces in a self-imposed buffer region in southern Lebanon.

The cost of the invasion is incalculable. The greatest losers were the Palestinians, who suffered at the hands of first the Israelis, then the Christian Phalangists, and finally the Shiite Muslims in Lebanon. The war also pitted the Israelis against the Shiites; the Shiites against the Maronite Christians and their army, the Phalangists; and a faction of the PLO (the rebels supported by the Syrians) against Arafat's faction. It produced the evacuation of the PLO guerrillas, the deaths of over six hundred Israeli soldiers, the de facto partition of Lebanon between Syria and Israel, and a deep emotional split within the population in Israel. The volatile political debates in Israel centered on whether the invasion had been necessary, for this was the first war initiated by Israel in which the survival of the state had not been an immediate issue.

There were still more costly consequences. Under UN auspices, a peace-keeping force made up of U.S., French, and Italian troops oversaw the evacuation of PLO fighters from Lebanon. Soon afterward, the U.S. and French peacekeeping forces ran head-on into an opposition of fury and anger few in the West were able to understand. Two suicide bombers blew up their trucks filled with explosives, killing 242 U.S. marines and 59 French soldiers. Nearly two decades later, the bloodletting continued as Israeli forces in southern Lebanon remained engaged in sporadic combat with Lebanese Shiites.

## ■ THE ISRAELI-PALESTINIAN IMPASSE

In the mid-1980s, the PLO was no closer than before to achieving its goal—the creation of a Palestinian state and the destruction of Israel. After the 1982 expulsion from Lebanon, the PLO was in disarray. For the next several years the nominal leader of the PLO, Yassir Arafat, now based in Tunisia, struggled to maintain the unity of the organization.

Nothing changed until December 1987, when the Palestinian population in Gaza and the West Bank took matters into its own hands. A Palestinian uprising, the *intifada* (literally, "shaking off" the Zionist yoke), began in Gaza when an Israeli truck collided with two cars, killing four Palestinian refugees. The protests escalated and spread to the West Bank. Israel put itself into the uncomfortable position of using armed soldiers against stone-throwing Palestinians. By early 1990, Israeli soldiers had killed more than six hundred Palestinians. Israeli hard-liners tried to deflect criticism by blaming the violence on the PLO.

The intifada spurred debate within Israel over the future of Gaza and the West Bank and produced a discussion within the PLO over strategy and tactics. In November 1988, the PLO convened in Algiers a meeting of the Palestinian National Council at which it passed a resolution proclaiming its willingness to recognize the state of Israel on the condition that Israel officially endorse UN Resolutions 242 and 338, which called for Israeli withdrawal—both its military and settlers now numbered seventy thousand—from the occupied territories and for the right of all parties in the Middle East to live in peace and security. For the PLO, this was a remarkably conciliatory position. Arafat also declared and repeated that "we [the PLO] totally and absolutely renounce all forms of terrorism."[13] Prime Minister Yitzhak Shamir and his party, the right-wing Likud, did not believe the peaceful protestations of his mortal enemies; there would be no talks with the PLO and no Palestinian state. Shamir could not forget that the PLO had vowed in the past to destroy the state of Israel and that, in fact, several of its factions still held this position.[14]

The end of the Cold War in 1990 led to significantly improved relations between Israel and the Soviet Union. The two nations reestablished diplomatic relations (which the Soviet Union had broken off after the Six Day War of 1967), and when Moscow opened its doors for the emigration of Jews, Israel welcomed them. The mass immigration of Jews to Israel (two hundred thousand in 1990 alone) had consequences beyond the domestic issues of providing housing and jobs. Many Soviet Jews were settled in the West Bank and Eastern Jerusalem, areas the Palestinians claimed. Although intifada violence had subsided, the influx of the Soviet Jews into the occupied lands inflamed Arab passions. Shamir, however, reiterated his pledge that he would keep intact for future generations the "Greater Israel," by which he meant all areas currently under Israeli control.

■ **THE SEARCH FOR A POLITICAL SOLUTION**

The Arab-Israeli dispute became more acute during the Gulf crisis occasioned by the invasion of Kuwait by Iraqi forces in August 1990 (see Chapter 20). Israel's most urgent concern was for its own security, since earlier in the year Iraqi ruler Saddam Hussein had threatened to "scorch half of Israel" in reprisal of any Israeli action against Iraq. In his efforts to secure Arab support, Hussein proclaimed his willingness to withdraw from Kuwait if Israel were to withdraw from all the occupied territories. Although most Arab leaders shunned this pretension, the PLO announced its support for Hussein.

The defeat of Iraq by the U.S.-led coalition in the Gulf War in early 1991 improved conditions for achieving a breakthrough in the Middle East. After the war, it was clearer than ever that Israel was a permanent fact of life in the Middle East. The PLO already had publicly contemplated recognition of Israel in exchange for some of the land taken by the latter in 1967. Syrian president Afez Assad, too, took a new tack in his quest to regain the Golan Heights. Deprived of Soviet backing, there was little point for Assad to continue to pretend he could force a military solution on Israel. Many Israelis, too, sought an end to the costly confrontation. The time had come to sit down and talk.

In June 1992, in a tight race, Labor Party leader Yitzhak Rabin defeated Shamir. Rabin had promised greater flexibility in the search for peace and was willing to trade some land for peace. Rabin was a military man who in January 1964 became the chief of staff of the Israeli army. His hawkish position had contributed to rising tensions in the years leading up to the Six Day War of 1967; during that war, he was as responsible as anyone for the Israeli conquest of Arab lands. Yet it was this man who now had to deal with the consequences of that war. Rabin declared that the most urgent task was to negotiate self-rule for Palestinians in the West Bank and Gaza, and toward that end he announced a curb on building new settlements in the occupied lands. Rabin was willing to trade land for peace; but he was not willing to return to the 1967 borders.

The Palestinian leaders with whom Israel was negotiating knew many Palestinians saw them as traitors negotiating away their patrimony. Syria demanded that any agreement with Israel must include the return of all, not just part, of the Golan Heights. To complicate matters, Israel now faced another Palestinian social, political, and military force, namely Hamas ("zeal" in Arabic), a militant Islamic organization based in Gaza, which had gained considerable support with its uncompromising call for the destruction of Israel. Hamas, the Palestinian branch of the Muslim Brotherhood (see Chapter 21) founded in Gaza in 1987 by its spiritual leader, Sheik Ahmed Yassin, launched suicide attacks against Israeli military and civilian targets and attacked suspected Palestinian collaborators with Israel as well. [15] Slowly but surely, particularly after the PLO accomplished little with its subsequent negotiations with Israel and its leadership increasingly became corrupt, Hamas became a powerful voice for the Palestinian community.

## ☐ The Oslo Agreements

At the end of summer 1993, secret talks in Oslo, Norway, between PLO functionaries and members of Israel's Peace Now movement (acting at first independently of the Rabin government) offered hope for a solution to the Arab-Israeli conflict. The negotiations produced a remarkable breakthrough when Arafat and Rabin accepted the broad outlines of an agreement. The signing ceremony for the agreement took place on the White House lawn in Washington, D.C., on September 13, 1993, where a reluctant Rabin shook Arafat's hand. The Oslo agreements called for an Israeli withdrawal from

Gaza (except for the Jewish settlements there) and from the West Bank city of Jericho, with further withdrawals sometime in the future. Political control of these regions would fall to a Palestinian Authority under Arafat.

The key defect of Oslo was that it failed to define the shape of a permanent peace. It said nothing about the fate of Jewish settlements in Gaza and the West Bank, a solution for East Jerusalem where the population was still almost exclusively Palestinian, the status of refugees, or the establishment of a Palestinian state. In fact, the two sides had different visions of what Oslo would achieve, something that became apparent at the signing ceremony. Rabin vaguely spoke of the two sides being "destined to live together on the same soil, in the same land." Arafat, however, spoke of the Palestinians' "right to self-determination" and "coexistence" with Israel on the basis of "equal rights." He called for the implementation of UN resolutions 242 and 338, which demanded an Israeli withdrawal from lands conquered in 1967.[16]

Not surprisingly, there was strong opposition to the agreement from radical elements in both Israel and the Palestinian community. As Rabin's foreign minister, Shimon Peres, later put it, "A peace negotiation is with your own people as well as with the other one."[17] Jewish militants, particularly those who had set up residence in the West Bank city of Hebron (which contains the tomb of Abraham, the revered patriarch of both Jews and Muslims), cried that Arafat remained a threat to Israel. Hamas charged that Arafat had obtained too little and had betrayed the Palestinian cause, and then initiated terrorist actions aimed at radicalizing public opinion in Israel, as well as among Palestinians. Israel and the PLO now became allies, each pinning its hopes on the other as they faced the same enemies—extremists who sought to derail the peace process.

The Oslo agreements prompted Jordan's King Hussein to act. Secret talks between representatives of Jordan and Israel soon produced a peace treaty, signed in Washington in July 1994, officially ending forty-six years of a state of war. The treaty also opened border crossings between the two countries.

In February 1994, a U.S.-born Zionist, Baruch Goldstein, shot to death twenty-nine Muslim worshipers at the Cave of the Patriarch (the resting place of Abraham) in Hebron. Goldstein was a member of an extremist organization whose attitudes were capsulized by a statement a rabbi made in a eulogy to the killer: "One million Arabs are not worth a Jewish fingernail."[18] As long as the Oslo peace process remained in force, the possibility continued that even the most intractable issues could be resolved. It was for this reason that the Nobel Peace Prize committee, as it had done several times in the past, offered its award to former enemies—Rabin, Arafat, and Peres—who had attempted to resolve their differences at the conference table rather than on the battlefield.

Arafat now had to shoulder the work of governing the Palestinians and improving their livelihood. Poverty was especially severe in Gaza, where the unemployment rate was around 50 percent. By the end of 1994, the World Bank and several nations contributed $180 million in developmental aid to the Palestinian Authority, but the amount was far less than was needed. In addition to having to fend off complaints about the economy, Arafat faced critics of his autocratic rule. Most serious was the challenge posed by Hamas. In October 1994, a Hamas suicide bomber blew up a crowded bus in Tel Aviv, killing twenty-one people. A rally in Gaza drew over twenty thousand Hamas supporters who praised the bomber as a martyr and denounced the PLO's agreement with Israel.

The struggle between the PLO and Hamas for the allegiance of the Palestinians continued unabated. In August 1995, Hamas carried out two more bus bombings, claiming twelve lives. Despite the violence, in September 1995, Arafat and Rabin affixed their signatures to a detailed plan that established a timetable for the withdrawal of Israeli forces from about 30 percent of the West Bank (including its major cities and about four hundred towns) and put the Palestinian Authority immediately in charge of public services for most of the residents of the West Bank. The new agreement also called for the election of a Palestinian president and legislature and for the release of five thousand Palestinian prisoners.

Hamas bombings produced in Israel ever-increasing hostility toward the peace process. Benjamin Netanyahu, the new leader of the opposition Likud Party, went so far as to accuse Rabin of treason. One of Netanyahu's campaign posters showed Rabin wearing the *kaffiyeh,* Arafat's trademark Arab headdress. In November 1995, a twenty-one-year-old Israeli extremist, Yigal Amir, assassinated Rabin. He justified his act on religious grounds: a Jew who harmed Jewish society must be killed. Rabin's successor was his foreign minister, Shimon Peres, one of the architects of the peace process who was committed to moving it forward, but first he had to face Netanyahu in an election.

☐ *Return to Impasse*

The first direct election of an Israeli prime minister took place in May 1996 under the shadow of escalating violence. Both Peres and his Likud Party opponent, Netanyahu, viewed the election as a referendum on the nearly three-year-long peace process. By a razor-thin margin, the victory went to Netanyahu, a hard-liner who had opposed the Oslo peace process agreements every step of the way. Netanyahu rejected Rabin's "land for peace" formula; he promised, instead, "peace with security."

After the election, prospects for a continuation of the peace initiatives looked dim. Netanyahu refused to make any commitments and for almost four months refused even to meet with Arafat, whom he still considered a terrorist and not a worthy negotiating partner. Instead of resuming negotiations with the PLO, Netanyahu demolished Palestinian homes, authorized the building of additional Jewish settlements and Jewish-only access roads in the West Bank, and delayed the previously agreed upon withdrawal of Israeli troops from Hebron.

After years of frequently fruitless wrangling and sporadic violence, the bright hopes in the afterglow of the Oslo accord had faded. Netanyahu showed scant interest in completing the Oslo process. Israel had granted the Palestinian Authority only 12 percent of the West Bank, land that consisted of enclaves that were not viable economically and surrounded by borders and roads controlled by the Israeli Defense Forces. All the while, however, Israel continued to build settlements in the West Bank, Gaza, and East Jerusalem. In the seven years after the signing of the Oslo accord, settlement construction had increased by more than 50 percent, the settler population by 72 percent, their numbers reaching 380,000 amid 3.4 million Palestinians.[19] Moreover, economic conditions for the Palestinians steadily declined. In February 2000, Egyptian president Hosni Mubarak warned that Palestine had become a time bomb.

In the May 1999 election, Ehud Barak, the centrist candidate of the Labor Party and a former career military man who had risen to the post of Israeli army chief of staff as a protégé of Rabin, defeated Netanyahu after promising to revive the stalled Oslo accords. But Barak was unable to come to a final agreement with Arafat. Instead, he focused on the withdrawal of Israeli troops from southern Lebanon where they had been since 1982. Once that had been achieved in July 2000, Barak then turned his attention to Syria in the hopes of coming to an understanding over the Golan Heights. Assad, however, showed little interest in negotiations and insisted, instead, on an unconditional withdrawal of Israel's eighteen thousand settlers and its military from the Golan.

Barak then returned to the Palestinian question. He convinced U.S. president Bill Clinton to convene a meeting at Camp David in July 2000, during which he offered Arafat concessions that went beyond the Israeli consensus. He promised Arafat much of the West Bank, the potential return of an unspecified number of the 3.5 million Palestinian refugees who had been displaced since 1948, and the withdrawal of an unspecified number of Israeli settlers from the West Bank and Gaza.

A sticking point again was the status of Jerusalem. Arafat continued to insist on Palestinian sovereignty over its eastern half. When Barak refused to discuss the issue, Arafat returned home to a hero's welcome. Before he left Camp David, he told Clinton: "If I make concessions on Jerusalem, I will be killed, and you will have to talk to Sheikh [Ahmed] Yassin," the spiritual head of Hamas.[20]

Barak and Clinton blamed Arafat for the breakdown. The head of Israel's military intelligence, however, concluded that Arafat did not dream of the destruction of Israel, as his critics charged, that he wanted a diplomatic solution, but that he could not accept the loss of 9 percent of West

Bank territory and of East Jerusalem. Nor could he ignore the Palestinian refugee problem.[21]

In September 2000, Ariel Sharon—the man primarily responsible for the 1982 Israeli invasion of Lebanon that resulted in the slaughter of Palestinians there, who had participated in a massacre of Palestinians in 1953, who once had referred to Palestinians as "cockroaches," and who as cabinet minister had overseen the building of Israeli settlements in the disputed territories—paid a visit to a most sensitive site, the Temple Mount in the Old City of Jerusalem, where it is thought the temple of Solomon once stood. The Western Wall—or Wailing Wall—of the mount is the holiest place of the Jewish faith. At the end of the seventh century A.D., however, Muslims had built on the top of the mount two mosques—the Dome of the Rock and the Al Aksa mosque—which they call the Haram al-Sharif or Noble Sanctuary. According to Muslim tradition, it was from there that the Prophet Mohammed took his "Night Journey" to heaven where he received Allah's command of five daily prayers. After the Six Day War, General Moshe Dayan, one of the architects of Israel's victory, had granted the Muslims sovereignty over the mount but at the same time had granted Israelis the right to visit it. Over the years, Israeli zealots had called for the establishment of a new temple on the mount.[22]

Under the heavy guard of a thousand Israeli soldiers and police, Sharon ascended the Temple Mount to underscore that it belonged to the Jews. Predictably, this incident touched off the time bomb Mubarak had predicted. Thus began the second intifada, which pitted mostly young Palestinians against Israeli soldiers and citizens. It featured the lynching of two Israeli soldiers and the death of a thirteen-year-old Palestinian boy caught in the crossfire, both acts caught on videotape and replayed endlessly on television.

Oslo was dead and Sharon, after he promised to restore order, became the next Israeli prime minister. Instead, violence continued. During the next four years, Palestinians carried out more than 170 suicide bombings attacks, most of them by Hamas; one-third of them, however, were carried out by the Al Aqsa Martyrs Brigade, an offshoot of Arafat's Al Fatah organization. Al Aqsa may have been out of Arafat's control, but he showed little interest in reigning it in.

Israel responded with helicopters, tanks, and bulldozers, demolishing Palestinian homes (243 in the West Bank and 2,508 in Gaza). In March 2004, Sharon ordered the assassination of Sheikh Ahmed Yassin, the founder of Hamas, and his immediate successor, and threatened the same fate for Arafat. All the while, the number of Jewish settlers in Gaza and the West Bank continued to increase. Between the beginning of 1997 and the end of June 2004, their numbers rose from 156,100 to 243,749. During the first four years of the second intifada, September 2000–September 2004, 1,002 Israelis and 2,780 Palestinians lost their lives.

Beginning with March 2002, the Israeli army took back most of the West Bank towns under Palestinian Authority control. Sharon and Arafat, two old men, were now engaged in their last battle. Arafat, seventy-five years old and suffering from Parkinson's disease, was trapped in his bombed-out compound in Ramallah threatened by expulsion by the seventy-six-year-old Sharon. Meanwhile, Hamas challenged him for the hearts and minds of the Palestinians.

In order to prevent suicide bombers from entering Israel, Sharon decided to build a wall separating Israel from the Palestinians on the West Bank. Arafat declared that he had no problem with such a wall provided it was built on Israeli territory. But the wall cut deep into the West Bank. Once completed, the wall was scheduled to run 410 miles and lead to the transfer of nearly 17 percent of West Bank territory to Israel. It would affect the lives of 38 percent of the West Bank population[23]—who would be cut off from other Palestinian communities, schools, hospitals, and farmland. What was left of Palestine, the Arabs complained, would remain in the form of a collection of *bantustans*, ghettos roped off by an "apartheid wall."

The administration of President George W. Bush in Washington, busy in the global war on terror and in Iraq, made a few pronouncements calling for a "roadmap" for peace, but then lost interest. It labored under the illusion that a political transformation in Iraq would force the Palestinians to accept whatever Israel had in store for them.

The "roadmap" had called for the dismantling of Israeli settlements as a step toward Palestinian nationhood. The only thing Sharon was willing to do, however, was to eliminate Jewish settlements in Gaza, where 8,100 settlers required the costly protection of six thousand soldiers. But the West Bank settlements would remain and there would be no Palestinian state. By the autumn of 2004, Sharon's chief negotiator in the "roadmap" talks declared it was already "dead" and went on to say that he had come to an understanding with the Bush administration that there would be no talks with the Palestinians until they "turn into [peaceful] Finns." The issue of a Palestinian state "has been removed indefinitely from our agenda . . . all with a [U.S.] presidential blessing and the ratification of both houses of Congress."[24]

In November 2004, Yassir Arafat, a man without a country, died in a Paris hospital. After the Egyptian government honored him with a state funeral, he was interred in his compound in Ramallah in the West Bank to which he had been forcibly confined during the last three years of his life.

## ■ RECOMMENDED READINGS

Avineri, Shlomo. *The Making of Modern Zionism: The Intellectual Origins of the Jewish State.* New York: Basic Books, 1981.
　　An explanation of the intellectual climate of the nineteenth century that produced the Zionist movement.
Elon, Amos. *The Israelis: Founders and Sons.* New York: Holt, Rinehart, and Winston, 1971.

A classic treatment of the roots of Zionism and the first two decades of the existence of Israel.

Kimmerling, Baruch, and Joel S. Migdal. *Palestinians: The Making of a People.* New York: Free Press, 1993.

How a clan-centered Arab population acquired a national collective character.

Lilienthal, Alfred M. *The Zionist Connection: What Price Peace?* Rev. ed. New Brunswick, N.J.: North American, 1982.

A critical explanation of the Zionist movement.

Oz, Amos. *In the Land of Israel.* New York: Random House, 1983.

By an Israeli novelist who dwells on Israel's dilemma.

Peters, Joan. *From Time Immemorial: The Origins of the Arab-Jewish Conflict over Palestine.* New York: Harper and Row, 1984.

An ambitious and controversial attempt to prove that the Jews did not displace the Arabs in Palestine but instead that Arabs had displaced Jews.

Rabinovich, Abraham. *The Yom Kippur War: The Epic Encounter That Transformed the Middle East.* New York: Schocken, 2004.

An Israeli journalist's definitive account of the war told from the Israeli side. The Arab view of the "Ramadan" War is covered only sketchily.

Reich, Walter. *A Stranger in My House: Jews and Arabs in the West Bank.* New York: Henry Holt, 1984.

An evenhanded and judicious attempt by a U.S. psychiatrist to understand the historical, sociological, and theological arguments of the inhabitants of the West Bank.

Ross, Dennis. *The Missing Peace: The Inside Story of the Fight for Middle East Peace.* New York: Farrar, Straus, and Giroux, 2004.

By the U.S. envoy to the Middle East who had served both Presidents George H. W. Bush and Bill Clinton.

Said, Edward W. *The End of the Peace Process: Oslo and After.* New York: Pantheon, 2000.

Collection of essays by a leading spokesman of the Palestinian cause, highly critical of both the Palestinian and Israeli leaderships.

———. *The Question of Palestine.* New York: Random House, 1980.

By a U.S. scholar of Palestinian descent, this is the classic study championing the Palestinian cause.

Segev, Tom. *One Palestine, Complete: Jews and Arabs.* New York: Henry Holt, 2000.

By an Israeli journalist and historian. A revisionist, also known as "post-Zionist," treatment of the British mandate period from the Zionist and Palestinian perspective.

———. *1949: The First Israelis.* New York: Free Press, 1985.

A controversial best-seller in Israel; a reinterpretation by an Israeli journalist of the early history of the state.

Shehadeh, Raja. *Samed: Journal of a West Bank Palestinian.* New York: Adama Publishers, 1984.

Life on the West Bank from a Palestinian's perspective.

Shipler, David K. *Arab and Jew: Wounded Spirits in a Promised Land.* New York: Times Books, 1986.

By a *New York Times* correspondent.

# ■ NOTES

1. Jewish nationalism has existed ever since the diaspora, the dispersion of the Jews that began in the sixth century B.C. with the destruction of Solomon's temple

and culminated with the destruction of the second temple in Jerusalem in A.D. 70 and the defeat of Bar Kochba in A.D. 135. British philosopher Bertrand Russell, in reminding his readers that modern nationalism is a relatively new concept, pointed out that at the end of the Middle Ages "there was hardly any nationalism except that of the Jews."

2. Quoted in Amos Elon, *The Israelis: Founders and Sons* (New York: Holt, Rinehart, and Winston, 1971), p. 106.

3. Palestinian Arab and Ben-Gurion cited in ibid., p. 155 (emphasis in the original).

4. "Balfour Declaration," in *Times* (London), November 9, 1917, p. 7.

5. In fact, when King Abdullah of Jordan, the great-grandfather of the current King Abdullah, sought to come to terms with the state of Israel (he met in secret with several Zionists in 1949), it cost him his life at the hand of a Palestinian assassin. The first Arab nation to exchange ambassadors with Israel was Egypt in 1979. For this, as well as for domestic reasons, Egyptian president Anwar Sadat suffered the fate of Abdullah when he, too, was assassinated.

6. As a result, 70 percent of the population of the Kingdom of Jordan consisted of Palestinians, from which came the argument in some quarters in Israel that a Palestinian state already existed.

7. Charles Glass, "'It Was Necessary to Uproot Them,'" *London Review of Books,* June 24, 2004, pp. 21–23.

8. "UN Resolution 242," *Yearbook of the United Nations: 1967* (New York: United Nations, 1969), pp. 257–258.

9. Moshe Dayan and King Hussein quoted in Dana Adams Schmidt, *Armageddon in the Middle East* (New York: John Day, 1974), p. 249. For a discussion of the positions of Dayan and Hussein, see Bernard Avishai, *The Tragedy of Zionism: Revolution and Democracy in the Land of Israel* (New York: Farrar, Straus, and Giroux, 1985), pp. 275–278.

10. Hosni Mubarak, Sadat's successor, jailed a number of suspects, among them Sheik Omar Abdel Rahman and Ayman al-Zawahiri, both of whom eventually were released. Once freed, they joined Osama bin Laden's al Qaeda. In 1993, Rahman led an attempt to blow up one of the towers of the World Trade Center in New York City; Zawahiri became one of the leading figures in al Qaeda.

11. "What can be done," Sharon told Habib, "and this is not actually a plan, but it is practicable, is a swift and vigorous strike of 24 to 48 hours, which will force the Syrians to retreat and inflict such heavy losses on the PLO that they will leave Lebanon." Sharon also expected the Lebanese government to regain control of the Beirut-Damascus highway, thus driving the Syrians further north. From a report of a U.S. diplomatic summary of the conversation between Sharon and Habib, published by the Israeli Labor Party newspaper, *Davar.* The U.S. ambassador to Israel, Samuel W. Lewis, and the State Department confirmed the basic outlines of the conversation. Thomas L. Friedman, "Paper Says Israeli Outlined Invasion," *New York Times,* May 26, 1985, p. 15.

12. John Fisk, *Pity the Nation: The Abduction of Lebanon* (New York: Thunder Mouth Press/Nation Books, 4th ed., 2002), chapter 11, "Terrorists," pp. 359–400. In 1983, an Israeli commission declared that Sharon was not fit as defense minister, that he bore personal responsibility for the massacres. Sharon subsequently headed the ministry of housing and construction from where he oversaw the expansion of settlements in the West Bank, and in 2001 he became prime minister.

13. Text of Arafat statement, *Baltimore Sun,* December 15, 1988.

14. Yitzhak Shamir, "Israel at 40: Looking Back, Looking Ahead," *Foreign Affairs* 66, no. 3 (1988), pp. 585–586.

15. U.S. State Department annual report on terrorism, *Patterns of Global Terrorism, 2000,* released April 2001.

16. The speeches of Rabin and Arafat, in Walter Laqueur and Barry Rubin, eds., *The Israel-Arab Reader: A Documentary History of the Middle East Conflict* (New York: Penguin, 5th rev. ed., 1995), pp. 613–614.

17. Peres cited in Connie Bruck, "The Wounds of Peace," *The New Yorker,* October 14, 1996, p. 64.

18. Cited in William Pfaff, "Victory to Extremists," *Baltimore Sun,* March 7, 1994, p. 14A.

19. According to the estimates of Arie Arnon of the Peace Now movement; Graham Usher, "Middle East Divide," *The Nation,* December 25, 2000, p. 6.

20. Cited by Ben Macintyre, "Arafat: If I Sign, I'll Be Killed," *Times* (London), July 27, 2000, p. 17.

21. Amos Malka cited in Robert Malley, "Israel and the Arafat Question," *New York Review of Books,* October 7, 2004, p. 23.

22. The bloody riots of 1929 had been the result of the Palestinians' belief that the Zionists were about to seize control of the Haram al-Sharif. In 1990, an Israeli group, the Temple Mount Faithful, sought to lay a cornerstone for a future temple. In the aftermath, Israeli forces killed seventeen Palestinians, whose memory is honored in the museum of the Haram al-Sharif.

23. From the website of B'Tselem, the Israeli human rights organization, http://www.btselem.org. See also John Ward Anderson and Molly Moore, "Israel Blunts Uprising's Impact," *Washington Post,* October 5, 2004, p. A22, and "A Bloody Vacuum," *Economist,* October 2, 2004, pp. 23–25.

24. Dov Weisglass, one of Sharon's closest advisers, cited in John Ward Anderson, "Sharon Aide Says Goal of Gaza Plan Is to Halt Road Map," *Washington Post,* October 7, 2004.

# PART 3

# THE SHIFTING SANDS OF GLOBAL POWER

From the outset the Cold War created a bipolar world in which the two contending superpowers pulled other nations toward one pole or the other. But gradually this bipolar East-West confrontation underwent a transformation marked by divisions within each camp and the emergence of other centers of power. The first eight years of the Cold War were marked by a straightforward adversarial relationship featuring the hard-nosed diplomatic combat of Joseph Stalin and Harry Truman. It also featured the U.S. containment policy, the division of Europe, the creation of two military alliances (NATO and the Warsaw Pact), a war in Korea, persistent ideological attacks and counterattacks, and the massive rearmament of both sides. Despite the conciliatory gestures by the successors of Stalin and Truman and talk of peaceful coexistence, the bipolar struggle carried over into the 1960s and grew even more intense as the two superpowers squared off in the Cuban missile crisis.

By that time, however, it was becoming clear to the superpowers that they could not make military use of their huge nuclear arsenals and that the day of direct confrontation had ended. Additionally, by the early 1960s, they could no longer take for granted the solidarity of their respective alliances. The bipolar world of the 1950s began to give way to multipolarity in the 1960s.

To understand this process, the political legacy of Joseph Stalin in the Soviet Union is our point of departure in Chapter 8. Here we trace the efforts of his successor, Nikita Khrushchev, to put to an end the excesses of Stalinism, the terror, and the arbitrary and abusive use of state power, and to institute reforms aimed at restoring orderly and legal procedures to Soviet rule and revitalizing the economy. The consequences of this reform effort and the pattern of Soviet politics under Khrushchev's successors are also discussed. Additionally, we examine the stresses and strains within the Communist bloc and particularly the impact of Khrushchev's reforms in Eastern Europe. The impact of de-Stalinization was controlled within the Soviet Union, but that was not the case in the satellite countries, especially in Poland and Hungary, where it rekindled nationalist sentiments and unleashed pent-up desires for political liberalization and liberation from Moscow's control.

But if the resulting revolts in Poland and Hungary and later in Czechoslovakia could be snuffed out by the Soviet Union, a recalcitrant Communist China could not so easily be dealt with. In Chapter 8, we analyze the causes and the course of the Sino-Soviet split, which divided the Communist world. Their bitter and long-lasting feud signified that ideological bonds are not stronger than national interests and that international Communism was not the monolithic movement it was generally thought to be.

Meanwhile, in the 1960s, the U.S. government, still convinced that Communism was monolithic, went off to war in distant Asia to stop its spread. In Chapter 9, we explain how and why the United States took up the fight in Vietnam. The staunch anti-Communist logic of U.S. leaders caused them to misread the revolution in that country, its causes and strengths, coming up with the erroneous conclusion that its source was Beijing-based Communist aggression rather than Vietnamese nationalism. We next offer an explanation of the prolongation and expansion of the war in Indochina and the difficulty the United States had in extracting itself from that war. We also examine the war's tragic consequences and impact on the remainder of Indochina, especially Cambodia, and the plight of the refugees, the "boat people."

In the late 1960s, despite the fact that the United States was still mired in Vietnam, progress was made in lowering East-West tension elsewhere. New leadership in West Germany, specifically that of Chancellor Willy Brandt, took bold steps seeking to break up the twenty-year-old Cold War logjam in Central Europe. In Chapter 10, we examine Brandt's conciliatory policy toward the Communist nations of Eastern Europe and the role it played in bringing détente—the relaxation of tension—to East-West relations. By the early 1970s, détente became the basis of Soviet-U.S. diplomacy.The new relations between Washington and Moscow left Beijing isolated as an enemy of both. In fact, the U.S.-Soviet détente at first brought jeers from China, which suspected an anti-Chinese conspiracy. But as we show in Chapter 10, Chinese leaders came to realize the dangers of China's continued isolation and judged that it had more to gain in terms of economic development and national security by normalizing its relations with the United States. In a dramatic diplomatic turnabout, the United States and Communist China, two nations that had been the most intransigent of ideological foes for over two decades, suddenly in 1972 buried the hatchet.

With U.S.-Soviet détente and the normalization of U.S.-Chinese relations, a new era of delicate tripolar power relations had arrived. Moreover, with the resurgence of Western Europe and the emergence of an economically powerful Japan, the international arena was now multipolar. The simpler world of East versus West, of the struggle between the "free world" and the "Communist world," gave way to a more complex world of power-balancing diplomacy, one calling for greater political flexibility.

# 8

---

# The Communist World After Stalin

When Stalin died in March 1953, he had ruled the Soviet Union for nearly thirty years and in the process left his imprint on the Communist Party and the nation. In the late 1920s, Stalin and his party had set out to initiate a program of rapid industrialization with a series of Five-Year Plans. In order to feed the growing proletariat (the industrial work force), he introduced a program of rapid collectivization whereby the small and inefficient individual farms were consolidated into larger collectives. In effect, it made the Soviet peasant an employee of the state. The state set the price the collective farms received for their agricultural commodities, a price kept low so that the countryside wound up subsidizing the cities, where an industrial revolution was taking place. In this fashion, agriculture became one of the "stepchildren" of the Communist revolution in the Soviet Union.

At the time of the Communist revolution of 1917, the peasants had realized an age-old dream, the private and unrestricted ownership of their land. Predictably, they resisted the Stalinist drive toward collectivization. Stalin, faced with intense opposition, had two choices: curtail the program of collectivization and industrialization or pursue it with force. He chose the latter. Collectivization became a bloody civil war during the late 1920s and early 1930s, in which several million peasants perished, and that witnessed widespread destruction of equipment and livestock. In such a wasteful and brutal manner, the countryside subsidized the industrial revolution and the growth of the city.

Stalin subordinated Soviet society to one overriding quest: to create an industrial state for the purpose of bringing to an end Russia's traditional economic backwardness, the root cause of its military weakness. In 1931, he spoke to a conference of factory managers on the question of whether the mad dash toward industrialization could be slowed. He offered his audience a capsule history of Russia:

> To slacken the tempo would mean falling behind. And all those who fall behind get beaten. . . . One feature of the history of old Russia was the continual beatings she suffered because of her backwardness. She was beaten by the Mongol khans. She was beaten by the Turkish beys. She was beaten by the Swedish feudal lords. She was beaten by the Polish and Lithuanian gentry. She was beaten by the British and French capitalists. She was beaten by the Japanese barons. All beat her—because of her backwardness, military backwardness, cultural backwardness, political backwardness, industrial backwardness. . . . Such is the law of the exploiters, to beat the backward and the weak. . . . Either we do it [catch up with the capitalist West], or we shall be crushed. . . . In ten years we must make good the distance which separates us from the advanced capitalist countries. . . . And that depends on us. Only on us![1]

Stalin's Five-Year Plans gave the Soviet Union a heavily centralized economy capable of withstanding the supreme test of fire, the German attack on the Soviet Union in 1941. In fact, during World War II the Soviet war economy, despite massive destruction at the hands of the Germans, outproduced that of Germany. Studies conducted after the war for the U.S. Joint Chiefs of Staff repeatedly paid tribute to Stalin's industrial revolution, which had transformed the Soviet Union from a weak, backward country into a formidable opponent that all too soon broke the U.S. nuclear monopoly (1949) and later was the first to venture into the frontiers of space (1957).

All of this did not come without a heavy price. Stalin contributed to the transformation of what initially had been meant to be a "dictatorship of the proletariat"[2] into a dictatorship of the party over the proletariat and the peasantry, and eventually into a dictatorship of the secret police over the proletariat, the peasantry, and the party itself. In 1937, Stalin initiated the bloodiest of a series of purges of the party by which he eliminated all opposition within the Communist Party. The Bolshevik Revolution of 1917, which had begun as an uprising by the proletariat, rank-and-file soldiers, and peasants, had become a monument to the triumph of the secret police.

## ■ KHRUSHCHEV AND STALIN'S GHOST

When Stalin died in 1953, the party immediately took steps to reassert the position of preeminence it had enjoyed in the days of Vladimir Lenin, the architect of the Bolshevik Revolution, who had led the Soviet Union until his death in 1924. Within a week after Stalin's death, the party forced Stalin's designated successor, Georgi Malenkov, to give up one of the two posts he held. The party told him to choose between the post of first secretary of the party (that is, the head of the party) or that of prime minister. Malenkov, inexplicably, decided to hold on to the position of prime minister. As a result, a lesser member of the ruling circle, the Politburo, Nikita

Khrushchev, became the new first secretary of the party in charge of its daily operations. The party then took another step to prevent the consolidation of power in the hands of one person. It officially established a collective leadership, a *troika* (Russian for a sled pulled by three horses) consisting of Malenkov as prime minister, Viacheslav Molotov as foreign minister, and Lavrentii Beria as the head of the secret police. Beria, who had been an agent of Stalin's terror, remained a threat to the party. In the summer of 1953, the party, with the help of the leadership of the Soviet army (which also had suffered greatly during the secret police's unchecked reign of terror), arrested Beria. It charged him with the abuse of power and then shot him.

The party continued in its attempts to come to terms with the Stalinist legacy. The reformers, however, repeatedly clashed with those who sought to prevent meaningful changes. Gradually, in the mid-1950s, the reformers gained the upper hand and some of the shackles of the Stalinist past were cast off. A general amnesty freed political prisoners. Writers, many of whom had been "writing for the desk drawer," succeeded in seeing their works in print. Détente with the West now became a possibility. Western visitors began to arrive in Moscow.

The most dramatic assault on the status of Stalin came in February 1956, at the Communist Party's Twentieth Congress, when Nikita Khrushchev

Soviet leader Nikita Khrushchev, flanked by Foreign Minister Andrei Gromyko and Marshal Rodion Malinovski, at a press conference in Paris, May 16, 1960. *(National Archives)*

delivered a scathing attack on Stalin's crimes. It became known as the "Secret Speech," but it did not remain secret for long—since an address before an assembly of hundreds of delegates, many of whom had much to gain by making it public, would certainly reach the light of day. The speech was the result of a commission the party had set up to report on Beria's and Stalin's crimes, mostly those committed against the party itself. Khrushchev told the assembled delegates that Stalin's terror, including the destruction of the party's role in the affairs of the state, had been an act of lawlessness, one which the party now sought to prevent in the future. "Socialist legality" was to take the place of one-person rule.

The speech was essentially an attempt by the party at self-preservation. And it was limited to just that. It did not address the larger question of Stalin's terror directed against the peasants, religious organizations, writers, and composers—in short, the public at large. One of Khrushchev's Western biographers wrote that the Secret Speech was a smokescreen as well as an exposure.[3] It did not tackle the question of one-party rule by the "vanguard of the proletariat," the Communist Party. Neither did it challenge the Stalinist system of agriculture, which the party admitted at the time was in ruin, nor the system of industrial organization, which still worked reasonably well. Instead, Khrushchev's speech focused on the dictatorship of the police over the party.

The Secret Speech signaled the end of the arbitrary terror of Stalin's time. The secret police was brought under the party's control and its wings were clipped, particularly in dealing with party members. Arbitrary arrests were largely ended. Censorship restrictions were partially lifted, breathing new life into the Soviet Union's intellectual community. Throughout his tenure Khrushchev repeatedly waged war against the memory of Stalin, particularly in 1957 and then in 1961, when he went so far as to remove Stalin's body from the mausoleum it shared with Lenin's remains and to rename cities and institutions that had been named in Stalin's honor. The city of Stalingrad, for example, the supreme symbol of the Soviet Union's resistance to Hitler, where an entire German army found defeat, became merely Volgograd, the "city on the Volga."

After Khrushchev's ouster in October 1964, the party made no concerted effort to rehabilitate Stalin's image, although overt criticism of Stalin was brought to an end. It was clear, however, that one day Soviet society again would have to come to grips with Stalin's legacy. The transformation of Stalin's image from a hero and generalissimo, to a murderous tyrant in violation of "Leninist legality," and finally to a shadowy figure who appeared scarcely to have existed, simply would not do. In 1961, the party published the long-awaited second edition of its *History of the Communist Party of the Soviet Union*. The first edition had been published in 1938 under Stalin's direct editorship and as such had heaped voluminous praise on Stalin. The second edition, in contrast, was an example of revisionist history with a vengeance. It never mentioned Stalin's name. It was Mikhail Gorbachev who in 1987 forced Soviet society once again to deal with its past and reopened the discussion of Stalin's role.

To many observers in the West, these changes were of little consequence. The Communist Party still retained its control and the economy remained unchanged. But in the context of Russian and Soviet history, these liberalizing changes were significant. This was something on which both Khrushchev and his opponents agreed. What Khrushchev needed to do was continue to introduce innovations without major repercussions, for, as Alexis de Tocqueville (the French political writer of the nineteenth century) wrote, the most difficult time in the life of a bad government comes when it tries to reform itself.[4] Khrushchev soon found that out.

Philosophically, Khrushchev expressed the view that art must not be censored. But the flood of writings that sought to portray Soviet reality as it in fact existed, warts and all, soon overwhelmed the party, and Khrushchev himself became a censor. In 1962, Khrushchev permitted the publication of Alexander Solzhenitsyn's exposé of Stalin's labor camps, *One Day in the Life of Ivan Denisovich,* the literary sensation of the post-Stalin age; yet, several years earlier, Khrushchev had supported "administrative measures" to prevent the publication of Boris Pasternak's *Doctor Zhivago,* admittedly without having read it. Late in life, a repentant Khrushchev wrote that "readers should be given a chance to make their own judgments" and that "police measures shouldn't be used."[5] As the first secretary of the party, however, Khrushchev never did manage to come to grips with his contradictions. The result was that he was unable to bring the restless writers under control. This task fell to his successor, Leonid Brezhnev.

By the early 1960s, Khrushchev had worn out his welcome. The majority of the party was increasingly beginning to view his erratic moves and innovations as hare-brained schemes. The classic case in point was the attempt to place nuclear missiles in Cuba in 1962, a rash impulsive act. Poorly thought out and hasty reforms in the areas of agriculture and industry also came back to haunt Khrushchev.

In 1958, Khrushchev demanded a drastic rise in meat production to surpass the United States. The ambitious first secretary of the party in Riazan, A. N. Larionov, publicly pledged a doubling of meat production in 1959. Khrushchev then ordered that other regions follow the Riazan example. In February 1959, before Larionov could even get started, Khrushchev went to Riazan to bestow on him personally the prestigious Order of Lenin. A desperate Larionov fulfilled his pledge by slaughtering whatever livestock was available. Eventually he went outside the region to purchase milk cows and breeding stock. In December 1959, Larionov declared a hollow "victory" for which, nevertheless, he was once again decorated. In 1960, meat production declined by 200,000 tons, a decline that took years to reverse. At the end of 1960, Larionov, a Hero of Socialist Labor, shot himself in his office.[6]

In October 1964, Khrushchev contemplated a shake-up in the party. It proved to be the last straw, for it threatened the exalted positions of many. By then Khrushchev had lost the support of the majority in the Central Committee, officially the major decisionmaking body of the Communist Party. The party, in a vote of no confidence, sent him out to pasture with the stipulation that he stay out of politics. Leonid Brezhnev succeeded him as the head of the party.

Khrushchev's demise proved to be his finest hour. He had dealt with his opponents within the bounds of "socialist legality," that is by using the rules and procedures written into the party's statutes and by using the support many in the party at one time gave him enthusiastically. But when his behavior became increasingly irrational, embarrassing, and reckless, the party then turned against him. Once he faced the cold, hard fact that he had lost the support of the majority, he stepped down. There was never a question of using the military or the secret police.

Khrushchev's successors gave the Soviet Union twenty years of stability, a significant increase in the standard of living, and rough military parity with the West. At the same time, this was an era when the status quo was maintained. A free-wheeling discussion of Stalin's role in Soviet history had no place in the scheme of the Brezhnev vision of Soviet society. The intellectuals were eventually brought under control by intimidation, jailing, and, in several cases, notably that of Solzhenitsyn, expulsion from the country. Brezhnev's prime minister, Alexei Kosygin, contemplated economic reforms but they were soon shelved when it became apparent that all too many factory managers had their fill of reforms under Khrushchev and fought for the retention of the status quo.

By the time Brezhnev died in 1982, the party was beginning to accept the need for another round of reform. Yuri Andropov and Konstantin Chernenko initiated the first modest steps, but both were hampered by what turned out to be incurable illnesses. In 1985, Mikhail Gorbachev, the new first secretary of the party, took on the nation's problems. In a direct challenge to Brezhnev's political, economic, and intellectual inertia, Gorbachev then committed his nation to a wide-ranging discussion of its shortcomings and to the restructuring of the economy (see Chapter 18).

## ■ EASTERN EUROPE: THE SATELLITES

As the Communist Party in the Soviet Union wrestled with Stalin's ghost, a similar drama began to unfold in Moscow's East European satellites. There, the conflict was fought with much more intensity and conviction. The reformers were willing to go much further than their counterparts behind the Kremlin walls. Although much of Eastern Europe subsequently moved further from the Stalinist model than the Soviet Union, Moscow always made clear that the reforms must remain within certain perimeters, which, although not rigidly defined and constantly shifting, must nevertheless not be transgressed. Moscow's position vis-à-vis Eastern Europe followed along the classic lines of the carrot, in the shape of a tolerance of reforms, and the stick, wielded by the Soviet army to maintain control.

The West considered the expansion of Soviet political and military power after World War II as a threat to its security and saw it as a source of Soviet strength. But Stalin saw it in a different light. He knew that the East European buffer offered his state a measure of security, but that it was also a potential source of headaches. At the Yalta Conference he had described the Poles as "quarrelsome." He well understood the volatile mix of nationalism, religion, and anti-Russian sentiments in Eastern Europe. Soviet occupation of Eastern Europe had strengthened his forward position in a future confrontation with the capitalist West, but it also promised to bring problems.

By 1948, Stalin appeared to have consolidated his position in Eastern Europe. The Communist parties of that region were for the most part the creation of the Soviet Union, and on the surface loyal members of the socialist camp lined up in solidarity against the capitalist threat. But the Communists of Eastern Europe were soon showing nationalist tendencies; it became clear they were more interested in championing the causes of their own nations instead of serving the interests of the men in the Kremlin.

## ☐ Yugoslavia

The classic example of such "nationalist deviation" was the case of Joseph Tito, the Communist ruler of Yugoslavia. In the late 1930s, Tito had spent time in Moscow under Stalin's tutelage, and during World War II he had fought with the Red Army (as well as the Western Allies) against Nazi Germany. His loyalty to Stalin and the cause of international Marxist solidarity appeared beyond reproach. Soon after the war, however, at the very moment the West and the Soviet Union were taking steps to consolidate their respective positions, the Yugoslav and Soviet Communists had a falling out over the question of who was to play the dominant role in running Yugoslavia. The upshot of this quarrel was that Tito established his independence from Moscow. He did not, however, move into the capitalist camp. He accepted aid from the West, but always maintained a position of neutrality between East and West.[7] The Tito-Stalin split pointed to a central problem the Soviets faced in Eastern Europe, the volatile force of nationalism.

The immediate consequence of Tito's defection was Stalin's reorganization of the Communist governments of Eastern Europe. He executed and jailed Communists (such as Poland's Wladyslaw Gomulka, of whom more later) whom he suspected of nationalist (or Titoist) tendencies. The loyalty of foreign Communists, Stalin had always insisted, must be to the Soviet

Union, not their native lands. Stalin's definition of a loyal Communist was one who faithfully served the interests of the Kremlin. An international *"revolutionary,"* Stalin wrote in 1927, is one "who is ready to protect, to defend the U.S.S.R. without reservation, without qualification."[8] In short, the interests of the Soviet Union outweighed the considerations of all other socialist governments. Stalin never budged on this definition of an international revolutionary. Only one Marxist was permitted to be a nationalist, namely, Stalin himself.

The damage Stalin did to Communist movements beyond the Soviet Union was seldom adequately appreciated or understood in the West. Not only did he subordinate the Communist parties to the interests of his state, but in doing so he tainted them with a brush wielded by a foreign power. As such, these movements found themselves struggling for support, their association with Moscow having become a millstone dragging them down, and their thunder stolen by reformist socialists in the West. After World War II, the shifts to the left were the result of wars, poverty, and disillusion with the old order, not the creation of Stalin; the left's demise, however, was in part Stalin's responsibility.

Stalin's brutal cleansing ("purging") of the East European Communist parties did have its desired effect. Until Stalin's death in March 1953, these parties were outwardly loyal to the Soviet Union, and Eastern Europe remained calm.

## ☐ Poland

But soon after Stalin's death, however, the East European Communist parties began to work toward partial independence from Moscow. This did not mean that they sought to leave the socialist camp or legalize capitalist political parties, but they did insist on dealing with their own internal problems without direct intervention by Moscow. An element of self-preservation played a large part in the restructuring of the relationship between the East European Communist parties and Moscow. The East Europeans sought to do away with Moscow's repeated and arbitrary purges of their ranks and interference in their internal affairs. The Polish party took the lead when it quietly released from house arrest (December 1954) and later readmitted (August 1956) into the party the nationalist Wladyslaw Gomulka.

Stalin had good reason to mistrust Gomulka. As early as 1945, Stalin's agents in Poland had warned him that the "deviationist" Gomulka had repeatedly and publicly advocated a "Polish road" to socialism, a "Polish Marxism." Gomulka's variation of Communism, unlike the Soviet version, sought a peaceful rather than a bloody transformation of society. It rejected the collectivization of agriculture, spoke of a "parliamentary democracy" for Poland, and even suggested that the Polish Communist Party had seized political power in 1945 in its own right—as it was "laying in the street" ready to be picked up—thus failing to show proper gratitude for the role of the Red Army. What we are dealing with here, the agents pointed out, is more a case of "Polish nationalism" than of Communism based on the Soviet model.[9]

The return to power of East European Communists who had been driven from power by Stalin was greatly speeded up when the new Soviet leader, Nikita Khrushchev, denounced Stalin's "mistakes" and "excesses," namely his crimes against members of the Communist Party in the Soviet Union itself. Khrushchev had sought to discredit his Stalinist political opponents at home, but his action had unforeseen and important repercussions in Eastern Europe.

When Khrushchev's first attack on the dead Stalin took place in his Secret Speech at the Twentieth Congress of the Communist Party of the Soviet Union in February 1956, the Polish Communist Party, which had sent delegates to the congress, leaked a copy of the speech to the West. Khrushchev later wrote in his memoirs: "I was told that it was being sold for very little. So Khrushchev's speech . . . wasn't appraised as being worth much! Intelligence agents from every country in the world could buy it cheap on the open market."[10] If Khrushchev could denounce Stalinism at home, the Poles reasoned, then they ought to be able to do the same. The Poles then used the speech to justify their attempt to travel their own road toward socialism without, however, leaving the Soviet camp.

At home the Polish Communist Party had its work cut out. The summer of 1956 saw rioting by workers, particularly in Poznan where seventy-five workers lost their lives in confrontations with police. To deal with this crisis, the party convened in October 1956 to initiate a program of reform and to elect Gomulka as its first secretary. Upon his election, Gomulka delivered a speech in which he affirmed Poland's right to follow a socialist model other than the Soviet example. He also insisted on his country's "full independence and sovereignty," as part of every nation's right to self-government. Polish-Soviet relations, he said, must be based on equality and independence.

What particularly had galled the Poles was that their defense minister, Konstantin Rokossovsky, was a Soviet citizen. Rokossovsky, a native of Poland, had left his country for the Soviet Union and had risen to the highest military rank, that of marshal of the Red Army. As Poland's minister of defense he thus served a foreign master. Understandably, Rokossovsky became one of the first casualties of Poland's peaceful "October Revolution" when he was dismissed as defense minister.

The behavior by the Polish Communists alarmed their Soviet comrades. In October, a high-level Soviet delegation, led by Khrushchev, arrived uninvited in Warsaw. The Poles refused to back down. They made clear they would continue to travel down the socialist road, yet at the same time, they insisted on the right to take care of their own internal problems. In addition, they pledged their loyalty to the Warsaw Pact, the Soviet-led military alliance.

The Soviet Union, here, gave tacit assent to the principle that there exist several different roads to socialism, that the Soviet model was not the only one and thus not necessarily the correct one. In effect, the Kremlin yielded and accepted the legitimacy of what once was a heresy, the right to nationalist deviation. If the Soviets had the right to find their own path to socialism, so did the other socialist countries. In fact, Khrushchev had already buried the hatchet in the ideological dispute with Tito. In May 1955, Khrushchev had gone to Belgrade on a state visit and when he and Tito embraced, it signaled an end to the intra-Marxist feud. The Soviet Union's monopoly on interpreting the writings of Marx and Engels was no more. The Italian Communist Palmiro Togliatti coined a word to describe the new reality, "polycentrism." The world now had several centers of Marxist orthodoxy.

The Poles, although still in the shadow of the Soviet Union, embarked on their own road to socialism, and the Communist Party took steps to placate the restless population. Workers gained concessions, and the gradual process of collectivizing farmland was halted and then reversed. (Unlike the Soviet Union where the state owned all land, most farmland in Communist Poland was in the hands of private farmers.) Political parties other than the Communist Party were permitted to exist and they received subordinate representation in the government. Gomulka released from jail the prelate of the Roman Catholic Church in Poland, Stefan Cardinal Wyszynski, and the Church regained the traditional right to administer its own affairs. In turn, Gomulka received the church's endorsement.

## ☐ Hungary

Across the border, the Hungarians watched the events in Poland with increasing intensity. If the Poles could eliminate some of the baleful effects of Stalinism, why could not they? Heated discussions took place in intellectual circles and within the Hungarian Communist Party. The upshot was that the Stalinists were forced to resign and Imre Nagy, Hungary's "Gomulka," took over.

Initially, events in Hungary paralleled those in Poland. But Nagy could not control the rebellious mood that was building up in his country. Reformers argued that it was not enough to rid the nation of the Stalinists; nothing short of independence from Moscow would do. A reformed Communist Party was not enough. Deep-seated Hungarian animosity toward the Russians had its historic roots in the intervention by the Russian army during the revolution of 1848, when Hungarians had sought to free themselves of Austrian domination. Also, the Stalinist secret police had bred deep

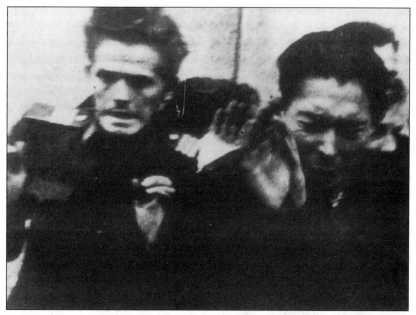

Hungarian secret police executed in the street by "freedom fighters," October 1956. (*National Archives*)

resentment. These factors, as well as economic grievances, led to massive street demonstrations and the lynching of secret police agents. Budapest had become unmanageable, and on November 1, 1956, Nagy suddenly announced that Hungary was now an independent nation. With this declaration came the pledge to hold free elections—elections that would no doubt bring an end to Communist Party rule in Hungary.

The events in Hungary left Nikita Khrushchev few choices, particularly when Radio Free Europe, a station operating out of Munich under the aegis of the CIA, encouraged the Hungarians by offering vague promises of U.S. aid. At this highly charged moment in the Cold War, a neutral Hungary was out of the question. John Foster Dulles, the U.S. secretary of state, had said earlier that neutrality in this holy war against the forces of absolute evil was the height of immorality.[11] The leaders in the Kremlin held a similar view. Hungary was thus destined to be but a pawn in an ideological and military tug-of-war. Its fate was to serve either the interests of Washington or those of Moscow. With the Soviet position in Eastern Europe beginning to disintegrate, Khrushchev acted.

For several days, the Soviets did not know what to do. At first, they saw the disturbances in Budapest as anti-Soviet (as had been the case in Poland) but not anti-Communist. They expected to work with Nagy and even discussed the possibility of withdrawing their troops from Hungary.

But then came the news that Communists were being lynched in the streets of Budapest. Any withdrawal, Khrushchev now argued, would "cheer up the imperialists." "We had to act," he declared in his memoirs, "and we had to act swiftly."[12]

The Soviet army attacked Budapest three days after Nagy's proclamation. After a week of savage fighting, the Soviets reestablished their control over Hungary. The Kremlin installed János Kádár as the Hungarian party's new first secretary, and he had Imre Nagy executed in 1958. Kádár, who came to power with blood on his hands,[13] proved in time to be a cautious reformer. Gradually over the next three decades, he introduced the most sweeping economic reforms anywhere in the Soviet bloc, culminating in the legalization of private enterprises in the early 1980s. This combination of the carrot (tolerance of reforms) and the stick (the Soviet army) lifted many restrictions, raised the standard of living, and kept Hungary quiet.

The United States could do little but watch with indignation the Soviet suppression of the Hungarian uprising and offer political asylum to many of the nearly two hundred thousand Hungarians who fled their country. John Foster Dulles, who in the past had repeatedly stated that the aim of the United States was the liberation of Eastern Europe and the rollback of the Soviet presence there, could do no more than watch in frustration. The events in Hungary offered him the opportunity to put his policy into operation, but President Eisenhower's cautious response revealed that Dulles's rhetoric was just that. The Hungarian rebellion also revealed that the United States would not challenge the Soviet Union in Eastern Europe; it would not start World War III over Poland or Hungary. The lesson was not lost on the Soviets when they had to deal with Czechoslovakia in 1968.

☐ *Czechoslovakia*

Events in Poland and Hungary did not affect Czechoslovakia during the 1950s. The country continued to be ruled by Antonin Novotny, whom Stalin had placed in power in 1952. In the late 1960s, Czechoslovakia, therefore, appeared to be the least likely candidate for social and political reform. Yet the unreconstructed Stalinist Novotny was bitterly resented by many in Czechoslovakia, particularly the writers but also members of his own party. When a writers' rebellion began late in 1967, Novotny found himself unable to deal with it because his own party did not support him. It asked him to resign, and he did so in January 1968. After the party dutifully checked with the Kremlin, Leonid Brezhnev responded that "this is your matter." The party then elected Alexander Dubcek as its first secretary.

The writers, many of whom were Communists, had raised a number of basic questions—those of civil rights, censorship, and the monopoly of the Communist Party in the political, economic, and social affairs of the nation. After Novotny's ouster, the party continued the discussions. Under Dubcek's stewardship, it introduced numerous reforms at breakneck speed. It attempted to create a "socialism with a human face," one that sought to combine Eastern-style socialism with Western-style democracy. One restriction after another was lifted. The results were freedom of the press, freedom to travel, freedom from fear of the police. An intense and open debate of the nature of the reforms took place in the uncensored pages of the press. The "Prague Spring" was under way. In the spring and summer of 1968, euphoria swept a nation that became oblivious to the inherent dangers of such radical reforms. Soon there was the inevitable talk of the possibility of leaving the Soviet bloc and of neutrality.

The Soviet leadership watched these developments intensely. Several high-ranking delegations arrived from Moscow and other East European capitals. The Communist parties of Eastern Europe urged Dubcek and his party to bring the movement under control before it completely got out of hand. Several of the East European governments (particularly those of Yugoslavia and Hungary) did not want to give the Soviet Union an excuse for intervention. But it was to no avail. Dubcek neither wanted to nor was he able to put an end to the discussions and experiments. The hopeful "Prague Spring" continued unabated. The border between Czechoslovakia and Austria became but a line on a map that Czechs—and visitors from the West—crossed without restriction. The Iron Curtain ceased to exist in this part of Europe.

Until August 1968, the Soviet leadership was divided on what course to take. The hard-liners in Moscow became convinced that Dubcek and his party were no longer in control. What was happening in Czechoslovakia was no longer a local matter. To the Soviets, a counterrevolution was in the making, one Dubcek was unable and unwilling to bring to an end. Dubcek was well aware of the inherent danger of this situation, that the Soviets had a contingency plan to use force. In a telephone conversation with Brezhnev on August 13, a week before the invasion, Dubcek said, "If you consider us traitors, then take the measures which your Politburo considers necessary."[14]

Events in Czechoslovakia also threatened to create repercussions in the Soviet Union. The non-Russian population of the Soviet empire—approximately half of the population—watched the events in Czechoslovakia with growing interest. The party chiefs in the non-Russian republics, particularly those of the Ukraine and Lithuania, took the lead in urging strong action. Brezhnev convened a plenary session of the party's Central Committee to inform the party that the Warsaw Pact was about to put an end to the "Prague Spring." On August 20, 1968, Brezhnev ordered the Soviet army into action. When the Soviet tanks rolled into Prague, the Czechs, as expected, did not resist to any appreciable degree. The Soviets then proceeded to replace Dubcek with Gustav Husak.

The Soviets justified their invasion by claiming that they had to protect Czechoslovakia against a counterrevolution. Moreover, Brezhnev declared that the Soviet Union had an inherent right to intervene in all socialist countries similarly threatened. This unilateral Soviet right of intervention in Eastern Europe became known in the West as the Brezhnev doctrine. In 1979, Brezhnev used it anew to justify intervention in Afghanistan, when he sent the Soviet army to bail out a bankrupt socialist government. And in 1980, Brezhnev resurrected it to warn Poland's Solidarity movement against going too far.

Ironically, the Soviet Union had been able to count on a certain measure of goodwill among the population of Czechoslovakia until the invasion of 1968. After all, it had been the Red Army in 1945 that had liberated Prague from the Germans, and only the Soviets had appeared to be willing to come to the aid of Czechoslovakia when Hitler had carved it up in 1938. But whatever goodwill had existed before 1968 became a thing of the past.

## ☐ East Germany

East Germany was unique among the Communist states in Eastern Europe. For one, it was the last of the Communist states Stalin established. It is not clear what Stalin had in mind for Germany after World War II, but after the West had formally created West Germany in May 1949, Stalin had little choice but to create his own state in October of that year. As late as March 1952, Stalin still proposed to the West a unified—but demilitarized and neutral—Germany. A West German historian concluded that East Germany was "Stalin's unloved child,"[15] a burden he wanted to be rid of. Stalin's proposal to unload East Germany came too late, however, as the Cold War by 1952 was in full bloom and attitudes had hardened. By then, West Germany was well on its way to rearmament as a member of NATO.

Second, East Germany was the Communist state with the least popular support. Its leaders understood only too well that without Soviet backing their state had no chance of existing. The politicians in Bonn considered it part of West Germany and bided their time until reunification. As a result, East German leaders, such as Walter Ulbricht and Erich Honecker, were the most hawkish of all the East European Communist rulers. They wanted the Soviets to dig in as deeply as possible in defiance of all Western aspirations. Shortly after Stalin died in March 1953, politicians in Moscow once again contemplated the abandonment of East Germany. But when widespread uprisings took place on June 17, 1953,[16] Moscow, after initial hesitation, came to the "fraternal" assistance of a Communist client in deep political trouble. It was Soviet army tanks that put an end to the disturbances in East Berlin and other cities.

Third, the Western challenge East Germany faced was not only political but also economic. As East Germany gradually rebuilt its economy under Soviet auspices, West Germany experienced a sustained economic boom. By the late 1950s, West Germany had reached its prewar standard of living, and it continued to improve. As a booming West German economy suffered from a shortage of skilled workers, many East Germans left their country to participate in the political and economic benefits in the West. East Berliners were able to travel by public transport to West Berlin, where they automatically received West German citizenship. Berlin had become the biggest hole in the Iron Curtain. By the early 1960s, the hemorrhage had become so serious for East Germany that Khrushchev repeatedly threatened war to drive the West out of Berlin.

The Berlin Blockade (1948–1949) and Khrushchev's saber rattling had proven to be ineffective in dislodging the Western powers; another solution had to be found. Khrushchev's solution was the erection of a 10-foot barrier around West Berlin. The Berlin Wall, built in August 1961, solved East Germany's most pressing problem when it sealed off the last remaining gap in the Iron Curtain. The East Germans left behind were shut off from the rest of the German-speaking world. The Berlin Wall thus became the supreme symbol of the division of Europe and the most visible manifestation of the Iron Curtain.

A view of the Berlin Wall and barbed wire right through Berlin, erected by the GDR regime on August 13, 1961. A border of death divided Germany into East and West. *(German Information Center)*

## ■ THE SINO-SOVIET SPLIT

After Stalin's death, the Soviet leaders faced another crisis within the Communist world. By the mid-1950s, the Communist rulers of the People's Republic of China (PRC) began to strike out on their own. Before long, it became apparent that the two Communist giants were at loggerheads. The rift between them became more serious with each passing year, and by the early 1960s, relations were openly hostile. The feud between the two Communist giants had a great impact on international relations. As the Sino-Soviet split emerged, the Cold War, initially a bipolar struggle between East and West, gave way to a triangular pattern of relations among the Soviet Union, China, and the United States.

From the time of its formation in October 1949, the People's Republic of China sought to establish and maintain close relations with the Soviet Union. At the time, Moscow and Washington were engaged in a potentially dangerous rivalry that already had turned into a nuclear confrontation. As early as 1950, Beijing sent its troops against the U.S.-led forces of the United Nations in Korea. Chairman Mao Zedong's mission to Moscow in early 1950 seemed to confirm the suspicion that Mao and Stalin were comrades united in the cause of international Communism and mutually dedicated to the defeat of the capitalist world. In Moscow, in February 1950, they signed a thirty-year military alliance aimed at the United States, and the Soviet Union took up the cause of seating the PRC in the United Nations to replace the Republic of China (Nationalist China). The Soviet Union also provided much-needed economic assistance to China in the form of loans, technicians, and advisers. The two nations also rallied in support of Communist North Korea during the Korean War. And of course they spoke the same Marxian language, which denounced U.S. imperialism. Moscow and Beijing thus faced a common foe and professed a common ideology. There was little reason to believe that their alliance would be short-lived. Yet, only six years after the PRC had come into existence, the two began to pull apart.

It was little wonder that the United States was skeptical about the early reports of difficulties between the two Communist states. The U.S. assumption, fostered by the Cold War, was that Communism was a monolith, a single, unitary movement directed by Moscow. This assumption was much slower to die than the reality of Communist unity.

In retrospect, we can recognize signs of friction between Beijing and Moscow from the very outset. The Chinese could hardly be pleased by the rather cavalier manner in which Stalin treated them. The terms of the Moscow agreement (1950) were not at all generous. Stalin offered Mao a development loan of no more than $300 million to be spread over five years and to be repaid by China in agricultural produce and with interest. As a price for that loan, China agreed to continued Soviet use and control of the principal railroads and ports in Manchuria and to the creation of joint Sino-Soviet stock companies to conduct mineral surveys in Xinjiang (Sinkiang), the innermost province of China. The paucity of Soviet aid and the concessions Stalin demanded from China suggest that Stalin's purpose was to accentuate Soviet supremacy and Chinese dependency. Indeed, it would seem that Stalin was wary of this new Communist friend and that he would have preferred dealing with a weaker, more vulnerable Nationalist China than with a vigorous new Communist regime in China. If the Chinese harbored ill feelings toward Stalin or resented the continued Soviet presence in Manchuria and Xinjiang, they prudently remained silent, publicly accepting Stalin's leadership and extolling their fraternal relationship with the Soviet Union. The backwardness of China's economy was such that Chinese leaders considered Soviet economic assistance and diplomatic support too important to sacrifice on the altar of national pride.

The unspoken Chinese misgivings during the early 1950s did not lead directly to the Sino-Soviet split later that decade. Nor is that feud to be explained as a direct consequence of earlier Sino-Russian troubles. One can surely trace the historical roots of animosity between the two countries back in time, to tsarist imperialism in the nineteenth century, or even to the Mongol invasions of Russia in the thirteenth century. But it would be too simple to argue that the conflict in the late 1950s was, therefore, the inevitable result of that history. The two sides dredged up the conflicts of the past, such as territorial claims, only after the dispute began to develop over other contemporary issues in the mid-1950s.

The first strains of conflict between Moscow and Beijing came in consequence of Soviet leader Nikita Khrushchev's famous Secret Speech in February 1956. The Chinese leaders were caught by surprise by this sudden, scathing attack on Stalin and by Khrushchev's call for peaceful coexistence with the capitalist world. Chinese Communists had no particular reason to defend the departed Stalin, but they feared that the attack on Stalin's "cult of personality" might, by implication, undermine Mao's dictatorship in China. Moreover, they questioned the wisdom of peaceful coexistence and they disputed the right of Moscow to unilaterally make such a major ideological shift with significant global implications. The Chinese leaders chafed at Khrushchev's bold reinterpretation of Marxist-Leninist doctrine, without so much as consulting with Mao in advance. Mao, who had led the Chinese Communist Party since 1935, was the world's senior ranking Communist leader, and he had reason to object to being ignored by the brash new leader of the Soviet Union. The Chinese were, in effect, questioning Khrushchev's authority to dictate policy to the Communist world.

The new Soviet line of peaceful coexistence soon became the major bone of contention between Moscow and Beijing. The Soviet leadership had become alarmed about the nuclear arms race and came to the conviction that the Soviet Union must avert a devastating nuclear war with the

United States, whose burgeoning nuclear arsenal posed a serious threat to the survival of their country. Khrushchev, therefore, concluded that it would be necessary to coexist peacefully with the capitalist superpower. However, at the same time that they were offering the olive branch to the other side, the Soviets worked feverishly to close the gap in the arms race, and in 1957, they made two remarkable technological breakthroughs. They launched their first ICBM (intercontinental ballistic missile) in August, and in October they stunned the world with *Sputnik,* the first artificial satellite sent into orbit around the earth. The enormous strategic significance of this Soviet advance in military technology was not lost on the Chinese. Mao, attending a meeting of world Communist leaders in Moscow in November 1957, contended that the international situation had reached a new turning point and that the Communist world had stolen the march on the capitalist world in the contest for global power. Mao asserted that "at present, it is not the west wind which is prevailing over the east wind, but the east wind prevailing over the west wind."[17] He argued that the Communist camp should put its newfound military superiority to work to attain the final victory over capitalism. Khrushchev strongly rejected these ideas and concluded the meeting with a reaffirmation of peaceful coexistence.

This was the origin of a dispute over global strategy that ultimately split the two Communist giants. The Chinese argued that, by making peace with the capitalists, the Soviet Union was departing from essential Marxist-Leninist doctrine. Peaceful coexistence might suit the Soviet Union, already an industrialized nation with secure borders and nuclear weapons, but it was unsuited to China, which had none of these. Mao well remembered that his army had fought a bloody war with the United States in the not too distant past, a war the imperialists in Washington were sure to resume. Mao argued that Communist nations should continue the international struggle by assisting Communist forces engaged in wars of national liberation. Moreover, the PRC sought assurances of Soviet support in its own unfinished war of national liberation: the civil war against Jiang Jieshi's Nationalist regime, which controlled the island of Taiwan. In 1958, Beijing intensified the pressure on Taiwan by launching a sustained artillery barrage against two off-shore islands, Quemoy and Matsu, which were occupied by the Nationalist forces. It seems that Mao's purpose was to test the resolve of the United States to defend Nationalist China and to test Soviet willingness to provide active military support to the PRC. The United States did make clear its commitment to the defense of Taiwan, but the Soviets, instead of pledging support, denounced China's actions as reckless. The Soviet Union would not allow itself to be drawn into a nuclear war with the United States over Taiwan.

In addition to disputing global strategy, the two Communist powers also disagreed on the means to attaining Communism. The Chinese had adopted the Soviet model for economic development when, in 1953, they put into operation a Soviet-style Five-Year Plan. But by 1957, the leaders in Beijing were beginning to question the appropriateness of the Soviet model for China. In early 1958, Mao called for scrapping the Second Five-Year Plan and replacing it with a new program known as the Great Leap Forward. Mao thus abandoned the Soviet model in favor of his own program designed to achieve industrial development and the collectivization of agriculture simultaneously. Boldly, Mao proclaimed that China had overtaken the Soviet Union in the quest to build a Communist society. But Mao was too quick to trumpet success, for within a year the Great Leap Forward, with its hastily created communes, produced an economic disaster (see Chapter 14). The Soviet leadership, concerned about the implications for the Eastern European satellites of China's departing from the Soviet model, was from the beginning critical of the new experiment in China. Indeed, Khrushchev heaped scorn on Mao's heralded Great Leap all the more when it failed.

In September 1959, Khrushchev gave Mao reason to suspect that the Soviet Union was plotting against China. At the invitation of President Eisenhower, Khrushchev made a two-week visit to the United States. Mao, who remained adamantly opposed to peaceful coexistence, took a dim view of this diplomatic venture, and he was left to speculate on what had transpired at Camp David during the private talks between Khrushchev and Eisenhower. He suspected that Khrushchev was making concessions at China's expense, specifically, striking a bargain that would trade Western concessions on the Berlin question for a Soviet commitment to oppose the PRC's use of force to settle the Taiwan question.

In 1960, the polemical feud between Moscow and Beijing became an open confrontation as each side, for the first time, made public their attacks on the other. The Chinese Communist Party struck first, in April 1960, with an article titled "Long Live Leninism" in *Red Flag,* an official organ of the Chinese Communist Party. It argued that peaceful coexistence was contrary to the precepts of Leninism:

> We believe in the absolute correctness of Lenin's thinking: war is an inevitable outcome of systems of exploitation and the source of modern wars is the imperialist system. Until the imperialist system and the exploiting classes come to an end, wars of one kind or another will always occur.[18]

The Soviet government responded quickly. In July 1960, it abruptly pulled out of China its 1,300 economic advisers, engineers, and technicians, who took their blueprints with them and left behind many unfinished projects. This was a serious blow to China's industrialization efforts. And at about this time, Moscow rescinded an earlier agreement to provide China nuclear technology to build the atomic bomb.

Khrushchev's purpose was not to terminate the alliance but to force Beijing back into line and to coerce its acceptance of Moscow's policies and position of leadership. In the year that followed, Beijing seemed to acquiesce while a more conciliatory Moscow seemed to be backing away from détente with the United States. But this proved to be only a brief respite, for in October 1961, at the Twenty-Second Party Congress of the Communist Party of the Soviet Union, Khrushchev again lashed out at the Chinese. He attacked China's economic policies and ideology and argued that modern industrial development must precede experiments with creating communes. Communism was to be achieved by following the Soviet lead. In response, Chinese foreign minister Zhou Enlai led the entire Chinese delegation out of the congress and back to Beijing.

In 1962, new diplomatic issues divided Moscow and Beijing and exacerbated their conflict. China and India engaged in a brief war in October over a border dispute, and Moscow, instead of supporting China (with which it had a military alliance), offered diplomatic support to India while joining the United States in condemning China for its reckless aggression. And shortly afterward, in the wake of the Cuban missile crisis, in which the United States and the Soviet Union came perilously close to a nuclear war, the Chinese scorned Khrushchev as weak-kneed for caving in to U.S. demands to pull out the Soviet missiles from Cuba.

The Chinese originally had hoped to draw from the strength of the Soviet-led Communist movement and specifically to attain from Moscow a firm commitment to provide military support for the "liberation" of Taiwan. Having failed in this, Beijing then sought to strengthen its position by cultivating its relations with other Communist and national liberation movements in Asia, Africa, and Latin America—that is, the Third World. China had already made a major step in identifying itself with the nonaligned nations of these parts of the world by its participation in the Bandung Conference in Indonesia in 1955.[19] Increasingly in the 1960s, the PRC sought to befriend leaders of revolutionary movements and those of newly independent nations in the Third World, even to the point of providing economic aid that China, with its own economic problems, could ill afford.

In the early 1960s, when the breach with China became wide open, Khrushchev seemed to have become as obsessed with the recalcitrant China as Mao had become obsessed with what he regarded as Soviet treachery. After publishing an open letter demanding Beijing's submission to Soviet leadership, Khrushchev began formulating plans for a meeting of world Communist leaders at which he would either force China back into the fold or force it out. Several Communist parties, however, declined invitations because they opposed Khrushchev's confrontational approach. Before this meeting could be arranged, Khrushchev himself was suddenly ousted from power in Moscow. And on the very day that this was reported in the world press, October 16, 1964, the PRC announced it had successfully tested an atomic bomb. Proudly, the Chinese proclaimed that the PRC too was now a superpower. They had successfully defied Khrushchev's efforts to dictate policy and his efforts to deny them nuclear weapons.

No significant change occurred in Sino-Soviet relations in consequence of the fall of Khrushchev and his replacement by Leonid Brezhnev. Nor did the escalation of the U.S. involvement in the Vietnam War in 1965 bring the two Communist powers together; instead, they rivaled one another for influence over the Communist regime in North Vietnam. In April 1965, Moscow proposed to Beijing that the two nations cooperate in support of North Vietnam. It asked the Chinese to allow Soviet aircraft use of Chinese airports and airspace. After lengthy debate within ruling circles in Beijing, Mao rejected the proposal. Mao feared not only a Soviet military presence in China but also the possibility of a full-scale war with the Soviet Union.

Mao Zedong's tirade against the Soviet Union reached new heights in the summer of 1966, when he launched the Great Proletarian Cultural Revolution, a campaign designed to revitalize the Chinese revolution by mass mobilization (see Chapter 14). This political program contained a strong anti-Soviet aspect, for Mao called upon the Chinese people to purge the party of leaders whom he condemned for trying to establish a Soviet-type Communism in China. He pronounced them guilty of the same crimes that he pinned on Soviet leaders: bureaucratic elitism, revisionism, sabotage of the Communist movement, and taking it down the capitalist road. The political and economic chaos caused by his Cultural Revolution gave the Soviet Union still more reason to ridicule Mao and Maoism. Nevertheless, despite the upheaval it caused, Mao proclaimed that he had set the revolution back on the track to true Communism, and he called upon all Communists and would-be Communists throughout the world to abandon the revisionist Soviets and turn instead to China for their model.

Tensions between the two Communist giants mounted even higher on yet another front: the Sino-Soviet border. From time to time during their feud, Mao had called into question the Soviet claim to territory north of the Amur River boundary between the two countries in Eastern Asia.[20] During the 1960s, as their feud heated up, both the Soviets and the Chinese fortified their common border with larger and larger forces. Within the Ussuri River, which separates China and the Soviet Maritime Province, were several disputed islands, and in February and March 1969, skirmishes between Chinese and Soviet armed forces suddenly broke out on the island of Damanskii. After the Chinese launched an assault, the Soviets retaliated with artillery, tanks, and aircraft and drove the Chinese back. The warfare left about eight hundred Chinese troops dead as compared with about sixty Soviet deaths.

Although a cease-fire was arranged, a war of nerves continued throughout the year. A full-scale war between China and the Soviet Union seemed imminent. It was in this context that leaders in Beijing began to consider ending their diplomatic isolation by improving their relations with the United States. Tension along the border continued into the 1980s as both sides reinforced their border security with greater military force. Ultimately, the Soviet Union deployed an estimated 2 million troops along its 2,700-mile-long China borders and armed them with the most modern of weapons, including tactical and intermediate-range nuclear missiles. China's border forces were thought to be as large as the Soviets', but not as well equipped.

One of the major consequences of the Sino-Soviet split, and specifically of the near war between the two Communist nations, was the normalization of relations between the PRC and the United States in the early 1970s. This had a profound effect on global power relations, supplanting the bipolar Cold War with what may be called a strategic triangle. Throughout the 1970s and 1980s, the PRC moved closer to the United States and still further away from the Soviet Union. It charged the latter with "socialist imperialism" and "hegemonism." In fact, "anti-hegemonism" became the main pillar of China's foreign policy in the 1970s, when it endeavored to attain the active support of the United States, Japan, and other nations in its standoff with the Soviet Union.

## ■ THE THIRTY-YEAR FEUD IS ENDED

The estrangement between the two Communist giants continued into the late 1980s. Although Moscow showed signs of desiring a thaw, Deng Xiaoping, the new Chinese Communist ruler who came to power after Mao's death in 1976, hunkered down with an inflexible policy. He insisted on three changes in Soviet foreign policy before relations could be normalized. He demanded a withdrawal (or at least a substantial reduction) of Soviet forces from the Chinese border, an end to the Soviet invasion of Afghanistan, and an end to Soviet support for the Vietnamese army in Cambodia. Although bilateral trade and diplomatic exchanges were gradually restored, further progress was blocked by Chinese and Soviet intransigence on the "three obstacles."

As both Beijing and Moscow focused their attention on economic reform in the 1980s, the prospects for Sino-Soviet rapprochement improved. Mikhail Gorbachev, who came to power in the Kremlin in 1985, brought a dynamic new pragmatism to Soviet diplomacy. Determined to regenerate the faltering economy, Gorbachev saw it necessary to reduce the size of the Soviet Union's military establishment, including the large deployment of forces in Asia. With this in mind, Gorbachev in July 1986 went to Vladivostok, the largest Soviet city in East Asia, to deliver a speech that boldly proclaimed a new Soviet initiative to establish peaceful relations with China and other Asian nations. In this conciliatory speech, Gorbachev addressed Beijing's three burning issues, declaring Soviet readiness to seek accommodation on all three. He indicated that steps were already being taken toward the evacuation of

Soviet forces from Afghanistan, that Soviet troops would be withdrawn from Mongolia on the Sino-Mongolian border, and that Moscow was prepared to discuss the issue of mutual reduction of military forces on the Sino-Soviet border and the Vietnam-Cambodia issue.

Deng Xiaoping reacted positively. In April 1987, Chinese and Soviet negotiators began addressing "regional issues," particularly border disputes, and the Cambodian question. Negotiations continued on various levels through the following year as both parties reciprocated with confidence-building gestures and agreements. By 1989, substantial improvement had been made toward the restoration of peaceful relations. The Soviet Union withdrew from Afghanistan, reduced its troops along the Chinese border,[21] and pressured Vietnam to begin evacuation of its troops from Cambodia. Placated by these conciliatory measures, Deng accepted Gorbachev's proposal for a summit meeting and extended an invitation to him to visit Beijing in May 1989.

Gorbachev's visit to China signaled the end of the thirty-year-long rift. He arrived in Beijing, however, in the midst of the mammoth student demonstrations in the Chinese capital, and his historic visit was upstaged by this tumultuous event (see Chapter 14). The summit meeting was, nonetheless, a success. Gorbachev, who acknowledged that the Soviet Union was partly to blame for the deep split between the two countries, proclaimed the summit a "watershed event." The two sides pledged to continue talks aimed at mutually reducing military troop strength along their long shared border "to a minimum level commensurate with normal, good-neighborly relations," to seek expanded trade and cultural relations, and to restore relations between the Communist parties of the two countries.[22] On Cambodia, they acknowledged a lack of agreement but pledged to continue efforts to avert a civil war in that country and to help it become independent and nonaligned. On the whole, the summit meeting advanced the new rapprochement between China and the Soviet Union and reflected their mutual objectives of lessening tensions and improving economic relations.

In 1992, the Russian parliament ratified Gorbachev's agreement with China. It recognized that Damanskii Island on the Ussuri River, where the fighting had broken out in 1969, was indeed Chinese territory. Russian historians estimated that Soviet troop deployment along the Amur and Ussuri Rivers from the onset of hostilities in 1969 to Gorbachev's visit to Beijing cost the state the massive sum of between 200 and 300 billion rubles (in 1960s rubles), roughly the equivalent of $200–$300 billion.[23]

## ■ RECOMMENDED READINGS

Bethell, Nicholas. *Gomulka: His Poland, His Communism.* New York: Holt, Rinehart, and Winston, 1969.
    An explanation of the Polish road to socialism.

Chen Jian. *Mao's China and the Cold War.* Chapel Hill, NC: University of North Carolina Press, 2001.
A thorough, detailed analysis.

Clubb, O. Edmund. *China and Russia: The "Great Game."* New York: Columbia University Press, 1971.
A comprehensive, detailed, and evenhanded analysis of the Sino-Soviet split by a U.S. diplomat-turned-scholar.

Crankshaw, Edward. *Khrushchev: A Career.* New York: Viking Press, 1966.

Deutscher, Isaac. *Stalin: A Political Biography.* Rev. ed. New York: Oxford University Press, 1966.
The classic biography by a Trotskyite.

Hinton, Harold C. *China's Turbulent Quest.* 2d ed. New York: Macmillan, 1973.
An analysis of the Sino-Soviet rift.

Kecskemeti, Paul. *The Unexpected Revolution: Social Forces in the Hungarian Uprising.* Stanford, Calif.: Stanford University Press, 1961.

London, Kurt, ed. *Eastern Europe in Transition.* Baltimore: Johns Hopkins University Press, 1966.
A study of the forces of nationalism in Eastern Europe.

Medvedev, Roy A. *Let History Judge: The Origins and Consequences of Stalinism.* New York: Knopf, 1971.
An indictment of Stalin by a Soviet "Leninist" historian.

Medvedev, Roy A., and Zhores A. Medvedev. *Khrushchev: The Years in Power.* New York: Norton, 1978.

Shipler, David K. *Russia: Broken Idols, Solemn Dreams.* New York: Times Books, 1983.
An explanation of Soviet society by a correspondent of the *New York Times.*

Solzhenitsyn, Alexander. *One Day in the Life of Ivan Denisovich.* New York: Praeger, 1962.
An exposé of Stalin's forced-labor camps; the novel that brought Solzhenitsyn international acclaim.

Tatu, Michel. *Power in the Kremlin: From Khrushchev to Kosygin.* London: William Collins Sons, 1968.
A well-received study of Soviet politics by a French expert.

Taubman, William. *Khrushchev: The Man and His Era.* New York: W. W. Norton, 2003.
The definitive biography.

Ulam, Adam. *Stalin: The Man and His Era.* New York: Viking Press, 1973.
A highly readable, detailed biography written from a Western perspective.

Valenta, Jiri. *Soviet Intervention in Czechoslovakia in 1968.* Baltimore: Johns Hopkins University Press, 1979.
A detailed explanation of the Kremlin's reasons for ending the Czechoslovak experiment in liberalization.

# ■ NOTES

1. J. V. Stalin, "The Tasks of Business Executives," February 4, 1931; J. V. Stalin, *Works* (Moscow: Foreign Languages Publishing House, 1955), vol. 13, pp. 40–41.

2. A proletarian—a member of the proletariat—is a wage-earner or, more commonly, a factory worker. In Marxist jargon, the words "proletarian" and "worker" are used interchangeably.

3. Edward Crankshaw, *Khrushchev: A Career* (New York: Viking, 1966), p. 228.

4. De Tocqueville quoted in Bernard B. Fall, *The Two Vietnams: A Political and Military Analysis* (New York: Praeger, 1963), p. 253.

5. N. S. Khrushchev, *Khrushchev Remembers: The Last Testament* (Boston: Little, Brown, 1974), p. 77.

6. Roy A. Medvedev and Zhores A. Medvedev, *Khrushchev: The Years in Power* (New York: Norton, 1978), pp. 94–101.

7. Tito's independence of both the Soviet Union and the West led him to take a "third" road. Tito, Nehru of India, and Nasser of Egypt became the early leaders of the Third World, that is, nations that refused to align themselves with either the Western or socialist blocs. The term later lost its original meaning, for it came to designate the world's underdeveloped nations.

8. J. V. Stalin, "The International Situation and the Defense of the U.S.S.R.," speech delivered on August 1, 1927, to the Joint Plenum of the Central Committee and Central Control Commission of the C.P.S.U. (b); J. V. Stalin, *Works* (Moscow: Foreign Languages Publishing House, 1954), vol. 10, pp. 53–54.

9. G. M. Adibekov, *Kominform i poslevoinnaia Evropa* (Moscow: Rossia molodaia, 1994), pp. 90–95.

10. Khrushchev, *Khrushchev Remembers*, p. 351; for the full text, pp. 559–618.

11. For a summary of Dulles's views on Communism, see his testimony before Congress, January 15, 1953; Walter LaFeber, ed., *The Dynamics of World Power: A Documentary History of United States Foreign Policy, 1945–1973*, vol. 2, *Eastern Europe and the Soviet Union* (New York: Chelsea House, 1973), pp. 465–468.

12. Khrushchev, *Khrushchev Remembers*, pp. 416–420. See also the documents made public at a conference in Budapest commemorating the fortieth anniversary of the uprising: Timothy Garton Ash, "Hungary's Revolution: Forty Years On," *New York Review of Books*, November 16, 1996, pp. 18–22; Reuters, "Soviets Almost Recognized Hungary Revolt, Data Show," *Baltimore Sun*, September 28, 1996, p. 7A; Jane Perlez, "Thawing Out Cold War History," *New York Times*, October 6, 1996, p. 4E.

13. "Blood on his hands" is a reference to Kádár granting safe conduct to Nagy (whom he nevertheless executed in 1958) and the bloody suppression of the rebellion. Kádár then became known as the "butcher of Budapest."

14. R. G. Pikhoia, "Chekhoslovakiia, 1968 god. Vzgliad iz Moskvy: Po dokumentam TsK KPSS," *Novaia i noveishaia istoriia* 1 (January–February 1995), p. 42.

15. Wilfried Loth, *Stalins ungeliebtes Kind: Warum Moskau die DDR nicht wollte* (Berlin: Rohwolt-Berlin, 1994).

16. That day became an official holiday in West Germany, the Day of Unity, commemorating the victims of the uprising and underscoring the commitment to unification. After Germany was unified in 1990, October 3 became the new official Day of Unity.

17. Mao cited in "At Present It Is Not the West Wind," *Survey of the China Mainland Press*, U.S. Consulate General, Hong Kong, no. 1662, December 2, 1957, p. 2.

18. Mao on Lenin, *Current Background*, U.S. Consulate General, Hong Kong, no. 617, April 26, 1960.

19. At this conference of twenty-nine African and Asian nations, China's representative, Zhou Enlai, shared the spotlight with India's neutralist prime minister, Nehru. China joined with these Third World nations in pledging peace and mutual noninterference.

20. In two separate treaties in 1858 and 1860, China relinquished to tsarist Russia territory north of the Amur River and east of the Ussuri River (the latter territory

known as the Maritime Province). But Mao now (the 1950s) contended that these were ill-gotten gains and that, since the treaties were forced on China by an imperialist government, they should not be honored or considered binding.

21. Gorbachev pledged in December 1988 at the United Nations to cut Soviet military forces by half a million, two hundred thousand of which would be from military units in Asia. He also announced plans to withdraw three-quarters of the Soviet troops in Mongolia and indicated that the first contingent of twelve thousand soldiers was already being taken out.

22. Scott Shane, "Gorbachev Returns Home from 'Watershed' Summit," *Baltimore Sun,* May 19, 1989.

23. Viktor Usov, "'Goriachaia vesna' na Damanskom," *Novoe vremia* 9 (1994), pp. 36–39.

# 9

## The War in Indochina

The Vietnam War, the United States' longest war, was one of the most tragic chapters in the history of the United States. It was even more tragic for Vietnam. The United States became engaged in a conflict in a distant Asian nation, confident that its great military capability could produce a victory and stop the spread of Communism in Southeast Asia. By getting involved in a war against an Asian people fighting in defense of their homeland, the United States ignored the lessons of the past—the Chinese resistance against an overpowering Japan in the 1930s and 1940s, and the success of the Viet Minh guerrillas in their eight-year-long battle against the French in Vietnam.

Massive U.S. intervention began in 1965, but continued to escalate until U.S. troops numbered well over half a million by 1968. This huge armed force with its modern weaponry was, however, denied victory by a resilient, determined Vietnamese enemy. In time, Washington learned that piling up the dead higher and higher would not necessarily bring victory. However, for political reasons, it would prove much more difficult to get out of Vietnam than it was to get in.

### ■ THE ESCALATION OF U.S. INVOLVEMENT

The Geneva Conference of 1954 called for France's withdrawal from Indochina after its defeat at Dien Bien Phu. The agreement established the independent states of Laos and Cambodia, and made a temporary separation of Vietnam into two zones divided at the 17th parallel. In the north a Communist government, the Democratic Republic of Vietnam, was already established with Hanoi as its capital and Ho Chi Minh its president. In the south, the French transferred power to the native monarch, Bao Dai, in Saigon. The Geneva Accords called for the unification of Vietnam on the basis of an internationally supervised election to be held two years later, in

July 1956. It also provided that, until unification, the people in Vietnam would be free to relocate across the dividing line, and that neither part of Vietnam would introduce foreign troops or make any military alliances.

The United States, which had already assumed the greater part of the financial burden of France's war in Vietnam, now took up the task of creating a client state in South Vietnam, financially, politically, and militarily. Even before the Geneva Accords had been signed (the United States never signed them, but did pledge to abide by them), U.S. Army officers arrived in Saigon to establish a military mission and prepare for paramilitary operations.

In the capital of South Vietnam, Saigon, the most effective political leader was not the playboy king, Bao Dai, known as the "Emperor of Cannes," but his prime minister, Ngo Dinh Diem. Diem, a Roman Catholic, had not been in his homeland during its struggle for independence against the French but was instead in the United States, where he cultivated important friendships, particularly with influential clergy and politicians. In October 1955, Diem deposed Bao Dai in a referendum and with it he became the president of the newly created Republic of Vietnam. It was a smashing electoral victory, for he won an incredible 98 percent of the votes cast, and in the city of Saigon he received 130 percent of the registered vote.[1] The French had little faith in Diem's ability to unify the country, but U.S. leaders saw in him the strongman needed to govern and defend South Vietnam. *Life* magazine called him the "Churchill of Southeast Asia," a decisive, staunchly anti-Communist leader who was determined to prevent the unification of Vietnam under Ho Chi Minh's Communist government and to suppress any resistance to his own government in the south.[2] So determined was he that he willfully ignored the terms of the Geneva agreement calling for the nationwide presidential election. With Washington's blessing, Diem defied the Geneva Accords on the matters of the elections and military alliances, and went on to entrench himself in the south with ever more U.S. aid.

At first, Diem went after organized crime and, having succeeded in that endeavor, he turned on others, such as former Viet Minh, Communists, liberals, and Buddhists. His rejection of the elections in 1956 had stirred protests, especially by former Viet Minh soldiers who had remained in the south in expectation of the reunification of the country. Diem sought to silence this protest by conducting a campaign of terror against the Viet Minh involving arrests, beatings, torture, and execution of suspected Viet Minh members. A second cause of the growing unrest in rural areas was the peasants' demand for land reform. A radical redistribution of farmland was being instituted in North Vietnam, and Diem's government had promised one in the south. The peasantry, which made up 85 percent of the population, felt betrayed by Diem's refusal to carry out a genuine land reform program. Instead, during Diem's tenure, the minority Catholics—10 percent of the population—became the largest landowners in South Vietnam.[3] This discontent

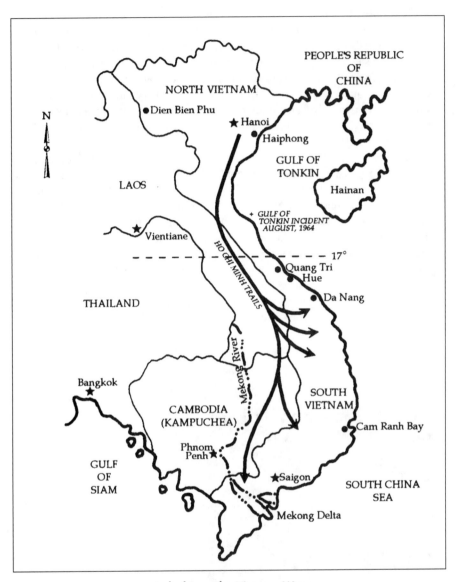

**Indochina: The Vietnam War**

was exploited by the Communist Party, which was formed mainly by Viet Minh veterans. It took the lead in organizing the antigovernment elements in the countryside and preparing them for a program of forceful resistance, which is to say, insurrection. When Diem began rounding up suspected dissidents—Communist and non-Communist alike—and placing them into detention camps, the new Communist-led revolutionary movement began to wage guerrilla warfare against his regime. Government terror was met with guerrilla terror, and the level of violence steadily increased in the late 1950s and early 1960s.

In December 1960, various opposition groups and parties, including the Communist Party, formed the National Liberation Front (NLF). The guerrilla forces of the NLF were commonly known as the Viet Cong, short for Vietnamese Communists. It was a derisive term Diem used to label his enemies. The more brutal Diem's regime became in its efforts to root out and destroy the insurrection, the stronger the NLF became. When Diem replaced local village headmen with his own bureaucrats in an attempt to control the countryside, these new village chiefs became targets for assassination by the Viet Cong. After trying several schemes to reorganize and secure the villages of South Vietnam, Diem finally resorted in 1962 to the drastic and expensive measure of resettling the villagers in compounds called "strategic hamlets." The peasants were strongly opposed to them and the NLF condemned them as concentration camps.

Ngo Dinh Diem, president of the Republic of Vietnam from 1955 to November 1963, when he was killed in a coup. *(National Archives)*

Diem's government was no more popular in the cities. He adopted a cult of personality, called "personalism," a doctrine steeped in the Confucian tradition. Diem demanded obedience; individual freedom must take second place to the collective betterment of society, which is achieved by dutiful loyalty to the morally superior ruler. In practice, it meant absolute obedience to Diem, even to the point of requiring all citizens to hang official photographs of him in their homes. It also made it impossible for him to understand the social, political, and economic forces the struggle against the French had unleashed. Meanwhile, he gathered around himself a tightly knit clique of loyal supporters, several of whom were his own brothers. The most notable among these was Ngo Dinh Nhu, who matched his brother in arrogance and who gained notoriety as the ruthless head of the secret police.

The Diem regime favored the Catholic minority, which brought him into a confrontation with the Buddhists. In May 1963, during the celebrations of Buddha's birthday, Catholic officials in Hue banned the flying of multicolored Buddhist flags. Demonstrators protesting the decree were gunned down. In protest, several Buddhist priests resorted to self-immolation. In a public square they were doused with a flammable liquid, and while seated in the posture for meditation, they ignited themselves. Madame Nhu, the wife of the chief of police, referred to the self-immolations as "barbecues." "Let them burn," she went on, "and we shall clap our hands."[3] This spectacle, seen around the world on television, signaled the degree to which Diem's government had alienated South Vietnamese society. Even before that, the South Vietnamese air force and army had turned against Diem; in 1962, the air force had bombed the presidential palace in an attempt to assassinate him.

Finally, U.S. officials in Saigon and Washington came to the conclusion that Diem must be replaced. A group of South Vietnamese army officers, encouraged by the U.S. embassy and CIA, staged a coup d'état in November 1963, murdering Diem and his brother Nhu in the process. They then formed a junta (a military ruling group) to govern in Saigon and to direct the military effort to crush the NLF.

The new government had the blessing of the United States, but it proved to be no more effective than the previous one. When it became apparent in the following year that the NLF was winning the struggle for control of South Vietnam, the Pentagon and State Department planners began laying plans for a greatly increased U.S. role. During the Kennedy administration, the U.S. presence grew from several hundred advisers to sixteen thousand "special forces." Lyndon Johnson, who succeeded the slain Kennedy as president in November 1963, confronted the prospect that the South Vietnamese government would soon be overthrown by a Communist-led insurrection.

The thinking in Washington at this time was that the NLF was completely controlled by the Communist regime in Hanoi, which in turn was under the control of Communist China. If South Vietnam were to fall to Communism, then other neighboring states would also fall one by one to this Beijing-directed Communist aggression. (This scenario was referred to as the "domino theory," a term that had been widely used in Washington since the Eisenhower administration.) Therefore, the U.S. commitment in South Vietnam was to defend this "free" (non-Communist) nation against "Communist aggression from outside." Officially, the Johnson administration saw the war in Vietnam as an international conflict, not a civil war between Vietnamese. Johnson told his nation in October 1964 that "we are not going to send American boys nine or ten thousand miles away from home to do what Asian boys ought to be doing for themselves," but at the same time he declared that he would "defend freedom" in South Vietnam and stop the "Communist aggression" from the north.[4] He was determined to prevent his administration from being charged with losing the battle against Communism in yet another Asian country. He feared, moreover, that such a major foreign policy setback would do political damage to his presidency and thus endanger the Great Society social program he had launched at home.

The NLF, whose voice was generally not heard in Washington, had a very different view of the realities in that country. It disputed the legitimacy of the Saigon government, protesting that the Diem regime and its successors in Saigon were merely puppets of U.S. forces. It called for the implementation of the 1954 Geneva Accords, the withdrawal of U.S. military forces from South Vietnam, and the creation of a coalition government. Ho Chi Minh's government in Hanoi took the same position. In April 1965, it set forth a four-point proposal that called for (1) withdrawal of U.S. forces, (2) an end of hostilities against North Vietnam, (3) honoring the Geneva Accords, and (4) allowing the Vietnamese to solve their own problems. Hanoi did not sway from its demands throughout the war and in the end obtained them.

Critics of President Johnson's policy—and they were still rather few at this stage—disputed the claim that the Saigon government was the victim of foreign aggression and raised the key question of the relationship between the NLF and the Communist government in Hanoi. The official U.S. position was that the NLF was a puppet of Hanoi, and thus Johnson consistently refused to recognize it in any formal capacity. His critics argued that the NLF was neither created nor controlled by Hanoi, but was the organized center of the revolution within South Vietnam and was essentially independent of Hanoi.

The relationship between Hanoi and the NLF is still debated by historians.[5] They had similar objectives and had the same enemies, and the NLF no doubt looked for and received guidance and supplies from Hanoi. However, it is fairly clear that the NLF fought its own battle, at least until the massive intervention by U.S. troops in 1965. In June 1966, Senator Mike

Mansfield (D-Montana) revealed that when sharp U.S. escalation began in early 1965, only 400 of the 140,000 enemy forces in South Vietnam were North Vietnamese soldiers. The Defense Department confirmed these figures. [6] *The Pentagon Papers* point to similar such low estimates of North Vietnamese forces during the years 1963–1964. Washington's panicky reaction to developments in Vietnam was in response to the weakness of South Vietnam's forces and fear of a Viet Cong victory.[7] It was not until 1965, after the sustained U.S. bombing of North Vietnam began in February of that year, that North Vietnam regulars entered the war in the south with military units.

In its effort to prepare the U.S. public for the escalation of the war, the U.S. State Department, headed by the hawkish Dean Rusk, sought to prove that the war in South Vietnam was the result of Communist aggression from the north. In early 1965 it published, with great fanfare, its famous white paper in which it sought to prove its case. It produced evidence that, among weapons captured from the NLF, a number were of Communist origin. But the number—179 out of 15,100—only proved that the NLF was depending more on weapons captured from the inept and demoralized Army of the Republic of [South] Vietnam (ARVN) than on outside Communist sources.[8]

## ■ THE AMERICANIZATION OF THE WAR

In early August 1964, during the U.S. presidential election campaign, Johnson found the pretext he needed for direct intervention and to do so with congressional support. The pretext became known as the Gulf of Tonkin incident. The U.S. government reported that one of its naval ships, the destroyer *Maddox,* had been attacked by North Vietnamese torpedo boats. Although Johnson claimed that the attack took place on the high seas (that is, in international waters) and that it was unprovoked, the destroyer was in fact within the twelve-mile limit of North Vietnam gathering intelligence electronically and providing support for covert military operations against North Vietnam by South Vietnamese commandos (which had been going on since January 1964). After an alleged second North Vietnamese "attack" two days later—one that was never confirmed by an investigation—President Johnson ordered retaliatory air strikes against targets in North Vietnam.[9] But more important, he also went to Congress for authorization to use military force in Vietnam. The result was the Gulf of Tonkin Resolution, which authorized the president to take "all necessary measures to repel any armed attacks against the forces of the United States and to prevent further aggression." The resolution was passed unanimously by the House of Representatives and by an eighty-eight to two vote in the Senate. Supporters of the war called it a "functional equivalent of a declaration of war."[10] Both President Johnson and his successor, Richard Nixon, used it as the legal basis for massive military operations in Vietnam and in neighboring countries.

Not until Johnson was elected and inaugurated for a new term of office, did he actually use his new powers. During the election campaign he appeared as a "dove" compared to his "hawkish" Republican opponent, Barry Goldwater. He repeatedly vowed that he was against committing U.S. boys to fighting a war in Vietnam. But after the election, on the advice of his political and military advisers, a group of men who had served under Kennedy, Johnson decided to step up the U.S. involvement in the war. It became evident that in order to save the South Vietnamese government, the United States had to take an active combat role. Johnson then, in February 1965, ordered Operation Rolling Thunder, a campaign of sustained bombing raids on North Vietnam, and in the weeks that followed, U.S. combat troops arrived in ever larger numbers in South Vietnam.

Meanwhile, in June 1965, another military coup in Saigon brought to power a new set of officers. The leaders of the new ruling group were Air Marshal Nguyen Cao Ky and Army General Nguyen Van Thieu. Their regime was quite willing to use force against any and all political opposition, and did so against the Buddhists in Hue in May 1966. They resolutely refused any negotiations or compromise with the NLF. In September 1967, a controlled election was held and Thieu was elected president and Ky vice-president. Only a military candidate had a chance to win. Ky declared that if a civilian won, he would respond "militarily" because in a "democratic country you have the right to disagree with the views of others."[11] As if this definition of democracy was not enough, Ky stated that he had but one hero and that was Adolf Hitler. The election served to provide the fiction that Washington was fighting in defense of South Vietnamese democracy.

The continued bombing of North Vietnam and its supply routes into the south (nicknamed the Ho Chi Minh Trail) and the heavy commitment of U.S. forces in search-and-destroy missions seemed to promise certain victory. In late 1967, General William Westmoreland, the commanding officer of U.S. forces in Vietnam, felt confident enough to state that "we have reached an important point, when the end begins to come into view."[12] Every week, U.S. television viewers were treated to higher and higher body counts of dead enemy soldiers. However, despite their increasing losses, the Viet Cong and the People's Army of [North] Vietnam (PAVN) grew stronger. Hanoi continued to infiltrate more supplies to arm the Viet Cong, who were able to recruit more soldiers to fight and die for their cause against the foreign army. Nationalism was surely on the side of the enemies the United States faced.

And so the weary war went on through 1967. No longer did South Vietnam carry the chief burden of the war; it had become Lyndon Johnson's war. And with North Vietnam now engaged in the fight in South Vietnam, it became an entirely different conflict, one that belied President Johnson's 1964 campaign promise that he sought no wider war. By the beginning of 1968, the optimism in Saigon and in Washington began to give way to pessimism. The war was becoming an escalated military stalemate. By this

Secretary of Defense Robert S. McNamara, on a visit to South Vietnam, with the commander of U.S. forces (1964–1968), General William C. Westmoreland, meeting with South Vietnamese officers, August 1965. *(National Archives)*

U.S. Army helicoptors on a "search-and-destroy" mission, Cu Chi province, May 1966. Cu Chi, located about 20 miles northwest of Saigon, was the most heavily bombed territory in history. *(National Archives)*

time, after three full years of large-scale warfare and increasingly volatile political protests at home, Johnson could hear voices even within his own administration and his own party suggesting that he consider getting out of Vietnam.

For the Vietnamese the cost of the war was death and destruction on an unprecedented scale. For the United States the cost was, in addition to the increasing number of war dead, a huge drain on the economy, strained relations with allies (many of which opposed the U.S. position), and loss of influence in the Third World. The war also caused serious political and social upheaval at home: it caused a deep split in U.S. society, it soon ruined Johnson's political career, and it contributed to the downfall of the next president, Richard Nixon. In 1968, both men—Johnson as he was leaving the presidency and Nixon as he campaigned for and prepared to assume the office—came to the conclusion that the United States must pull out of this costly war.

That realization came to Johnson in the wake of the Tet Offensive, which began at the end of January 1968. After a lull in the fighting, which the United States interpreted as a sign that the enemy had finally been worn down, the Viet Cong and the PAVN launched a surprise offensive throughout South Vietnam during Tet, the lunar New Year holiday. They were able to take thirty-six of the forty-four provincial capitals in the country, and most surprising of all, they staged a major attack on Saigon, where suicide commandos even penetrated the grounds of the U.S. embassy. The impact of the Tet Offensive, as Communist forces had calculated, shattered the popular illusion the U.S. leaders had created that they were on the verge of victory.

The U.S. military command in Vietnam launched a furious counter-attack making full use of its massive firepower. Enemy losses were staggering as they were driven out of Saigon and the other cities and towns they had taken. Within a month General Westmoreland could claim that the Tet Offensive had been a military disaster for the enemy forces, that they had wasted their remaining strength. This was not an empty claim, for subsequent evidence has made clear that the U.S. counterattack all but eliminated the Viet Cong as a fighting force, leaving primarily PAVN forces to fight the war from this point on.

Particularly harsh were the fates of the old imperial city of Hue and of Ben Tre, a provincial capital in the Mekong Delta. After the North Vietnamese conquered Hue, they immediately rounded up and executed an estimated three thousand residents of the city suspected of collaboration with Saigon and U.S. forces. The U.S. military command, in an effort to drive the North Vietnamese out of Hue, subjected the city, particularly its huge citadel, to sustained bombardment. In all, ten thousand soldiers and civilians died in the battle for Hue. In late February 1968, U.S. Marines reoccupied a city largely in ruins.[13]

Vietnamese president Nguyen Van Thieu and vice-president Nguyen Cao Ky meet with U.S. president Lyndon Johnson, Honolulu, Hawaii, February 7, 1966. *(National Archives)*

Viet Cong prisoners under U.S. military guard. *(National Archives)*

Ben Tre suffered a worse fate. U.S. artillery destroyed it completely. When asked why the city had been leveled, a U.S. major offered what became his country's epitaph in Vietnam: "It became necessary to destroy the town to save it."[14] It was the only answer he could give. The U.S. military involvement in Vietnam no longer made sense.

The Tet Offensive was a military setback for the enemy. It was, however, a psychological and political victory for them, because of its impact on the people of the United States and on the Johnson administration. Hanoi was well aware that 1968 was an election year in the United States. In addition to seeking a sudden military victory, Hanoi's purpose was also to give notice that the war was far from over, despite the optimistic pronouncements by U.S. generals and politicians. In this Hanoi was quite successful. Johnson, faced with mounting opposition to his Vietnam policy even in his own party, was forced to reassess the war.

In March 1968, Johnson received from General Westmoreland in Vietnam a request for 206,000 additional soldiers, this despite Westmoreland's consistent claims that his troops were winning the war. In a presidential election year, Johnson's options were limited. At the end of March, he spoke to the nation, announcing that he would call a halt to the bombing of North Vietnam as an inducement to Hanoi to seek a negotiated settlement and—the real surprise—that he would not seek reelection.

The winner of the 1968 presidential election, Richard Nixon, proclaimed during the campaign that he had a secret plan to end the war. But he still wanted to win the war. Years later he admitted that he had no such plan and once in office he devised a strategy designed to gradually end the U.S. involvement in Vietnam, but it also kept U.S. soldiers in combat for four more years. Nixon's strategy called for the "Vietnamization" of the war, whereby the United States would gradually disengage while strengthening the ARVN. This would allow him to placate his domestic opponents of the war by announcing periodic withdrawals of U.S. troops, and—he hoped—would still produce a victory. But this plan took time to implement, and in the meantime the war raged on, as did opposition to it at home. Subsequently, tens of thousands more U.S. and Vietnamese soldiers died in battle during the years of Vietnamization, from 1969 to 1973. Ultimately, Vietnamization failed, despite the enormous amount of military provisions supplied by the United States, mainly because, no matter how well equipped, the corrupt and undisciplined ARVN was no match for its more determined foes.

## ■ THE U.S. EXIT

Johnson had tried persistently to persuade Hanoi to come to the bargaining table, but Hanoi just as persistently refused his terms. North Vietnam had presented its peace plan in April 1965, a four-point proposal calling for the withdrawal of U.S. forces from Vietnam, the end of hostilities against North Vietnam, adherence to the Geneva Accords, and allowing the Vietnamese alone to settle their problems. It also insisted, as a condition for negotiations, that the NLF be recognized and be allowed to take part in the negotiations. But the Johnson administration and the Thieu-Ky government in Saigon steadfastly refused to have any dealings with the NLF. In the end, Johnson yielded on that issue, and in October 1968, the two sides agreed to begin peace talks in Paris, with the NLF and Saigon represented as well as Hanoi and Washington.

The four-party peace talks began in January 1969, just as the Nixon administration took office in Washington. The Communist side demanded a commitment by the United States on a timetable for the complete withdrawal from Vietnam and the replacement of the Saigon regime by a coalition government made up of all parties, including the NLF. Nixon rejected these demands, and further talks were postponed. However, in 1971, the U.S. negotiator, Henry Kissinger, and the North Vietnamese representative, Le Duc Tho, met in Paris to conduct secret negotiations that, however, produced no results.

Even though U.S. troop levels were reduced from 542,000 soldiers in February 1969 to 139,000 in December 1971, the warfare did not diminish; in fact, it was expanded into Laos and Cambodia. Richard Nixon, as Lyndon Johnson before him, was determined not to be the first president to lose a war. He counted on the destruction of North Vietnam's sanctuaries and supply routes in the neighboring countries to bring victory in Vietnam.

The prelude to the entry of ARVN and U.S. forces into Cambodia was the overthrow of the ruler of that country, Prince Norodom Sihanouk, in March 1970. Sihanouk had managed to keep his country out of the Vietnam conflict by professing a policy of neutrality while in fact allowing Vietnamese Communist forces to make use of Cambodian jungle areas along the eastern border and accepting U.S. retaliatory air strikes against them. He was overthrown by his own prime minister, General Lon Nol, who then turned to the United States for military aid. In April 1970, Nixon authorized joint U.S.-ARVN attacks into Cambodia to clean out enemy bases there. For over a month U.S. and ARVN troops, numbering over fifty thousand, searched the jungles of eastern Cambodia in a futile effort to find the headquarters for the Communist Operations in South Vietnam (COSVN).[15] The widening of the war caused an uproar of protest from antiwar activists in the United States. It was at this juncture that antiwar students at Columbia University and other colleges in the United States sought to forcibly shut down their schools in protest. They were intent on "bringing the war home," and in a sense that is what happened on the campus of Kent State University, where four students were shot to death at an antiwar rally by the National Guard on May 4, 1970.

An incursion into southern Laos in March 1971 demonstrated the failure of Vietnamization. ARVN forces who had sought to gain control of the Ho Chi Min Trail, and who had entered Laos with U.S. air support, were badly routed by the PAVN. Television crews sent back images of panic-stricken ARVN troops hanging on the skids of evacuation helicopters in a desperate effort to escape the North Vietnamese counterattack.

As the 1972 election rolled around, the Vietnam War was still raging; more than twenty thousand additional U.S. soldiers had died since Nixon had come to office. Nixon intensified his effort to achieve a negotiated settlement. Henry Kissinger and Le Duc Tho resumed secret talks in Paris in April 1972. Meanwhile, both sides sought to strengthen their bargaining positions. While Hanoi launched an offensive on the ground, U.S. B-52 bombers pounded North Vietnam with the heaviest bombing yet, and U.S. ships blockaded and mined the Haiphong harbor. On the eve of the U.S. election, Kissinger was able to announce that "peace is at hand."[16] He and Le had hammered out a preliminary agreement for ending the war. Its terms stipulated that within sixty days after the cease-fire the United States would complete the withdrawal of all of its troops from Vietnam, Hanoi would release all U.S. prisoners (mostly downed airmen), and the political settlement in South Vietnam would be left for the Vietnamese to work out. The contending Vietnamese factions were to form a "National Council of Reconciliation and Concord" with equal representation for the Thieu regime, the NLF, and neutral parties. But one major problem remained: Thieu refused to accept these terms. To win him over, Kissinger traveled to Saigon carrying with him President Nixon's pledge of continued U.S. protection for his government and a billion dollars worth of additional armaments.

Before the agreement was signed, Nixon delivered one final, savage punishment to North Vietnam. To demonstrate his continuing commitment to defend Thieu's government, Nixon, who had recently been reelected in a landslide victory, ordered another bombing of Hanoi and Haiphong. The around-the-clock bombing raids (dubbed by his critics the "Christmas bombings"), which began on December 18 and continued until the end of the month, turned large parts of these two cities into rubble. The bombings did not bring any significant change in the terms of the peace agreement finally signed in January 1973; its terms were essentially those agreed to by Kissinger and Le the previous October.

With the signing of the agreement on January 27, 1973, the United States finally exited from the Vietnam War. This long-awaited event brought great relief to the United States, but it did not bring an end to the war in Vietnam. ARVN forces, despite their arsenal of U.S.-made weaponry, proved to be no match against the PAVN. Reintervention by the United States was impossible once its troops had been withdrawn; public opinion would not tolerate it. Moreover, the Nixon administration was by this time in shambles over the Watergate affair,[17] and Congress, reflecting the will of the

Refugees on Route 1 near Quang Tri, South Vietnam, 1972. *(National Archives)*

President Lyndon Johnson meets with General Creighton Abrams and key cabinet members at the White House for a discussion of the war, October 29, 1968. *(National Archives)*

nation, cut off further aid to South Vietnam. Finally, in January 1975, ARVN collapsed when a North Vietnamese attack in the northern highlands produced a panic that spread throughout the country. The expected battle for Saigon never took place. In April 1975, North Vietnamese forces entered the city unopposed and in triumph. The U.S. embassy in Saigon was the scene of a frantic airlift of the remaining U.S. personnel and as many of their Vietnamese cohorts and friends as they could crowd onto the last departing helicopters.[18]

The final cost of the war for the United States includes more than 58,000 soldiers killed and more than 300,000 wounded. The war cost an estimated $165 billion. Indirect economic consequences are beyond estimation, but the huge expenditures for the prolonged war surely contributed to the inflation, the deficit, and the balance-of-payments problems that plagued the United States during the 1970s. The social, political, and psychological damage of the Vietnam tragedy is also incalculable. U.S. society was divided as it had not been since the Civil War a century earlier. Antiwar protests led directly to strong-arm police actions against antiwar activists. The war also generated a political awakening for the country's young people—a new activism and a heightened political consciousness. But later, as it dragged on and on, the war, together with the Watergate scandal, caused deep feelings of mistrust, apathy, and skepticism toward government.

In 1995, over three decades after the Americanization of the war, Robert McNamara, who had been the U.S. secretary of defense and one of the principal architects of the U.S. involvement in Vietnam, published his memoir in which he confessed that the United States "could and should have withdrawn from South Vietnam" in late 1963. At that point, only seventy-eight U.S. soldiers had died there. McNamara, looking back, saw things much clearer than he had when he played a leading role in the escalation of U.S. forces. He listed eleven major errors on the part of the United States, including misjudging the strength of North Vietnam, underrating nationalism as a force in Vietnam, failing to understand the history and culture of Vietnam, and failing to recognize the limitations of modern technological warfare.[19]

The cost of the war to the peoples of Indochina was greater yet. The U.S. estimate of ARVN deaths was over two hundred thousand, and for enemy forces—both NLF and PAVN—almost five hundred thousand. We will never know how many civilians died or how many became refugees. In an interview in 2002, McNamara put the number of dead at 3.4 million.[20] The physical mutilation of the country was also staggering. The United States dropped three times more bombs on Indochina than it dropped on its enemies in World War II. In addition, it defoliated over 5 million acres with chemicals such as Agent Orange, a powerful, cancer-causing herbicide.

# ■ THE CONTINUING TRAGEDY OF INDOCHINA

The idea that a Communist victory in Vietnam would be a victory for Communist China proved entirely wrong. After the war, Chinese-Vietnamese relations deteriorated, becoming so hostile that the two nations became engaged in a border war four years after the fall of Saigon.

In the wake of the Communist military victory, the South Vietnamese braced themselves for the terrible, vengeful "bloodbath" that Nixon had predicted, but it did not come. Hanoi initially allowed South Vietnam to retain its separate identity under a provisional revolutionary government. It adopted a policy of gradualism in imposing its system on the south and was much less forceful and heavy-handed than expected. To be sure, those identified as high-ranking former government or military officers of the overthrown Saigon regime were singled out for severe punishments, usually involving confiscation of property, arrest, and long sentences to hard labor in remote rural "reeducation" camps. The new order in the south also meant a transformation of the city of Saigon, renamed Ho Chi Minh City. Quickly, the bars and dance halls were closed and the prostitutes disappeared, as did other traces of the twenty-year-long U.S. presence. But beyond this and the introduction of revolutionary broadcasts and music over street loudspeakers, change in the city was rather minimal.

Within a year, severe economic problems gripped Vietnam, and conditions steadily worsened. The government's plan to quickly restore the agricultural productivity of the south to complement the industrial development of the north proved too optimistic. In part, the failure at economic recovery was the result of legacies of the war. Not only were the cities blighted, but vast areas of the countryside were no longer under cultivation due to the flight of peasants and the defoliated and bomb-cratered land. Hundreds of thousands of unemployed city dwellers were lured to rural "New Economic Zones" with promises of houses, land, and food. Many of these people would soon flee from the harsh, primitive rural conditions, causing the government to resort to forced relocation in the New Economic Zones. To compound matters, southern Vietnam experienced three successive years of natural disasters, including both droughts and devastating floods.

Nor was there international deliverance. Vietnam was unable to attract foreign investment, without which its hopes of economic recovery were dim. It had hoped for reparation payments from the United States, such as President Nixon had once promised, but Washington was not so forgiving or generous. Instead, it refused to provide either economic aid or investment, and it pressured international lending agencies to reject Vietnam's pleas. Other Western and Asian nations were also unsympathetic. Increasingly, Hanoi was forced to turn to the Soviet Union for economic assistance. Reliance on the Soviet Union contributed to a worsening of relations with China, which until 1978 had provided a modicum of aid to Hanoi. Vietnam's economic and diplomatic difficulties worsened in 1979, when it sent its military forces into Cambodia.

## ☐  *The Plight of Cambodia*

The anticipated bloodbath occurred not in Vietnam but in neighboring Cambodia. When the United States disengaged from Vietnam in early 1973, it also terminated its military support for the Lon Nol government in Cambodia, which was embattled by the Khmer Rouge, a native Communist force. In April 1975, at the same time that Saigon fell to the North Vietnamese, the Khmer Rouge defeated Lon Nol's forces and swept into Phnom Penh, the Cambodian capital.

Cambodia braced itself for a new order under the Communist government led by Pol Pot, who immediately began a reign of revolutionary terror. Unlike most other revolutionaries, Pol Pot did not merely advocate a revolutionary transformation; he was willing to eradicate completely the old order, root and branch, and to reorganize society to a degree no revolutionary regime had ever attempted. Pol Pot's ideal was to create a nation of industrial workers and peasants. The entire urban population was evacuated to the countryside, where it was placed in armed work camps. Those who resisted—members of the old regime, the Western-educated elite, city dwellers, and all real or suspected "enemies" of the revolution—were exterminated. In the space of three years, an estimated 1.5 million Cambodians—almost one-fifth of the population—were murdered.

Pol Pot also initiated attacks against neighboring Thailand and Vietnam, his former supporter. He was vehemently anti-Vietnamese, regarding Vietnam as the greatest threat to the independence of the Cambodian revolution. He saw a rebellion brewing in the eastern part of the country, which had a substantial ethnic Vietnamese population. In 1978, he unleashed a furious attack against the Vietnamese, slaughtering thousands of them. The Khmer Rouge army then clashed with Vietnamese forces in the Parrot's Beak border area. The purpose of these attacks was not only to eliminate native resistance, but also to assert Cambodia's claim to certain disputed borderlands.

In retaliation, Vietnam, with its superior, battle-tested army, drove into Cambodia in January 1979, scattered the forces of the Khmer Rouge, took control of Phnom Penh, and installed a former Khmer Rouge officer, Heng Samrin, as head of a new pro-Vietnamese government. The Vietnamese conquest of Phnom Penh, however, did not bring peace to Cambodia. A Vietnamese army of about 170,000 occupied the country and continued to battle remnants of Pol Pot's forces.

The military occupation of Cambodia and the continuing struggle against the Khmer Rouge in remote jungle encampments near the Thai border put a strain on an already exhausted Vietnamese nation. It meant withdrawing its army from food production and reconstruction of Vietnam and diverting dwindling treasury funds to the military.

Even though Hanoi had ended the genocidal fury of the Pol Pot regime, it was nevertheless rebuked by the United States and most strongly by China. In response to Vietnam's "invasion" of Cambodia, China invaded Vietnam in February 1979 in order to "teach it a lesson." The Chinese incursion into Vietnam proved inconclusive; Beijing withdrew within a month, leaving Hanoi in control of Cambodia. The Chinese, however, continued to support the deposed Pol Pot. Washington strengthened its resolve not to extend official recognition to the government of Vietnam or to provide it desperately needed economic assistance. The administrations of Jimmy Carter and Ronald Reagan did, however, provide diplomatic and economic assistance to the genocidal Pol Pot.

Conditions that had sustained the civil war in Cambodia since its beginning in 1979 began to change about a decade later. The new Soviet leader, Mikhail Gorbachev, made clear that his nation would disengage from the Third World, thus ending economic and military assistance to Vietnam. The Vietnamese government, having installed a pro-Vietnam regime in Phnom Penh, ended in 1989 its costly occupation of Cambodia. By the summer of 1991, the Soviet Union began to unravel. With the Soviet threat disappearing and Washington and Beijing losing interest in Cambodia, the United Nations was able to work out a political solution. In the same year, King Norodom Sihanouk returned from exile and was reinstated as king. In 1993, the United Nations oversaw a nationwide election—won by the royalist party led by Sihanouk's son, Ranariddh—giving Cambodia a modicum of stability. Pol Pot, by now aged and in ill health, was still holed up in the jungle near the Thai border. In April 1998, just as a rebel faction of the Khmer Rouge was about to hand him over to the government to stand trial for his crimes, Pol Pot cheated the hangman when he died of an apparent heart attack.

☐  *The Refugees of Indochina*

Another dimension of the continuing tragedy of Indochina was the desperate flight of refugees from Cambodia, Laos, and primarily from Vietnam, which saw 1.5 million of its citizens escape the country by boarding vessels and taking to the sea. Two hundred thousand of these "boat people" died on the South China Sea from exposure, drowning, and attacks by pirates.

The first wave of "boat people" came in 1975 at the time of the fall of Saigon, when about a hundred thousand people fled the country. The exodus diminished during the next three years, but in 1978 and 1979, when the war between Cambodia and Vietnam occurred, a second and much larger wave of refugees fled Vietnam. They arrived in neighboring countries at the rate of over 12,500 a month, quickly causing an international crisis when nations such as Malaysia (where most of them landed), Thailand, and Singapore refused to accept them. In July 1979, a UN Conference on Refugees was called at Geneva to deal with this issue. The UN secured an agreement from Vietnam to limit the refugee outflow, provided relief to the nations of "first asylum" such as Malaysia, and received promises from other nations to open their doors to the refugees.

The majority of those who left Vietnam were ethnic Chinese, who had long dominated private business in southern Vietnam and fell victim to government policies in early 1979 that abolished "bourgeois trade" and introduced a currency reform that rendered their accumulated savings almost worthless. Curiously, many were assisted in their flight by the Communist authorities, who collected exit fees of $2,000 in gold from each departing refugee. In northern Vietnam the exodus of the Chinese amounted to expulsion. About 250,000 of the approximately 300,000 ethnic Chinese in northern Vietnam fled northward to find sanctuary in China.

## ■ RECOMMENDED READINGS

Appy, Christian G. *Patriots: The Vietnam War Remembered from All Sides.* New York: Penguin, 2003.
An oral history, consisting of approximately 140 interviews of participants, U.S. as well as Vietnamese.

Arnett, Peter. *Live from the Battlefield: From Vietnam to Baghdad: 35 Years in the World's War Zones.* New York: Touchstone, 1994.
By a reporter from New Zealand who first made his mark as a correspondent for AP in Southeast Asia and more recently as the CNN correspondent in Baghdad during the Gulf War.

Caputo, Philip. *A Rumor of War.* New York: Holt, Rinehart, and Winston, 1977.
The reminiscences of a loyal marine who, by the end of his tour of duty, questioned the purpose of the U.S. involvement.

Fall, Bernard B. *Vietnam Witness, 1953–1966.* New York: Praeger, 1966.
By the French historian who was widely considered the West's leading authority on Vietnam.

FitzGerald, Frances. *Fire in the Lake: The Vietnamese and the Americans in Vietnam.* New York: Random House, 1972.
An award-winning study that places the U.S. intervention in a context of Vietnamese history.

Halberstam, David. *The Best and the Brightest.* New York: Random House, 1972.
A critical account of how the leaders in Washington drifted into a war on the other side of the globe.

Herring, George C. *America's Longest War: The United States and Vietnam, 1950–1975.* New York: John Wiley and Sons, 1979.

Herrington, Stuart A. *Peace with Honor: An American Report on Vietnam, 1973–75.* Novato, Calif.: Presidio Press, 1983.
A critical view of U.S. responsibility for the fall of Saigon to North Vietnamese forces.

Hersh, Seymour. *My Lai Four: A Report on the Massacre and Its Aftermath.* New York: Random House, 1970.

Isaacs, Arnold R. *Without Honor: Defeat in Vietnam and Cambodia.* Baltimore: Johns Hopkins University Press, 1983.

Just, Ward, ed. *Reporting Vietnam: American Journalism, 1959–1975.* New York: Library of America, 1998.
  Excellent selection of articles.

Kaiser, David. *American Tragedy: Kennedy, Johnson, and the Origins of the Vietnam War.* Cambridge, Mass.: Belknap Press, 2000.
  The definitive study on the U.S. involvement in Vietnam.

Karnow, Stanley. *Vietnam: A History.* New York: Viking, 1983.
  A major work by a noted journalist who served as the consultant for a thirteen-part television documentary on the Vietnam War.

Langguth, A. J. *Our Vietnam: The War, 1954–1975.* New York: Simon and Schuster, 2000.
  A definitive, detailed treatment of the war.

Mangold, Tom, and John Penycate. *The Tunnels of Cu Chi.* New York: Berkley Books, 1986.
  An account of the 200-mile-long tunnel complex stretching from the outskirts of Saigon to the "free-fire zone" known as the "Iron Triangle."

McNamara, Robert S. *In Retrospect: The Tragedy and Lessons of Vietnam.* New York: Times Books/Random House, 1995.
  The mea culpa of the secretary of defense for Presidents Kennedy and Johnson.

Shawcross, William. *Sideshow: Kissinger, Nixon and the Destruction of Cambodia.* New York: Simon and Schuster, 1979.
  An analysis of the widening of the war into Cambodia, faulting the policy of President Nixon and Henry Kissinger for causing the bloodbath that occurred subsequent to the U.S. withdrawal from that country.

Sheehan, Neil. *A Bright Shining Lie: John Paul Vann and America in Vietnam.* New York: Random House, 1988.
  A critical account of the U.S. conduct of the war in Vietnam.

Sheehan, Neil, et al. *The Pentagon Papers.* New York: Bantam, 1971.
  A most useful collection of primary sources on the U.S. involvement in the Vietnam War, revealing the plotting and planning of Washington decisionmakers.

Summers, Harry G. *On Strategy: A Critical Analysis of the Vietnam War.* Novato, Calif.: Presidio Press, 1982.

# ■ NOTES

1. Bernard B. Fall, *Last Reflections on a War* (Garden City, N.Y.: Doubleday, 1967), p. 167. In Saigon, Diem received 605,025 votes from 450,000 registered voters.

2. Vice-President Lyndon Johnson's characterization of Diem, cited in Frances FitzGerald, *Fire in the Lake: The Vietnamese and the Americans in Vietnam* (Boston: Random House, 1972), p. 72; also John Osborne, "The Tough Miracle Man of Vietnam: Diem, America's Newly Arrived Visitor, Has Roused His Country and Routed the Reds," *Life,* May 13, 1957, pp. 156–176.

3. Stanley Karnow, *Vietnam: A History* (New York: Viking, 1983), p. 281.

4. Quoted in Richard J. Barnet, *Intervention and Revolution: The United States in the Third World* (New York: New American Library, 1968), p. 216.

5. As late as 2000, scholars such as David Kaiser and William Duiker acknowledged that their understanding of Hanoi's policies at the time was "quite limited." David Kaiser, *American Tragedy: Kennedy, Johnson and the Origins of the Vietnam War* (Cambridge, Mass.: Belknap Press, 2000), p. 7.

6. Theodore Draper, "The American Crisis: Vietnam, Cuba and the Dominican Republic," *Commentary* (January 1967), p. 36.

7. Neil Sheehan et al., *The Pentagon Papers* (New York: Bantam, 1971), documents 61–64, pp. 271–285.

8. For the white paper, "Aggression from the North," and I. F. Stone's reply, see Marcus G. Raskin and Bernard B. Fall, eds, *The Vietnam Reader: Articles and Documents on American Foreign Policy and the Viet-Nam Crisis,* rev. ed. (New York: Vintage, 1967), pp. 143–162.

9. More than thirty years later, even then-Secretary of Defense Robert McNamara did not know precisely what had taken place at the Gulf of Tonkin. In his memoirs he concluded, however, that it appeared no second attack had taken place. See Robert S. McNamara, *In Retrospect: The Tragedy and Lessons of Vietnam* (New York: Times Books/Random House, 1995), pp. 128–142.

10. First used by Johnson's acting attorney general, Nicholas Katzenbach; Karnow, *Vietnam,* p. 362.

11. AP, *New York Times,* May 14, 1967, p. 3.

12. Karnow, *Vietnam,* p. 479.

13. One hundred and fifty U.S. Marines, four hundred ARVN, an estimated five thousand PAVN, and the rest civilians. Karnow, *Vietnam,* p. 534.

14. Peter Arnett, *Live from the Battle Field: From Vietnam to Baghdad—35 Years in the World's War Zones* (New York: Touchstone Books, 1994), p. 256.

15. President Nixon was already conducting a secret war in both Laos and Cambodia prior to the entry of U.S. ground forces into Cambodia in April 1970— secret only in the sense that the Nixon administration did not make public U.S. military operations (mainly heavy bombing by B-52s) in these two countries and, in fact, repeatedly denied reports of such operations.

16. Transcript of Kissinger's news conference, *New York Times,* October 27, 1972, p. 18.

17. Watergate was a direct outgrowth of the war in Vietnam. In June 1971, Daniel Ellsberg, who had once served as a zealous administrator of official U.S. policy in Vietnam and who had since become an equally zealous opponent of the war, leaked to the *New York Times,* the *Washington Post,* and other newspapers copies of a study of the war, the "Pentagon Papers," as they became popularly known, that had been commissioned by Johnson's secretary of defense, Robert McNamara. Nixon, furious at this and other leaks of classified information, created a group, the White House "plumbers," whose task it was to plug intelligence leaks and to investigate Ellsberg and other "subversives" undermining his presidency and conduct of the war. For reasons still not clear, in June 1972, the "plumbers" broke into the national headquarters of the Democratic Party at the Watergate apartment complex in Washington, D.C. As evidence of wrongdoing began to implicate Nixon himself, he ordered his subordinates to commit perjury, that is, lying under oath. Unfortunately for Nixon, he had taped his own crime, and for reasons also still not clear, he had not destroyed the evidence. The upshot was the preparation for an impeachment trial in the Senate. When it became obvious to Nixon that his removal from office was all but a certainty, he resigned; Vice-President Gerald Ford then became the nation's chief executive.

18. During the war, the United States had turned Saigon's Tan Son Nhut Airport into one of the busiest and Cam Ranh Bay into one of the largest naval supply bases in the world, but, ironically, in the 1980s they were both used mainly by the Soviet Union to supply Vietnam.

19. McNamara, *In Retrospect.* McNamara's doubts about the war were not new; they go back to as early as 1967, when he began to reevaluate the U.S. position in

Vietnam. For that reason President Johnson replaced him with Clark Clifford who, too, eventually concluded (during the Tet Offensive of 1968) that the United States had reached a dead end and the time had come to find a way out of Vietnam.

Ironically, Johnson had doubted the wisdom of any and all involvement in Vietnam as early as May 1964. In a telephone conversation with his former Democratic colleague in the Senate, Richard B. Russell, Johnson questioned a continued involvement in Vietnam: "It is the damndest worst mess that I ever saw . . . and it's going to get worse." "How important is that [Vietnam] to us?" Russell wanted to know. Johnson replied that neither Vietnam nor Laos, so important to the Kennedy administration, were worth "a damn." The Republican Party, however, he went on to say, would make political hay of a withdrawal. "It's the only issue they've got." Johnson's telephone conversation with Russell, May 27, 1964, Lyndon B. Johnson Library, Tape WH6405.10, Side A.

20. Errol Morris (director), documentary, *The Fog of War: Eleven Lessons from the Life of Robert S. McNamara* (2003).

# 10

---

# Détente and the End of Bipolarity

Ironically, the years of U.S. military involvement in Vietnam, 1965–1973, which represented a crusade against international Communism, saw a gradual improvement in relations between Washington and the two great Communist states. Toward the end of that period, the Cold War took on several unexpected turns. First, détente eased the tensions between Moscow and Washington. Second, the early 1970s saw the normalization of relations between the United States and the People's Republic of China (PRC). In the end, President Richard Nixon, the quintessential anti-Communist who had always urged strong measures against the Vietnamese, Soviet, and Chinese Communists—all part of a great conspiracy—visited Moscow and Beijing. The bipolar world, with Moscow and Washington at center stage, was at an end.

## ■ THE UNITED STATES AND CHINA:
## THE NORMALIZATION OF RELATIONS

The split between the Soviet Union and the People's Republic of China gave the United States a golden opportunity. Monolithic Communism, or "international socialist solidarity" as its proponents frequently called it, proved to be an ideological quest that ran aground on the shoals of nationalist interests. A succession of governments in Washington, tied to the principle of an international Communist conspiracy, had been slow in taking advantage of the falling-out between the two most important Communist states. But by the early 1970s, the time had come to cash in on what clearly had become a windfall for Washington.

Rapprochement between the United States and the vast Chinese empire could only give the Soviets a headache. At first, it had been Moscow that had been able to play the "China card." With it, the Soviet Union's first line of defense in the East had been on the shores of the Yellow Sea. Washington's

228

ability to play the same card promised to pay immeasurable dividends. The Chinese in their turn, however, a proud and ancient people, had no intentions of playing the pawn and instead sought to carve out their own niche as a major player in the superpower game. When Beijing and Washington took the first steps toward the normalization of relations in the early 1970s, the result was an end to great-power bipolarity and increased complexity in international relations.

For more than twenty years the United States and the PRC had no official relations; instead, they were hostile adversaries. Successive U.S. presidents denounced "Red China" as a menace to the peace-loving peoples of Asia, as a reckless, irresponsible, aggressive regime, unworthy of diplomatic recognition or United Nations membership. The United States maintained relations instead with the Nationalist regime on Taiwan, adhering to the fiction that it was the only legitimate government of China and pledging to defend it against "Communist aggression." It did not immediately commit itself to the defense of the government on Taiwan, but it did so in 1954, after having engaged Chinese Communist forces in battle for three years in Korea. Beijing denounced the U.S. military alliance with Jiang's Nationalist government and the U.S. military presence on Taiwan as "imperialist aggression" and as interference in the internal affairs of China. Meanwhile, the United States effectively blocked the PRC from gaining admission into the United Nations, contained it with an arc of military bases, maintained a rigid embargo on all trade with China, and permitted no one from the United States to travel to China.

Nor was this merely a bilateral feud, since both antagonists called upon their respective Cold War allies for support. Supporting China, at least in the first decade of the Beijing-Washington clash, was the Soviet Union, its satellite states in Eastern Europe, and Communist parties in other parts of the world. The Soviet Union had supported from the outset the PRC's bid to replace the Republic of China (Jiang's government) in the United Nations. The United States, which perceived itself as leading and speaking for the "free world," applied diplomatic pressure on its allies for support of its uncompromising China policy. And Washington also pressured its friends to stand united against diplomatic recognition of the PRC and against its entry into the United Nations. The United States reacted negatively, for example, when in 1964 the independent-minded French government broke ranks and extended formal recognition to the PRC.

While Washington tirelessly denounced "Red China" and condemned Mao and the Chinese Communists for their brutal enslavement of the Chinese people, Beijing regarded the United States, the most powerful capitalist nation in the world, as its "Number One Enemy" and argued persistently that U.S. imperialism was the major threat to world peace. The United States pointed to the Chinese intervention in the Korean War and China's border war with India in 1962 as examples of Chinese aggression. But Beijing (and some observers in the West) countered that in both cases China acted legitimately to protect its borders. The Chinese pointed to the ring of U.S. military positions on China's periphery—from Japan and Korea in the northeast, through Taiwan and the Philippines to Vietnam and Thailand in the south—as proof of the aggressive imperialism of the United States. So intense was this ideological conflict between the two countries that any reduction of tensions seemed impossible.

The Sino-Soviet split that became manifest in the late 1950s did not bring about an improvement in Sino-U.S. relations. Instead, relations worsened since it was China, not the Soviet Union, that argued for a stronger anti–United States line. When the United States and the Soviet Union began to move toward détente in the late 1960s, Beijing's anti-imperialist, anti–United States rhetoric became even more shrill as it sought to make its point: the Soviet Union had grown soft on capitalism, while China had not. China complained bitterly of Soviet "socialist imperialism," arguing that it was linked with U.S. "capitalist imperialism" to encircle China. Mao spoke fervently of China's support for revolutionary movements throughout the world and support for wars of national liberation such as that waged by Communist forces in Vietnam. He even taunted the United States to make war on China, saying that the atomic bomb was merely a "paper tiger" and that China would prevail in the end. Mao's inflammatory rhetoric made it easy for both superpowers to condemn China as a reckless warmonger, the greatest threat to world peace.

The seemingly interminable hostility between China and the United States ended quite suddenly in the early 1970s, in one of the most dramatic turnabouts in modern diplomatic history. On July 15, 1971, President Richard Nixon made an unanticipated announcement that stunned the world. He stated that he intended to travel to China within six months, at the invitation of the Chinese government, for the purpose of developing friendly relations with that government. He revealed that his secretary of state, Henry Kissinger, had just returned from a secret trip to Beijing where he and Chinese premier Zhou Enlai had made arrangements for this diplomatic breakthrough.

The Nixon administration had begun making subtle overtures to the PRC in the previous year. In Warsaw, Poland, where the U.S. and Chinese ambassadors had periodically engaged in secret talks, the U.S. side intimated its desire for improved relations. In his State of the World speech before Congress in February 1971, President Nixon referred to the Beijing government as the People's Republic of China, instead of the usual "Red China" or "Communist China," and Chinese leaders took note of the fact that for the first time the U.S. government had publicly used the proper name of their government. This opened the door to what became known as "ping-pong diplomacy." A U.S. table-tennis team was invited to play an exhibition tournament in Beijing, and Premier Zhou gave them a warm reception and noted that their visit "opened a new page in the relations between the Chinese and U.S. peoples."[1] President Nixon responded by announcing a relaxation of the U.S. trade embargo with China, and this was followed by Kissinger's secret trip to Beijing in early July 1971 that prepared the ground for President Nixon's dramatic announcement.

The following February, President Nixon made his heralded two-week visit to China. He was welcomed with great fanfare by Chinese leaders. At the Beijing airport he extended a hand to Premier Zhou, the same Chinese leader whom John Foster Dulles had pointedly snubbed eighteen years earlier at Geneva by refusing to shake hands. In addition to his own large staff, Nixon was accompanied by a large retinue of journalists and television camera crews who recorded the historic event and gave the U.S. people their first glimpse of life in Communist China. For two weeks the United States was treated to pictures of China and its friendly, smiling people. And they were treated to the spectacle of the U.S. president, a man known for his trenchant anti–Chinese Communist pronouncements in the past, saluting the aged and ailing Chairman Mao Zedong and toasting the new bond of friendship with China's most able diplomat, Premier Zhou Enlai. For the United States and China alike, it was a mind-boggling, 180-degree turnabout.

It was ironic that Nixon, a conservative, Communist-hating Republican, would be the one to go to China and establish friendly relations with

U.S. president Richard Nixon and Chinese premier Zhou Enlai at a reception banquet in Beijing, February 21, 1972. *(National Archives)*

its Communist government. But the task required just such a politician. A Democratic president would have found it impossible to do so, because the Democratic Party still carried the scars of allegedly having "lost China" to Communism in the first place. But a Republican president like Nixon, whose anti-Communist credentials were beyond question, would encounter much less opposition for reversing U.S. policy toward Communist China.

In any case, the normalization of U.S.-PRC relations was an event whose time had come. Indeed, it was long overdue. Both sides finally came to the realization that they had much more to gain by ending their mutual hostility than by continuing it. The Chinese needed to end their isolation in the face of a growing Soviet threat after the Ussuri River border clash in March 1969. The Soviets had greatly increased their ground forces along the Chinese border and equipped them with tactical nuclear weapons. Menaced by a superior Soviet force on their border, the Chinese leaders came to view closer ties with the United States as a means to decrease the possibility of a preemptive Soviet nuclear attack. By ending its isolation and reducing tensions with the United States, the PRC stood to gain greater security against becoming engaged in a war with either of the two superpowers, much less with both of them in a two-front war. The PRC also saw it as a means to gain entry into the United Nations and to solve the Taiwan question. China's international prestige would be greatly enhanced by its new relationship with the United States, while that of its rival, the Nationalist government on Taiwan, would be diminished. In addition, China had much to gain economically from trade opportunities that would come with normalization of relations with the United States and its allies.

The United States stood to benefit from normalization as well. President Nixon and his ambitious secretary of state, Henry Kissinger, had developed a grand design for achieving a new global balance of power. They postulated that the bipolar world dominated by the two opposing superpowers was giving way to a world with five major power centers: the United States, the Soviet Union, Western Europe, Japan, and China. In order to achieve an international power balance it was necessary to end the isolation of one of those new centers of power, the PRC. Détente with the Soviet Union was already well under way, but now the United States sought to "play the China card" when dealing with Moscow. By cautiously drawing closer to China, the United States sought to gain greater leverage in its diplomacy with Moscow. The Nixon administration saw that détente with the Soviet Union and normalization of relations with China were possible at the same time and that together these policies would perhaps constitute a giant step toward ending the Cold War. The result would be greater national security for the United States at a reduced cost. Nixon and Kissinger also calculated—incorrectly it turned out—that Beijing could bring influence to bear on Hanoi to negotiate an end to the Vietnam War. The opportunity for trade with China was also a motivating factor, but not as important as the diplomatic factors.

The major obstacle to improvement of relations between the two countries was—as had always been the case—Taiwan. The United States had stood by the Nationalist regime on Taiwan, recognizing it as the sole legitimate government of China, and had made a commitment to defend it. The only compromise solution to the Taiwan question that U.S. leaders had ever been willing to discuss was the so-called "two-China formula," which called for formal diplomatic recognition of two separate Chinese governments, one on the mainland, the other on Taiwan. But this proved to be impossible since both Chinese governments firmly refused to accept that formula. Neither would give up its claim as the sole legitimate government of the whole of China.

When President Nixon first communicated his desire for talks aimed at improving relations with the PRC, Zhou Enlai replied that he was ready to join in that effort on the condition that the United States was prepared for serious negotiations on the Taiwan issue. Beijing was not willing to bend on that question, but the U.S. government was finally willing to do so. The first step toward a solution of this issue came with the U.S. government's ending its objection to the PRC's entry into the United Nations.[2] In October 1971, the PRC was admitted to the United Nations on its terms, namely, as the single legitimate government of China and as the rightful claimant of the seat that had been occupied by the Republic of China.

It was a test of the diplomatic skills of Henry Kissinger and Zhou Enlai to arrive at an agreement on Taiwan that would recognize the PRC's claim to Taiwan and yet would be less than a complete sellout of the Nationalist government on Taiwan by its U.S. ally. They reached a tentative agreement on Taiwan in the carefully worded Shanghai Communiqué at the end of Nixon's visit to China in February 1972. In it, the United States acknowledged that all Chinese maintain "there is but one China and that Taiwan is part of China" and that the United States does not challenge that position. In the communiqué, the U.S. side reaffirmed "its interest in a peaceful settlement of the Taiwan question by the Chinese themselves." The United States also agreed to reduce its military forces on Taiwan "as tension in the area diminishes." (This was in reference to the war in Indochina from which U.S. forces were gradually withdrawing.) The PRC obtained important concessions on the Taiwan issue—namely, the U.S. acknowledgment that the island is part of China proper and a U.S. promise to withdraw its military force from that island. The United States conceded more than it gained, but came away with an understanding that the PRC would not attempt to take over Taiwan by military means and with the satisfaction that its new friendship with China would serve to enhance stability in Asia.

This was not the end, but the beginning of the normalization process. Full normalization of relations, involving the formal recognition of the PRC by the United States and the breaking off of U.S. diplomatic ties with Nationalist China, was yet to be achieved. However, in accordance with the Shanghai Communiqué, the two countries established liaison offices in each other's capital; began a series of exchanges in the fields of science, technology, culture, journalism, and sports; and initiated mutually beneficial trade relations that grew steadily in subsequent years.

It was not until January 1979 that full diplomatic relations between the two countries were achieved. There were two main reasons for the seven-year delay: political leadership problems in both countries in the mid-1970s, and the still unresolved Taiwan issue. In the United States, President Nixon was suffering from the Watergate scandal and finally resigned in disgrace in August 1974. And in China, both Chairman Mao and Premier Zhou died in 1976, leaving behind a succession problem that was not resolved until Deng Xiaoping consolidated his leadership in 1978. It was left to new political leaders, Deng and President Jimmy Carter, to settle the Taiwan question. Deng came to the view that establishing diplomatic ties with the United States was of greater importance than liberating Taiwan and that a formula could be found to achieve the former by postponing the latter. Secret negotiations produced an agreement in December 1978, the terms of which included restoration of full diplomatic relations between the United States and the PRC and the termination of U.S official relations and defense pact with the Republic of China. It did allow, however, for continued U.S. commercial and cultural ties with Taiwan and continued U.S. arms sales to Taiwan. On the latter point, the Chinese government agreed to disagree, which is to say that it did not formally agree to such arms sales but would set aside that issue so that the normalization agreement could be made without further delay. To further strengthen the new diplomatic relations, Deng Xiaoping accepted an invitation to visit the United States, and he was given a warm reception during his nine-day visit that began less than a month after the normalization agreement had gone into effect on January 1, 1979.

The agreement was a severe blow to Taiwan, which remained in the hands of the anti-Communist Nationalist government now headed by Jiang Jingguo (Chiang Ching-kuo), son of Jiang Jieshi, who had died in 1975. The U.S. government attempted to soften the blow by passing the Taiwan Relations Act, which affirmed the resolve of the United States to maintain relations with the people (not the government) of Taiwan and to consider any effort to resolve the Taiwan issue by force as a "grave concern to the United States."

The consequences of the normalization of Chinese-U.S. relations were immense. The United States ended the anomaly of recognizing a government that ruled only 17 million Chinese in favor of one that governed over 900 million. Normalization resulted in a significant reduction of tension between the two nations and it provided greater stability in Asia. Both countries attained greater security, and at the same time they gained greater maneuverability in dealing with other powerful nations, notably the Soviet Union. Normalization opened the way to a vast increase in trade, which provided China with much-needed capital and technology for its ongoing economic modernization. In the United States it was hoped that China's large market might serve to offset the mounting U.S. trade deficit in other world markets.[3]

One of the most important consequences of the normalization of Sino-U.S. relations was the ending of China's diplomatic isolation. Not only did the PRC gain a permanent seat in the UN Security Council, but many nations of the world that had formally withheld formal ties with the PRC now followed the U.S. lead by breaking off official ties with Taiwan and recognizing the PRC instead. In 1969, sixty-five countries had recognized Taiwan as the legal government of China, but by 1981 only twenty countries did so.

The breakthrough in Sino-U.S. relations brought in its wake an equally abrupt turnaround in Sino-Japanese relations, which was of great significance to both countries and for peace and stability in Asia. Initially, the Japanese were stunned by President Nixon's surprise announcement in July 1971, not because they opposed the move but because they were caught off guard by it and felt that they should have been consulted beforehand.[4] But once they got over the "Nixon shock," as they referred to it, the Japanese hastened to achieve their own rapprochement with China. Japan's prime minister, Tanaka Kakuei, responded to mounting public pressure within Japan for normalization of relations with China by arranging a visit to Beijing at the invitation of the Chinese government. His trip, which took place in September 1972, was of great historical importance, being the first visit to China by any Japanese head of state and coming after almost a century of hostile Sino-Japanese relations. In Beijing, the Japanese prime minister contritely expressed his regret over the "unfortunate experiences" between the two nations in the past and stated that "the Japanese side is keenly aware of Japan's responsibility for causing enormous damage in the past to the Chinese people through war and deeply reproaches itself."[5]

The product of Tanaka's talks with Zhou Enlai in Beijing was an agreement on the restoration of full diplomatic relations between the two countries on the following terms: Japan affirmed its recognition of the PRC as the sole legal government of China and agreed to the claim that Taiwan was an inalienable part of the territory of the PRC. China waived its claim to a war indemnity of several billion dollars and agreed to discontinue its protest against the U.S.-Japan Mutual Security Pact and to drop its insistence that Japan end its trade relations with Taiwan. The two countries also agreed to negotiate a new treaty of peace and friendship in the near future. Both China and Japan reaped enormous benefits from their improved relations, particularly from the huge volume of two-way trade that developed between them in the following years. The two countries are natural trading partners; China had various raw materials to offer resource-poor Japan in exchange for Japan's technology, machinery, and finished goods. The diplomatic rewards of the Sino-Japanese détente were probably even greater, for relations between these two major Asian nations had never been better than this since the nineteenth century, and the new relationship between these once hostile neighbors brought an era of stability and security to East Asia.

The government most disaffected by the PRC's new diplomatic achievements was, of course, the Republic of China on Taiwan. It bitterly denounced its former allies—the United States, Japan, and others—for abandoning a friend and argued that leaders in Washington and Tokyo had been duped by the Communist government in Beijing, toward which Taiwan leaders directed their strongest attacks. Although it was becoming isolated diplomatically, Taiwan carefully sought to retain ties with the United States, Japan, and other Western nations with whom it still maintained a lucrative commercial trade. And despite its diplomatic setback, Taiwan continued to maintain a high rate of economic growth, which produced a far higher standard of living for its people than the Chinese on the mainland. Stubbornly, its government, still dominated by the Nationalist Party, rebuffed every overture by the PRC for a peaceful reunification. Meanwhile, the PRC, careful not to risk damaging its good relations with the United States, patiently refrained from forceful gestures toward Taiwan and waited for a softening of Taiwan's position. But, insofar as the very raison d'être of the Nationalist government on the island was to overthrow the Communist rulers of the mainland, it neither wavered in its resolute anti-Communist policy nor moderated its strident anti-Beijing propaganda. Not until the late 1980s, when the global Cold War ended, did the Taiwan government retreat from its rigid Cold War stance.

## ■ DÉTENTE BETWEEN EAST AND WEST

The rapprochement between Washington and Beijing took place in an era of thawing of frozen relations across a wide front. It pointed to significant changes in the Cold War mentality in both camps. Originally, both sides had taken the position that there could be no improvement of relations until such issues as Taiwan, Germany, and the like had been resolved. In the mid-1960s, however, the belligerents backtracked when they took the position that a normalization of relations—such as in the areas of trade, international travel and contact, and arms limitations—could contribute ultimately to resolving the greater issues—the unification of divided nations, the nuclear arms race—and perhaps even put an end to the Cold War. The result was a period of lessening tensions in international relations.

\* \* \*

The Cold War of the late 1940s had created two German states—a West German state aligned with the West and ultimately with the North Atlantic Treaty Organization, and an East German state whose government had been installed by the Red Army and which later joined the Soviet Union's military organization, the Warsaw Pact. The conservative anti-Communist West German governments of the 1950s and the early 1960s, particularly that of Chancellor Konrad Adenauer, considered the Soviet creation of East Germany as illegitimate and refused to recognize or deal with it. The West German leaders treated Germany as a whole, claimed to speak for all Germans, and automatically granted citizenship to East Germans who made it across the border into West Germany. The West German capital, Bonn, was the provisional seat of a provisional state; the true political heart of Germany was Berlin.

Adenauer stated his position forcibly when his government issued the Hallstein Doctrine (named after the state secretary of the West German Foreign Office) in 1955. The Hallstein Doctrine emphasized that West Germany would not recognize any state (with the exception of the Soviet Union) that had diplomatic relations with East Germany. In practical terms it meant that West Germany would have no dealings with the Soviet client states of Eastern Europe. It would make no attempt to raise the Iron Curtain.

But in 1966, Willy Brandt, West Germany's new foreign minister, reversed Adenauer's stand when he took the first steps to establish contact with the socialist nations of Eastern Europe. He was willing to recognize the political realities now that more than two decades had elapsed since the Red Army had rolled into the center of Europe. The president of the United States, Lyndon Johnson, anticipated Brandt's new position when he stated that the reunification of Germany could only come about as a result of détente. In other words, Brandt and Johnson took the position that détente was a precondition for a unified Germany, whereas Adenauer and Hallstein had earlier argued that there must first be a unified Germany before there could be talk of improved relations with the Soviet bloc. Brandt and Adenauer sought the same end; they only differed over the means.

Brandt's departure from Adenauer's stance also meant that he was willing to grant de facto recognition to the existence of East Germany, as well as to the borders of the two Germanies resulting from Germany's defeat in World War II. To achieve the normalization of relations between East and West, Brandt's government was willing to recognize the Oder-Neisse Line as the border between East Germany and Poland. The new border had been in existence since the end of the war, when the Soviet Union moved Poland's western border about 75 miles (into the region of Silesia, which before the war had been German territory) to the Oder and Western Neisse Rivers. Of the 6 million former German inhabitants of the area lost to Poland, many had been killed during the war, others had fled before the advancing Red Army, and the remaining 2 million were expelled. The Germans also had lost East Prussia, the easternmost province of the German Reich, to the Soviets, who took the northern half, and to the Poles, who took the southern. And in Czechoslovakia, the Germans had lost the Sudetenland, which the British and the French had granted Hitler in 1938. The Czechs, of course, wasted little time after the war in expelling what was left of the 3 million Sudeten Germans.[6]

The Adenauer government had been most adamant in its refusal to accept the loss of German territory to Poland. Willy Brandt, however, acknowledged that the Oder-Neisse Line had existed as the new German boundary for over twenty years and had few Germans living east of it. Brandt also stopped believing that his government could ever hope to reclaim East Prussia. Any attempt to do so would lead to another war in Europe and only drive Poland and the Soviet Union into each other's arms. (In 1945, the Poles and the Soviets had been able to agree on only one thing, that Germany must pay for the war with the loss of territory.) Brandt also abandoned all claims to the Sudetenland. This was the least-controversial of the steps Brandt was willing to take, for the region had been Czechoslovakia's before the war and its transfer to Hitler's Reich was one of the most significant events leading to World War II. That the Sudetenland would be returned to Czechoslovakia after the war had been a foregone conclusion.

The Soviet Union and East Germany, however, wanted more than a mere West German recognition of the borders. They also wanted West German recognition of the East German government, which of course would legitimize it. Such recognition, however, would also undermine the West German government's claim that it spoke for all Germans. This, however, Brandt—or any other West German leader—was not willing to do.

Still, the two German governments did begin to talk to each other. On March 19, 1971, a historic meeting took place in Erfurt, East Germany, between Willy Brandt, who by then was West Germany's chancellor, and the head of the East German Communist Party, Walter Ulbricht. This event led to the Basic Treaty of 1972 between the two German states. East Germany did not obtain full diplomatic recognition from West Germany, but the treaty did call for "good neighborly" relations and it led to increased contacts of a cultural, personal, and economic nature. The Iron Curtain was partially raised.

Brandt's attempts to establish contacts with Eastern Europe became known as *Ostpolitik* (an opening toward the East, literally "eastern politics"). It included a partial thaw in relations with the Soviet Union and other East European countries. In 1968, West Germany established diplomatic relations with Yugoslavia. In 1970, the governments of West Germany and the Soviet Union signed a nonaggression treaty in Moscow. Later that year, Brandt went to Warsaw to sign a similar treaty with the Polish government, and his government accepted the Oder-Neisse Line.

But Brandt's de facto recognition of that line merely meant that he would not permit it to stand in the way of better relations with the East. A central feature of the West German position—one spelled out during the early 1950s—had not changed, however. There could be no final, legal acceptance of Germany's borders until it signed peace treaties with the nations involved. The Helsinki Agreement (see below) was not a legally valid substitute for such treaties. Until the treaties were ratified there could be no de jure recognition of the postwar borders. With the deterioration of East-West relations during the late 1970s, West German conservatives, including Chancellor Helmut Kohl, dusted off this argument. They refused to consider Germany's borders a closed issue.[7]

Détente and Brandt's *Ostpolitik* made possible a series of U.S.-Soviet arms limitation talks, including SALT I and SALT II (see Chapter 19), which led directly to the European Security Conference of August 1975 in Helsinki, Finland. The Soviets had proposed such a conference as early as 1954 and again in the late 1960s to ratify the consequences of World War II. The Soviet proposals were to no avail. Since no formal treaty or conference had recognized the redrawn map and the new governments of Eastern Europe, the Soviet leaders continued to press for such a conference. At Helsinki in 1975, thirty years after the fact, they hoped to obtain such recognition.

The participants at Helsinki included all European states (except Albania) as well as the United States and Canada. The agreement signed at Helsinki recognized the postwar borders of Europe, but it left open the prospect that the borders could be changed, although only by peaceful means. West Germany renounced its long-standing claim as the sole legitimate German state. East and West agreed to observe each other's military exercises to avoid the misreading of the other's intentions. Lastly, all signatories of the Helsinki Agreement promised greater East-West contact and to guarantee the human rights of their citizens. In Eastern Europe, however, the rights of citizens were defined differently than in the West, and this point later become a central issue when détente was shelved by the United States during the late 1970s.

Détente between East and West also produced the first steps on the road to limit the unchecked nuclear arms race. Until 1972, there were no limits on the nuclear arsenals of the United States and the Soviet Union. Both had more than enough firepower to destroy each other several times over, and there was little point in adding to stockpiles already of grotesque proportions. By 1970, the Soviet Union had concluded its concerted effort to catch up with the United States and had achieved a rough sort of parity. The U.S. strategic nuclear arsenal consisted at that time of 3,854 warheads; the Soviet total was 2,155.[8]

The year 1975 with its Helsinki Agreement saw the high point of détente. After that, relations between the United States and the Soviet Union began to deteriorate, and by 1980, détente was a thing of the past. A number of factors contributed to the new climate.

Détente had never set well with a number of influential U.S. policymakers. To them, détente was always a snare and a delusion. One cannot do

West German chancellor Willy Brandt after placing a wreath at the Tomb of the Unknown Soldier in the Polish capital of Warsaw, December 1970. *(German Information Center)*

Soviet leader Leonid Brezhnev and U.S. president Richard Nixon at the White House, Washington, D.C., June 19, 1973. *(AP/Wide World Photos)*

business, they warned, with an ideological system that professes world revolution. They seized every opportunity to sabotage détente. Eventually, a number of liberals joined their chorus. These liberals—together with the old hard-liners—became known as the neoconservatives, or simply "neocons," who were responsible for the foreign policy of President George W. Bush more than twenty years later.

With the intensification of the Cold War came a reassessment of Soviet military strength and intentions. In 1976, the head of the CIA, George H. W. Bush, brought in a group of Cold War warriors (known as the "B Team") who overruled a CIA estimate of Soviet military spending. According to the B Team's interpretations, the Soviets were spending nearly twice as much on their military as the CIA had reckoned. These ominous interpretations placed Soviet intentions and capabilities in a new light. Reporters, editorial writers, politicians, and academicians quickly accepted these new figures, which then became part and parcel of the new orthodoxy during this latest phase of the Cold War.[9] This was not the last time the neocons would challenge CIA orthodoxy. Their greatest success came when they beat the drums for war against Iraq in 2003.

With these new estimates of Soviet military spending came a reevaluation of the nuclear arms race and the charge that the Soviets had opened up a lead on the United States. Between 1976 and 1980, presidential candidate Ronald Reagan got considerable mileage out of this argument. He also promised to restore U.S. military might, a pledge that, probably more than anything else, gained him the presidency in 1980 after the incumbent Jimmy Carter proved impotent in gaining the release of the U.S. hostages in Iran (see Chapter 20). The seizure of the hostages and the burning of U.S. flags in full view of television cameras had a profound effect. A new militancy set in.

The Soviets, too, contributed to the scuttling of détente. Their definition of détente had always been different than that of the West. They insisted on the right to continue to conduct their foreign and domestic affairs as they had in the past. For example, what they did in Africa, they insisted, had nothing to do with Soviet-U.S. relations. But many in the United States perceived the Soviet activities in Africa differently. In 1975, the Soviet Union began sending arms to clients in Angola, Somalia, Ethiopia, and Mozambique, and Cuban soldiers arrived in Soviet planes in Angola and Ethiopia to train African soldiers. In the early 1970s, the Soviet Union had established close ties with the Marxist leader of Somalia, Siad Barre. Then, in late 1976, the Soviet Union began to send arms shipments to the Marxist head of Ethiopia, Mengistu Haile Miriam. In 1978, the governments of Somalia and Ethiopia went to war over a stretch of desert in the Somalian border province of Ogaden. The Soviets had to choose, and they decided to stay with Ethiopia. The United States then became the supplier of weapons to Siad Barre. In addition, Moscow had a client in Vietnam who, in

1979, marched into Phnom Penh, the capital of Cambodia. And in December 1979, the Soviet army moved into Afghanistan to prop up a bankrupt and brutal Communist government. Then, in 1981, the head of the Polish state invoked martial law in an attempt to destroy the only independent labor union in the Soviet bloc. To many in the West, Moscow and its surrogates appeared to be on the march.

At home, the Soviets also undermined the spirit of détente. Jewish emigration from the Soviet Union was drastically curtailed. Jews who wished to leave the Soviet Union had been bargaining chips in East-West relations during the 1970s. In all, about 270,000 Jews emigrated. Afterwards, emigration slowed to a trickle. Dissidents, the most famous of whom was the nuclear physicist Andrei Sakharov, were either jailed or exiled, in violation of the Helsinki Agreement. Under these conditions, détente had little chance of survival.

## ■ RECOMMENDED READINGS

Bueler, William M. *U.S. China Policy and the Problem of Taiwan.* Boulder, Colo.: Colorado Associated University Press, 1971.
    An analysis of the Taiwan issue on the eve of Nixon's visit.
Fairbank, John K. *The United States and China.* 4th ed. Cambridge, Mass.: Harvard University Press, 1981.
    A standard work that provides a historical account of Sino-U.S. relations as well as a survey of Chinese history.
Garthoff, Raymond. *Détente and Confrontation: American-Soviet Relations from Nixon to Reagan.* Washington, D.C.: The Brookings Institution, 1985.
    A most detailed analysis of the topic.
Griffith, William E. *Peking, Moscow, and Beyond: The Sino-Soviet Triangle.* Washington, D.C.: Center for Strategic International Studies, 1973.
    Discusses the implications of Nixon's visit to Beijing.
Hersh, Seymour M. *The Price of Power: Kissinger in the Nixon White House.* New York: Summit Books, 1983.
    A devastating analysis of Kissinger's foreign policy.
Schaller, Michael. *The United States and China in the Twentieth Century.* New York: Oxford University Press, 1979.
    A useful study that takes the story well beyond the Nixon visit to China.
Ulam, Adam B. *Dangerous Relations: The Soviet Union in World Politics, 1970–1982.* New York: Oxford University Press, 1983.
    Discusses the rise and fall of détente.

## ■ NOTES

1. Immanuel C. Y. Hsu, *The Rise of Modern China,* 3d rev. ed. (New York: Oxford University Press, 1983), p. 373.
2. In the past, the United States had voted against the PRC replacing the Republic of China in the United Nations but now made it known that it would not

block this move as it had for over two decades. The U.S. vote was essentially a face-saving gesture.

3. By 1996, that hope vanished when China (overtaking Japan) ran up the largest trade deficit of any nation with the United States for that year and would continue to do so for years to come.

4. The Japanese prime minister, Sato Eisaku, had for years stressed the mutual trust between his government and Washington, and, in order not to jeopardize the strong ties with the United States, he had consistently resisted the popular pressure for normalization of relations with China. For the United States to suddenly reverse its China policy without consulting its major Asian ally was considered by the Japanese as a diplomatic slap in the face.

5. Cited in Hsu, *The Rise of Modern China*, p. 751.

6. For a map of the transfer of land after World War II, see the one on p. 37 in Chapter 2, "The Cold War Institutionalized."

7. Bernt Conrad, "How Definite Is the Oder-Neisse Line?" *Die Welt*, December 24, 1984; reprinted in *The German Tribune: Political Affairs Review* (a publication of the West German government), April 21, 1985, pp. 15–16. See also *The Week in Germany*, a weekly newsletter of the West German Information Center, Washington, D.C., June 21, 1985, p. 1.

8. For details of negotiations between Washington and Moscow, see Chapter 19, "The Nuclear Arms Race."

9. In 1983, the professionals in the CIA, in a report to a congressional committee, cast off the shackles of Bush and the B Team when they restated the validity of their original estimates of Soviet military spending. They cut the B Team's estimates by more than half. While the B Team's findings had received much publicity, the CIA's declaration of independence from meddling outsiders received scant attention. In January 1984, a NATO study concluded that Soviet military spending since 1976 had been at less than 2.5 percent of the nation's GNP, as compared to 4–5 percent during the early 1970s.

# PART 4

# THE THIRD WORLD

T he East-West confrontation was surely the dominant theme in international relations in the postwar period, but since the 1970s, another
cleavage, the North-South divide, became increasingly important.
"North" refers to the modern industrialized nations, most of which happen to
be located in the temperate zones of the Northern Hemisphere, and "South"
signifies the poorer nations, most in the equatorial region or in the Southern
Hemisphere. The nations of the South are scattered throughout Asia, Africa,
and Latin America. They are sometimes euphemistically called "developing
countries," even though some have hardly been developing at all, or "underdeveloped countries." More commonly, they are referred to collectively as
the "Third World."

By the end of the twentieth century, the Third World as a large, non-
Western, poverty-stricken entity had largely ceased to exist. The term,
however, continued to be used—as we use it here—to describe nations
lacking sustained economic development, notably in the area of industrialization. Indeed, the principal identifying characteristic of Third World
nations was and remains poverty.

The economic dilemma of the Third World is the theme of Chapter
11. First we examine the gap between North and South and the various
reasons for the retarded economic development of the latter. We particularly focus on the population factor and problems in agricultural and
industrial development. In the remainder of the chapter, we examine a
global economic dilemma that strongly affected many Third World nations
and became especially acute in the 1990s: the crisis of debt. Many of the
nations of the Third World—even those with an industrial base such as
Brazil, Mexico, and Argentina—amassed foreign debts so large that they
were unable to pay either the principal or the interest on their loans.

Economic and political development are interrelated, one being a
function of the other, and this was surely the case in Africa, which is

the focus of Chapter 12. It is necessary, therefore, to seek political reasons for the economic problems in the Third World and economic reasons for its political problems. We examine the political patterns of postindependence sub-Saharan Africa, where the demise of fledgling democratic governments and the rise of militarism were common. We also take note of a new push for democracy in the early 1990s that ultimately bore little fruit. We also examine in this chapter South Africa, which stood apart from its northern neighbors, not so much because it was more prosperous but because it alone among African nations continued to be ruled until 1994 by a white minority. After explaining the policy of apartheid in South Africa, we relate the story of abolishing apartheid and the role of Nelson Mandela in the creation of a nonracial democratic South Africa.

The militarization of politics, new to Africa after independence, had long been a reality in Latin America. In Latin American countries, large and small, postwar economic development was disappointing, and the disaffected classes in these countries—mainly laborers and landless farmers—continued to be victimized by an elitist system that has endured for centuries. In Chapter 13, we examine the patterns of politics—the swings between democratic rule and militarism in Latin America, particularly in Argentina, Brazil, Chile, and Peru. Next we turn to the struggle for economic and political modernization in Mexico. Economic problems and political struggle were even more acute in Central America, where several Central American nations became hotbeds of revolution, and in this chapter we focus particularly on Nicaragua and El Salvador. We also treat the U.S. intervention in Panama here. Finally, we take up the issue of Latin American narcotics trade, centering on Colombia.

In Chapter 14, we turn to Asia to study the twists and turns of the Communist rule in the People's Republic of China as it attempted to put that huge Third World nation on the track of economic development. China, the world's largest nation—with over 1 billion people in 1990—faced the problems of feeding a burgeoning population and maintaining political order. China is unique not only because of its great size but because for almost three decades, while under the rule of Mao Zedong, the political goal of creating a Communist society was given higher priority than the economic goal of industrial development. From the late 1970s, however, China's new leader, Deng Xiaoping, gave priority to economic growth. We relate the remarkable success of Deng's policies as well as the lack of corresponding political liberalization, as seen in the crushing of the prodemocracy demonstration in Tiananmen Square in Beijing in 1989. Next we turn to the other China—Taiwan—and its economic and political development and its ongoing rivalry with Communist China.

The focus shifts in Chapter 15 to South Asia and Southeast Asia, where the trials and tribulations of India—the world's second-largest nation—Pakistan, and Bangladesh are given primary attention. In the same chapter, we examine briefly the politics and the economic surge of the Southeast Asian countries of Indonesia, Thailand, and Malaysia, and the problems of the Philippines, where a corrupt dictatorship was overthrown in 1986.

# 11

# Problems of Economic Development in the Third World

A mong the nations of the world, a gulf has always existed between the rich and the poor, but was never as wide as it became in the postwar era. About three-quarters of the world's wealth was produced and consumed by a relatively small proportion of its people, those of the North. Conversely, the large majority of the earth's people, those in the South,[1] alternatively known as the Third World, produced and consumed but a small proportion of the world's wealth. This disparity in wealth between the North and the South is revealed by the figures on per capita GNP (gross national product) in Table 11.1.

**Table 11.1 Per Capita Gross National Product, 1990**

| | |
|---|---|
| North | |
| United States | $21,790 |
| Switzerland | $32,680 |
| Japan | $25,430 |
| West Germany (before unification) | $22,320 |
| OECD members | $21,170 |
| South | |
| Sub-Saharan Africa | $340 |
| East Asia and the Pacific (without Japan) | $600 |
| South Asia | $330 |
| Middle East and North Africa | $1,790 |
| Latin America and the Caribbean | $2,180 |
| World | $4,200 |

*Source:* World Bank, *World Development Report 1992*, pp. 196, 218–219.

During the 1950s, French journalists coined the phrase "Third World" to describe nations that were neither part of the Western world nor of the

Communist bloc. In 1955, the leaders of these nations met for the first time at an Afro-Asian conference in the Indonesian city of Bandung. The spiritual father of the nonaligned Third World movement was the prime minister of India, Jawaharlal Nehru. As early as 1947, at a time when India had just gained its independence from Great Britain and the Cold War was already in full bloom, Nehru had declared that "we will not attach ourselves to any particular group," neither the Communist nor the Western camp.[2] At Bandung, seven years later, he called for an "unaligned area" as a buffer between the two camps, if only to lessen the danger of war between them.[3] The Bandung Conference criticized "colonialism in all of its manifestations," a direct swipe at the remaining Western colonial presence in the Third World as well as the Soviet Union's presence in Eastern Europe.

Among the other leaders in attendance were Gamal Abdel Nasser (Egypt), Kwame Nkrumah (Ghana), Achem Sukarno (Indonesia), and Zhou Enlai (China). Eventually they were joined by Joseph Tito of Yugoslavia, the head of a European Communist nation that had, however, taken a neutral stance in the Cold War. Collectively, the representatives of twenty-nine African and Asian nations spoke for more than one-half of the world's population. They had much in common; they had participated in the postwar struggle for independence from colonial control and now sought to resolve the host of problems of their newly independent nations. They tended to reject capitalism, the economic model of the former colonial powers, and instead opted for some variant of socialism. Officially, they were nonaligned in the Cold War, although some leaned toward the Soviet bloc and some toward the Western bloc. The tilt to one or the other bloc often depended on the assistance they received from either Washington or Moscow. Genuine neutrality was difficult to maintain, particularly because the superpowers constantly bid for the nonaligned nations' loyalty.

The alarming increase in the gap between the impoverished South and the more prosperous North was the focus of an international conference in Cancún, Mexico, in September 1981. Figures presented at this conference indicated that the 140 countries that classified themselves as "developing nations" comprised 75 percent of the world's population but had only 20 percent of the world's income. These nations were developing, yet the gap between the North and South continued to grow larger in the 1980s. (See Table 11.2.)

The statistical average of $700 annual per capita GNP for the Third World in 1985 masked the great disparity in wealth among Third World nations. In fact, per capita GNP for most sub-Saharan African countries was far below $700. According to World Bank figures, in 1984 Ethiopia had a per capita GNP of only $110—the lowest among African nations—followed by Mali ($140), Zaire ($140), and Burkina Faso ($160).[4] Moreover, most of the nations of Africa had low economic growth rates. Indeed, at least fourteen African nations registered "negative growth," or decline of per capita GNP.

**Table 11.2  North Versus South, 1985**

|  | North | South |
|---|---|---|
| Population | 1.18 billion | 3.76 billion |
| Annual per capita GNP | $9,510 | $700 |
| Life expectancy | 73 years | 58 years |
| Annual rate of population growth | 0.6% | 2.0% |

*Source:* Population Reference Bureau, *1986 World Population Data Sheet.*

World Bank figures revealed that Zaire, for example, had a negative growth rate of −1.2 percent and Uganda one of −3 percent for the decade between 1972 and 1982. This meant that in those countries the population grew faster than the economy. And in real terms, this meant continued dismal poverty, hunger, and misery.

Within each impoverished nation of the South, a great disparity existed between the relatively wealthy and the poor. The maldistribution of wealth in the underdeveloped nations of the Third World was greater than that in industrialized nations of the North.[5] The majority of people in Third World nations, mainly peasants but many city dwellers as well, had far less than the national average per capita income. Taking this fact into account, as well as considering the increasing population and low per capita income figures for the poorest nations, we can begin to fathom the dimensions of poverty and hunger in the Third World. At least one-fifth of the earth's inhabitants live in dire poverty and suffer from chronic hunger and malnutrition.

## ■ THE POPULATION FACTOR

Unquestionably, population growth was a major factor in the persistence of poverty. In the twentieth century, the population of the world grew at an increasing rate and at an especially alarming rate in the Third World. It took about 5 million years for the world's population to reach 1 billion, around 1800. The second billion mark was reached in about 130 years, by 1930; the third billion in 30 years, by 1960; the fourth billion in 15 years, by 1975; and the fifth billion in only 11 years, by 1986. The rate of population growth, however, has decreased since the mid-1960s, as witnessed by the fact that the sixth billion was reached after 14 years. (See Figure 11.1.) The rate of growth of world population peaked at 2.4 percent annually in 1964 and by the mid-1990s had fallen to about 1.5 percent.

The pressure of overpopulation was much greater in the Third World, where population growth rates remained high compared with the developed nations of the North. After World War II, Third World population grew at a historically unprecedented rate. During the late 1980s, in Africa, for example, many nations had growth rates of more than 3 percent, and some even reached more than 4 percent. In contrast, the industrialized nations had a much lower rate of growth, and—notably East Germany, West Germany, and Austria—attained a stable population (no growth at all) or even a negative growth rate. (See Figure 11.2.)

Because of their huge population growth rates, many Third World nations were on a treadmill. The increase in economic output, never large to begin with, was all too often swallowed up by the relentless growth in population. During the 1970s and 1980s, Africa's population growth rate of about 3 percent was about nine times that of Europe and about three times that of the United States and Canada. These ominous statistics meant that unless the trend was reversed, the continent's population of 450 million would double in only twenty-three years. The growth rate in Kenya throughout the 1970s stood at 3.5 percent, and by the mid-1980s it had risen to 4.2 percent. Kenya's fertility rate (the average number of children born to a woman) was 8.0. These figures were among the highest in recorded history. But Kenya was not alone, for all of these African countries had population growth rates approaching 4 percent: Rwanda, Burundi, Zimbabwe, Tanzania, Uganda, Ghana, and Libya.

How is the population explosion in the Third World to be explained? In briefest terms, the death rate fell while the birth rate either rose or remained constant. The introduction of modern medicines, the eradication of communicable diseases (such as smallpox), and improved public health and education all contributed to a reduced rate of infant mortality and an increased life expectancy. But there was no corresponding decrease in fertility. In most developing countries, most families had at least four children and in rural areas often more than five. In these countries—similar to the developing European countries in the nineteenth century—the larger the number of children in a family, the greater the number of hands in the fields or in the factories, where they were able to earn money to supplement their parents' meager income. Having large families was a means to escape poverty and was, therefore, considered economically rational. The responsibility for overpopulation in the Third World is often attributable to men, who tended to disdain all artificial birth control methods and for whom having many children was a sign of virility and moral rectitude. Yet, it was the women who bore the children and wound up caring for the large families. But it was also true that in most of the Third World, women also typically shared the men's desire for many children.

Programs of governments and international agencies to control population growth in the Third World initially met with mixed success. The most dramatic reduction of the birth rate occurred in China, where the Communist government instituted a stringent birth control program that included paramedical services, free abortions (even at near full term), public education,

**Figure 11.1  Past and Projected World Population, A.D. 1–2150**

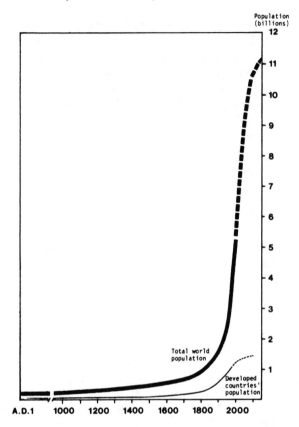

**Figure 11.2  Population Growth Rates, 1950–1985 (World Bank, 1986)**

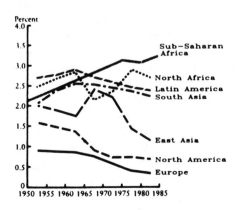

social pressure, and economic sanctions. Government-supported family-planning programs were moderately successful in other Third World countries, notably South Korea, Colombia, Mauritius, Sri Lanka, Argentina, Uruguay, and Egypt. In many other countries, governments were less active in, or were slow to begin, birth control efforts. In India, birth control programs had mixed results but were generally more effective in regions where public education was more widespread. Until the 1960s, such programs had little impact on many countries in Latin America (especially Central America) and in sub-Saharan Africa.

The problems of overpopulation in the Third World were compounded by an ongoing exodus of people from the surrounding countryside migrating into already overcrowded cities in quest of a better life.[6] The result was a phenomenal growth of Third World cities, many of which became the largest in the world—for example, Mexico City, São Paulo, Buenos Aires, Seoul, Calcutta, and Cairo. In Africa, only three cities had a population of five hundred thousand in 1950; thirty-five years later there were twenty-nine cities of at least that size. The urban population of Kenya doubled in a decade. The population of Lagos, Nigeria, grew incredibly from three hundred thousand in 1970 to over 3 million in 1983.

Although the cities typically offered more and better employment opportunities, medical services, and education than the villages, they could not accommodate the massive influx of newcomers. They did not provide adequate employment, housing, sanitation, and other services for the numerous new inhabitants—many of whom remained unemployed, impoverished, and homeless. Mexico City was the most extreme case. Its population doubled in a decade to over 18 million. More than one-third of these people lived in squatter settlements in the world's largest slum. This scene was duplicated in most other Third World cities, such as Cairo, where many thousands lived in the city's cemeteries and refuse dump, and Calcutta, where nearly 1 million of the city's 10 million inhabitants lived in the streets. The concentration of such huge numbers of disaffected peoples, living in the shadows of the edifices of the more opulent class and often within marching distance of the centers of political power (many of the largest Third World cities are capital cities), heightened the potential for massive political revolts.

One of the most critical problems associated with overpopulation was how to feed the people. In the 1960s, television began to bring home to people in the North the tragedy of mass starvation in Ethiopia and Somalia, but most viewers remained unaware that hundreds of thousands of people in other African countries—Sudan, Kenya, Mozambique, Chad, Mali, Niger, and others—also suffered from starvation. Estimates of the extent of world hunger varied greatly, depending in part on how hunger was defined, but there was little doubt that an enormous number of Third World people—perhaps 1 billion—were chronically malnourished.

In the late 1980s, a number of international agencies began to single out overpopulation as a leading factor threatening the quality of life in the twenty-first century. The UN Population Fund, in its Amsterdam Declaration of November 1989, urged a recognition of responsibility to future generations. It stressed that men must recognize that "women are in the center of the development process" and that their freedom to make choices "will be crucial in determining future population growth rates." Without rights for women—legal, social, educational, and reproductive—there would be little hope of solving the problem of rapid population growth.[7]

Similarly, the Development Assistance Committee of the Organization for Economic Cooperation and Development (OECD), at its annual conference in 1989, argued that "women must be fully involved in the planning and implementation of population programmes" because thus far they "have often been designed in a way which takes insufficient account of women in their reproductive role and as decision-makers, producers, and beneficiaries."[8] The committee concluded that one of the priorities for international assistance should be the slowing of population growth. The World Bank's fifteenth annual *World Development Report* (1992) emphasized for the first time the link between unchecked population growth and environmental degradation, slow economic growth, declining health care, and declining living standards.

The international organizations understood that the implementation of effective family-planning programs would not be easy because they frequently clashed with deeply entrenched cultural and religious values held particularly (but not exclusively) by adherents of Islam, Hinduism, and Roman Catholicism. Pope John Paul II, for instance, in his encyclical "On the Hundredth Anniversary of Rerum Novarum" (May 1991), denounced, as he had done before, all measures "suppressing or destroying the sources of life." "Anti-childbearing campaigns," he argued, rested "on the basis of a distorted view of the demographic problem." The pope went on to restate his position that new birth control techniques were responsible for "poisoning the lives of millions of defenceless human beings, as if in a form of 'chemical warfare.'"[9]

For the first two decades after 1945, the world witnessed a veritable population explosion unprecedented in history. But from the mid-1960s on, it witnessed another demographic trend, a considerable *decline* in the population growth rate, from 2.4 percent to 1.5 percent by the end of the century. The world was slowly moving toward the zero-growth fertility rate of 2.1 infants per female.

Conventional wisdom declared that a falling birth rate was necessarily tied to prosperity, but the increasingly wider availability of birth control in many poorer countries upset this theory. One example was Bangladesh, which not only ranked among the poorest nations but was also overwhelmingly Muslim. The tenets of Islam prohibit family planning, yet 40 percent of that country's women used some sort of birth control. This trend produced a shift from the view that "development is the best contraceptive" to "contraceptives are the best contraceptives."[10] In addition, Third World feminists stressed that birth control frequently was tied to levels of education. At a UN conference on population control in April 1994, they produced statistics pointing to the correlation between higher female education and a lower fertility rate.[11]

# ■ THE AGRARIAN DILEMMA

Food production in the South increased at about 3.1 percent annually from the late 1960s to the late 1980s, but population growth ate up this increase almost entirely. Although most Asian nations made considerable progress in agricultural production, fifty-five Third World nations—again most of them in Africa—registered a decline in food production per capita after 1970. In the early 1970s, the nations of the South collectively were net exporters of food, but by the early 1980s they had become net importers.

Why were the nations of the Third World, almost all of which were agrarian, unable to increase their food production to a level of self-sufficiency? This complex question defies a simple explanation, but there are several major causal factors.

1. *Natural causes.* Most Third World nations are in the tropics where the climate is often very hot and where both extended droughts and torrential rainstorms occur. Desertification is a major problem in Africa, where the Sahara Desert has pushed its frontier southward into West Africa and eastward into Sudan. Indeed, much of that continent suffers from prolonged drought. In addition, Third World areas also suffer from other natural catastrophes such as flooding, cyclones, and earthquakes.

2. *Abuse of the land.* Great amounts of topsoil are lost to wind and water erosion every year, in part because of human causes such as deforestation and overgrazing. Another problem is overcultivation, which results in the exhaustion of the land's nutrients.

3. *Primitive farming methods.* Most Third World peasants work with simple tools, many with nothing more than a hoe, and most plowing is still done with draft animals. Peasants are usually too poor to afford modern equipment. In some instances, intensive farming with traditional methods and tools is efficient, especially in the case of paddy farming in Asia, but in many other areas—especially in Africa—toiling in parched fields with hand tools is an inefficient mode of production. In some parts of Africa, most of this toil is done by women.[12]

4. *Inequality of land holdings.* Throughout the Third World, agricultural production often suffers because the majority of the peasants have too little land and many are tenants burdened with huge rent payments. Impoverished, debt-ridden peasants are forced to become landless laborers. In 1984, an international study concluded that in Latin America 80 percent of

Ethiopian famine victims, 1984.
*(AP/Wide World Photos)*

Cambodian children receiving relief food at a refugee camp in Trat, Thailand,
June 4, 1979. *(AP/Wide World Photos)*

the farmland was owned by 8 percent of landowners, and the poorest peasants—66 percent of all owners—were squeezed onto only 4 percent of the land.[13] Land reform, that is, redistribution of land, paid off with significantly increased agricultural output for nations such as Japan.

5. *Lack of capital for agricultural development.* Third World food-producing farmers need irrigation works, better equipment, chemical fertilizers, storage facilities, and improved transport. Yet all too often, their governments are unwilling or unable to supply the capital needed to provide these essentials.

6. *One-crop economies.* In many Third World nations, the best land with the best irrigation belongs to wealthy landowners (and sometimes to multinational corporations) who grow cash crops—peanuts, cocoa, coffee, and so on—for export rather than food for domestic consumption. Generally, Third World leaders accept the dogma that the progress of their countries depends on what they produce for sale to the developed countries. Dependence on a single cash crop for export, however, places the developing nations at the mercy of the world market, where competition is fierce and where prices for that reason fluctuate greatly. This situation proves disastrous for Third World countries when prices of agricultural exports drop sharply while prices of necessary imports (especially petroleum, fertilizers, and finished goods) rise. Meanwhile, Third World leaders neglect the needs of the majority of the food-producing farmers in favor of support for the cash-crop farmers. In many cases, governments—out of political considerations—keep food prices artificially low to the benefit of the growing number of city dwellers and to the detriment of the farmers who grow the food.

Many of these problems were caused by the political leaders rather than the farmers. The solution to these problems consists of land redistribution, diversification of agriculture, and the building of irrigation systems, roads, storage facilities, fertilizer plants, and agricultural schools. But these efforts require a large amount of capital, political stability, and strong and able political leadership—all of which are frequently lacking.

A number of Third World nations obtained relief in the form of large shipments of food to feed starving people. Although such aid is beneficial and humane, it does not go to the root of the problem (and, in fact, it often does not reach those who need it most). Subsequently, donor nations and international financing institutions increasingly channel their aid into long-term agricultural development programs for which they provide expertise, training incentives, and capital.

## ■ PREREQUISITES FOR INDUSTRIALIZATION

Upon gaining independence from Europe, Third World nations tended to blame their economic backwardness on their former colonial masters. They looked forward to rapid progress as independent nations, hoping to close the gap that separated them from the economically advanced nations. They saw industrial development as the primary road to economic modernization. By giving priority to industrial growth, however, they tended to neglect agriculture and its role in economic development. Moreover, their efforts at rapid industrialization were often met with frustration and failure. They expected rapid progress but found, to their dismay, that industrial development is a difficult process. Economists long have argued over the prerequisites for industrial development, but the following are generally considered minimal necessary conditions.

1. *Capital accumulation*. Money for investments to build plants and buy equipment has to come from somewhere: the World Bank, foreign powers (which usually seek to gain political or military leverage), heavy taxation (often falling upon people who can least afford it), or the export of cash crops or raw materials. This last method of capital accumulation often leads to an anomaly: the agrarian nations of the Third World find themselves importing food, often from the developed nations, in ever-increasing amounts and at ever-increasing cost; thus, money tends to flow out of their economies rather than in.

Third World nations are in great need of foreign aid, but such aid is not necessarily the answer to their problems. They received substantial aid from abroad for many years, but too often the money was mismanaged, squandered on unproductive projects, or simply siphoned off by corrupt leaders. Moreover, overreliance on outside financial aid produced its own hazards. Third World leaders were wary of political strings attached to foreign loans, which they saw as intrusions into their national sovereignty or as threats to their personal power. The loans also produced excessive indebtedness (see Chapter 17). After having struggled to win political independence from the developed nations of the North, the leaders were (and are) loath to become economic dependencies of those same nations.

2. *Technology*. To compete with the highly sophisticated industries of the economically advanced nations, developing nations must rapidly incorporate new technology. But technology transfer is a complicated matter, and its acceptance and implementation in tradition-bound societies has at best been a slow process. Meanwhile, technological change in developed nations was rapid, and developing countries too often fell further behind.

3. *Education*. Technology, even when borrowed from abroad, requires educated technicians and workers. An industrialized society requires a literate working class, as well as educated managers and engineers. Industry needs skilled labor, and literacy is essential for training such a work force. The attainment of mass education is a long-term and costly undertaking.

4. *Favorable trading conditions*. In general, the system of free trade erected by the industrially advanced nations of the world after World War II served both developed and developing nations well, but the latter needed

preferential treatment to compete with the former in the global marketplace. Third World nations sought new trade agreements that would, in some manner, underwrite their exports with guaranteed minimum purchases at prices not to fall below a fixed level. At the same time, they wanted to maintain higher tariffs on imports to protect their native industries.

5. *Political stability.* Capital accumulation and the conduct of business require safety and stability. Domestic strife and international wars are disruptive and costly, draining off the meager resources for industrial development. (Nearly all of the wars since 1945 were fought in Third World countries. The list seems endless: China, Korea, Vietnam, Iran, Iraq, Ethiopia, Angola, Chad, Nigeria, Lebanon, India, Pakistan, El Salvador, Nicaragua, and so on.) Even developing nations not engaged in external or civil wars spent an extraordinary amount on sophisticated weapons, which they were ill able to afford and which were purchased from the industrialized powers—primarily the United States and the Soviet Union.

6. *Capital investment.* The economies of the Third World tend to be exploitative of their own people. Available capital from whatever source is often spent on luxury imports for the elite, the building of showcase airports, hotels, and the like, and not on the development of the economic substructure for industrial and agricultural growth—an activity that would benefit the population as a whole. Thus, we see in Third World cities great contrasts of wealth coexisting with grinding poverty—elegant mansions in one part of town and tin-roof hovels in another.

After independence, the hard realities of economic development began to set in as Third World countries struggled to overcome their economic deficiencies and to come to terms with the problems of feeding their people and improving the quality of life. In this endeavor, some countries, mainly in Asia, met with considerable success, but others, mainly in Africa and Latin America, continue to find themselves in a perilous condition.

## ■ THIRD WORLD DEBT: AFRICA AND LATIN AMERICA

The 1970s saw the emergence of a phenomenon with potentially serious international repercussions: the increasing indebtedness of the Third World to the industrial First World. Traditionally, nations seeking to develop their economies rely upon capital from abroad. This was true, for example, of the industrial revolutions in England, the Netherlands, the United States, and Russia.[14] Foreign capital—in the form of profits from sales abroad, loans, or capital investments—has long been a catalyst for speeding up the difficult process of industrialization.

The emerging, developing economies of the Third World sought this shortcut after World War II. But until the oil crises of the 1970s, the reliance on foreign money had been kept in bounds. The money borrowed from the First World was doled out in reasoned, and at times sparse, amounts—until the surfeit of "petrodollars" (that is, money invested in Western banks by the oil-rich nations) created a binge of lending by these same banks and an orgy of borrowing by the nations of the Third World. There appeared to be no limit to the banks' willingness to extend credit and the recipients' willingness to take it. Foreign capital seemed to promise the road out of the wilderness: rapid economic development and, with it, the ability to repay the loans. By the mid-1980s, the consequence was a staggering debt of Latin American and African nations in excess of $500 billion, a sum far beyond the capacity of the debtor nations to repay.[15] Many were staring bankruptcy in the face, and if they defaulted, they threatened to take the lending institutions and the international banking system itself down the road to ruin.

## ☐ Africa

The African debt had its roots in the political instability that followed independence, which resulted in frequent government turnovers, secessionist movements, and civil wars. Among the first casualties were the budding democratic institutions. Political and military considerations quickly began to take precedence over economic development, for the first priority of dictatorships is the retention of power. As such, precious resources were diverted to the military, whose main task was not so much the defense of the nation against a foreign foe, but the suppression of domestic opposition.

One consequence of political instability in Africa was the flight of Europeans, who took with them their skills and capital. This was the case particularly in the new states where independence was won by force and where a legacy of bitterness and mistrust remained after the violence had subsided. Algeria, Mozambique, Angola, Zimbabwe (formerly Southern Rhodesia), and Kenya readily come to mind. South Africa, too, saw the flight of whites as racial tensions were beginning to mount during the early 1980s. The result of this exodus left many African nations with a badly depleted industrial base and a continued reliance on the agricultural sector. Yet, Africa's agriculture remained the world's most primitive. Most of it consisted of subsistence farming with women doing most of the work.

Until the late 1970s, the African economies limped along, but then the roof began to cave in when a number of conditions came together. The result was that much of the continent was bankrupted. First came the oil crisis with its accompanying rise in the cost of crude oil. The crisis had a greater impact on the poorer nations than on the industrial West, which had the means of meeting the higher payments. (Although several oil-producing nations of sub-Saharan Africa, such as Nigeria and Cameroon, benefited from the new, higher price tag on oil, most suffered greatly. And when oil prices began to fall in the early 1980s, Nigeria was among the hardest hit, having become saddled with mounting debts and attendant political instability.) In the West, the oil crisis contributed to a global recession, which in turn lessened the demand for raw materials. The prices for copper, bauxite (aluminum ore), and diamonds fell. Prices for agricultural exports fell similarly, as a result of a worldwide surplus. The glut in agricultural commodities played havoc with the African economies. Cacao, coffee, cotton, peanuts, and such no longer brought the prices African exporters had been accustomed to. After 1979–1980, prices for African commodity exports declined by as much as 30 percent. All the while, prices for crude oil and for goods manufactured in the West—such as machinery, tools, electronics, and weapons—continued to rise.

Appreciation of foreign currencies, particularly the U.S. dollar, added to the dilemma. Since the debts of nations were calculated in U.S. dollars, the increasing purchasing power of the dollar in the early 1980s played havoc with the pay rate of debtor nations. Debts now had to be repaid in dollars with greater purchasing power; this meant that Third World nations had to export more. In effect, this condition forced African governments to repay more than they had borrowed.

As Africa's indebtedness to the industrial world increased during the first half of the 1980s, the poorest continent became a net exporter of capital. In 1985 alone, African nations were required to pay $7 billion to banks and governments of the developed world. On average, African nations used 25 percent of their foreign currency earnings to repay their foreign debts. They were reaching the point where they were dismantling their social and economic development plans in order to meet their debt obligations. They were, in effect, cannibalizing their economies to meet their interest payments. Hope for a future resolution of the continent's dilemma faded.

The African nations listed in Table 11.3 increased their foreign debts between 1987 and 1990.

**Table 11.3  African Nations with Foreign Debt Increases, 1987–1990**

| Nation | Debt in 1987 (billions) | Debt in 1990 (billions) | Percentage of Increase 1987–1990 |
|---|---|---|---|
| Nigeria | $28.7 | $36.1 | 26% |
| Ivory Coast | 13.5 | 17.9 | 33 |
| Sudan | 11.1 | 15.4 | 39 |
| Zaire | 8.6 | 10.1 | 17 |
| Zambia | 6.4 | 7.2 | 13 |
| Kenya | 5.9 | 6.8 | 15 |
| Tanzania | 4.3 | 5.9 | 37 |

*Sources*: World Bank, *World Development Report, 1989*, p. 205; *World Development Report, 1992*, p. 258.

In the mid-1980s, Africa's foreign debt stood between $150 billion and $170 billion. As such, its debt was about half that of Latin America's, which was over $360 billion. But Latin America's condition, as grim as it was, was not as hopeless as Africa's because of its stronger economic base. Africa reached a point where it could neither repay its debt nor borrow any appreciable sums of money. (Not surprisingly, Nigeria, a major oil-exporting nation, ran up the largest debt on the basis of its projected ability to repay its obligations.) On top of this, there was no significant foreign investment in Africa after 1980. The continent was on a treadmill, pledged to come up with interest payments over an indefinite period to the industrialized West and its banks. Under such circumstances, the indebtedness to the West remained indefinite, since there was no question of making a dent in the principal (i.e., the debt itself).

Predictably, African leaders were pointing an accusing finger at the international banking system. In July 1985, the African heads of government met under the aegis of the Organization of African Unity (OAU) in Addis Ababa, Ethiopia's capital, to address this bleak situation in the hope of finding economic and political solutions. The meeting ended with a surprisingly frank declaration that most African countries were on the brink of economic collapse. The declaration placed part of the blame on an "unjust and inequitable [international] economic system," but it also acknowledged that natural calamities such as droughts, as well as "some domestic policy shortcomings," had contributed to Africa's problems.

The chair of the OAU, Tanzanian president Julius Nyerere, hinted at the creation of a defaulter's club, which promised to seek, among other things, the cancellation of government-to-government loans and the restructuring of interest rates—all for the purpose of avoiding default and with it national bankruptcy.

☐ *Latin America*

Other economies took sharp downward turns during the late 1970s, and the reasons were not unlike those that caused difficulties in Africa. Latin American nations, too, remained heavily dependent on agricultural exports. The rapid increase in oil prices in the 1970s and the drop in agricultural commodity prices produced a sharp decline in the standard of living.

Latin America has long been a region of economic promise. This was especially the case with Brazil, a land of seemingly unlimited potential, resources, and workers. On the basis of future earnings, the Brazilian government was able to borrow huge sums of money during the 1970s, an action that later came back to haunt it. By 1987, the foreign debt of Brazil was well over $120 billion and in 2003, more than $220 billion, sums beyond the country's capacity to repay. The best that Brazil could do was merely make the interest payments and in this fashion avoid a declaration of bankruptcy. The country's potential bankruptcy threatened the international banking system, and for this reason, despite its staggering debt, Brazil was able to demand additional loans until the time—sometime in the distant, nebulous future—when it would be able to begin to repay the principal. In the meantime, Brazil remained beholden to the Western banks and governments.

Argentina was another Latin American nation that accumulated a large foreign debt. It had traditionally been a nation with a strong and vigorous economy, which made it relatively easy for its governments to borrow money from abroad. But a succession of military regimes (1976–1983) contributed to the ruination of the nation's economy. The regimes' brutality (see Chapter 13) and a losing war with Great Britain over the Falkland Islands in 1983 brought about the return to civilian rule that year. At that time, Argentina's foreign debt was thought to have been at about $24 billion—a large sum by anyone's yardstick. The new civilian government discovered, however, that the military had in fact run up a debt of twice that figure, an obligation of $48 billion, the third-largest foreign debt (after Brazil and Mexico) among the developing countries.

In contrast to most Third World nations, the oil shortages of the late 1970s did not initially harm Mexico's economy. Instead, the shortages appeared to work to its benefit, for Mexico's oil reserves were potentially the world's largest. It was oil that promised to solve Mexico's economic problems, caused in part by its large and rapidly growing population, weak industrial base, and inefficient agricultural system. Mexico, too, was able to borrow large sums of money in the expectation that oil shortages and high oil prices would make it possible to repay the loans. In short, Mexico borrowed against future income. At the end of 1981, Mexico's foreign debt was at about $55 billion. Four years later, that figure had risen to well above $100 billion. By 1990, Latin America's leading debtors, unlike those of Africa, had a measure of success in reducing their debts—by a combination of increasing exports, selling off equity, and debt cancellation by lenders.

## ■ THE THIRD WORLD'S CONTINUING POVERTY

In the 1960s, when many Third World nations gained their independence, there already existed a huge gap between their level of economic development and wealth and that of the industrialized world. For much of the Third World, however, the gap was even wider at the end of the century. The 1990s was a time of vastly increasing wealth in the industrialized world, but many of the poorest nations became even more deeply in debt to the rich. Saddled with enormous debt payments that squeezed national budgets, Third World nations lacked the means to dig themselves out of the hole. While per capita GNP figures for most industrialized countries rose ever higher over the past forty years, the figures for most Third World countries rose only slightly, if at all. The per capita GNP for the former remained as much as a hundred times higher than that for the poorest of Third World countries.

It should be pointed out that GNP figures do not give a complete picture of the standard of living in a developing nation since much of its economy is informal. GNP statistics tend to understate real income in Third World nations, because many of the people meet their needs by barter or may be paid for by labor in kind—such as in a sharecropping arrangement—and these informal arrangements are not measured and do not enter into GNP figures. To go beyond economic statistics and assess the quality of life, the UN conducted a "human development" survey, assessing and ranking 174 nations on such things as health care, life expectancy, education levels, and access to clean water, as well as income. But even in this assessment, published in the annual UN *Human Development Report* released in June 2000, Third World nations were generally at the bottom half of the ranking. At the very bottom of the list were twenty-four African countries.[16]

Not all Third World countries, however, remained mired in poverty at the end of the century. Some had made moderate economic progress and a few others, particularly in Asia, had made much significant progress and were able to climb from Third World status to become newly industrializing countries.

## ■ RECOMMENDED READINGS

Barnet, Richard J. *The Lean Years: Politics in the Age of Scarcity.* New York: Simon and Schuster, 1980.
    A study of the political factors involved in sharing limited global resources.
Brown, Lester R., et al. *State of the World, 1986.* New York: W. W. Norton, 1987.
    An annually updated reference on food and environmental issues around the globe.
Ehrlich, Paul E., and Anne H. Ehrlich. *The Population Explosion.* New York: Simon and Schuster, 1990.
    This sequel to Paul Ehrlich's *The Population Bomb* (1968) warns of the dangers of rampant population growth.
Emerson, Steven. *The American House of Saud: The Secret Petrodollar Connection.* Danbury, Conn.: Franklin Watts, 1985.
    An account of the link between the U.S. oil companies and Saudi Arabia.
George, Susan. *Ill Fares the Land: Essays on Food, Hunger and Power.* Rev. and expanded ed. London: Penguin, 1990.
    A sociological inquiry into what went wrong with agricultural planning in the Third World.
Harrison, Paul. *Inside the Third World.* 2d ed. New York: Penguin, 1984.
    An excellent comprehensive description and analysis of the dilemmas of the Third World.

Kapuscinski, Ryszard. *The Soccer War.* New York: Alfred A. Knopf, 1991.

　　A Polish journalist's explanation of the political problems of the Third World.

Lacey, Robert. *The Kingdom: Arabia and the House of Sa'ud.* New York: Avon, 1983.

　　Another look at the oil crisis.

Sampson, Anthony. *The Sovereign State of ITT.* 2d ed. New York: Fawcett, 1974.

　　By an English muckraking reporter who has written several popular books on the world of international finance, this book discusses ITT's foreign operations, particularly in Latin America.

————. *The Seven Sisters.* New York: Viking Press, 1975.

　　A chronicle of the activities of the major international oil companies.

————. *The Money Lenders: The People and Politics of International Banking.* New York: Penguin, 1982.

　　A look at the international banking community and its involvement in the Third World.

World Bank. *World Development Report: Development and Environment.* New York: Oxford University Press, 1992.

　　Fifteenth in an annual series, this report discusses the link between economic development, population pressures, and the environment.

# ■ NOTES

1. The concept of a North-South division of the world was popularized by the West German foreign minister (and later chancellor) Willy Brandt, who argued that the East-West division (between the Western and Soviet blocs) can readily be overcome. The division between the haves and the have-nots, however, was a much more difficult matter.

2. Nehru's foreign policy address to India's Constituent Assembly, December 4, 1947, in Dorothy Norman, ed., *Nehru: The First Sixty Years* (New York: John Day, vol. 2, 1965), pp. 353–356.

3. See Nehru's address to the Bandung Conference, in G. M. Kahin, *The Asian-African Conference* (Ithaca: Cornell University Press, 1956), pp. 54–72.

4. GNP, or gross national product, is the wealth—the total goods and services—a nation produces per year. The per capita GNP is calculated by dividing the figure for wealth generated (calculated in U.S. dollars) by the nation's population.

5. See Paul Harrison, *Inside the Third World,* 2d ed. (New York: Penguin, 1984), pp. 414–415. Harrison shows that the gap in income between the richest and the poorest people in Third World countries is, on average, greater than the income gap between rich and poor in the world's developed countries.

6. Ibid., p. 145, notes that 185 million people lived in Third World cities in 1940, but by 1975 the number had risen to 770 million. In the early 1970s, 12 million people a year—33,000 a day—were arriving in these cities.

7. For the text of the Amsterdam Declaration, see *Population and Development Review* (March 1990), pp. 186–192.

8. For the text of the OECD's statement, see "Population and Development—DAC Conclusions," *Population and Development Review,* September 1990, pp. 595–601.

9. "Pope John Paul II on Contemporary Development," *Population and Development Review,* September 1991, p. 559. The citations are from Chapter 4 of the encyclical.

10. The statement is by Bryant Robey of the Johns Hopkins School of Hygiene and Public Health and the editor of *American Demographics,* cited in William K. Stevens, "Poor Lands' Success in Cutting Birth Rate Upsets Old Theories," *New York Times,* January 2, 1994, p. 8.

11. Susan Chira, "Women Campaign for New Plan to Curb the World's Population," *New York Times,* April 13, 1994, pp. A1, A12.

12. Traditionally, African men were primarily hunters and herdsmen, and women were left to work in the fields. The tradition has changed only to the extent that with the depletion of wild game, few men still hunt. But too proud to toil in the fields, men either supervised women who do that work, or sought other employment. Exact figures are difficult to obtain, but a UN report, *State of the World's Women,* 1985, estimated that between 60 and 80 percent of farm work in Africa was still done by women. Barber Conable, president of the World Bank, at a joint World Bank–International Monetary Fund meeting, stated that women did two-thirds of the world's work, earned 10 percent of the world's income, and owned less than 1 percent of the world's property. "They are the poorest of the world's poor" (Clyde Farnsworth, "World Bank Chief Outlines Strategy," *New York Times,* October 1, 1986, p. D23.)

13. Harrison, *Inside the Third World,* p. 455.

14. Prerevolutionary tsarist Russia drew heavily upon foreign capital and foreign engineers to begin the industrialization process. Stalin's industrial revolution of the 1930s, in contrast, accomplished largely without foreign assistance, became in the early 1960s one of the models considered by a number of newly independent nations of the Third World. Their economic planners found out, however, that their economic base was so primitive, in contrast to what Stalin had inherited from the tsars, that they had little choice but to turn to economic assistance available from the industrialized First World.

15. All dollar amounts are in U.S. dollars.

16. Cited in "Rankings of World's Nations in Human Development." UN, June 29, 2000. *AOL News.* Among Third World nations Cuba ranked highest (56th), followed by Belize, Panama, Venezuela, Colombia, and Brazil.

# 12

# Africa

In the early 1960s, when most African nations gained their independence, proud African leaders heralded the dawn of a new age. Freed from the shackles of European colonialism, they looked confidently to a new political and economic order that promised an end to the continent's economic backwardness and dependence on the West. But the euphoria of the early 1960s soon gave way to a more somber reality, for as years went by, African leaders' shared goals of economic growth, of national self-reliance and dignity, and of African unity remained elusive. Indeed, forty years later those dreams were in shambles, as most African countries had become increasingly impoverished and more dependent on foreign aid than ever before. Across the continent one found declining economies, grinding poverty, civil strife, corruption, crop failures, hungry and starving people, spreading disease, overcrowded and deteriorating cities, massive unemployment, and growing numbers of refugees.

The plight of Africa was exacerbated by the political turmoil that became common throughout Africa. In one African country after another, democratic rule gave way to military rule, and several countries experienced a series of military coups. Many countries were torn apart by civil wars, which were often internecine struggles among ethnic groups. Often the flames were fanned by the rival superpowers who armed the combatants. Political stability necessary for economic growth was sorely lacking.

Africa had the world's lowest economic growth rates, highest infant mortality rates, and highest rates of population growth. In the 1970s, the population of Africa grew at about twice the rate of increase in food production. Chronic malnutrition and starvation became more common in subsequent years. Perhaps as many as two hundred thousand people succumbed to starvation in the Ethiopian famine in the early 1970s, and another famine a decade later—more publicized than the earlier one—took an equally large toll.[1] Media attention focused on Ethiopia diverted attention from the hundreds of thousands of people malnourished and on the verge of starvation in Sudan, Chad, Niger, and Mali, nations most affected by the relentless expansion of the Sahara Desert. Further south, countries such as Kenya, Uganda, Gabon, and Mozambique were also drought-stricken. The Economic Commission for Africa, a UN agency, reported that from 1960 to 1975 there was no significant improvement in most African nations' economies. In 1960, Africa had been 95 percent self-sufficient in food, but twenty-five years later every African country except South Africa was a net importer of food.

The nations of sub-Saharan Africa were not equally impoverished. By far the most prosperous nation on the continent was South Africa, which stood as an exception to the economic decline characteristic of the remainder of sub-Saharan Africa.[2] Nigeria, burdened with Africa's largest population and yet blessed with large deposits of oil, prospered greatly following independence, only to find its economy in collapse as a result of political corruption and plummeting world oil prices in the early 1980s. An examination of per capita GNP growth rates in the decade after 1973 reveals that black African nations were either struggling to maintain marginal economic progress, marking time, or actually declining. According to World Bank figures, only Benin, Botswana, Cameroon, the People's Republic of Congo, Ivory Coast, and Rwanda had marginal growth. Fourteen countries had a decline in per capita GNP.[3] Most tragic were those states that had displayed the potential for economic growth and had made progress in the first decade of independence only to slide backward since then. Ghana, Nigeria, Kenya, Uganda, and Zaire particularly come to mind.

## ■ POLITICAL INSTABILITY IN SUB-SAHARAN AFRICA

Africa's problems were both economic and political. Indeed, an interrelationship existed between economic and political problems. Political chaos often followed economic disaster; conversely, political problems often contributed to the economic woes of African nations.

Following independence, Africa witnessed the steady erosion of democratic institutions and the steady militarization of politics. After initial trial runs in parliamentary democracy, elected governments often retained power by eliminating the electoral process and political opposition. Subsequently, military coups—not popular elections—were the primary vehicle for the transfer of power. Dictatorships became common throughout Africa, where about three-quarters of the governments were controlled either by one-party regimes or military men. Only about half a dozen states in sub-Saharan Africa permitted opposition parties to engage in the political process, and no African head of state was voted out of office until 1990. Political repression became the order of the day, especially in countries such as Uganda, Zimbabwe, Zaire, and Guinea, where political leaders massacred many thousands of opponents. And more often than not, African leaders were as corrupt as they were repressive.

## ☐ The Colonial Legacy

Many African leaders were quick to blame a century of European colonialism for many of Africa's problems. Colonialism was exploitative and disruptive, and its impact on Africa was enormous, but the nature of the impact is not easily determined. Still, it is possible to discern certain consequences of colonialism that left Africans ill prepared for the task of nation building. One may question whether the political and economic models Europeans provided Africa were suitable for African society. It might also be argued that the Europeans left too abruptly, leaving the Africans with political institutions that few, beyond a small circle of Western-educated elites, appreciated or understood. The European powers did little to develop national economies in their colonies; instead, they had mainly built up enterprises focused on export commodities, such as coffee, cacao, copper, or bauxite. The economic system inherited by the new African nations had been designed for export rather than for producing goods and services for domestic consumption. Moreover, the export-oriented economy of each colony was directly linked with the former colonial power instead of with its African neighbors.

Perhaps the most baleful legacy of European colonialism was the artificiality of the national boundaries it had created. In the nineteenth century, the European imperialists often hastily drew boundaries as they divided Africa into colonies, and these arbitrary boundaries—drawn with little or no recognition of the ethnic makeup of Africa—remained the root of many of Africa's problems after independence. One British commissioner later joked: "In those days we just took a blue pencil and a rule, and we put it down at Old Calabar, and drew that blue line up to Yola. . . . I recollect thinking when I was sitting having an audience with the [local] Emir . . . it was a very good thing that he did not know that I . . . had drawn a line through his territory."[4] It was not so much that the new African nations disputed the boundaries, for border conflicts were not as serious a problem as ethnic conflicts and secessionist wars within the new African nations. As a result of the political boundaries created by the Europeans, however, most African states were much larger than the precolonial political units and contained within them many ethnic groups. Only two countries in sub-Saharan Africa—Lesotho and Swaziland—had ethnic uniformity. All others had populations made up of numerous ethnic groups. The most extreme cases, such as Nigeria and the former Belgian Congo, include within their borders over two hundred distinct ethnic groups. The new nations were in many instances artificial constructs, and their rulers had the task of superimposing a new national identity over the existing ethnic configuration. In most instances, however, ethnic identity prevailed over nationalism—a relatively

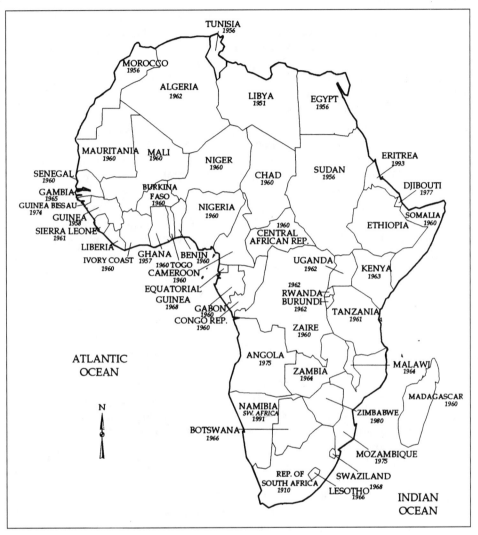

**Africa After Independence**

new and foreign concept—to the detriment of the process of nation building. The result was ethnic conflicts ranging from political contention to
bloody civil wars, secessionist wars, and even genocide. Ethnic strife
claimed a frightful toll of lives in the two small Central African nations of
Rwanda and Burundi in the 1960s and 1970s. Even more lives were lost in
Nigeria in the 1960s in the Biafran War.

Tribalism is a legacy not of colonialism but of African history. It persisted through the colonial era—in some places strengthened by colonial
policy, in others diluted—and remained strong after independence. Typically, an African's strongest loyalties were to family and ethnic group
(tribe). Given the relative lack of geographic mobility in Africa, people of
one ethnic group maintained local roots and mixed little with people of
other ethnic groups. Governments in Africa often represented one dominant
ethnic group to the exclusion of others, and the discontent of the excluded
ethnic groups was often the source of instability and repression. In countries ruled by leaders from a minority ethnic group, such as Kenya, Uganda,
and Zambia in the mid-1980s, the ruler maintained order only as long as the
country's largest ethnic groups were satisfied.

Tribalism relates to another aspect of African heritage that plagued
African politics: corruption. In kinship-based societies such as those in
Africa, communal elders were entrusted with authority not only to make
decisions binding for the group but also to divide the wealth among its
members. Gifts and favors were parceled out by the leader, who expected to
be favored with gifts in return. Self-aggrandizement and corruption on an
immense scale were often the result. There was usually little dissent, except
from members of other ethnic groups whose opposition to the corruption
was based more on jealousy than on ethical considerations. Thus, African
politics often degenerated into ethnic contests for the spoils of power.

The combination of unbridled corruption and the cult of personality in
Africa produced some of the world's most outrageous displays of extravagance. Not a few African rulers lived in regal splendor in fabulous palaces,
owned fleets of luxury cars, and stashed vast amounts of money in Western banks. For bizarre extravagance none exceeded Colonel Jean-Bedel
Bokassa, emperor of the Central African Republic, who spent about $20
million—one-quarter of his nation's revenue—on his coronation ceremony
in 1977. He wore a robe bedecked with 2 million pearls that cost $175,000
and donned a $2 million crown topped with a 138-carat diamond. This in a
country that had no more than 170 miles of paved roads. Two years later,
Bokassa was deposed.

Most of the newly independent nations of Africa began with inherited
parliamentary systems in which executive power was in the hands of a prime
minister who was elected by and responsible to a popularly elected legislative body. Typically, the African prime ministers revised the constitutions to
allow themselves to become presidents with broadened executive powers
and longer terms of office. (A prime minister is elected by and responsible

to the parliament and may be called to resign at any time by a vote of no confidence in the parliament. But a president is elected by the people for a fixed, usually longer term and is not so easily expelled from office.) Without an effective check on their new powers, the presidents began exercising them in a dictatorial manner and no longer tolerated political opposition. They argued that opposition parties were divisive, a threat to political stability, even unpatriotic; on these grounds the presidents abolished them, thus creating one-party states. The notion of the "loyal opposition," an out-of-power political party opposed to the party currently in power but loyal to the nation and qualified to govern if elected, remained foreign to Africans, especially to those in power.

African presidential dictators also took steps to strengthen the central governments by bringing local administration and all levels of civil service under their direct control. They replaced local officials with ruling party members and cronies loyal to them. They made use of state wealth and especially foreign loans to buy off or secure the loyalties of others. To win popular support, they used other instruments of modern state power, such as media control and propaganda, in which loyalty to nation and loyalty to the ruler were equated. They also relied on military force to guard their power, to suppress dissent, and sometimes to terrorize the population.

## □ The Militarization of African Politics

Presidential dictators in Africa, however, could not be certain of the loyalty of the military, and this proved to be the Achilles heel for many of them. In many African nations, military revolts supplanted presidential dictators with military dictators. Many of Africa's first line of rulers were overthrown by their own armies.[5] The overthrow of Ghana's Kwame Nkrumah in 1966 gave rise to a wave of military coups across Africa, and by 1980, no fewer than sixty coups had taken place. In Benin (formerly Dahomey), there were five military coups and another ten attempted coups between 1963 and 1972. Military officers with their own ésprit de corps and political ambitions had little difficulty in finding cause to overthrow unpopular corrupt rulers. Some of the new military rulers promised to restore rule to civilian politicians, but few actually did so. Some, like Zaire's Joseph Mobutu, retired their military uniforms and became presidents, whereas others became victims of later military coups. Most of the earlier coups were carried out by high-ranking officers, but as time went on, lower-ranking officers and even noncommissioned officers thrust themselves into power using the barrel of a gun. In Sierra Leone, army generals took power in 1967 but were overthrown several months later by other army officers, who in turn were soon ousted by a sergeants' revolt.

New military regimes were often welcomed by a disillusioned people, but because the military rulers were usually less prepared than the ousted politicians to cope with the problems of poverty, economic stagnation, and political unrest, they seldom succeeded. As they became more tyrannical and as corrupt as those of the civilian rulers they had overthrown, they quickly lost popular support and became ripe for overthrow by still other ambitious military officers.

The process of militarization in African politics was demonstrated by the experience of Ghana, a nation once looked upon as the pacesetter in Africa's drive for modernization. The charismatic Kwame Nkrumah, who had led the fight for independence, provided vigorous leadership as prime minister for a nation that, in the early 1960s, had the second-highest per capita income in Africa. As the most outspoken champion of pan-Africanism, Nkrumah became the spokesman for the liberation of other African colonies. He adopted a socialist program for Ghana that entailed nationalization of industries and state planning, but he did not attempt a social revolution involving land redistribution. Nkrumah was an inspirational nationalist who placed special emphasis on education as a vehicle for Ghana's development. But before his reorganization programs produced significant economic progress, Ghana was victimized by a drastic decline in the world price for cocoa, its principal cash crop. In the decade following independence, the price fell to a third of its previous level. Nkrumah's own corruption and extravagance became targets of criticism. Nkrumah did not tolerate dissent and became increasingly repressive. With the pressures of a bankrupt economy and popular unrest mounting, the volatile Nkrumah, now a dictator, jailed the opposition and silenced dissent. Finally, in February 1966, when he was away on a visit to China, the army toppled his regime.

In the years that followed, Ghana became the epitome of political instability as coup followed coup. The officers who grasped power in 1966 made good on their promise to restore civilian rule, but after a brief period of civilian rule a group of junior officers staged another coup in 1969, eliminating by firing squads former government leaders. After still another coup in 1972, Ghana remained under military rule through the 1970s. In 1979, a youthful flight lieutenant, Jerry Rawlings, shot his way to power and carried out another wave of executions. In 1980, however, he made good on his promise to give democracy another chance in Ghana. This, too, proved short-lived when, at the end of 1981, Rawlings once again seized power by force. Despite a host of problems, Rawlings remained popular, however; in 1992 and again in 1996, he won multiparty elections. In 2000, he decided to leave office—in compliance with the constitutional restriction of two terms—provided the election was "fair, genuine and sincere."[6] All the while, however, Ghana's economic and social woes continued to worsen.

Many of Africa's military leaders have been brutal, but few have exceeded the brutality of Idi Amin of Uganda. In 1971, Amin—an army officer—staged a coup, overthrowing the dictatorship of Milton Obote. Soon Amin found scapegoats for the economic and social ills of Uganda in several minority tribes and in the community of Asian (mainly Indian) residents of the country. In 1972, Amin forcefully expelled some fifty thousand Asians, an act most detrimental to the economy since many of them were merchants and professionals. As conditions worsened, Amin resorted to torture, public executions, and assassinations. Meanwhile, he launched an attack on neighboring Tanzania and used the pretext of war to further terrorize his own people. After surviving a number of plots on his life, he was finally overthrown in 1979 by a force from Tanzania, which then installed a civilian government. Before his removal from power, Amin had massacred an estimated 250,000 of his own people, caused about as many to flee the country, and left Uganda in shambles. In 1980, Milton Obote returned to power as dictator. His regime continued military "cleanup operations" but never succeeded in restoring order. In the end, he eventually killed almost as many people as Amin had and caused another wave of refugees fleeing the stricken country.

## ■ THE BIAFRAN WAR

Nigeria provides another case of militarization and offers an example of the consequences of ethnic conflict. During the early years of independence, no country made greater efforts to overcome ethnic disunity, yet none subsequently spilled more blood in ethnic strife. At the time of independence, Nigeria, Africa's most populous nation and one of its wealthiest, was a federal republic of three self-governing regions, each dominated by a major ethnic group—the Hausa-Fulani in the northern region (approximately 15 million strong), the Yoruba in the western region (15 million), and the Ibo in the southeastern region (10 million). Tensions remained high among these groups since each feared domination by the other. The first census in independent Nigeria only added to the suspicion that the northerners were about to abolish the federal system of power sharing. The census, manipulated by northerners, declared that the northern region contained an absolute majority of the population and thus could create a government dominated by Hausa and Fulani. The census upset the balance of power, charged the political atmosphere, and set the stage for the political crisis that followed.[7]

In January 1966, military officers—mainly Ibos—staged a coup and established a military regime under General J. T. Ironsi. The northerners, who were mainly Muslims, feared and resented the largely Christian and better-educated Ibos, who had enjoyed commercial and political privileges under British rule and during the early years of independence. The northerners saw the coup as an attempt to destroy the power of the Hausa-Fulani oligarchy.

At the end of May 1966, the northern general, Yakubu Gowon, staged his own coup and kidnapped (and later murdered) Ironsi and members of his government. It was at this point that the first wave of assaults against the Ibos took place, first in the north where tens of thousands were massacred and 2 million were driven to flight. In July 1966, Ibo soldiers in the Nigerian army were massacred. Additional attacks on Ibos followed. An Ibo brotherhood called upon Ibos throughout the country "to come home." On May 30, 1967, at the regional capital of Enugu, an Oxford-educated lieutenant colonel, C. O. Ojukwu, issued the declaration of independence of the Republic of Biafra. The declaration denounced the "evils and injustices"—not the least of which were the "premeditated and planned" pogroms—carried out by the military government.[8] Now came the difficult task of defending the independence of Biafra.

The Biafran rebels quickly found out that they stood alone. Only four of Africa's fifty-odd nations and one European state, France, recognized Biafra. France did so because Biafra was located in the oil-rich southeastern corner of Nigeria and contained the nation's largest oil field and its only refinery. The African nations, even though they had denounced repeatedly the arbitrary borders the European colonialists had carved out, did not want to see a dangerous secessionist precedent take place.

General Gowon treated the rebellion as a Nigerian matter that was not the business of others. The United Nations and the rest of the world accommodated him. When the great powers did become involved, notably Britain and the Soviet Union, they did so in support of a united Nigeria. Britain sought to maintain its political and economic influence in Nigeria. Moreover, within a week after the Biafran declaration of independence, the Six Day War in the Middle East closed the Suez Canal, and Nigeria's oil suddenly became more important for Britain. The Soviets, in turn, sought to increase their influence in Africa and thus provided Gowon's army—the likely winner—with modern weapons. This was the first time in modern history an African nation fought a war using weapons provided by outside powers, but it would not be the last. Civil wars and secessionist movements armed by outside powers were later responsible for the destruction of much of Angola, Mozambique, Ethiopia, and Somalia.

Biafra's resistance ended after thirty months. Defeats on the battlefield, bombing raids, and widespread starvation took their toll. In January 1970, the Ibos surrendered. Gowon insisted that no retribution be taken and that the Ibos be reintegrated into Nigerian society. A Nigerian colonel described the aftermath to a U.S. reporter: "It was like a referee blowing a whistle in a football game. People just put down their guns and went back to the business of living."[9]

## ■ FOREIGN INTERVENTION

Political instability and economic disaster following independence made African nations ripe for exploitation and intervention by outside powers. At the outset of independence, African leaders sought to eliminate dependence on foreign powers and insisted on "African solutions to African problems." It was largely in quest of this ideal that the Organization of African Unity (OAU) was formed in 1963. This body never achieved a meaningful concert of Africa, as the nations tended to pull apart and most maintained closer ties with their former colonial masters in Europe than with their neighbors. They continued to rely on the Europeans for economic aid and sometimes military assistance as well, and the Europeans continued to invest in Africa and to protect their investments. France, in particular, maintained a military presence of more than fifteen thousand troops, including its highly mobile *force d'intervention.* As the gap between African economic development and that of the industrialized nations widened, especially after the oil crises in the 1970s, the Africans were forced all the more to depend on foreign aid and became even more vulnerable to meddling by outside powers. These powers were not limited to the former colonial powers of Europe but came to include the United States and the Soviet Union, which, in their global struggle, were eager to make themselves indispensable to new African friends and to check the spreading influence of the other.

China, too, competed for influence in Africa. Its boldest undertaking in Africa was the building of the 1,200-mile Tanzam "Great Freedom" railroad in the mid-1970s, linking landlocked Zambia with the Tanzanian port city of Dar es Salaam. The $500 million project—which employed some twenty thousand Chinese and fifty thousand African workers—was undertaken after Britain, Canada, and the United States declined the project. The United States had earlier missed an opportunity to expand its influence in northern Africa when, in 1956, it rejected Egypt's request for financial backing to build the Aswan Dam on the Nile River. The Soviet Union moved in within a year to build the dam and temporarily won Egypt as a client state.

The United States offered security arrangements, weapons, and economic aid to its African clients; the Soviet Union similarly supplied weapons and economic assistance, especially to those nations whose leaders paid lip service to Marxism. Although the United States provided much more developmental aid to African nations than did the Soviet Union, it did not win more friends. Nowhere was this more evident than in the United Nations, where African nations and the Soviet Union—sharing an anticolonialist viewpoint—often voted the same way, whereas the United States was seldom able to count on the votes of these nations.

Advocacy of Marxism by an African leader, however, did not necessarily signify successful Soviet intervention. Marxism-Leninism was in vogue in the early postindependence years, as new African leaders were attracted to the ideology for its explanation of past colonial exploitation and neocolonialism. (Neocolonialism, as Ghana's Nkrumah explained, was domination—mainly economic—that the Western colonial powers continued to exercise over their former colonies.)[10] They also found in Marxism-Leninism a model for political organization and state planning for economic modernization. But nations that adopted Marxism and established close ties with Moscow, such as Guinea and Angola, found developmental aid from the Soviet Union to be disappointingly meager. Some African leaders, such as Nkrumah and Tanzania's Nyerere, conjured up their own brands of "African socialism," a blend of Marxist ideas and indigenous African notions, which were usually vague and had little resemblance to either Marxism or the Soviet system. In any case, it was difficult to distinguish between those African states that were nominally socialist and those that claimed to be capitalist, for in all of them state planning and control of the economy were common. "The distinction between socialist and capitalist states in Africa," two noted African specialists have explained, "has often proved to be more one of rhetoric than reality. . . . In the last resort, the socialist or capitalist jargon employed in any individual state is often a reflection of where external aid was coming from at a particular time."[11]

It was not until the mid-1970s, with the end of Portuguese colonial rule in southern Africa, that a direct confrontation between the superpowers occurred in Africa. The departure of Portugal created a volatile situation across southern Africa, not only because power was up for grabs in Portugal's former colonies but also because the buffer between black African nations and the white supremacist regime of South Africa had been removed. South Africa now found itself threatened by the accession of a Marxist regime in Mozambique in 1975, the transfer of power to a black government in Zimbabwe (formerly Rhodesia) in 1980, and the increasing resolve of Botswana, Zambia, and other black African nations to oppose its racist policies. As a consequence, South Africa resorted increasingly to military force, intervening in Angola, Mozambique, and Lesotho.

In defiance of the United Nations, South Africa continued to dominate Namibia,[12] occupying it militarily and thwarting its demand for independence. In 1975, it installed a puppet black government in Namibia and promised to grant it independence. The left-leaning South-West Africa People's Organization (SWAPO), the largest Namibian party, was left out of the government and, supported by black African nations, it continued guerrilla resistance in its fight for Namibian independence.

The focal point of international struggle in sub-Saharan Africa between 1975 and 1990 was Angola, where the largest buildup of foreign military forces in Africa in postcolonial times took place. The outside forces were from nations such as the United States, the Soviet Union, the People's Republic of China, Cuba, Zaire, and South Africa. When Portugal withdrew in April 1975, three separate Marxist Angolan revolutionary groups rivaled each other for power. The Popular Movement for the Liberation of Angola (MPLA), a group founded in 1956 and the one engaged longest in the fight for independence, was in control of the capital city of Luanda. The National

Front for the Liberation of Angola (FNLA), established in 1962, held control of the mountainous region in the north. And the National Union for the Total Independence of Angola (UNITA), founded in 1966, representing the Ovimbundu—the largest ethnic group in Angola—ruled in the central and southern regions. The transitional government established by the Portuguese collapsed in June 1975, and foreign powers intervened in support of rival revolutionary groups.

Typically, the United States and the Soviet Union accused each other of meddling in Angola and claimed their own involvement was justified by the aggression of the other. By the time fighting began in mid-1975, the MPLA had received Soviet financial support and was assisted by Cuban advisers and a Zairean military unit, and the FNLA and UNITA were receiving financial support and covert military assistance from the CIA. By September, the MPLA had won a decisive victory against the FNLA, and it then battled a UNITA force backed by South African troops. The South African entry into the conflict led to stepped-up CIA action in Angola, as well as a huge increase in Soviet and Cuban assistance for the MPLA. In November 1975, the scales were tipped heavily in favor of the MPLA with the arrival of a massive amount of Soviet and Cuban armaments and several thousand Cuban troops. By the end of the year, the MPLA's victory appeared complete, and it formed a new Angolan government.

In Washington, the administration of Gerald Ford and its secretary of state, Henry Kissinger, refused to accept what they considered a Soviet victory. Continued U.S. military aid to UNITA rebels and South African military involvement in the years that followed served to keep the Angolan situation alive as an international issue. Indeed, this issue was one of several that brought, by the end of the 1970s, an end to the era of détente between the United States and the Soviet Union.

## ■ THE WORSENING ECONOMIC PLIGHT OF SUB-SAHARAN AFRICA

The 1980s saw an increase in the living standard throughout much of the globe, except for nations at war, such as Afghanistan, Nicaragua, El Salvador, Cambodia, Iran, and Iraq. The most important exception, however, was sub-Saharan Africa, the region that covers all of Africa with the exception of the Arabic-speaking belt along the shores of the Mediterranean Sea in the north.

From 1965—that is, shortly after independence—through the 1980s, per capita income in sub-Saharan Africa grew a mere 0.6 percent.[13] Overall, economic growth averaged 3.4 percent per year, barely above the increase in population. Between 1970 and 1987, the rate of growth of agricultural production declined; it grew at a pace of less than half of the rate of population growth, 1.4 percent against 3.3 percent. Droughts and the increasing drying-up of the Sahel, the belt directly south of the Sahara, were in part to blame for the decline in agricultural production. Whatever economic gains sub-Saharan Africa had enjoyed during the preceding thirty years were eaten up by the phenomenal rise in population. A World Bank report concluded that "never in human history has population grown so fast." By the year 2010, the region's population was expected to more than double, to over 1 billion. Often the result of such growth is hunger. Nearly one-quarter of the population faced "chronic food insecurity." Family planning was needed to reduce the threat of hunger and to improve health care. Sub-Saharan Africa had the highest rates of maternal and infant mortality in the world. In the poorest countries (Burkina Faso, Ethiopia, and Mali), one-quarter of the children died before they reached the age of five.

The 1980s saw further deterioration. Per capita income and food production continued to decrease; the share of sub-Saharan Africa's exports in world markets declined from 2.4 percent in 1970 to 1.3 percent in 1987; and the region witnessed, in the terse language of a World Bank report, "accelerated ecological degradation." Several countries—among them Ghana, Liberia, and Zambia—had slipped from the middle-income to the low-income group. In 1987, the region's population of 450 million produced only as much wealth as Belgium's 10 million. The world's per capita GNP in 1987 stood at $3,010; for sub-Saharan Africa, the figure was $330.[14]

Another problem, one that went back to the 1960s, was the high level of public expenditures for government, schools, and the military. The World Bank stressed that a direct link existed between low military spending and good economic performance, as in Botswana and Mauritius. It addressed here for the first time the question of official corruption, although only briefly and gingerly. "Bad habits," it noted, "are hard to undo," such as the siphoning of millions of foreign aid dollars into private overseas accounts. An unfettered and vigilant press, playing the role of a watchdog, was all too rare. The nations with the best economic performance—Botswana and Mauritius—had parliamentary democracies and a free press.

Meanwhile, the nations of sub-Saharan Africa were increasingly unable to pay off their mounting debts. The region was overburdened by an external debt that totaled nearly $106 billion in 1987, up from $5.3 billion in 1970 and $41.2 billion in 1980.

## ■ AFRICA IN THE EARLY 1990S: THE CALL FOR DEMOCRACY

In the early 1990s, a number of factors came together. For one, the Cold War had ended, and the countries of that region were no longer considered important after the superpower rivalry had come to an end. It was no longer necessary for either Moscow or Washington to prop up African dictators. Second, it became possible, therefore, for political factions to try to resolve their problems without outside interference. Third, the world's leading international financial institutions, notably the International Monetary Fund (IMF) and the World Bank, had come to the realization that the region's economic plight could not be resolved without governments becoming accountable for their actions. Britain's foreign secretary, Douglas Hurd, declared in 1990 that "governments which persisted with repressive policies, corrupt management and wasteful, discredited economic systems should not expect us to support their folly with scarce aid resources."[15] French president François Mitterand delivered the same message at a Franco-African summit meeting when he stated that there could be "no development without democracy and no democracy without development."[16]

The year 1990 saw the rise of protest from below as political discontents—students and scholars, labor unions (often including government employees), and the impoverished masses—railed against oppressive government, corruption, and deprivation. Strikes, protest marches, and riots suddenly had an effect on dictators who for many years had been impervious to criticism. The main instrument for political change in Africa in the early 1990s was the "national conference." Opposition leaders demanded the convening of these conferences, where the political future of the nation was to be deliberated and political groups could present their demands and proposals for multiparty elections.

One of the first nations to undergo such a political transformation was Benin. In 1990, Benin's President Mathieu Kerekou—military dictator for seventeen years—bowed to political pressure and convened a national conference, which proceeded to strip him of his powers, appoint an interim president, call for a presidential election, and draft a new constitution. Kerekou accepted the decisions of the national conference and, after being defeated by his opponent by a two-to-one margin in the March 1991 election, he became the first African ruler to be voted out of office. Benin's national conference became a model for political change in Africa, particularly in the former French colonies.

Not all of Africa's strongmen succumbed to the demands for democratic change, nor did all those promising to hold free elections keep their promises or abide by their results. A case in point was Mobutu, the heavy-handed dictator of Zaire since 1965. In April 1990, he announced an end to one-party government and promised to accept the verdict of a free, multiparty election. When elections were finally held, Mobutu received over 99 percent of the votes, hardly the hallmark of a free election. In the Central African Republic, strongman President André Kolingba authorized opposition parties and scheduled an election in October 1992, but then abruptly halted the election in progress and arrested the opposition. Another holdout was President Daniel arap Moi of Kenya, who denounced the movement for multiparty elections as "garbage" and an invitation for chaos. His police then gunned down protesters.[17] After a year and a half of continued political agitation and after Western governments had terminated aid to Kenya, arap Moi finally consented to legalize opposition parties in December 1991 and to call an election a year later. He then manipulated the election to make certain he remained in power.

Most of the dictators had no intention of relinquishing power. Instead, they participated in "democratic" reforms in order to legitimatize and extend their own rule, to pacify the opposition and foreign critics, and to avoid economic retribution at the hands of aid-granting nations. Not all of the widely proclaimed elections, therefore, were free or fair. Several erstwhile rulers, including Ivory Coast's President Félix Houphouët-Boigny, one of Africa's more benevolent dictators who had been in power since the early 1960s, were not beyond rigging elections to stay in power. In October 1990, demonstrations forced him to legalize opposition parties and call an election, which, however, he took every precaution to win decisively.

In many African countries, claims of successful democratization proved either premature or baseless. By the end of the twentieth century, freedom of the press existed in only three of Africa's fifty-five states: South Africa, Senegal, and Mali.[18] Not until 1986 did the OAU come up with an African Charter of Human Rights and the Rights of Peoples. The charter's interpretation of human rights, however, differed from the Western definition, which stresses the protection of the individual against the powers of the state. In Africa the traditional group—whether family or state—is more important and the rights of individuals are limited. The right of assembly, for example, is subject to "necessary limitations," and individual liberties have to be reconciled with the rights of others, i.e., collective security, customs, and social interests. The OAU was hesitant to condemn member states, even in the case of systematic human rights violations such as in the case of Emperor Bokassa of the Central African Republic, who in 1972 led his soldiers into a prison to quell a disturbance and ended up maiming and murdering prisoners and then displaying the dismembered bodies to the crowds.[19]

## ■ FLASHPOINTS IN AFRICA IN THE 1990S

### □ Namibia, Angola, and Mozambique

The impact of the end of the Cold War was felt quickly in three war-torn countries in southern Africa: Namibia, Angola, and Mozambique. Soviet ruler Mikhail Gorbachev withdrew financial support for the leftist government in Angola and for the maintenance of Cuban troops deployed in that country and in neighboring Namibia. U.S.-sponsored and Soviet-supported negotiations produced an agreement in December 1988 that led to the evacuation of

Cuban troops from Angola in exchange for a South African troop withdrawal from Namibia. UN negotiators brought together opposing revolutionary groups who (again with U.S. and Soviet support) drafted one of Africa's most democratic constitutions and then held one of Africa's freest and fairest elections. In March 1990, the Namibian government, headed by SWAPO leader Sam Nujoma, celebrated the end of seventy-five years of colonial rule and twenty-three years of guerrilla warfare.

Gorbachev's withdrawal from the Third World affected Angola as well, but the impact was delayed because of the unrelenting civil war. The conflict pitted the Soviet/Cuban–supported MPLA government headed by José Eduardo dos Santos against the U.S./South African–supported UNITA guerrilla forces of Jonas Savimbi, a former self-proclaimed Maoist who compared his military campaigns to Mao's "long march." Neither this nor his brutality (Human Rights Watch reported incidents of witches burned alive) prevented Savimbi—since he was fighting the Soviet-backed Cubans—from becoming a darling of the political right in the United States. In 1986, President Ronald Reagan had invited him to the White House and praised his struggle "for freedom." The inconclusive war had exhausted both sides. With Portugal, the former colonial ruler, serving as peace broker and Washington and Moscow cooperating in applying pressure on the two sides to resolve their differences, a settlement was finally signed in May 1991. The agreement called for the adoption of market-oriented economic reforms, the demobilization and integration of the two military forces, and an election by the end of 1992. The breakthrough promised to end the sixteen years of continuous and crippling warfare that had devastated the country, claimed over three hundred thousand lives, and given Angola the morbid distinction of having the world's highest per capita of amputees.[20]

The new armistice held as both sides prepared for the impending elections. Angola's first free multiparty presidential election took place in September 1992 and was relatively free of irregularities. The victor was dos Santos, but Savimbi, charging election fraud, disputed the election even before the results were in. Gunfire once again rang out in the streets of Luanda. The United States, the United Nations, and African leaders urged the recalcitrant revolutionary to lay down his arms and accept the election's verdict. Savimbi, however, by now an isolated international pariah, remained defiant, and his armed resistance continued until government troops hunted him down and shot him to death. The civil war was over.

At the same time, a similar sequence of events unfolded in Mozambique, another former Portuguese colony in southern Africa. There, too, a long, bloody civil war between a Soviet-backed Marxist government and a South African–supported right-wing rebel force, Renamo (the Mozambique Nationalist Resistance), ended with a negotiated settlement. The peace agreement between Renamo and the government in September 1992 terminated an extraordinarily brutal war that had claimed nearly a million lives.

It also set the stage for UN-supervised elections and opened the way for desperately needed foreign aid to reach the people of this blighted country, where about one-quarter of the population of 15 million had become refugees, over 3 million people faced starvation, and in 1990, Mozambique's per capita GNP of $80 was the world's lowest.[21]

## ☐　Sudan, Ethiopia, and Somalia

The most war-ravaged and famine-stricken nations in Africa were Ethiopia and Somalia, where starvation, disease, and the displacement of peoples were endemic. In 1990, drought returned to Sudan and Ethiopia, causing crop failures and famine and forcing farmers to eat their remaining animals and seed grain. The main cause of misery, however, was the ceaseless civil wars.

In Sudan, war between the government in the north and the Sudan People's Liberation Army in the south had deep-seated ethnic and religious roots. In the heavily Muslim north, Arab and Egyptian Mamluk influence was strong; in the south, darker-skinned Africans, many of them Christians, resisted northern domination. Prospects for a peaceful resolution of the conflict were set back in 1989 when a military junta took power in the capital of Khartoum and announced plans for establishing an Islamic state. As the fighting continued, some 8 million Sudanese were in desperate need of food, many becoming wandering refugees in regions beyond the reach of overland food shipments. Additionally, the darker-skinned people in the south were subjected to slavery by northerners, even though the government in Khartoum denied it when it was brought to international attention.

In April 2003, five weeks after U.S. president George W. Bush invaded Iraq, ostensibly to bring human rights to that nation, the world's largest human catastrophe began to unfold in Sudan. Between April 2003 and the end of 2004, at least seventy thousand black African Sudanese had been murdered and another million and a half had become refugees surviving on the edge of starvation.

The conflict took place in Darfur (literally, "the land of the Fur,"), the western provinces of Sudan. It pitted nomadic Arabs against the indigenous Fur who had long cultivated the land. The two had long coexisted; they had intermarried and the Fur had become Muslims centuries ago. In the mid-1970s, however, as a prolonged drought ravaged Darfur accompanied by a population explosion,[22] farmers and herders began to engage in sporadic clashes.[23] The military regime in Khartoum, dominated by Arabs, took the side of the herders. In April 2003, the conflict took another bloody turn when Darfur rebels, organized as the Sudanese Liberation Army, claiming governmental discrimination and exploitation, attacked military garrisons destroying helicopters and airplanes, and killing approximately one hundred soldiers. At the time, the government was still seeking to resolve a bloody twenty-one-year-long conflict in the south that pitted northern Muslim Arabs against indigenous Christians. To complicate matters for the government, 40 percent of its armed forces came from Darfur who, understandably, were reluctant to fight against the rebels.

To solve this problem, it turned to Musa Hilal, an Arab sheik whose family had long been in conflict with blacks in Darfur. During the 1990s, the government had imprisoned Hilal for murder, armed robbery, and tax evasion. Still, it released Hilal who then, with government support, created an army of marauders, the *janjaweed* (literally, "evil horsemen" or simply "bandits"), who were not only given governmental immunity to engage in ethnic cleansing and to plunder, murder, and rape, but were in fact supported by it.

The conflict, however, was more than just over land. Since the late 1980s, under the influence of Muammar Qaddafi of Libya, Arabs had been attempting to establish an "Arab belt" south of the Sahara. "Arabism" was to become the political ideology of sub-Saharan Africa. The violence in Darfur was thus fueled by economic, ethnic, and religious causes—even though both sides were Muslim. The *janjaweed* argued that they—and not the black Africans—were the original settlers of the land, that Arabs had brought civilization to the region, and that they were hardly bandits, but *mujahidin* (freedom fighters) protecting they own people.

By April 2004, the ongoing tragedy began to make headlines around the world, at a time when the United Nations commemorated the ten-year anniversary of the slaughter in Rwanda (see below). In April 2004, U.S. president Bush insisted that "the government of Sudan must not remain complicit in the brutalization of Darfur." Kofi Annan, the UN's secretary-general, spoke of the prospect of "military action."[24] And in July 2004, the U.S. Congress, under the influence of evangelical Christians who had long sought to drum up international support against Khartoum's atrocities against fellow Christians in the south of Sudan, played a leading role in passing a resolution condemning "genocide" in Darfur. This marked the first time that the U.S. Congress had used the word to discuss the ongoing massacre. The U.S. State Department would not go so far as to call it officially genocide, but in September 2004, Secretary of State Colin Powell did for the first time speak of genocide. In August 2004, the UN Security Council gave Khartoum thirty days to disarm the *janjaweed,* threatening it with sanctions. Khartoum responded that the demand was unreasonable, comparing it with the inability of the United States to disarm militants in Iraq. After the thirty days had expired, neither the Bush administration—militarily overextended in Iraq—nor the United Nations had an answer to the violence in Darfur.

Ethiopia witnessed Africa's longest civil war, between the government in Addis Ababa and Eritrean rebels. After the overthrow of Emperor Haile Selassie in 1974 by a brutal Marxist junta headed by Mengistu Haile Miriam, the Soviet Union provided over \$11 billion in military and economic aid. Arrayed against him were ethnic-based rebel armies such as the People's Revolutionary Democratic Front in Tigre Province and the Eritrean People's Liberation Front. The Eritrean fight for independence began in 1952, shortly after the United Nations had transferred Eritrea (previously an Italian colony along the shores of the Red Sea) to Ethiopia. Ironically, the Eritrean rebel leaders were Marxists who fought the Marxist government and many of the Tigre rebels were also Marxist.

In 1990, the Soviet Union shut off military aid to the Ethiopian government, and soon thereafter rebel forces gained the upper hand. In April 1991, as rebel armies closed in on Addis Ababa and Eritrean forces liberated their homeland in the north along the coast of the Red Sea, Mengistu fled the country and with it down came the statues of Lenin in Addis Ababa. With the restoration of order, urgently needed international food relief and developmental aid began to arrive.The new Ethiopian government of Meles Zenawi and the Eritrean People's Liberation Front agreed to accept the results of an internationally supervised referendum on independence held in May 1993. The outcome of the referendum was a foregone conclusion. The Eritreans' long war for independence was finally crowned with victory.

In neighboring Somalia, the superpower rivalry left behind a devastated nation. Its ruler, Mohammed Siad Barre, had maintained a semblance of order in that country for twenty-one years by force of arms (supplied first by the Soviet Union and then by the United States), but in January 1991, he was forced by opposing clans to flee the capital of Mogadishu. Various rebel forces then fought for control of the capital. It was a clan feud, a fight for power by forces armed with a wide array of U.S. and Soviet weapons. Somalia quickly became a lawless land wracked by savage fighting, fear, looting, and starvation. Jeeps roamed the streets of Mogadishu mounted with recoilless rifles, many of them manned by teenage soldiers. In a three-month period at the end of 1991, an estimated twenty-five thousand people— mostly civilians—were killed or wounded in the fighting, and a quarter of a million residents of the capital were expelled.

The combination of drought and warfare produced a famine as severe as any in modern times. Nongovernmental relief agencies such as the Red Cross, CARE, and Save the Children (a British-based charity) managed to deliver thousands of tons of food a day, but many interior areas of Somalia and even some sections of Mogadishu were beyond reach. All too often, warring forces stole the food. In mid-1992, the UN Security Council sent emergency food airlifts into Somalia protected by a token UN force of five hundred armed guards. The UN relief missions frequently came under armed attack at the airport and ships laden with UN relief food were denied permission to unload at the docks. Finally, in December 1992, the United Nations sanctioned a request from U.S. president George H. W. Bush to send a UN military operation led by twenty-eight thousand U.S. troops to ensure the distribution of food and medicines. By the time the world's largest armed humanitarian rescue mission was launched, an estimated three hundred thousand Somalis already had died of starvation, and as many as one-third of the 6 million people of Somalia were in danger of succumbing to the same fate.

Bush envisioned a purely humanitarian mission of short duration; UN secretary-general Boutros Boutros-Ghali, however, proclaimed a larger mission: to disarm the Somali warlords and establish political stability in the country. The new U.S. president, Bill Clinton, accepted this expanded mission to eliminate the political source of mayhem and famine in Somalia.

Initially, the U.S.-led intervention in Somalia was an admirable success, making possible the delivery of life-saving food to hundreds of thousands of people, but this achievement was soon overshadowed by military failure. Clinton authorized U.S. soldiers to engage in a manhunt for the Somalian warlord considered most responsible for the continued violence, General Mohammed Farah Aidid. His capture was deemed all the more important after his troops had ambushed and killed twenty-four Pakistani UN soldiers in June 1993. Meanwhile, opposition to the extended military operations in Somalia was mounting in Washington. In October 1993, an unsuccessful U.S. Army Ranger raid on Aidid's headquarters led to a furious day-long firefight that left eighteen U.S. soldiers dead and eighty wounded. Worse yet was the spectacle of Aidid's troops dragging the corpse of a U.S. soldier through the streets of Mogadishu. The Clinton administration quickly decided to cut its losses and, instead of fighting Aidid, the United States accepted him as a political leader who held one of the keys to restoring peace and order in Somalia.

Peace and political order remained elusive, however. Sporadic warfare between Aidid's clan and various rivals continued during the remaining year and a half of the UN operation in Somalia. In the end, the operation—which cost over $2 billion (30 percent of which was borne by the United States) and hundreds of casualties—was a political and military failure. The operation, coupled with a plentiful harvest in 1994, however, did bring to an end the famine.

## ☐ Ethnic Violence in Burundi and Rwanda

The bloodiest confrontations between blacks in postcolonial Africa took place between the Tutsis and the Hutus in the center of the continent, the Great Lakes region in Burundi and Rwanda. Widespread violence, the consequence of ethnic and class divisions, began as the Belgians granted independence to their colonies in 1960.

The origins of the two peoples are not clear. The Hutus arrived in the Great Lakes region well before the Tutsis, who came from around the Horn of Africa, perhaps from Ethiopia, 400–500 years ago. The Tutsis were cattle herders, the Hutus were cultivators. By the mid-nineteenth century, when the first reliable records were kept, the two groups had developed a common culture (spirit faiths, cuisine, folk customs) and languages. Occasionally, they also intermarried. By that time, there were so few ethnic distinctions that one could not readily call them two different ethnic groups; the division was made mainly on the basis of class.

The Europeans helped to intensify the class and ethnic divisions between the Tutsis and the Hutus. The Belgians had stressed the differences between them and issued ethnic identity cards. They treated the minority Tutsis (15 percent of the population) as a separate, superior ethnic entity and favored them for educational, professional, and administrative opportunities. The majority Hutus (85 percent) were treated as an inferior group.

By the time the Belgians withdrew in 1962, the divisions were deep. The colonial system of using ethnic identity cards remained in force. Ever since, the history of Rwanda and Burundi has been marked by Hutu uprisings and massacres of Tutsis, followed by brutal Tutsi repression. In Rwanda in 1965, after Tutsi extremists had assassinated the Hutu prime minister three days after he had been appointed, Hutu military officers attempted a coup. Tutsi reprisals were extremely brutal in an attempt to wipe out the first generation of postcolonial Hutu political leaders. In 1972, following another Hutu rebellion—this one in Burundi—the Tutsis responded with what can only be called a genocidal fury. In a span of three months, they killed approximately 250,000 Hutus and purged the army, the government, and the economy of Hutu elements. In fact, both sides practiced murder and ethnic cleansing in a way that was unambiguously genocidal in nature. By this time, the Belgian myth of two different tribes had been turned into reality. The Tutsis and Hutus feared each other and began to construct their own mythical versions of their past, which only further solidified the divisions, fear, and hatred.[25]

In Burundi in 1987, Tutsi general Pierre Buyoya attempted to bring about a reconciliation between the two groups. But suspicion ran so deep that reconciliation proved impossible. In August 1988, a confrontation between Tutsi administrators and Hutu civilians in northern Burundi sparked a renewal of violence. Hutu and Tutsi mobs once again began to slaughter each other indiscriminately. Many anticipated violence and responded with preemptive violence. Tutsi control of Burundi continued until June 1993, when the country elected its first Hutu president, Melchior Ndadaye. Six months later, in December 1993, the Tutsi military assassinated him. This event touched off another round of bloodletting. In the first six months alone, the estimated death toll was between 50,000 and 100,000, and 600,000 refugees fled into neighboring countries.

Ethnic violence in Burundi was soon overshadowed by a far greater massacre in neighboring Rwanda. Under the banner of "Hutu Power," President

Juvenal Habyarimana, who had ruled Rwanda since 1973, forced many Tutsis into exile in neighboring Zaire. In 1990, exiled Tutsis in Zaire formed the Rwandan Patriotic Front (RPF), whose aim was to reclaim power in Rwanda. An RPF invasion of Rwanda in October of that year provoked the government to step up its Hutu Power campaign of violence against the Tutsis. The immediate cause for the outbreak of violence was the assassination of President Habyarimana in April 1994, when his plane was shot down over Kigali, the Rwandan capital. Hutu soldiers blamed the incident on Tutsis and immediately began to avenge Habyarimana's death with indiscriminate massacres of any and all Tutsis, as well as moderate Hutus—particularly those who had married Tutsis. The militants forced other Hutus to join in this orgy of murder or be killed themselves. Mobs conducted house-to-house searches, hunting down and killing their victims with whatever weapons they had at their disposal—machine guns, machetes, spears, knives, and clubs. People were herded into buildings, including churches, which were then set ablaze.

In the end, the Tutsis, true to their military tradition, fought back and took revenge. They rallied to the RPF, which fought its way into the capital and expelled the Hutu government and its army. In July 1994, RPF leader Paul Kagame set up a new government with a moderate Hutu as a figurehead president and himself as vice-president and defense minister. Kagame, who retained actual power, took effective measures to halt the violence—including Tutsi crimes of vengeance against Hutus—and before long assured the Hutu refugees that it was safe to return home. When the carnage ended in Rwanda, a country of 8 million people, between eight hundred thousand and 1 million Rwandans lay dead, murdered in less than two months, the greatest ever slaughter during such a short period.[26] In the capital city of Kigali alone, a hundred thousand had been slaughtered.

The refugee problem generated by the bloodletting was of immense proportions. Between 1.1 and 1.5 million refugees—mainly Hutus, fearing for their lives—streamed into neighboring Zaire, and another 350,000 poured into Tanzania. Besieged relief workers were overwhelmed. Donor nations and international relief agencies sent food and medicine, but even though a total of over $1.4 billion in aid was sent (one-fourth of total worldwide relief aid in 1994), it proved insufficient and tardy. Thousands of refugees died from hunger and disease in refugee camps. The UN High Commissioner for Refugees negotiated a repatriation agreement with the new government of Rwanda, which again gave assurances to the Hutu refugees that it was safe to return home, but few were persuaded to do so.

Only when the slaughter was over, did the United Nations act. At the end of 1994, it established in Arusha, Tanzania, a court of justice modeled after the Nuremberg and Tokyo war crimes tribunals after World War II. An international tribunal was commissioned to undertake the herculean task of trying more than a hundred thousand genocide suspects in Rwanda. After three years of taking testimony, in September 1998 it obtained its first convictions, that of a small-town Hutu mayor, Jean-Paul Akayesu, for inciting fellow Hutus to kill Tutsis. It then convicted former Rwandan prime minister, Jean Kambanda, who became the first head of any government to be convicted of genocide. It also established a precedent in international law when it ruled that rape could be an aspect of genocide. In June 2001, a court in Belgium also convicted two Rwandan Catholic nuns of war crimes, making it the first time that a court from one country had judged defendants for crimes committed in another.

The judicial process in Arusha was maddeningly slow and limited in scope. Tutsis complained that the prosecutions took too long and that only sixty-three individuals had been charged with genocide; moreover, Tutsis refused to permit the tribunal to investigate its Rwandan Patriotic Front for any crimes it may have committed.

☐  *Conflict in Zaire*

In 1996, the Hutu-Tutsi war spilled beyond the borders of Rwanda and Burundi. By this time, the Rwandan Hutu militants in Zaire had linked up with the Zairean army in an effort to oust Tutsis indigenous to the eastern region of Zaire. The Zairean Tutsis, in turn, were armed and supported by Tutsis from Rwanda and Uganda. The chaotic fighting caused many Hutu refugees to take flight from their camps into the surrounding bush in search of safety. At the end of 1996, as a consequence of continued Hutu-Tutsi fighting in Zaire, large numbers of desperate Hutu refugees were finally persuaded to return to Rwanda. Once again, roads were clogged with hundreds of thousands of refugees, balancing on their heads bundles containing their only belongings—this time heading home to Rwanda and an uncertain future.

The violence in eastern Zaire soon became a full-scale civil war when the Tutsis were joined by Laurent Désiré Kabila who for more than thirty years had sought Mobutu's overthrow. As a young man, Kabila had been a Marxist and a supporter of Patrice Lumumba and had gotten to know the Cuban revolutionary Ché Guevara. Guevara, however, had come away disenchanted from their meeting, noting in his diary that Kabila's forces lacked discipline and that Kabila himself was "too addicted to drink and women."[27] After Mobutu's rise to power in 1965, Kabila fled to eastern Zaire from where he launched a number of unsuccessful raids to overthrow Mobutu while receiving some support from the Soviet Union and Communist China. In the meantime, he became engaged in the trafficking of precious materials such as ivory, gold, and diamonds, as well as alcohol and prostitution.

By the mid-1990s, the corrupt regime of the aged and ailing Mobutu had scant popular support. Under Mobutu, *The Economist* noted, Zaire had "experienced more than corruption. . . . It saw the systemic theft of the state, from top to bottom . . . his bank account [being] indistinguishable from the national treasury."[28] Since 1965, Zaire's economy had hit rock bottom. Zaire, the size of Western Europe, had only 200 miles of paved roads; in the capital of Kinshasa 90 percent were unemployed. In the spring of 1997, Mobutu's regime collapsed like a house of cards.

Kabila promised to bring freedom and democracy and disavowed his Marxist past, declaring "that was 30 years ago. Yeltsin was a Marxist 30 years ago." In May 1997, his troops entered Kinshasa where he proclaimed a new order and a new name for the country: the Democratic Republic of Congo. The long-suffering people welcomed the deliverance from thirty years of misrule and expected something better. The joy did not last long, however. Kabila compared his long struggle against Mobutu to "spreading fertilizer on a field" and that the "time to harvest" had come.[29] It was now the turn of Kabila and his men to collect the spoils of victory and to engage in human rights violations. Within a year, Kabila faced a rebellion out of the eastern provinces. Congolese Tutsis, now supported by Uganda and Burundi as well as Rwanda, turned on Kabila's forces. In Kinshasa, soldiers sympathetic to the rebels clashed with troops loyal to Kabila, who soon became dependent on troops from Angola, Namibia, and Zimbabwe to keep him in power. It became the most complicated of all African wars since independence, dubbed "Africa's first world war."

By the end of 2000, Kabila lost the eastern half of his nation to rebels and foreign invaders. The lion's share of partitioned Congo fell to Uganda. Rwanda, too, benefited financially; its capital, Kigali, became a market for gold and diamonds from Congo's Kivu Province.[30] The war, however, continued because it had become a more lucrative enterprise than peace.

In January 2001, Kabila was assassinated by palace guards and his son, Joseph, took over a divided nation wracked by a continuing civil war that, between 1998 and 2004, already had taken the lives of an estimated 3 million Congolese. UN peacekeepers proved to be ineffective as they could barely defend themselves.

☐ *Nigeria*

In oil-rich Nigeria, General Sani Abacha seized power in a coup in 1993, crushing all dissent. His greed knew no limit. His family fortune was estimated at $3 to $6 billion. In 1998, the general, bowing to foreign pressure, announced elections and his intention to run for president. He authorized five "opposition" parties and funded them once they each declared their support for his candidacy. Real political opponents—some seven thousand of them—were in prison, and several were sentenced to death by firing squads.

Nigeria was the world's sixth-largest exporter of oil; still it had to import refined fuel and ration gasoline because corruption had put the nation's refineries out of business.[31] Most of its people were without clean water, adequate health care, or reliable electricity. Before the scheduled election, Abacha died of a heart attack. His death made possible a free presidential election. The winner of the election in February 1999 was a retired general, Olusegun Obasanjo, who had the distinction of being the only Nigerian ruler to have given up power voluntarily. Obasanjo vowed to restore democracy and end corruption, but this would be a tall order. Since independence, Nigeria had been under military rule for all but ten years, and the legacy of military rule would be difficult to set aside. To complicate Obasanjo's task was the endemic poverty (approximately 90 percent of the population lived on $2 a day or less). There was also ethnic violence to contend with. In February 2000, violence in the northern province of Kaduna claimed four hundred lives, mostly Christians. It was the result of the imposition of Islamic religious law—the *sharia*—in the predominantly Muslim north by the cronies of the late dictator Abacha. The law provided for Islamic curricula in the public schools as well as the amputation of a hand for theft and public flogging for other crimes. It also forbade women from working outside the home or sharing public transportation with men.[32]

## ☐ Zimbabwe

In the 1960s, under the leadership of Ian Smith, the whites of Southern Rhodesia resisted as long as possible the "wind of change" calling for independence. The result was a war of nearly twenty years' duration that claimed approximately thirty thousand lives. In the end, the independence movement led by Robert Mugabe triumphed and, after promising black-white reconciliation, a black majority government under Mugabe took power in 1980.

At the time of independence, the presidents of neighboring Mozambique and Tanzania told Mugabe, "You have the jewel of Africa in your hands. Now look after it." Zimbabwe, as the country became known, had a fine railroad system, good roads, and a functioning hydroelectric system, and produced vast amounts of food (maize, peanuts, pineapples, mangoes, apples, etc.) and raw materials (gold, chromium, platinum, etc.). Blacks had done fairly well economically, although they had no political power.[33]

The white settlers eventually lost their political dominance, and their numbers declined from 278,000 in 1975 to 70,000 by 2000. Those who remained, however, retained their vast landholdings. An agreement in 1979 between the British government and Mugabe had stipulated that the white farmers were not to lose their land without compensation, that all land transfer was to be based on the principle of a "willing buyer, willing seller," and that London would help finance the transfer of land to impoverished black workers. It soon became apparent, however, that the transfer funds disappeared into the coffers of Mugabe and his allies.

Mugabe and his supporters focused on enriching themselves at the expense of the economy at large, which by the end of the 1990s was in

ruins from neglect. The telephone system, once the best in Africa, func-
tioned only sporadically. The indigenous agricultural sector remained primitive; 36 percent of the population lived in poverty—their income being less
than one dollar a day—and 26 percent between the ages of fifteen and
forty-nine years suffered from AIDS; per capita GNP stood at $620; infla-
tion ran at over 25 percent; unemployment stood at 30 percent, while wages
had fallen by one-third during the 1990s.[34] In August 1998, Mugabe committed scarce resources to the conflict in the Congo, the number of Zimbabwe's troops eventually reaching eleven thousand.

In November 1998, labor leaders protested against corruption and
intervention in the Congo, and in March 1999, they formed an opposition
party. To shore up his sinking popularity, Mugabe conducted a referendum
in February 2000 asking voters to give him additional powers, primarily to
dispossess—without compensation—the remaining white farmers, who still
controlled 4,500 large farms encompassing one-third of the nation's land.
These farmers, however, also represented the most productive segment of
Zimbabwe's economy: they produced 70 percent of the nation's agricultural
exports and they employed approximately three hundred thousand black
workers. When the predominantly black voters rejected the referendum,
Mugabe declared the white farmers "enemies of Zimbabwe" and encouraged veterans of the war of liberation to seize white-owned farms, drive out
their owners, intimidate the black workers, and, if need be, kill those who
resisted. The veterans reponded by murdering a number of white settlers as
well as Mugabe's black political opponents. Neither repeated supreme court
decisions declaring that the land seizures were illegal nor the appeal by
Kofi Annan, the UN secretary-general, had an impact on Mugabe. Instead,
he invited the whites to leave the country. By 2004, there were scarcely any
white farmers left.[35]

## ☐ Sierra Leone and Liberia

While the Western world's attention was riveted on the fate of a small number of white settlers in Zimbabwe, a more gruesome spectacle, largely
ignored, continued in Sierra Leone. It began in 1991, when Foday Sankoh
created the Revolutionary United Front (RUF). Sankoh, with Charles Taylor of Liberia, in the face of feeble resistance from the Sierra Leonean government, gained control of the region rich in gold and diamonds. In January
1999, it torched one-third of the capital city of Freetown and massacred six
thousand people. A UN force of 8,700 soldiers failed to disarm the rebels;
in fact, the RUF captured 500 of them before eventually releasing them. It
was British paratroopers who stood between the rebels and Freetown.

Sankoh's forces engaged in systematic atrocities as torture, rape, arson,
wholesale slaughter, and mutilation became commonplace. The men under
Sankoh, a visionary who claimed to have supernatural powers, hacked off

the arms and legs of an estimated ten thousand children. They also pressed children (as young as ten years of age) into military service. Fankoh dubbed one of his campaigns as "Operation Pay Yourself," encouraging his men to loot anything they could find. By 2000, an estimated 100,000–200,000 people had perished in the conflict.[36]

None of that caused much of an outcry abroad. U.S. president Bill Clinton—burned by the U.S. military setback in Somalia in 1993 and then engaged in Kosovo—and most of the rest of Africa and the West showed little interest in being drawn into Sierra Leone. It was up to Great Britain to see what it could do to restore order in one of its former colonies. British troops with shoot-to-kill orders routed the RUF in 2000. Britain charged Fankoh with seventeen counts of war crimes, but before the trial began, Sankoh died of a stroke.

Sankoh had not acted alone in his murderous campaign. He had the support of Charles Taylor of neighboring Liberia, a country with its own recent tragic history. In April 1980, a revolt led by Master Sergeant Samuel K. Doe, overthrew the government of William Tolbert, a descendant of Americo-Liberians, former slaves from the United States who had ruled Liberia since its formation in 1847. The former U.S. slaves had become the colonizers and oppressors of the native majority. When Doe, a native Liberian (from the Krahn ethnic group), murdered Tolbert, it marked the first time that a native Liberian had ruled the country. Sergeant Doe quickly promoted himself to general and then launched a reign of terror replete with mass exections and grand theft, as he and his Krahn helped themselves to the spoils of war.

When in 1989, the soldier of fortune Charles Taylor, another Americo-Liberian, challenged Doe, Liberia was plunged into a civil war that ended in September 1989 with Doe's brutal torture and execution (at the hands of yet another rival faction). Now it became Taylor's turn to plunder and terrorize Liberia. It touched off yet another civil war, this one lasting six years, during which an estimated 150,000–200,000 people died and one-third of the population became refugees. UN economic sanctions in 2001 and the advance of seven rebel factions steadily weakened Taylor's hand. In July 2003, he was on the ropes. A UN-backed war crimes court had indicted him for war crimes and his enemies controlled two-thirds of the country. In the end, Taylor accepted political asylum from the military rulers in Nigeria, leaving behind his devastated native land.

■ **AIDS IN SUB-SAHARAN AFRICA**

During the 1990s, in addition to genocide, wars, economic decline, and ecological degradation, sub-Saharan Africa was ravaged by an AIDS (acquired immune deficiency syndrome) epidemic of unprecedented proportions.

Between the early 1980s and the end of 2000, more African people had died of AIDS (19 million) than in all the wars fought across the globe. About six thousand Africans died from AIDS each day and millions were infected by the human immune-deficiency virus (HIV), which weakens the natural immune system and is the root of AIDS.[37] Sub-Saharan Africa contained 10 percent of the world's population, yet had 70 percent of the world's population (24.5 out of 34.3 million) infected with HIV.[38] Hardest hit were Zimbabwe, Zambia, Botswana, and South Africa. Botswana had the world's highest rate of infection—35 percent of the population.

South Africa was the last sub-Saharan African nation to be visited by the epidemic. In the 1980s, AIDS in South Africa was considered an illness that affected primarily white homosexuals. Within a decade, however, it had spread to more than a tenth of the population and nearly all of the victims were black. By 2000, South Africa had more people infected than any nation in the world. During his five years as president, Nelson Mandela paid scant attention to the problem. When he finally did, in 1998, 20 percent of South Africa's pregnant women were already infected. Mandela's successor, Thabo Mbeki, as well as Mbeki's health minister, rejected the explanation that the HIV virus caused AIDS and blamed it instead on drug and alcohol misuse, poverty, and underdevelopment. In the meantime, each hour witnessed seventy new HIV infections in South Africa. One of the breeding grounds of the virus was the communal residences of miners separated from their families for months at a stretch. There, sexual contact, the most common route of AIDS transmission, infected more than a third of the young adults—both men and women. When the men returned home, they spread the disease. The HIV virus also contributed to the rapid spread of tuberculosis, particularly among miners, and a host of other illnesses. All the while, the topics of sex and AIDS remained taboo.

Mbeki's government refused to provide funds for AZT (Azidothymidin), a drug that suppresses the impact of the virus and which in most cases prevents the transmission of the disease to children born of infected women. It is, moreover, an expensive drug that must be taken in combination with other expensive drugs to be effective.

In January 2000, AIDS became for the first time a topic at the UN Security Council, and in April, the IMF linked its economic development programs with the fight against the disease. In May, the U.S. government went so far as to declare it a potential threat to national security. The bitter truth was that it threatened first and foremost the poorer countries where the work force—those between the ages of fifteen and forty-nine—was most at risk. Ninety-five percent of individuals affected by the HIV virus lived in underdeveloped nations. The International Labour Organization estimated that, unless the epidemic was checked, by 2020 sub-Saharan Africa would suffer from a shortage of at least 24 million workers. UN studies predicted that eventually half of all fifteen-year-olds in sub-Saharan

Africa will die of the disease. The AIDS epidemic in Africa also reduced life expectancy, raised mortality rates, lowered fertility, and produced millions of orphans. By the onset of the twenty-first century, with the fate of the next generation at stake, AIDS education and preventive programs were finally becoming priorities for many of the governments of sub-Saharan Africa.

## ■ APARTHEID IN SOUTH AFRICA

Between 1949 and 1994, South Africa stood apart from the rest of Africa, not only as the most economically developed nation but also as one ruled by an intransigent white minority. In defiance of world opinion, the expressed will of the rest of Africa, and the demands of the black majority, the rulers of South Africa maintained political power by means of a racist policy known as apartheid, literally "apartness." It was a legal system that demanded the most rigid form of racial segregation anywhere. The laws forbade the most elementary contact among the four racial groupings in South Africa: the blacks (also known as Bantus), the whites (mostly of Dutch, French, and English descent), the coloreds (of mixed black-white parentage), and the Asians (largely Indians).

In 1948, the whites of Dutch (and in part of French)[39] origin replaced another group of European settlers, the English, as the dominant political force in shaping the destiny of a country they considered to be theirs. The Dutch, having settled on the South African coast as early as 1652, eventually came to consider it their native land. In fact, they called themselves "Afrikaner," Dutch for Africans. (They also called themselves "boers," or farmers, and are often referred to by that name.) They argued that their claim to the land rested on discovery, conquest, economic development, and, ultimately, on the will of God.

Apartheid was steeped in the teachings of the Dutch Reformed Church, which saw the Afrikaner as God's chosen people, destined to dominate the land and others who inhabited it. Apartheid, the Afrikaners argued, was specifically sanctioned in the Bible. The most fervent defenders of apartheid were frequently ministers of the Dutch Reformed Church. Apartheid was also based on the primitive principle of racial superiority. The Bantus, the Afrikaners argued, had contributed nothing to civilization; their existence was one of savagery. The twin pillars of apartheid—religious determinism and racial superiority—were the consequence of the Afrikaners' long struggle against heresy, Western liberalism, and the black native population of South Africa.

By the end of the eighteenth century, the Dutch had deep roots in the South African soil. In 1795, however, the British gained control of the South African cape. The result was a struggle for political supremacy between the established Dutch and the newly arrived, victorious English who had settled largely around the Cape of Good Hope. It was a contest the

Afrikaners could not win, and it led to their decision to move into the hinterlands to escape the discriminatory English laws. Moreover, the Afrikaners opposed the English ban of slavery, which in 1833 became the law of the British empire. In 1835, the Boers set out on the Great Trek northward into the high plains of Natal and Transvaal. The journey was filled with bitterness and determination, coupled with a deep religious fervor. The trek became a triumphant religious procession by which God's elect, a people with a very narrow view of salvation, set out to build a new Jerusalem. And God's favor clearly seemed to shine on the "righteous" when, on December 16, 1838—in a scene straight out of the Old Testament—470 Boers decisively defeated a force of 12,500 Zulu warriors, killing 3,000 of them, on the banks of what became known as the Blood River.[40] After the Afrikaners came to power, December 16 became a national holiday, the Day of Covenant between God and the righteous.

Later in the century, when the British once again encroached on Boer territory, the Boers stood and fought two bloody and brutal wars; by 1902, however, the British emerged victorious. From that day, they prepared for the day of liberation to redress their defeat and to reestablish the social and religious principles of the Great Trek. That day came in 1948, when their National Party, under the leadership of D. F. Malan—a former minister of the Dutch Reformed Church—won a narrow electoral political victory. At this juncture, British efforts to maintain racial harmony in South Africa were abandoned, and the segregation laws came into being. The Afrikaners, driven by an intense sense of religious and cultural self-preservation, rejected all previous proposals for social and racial integration. Instead, the Afrikaners insisted that the races must be kept apart by law and that no one had the right to cross the color line. The upshot of this militant position was the political isolation of South Africa. Yet, such isolation only bred defiance and reinforced the outlook of a people long accustomed to adversity and determined to go it alone. A stiff-necked people, the Boers had stood up to the British, the blacks, and now the world.

The first of the segregation laws, enacted in 1949, forbade miscegenation—the marriage or cohabitation of persons of different color. Other segregation laws followed in rapid succession. Schools, jobs, and pay scales were all determined by the segregation laws. The Population Registration Act listed individuals on the basis of race; another law demanded residential segregation and limited the rights of blacks to remain in designated cities. Political organizations and strikes by nonwhites were outlawed. All public facilities—from hospitals to park benches and beaches—became segregated. Whites and nonwhites were not permitted to spend the night under the same roof. Every aspect of sexual, social, religious, and economic intercourse between the races was regulated, among both the living and the dead—even the cemeteries were segregated. The number of apartheid laws ran well over three hundred.

The issue of race and segregation became an obsession in South Africa. A classification board first had to assign a racial category for every individual, but the science of distinguishing skin color, facial features, and hair texture is not exact. Often the result was as follows:

> In one typical twelve-month period, 150 coloreds were reclassified as white; ten whites became colored; six Indians became Malay; two Malay became Indians; two coloreds became Chinese; ten Indians became coloreds; one Indian became white; one white became Malay; four blacks became Indians; three whites became Chinese.[41]

Apartheid turned the once oppressed Afrikaners into oppressors of the majority. In 1980, in this nation of 28 million, blacks outnumbered whites by a ratio of three to one, 18 million to 6 million. The coloreds numbered about 3 million, the Asians nearly 1 million. It was little wonder that a siege mentality permeated white society. And, in fact, white settlements were frequently referred to as *laagers,* literally "camps," a term taken from the Great Trek of the 1830s.

The segregation laws were also the linchpin of economic exploitation. The laws excluded nonwhites from the better-paying jobs and positions of authority. In the construction industry in the late 1980s, for instance, whites earned twice the salary of Asians, three times that of coloreds, and five times that of blacks. A white miner earned $16,000 a year, a black miner $2,500. The combination of rich natural resources, industrial planning, and cheap labor provided by the black work force turned the nation into the African continent's only modern, industrialized state—but only for the white population. The defenders of apartheid pointed out that the wealth of the nation also trickled down to the black population, whose standard of living was the highest of any blacks in Africa. Blacks regarded this argument as irrelevant. Apartheid— a philosophy of psychological oppression, economic exploitation, and political domination—became a way of life that only force could maintain.

## ☐ The Struggle Against Apartheid

In 1959, the National government set aside ten regions (Bantustans, or "homelands") for the black population that constituted 13 percent of the nation's land. The "homelands" became the centerpiece of apartheid, for they denied native blacks unrestricted access to the rest of South Africa. They became the sole legal residences for the nation's black population. Blacks, who made up much of the nation's essential work force, thus had no right to be in, say, the city of Johannesburg. It also meant that although black fathers could find work in areas set aside for whites, their families had to remain behind. In this fashion, many black families were divided, frequently for eleven months at a stretch. Blacks were but temporary visitors at the

Nelson Mandela, leader of
the African National Congress
and first nonwhite president of
the Republic of South Africa.
*(Courtesy of the Embassy of the
Republic of South Africa)*

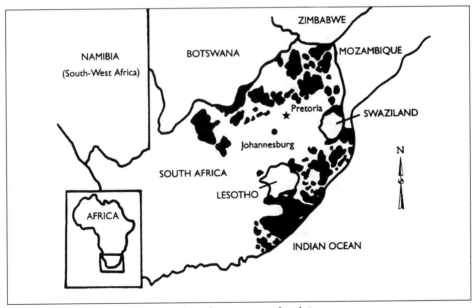

**South Africa's "Homelands"**

pleasure of the white hosts, aliens in their native land. The creation of the "homelands" signaled the completion of the system of apartheid. The South African government hoped to obtain international recognition of the Bantustans as the national homes of the blacks of South Africa, yet no country recognized them as independent. They acquired no legal international standing, for none of the "homelands" was ever viable; they remained financially dependent on the South African government.

The government's position became more rigid still in 1960, the UN's "Year of Africa," during which a number of sub-Saharan African nations gained independence. In February, British prime minister Harold Macmillan went to Capetown to address the South African parliament, where he delivered his "wind of change" speech in which he warned that black nationalism was a force that had to be recognized or the newly independent African nations would be drawn into the Communist camp. The government of Hendrik Verwoerd ignored whatever winds were blowing through Africa and made clear that there would be no accommodation with African nationalism in South Africa. Six weeks later, on March 21, Verwoerd's government replied to Macmillan with the Sharpeville massacre, in which the police killed sixty-nine demonstrators who had protested the creation of the Bantustans and the "pass laws" that required them to carry documents granting them permission to be in places reserved for whites.

The Sharpeville massacre had an extraordinary psychological impact on black Africans, who viewed it as a watershed; the time had come to move from peaceful agitation to armed revolution. The laws of South Africa left them two choices: accept the status of second-class citizenship or rebel. In addition to Sharpeville, highly publicized disturbances also took place in Soweto (short for South-West Township), a black ghetto of 1 million people thirty minutes from Johannesburg, the elegant financial capital of South Africa. In April 1960, the government banned the still moderate African National Congress (ANC) and the militant Pan-Africanist Congress.

It was at this juncture that South Africa's oldest and most influential civil rights organization, the African National Congress—an umbrella organization of blacks, whites, Asians, coloreds, and liberals—reassessed its strategy. Since its formation in 1912, the ANC had sought the peaceful establishment of a nonracial democracy. As its leader, Nelson Mandela, explained at his trial in 1964, until the advent of apartheid the organization had "adhered strictly to a constitutional struggle."[42] But the events between 1959 and 1961 made clear that this approach had reached a dead end.[43]

In 1961, the ANC, having concluded that all legal venues were now closed, adopted armed struggle as one of the means to bring an end to apartheid. It formed its armed wing, Umkhonto we Sizwe—the "Spear of the Nation"—because as Mandela, one of the founders of Umkhonto, explained, "fifty years of nonviolence had brought the African people nothing but more and more repressive legislation, and fewer and fewer rights." On December 16, 1961, Umkhonto responded with acts of sabotage throughout South Africa. The ANC marked December 16 as Heroes' Day to honor those who had lost their lives in the struggle against apartheid; it was the same calendar day declared by the Afrikaners as the Day of Covenant that commemorated the defeat of the Zulus at Blood River in 1838.

The armed conflict between Umkhonto and the government had precisely the effect Macmillan had feared. The ANC made common cause with the country's Communist Party, and consequently South Africa was drawn into the global Cold War. The Soviet Union provided money and weapons to the ANC, and the United States tilted toward the South African apartheid regime. In the eyes of many Westerners, the fact that the ANC included some Communists in its ranks made it a Soviet front organization. The ANC, however, did not espouse Marxist economic theory; in fact, it advocated a capitalist South Africa but one in which private property was more equitably distributed.

A tip from the CIA led to the police arrest of Nelson Mandela in 1963. At his trial in 1964, Mandela justified the formation of Umkhonto by pointing to the repeated acts of violence by the government against the black population. The court rejected his argument and sentenced him to life in prison at hard labor.

## ☐ Black Consciousness and Zulu Nationalism

The early 1970s saw the emergence of the "black consciousness" movement, a phenomenon influenced in part by the U.S. civil rights movement. Its leading advocate was Steve Biko, who insisted that South African blacks must no longer rely on liberal whites to speak for them but must deal with all whites as equal. "Whites must be made to realize that they are only human, [and] not superior," he declared, and blacks "must be made to realize that they are also human, [and] not inferior."[44] The very thought of a black man demanding racial equality as his birthright made Biko a dangerous and marked man. No sooner than his star had risen as an antiapartheid leader, he was arrested on a pass violation; soon afterward he died in police custody in September 1977, his skull fractured. After Biko's death, the radical Azanian People's Organization (Azapo), the militant wing of the Pan-Africanist Congress, declared itself the heir of Biko's "black consciousness" and then went further than the position he had taken. It demanded the expulsion of all whites and declared war on them under the slogan "one settler, one bullet." Azapo also became engaged in an ideological—and soon bloody—conflict with the ANC and its allies who promoted a nonracial democracy.

At the same time, the ANC faced opposition from still another black organization, the Inkatha Freedom Party, the political base of Zulu chief

Mangosuthu Buthelezi. In their younger days, Buthelezi and Mandela had been comrades in their opposition to apartheid, but over the years Buthelezi had become the champion of narrow Zulu, rather than national, interests. He became a defender of the Zulu "homeland," KwaZulu, in the province of Natal. An integrated South Africa threatened Buthelezi's base of power, and thus he sought to perpetuate the continued existence of KwaZulu or the creation of an entirely independent Zulu state. Biko and Mandela both charged Buthelezi with accepting the Bantustans and thus adopting the Afrikaner formula for separation of the races.

## ☐  The Dismantling of Apartheid

In the mid-1980s, the government slowly began to question the wisdom of continuing with apartheid. The financial, psychological, and human costs were becoming too high. June 1976 saw an uprising in Soweto that the police put down by killing several hundred residents. In 1985, during demonstrations commemorating the twenty-fifth anniversary of the Sharpeville massacre, the police killed nineteen people at one demonstration alone, and scores of others died in other clashes. The funeral processions for those killed served as protest demonstrations and brought more violence. At summer's end, for the first time white residential areas became the scenes of racial confrontations. There were 1,605 outbreaks of political violence in January 1986, and the numbers kept climbing in subsequent months. The antiapartheid uprising of the mid-1980s claimed 1,650 lives and nearly 30,000 detainees.[45]

In 1985, as violence escalated, the government began to consider the unthinkable: the establishment of a political dialogue with the banned ANC and its leader. Mandela, however, refused a deal to gain freedom on the conditions that the ANC pledge to refrain from violent activity and that he live in the "homeland" set aside for the Xhosa, the Transkei. At the same time, another voice in opposition to apartheid came to national and international attention, that of Episcopalian bishop Desmond Tutu, who in 1984, received the Nobel Peace Prize in recognition of his attempts to work out a peaceful solution.

By 1985, President P. W. Botha came to acknowledge the reality of the permanence of blacks in "white" South Africa, a permanence that ultimately would have to be granted legality. His slogan became "adapt or die." Demographics alone, in a nation where the black population was growing more rapidly than the ruling white population, demanded such a concession. At the same time, South Africa witnessed a growing split in the government between the "enlightened" ministers and the conservatives fearful of any change.

Determined to quell racial disturbances and to put an end to worldwide press and television coverage of the carnage occurring in its streets, the

Botha government imposed a nationwide state of emergency on June 12, 1986. Under this decree, a black protester could be imprisoned without trial for up to ten years for statements interpreted to "weaken or undermine" confidence in the government. Botha, however, did scrap the hated pass laws, and thereby abandoned the Boer fiction that a purely white South Africa was a possibility. Botha made clear that the old days were over, without having a clear idea of what would come next.

International pressure began to have a telling effect. Under the aegis of the United Nations, the United States and most European governments imposed trade sanctions, and many foreign corporations began withdrawing capital from South Africa. Between 1986 and 1988, the country suffered a net capital outflow of nearly $4 billion; consequently, unemployment, inflation, and interest rates all increased and economic growth declined from 5 to 2 percent. The price of apartheid had become too high.[46] A growing number of whites, especially in the business community, began urging change. Many whites also felt a sense of isolation from the world community. Since the late 1960s, South Africa, a nation proud of its world-class athletes, had been banned from the Olympic Games and other venues of international competition, such as the World Cup in soccer.

In response to these pressures, Botha began gradually to moderate the apartheid system in 1988 and 1989. Some of the more superfluous apartheid restrictions were lifted. Certain public facilities—such as drinking fountains, movie theaters, and public parks and swimming beaches—were desegregated, and mixed residency was permitted in certain previously segregated urban residential areas.

## ☐ De Klerk and Mandela

In September 1989, Frederik W. de Klerk succeeded Botha as president of South Africa. In his inauguration speech de Klerk pledged to work for "a totally changed South Africa . . . free of domination or oppression in whatever form."[47] He went on to declare his intentions of bridging the deep gulf of distrust and fear among the races and finding a "completely new approach" to negotiations with black leaders.

A major sign of the changing attitudes in the country under the leadership of de Klerk was his remarkably conciliatory policy toward the outlawed ANC. Antiapartheid protesters were permitted to hold a mammoth rally in Soweto at which released ANC leaders were allowed to address a throng of some sixty thousand people. Even more surprising were the lifting of the political ban on the ANC and the unconditional release of its seventy-one-year-old heralded leader, Mandela, in February 1990. De Klerk also declared an end to the state of emergency Botha had declared in June 1986 and promised to free all political prisoners. International investors responded swiftly by making money available to the South African economy, and the Johannesburg Stock Exchange industrial index rose 7.2 percent in two days.

As the newly freed Mandela began to take the first tentative steps to negotiate an end to apartheid with the de Klerk government, old issues came to the fore. One was the continued political rivalry between Mandela's ANC and Buthelezi's ethnic Zulu-based Inkatha movement. In contrast to Buthelezi, Mandela, although a descendant of Xhosa kings, had long since moved beyond ethnic politics and was committed to the abolition of all Bantustans.

Mandela's stature was greatly elevated after his release from prison, but he was unable to halt the violence between the black-on-black bloodletting. Between 1985 and 1996, ANC-Inkatha fighting cost 10,000–15,000 lives. Much of the violence was carried out by young radical blacks, the "Young Lions," who sought to establish bases of economic and political power in the townships. The Young Lions had gained notoriety by "necklacing" their victims (placing tires around their necks and setting them on fire). They were impervious to pleas for moderation. Mandela's appeal to the Young Lions to throw their guns and knives into the sea fell on deaf ears.

In 1991, de Klerk took decisive steps to abolish the apartheid laws (including the Population Registration Act, the legal underpinning of apartheid) to clear away obstacles to the negotiation of a new constitution. The ANC, as always, insisted on "one man, one vote"—that is, majority rule. Such a solution meant the election of a black majority government and, therefore, would produce a strong reaction from the Afrikaner right wing, such as the Conservative Party and the Afrikaner Resistance Movement. A national referendum by the white voters gave de Klerk a mandate (68 to 32 percent) to continue his negotiations with Mandela.

In 1992, the last remnant of the apartheid laws, the ten "homelands," became a focal point of the ANC's political agenda. Pretoria still considered four of them—Ciskei, Bophuthatswana, Transkei, and Venda—independent entities. The ANC did not recognize their independence and insisted they be reincorporated into South Africa and that they participate in the national political process. The leaders of these "homelands," where elections and opposition parties (including the ANC) had been banned, insisted on maintaining their autonomy and made clear that they would defend that autonomy by force if necessary. Only after repeated, bloody clashes with ANC supporters did they finally yield to incorporation into a unified South Africa. Buthelezi and KwaZulu remained defiant, however.

Meanwhile, the ANC and the National Party scheduled South Africa's first free multiracial election that, everyone knew, would mean the transition from white minority rule to black majority rule. They set April 27, 1994, as the date for nationwide elections for a four-hundred-seat National Assembly. At this point, Mandela joined de Klerk in calling for an end to international economic sanctions, stating that they had served their purpose.

But not all parties were on board. Zulu leader Buthelezi continued to hold out for the independence of KwaZulu, with its Zulu population of 7.5 million, South Africa's largest ethnic group. Not until the very eve of the April elections did Buthelezi finally direct his Inkatha Freedom Party to participate. Another holdout was Lucas Mangope, president of Bophuthatswana, but he, too, was won over at the eleventh hour.

## ☐ Mandela's Victory

Mandela's ANC was, as expected, the big winner in the historic election—the first free multiparty and multiracial election in South Africa. The ANC garnered 62 percent of the vote and won 252 seats in the National Assembly, whereas the National Party obtained 20 percent of the vote and 82 seats. On May 27, 1994, the seventy-five-year-old Mandela, who had spent twenty-seven years of his life as a political prisoner, was elected by the National Assembly as the first nonwhite president of his country. Mandela marked the profound historical importance of South Africa's accomplishment in these words: "The time for the healing of wounds has come. . . . Never, never, and never again shall it be that this beautiful land will again experience the oppression of one by the other. . . . Let freedom reign. God bless Africa!"[48]

This remarkable turn of events was the result of several coinciding factors: the South African government's inability to produce a stable society under apartheid; the enactment of effective international economic sanctions; the end of the Cold War, which ended direct outside meddling by the superpowers; and the roles of de Klerk and Mandela. For their efforts, de Klerk and Mandela shared the Nobel Peace Prize in 1993. Nor should the roles of old-guard National Party leaders, who began behind-the-scenes initiatives for change a decade earlier, be overlooked. At the time of the 1994 elections, several members of the former Botha government revealed that they had become convinced in the 1980s that apartheid could not be sustained for long and that they should strike a deal with leaders in the ANC to work out a peaceful transition to majority rule. It took another two and a half years after the election to reach an agreement on a permanent constitution. When the time came to sign this document in December 1996, it was only appropriate that the signing take place at Sharpeville in the presence of survivors of the 1960 massacre.

Mandela's inauguration, however, could not disguise the hard realities of unresolved divisive political issues and persistent economic and social inequalities. The dismantling of apartheid and the changing of the guard did not miraculously erase the miserable living conditions for the bulk of the black population or provide the education needed for their advancement.

One of the most difficult tasks was determining how to deal with those who were guilty of political violence since 1960 (the year of Sharpeville and the banning of the ANC). Under Mandela's persistent demand, South

Africa, which had one of the world's highest rates of capital punishment, abolished the death penalty. In July 1995, the government set up a Truth and Reconciliation Commission, which sought—as its name implied—not to punish the guilty but to try to bring about national reconciliation between peoples who only recently had been killing each other. The head of the commission was retired Episcopalian archbishop Desmond Tutu, the recipient of the Nobel Peace Prize for 1984—a man whose life had been dedicated to the idea of peaceful reconciliation.

The commission operated on the principle of granting amnesty to all who acknowledged their past crimes. The families of the victims—understandably—were generally opposed to amnesty, but there appeared to be no workable alternative to the commission's solution. If punishment were to be meted out, then to whom? The defense minister, Joe Modise, who had been the head of Umkhonto? Former Defense Minister Magnus Malan, who had organized anti-ANC death squads manned by Zulus? The guilty parties in the ANC-Inkatha violence that had claimed as many as fifteen thousand lives in a ten-year span and who continued to kill each other even as the commission was holding its hearings? Could the state, even if it wanted to, bring some of the Inkatha leaders—not to mention Buthelezi—into the dock? And what was one to do about the charges that directly implicated P. W. Botha in acts of violence?[49]

In October 1998, after two and a half years of hearings, the Truth and Reconciliation Commission issued its long-awaited final report. The 2,750-page document presented in gruesome detail thousands of instances of human rights violations perpetrated by both blacks and whites. Many whites, especially those associated with the National Party and right-wing organizations, denounced the report as biased against the white minority. Some blacks denounced the report for finding the ANC guilty of abuses. The report did not implicate former President de Klerk for apartheid-era abuses, but did implicate former President Botha, who denounced the commission as a witch hunt and repeatedly refused to testify. The report offered recommendations, such as the creation of human rights bureaus in every government ministry, restitution for those who suffered from apartheid discrimination, apologies to all whose human rights had been violated, and the prosecution of human rights violators who did not seek amnesty.

In the meantime, although the government had to tackle the daily tasks of governance, the authority of the state was weak. Crime was the biggest problem: many South Africans seemed to believe they were able to break the law at will. Police were often poorly trained and affected by corruption, absenteeism, and lack of discipline. Many crimes were not properly investigated; only 32 percent of murder suspects were convicted, this in a country with the highest murder rate in the world. Another urgent problem was the AIDS epidemic. In 2000, the Health Ministry calculated that AIDS already had claimed 250,000 lives and that the nation faced 1,600 new

AIDS cases daily. In sum, the ANC's accomplishments after six years in power consisted of mixed results.

In December 1998, Mandela turned over the reins of the ANC to his old comrade-in-arms, Thabo Mbeki; six months later Mbeki succeeded Mandela as president of South Africa. The eighty-year-old Mandela thereby effected a peaceful transfer of power in contrast with all too many African leaders who clung to power until their dying breaths. Mandela left behind an impressive legacy of leading the fight against apartheid and achieving the transfer of power to the black majority and laying the foundation for a free society: a critical free press, universities, a blooming civil society, political pluralism, and a private economy. In his words, "We have confounded the prophets of doom and achieved a bloodless revolution. We have restored the dignity of every South African."[50] The revolution had not been really bloodless, but there had been far less violence than thought possible. Mandela, however, also left behind a nation still troubled by great economic disparity and poverty, racial tensions, and unabated violent crime.

Since 1994, the National Party, the party of apartheid, had no reason for existence. In August 2004, its leader announced he was joining the ruling ANC and advised his followers to do the same, explaining that "the real debate about the future of the country is within the ANC and not outside."[51]

## ■ RECOMMENDED READINGS

### ☐ Sub-Saharan Africa

Bayart, Jean François, and Stephen Ellis. *The Criminalization of the State in Africa.* London: Oxford University Press, 1999.
    A critical look at one of Africa's problems.
Gourevitch, Philip. *We Wish to Inform You That Tomorrow We Will Be Killed with Our Families: Stories from Rwanda.* New York: Farrar, Straus, and Giroux, 1998.
    A reporter's account of the genocide in Rwanda.
Hochschild, Adam. *King Leopold's Ghost: A Story of Greed, Terror, and Heroism in Colonial Africa.* Boston: Houghton Mifflin, 1998.
    An indictment of the legacy of colonialism in Central Africa.
Kapuscinski, Ryszard. *"The Shadow of the Sun": Africa, a Mosaic of Mystery and Sorrow.* New York: Alfred A. Knopf, 2001.
    The reminiscences of a veteran Polish journalist who covered Africa from the beginning of the independence movement until the end of the twentieth century.
Leys, Colin. *Underdevelopment in Kenya: The Political Economy of Neo-Colonialism.* Berkeley: University of California Press, 1975.
Mazrui, Ali A. *Africa's International Relations: The Diplomacy of Dependency and Change.* London: Heinemann, 1977.
    A study by a noted specialist who presents his case from the Africans' viewpoint.
Neuberger, Ralph Benyamin. *National Self-Determination in Postcolonial Africa.* Boulder, Colo.: Lynne Rienner Publishers, 1986.

A theoretical and comparative analysis of the impact of colonial experience on postcolonial African nationalism and secession.

Oliver, Roland, and Anthony Atmore. *Africa Since 1800.* 3d. ed. New York: Cambridge University Press, 1981.

Soyinka, Wole. *The Open Sore of a Continent: A Personal Narrative of the Nigerian Crisis.* New York: Oxford University Press, 1996.

By the Nigerian Nobel laureate for literature.

☐  South Africa

Boraine, Alex. *A Country Unmasked: Inside South Africa's Truth and Reconciliation Commission.* New York: Oxford University Press, 2001.

By the former president of the Methodist Church of South Africa and antiapartheid activist who served as deputy chair of the commission. It discusses the difficult process of South Africa's attempts to come to grips with its past.

Breytenbach, Breyten. *The True Confessions of an Albino Terrorist.* New York: Farrar, Straus, and Giroux, 1984.

An autobiographical account by a poet from a well-known Afrikaner family who became a revolutionary activist.

Lelyveld, Joseph. *Move Your Shadow: South Africa, Black and White.* New York: Times Books, 1985.

A *New York Times* reporter explains the racial realities of South Africa.

Malan, Rian. *My Traitor's Heart: A South African Exile Returns to Face His Country, His Tribe, and His Conscience.* New York: Atlantic Monthly Press, 1990.

Mandela, Nelson. *The Long Walk to Freedom: The Autobiography of Nelson Mandela.* Boston: Little, Brown, 1995.

———. *The Struggle Is My Life.* New York: Pathfinder Press, 1986.

Collection of Mandela's speeches and writings.

Shea, Dorothy. *The South African Truth Commission: The Politics of Reconciliation.* Washington, D.C.: United States Institute of Peace, 2000.

Thompson, Leonard. *The Political Mythology of Apartheid.* New Haven, Conn.: Yale University Press, 1985.

An account of the origins of, and a justification for, that racial policy.

Woods, Donald. *Biko.* New York: Paddington Press, 1978.

A white South African's sympathetic account of the antiapartheid struggle, focusing on Steve Biko, founder of the black consciousness movement, who died in police custody in 1977.

# ■ NOTES

1. Ethiopia's aged emperor, Haile Selassie, did little to avert the earlier famine and instead went to great lengths to suppress news of it. After he was overthrown in 1974, a new Marxist regime attempted to carry out an extensive land reform program, only to reap another agricultural disaster that was the consequence not so much of the reforms as of past years of deforestation, overcultivation, and the hostile forces of nature.

2. In the 1980s, South Africa had a per capita income of more than $12,500, far higher than that of any other African country. It should be pointed out , however, that blacks, who outnumbered whites by five to one, earned only about one-sixth of what white workers were paid. In contrast to the standard of living of South

African whites, which was among the highest in the world, that of the blacks was substantially lower.

3. *The World Bank Atlas, 1985* (Washington, D.C.: World Bank, 1985).

4. Cited in Arthur Agwuncha Nwankwo and Samuel Udochukwu Ifejika, *Biafra: The Making of a Nation* (New York: Praeger, 1970), p. 11.

5. The most notable exceptions include such rulers as Léopold Senghor of Senegal, Félix Houphouët-Boigny of the Ivory Coast, Jomo Kenyatta of Kenya, Julius Nyerere of Tanzania, Kenneth Kaunda of Zambia, Sekou Touré of Guinea, and Seretse Khama of Botswana—all of whom remained in power for fifteen years or more.

6. Reuters, "Ghana's Opposition Ahead in Early Election Returns," *New York Times,* December 8, 2000.

7. Moyibi Amoda, "Background to the Conflict: A Summary of Nigeria's Political History from 1919 to 1964," in Joseph Okpaku, ed., *Nigeria: Dilemma of Nationhood: An African Analysis of the Biafran Conflict* (New York: Third Press, 1972), p. 59.

8. "Proclamation of the Republic of Biafra," Enugu, May 30, 1967, in Nwankwo and Ifejika, *Biafra,* pp. 336–340.

9. David Lamb, *The Africans* (New York: Random House, 1982), p. 309.

10. Kwame Nkrumah, *Neo-Colonialism: The Last Stage of Imperialism* (New York: International Publishers, 1966), "Introduction."

11. Roland Oliver and Anthony Atmore, *Africa Since 1800* (New York: Cambridge University Press, 1981), p. 330.

12. Namibia had been the German colony of South-West Africa until World War I, when it was conquered by South African forces. After the war, it was placed under a League of Nations mandate administered by South Africa. The mandate was assumed by the United Nations after World War II, but by that time the South African presence in Namibia was deeply entrenched politically and militarily.

13. World Bank, *Sub-Saharan Africa: From Crisis to Sustainable Growth: A Long-Term Perspective Study* (Washington, D.C.: World Bank, 1989). All data are from this source.

14. The figures are for all "reporting countries," which excluded the Soviet Union and most of its bloc—the inclusion of which, however, would not appreciably change the figures. See World Bank, *World Development Report, 1989* (Washington, D.C.: World Bank, 1989), p. 165.

15. Cited in "Democracy in Africa," *The Economist,* February 22, 1992, p. 21.

16. Cited in "Under Slow Notice to Quit," *The Economist,* July 6, 1991, p. 43.

17. "Lion's Den," *The Economist,* July 4, 1990, pp. 36–37. In July 1990, Kenyan police opened fire on several hundred dissidents during a peaceful demonstration for the legalization of opposition parties, killing at least twenty-six and jailing over a thousand.

18. Interview with the dissident journalist Charles Gnaleko from Ivory Coast, "Pressefreiheit gibt es nur in drei von 55 Staaten, *Frankfurter Rundschau,* April 13, 2000, p. 11.

19. Reinhard Muller, "Die Gruppe ist wichtiger: Die afrikanische Charta der Menschenrechte," *Frankfurter Allgemeine Zeitung,* May 24, 2000.

20. "Angola Moves to Put Aside the Devastation of War," *U.S. News and World Report,* May 13, 1991, p. 50. During the sixteen-year war, Moscow had poured in 1,100 advisers, 50,000 Cuban troops, and between $500 million and $1 billion annually to prop up the leftist government; the United States provided at least $60 million a year to support Savimbi's guerrillas. Christopher Ogden, "Ending Angola's Agony," *Time,* June 3, 1991, p. 22.

21. World Bank, *World Development Report, 1992* (Washington, D.C.: World Bank, 1992), pp. 211, 218.

22. Sudan had one of the highest birth rates in the world; the CIA estimate for 2004 was 2.64 percent per year; CIA, *World Fact Book* (Washington, D.C.: CIA, 2004.)

23. Between 1987 and 1989, 2,500 Fur and 500 Arabs died in clashes. Samantha Power, "Dying in Darfur," *The New Yorker,* August 30, 2004, p. 61.

24. Power, "Dying in Darfur," p. 68.

25. Philip Gourevitch, "The Poisoned Country," *New York Review of Books,* June 6, 1996, pp. 58–60.

26. "Judging Genocide," *The Economist,* June 14, 2001.

27. "Laurent Kabila," *The Economist,* January 18, 2001.

28. "The Last Days of Mobutu," *The Economist,* March 22, 1997.

29. "Laurent Kabila," *The Economist,* January 18, 2001.

30. Karl Vick, "Congo Looks for Leadership," *Washington Post,* October 30, 2000, pp. A1, A22.

31. Ian Stewart, "Nigeria Boss Remakes His Leadership," April 21, 1998, Associated Press, *AOL News Profiles.*

32. Douglas Farah, "Islamic Law Splits Nigeria," *Washington Post,* August 31, 2000, pp. A24, A28.

33. Samora Machel of Mozambique and Julius Nyerere of Tanzania, cited in Doris Lessing, "The Jewel of Africa," *New York Review of Books,* April 10, 2003, p. 6.

34. "Poorer and Angrier," *The Economist,* August 15, 1998; Simon Robinson, "Power to the Mob," *Time,* May 1, 2000, pp. 42–46.

35. The exodus between 2000 and 2003 led to a precipitous drop in agricultural output and with it foreign-currency earnings. The harvest of maize, for example, declined by 67 percent, that of wheat by 91 percent, and that of tobacco by 75 percent. In 2003, one-third of the population was infected by HIV, resulting in 3,800 deaths per week. Samantha Powers, "How to Kill a Country," *Atlantic Monthly* (December 2003), pp. 86–100.

36. "Human Rights Watch Report 2000," letter to Kofi Annan, November 29, 2000; Udo Ulfkotte, "Kurzsichtigkeit ist die Amme der Gewalt," *Frankfurter Allgemeine Zeitung,* May 20, 2000, p. 1.

37. Associated Press, *AOL News Profiles,* October 31, 2000.

38. UN figures. Marion Aberle, "Sog des Verderbens," *Frankfurter Allgemeine Zeitung,* July 8, 2000. See also Brigitte Schwartz, "Fluch der Jungen," *Der Spiegel,* July 3, 2000. In contrast, North America and Europe combined had less than 1 percent of those infected.

39. In the late 1680s, French Calvinists, the so-called Huguenots, left France after their government revoked in 1685 the Edict of Nantes of 1598, a decree of religious toleration. The Huguenots were shortly absorbed into the Dutch Afrikaner community.

40. C. F. J. Muller, ed., *Five Hundred Years: A History of South Africa* (Pretoria: Academia, 1969), pp. 166–167.

41. David Lamb, *The Africans* (New York: Random House, 1982), pp. 320–321. The official absurdity knew no end. Chinese were classified as a white subgroup and Japanese as "honorary whites."

42. This and other statements by Mandela later in the chapter are from his defense from the dock in Pretoria Supreme Court, April 20, 1964, cited in *Nelson Mandela: The Struggle Is My Life* (New York: Pathfinder Press, 1986), pp. 161–181.

43. The Nobel Peace Prize committee acknowledged the peaceful nature of the ANC when in 1960 it awarded its medal to Chief Albert J. Luthuli, the ANC's president since 1952.

44. Biko cited in Donald Woods, *Biko* (New York: Paddington Press, 1978), p. 97.

45. Rian Malan, *My Traitor's Heart: A South African Exile Returns to Face His Country, His Tribe, and His Conscience* (New York: Atlantic Monthly Press, 1990), p. 333. For black-on-black violence, see pp. 323–334.

46. World Bank, *World Development Report, 1989* (Washington, D.C.: World Bank, 1989), pp. 165, 167, and 179, has the following figures: the percentage of average annual growth rate, 1965–1987, stood at a mere 0.6 percent; the average rate of inflation, 1980–1987, was 13.8 percent. During the years 1980–1987, there was a decline in average annual growth rate in industry and manufacturing of –0.1 and –0.5, respectively. Gross domestic investment, 1980–1987, declined by 7.3 percent.

47. Peter Honey, "De Klerk Sworn In, Promises 'Totally Changed' S. Africa," *Baltimore Sun,* September 21, 1989.

48. "Mandela's Address: 'Glory and Hope,'" *New York Times,* May 11, 1994, p. A8.

49. Tina Rosenberg, "Recovering from Apartheid," *The New Yorker,* November 18, 1996, pp. 86–95.

50. Terry Leonard, "Mandela Has a Legacy of Peace," Associated Press, June 1, 1999. *AOL News.*

51. Cited in "The Party of Apartheid Departs," *The Economist,* August 14, 2004, p. 44.

# 13

## Latin America

Latin America embraces the thirteen countries of the South American continent, Mexico, the six countries that make up Central America, and the various islands that dot the Caribbean Sea. In the first part of this chapter, we offer generalizations about the entire region; then the focus shifts to South America, next to Mexico, and then to Central America.

Latin America is a part of the Third World and shares many of its features: economic underdevelopment, massive poverty, high population growth rates, widespread illiteracy, political instability, recurrent military coups, dictatorial regimes, intervention by outside powers, and fervent nationalistic pride. A wide range of economic development exists, however, within Latin America. For example, several large nations such as Mexico, Brazil, and Argentina have sustained impressive industrial growth and attained GNP levels that may qualify them as middle-income nations. Unlike most other parts of the Third World, the nations of Latin America are not newly independent states struggling to meet the challenges of nation building after World War II. On the contrary, most won their independence from Spain early in the nineteenth century and had by 1945 experienced almost a century and a half of nationhood.

### ■ THE COLONIAL HERITAGE

Although Latin America's colonial experience lies in the distant past, it still conditions the present, much as other Third World nations are conditioned by their more recent colonial past. The legacy of Spanish rule has persisted over the centuries and is still embodied in the culture and social fabric of Latin American countries. They inherited from their Spanish colonial experience complex multiracial societies with pronounced social cleavages between a traditional aristocracy and the underprivileged lower classes. The prosperous and privileged elite, mainly the white descendants of the European conquerors later joined by newer immigrants from Europe, preserved for themselves vast wealth and political power and thoroughly dominated the remainder of the population, which consists mainly of *mestizos* (racially mixed peoples), native Indians, and descendants of African slaves. The traditional social structure continued to influence political and economic patterns, even in the post–World War II period.

The great gulf between the privileged class, who may be thought of as an oligarchy, and the dispossessed lower classes is best seen in the landholding patterns in Latin America. Nowhere in the world was the disparity in land ownership as great. Traditionally, over two-thirds of the agricultural land was owned by only 1 percent of the population. The *latifundio,* huge estates owned by the elite, were so large—often over a thousand acres—that they were not fully cultivated; as a result, much of that land lay fallow. A 1966 study, for example, revealed that in Chile and Peru, 82 percent of the agricultural land was latifundio, and that the average size of the latifundio was well over five hundred times larger than the *minifundio,* the small farms of most farmers.[1] Minifundio were often too small to provide subsistence even for small families. In Ecuador and Guatemala, for example, nine out of ten farms were too small to feed the owners' families. Moreover, in many Latin American countries the majority of the rural population owned no land; they were peons whose labor was exploited by the owners of the latifundio. Even after years of land reform efforts, the imbalance remained. Several Latin American countries (such as Mexico and Chile) enacted modest land reform programs, but they were seldom fully implemented; consequently, very little agricultural land was redistributed.

Many of Latin America's persistent economic problems stem from this inequity of land ownership and its inherent inefficiencies. The wastefulness of the latifundio is a major cause of the failure of Latin American agriculture to meet the food needs of its people. Consequently, Latin America imported an increasing amount of foodstuffs, and the high cost of such imports had a baleful effect on the economies of the region. Moreover, the depressed state of agriculture and the impoverishment of the rural population militated against industrial development because the majority of the people were too impoverished to be consumers of manufactured products.

## ■ "YANQUI IMPERIALISM"

The colonial heritage is but one of two major outside influences on the economic and political life of contemporary Latin America; the other is the "Colossus of the North," the United States. Ever since Spain left the continent in the early 1800s, the United States cast its long shadow over its neighbors to the south, especially in the twentieth century. In many ways, the role played by the United States in Latin America was analogous to that played by European colonial powers in other parts of the Third World. Whereas the nationalism of Asian and African countries was directed against their former European colonial masters, nationalism in Latin America characteristically focused on "Yanqui imperialism," an emotive term referring to the pattern of U.S. (Yankee) domination and interference in Latin America.

With the Monroe Doctrine of 1823, the United States claimed for itself a special role in the Western Hemisphere as the protector of the weaker countries to the south. Beginning with the 1890s, however, Washington extended its claim (notably with the Roosevelt Corollary of 1904) by which it asserted the right to intervene in Latin American countries to maintain political order. By the 1920s, the corollary had been invoked several times, and a pattern of military intervention to prop up tottering regimes and protect U.S. investments was firmly set. Inevitably, this intervention produced fear and resentment at "Yanqui" interventionism. The strains in U.S.–Latin American relations were somewhat ameliorated, however, by President Franklin Roosevelt's "good neighbor" policy and by the exigencies of World War II, during which the two cooperated as allies.

After the war, Washington sought to strengthen its bonds with Latin American countries by plying them with military and economic aid, taking the lead in forming an organization for regional collective security, and creating bilateral defense agreements. Latin leaders welcomed U.S. aid but were disappointed at being left out of the generous Marshall Plan, which pumped far greater amounts of aid to the European Cold War allies of the United States. Meanwhile, Washington's increasing preoccupation with the Cold War gave its hemispheric relations a distinct anti-Communist ideological cast; consequently, it pressured Latin American governments to cut ties with the Soviet Union and outlaw local Communist parties, and it altered its aid program to give greater priority to bolstering the armies in Latin American countries than to economic development. Whereas Latin American military leaders stood to gain by this shift, politicians—who were generally more interested in economic assistance, especially in modern technology—had misgivings. Still, when an economic aid package was as generous as President Kennedy's 1961 Alliance for Progress program, Latin leaders were eager to accept it, even with its Cold War–oriented political and military components.

The Alliance for Progress offered $20 billion to Latin American governments over ten years if they instituted fundamental social and economic reforms, including land reform, and developed counterinsurgency programs designed to thwart Cuba-type revolutionary movements. Despite the initial enthusiasm for this program, it eventually proved a failure. The alliance produced increased financial dependency and indebtedness of Latin American countries and caused confusion over priorities, whether to focus on industrial projects, bolster the military to suppress leftist rebels, initiate social reform, or administer relief for the poverty-stricken.

Corporate U.S. business interests added to U.S. influence in Latin America. Businesses invested heavily, buying Latin American land, mines, and oil fields, establishing industries (exploiting cheap labor), and selling arms. As a consequence, in Brazil, for example, in the 1960s, thirty-one of the fifty-five largest business firms were owned by foreigners, mainly from the United States. In the 1970s, eight of the ten largest firms and 50 percent of the banks in Argentina were foreign owned.[2] U.S. business interests assumed that, as in the past, the U.S. flag followed the dollar, and they lobbied for and expected U.S. diplomacy to protect their investments. Business interests usually coincided with Washington's ideological and strategic goals insofar as both gave priority to the maintenance of political stability and support to military strongmen—by U.S. troops if necessary.

## ■ ECONOMIC AND POLITICAL PATTERNS

Industrialization became an obsession for many Latin American countries after World War II, and the postwar industrial progress of several of the larger countries was indeed impressive. Governments began playing an important role in this endeavor, investing in heavy industry and erecting high import tariffs. Argentina particularly exhibited a strong economic nationalism aimed at ending foreign dependency. Industrial progress was, however, limited to only a few countries (Argentina, Brazil, and Mexico accounted for 80 percent of Latin America's industrial output in the late 1960s) and to just a few cities in those countries, such as Buenos Aires, São Paulo, and Mexico City.

Although industrial growth did produce higher GNP figures and contributed to a modest increase in the standard of living, it also produced frustration as it failed to meet expectations. It contributed to the growth of the middle class and an urban working class, both of which sought a larger share of the nations' wealth and a larger role in the political process. The emerging middle class, which found political expression through political parties, provided support for democratic movements. It remained, however, generally too weak politically to challenge the traditional landowning elite.

The new urban working class grew in size but remained largely impoverished. It sought to advance its cause for higher wages through both trade unions and political parties. The growing radicalism of organized labor, however, tended to arouse fears of the middle class and caused it to side with the more conservative elements: the oligarchy and the military. Given the frailties of the middle class, the entrenchment of the oligarchy, the lack of political involvement of the impoverished rural masses, and the potential radicalism of the growing labor class, it was little wonder that democratic governments did not become firmly rooted in Latin America.

Military intervention in politics has a long history in Latin America. Since World War II, there have been scores of military coups, and in one short span of less than three years (1962–1964) eight countries fell victim to military takeovers. The military, with few foreign wars to fight, tended to assume a domestic role as the guardian of the state. Officers, traditionally nationalistic and conservative, could be counted on to defend the status quo and maintain order. Military rule was reinforced by still another enduring colonial legacy: the rule by a *caudillo,*[3] a strongman, such as Juan Perón of Argentina, Augusto Pinochet in Chile, Rafael Trujillo in the Dominican Republic, and a host of others.

## ■ SOUTH AMERICA: OSCILLATION BETWEEN MILITARY AND CIVILIAN RULE

### □ Argentina

Postwar Argentina went through four distinct political phases: a decade of the dictatorship of Juan Perón (1946–1955), a decade-long—largely unsuccessful—attempt to establish democratic government (1955–1965), seventeen years of military dictatorship and the brief interlude of the return of Perón (1965–1982), and a return to a semblance of democracy in 1983. The rule of Perón was rather distinctive, for it simultaneously contained elements of populism, dictatorship, capitalism, and national socialism. Perón, a former army officer, was elected to the presidency of Argentina in 1946 largely on the strength of the votes of the working class, whose support he had cultivated in his previous post as labor minister. Perón's nationalistic policies aimed at ridding his country of foreign domination and attaining Argentine self-sufficiency were initially successful, and as a result his popularity soared. He bought out foreign businesses, created a government board for marketing agricultural produce, subsidized industrial development, extended social services, expanded education, and strengthened labor's rights. Meanwhile, he took steps to increase greatly his personal power by impeaching the supreme court, enacting a new constitution that broadened the powers of the president, and purchasing the support of the army by vastly increasing the military budget. He also benefited from the immense popularity of his young, beautiful wife, Eva Perón, who was given a large budget for building hospitals and schools and dispensing food and clothing to the needy.

Perón's economic program, however, began to sputter by 1950, and within a year was plunged into an economic crisis marked by falling agricultural and industrial production, wage reductions, worker layoffs, and runaway inflation. In response to protests, Perón became more dictatorial, silencing the press and political opposition. Frustrated by his loss of public support (occasioned in part by the death of Eva in 1952) and the mounting economic chaos, he became more erratic. Perón feuded with the Roman

**South America**

Catholic Church, which caused him a still greater loss of support.[4] Finally, in September 1955, the military, too, abandoned him and forced him into exile in Spain.

The army sought—with limited success—to purge Argentina of all Peronista influence. It outlawed the Peronista constitution and the party itself and arrested its leaders. Elections were held in February 1958, and a democratically elected president, Arturo Frondizi, took office. His government inherited a politically fragmented country with a still struggling, inflation-ridden economy. Although Perón himself remained in exile for the next seventeen years, he continued to cast a shadow over Argentine politics, since his Peronista Party—although officially outlawed—remained a force to be reckoned with. Frondizi's economic policies, specifically his invitation to foreign interests to take control of the stalled oil industry, provoked a nationalistic outcry. His relations with the military were strained, and when he began to look to the left for support, army leaders known as the *gorillas* began to stir. In desperate need of support during the 1962 election, Frondizi legalized the Peronista Party. After the Peronistas won a smashing electoral victory, the army intervened. It seized power once again, arrested Frondizi, and again banned the Peronistas.

The parade of military rulers was broken in 1972 by none other than Perón, whose regenerated party once again won an electoral victory. The Perón spell, however, was insufficient to remedy the country's economic ills. He died in office in July 1974, leaving power in the hands of his third wife, Isabel, who just happened to be his vice-president. But she, too, proved unequal to the immense task of governing a troubled nation, and in 1976, the army again stepped in.

The new military regime, headed by General Jorge Rafael Videla, was more ruthless than any of its predecessors. Videla suspended congress, the courts, political parties, and labor unions and vested all power in a nine-man military commission. Determined to end all opposition, his regime imposed a reign of terror that not only filled the jails but also took untold lives. The army engaged in a witch-hunt against any and all critics. Only several hundred of those killed were guerrillas; the vast majority were peaceful left-wing activists.[5] The military murdered up to thirty thousand; many of them were tortured and some of them simply "disappeared" as they were pushed out of airplanes over the Atlantic Ocean.

As if to draw people's attention from economic woes and the "dirty war" and to arouse their patriotism, in 1982 the military took the nation to war in defense of Argentina's historical claim to the Falkland Islands, a British possession known in Argentina as the Malvinas, located some 300 miles off its coast. The costly defeat suffered by the Argentine forces at the hands of the British further discredited the military; consequently, it was forced to call elections and relinquish power to a new civilian government in October 1983.

Argentina's new president, Raul Alfonsín, head of the Radical Party, was the first to defeat the Peronistas in an open election, and his election was considered a mandate to restore order and civility. Cautiously, Alfonsín set in motion criminal proceedings against his military predecessors. He put the junta leaders on trial, and those convicted of various crimes committed in the "dirty war" were sentenced to long jail terms. Alfonsín also succeeded in retiring fifty generals. But a series of barrack revolts led to laws ending further prosecutions. One of the laws passed even granted the accused the right to argue they had been "obeying orders," a spurious defense used by Nazi war criminals at the Nuremberg trials. During 1989–1990, the next president, Carlos Menem, in what he called an "act of reconciliation," declared a general amnesty. In October 1989, Menem went so far as to grant the military a blanket pardon. With a stroke of the pen he undid attempts at holding the military accountable for its crimes. Among those pardoned was the chief architect of the "dirty war," General Videla, who had been sentenced to life in prison.

But the issue would not go away. In June 1998, the courts overturned Menem's pardon, ruling that the pardons did not extend to officers such as Videla, who—among his other crimes—had been charged with the abduction of children and the murder of their mothers. Survivors of the "dirty war"—mainly mothers and wives of the disappeared—continued through the years to demand justice as they sought to reclaim their children stolen from them over thirty years earlier and then adopted by couples with connections to the military.[6]

Alfonsín had to face an even greater challenge: an economy saddled with one of the world's highest rates of inflation and highest debts. Between 1976 and 1989, the income per person had shrunk more than 1 percent each year.[7] At the end of Alfonsín's presidency in 1989, inflation had risen to an incredible 7,000 percent annually—and the debt crisis remained unresolved.

A temporary economic turnaround came under Menem, who, following the advice of the International Monetary Fund (IMF), (1) proceeded to peg the Argentine peso to the U.S. dollar—backed by the country's hard currency reserves—and (2) sell off government property, such as the telephone system, airlines, railroads, electricity, water system, and even pensions. At the same time, Menem opened the Argentine economy to the international free market. In return, the IMF provided new credits to assist Argentina to restructure its massive foreign debt. Between 1991 and 1997, the economy grew at an average of 6.1 percent, the highest in the region. Argentina became the poster child for globalization. Its economy, with IMF help, appeared to be on the right track.

The debt restructuring, however, had little effect because its foreign debt increased to a whopping $155 billion in 1998. At the same time, the public debt rose steadily. Entry into the global economy produced a raft of bankruptcies of Argentine companies that could not compete with foreigners. The result was a rising tide of unemployment. Menem had privatized the pension system, but the state still had obligations to its remaining pensioners as well as the unemployed. Moreover, Argentina had an inefficient system of tax collection. The state eventually ran out of money. The peso began a precipitous drop in 2001, as it was no longer backed by hard currency reserves and as the government began to withdraw money from the banks. By February 2002, it had lost half of its value, selling two pesos to the dollar. The middle class lost much of its savings. There were desperate runs on the banks, which did not have the means to fulfill their obligations to depositors. Income per person dropped from $7,000 to $3,500 and unemployment stood at 25 percent. Among the consequences were a higher crime rate, the spread of *villas miserias* (shantytowns), higher divorce rates, and hunger. By February 2003, 58 percent of the population, according to the government's own figures, was designated as poor.[8] All this resulted in the biggest default on foreign debt in history.

Argentina, which in 1913 had ranked among the ten richest nations—ahead of France and Germany—had hit rock bottom. It was an economic calamity without parallel, one of the steepest declines in recent history.

## □ Brazil

Brazil stands out among the nations of South America both because of its Portuguese (rather than Spanish) background and because of its immense size. In 1990, its population of 150 million occupied one-third of the continent. With its extensive resources, its potential is vast.

Brazil, like Argentina, experimented with democracy, but when democratically elected governments proved unable to cope with economic decline or attempted radical reforms, they gave way to military leaders. In both Argentina and Brazil, military rule lasted from the mid-1960s to the early 1980s and finally yielded to popular pressure for the return to democracy. The major difference between the two countries' experiences was that the Brazilian military regimes proved somewhat more successful in dealing with economic problems.

In the first decade after World War II, successive democratically elected presidents wrestled with inflation and heavy government borrowing. A case in point was the administration of Juscelino Kubitschek, who aggressively pursued the goal of economic modernization with lavish spending programs. His most extravagant project was the founding of a spectacular new capital city, Brasilia, located in the interior of the country. This project was designed to spur the development of the interior region and to stimulate national pride.

Kubitschek, however, lost the election of 1960 to João Goulart, who brought a new approach to the nation's economic problems. Goulart proposed extensive land reform, election reform to enfranchise the nation's illiterate (40 percent of the population), and tax reform to increase government revenues. In 1964, he ordered the expropriation of some of the nation's largest estates. Such programs earned him the support of the peasantry and the working class but incurred the wrath of the landowning elite, the middle class, and the military. Goulart also proclaimed a neutralist foreign policy, established diplomatic relations with the Soviet Union, legalized the Brazilian Communist Party, and began to woo that party's support. Goulart's free-spending policies, like those of Kubitschek, caused inflation, and this, in addition to Goulart's move to the left, resulted in an erosion of support from the middle class. Army leaders, who had secured U.S. support in advance, forced his resignation in April 1964.

This time the military junta came to stay; it governed Brazil with a heavy hand for the next twenty years. Blaming free-spending civilian politicians for Brazil's ills, the generals silenced all opponents and forced an austerity program on the nation. They banned the Communist Party and carried out mass arrests of Communists and those suspected to be Communists. They then issued a series of "institutional acts" that incrementally restricted the powers of the congress, arrogated greater powers to the presidency, disenfranchised other political parties, repressed political freedoms, and sought to crush the labor unions.

However, the Brazilian economy responded to the stringent austerity program; in fact, during the twenty years of military rule, Brazil realized its highest economic growth rates. In 1966, Brazil's annual rate of growth of GNP was 4 percent; it rose steadily and reached 10 percent in the early 1970s. The growth of both agricultural and industrial production made possible a favorable balance of trade for the first time since World War II. But this economic success story had a dark side. On the one hand, it could not be sustained, partly because of the severe impact of the oil crises of the 1970s and partly because of the gigantic foreign debt the military leaders ran up. On the other hand, the growth of the GNP had not produced a higher standard of living for the majority of Brazilian people. Industrial growth was made possible by keeping wages low, and the rise in the cost of living continued to exceed the growth in wages. In addition, the military undertook no land reform and did nothing to improve the lot of the rural poor.

By the late 1980s, military rule gave way to democratic elections. Brazil's first free election in twenty-nine years, in March 1989, was won by Fernando Collor de Mello, a young, winsome, articulate, conservative politician who defeated the candidate of the left, Luiz Ignacio da Silva. Collor de Mello promised democratic reform and economic prosperity, but what he brought to Brazil, instead, was the largest scale of personal corruption the country had ever witnessed. In 1992, Collor de Mello was forced to resign.

The rule of the Brazilian military had been moderate by South American standards. Only two hundred were executed (as compared to up to thirty thousand in Argentina) and hundreds were driven into exile. In 1995, the government of Fernando Henrique Cardoso finally offered compensation for the relatives of the victims.

For more than a dozen years, the conservatives ruled Brazil. But in October 2003, da Silva—commonly known as Lula—in his fourth bid for the presidency, won by a wide margin a runoff election. Lula's rise to power was literally from rags to riches. One of twenty-two children of an illiterate farm worker, Lula rose from shoe-shine boy to the leader of São Paulo's militant car workers' union. He then organized the Workers's Party, Latin America's largest left-wing party.

Lula inherited an economy in deep trouble. In 2003, the *real,* Brazil's currency, had lost 40 percent of its value, and as a consequence the public debt spiraled upward. The international financial community feared that Brazil would follow Argentina and default on its debt. Immediately after the election, Lula put on a tie and suit and stepped back from his pledge to renege on Brazil's heavy debt. He had already brought under control the radicals in his party and had made an alliance with the center-right Liberal Party. He agreed to work with the IMF to try and bring the international debt under control, reminding the Brazilians that "there is no miraculous solution for such a huge social debt."9

## ☐ Chile

Chile presents still another variation on the theme of oscillation between civilian and military governments. Chile, however, did not succumb to military rule until 1973. The army had stayed out of politics until 1973, but when it did intervene, it did so with a vengeance. Between 1945 and 1973, Chile was the most orderly and democratic country in Latin America and its army was "exceptionally apolitical by Latin American standards."10 Chile also stood out as the most flagrant example of U.S. interference in South America.

Nowhere in South America were U.S. business interests more substantial than in Chile. Early in the twentieth century, Chile became the main source of copper for the United States, and its copper mines and many of its industries were owned by U.S. firms. Thus, when Chilean politics moved to the left, it was not only conservative elements in Chile that were alarmed. Washington would not sit still as another Latin American country, especially one as economically important as Chile, edged closer to Communism.

Washington favored conservative governments in Chile, and under the moderate Eduardo Frei, the head of the Christian Democratic Party, Chile received generous amounts of U.S. Alliance for Progress loans, which financed industrial expansion but also increased the nation's indebtedness. The Chilean elite and conservative parties considered Frei's gradualist

Chilean president Salvador Allende, who died in the presidential palace during the September 1973 coup. *(Organization of American States)*

General Augusto Pinochet, who led the military coup against Allende in 1973 and remained in power in Chile afterward. *(Organization of American States)*

reforms—education initiatives to reduce illiteracy, expansion of social services, and a modest agrarian program—as too radical, while the working class and the parties on the left saw them as too modest. Only the middle class and Washington seemed happy with Frei.

The polarization of Chilean politics was evident in the 1970 election. The Marxist Salvador Allende, the candidate of a leftist coalition Popular Unity, squeaked by with a narrow victory and became the world's first freely elected Marxist head of state. Allende, whose cabinet consisted mainly of socialists and Communists, called for a peaceful transition to socialism. He went right to work to achieve that end, nationalizing both U.S. and Chilean copper and nitrate companies and banks, extending the land reform begun by Frei, and placing a ceiling on prices while raising workers' wages. These measures were immensely popular with the majority of people in Chile, but they alarmed Allende's opponents, as well as the Nixon administration in Washington.

Chile was already in an economic depression when Allende took office. By the second year of his term, the economy was in a tailspin, with inflation running out of control. Allende's policies contributed to these problems, but the major blow to the Chilean economy was a drastic fall in the international price of copper. By mid-1972, Allende's base of support had dwindled to little more than the working class and the poor. Conservative elements—notably the military—began to organize in opposition to Allende and carried out actions such as a crippling, nationwide truckers' strike—a measure secretly supported by CIA funds. The polarization of the nation became extreme, and a violent clash seemed imminent. Allende and his Communist supporters began arming workers, and the army began plotting a coup. That coup took place in September 1973 when the air force bombed the presidential palace, where, in the end, Allende committed suicide as the army moved in.

The United States was not an innocent bystander. It was involved initially in efforts to prevent Allende from coming to power, and having failed that, it participated in the efforts to destroy his government. President Nixon and National Security Adviser Henry Kissinger regarded Allende as a threat to the entire region. Kissinger later declared that "I don't see why we have to let a country go Marxist just because its people are irresponsible."[11]

Nixon used two levers to force Allende's downfall: it funneled some $8 million through the CIA to Allende's opponents, and it took steps to cut off all loans, economic aid, and private investments to Chile. Speculation was rife at the time that there was direct U.S. involvement in the military coup, but Washington admitted nothing and kept its relevant documents classified until the late 1990s, when the Clinton administration declassified evidence supporting such speculation.[12] Moreover, a number of the Chilean military officers who led the coup—like many others from Latin American countries—had received training at the School for the Americas, a facility in Panama established by the U.S. Army to train Latin American military officers.

The new government, headed by General Augusto Pinochet, swiftly carried out a relentless campaign against leftists and anyone suspected of having been associated with the deposed regime. The military crammed the jails and even a huge stadium with political prisoners and killed three thousand of them and then later at least a thousand others. After the coup, the military formed a "Caravan of Death," whereby soldiers traveled throughout the country to carry out summary executions. And it was under Pinochet that Latin America experienced the first cases of people simply "disappearing," a practice that subsequently spread through the region. Pinochet became the guiding force of Operation Condor, an effort on the part of military strongmen in six participating countries (Chile, Argentina, Brazil, Uruguay, Paraguay, and Bolivia) to track down opponents, not only in Latin America but also in Europe and the United States. In 1976, Chilean operatives assassinated the former foreign minister Orlando Letelier in the streets of Washington, D.C. Kissinger knew of Operation Condor and, in fact, supported the campaign against leftist Chilean exiles in Argentina. He told the Argentine foreign minister that it should act "quickly" and then "get back quickly to normal procedure."[13]

Pinochet invited U.S. copper companies back in, halted the land reform program, broke up labor unions, banned all leftist parties, and dissolved congress. All the while, Pinochet continued to enjoy the support of the United States, which preferred the secure climate for investment and the anti-Communist partnership that Pinochet provided to the political instability his overthrow might bring.

In the late 1980s, despite the ban against antigovernment demonstrations, thousands of protesters went into the streets to demand change. Finally, in 1990, Pinochet relented by allowing a referendum on whether military rule should continue. In the first free election in twenty years, the people voted overwhelmingly to restore civilian rule. Pinochet, however, remained army commander by virtue of a clause in the constitution he had written, preventing the elected president from dismissing him until 1997. The constitution also made the armed forces the "guarantor of institutionality";[14] in other words, it gave them the right to step in whenever they felt Chile's interests were threatened.

Pinochet relinquished his command of the army in March 1998 and was made "senator for life," a position that would grant him immunity from criminal charges for atrocities committed under his seventeen-year rule. Gradually he faded into the background, but suddenly he returned to the front pages of the world press when he was arrested in October 1998 in London at the request of Spain, which wanted him extradited to be tried on charges of human rights abuses against Spanish citizens in Chile. The eighty-three-year-old ex-dictator languished in London under house arrest for over a year until, in January 2000, a team of British physicians found him too ill to stand trial, thus permitting him to be flown back to Chile.

In August 2004, Chile's supreme court, by a vote of nine to eight, ruled that the now eighty-eight-year-old Pinochet was not immune from the murders committed during the 1970s. But first, doctors would have to certify that Pinochet, suffering from mild dementia, was fit to stand trial. By the end of the 1990s, some twenty soldiers and police had been convicted of crimes committed after 1978, after the worst excesses had already been committed. The notable exception was the prison term set down for Colonel Manuel Contreras, the former head of the secret police, the Department of National Intelligence, for his role in the 1976 murder of Letelier. The court did not accept Contreras's defense that he only followed Pinochet's orders.

□ Peru

Perhaps nowhere in South America were social and economic inequities as wide as in Peru. A small, wealthy elite kept the Peruvian masses—mainly of native Indian stock—in dismal poverty. About 80 percent of the land was owned by a mere 1 percent of landowners, and the richest owned over 1 million acres. Landless Peruvian peasants sporadically rose in revolt, seeking to grasp some of the largely unused latifundio of the elite, only to be crushed by the Peruvian army. Neither the early postwar military regime in Peru (1946–1956) nor the civilian administrations that followed attempted land reform. All the while, the country was seething with peasant unrest, and a rural-based Communist movement began to spread. In October 1968, President Fernando Belaunde's government was floundering amid economic chaos and corruption scandals, when the military interceded and replaced him with one of their own.

The new leadership, headed by Juan Velasco, unlike the military governments in the rest of Latin America, became an agent of reform. In quick order, it introduced state planning and modest social and economic reforms enforced by the army. Most noteworthy was land reform, which within seven years expropriated and redistributed some 25 million acres—about 72 percent of Peru's arable land. The government also undertook a program of land reclamation to increase agricultural output and meet the needs of the land-starved Indians. The Velasco regime also nationalized foreign properties, including U.S.-owned copper, petroleum, and sugar companies. Private enterprise remained legal, but industries were required to share profits with their workers. Although a modest increase in agricultural production resulted from the agrarian reforms, the economy slumped badly, especially after the 1973–1974 oil crisis. Still, the military rulers, despite their reformist efforts, failed to achieve either a fundamental social transformation or a significant improvement in the standard of living for most Peruvians.

By 1980, the generals stepped back and permitted civilian rule once again. Belaunde, whom the generals had ousted in 1968, won the election but he was no more capable of resolving Peru's economic problems than he had been twelve years earlier. The July 1990 presidential election was won by an unlikely candidate, Alberto Fujimori, an inexperienced politician of Japanese ancestry. When Fujimori took office, Peru had not made a payment for two years on its $23 billion debt; the inflation rate was over 40 percent a month; and the central government was unable to govern outlying areas, where hostile guerrillas stalked the countryside. Fujimori first attacked the economic problem. Through such stringent measures as slashing government payrolls and subsidies and overhauling the tax system, he managed to break the inflationary cycle within six months.

The unorthodox Fujimori then formed an alliance with the military. In April 1992, he carried out a political coup, suspending the constitution, closing the legislative assembly, and assuming emergency executive powers. For this he was denounced not only by the unseated Peruvian politicians but also by governments throughout the hemisphere. But Fujimori's bold housecleaning measures were, at first, popular with most Peruvians, even though they cost the country much-needed foreign aid and thus crimped economic development.

Fujimori also won acclaim at home and abroad by winning a surprising victory in Peru's twelve-year war against the Sendero Luminoso, the "Shining Path," a Maoist-Marxist movement that had combined violent revolution with drug trafficking. His government arrested and sentenced to life in prison the leaders of the Shining Path, including its charismatic founder, Abimael Guzman Reynoso, a former philosophy professor. The Shining Path had organized poverty-stricken peasants to protect them against brutality at the hands of the police and the military, with the aim of ultimately bringing down the government. The result was a civil war with extraordinary brutality on both sides. The war threatened to bankrupt the government; it caused an estimated $22 billion in damages. Sixty-nine thousand Peruvians were killed or simply "disappeared," being impoverished native Quechua in the high Andes.[15] Fujimori's stunning victory against the revolutionaries, combined with a measure of economic progress, won him considerable popularity within Peru. He handily won reelection in 1994.

But success came at a price. Fujimori's austerity program benefited only small segments of the population—among them the financial sector and international investors. Fujimori's first task was to meet Peru's financial obligations as spelled out by the IMF, one of the pillars that sustained his regime. Meanwhile, real wages fell by 10 percent and the majority of Peruvians—about two-thirds of them—remained mired in poverty.

Fujimori continued to present himself as the champion of "true democracy" and the common man, but all along he was doing the army's bidding.[16] After all, it was the army that was his main pillar of support. In July 1992, a military death squad operating under the direct orders of commander-in-chief of the army, General Nicolas Hermoza—and ultimately under Fujimori's orders—abducted and murdered nine students and a professor. When the courts eventually convicted and sentenced twelve soldiers for the crime, Fujimori pushed through a pliant congress a blanket amnesty for those convicted of human rights crimes between May 1980 and June 1995.[17] The amnesty cemented a symbiotic relationship between the president and the armed forces.

In December 1996, yet another leftist organization, the Tupac Amaru, which Fujimori claimed had been defeated, resurfaced when it took approximately four hundred hostages at a Christmas party hosted by the Japanese ambassador. Tupac Amaru demanded the release of its imprisoned comrades, many of whom had been engaged in acts of violence and had been sentenced by Peruvian military tribunals. The hostage crisis continued unresolved into April 1997, in part because the Japanese government insisted on a negotiated settlement. In the end, Peruvian commandos stormed the building, killing all members of the Tupac Amaru inside while losing one hostage and two commandos. For Fujimori, it was another feather in his cap.

In 1996, the Fujimori majority in congress reinterpreted the constitution, which had restricted a president to two five-year terms. The obedient congress granted Fujimori another term. Judges who ruled against the legitimacy of a third term were dismissed. Newspapers were turned into apologists of the Fujimori regime. Editors who refused to fall into line felt the wrath of Vladimiro Montesinos, head of the National Intelligence Service, who controlled the army as well as death squads that operated out of his headquarters, the "Little Pentagon." Critics disappeared or were slandered, stripped of their citizenship, blackmailed, and tortured. Peru withdrew from the jurisdiction of the Inter-American Court of Justice in order to escape the court's scrutiny.

Montesinos had been on the CIA payroll, despite the fact that the agency knew that he and Fujimori had long been engaged in extortion, larceny, drug trafficking, torture, and murder.[18]

In the election of April 2000, Fujimori faced a surprisingly strong contender in the person of Alejandro Toledo, a U.S.-trained economist. Toledo came in a strong second, forcing a runoff election. Toledo accused Fujimori of election fraud and refused to participate in the runoff unless it contained safeguards against rigging it. Fujimori refused to oblige him and went ahead with his third term, despite daily protest demonstrations by the Toledo-led opposition and criticism from neighboring countries, the Organization of American States, and the United States, which heretofore had supported Fujimori.

Fujimori's grip on the nation slipped in September 2000, when his right-hand man, Montesinos, was caught on videotape attempting to bribe an opposition politician. Ten days later, Montesinos flew to Panama to seek political asylum, only to be turned away. Upon returning to Peru a week later, he went into hiding and rumors of an impending coup were rife again. Two weeks later, in November 2000, Fujimori fled to Tokyo from where he resigned by fax. The Peruvian congress would not let him resign; instead, it invoked a constitutional provision declaring him morally unfit to govern. Japan granted Fujimori citizenship, through which he escaped the long arm of Peruvian law. The Peruvian government then launched an investigation of charges of corruption by Fujimori in exile and Montesinos, whom it managed to apprehend.

When Fujimori began his political career, he had identified with the nation's poor. He emphasized his own humble origins and campaigned in the garb of the rural Indian people. He did manage to bring inflation under control, but in the end did little to end the country's economic woes. The extent of poverty remained essentially unchanged; during the 1990s, the national poverty rate hovered around 50 percent, and 41 percent of the people lived on $2 a day or less.[19] Montesinos and Fujimori, however, had no difficulty in making ends meet. Transparency International concluded that the two had been engaged in "unprecedented looting of the resources" of

Peru. Montesinos siphoned off an estimated $2 billion; Fujimori escaped with $600 million.[20]

# ■ MEXICO

The roots of many of the problems Mexico faced at the end of the twentieth century date back to the political and economic consequences of the revolution of 1910–1917. That revolution disintegrated into a bloody civil war in which 1.5 million people—approximately 10 percent of the population—lost their lives. Not until the late 1920s did the country begin to enjoy a measure of stability. It was then that a new party, the Partido Revolucionario Institucional (the Institutional Revolutionary Party, or PRI), came to power and began to organize diverse groups in support of the state. It encouraged workers, peasants, bureaucrats, big-business executives, owners of small enterprises, teachers, and other groups to bargain with the party, which then acted as the arbiter for these various interest groups. To maintain power, the PRI skillfully formed political alliances, doled out patronage jobs, co-opted its opponents, occasionally carried through reforms within the party, controlled the media, and, when necessary, resorted to fraud and violent repression. Incumbent presidents usually chose their successors behind closed palace doors. Thus, the PRI-dominated Mexican government produced a surface calm, but it did not address the underlying causes of social discontent that periodically became visible.

The revolution of 1910 had begun as a liberal challenge to the dictatorship of Porfirio Díaz, but it soon became more radical when the *campesinos* (the peasantry), under the slogan "Land and Liberty" and such leaders as Emiliano Zapata and Pancho Villa, demanded the redistribution of land. At the time, 96 percent of the rural households owned no land, and fewer than 850 families owned 97 percent of Mexico's arable land.[21] The 1917 Constitution promised a redistribution of land, but prior to the presidency of the populist Lazaro Cárdenas (1934–1940), only about 10 percent of the rural population had benefited from land reform.

Cárdenas distributed more land than any other Mexican president. During his tenure, the campesinos' irrigated landholdings increased fourfold,[22] but even under Cárdenas land distribution came to a halt after 1937. When army generals complained that his populist reforms had gone too far, Cárdenas shifted, in March 1938, his focus of attack to "imperialist intervention," that is, foreign—U.S. and European—corporations that controlled sectors of the Mexican economy, notably oil. The time was ripe, he declared, for the nationalization of these companies. There was a massive outpouring of support; millions of Mexicans contributed to a national indemnity fund to help pay off the $200 million the oil companies eventually received in compensation.[23]

One of the PRI's functions was to oversee the development of state capitalism, which gave Mexico decades of sustained growth. Between 1940 and 1960, manufacturing rose by 365 percent, steel production by 934 percent, motor vehicle production by 451 percent, and agricultural output by 218 percent; during the same period, the population increased by 78 percent. Per capita government expenditures increased fourfold.[24] Yet the gap between the rich and the poor grew after World War II. Mexico witnessed a potentially volatile mix of economic growth, raised expectations, a pattern of growing social inequalities, and dissent.

The economic downturn of the late 1960s had severe social and political repercussions. On October 2, 1968, tens of thousands of demonstrators—mostly young students—congregated in Mexico City's Tlatelolco Plaza to protest police brutality, political corruption, and economic hardship. The army promptly put an end to this challenge to the PRI by fatally shooting at least three hundred civilians. Ten days later, the Mexico City Olympic Games began, the first such showcase in a developing country. As the torch was lit in Aztec Stadium, troops and tanks were deployed outside the view of television cameras.

The massacre did not solve the PRI's problems; it triggered instead a crisis of legitimacy for the PRI. During the 1970s and 1980s, the government conducted Mexico's "dirty war" against opponents, many of whom traced their anger back to the massacre. For thirty years, the PRI denied that this, and other massacres, had taken place. Eventually, Mexico, as other Latin American nations had done, began to come to terms with its past. In February 2002, pictures of the Tlatelolco Square massacre appeared in newspapers, and in October 2004, Mexico's supreme court issued an arrest for the now eighty-two-year-old former president, Luis Echeverría, for the June 1971 murder of thirty students.[25]

In 1970, when Echeverría, the interior minister during the 1968 massacre, became president, dissidents—among them students, reporters, guerrillas, and practitioners of "liberation theology"—sought to build grassroots social bases in the barrios and among the campesinos. Echeverría, under pressure to create more jobs, borrowed both time and money. The government bought bankrupt enterprises in an attempt to save jobs, and the legislature passed even more restrictive laws against foreign investors. It then began to borrow increasing amounts of foreign money—without the revenue to finance the borrowing binge. When Echeverría took office in 1970, the nation's foreign debt stood at $5 billion; by the time his successor, José López Portillo (1976–1982), took office, the debt had risen to $20 billion. López came to power in the midst of the oil boom of the 1970s, which made it possible for Mexico—sitting on top of vast oil reserves—to borrow still more money. During López's presidency, the public and private sectors borrowed another $60 billion. By August 1982, Mexico was unable to pay off its massive foreign debt, a condition that triggered a Latin American debt crisis.

In the early 1980s, elections in northern Mexico—free of the usual tampering by PRI functionaries—showed the weakness of the PRI, which lost several local races to the Partido Acción Nacional (National Action Party, or PAN), a center-right, business-based party. In the mid-1980s, an environmental protest movement emerged partly in response to Mexico City's horrendous air pollution. Then came the massive earthquake of September 19, 1985, which buried more than ten thousand people. In its aftermath, Cuauthemoc Cárdenas (the son of the revered Lazaro Cárdenas) broke with the PRI and became the candidate of a center-left coalition, and in the 1988 presidential election, he challenged the PRI candidate, Carlos Salinas de Gortari. Cárdenas had a substantial following, but two days before the election two of his key aides were murdered (crimes that were never solved), and a few hours after the voting ended, the computer counting the votes crashed. When the computers came back on-line, Salinas had won the election with just over 50 percent of the vote. A few months later, the PRI destroyed the ballots.

By now, Mexico's economy was treading water during what became the country's worst recession in sixty years. Between 1980 and 1993, annual output had declined by an average of 0.5 percent. Salinas, in an attempt to revive the economy, continued Mexico's venture into the minefields of the global economy. Mexico worked out agreements with multilateral international lending institutions (such as the World Bank and the IMF) that gave it access to additional credits; simultaneously, it negotiated with Canada and the United States the terms of the North American Free Trade Agreement (NAFTA). Lazaro Cárdenas's "anti-imperialist" campaign of the 1930s was now but a dim memory.

The social price of admission into the global economy was high. It consisted of deep structural adjustments to satisfy the creditors—the elimination of tariffs, deregulation of the economy, privatization of state enterprises, and labor "flexibilization" (literally, making labor more flexible, more amenable to the demands of factory owners) with the object of increasing productivity and international competitiveness. In short, workers were expected to work harder for lower wages. The state took steps to deny unions the right of free association and repeatedly used police and the army against workers and their unions. With economic restructuring and flexibilization, the unions lost both economic and political power.

## ☐ Chiapas

On January 1, 1994, Mexico faced yet another crisis. In the state of Chiapas, in the southeastern corner of the nation along the border with Guatemala, campesinos, mostly Indians, suddenly rose in rebellion. They called themselves the Zapatista National Liberation Army in memory of Emiliano Zapata, one of the heroes of the revolution of 1910. They seized control of a number of cities and latifundio, which they turned into communal farms and insisted that the land they worked had been granted to them by the 1917 Constitution.

The Zapatistas of 1994 saw land as the core issue. Since the move toward privatization of the economy during the mid-1980s, the campesinos—who had little land to begin with—had been losing land to the latifundistas. When the Zapatistas seized the courthouse in San Cristobal de las Casas, they promptly burned the municipal archives that held the land titles. They denounced the government's electoral fraud;[26] demanded regional autonomy; and declared that they would no longer endure abuse at the hands of the police, the army, and the terrorist *guardias blancas* ("white guards") deployed by the latifundistas.

Chiapas was the poorest state in a poor country. The federal government spent less than half the amount of development money per capita in Chiapas than it did in the nation as a whole. Chiapas needed paved roads, adequate schools, electricity (the state contained large dams that exported energy to other states), and health facilities. A large percentage of the population was of Mayan Indian origin (26.4 percent, compared to the national average of 7.5 percent); a third of the people did not speak Spanish. The national minimum daily wage of workers in 1990 was $3.33; in Chiapas, nearly 60 percent earned less than that amount. Nineteen percent of the labor force had no income, working as peasants and existing at a bare subsistence level. Food production had barely kept up with a population that had doubled over the past two decades,[27] and prices for the main cash crop, coffee, had fallen drastically.

The rebellion broke out the very day NAFTA went into effect—the final indignity. The Zapatistas saw the treaty with the United States as a "death certificate" for the Indians of Mexico, who would not be able to compete with manufacturers and food producers in the United States and Canada. Led by the charismatic and mysterious Subcomandante Marcos, his face hidden by a ski mask, the Zapatistas declared that they spoke for all of Mexico in a struggle for democracy, land, economic change, and autonomy. The Salinas administration, hamstrung by repeated scandals and mistrusted by the majority of its people, deployed the army in an attempt to end the rebellion. Within the context of Mexican history, however, the government showed remarkable restraint; estimates of fatalities varied widely, from 145 to 400. In the end, Salinas agreed to negotiations with the rebels, whose strength lay not so much in their military power but in their manifestos, through which they rallied public support.

## ☐ The PRI Defeated

The Zapatistas were hardly alone in venting their anger against the system. Two million members of the middle class—small shopkeepers, merchants, and farmers, hard hit by the recession of the mid-1990s—had already formed their own resistance movement, El Barzon. They, too, had a program of legal action and civil resistance, such as showing up in large numbers at foreclosure hearings. Another group, the Civic Alliance, sent election observers to polling stations to prevent the PRI's rampant election fraud. And the National Episcopal Conference sided with the Roman Catholic Church in Chiapas, headed by Bishop Samuel Ruíz García, who played the role of intermediary in the talks between the rebels and the authorities.

The PRI no longer fulfilled the functions for which it had been created—to arbitrate disputes among competing interest groups. Its political monopoly was crumbling. In 1996, PAN, the right-center party, elected four state governors and ruled about one-third of the population. Continued widespread corruption—including theft from the national treasury—and unresolved political murders in 1994 and 1995 further undermined the legitimacy of the PRI.

The Mexican people's growing dissatisfaction with, if not utter contempt for, the PRI was expressed clearly in the presidential election in July 2000. Vicente Fox, candidate of the National Action Party and a businessman who campaigned for sweeping political and economic reforms, won a resounding victory against the PRI candidate, thus ending the PRI's seventy-one-year monopoly on power. At least one factor determining the outcome was that for the first time the presidential election was run by an independent commission that kept the PRI from rigging it. After his inauguration, Fox declared his intention of negotiating an end to the standoff in Chiapas.

## ■ REVOLUTION AND COUNTERREVOLUTION IN CENTRAL AMERICA

In Central America, political struggles, recurrent since the days of colonial occupation, resurfaced with a vengeance during the 1970s and attracted worldwide attention. These conflicts, fueled by deep social divisions, quickly became part and parcel of the global struggle between the United States and the Soviet Union. On one side were the landowners, who enjoyed political power and had the backing of the army. Opposing them was the majority of the population, which possessed little land and even fewer political rights.

Direct U.S. involvement in Central America began in the 1890s and increased after the Spanish-American War of 1898, when the United States took on the role of police officer of the Western Hemisphere, especially in the Caribbean. The United States, in the words of Teddy Roosevelt, would not permit "chronic wrongdoing" in a region some in the United States considered its "backyard."[28] The region became a U.S. sphere of influence where the protection of U.S. interests—political, economic, and military—became of paramount concern.

Officially, the U.S. goal in Central America was to bring the blessings of democracy to its people. In 1913, President Woodrow Wilson went so far as to declare that he would "teach the South American republics how to elect good men."[29] The military regimes in Latin America, however, had other ideas. Moreover, U.S. commitments to the cause of democracy often took a backseat to what became the primary quest: political stability and the protection of U.S. interests. In the early 1960s, President John Kennedy described the U.S. dilemma in Central America:

> There are three possibilities in descending order of preference: a decent democratic regime, a continuation of the Trujillo regime [a right-wing dictatorship in the Dominican Republic] or a Castro regime [a left-wing dictatorship in Cuba]. We ought to aim at the first, but we really can't renounce the second until we are sure that we can avoid the third.[30]

Washington's problem was the absence of Kennedy's "decent democratic regimes" in Central America. Successive U.S. administrations had to choose between the likes of a Trujillo or a Castro. They were also unable to reconcile their official creed of political liberty with support of dictators who, miraculously, were now part of the "free world." At the same time, the United States did little to assist democratically elected, reformist governments such as that of Jacob Arbenz in Guatemala in the early 1950s.

The Cuban revolution of 1959 provided the rationale for U.S. policy in Central America. Fidel Castro, unlike other revolutionaries in Latin America, refused to accept the unequal relationship between Cuba and the United States, one that dated back to 1898 when the United States seized Cuba from Spain. U.S. companies controlled large portions of the Cuban economy, and the U.S. ambassador to Havana wielded great power. To rectify this condition, Castro insisted on the nationalization (governmental takeover) of U.S. property—with compensation[31]—and the reorganization of the Cuban economy along socialist lines. Moreover, Castro worked out a trade agreement with the Soviet Union, trading Cuban sugar for Soviet oil and machinery.

The United States, unaccustomed to such a brazen show of defiance, initiated economic warfare against Castro and broke off diplomatic relations. It then moved to overthrow Castro, an attempt that resulted in the fiasco at the Bay of Pigs in 1961 (see Chapter 4). Other attempts followed, but Castro survived and, with the help of the Soviet Union, consolidated his power. The Cuban missile crisis in 1962 led to a U.S. pledge not to invade Cuba, but successive U.S. governments, whether Democratic or Republican, were in no mood to tolerate other radical regimes in their "backyard." One Cuba was enough.

## ☐ *Nicaragua*

The next serious outbreak of revolutionary violence in Central America began in Nicaragua during the late 1960s. It came on the heels of a devastating earthquake in 1972 that leveled much of Managua, the nation's capital. Nicaragua at the time was ruled by the Somoza family, which had come to power in the early 1930s with the help of U.S. Marines (an occupation force in Nicaragua, off and on, from 1911 to 1932). President Franklin Roosevelt once remarked that Anastasio Somoza García, the founder of the dynasty, was an "s.o.b., but [he is] our s.o.b."[32] The greed of the Somozas became legendary. When the last of the Somozas, Anastasio Jr. ("Tachito"), fled the country in 1979, he took with him an estimated $100–$400 million, most of it from the national treasury.

The 1972 earthquake highlighted the greed of Anastasio Somoza Jr. and the National Guard, his private army. They had long been involved in the seizure of land and the control of many sectors of the economy—construction kickbacks, prostitution, gambling, taxation. When the devastation hit the capital, all discipline in the National Guard broke down, as its soldiers looted publicly. Somoza and his officers handled the foreign contributions for the relief of the earthquake victims, siphoning off large sums of money and selling relief supplies.

By 1974, Somoza had created powerful enemies, including the Roman Catholic Church and the middle class, neither of which had forgiven him for his conduct after the earthquake. In January 1978, Somocista killers assassinated Pedro Joaquín Chamorro, an outspoken critic and the editor of the newspaper *La Prensa*. This act sparked the first mass uprising against Somoza. Once Jimmy Carter became president in 1977 and made human rights a priority, Somoza could no longer count on the United States to bail him out (although it continued to sell him arms). The National Guard executed thousands, but it was too late. The rebellion gathered in strength; no amount of bloodshed could save Somoza's regime.

The violence in Nicaragua was brought home to the U.S. public in June 1979, when the National Guard arrested ABC newsman Bill Stewart, forced him to kneel, and executed him. Stewart's camera crew recorded the murder on film, and hours later the scene was reproduced on U.S. television screens. Only then did the Carter administration cut off arms sales to Somoza. A month later, in July 1979—after having looted the national treasury—Somoza fled Nicaragua, leaving behind a devastated country. The death toll was between forty and fifty thousand, 20 percent of the population was homeless, and forty thousand children were orphaned. The industrial base was in ruins; the Somocistas, having plundered the country, left behind a foreign debt of $1.5 billion.

In Somoza's place, the Sandinistas, a coalition of revolutionaries, seized power. The Sandinistas had taken their name from the revolutionary

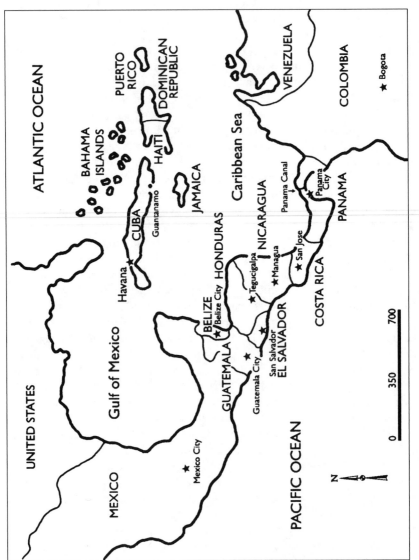

**Central America**

Augusto Sandino, whom the first Somoza had murdered nearly fifty years previously. Carter did not like the leftist orientation of the Sandinistas, but eventually he provided a modest amount of foreign aid in order to retain a bit of leverage over them. But as the Nicaraguan revolution continued to shift to the left, a disillusioned Carter suspended all economic aid.

The Sandinistas then proceeded to solidify their position and establish a new order that included the nationalization of land, press censorship, political prisoners, the nationalization of segments of industry, a militarized government, and a restricted electoral process. But it also included extended health care for the population, a fair measure of freedom of speech, a literacy campaign, the redistribution of land, and an economy of which half remained in private hands. In short, the Sandinista government became a typical example of a revolution seeking to consolidate its power while at the same time seeking to resolve the nation's most pressing social and economic problems.

The war of nerves between Washington and Managua escalated in 1981, after President Ronald Reagan took office. Reagan canceled all aid to Nicaragua and launched covert CIA actions against the Sandinistas, who had committed the unpardonable sin of becoming recipients of aid from the Communist states of Eastern Europe, notably the Soviet Union (but also from West European states such as France and West Germany). Moreover, prior to March 1981, they had even sent a small amount of arms to the leftist rebels in neighboring El Salvador. In the eyes of the Reagan administration, the

Daniel Ortega, Sandinista leader and one-time president of Nicaragua. *(Organization of American States)*

Sandinistas had become a spearhead of Soviet expansionism in Central America.

The CIA then proceeded to organize and arm the Contras, the counter-revolutionary opponents of the Sandinistas. Headed by former members of the National Guard—Somoza's army—the Contras were tainted by their past association with Somoza and therefore had little support in Nicaragua. Reagan had a difficult time selling his assistance to the Contras to Congress and the U.S. public, who—after the Vietnam War—were leery of being drawn into another civil war in a land of which they knew little. But when Daniel Ortega, the dominant figure in the Sandinista government, flew to Moscow seeking economic aid, Congress approved financial assistance to the Contras, but that aid was to be used only for "humanitarian" rather than military purposes.

Reagan threatened to tighten the screws on the Sandinistas until they "cried uncle." A number of Latin American countries, the so-called Contadora group—Mexico, Panama, Colombia, and Venezuela—called for a political settlement instead. It proposed a mutual disengagement of all foreign advisers and soldiers—Cuban, Soviet, and U.S.—from Central America, in short, the political and military neutralization of the region. It pointed to the counterproductive nature of Washington's Central American containment program: the Sandinista army had doubled in size since 1981 and the Salvadoran revolutionaries had tripled their forces. Reagan carried out his own escalation when he directed the CIA to arm and assist the Contras and began to conduct military exercises in nearby Honduras. Central America had become another Third World battleground in the East-West confrontation.

The Sandinistas proclaimed their willingness to abide by the Contadora solution; the Reagan administration, however, rejected this solution because it would permit the Sandinista regime to remain in power. In his address to Congress in April 1983, Reagan tied the fate of the Nicaraguan revolution to the global Cold War:

> If Central America were to fall [to Communism], what would be the consequence for our position in Asia and Europe and for alliances such as NATO? If the United States cannot respond to a threat near our own border, why should Europeans and Asians believe we are seriously concerned about threats to them? . . . Our credibility would collapse, our alliances would crumble.[33]

To complicate matters for Reagan, the Contras had made no significant military progress, had no base of popular support in Nicaragua, and had virtually no prospect of defeating the Sandinista army. When Congress, in response to the public's distaste for becoming involved in Nicaragua, suspended further military aid to the Contras in 1984 and again in early 1985, Reagan resolved to find other ways to fund the Contras. Thus began what came to be known as the "Iran-Contra affair." Officials in the president's National Security Council worked out a complex scheme whereby profits from covert and illegal sales of arms to Iran—through Israeli intermediaries—would be turned over to the Contras. Colonel Oliver North, who conducted this operation from the basement of the White House, also sought money from political donors within the United States and from friendly foreign governments—all in violation of congressional laws prohibiting further military aid to the Contras. These illegal and covert operations, detected in November 1986, remained the national focus for several years—much like the Watergate scandal in the Nixon era—for they raised many questions about ethics, law, and power. Where Nicaragua was concerned, the Iran-Contra affair had a ruinous effect on Reagan's policy. Congress, which earlier had vacillated on the issue of Contra aid, now firmly rejected any further military support despite Reagan's persistent pleas. Another setback for Reagan came in June 1986, when the World Court (the International Court of Justice in The Hague, Netherlands) ruled—for the first time against the United States—that it had violated international law by mining Nicaraguan harbors in 1984 and had sought to overthrow the sovereign government of Nicaragua.

In 1987, Costa Rica's president, Oscar Arias, launched a new peace initiative that won the endorsement of the rulers of all five Central American nations—including Sandinista leader Daniel Ortega. The Arias plan committed the Central American nations to a cease-fire, a general amnesty, freedom of the press, free elections, the suspension of all foreign military aid, and a reduction in the level of arms. Ortega's unconditional acceptance of the Arias peace plan offered him a diplomatic victory over Washington and spelled doom for the Contras, who now stood isolated.

But Ortega's problems were by no means over. The Sandinistas now had to deal with a crisis more threatening to their survival than either the Contras or the United States: the failing economy. The looting of the treasury by Anastasio Somoza, the war against the Contras, the U.S. trade embargo, the loss of foreign credits, hyperinflation, and their own mismanagement all had left their mark. Nicaragua's per capita gross national product had fallen from over $1,000 in 1980 to $830 in 1987 and to $340 in 1993.[34]

In 1989, the Sandinistas took a calculated risk when they agreed to hold and abide by free elections in February 1990. The result of the election was not what they—nor Washington—had expected. A coalition of fourteen anti-Sandinista parties led by Violeta Chamorro—the widow of the publisher of *La Prensa* whom Somoza had murdered in 1978—won fifty-two of the National Assembly's ninety seats. Nearly a dozen years of war and deprivation had taken their toll on the Sandinista revolution when the voters cast their ballots for a change. Ortega grudgingly accepted the electoral defeat and agreed to transfer his movement's base of power, the seventy thousand troops of the army, to the authority of the new government.

The Chamorro government in Nicaragua adopted a centrist and conciliatory policy, keeping a wary eye on both the army, which was still led by
Sandinista officers, and the former Contras. Although peace—or at least the
end of overt warfare—had its benefits, the new government was unable to
reverse the fortunes of the exhausted nation.

There were no effective economic reforms, and neither production nor
the standard of living increased. The country remained heavily dependent
on external financial aid, which remained meager. Meanwhile, incessant
political violence continued as bands of retread revolutionaries—ex-San-
dinista soldiers on the left and former Contras on the right—continued to
fight each other. Nicaragua remained a blighted country with an estimated
60 percent of its people living in poverty. At the end of the century, it was
among the the poorest countries in the Western Hemisphere.

## ☐ El Salvador

In El Salvador, a scenario similar to the one in Nicaragua began to unfold
in the early 1980s. A rebellion in the countryside threatened to oust the oligarchy that governed the country. The oligarchy was composed largely of
*las catorce familias,* the Fourteen Families. Jorge Sol Costellanos, an oli-
garch and a former minister of the economy, defined the class structure in
El Salvador as follows:

> It's different from an aristocracy, which we also have. It's an oligarchy
> because these families own and run almost everything that makes money
> in El Salvador. Coffee gave birth to the oligarchy in the late 19th century,
> and economic growth has revolved around them ever since.[35]

Sol went on to say that, in fact, the Fourteen Families (or, more accurately,
clans) controlled 70 percent of the private banks, coffee production, sugar
mills, television stations, and newspapers. In contrast to the oligarchy was
the impoverished peasantry of El Salvador who made up the bulk of the
population but received a disproportionately small share of the nation's
meager wealth. In 1984, the annual per capita GNP of El Salvador was
around $710, about 6 percent of the U.S. figure.

The revolution that broke out in El Salvador in the early 1970s had its
roots in events forty years earlier. In 1932, deteriorating economic conditions—brought about by the Great Depression and falling farm prices—and
Communist activities under the leadership of Augustín Farabundo Martí led
to peasant uprisings. A lack of organization and arms proved to be fatal for
the peasants, for machetes were no match against a well-equipped army. In
a matter of days, the armed forces, led by General Maximiliano Hernández,
slaughtered thirty thousand campesinos. Martí was captured and executed.
The revolution was over, but its impact remained deeply etched into the
collective memory of the nation. Hernández became the symbol of both
deliverance and oppression, and his ghost continued to haunt El Salvador.

The 1932 massacre produced an uneasy stability in El Salvador until the 1972 national elections, when the civilian candidates of the Christian Democratic Party (PDC)—José Napoleón Duarte and his running mate, Guillermo Ungo—defeated the military candidate. The PDC had called for reforms, particularly the redistribution of land, but the oligarchy and the generals wanted no part of it. The military arrested Duarte, tortured him, and sent him into exile.

The military, as it had done in the past, resorted to terror. Death squads went on a rampage of indiscriminate violence. They summarily killed thousands of men, women, and children. In March 1980, the Roman Catholic archbishop of San Salvador, Oscar Arnulfo Romero—a critic of the military—was gunned down at the altar while saying mass. The assassins were members of a death squad under the command of Roberto d'Aubuisson. The CIA informed the Reagan administration that d'Aubuisson was the "principal henchman for wealthy landowners and a coordinator of the right-wing death squads that have murdered several thousand suspected leftists and leftist sympathizers during the past year." The agency went on to say that he was also involved in drug trafficking, arms smuggling, and the death of Romero—even providing details of how the men were selected to carry out the murder.[36] The Reagan administration did not condone d'Aubuisson's activities, but it continued to work with him as part of its strategy to deal with the insurgency.

*Liberation Theology.*  The assassination of Romero put into sharp relief a major change in the political life of Latin America that had occurred during the previous decade. Since the 1960s, the Roman Catholic Church, traditionally the champion of the status quo, had begun to reexamine its mission. Many of its clergy had moved toward a renewed commitment to improve the lot of the faithful on this earth. Village priests in particular found they could not preach eternal salvation and at the same time ignore the violence visited upon their parishioners. The upshot was a split between the traditional wing of the clergy and those, such as Romero, who championed what became known as liberation theology. Liberation theology may be traced to the encyclicals of Pope John XXIII and Pope Paul VI and to the Second Vatican Council (1963–1965), and was subsequently embraced by the 150 Latin American Roman Catholic bishops in attendance at the Second General Conference in 1968 in Medellín, Colombia. The bishops focused their attack on the "institutionalized violence" that condemned the lower classes to poverty and hunger. They also denounced foreign investors who benefited at the expense of the local population. The Church thus combined its spiritual mission with one for social change and justice. Marcos G. McGrath, archbishop of Panama, explained that the Church's mission was meant to "integrate eternal salvation and revolutionary action for a just order in this world."[37] The bishops denounced both capitalism and Marxism and looked for a third way:

The liberal capitalist system and the temptation of the Marxist system appear as the only alternatives in our continent. . . . Both these systems are affronts to the dignity of the human person. The first takes as a premise the primacy of capital, its power, and the discriminating use of capital in the pursuit of gain. The other, although ideologically it may pretend to be humanist, looks rather to the collective man, and in practice converts itself into a totalitarian concentration of state power.[38]

The Church began to work on the local level to establish base communities and cooperatives in an attempt to ameliorate the consequences of police and army brutality, poverty, illiteracy, and the lack of medical facilities. When the Third Conference of Latin American Bishops convened in Puebla, Mexico, in 1979, a radicalized Church was already a fact of political life in much of Latin America. Church leaders repeatedly condemned state and guerrilla violence, capitalism, and Marxism. But they directed their harshest attacks toward multinational corporations and their "stages of growth" that predicted that poverty in the Third World was but a temporary phenomenon and that capitalism would eliminate poverty.

Maryknoll Sister Ita Ford, shortly before she and three other nuns were murdered in El Salvador in 1980, stated that "the Christian base communities are the greatest threat to military dictatorships in Latin America," a view the military dictatorships—particularly that of El Salvador—readily shared. As early as 1972, Salvadoran death squads began to murder members of the clergy, at times leaving their bodies dismembered as warnings. The oligarchs denounced the clergy as Communists and urged citizens "to be patriotic—kill a priest!" In the years between the Medellín and Puebla conferences (1968–1979), military governments or their henchmen murdered, tortured, arrested, or expelled an estimated 850 nuns, bishops, and priests in El Salvador. The murder of Archbishop Romero was but the most dramatic act of violence visited on the champions of liberation theology.[39]

\* \* \*

U.S. policymakers ignored the social, economic, and political roots of Salvadoran revolutionary violence and insisted that it was inspired from the outside. Washington saw the rebels, organized as the Farabundo Martí National Liberation Front (FMLN), as an extension of Nicaragua, Cuba, and, ultimately, the Soviet Union.

The United States pursued a two-track policy. On the one hand, it strengthened the military; on the other, it sought a political solution. Under U.S. supervision, El Salvador went through the motions of holding a presidential election that returned Duarte to power in 1979. Duarte, however, ruled at the pleasure of the generals who needed him, because without Duarte Washington could hardly justify its support of the Salvadoran military. Duarte's election enabled the Reagan administration to argue that reforms were taking hold and that the army's human rights record was improving. The violence, however, continued after the election of Duarte, who was powerless to stop it. The death squads continued about their grisly work.

By 1989, after nine years of fighting, some seventy thousand Salvadorans had been killed. Despite $3.3 billion in U.S. economic and military aid, little had changed. The guerrillas, regarded by one observer as "the best trained, best organized and most committed Marxist-Leninist rebel movement ever seen in Latin America,"[40] controlled about one-third of the country and made their military power felt through periodic attacks in the capital and elsewhere.

In November 1989, the army committed yet another atrocity. A right-wing death squad burst into the rooms of six Jesuit priests who taught at the Catholic University and murdered them, their cook, and her daughter. The newly elected president, Alfredo Cristiani, the candidate of the rightist ARENA party (National Republican Alliance), whose government still received U.S. military aid, assured Washington that it would conduct a thorough investigation and bring the killers to justice. In January 1990, his government arrested and officially charged eight military men, including a colonel who allegedly had ordered the murder of the priests.[41]

Peace finally came to El Salvador. In March 1989, the FMLN agreed to participate in the electoral process. An FMLN offensive in November of that year showed the George H. W. Bush administration that military victory was beyond its reach. The end of the Cold War was another factor. ARENA could count on U.S. military aid only so long as its army was seen as holding Communism at bay. With the global Communist menace suddenly gone, Washington's threat to discontinue aid to El Salvador unless accompanied by political reform became more credible, and ARENA became more amenable to compromise.

In May 1990, Moscow and Washington agreed to back UN-arranged Salvadoran peace talks, which finally produced a peace agreement in January 1992. It ended a brutal war that had claimed approximately eighty thousand lives over twelve years. In exchange for an agreement to dissolve their military forces, the rebels secured government pledges to legalize the FMLN as a political party and to reduce by one-half the number of troops in the Salvadoran army within two years. The agreement also called for implementation of land reform, as well as judicial and electoral reforms and the creation of a UN Truth Commission to investigate cases of human rights violations. The most appalling of these was the December 1981 massacre of more than seven hundred peasants—evangelical Christians who did not support the rebels—by the U.S.-trained elite Atlacatl Battalion in the remote village of El Mozote. In 1982, the Reagan administration had angrily and repeatedly denied—although it knew better—that such a massacre had taken place. In El Salvador, El Mozote remained a metaphor for the army's ability to avoid responsibility for human rights abuses.[42] These investigations produced reports replete with damning evidence of massacres by army officers and right-wing death squads, but its recommendations were not carried out by the ARENA government. To the contrary, in 1994, it passed a law granting full amnesty to all army officers, despite the incontrovertible proof of massacres such as that of El Mozote. Civilian control of the military—a fundamental principle of democratic government—remained out of reach in El Salvador.

In May 1984, under pressure from the U.S. Congress, which threatened to withhold aid, five enlisted members of the National Guard were convicted of the 1980 murder of the four U.S. nuns. It marked the first time in the nation's history that a member of the military had been found guilty of such a crime. Still, the officers at the top who had given the orders, the director of the National Guard, Eugenio Vides Sasanova, and the minister of defense, Jose Guillermo Garcia, escaped prosecution under a general amnesty. After they had retired in Florida, however, they were tried under U.S. law, but the prosecution was unable to establish a direct link between the generals and those who had committed the murders.

## ■ LATIN AMERICAN DRUG TRAFFIC

In the late 1980s, the increasing volume of illicit drugs flowing from South America—particularly to the United States and Western Europe—and the rising level of violence attendant to this drug traffic became an issue of concern. In 1989, President George H. W. Bush proclaimed an all-out war against drugs, aimed at eliminating the global demand and the supply in South America. Despite the resounding fanfare with which the plan was proclaimed, it had little success.

Latin American drug traffic was centered in Colombia, where powerful drug cartels in the late 1980s managed operations responsible for about 80 percent of the cocaine entering the United States. Coca plants, from which cocaine is extracted, and marijuana grow abundantly in the equatorial climate of Colombia, Bolivia, and Peru. The farmers on the slopes of the Andes Mountains and in the Amazon Valley earned far more from growing these plants than from growing food crops. Drug money was the salvation of farmers, the road to fabulous wealth for criminal organizations, and a windfall for corrupt local police and politicians. One cartel, based in the city of Medellín, operated like a large multinational corporation. U.S. Drug Enforcement Agency officials estimated that its profits were as high as $5 billion a year and that tens of thousands of people were on its payroll. The Medellín cartel and its rival in Cali were well prepared to offer enormous bribes to Colombian military, political, and judicial officers to protect their operations. When bribes failed to achieve their purpose, they readily resorted to intimidation and violence.

The Colombian government launched its own war on the drug cartels in August 1989, when President Virgilio Barco Vargas ordered military forces into action. It set crops ablaze, destroyed production facilities, and seized the homes and properties of several major drug kingpins. The drug cartels responded with a counteroffensive of terrorism. They carried out hundreds of bombings and gunned down politicians and judges. In December 1989, the Medellín cartel bombed the headquarters of the Department of Security, the agency most involved in the effort to destroy their drug operations. Half a ton of dynamite destroyed the six-story building, killing 52 people and injuring 1,000. It also claimed responsibility for the bombing of a Colombian jetliner ten days earlier, killing all 107 people aboard. The drug cartels appeared to be winning the war. In the end, Barco was able to claim some success, as the flow of drugs from Colombia was reduced—at least temporarily—by about 30 percent in 1990.

A central issue in the drug war was the extradition treaty Colombia had signed with the United States in 1979, according to which a captured Colombian drug boss could be sent to the United States to stand trial. In February 1987, Carlos Lehder, a major drug figure, was captured and extradited to the United States, where a year later he was found guilty of drug smuggling and sentenced to life plus 135 years. The drug lords exerted enormous pressure on judges and politicians to overturn the extradition law, in some cases offering them a choice between fantastically large bribes or death.

In June 1989, the authorities managed to apprehend Pablo Escobar, the most powerful Medellín kingpin. Escobar, however, had surrendered on his own terms. He had accepted the government's offer to surrender in exchange for immunity against extradition to the United States, where he was under indictment, and a greatly reduced prison sentence. Moreover, he was allowed to select his own "jail"—a comfortable rural villa in his home province replete with Jacuzzi, fax machines, cellular telephones, computers, and even guns—and allowed to dictate the security arrangements, such as selecting his own guards. This arrangement protected Escobar from Colombian police and U.S. prosecutors and allowed him to continue to run his drug empire from "prison."

In July 1992, an embarrassed Colombian government reported that Escobar had escaped. In December 1993, Colombian police, with the help of U.S. advisers, finally cornered Escobar and killed him in a shoot-out. The death of Escobar changed little. The chief beneficiary was the Cali cartel.

The Medellín and Cali cartels were not alone in selling drugs; leftist guerrillas, too, had succumbed to the lure of this profitable enterprise. The largest of the guerrilla groups was the Armed Revolutionary Force (FARC), which was seventeen thousand strong and controlled large areas of rural Colombia and several hundred thousand people. FARC was initially founded in 1964 as a leftist movement seeking social change, but since then it had found a new calling: the sale of protection to coca, marijuana, and poppy (the source of heroin) growers and the lucrative business of kidnapping. By the end of the 1990s, its activities netted an estimated half-billion dollars annually.[43] Another, smaller guerrilla group with the same agenda was the National Liberation Army (ELN). Colombia's eleven-thousand-man army proved ineffective against the well-financed guerrillas.

The early 1990s, however, saw another force, the Colombian Self-Defense Force, rightist paramilitary death squads between five and seven thousand strong, that ranged widely in the country fighting their own war against the leftists. They, too, became involved in the drug trade and kidnapping. The rightist vigilantes were responsible for their own reign of terror as they murdered tens of thousands of individuals—mostly civilians—thought to be sympathetic to the guerrillas.[44] To add to Colombia's misery, the army, too, was engaged in the torture and murder of civilians.[45]

In the late 1990s, the Clinton administration was drawn into the civil strife in Colombia. Congress, however, raised questions about Colombian human rights violations and about the possibility of the United States getting involved in another Vietnam-like situation. Clinton, after obtaining a bipartisan consensus, traveled to Colombia in August 1999 to present its government an antidrug aid package of $1 billion, replete with five hundred military advisers and transport and attack helicopters. During his visit, however, Clinton carefully avoided the capital city of Bogotá; his eight-hour stay was limited to the coastal city of Cartagena under a heavy military guard of 5,500 government troops, 350 U.S. agents, four frigates, and eighteen patrol boats. Nonetheless, he expressed confidence that this new round in the war on drugs would succeed where previous efforts had failed, namely to reduce the supply in the West.

The magnitude of the profits from the drug business spoke against this kind of optimism. At its source, a kilogram of coca paste already fetched $2,500; in Miami, after changing hands several times, the price was $20,000; by the time it reached New York City it was $80,000; and in Europe $120,000.[46]

In 2003, the Colombian government—with U.S. support—launched an offensive, the "Patriot Plan," against the FARC. The defense minister announced a string of victories. "The tide has turned," he announced, "and there is an end in sight," only to add that one "cannot expect a big [final] battle, a Waterloo."[47]

## ☐    The Panama Connection

The first year of the George H. W. Bush presidency (1989) saw a puzzling war of words with Manuel Noriega, the military strongman of Panama, who had previously been an ally of the United States but was now suspected of being a conduit for Colombian drugs en route to the United States. In fact, he had been on the payroll of the CIA, which had paid him $250,000 a year for Caribbean intelligence during the war against the Sandinistas in Nicaragua. In the process, the Reagan administration had turned a blind eye to human rights abuses by Noriega. Torture, murder, rape, plunder, prostitution, drug trading, and the theft of elections—such as that in 1984—did not faze Washington. It continued to fund Noriega's army, now renamed the Panamanian Defense Forces, as it contemplated the military withdrawal from the Canal Zone before the year 2000, as stipulated by the treaty of 1979. But in 1987, Washington became aware that Noriega had transgressed the bounds of propriety when it learned he was also offering intelligence to Castro's Cuba. Ambler Moss, President Carter's envoy to Panama, explained that Noriega was "dealing with everybody—us, the Cubans, other countries. We used to call him the rent-a-colonel."[48] The betrayal became too much for President Bush to bear. He accused Noriega of being part of the international drug cartel. But the episode was reminiscent of Claude Rains's discovery of gambling in Rick's place in the movie *Casablanca*. After all, knowledge in Washington of Noriega's drug connections went all the way back to the Nixon administration.[49]

Noriega resisted U.S. pressure to step down and presented himself instead as the champion of small Latin American nations bullied by the "Colossus of the North." In 1987, grand juries in Tampa and Miami indicted him on drug-trafficking charges. Just before Christmas 1989, Bush sent a posse of twenty thousand U.S. soldiers to bring Noriega to justice. Operation "Just Cause" got its man, but the cost was high. Several hundred Panamanians—mostly civilians—and twenty-three U.S. soldiers died in the fighting. In addition, the collateral damage of property and subsequent looting of stores in Panama City resulted in losses to small businesses totaling $1 billion.

The invasion of Panama was also the first instance of U.S. military intervention abroad since 1945 in which the anti-Communist theme was not central. As such, it was a sign of the times that the Cold War was winding down. Bush defended his action as part of his war on drug dealers and as his duty to defend the Panama Canal. As another sign of the times, he stood in direct contrast to Soviet leader Mikhail Gorbachev, who had declared at about the same time that no nation had a legal or moral right to interfere in the internal affairs of another.

In Miami, before a federal judge, Noriega—dressed in his general's uniform—presented himself as a "prisoner of war." The judge, however, held that he was dealing with a common criminal. U.S. foreign policy was acquiring a new focus—the international drug connection—and Noriega's arrest became Exhibit A of the federal prosecution's commitment to a new war. In April 1992, when Noriega was found guilty on numerous charges, including the acceptance of millions of dollars in bribes from the Medellín cartel, and sentenced to forty years in prison, he became the first head of a foreign state to be convicted of criminal charges in a U.S. court.[50]

# ■ RECOMMENDED READINGS

## ☐ *Latin America—General*

Burns, Bradford. *Latin America: A Concise Interpretive History.* 3d ed. Englewood Cliffs, N.J.: Prentice-Hall, 1982.

Gill, Leslie. *The School of the Americas: Military Training and Political Violence in the Americas.* Durham, N.C.: Duke University Press, 2004.

Lewis, Paul H. *The Governments of Argentina, Brazil, and Mexico.* New York: Crowell, 1975.

Rosenberg, Tina. *Children of Cain: Violence and the Violent in Latin America.* New York: Penguin, 1991.

Skidmore, Thomas E., and Peter H. Smith. *Modern Latin America.* New York: Oxford University Press, 1984.

Wolf, Eric R., and Edward C. Hansen. *The Human Condition in Latin America.* New York: Oxford University Press, 1974.

## ☐ *South America*

Alexander, Robert J. *The Tragedy of Chile.* Westport, Conn.: Greenwood Press, 1978.

———. *Juan Domingo Perón: A History.* Boulder, Colo.: Westview Press, 1979.
An authoritative biography of the most important political figure in modern Argentine politics.

Blanco, Hugo. *Land or Death: The Peasant Struggle in Peru.* New York: Pathfinder Press, 1972.
A longtime revolutionary strongly argues his case for radical land reform.

Burns, E. Bradford. *A History of Brazil.* 2d ed. New York: Columbia University Press, 1980.

Valenzuela, Arturo. *The Breakdown of Democratic Regimes: Chile.* Baltimore: Johns Hopkins University Press, 1978.
Strongly critical of the militarist intervention in Chile.

Wesson, Robert. *The United States and Brazil: Limits of Influence.* New York: Frederick A. Praeger, 1981.

Whitaker, Arthur P. *The United States and the Southern Cone: Argentina, Chile, and Uruguay.* Cambridge, Mass.: Harvard University Press, 1976.

## ☐ *Central America*

Berryman, Phillip. *Inside Central America: The Essential Facts Past and Present on El Salvador, Nicaragua, Honduras, Guatemala, and Costa Rica.* New York: Pantheon, 1985.
The observations of a man who for four years served as the Central American representative of the American Friends Service Committee.

Chace, James. *Endless War: How We Got Involved in Central America and What Can Be Done.* New York: Vintage, 1984.
Offers a brief, popular, but insightful historical analysis.

Danner, Mark. *The Massacre at El Mozote.* New York: Random House, 1993.

Diedrich, Bernard. *Somoza and the Legacy of U.S. Involvement.* New York: Dutton, 1981.

LaFeber, Walter. *Inevitable Revolution: The United States in Central America.* Expanded ed. New York: W. W. Norton, 1984.
By a well-known revisionist historian of the role of the United States in the Cold War.

Langley, Lester D. *Central America: The Real Stakes, Understanding Central America Before It's Too Late.* New York: Crown, 1985.

Lopez Vigil, José Ignacio. *Rebel Radio: The Story of El Salvador's Radio Venceremos.* Willimantic, Conn.: Curbstone Press, 1995.
An oral history of the "Voice of the Voiceless," which broadcast from the mountains of El Salvador each night from 1981 until the peace accord of 1992.

Montgomery, Tommie Sue. *Revolution in El Salvador.* Boulder, Colo.: Westview Press, 1982.

Schlesinger, Stephen, and Stephen Kinzer. *Bitter Fruit: The Untold Story of the American Coup in Guatemala.* Garden City, N.Y.: Doubleday, 1982.
The best-seller on the CIA's 1954 coup in Guatemala.

# ■ NOTES

1. Paul Harrison, *Inside the Third World: The Anatomy of Poverty,* 2d ed. (New York: Penguin, 1984), cites a survey by the Inter-American Commission for Agricultural Development, pp. 108–109.

2. E. Bradford Burns, *Latin America: A Concise Interpretive History,* 3d ed. (Englewood Cliffs, N.J.: Prentice-Hall, 1982), p. 214.

3. *Caudillos* first appeared in the early nineteenth century during the wars for independence. At first they had no particular political philosophy; their strengths lay in their personal magnetism and their military abilitites. Their power was extra-constitutional, i.e., outside the law and thus unchecked by any law.

4. Perón was angered by the Catholic Church's refusal to canonize Eva. The Church, in turn, opposed his efforts to require the teaching in schools of his ideology, which deified the state and himself as its head. Perón accused the Church of organizing a mass movement against him and responded by censoring Catholic newspapers, arresting priests, and forbidding Church processions. Pope Pius XII retaliated by excommunicating him.

5. "Crimes Past, Crimes Present," *The Economist,* June 3, 2004.

6. Luis Marcus Ocampo, "Beyond Punishment: Justice in the Wake of Massive Crimes in Argentina," *Journal of International Affairs* (spring 1999); "The Challenge of the Past," *The Economist,* October 22, 1998.

7. "A Decline Without Parallel," *The Economist,* February 28, 2002.

8. Ibid. Also, "Argentina's Bottomless Pit," *The Economist,* August 8, 2004, and Peter Greste, "Argentina's Poor Hit New Record," *BBC News,* February 1, 2003.

9. "From Pauper to President: Now Lula's Struggle Really Begins," *The Economist,* October 31, 2002.

10. Arthur P. Whitaker, *The United States and the Southern Cone: Argentina, Chile, and Uruguay* (Cambridge, Mass.: Harvard University Press, 1976), pp. 301, 309.

11. Cited in Walter Isaacson, *Kissinger: A Biography* (New York: Touchstone Books, 1993), p. 290.

12. Between 1998 and 2004, sixteen thousand documents in the U.S. Archives relating to Pinochet's reign were declassified. See Peter Kornbluh, director, "Chile Documentation Project," http://www.gwu.edu/~nsarchiv/.

13. Knight Ridder/Tribune, "Pinochet Is Not Immune, Chile's High Court Rules," *Baltimore Sun,* August 27, 2004, p. 18A.

14. Tina Rosenberg, "Force Is Forever," *New York Times Magazine,* September 24, 1995, p. 46.

15. "The Shining Path Revisited," *The Economist,* September 4, 2003.

16. Guillermo Rochabrun, "The De Facto Powers Behind Fujimori's Regime," *NACLA Report on the Americas* (July–August 1996), pp. 22–23. For the impact of economic reform on the population at large, see Manuel Castillo Ochoa, "Fujimori and the Business Class: A Prickly Partnership," ibid., pp. 25–30.

17. Enrique Obando, "Fujimori and the Military: A Marriage of Convenience," *NACLA Report on the Americas* (July-August 1996), pp. 31–36; also "Anatomy of a Cover-Up: The Disappearances at La Cantuta," a summary of a report by Human Rights Watch/Americas, ibid., pp. 34–35.

18. Kevin G. Hall, "CIA Paid Millions to Montesinos," *Miami Herald,* August 3, 2001.

19. *World Bank Development Report 2000/2001: Attacking Poverty* (New York: Oxford University Press, 2000), p. 281.

20. Press release, "Transparency International Calls on Japanese Government to Extradite Fujimori," August 27, 2003; "Cleaner-Than-Thou," *The Economist,* October 7, 2004.

21. Judith Gentleman, "Mexico: The Revolution," in Barbara A. Tenenbaum, ed., *Encyclopedia of Latin American History and Culture,* vol. 4 (New York: Charles Scribner's Sons, 1996), p. 15; Alma Guillermoprieto, "Zapata's Heirs," *New Yorker,* May 16, 1994, p. 54.

22. James W. Wilkie, *The Mexican Revolution: Federal Expenditure and Social Change Since 1910* (Berkeley: University of California Press, 1970), pp. 193–194.

23. James D. Cockcroft, *Mexico: Class Formation, Capital Accumulation, and the State* (New York: Monthly Review Press, 1983) pp. 136–138.

24. Wilkie, *The Mexican Revolution,* pp. 222–225, 128–129, 195–197.

25. Kevin Sullivan, "Memories of Massacre in Mexico: Long-Hidden Photos Detail '68 Army Shootings of Students," *Washington Post,* February 14, 2002, p. A21. Letta Tayler, "Judges to Review Genocide Cases Against Mexican ex-President," *Baltimore Sun,* October 14, 2004, p. 19A.

26. Paco Ignacio Taibo II, "Images of Chiapas: Zapatista! The Phoenix Rises," *The Nation,* March 28, 1996, pp. 407–408.

27. Figures are from the 1990 Mexican census and the president's report to Congress; "The Mexican Rebels' Impoverished Home," *New York Times,* January 9, 1994, p. 6E.

28. Theodore Roosevelt, "Annual Message to Congress," December 1904, in Robert H. Farrell, *American Diplomacy: A History* (New York: W. W. Norton, 1959), p. 251.

29. From conversation with Sir William Tyrell, a representative of Britain's Foreign Office, November 13, 1913. Arthur S. Link, *Wilson, II, The New Freedom* (Princeton, N.J.: Princeton University Press, 1956), p. 375.

30. Quoted in Arthur M. Schlesinger Jr., *A Thousand Days: John F. Kennedy in the White House* (Boston: Houghton Mifflin, 1965), p. 769.

31. Castro offered to pay for U.S. property, but only on the basis of a low assessment the companies themselves had submitted for tax purposes. The U.S. companies, however, had other figures in mind. Stephen E. Ambrose, *Rise to Globalism: American Foreign Policy, 1938–1970* (New York: Penguin, 1971), p. 269n.

32. "I'm the Champ," *Time* cover story on Somoza, November 15, 1948, p. 43.

33. Ronald Reagan to a joint session of Congress, *New York Times,* April 28, 1983, p. A12.

34. World Bank, *World Development Report: Workers in an Integrating World* (New York: Oxford University Press, 1995), p. 162.

35. Paul Heath Hoeffel, "The Eclipse of the Oligarchs," *New York Times Magazine,* September 6, 1981, p. 23.

36. Clifford Krauss, "U.S. Aware of Killings, Kept Ties to Salvadoran Rightists, Papers Suggest," *New York Times,* November 9, 1993, p. A9.

37. Marcos G. McGrath, "Ariel or Caliban?" *Foreign Affairs* (October 1973), pp. 85, 87.

38. From the bishops' "Document on Justice," ibid., p. 86.

39. Walter LaFeber, *Inevitable Revolutions: The United States in Central America,* expanded ed. (New York: W. W. Norton, 1984), pp. 219–226; Tina Rosenberg, *Children of Cain: Violence and the Violent in Latin America* (New York: Penguin, 1992), pp. 219–270.

40. James Le Moyne, "El Salvador's Forgotten War," *Foreign Affairs* (summer 1989), p. 106.

41. One month later, however, a witness to the murders complained to Church officials of "coercive interrogation" by Salvadoran and U.S. officials, who were attempting to get her to change her story. Neither Cristiani nor the Bush administration wanted the Salvadoran army to be found responsible for the atrocity, which threatened to bring about congressional suspension of further military aid to the country.

42. Mark Danner, "The Truth of El Mozote," *New Yorker,* December 6, 1993, pp. 50–133; eventually published in book form as *The Massacre at El Mozote* (New York: Random House, 1994).

43. Almo Guillermoprieto, "The Children's War," *New York Review,* May 11, 2000, p. 37; Patrick Symmes, "Miraculous Fishing: Lost in the Swamps of Colombia's Drug War," *Harper's* (December 2000), p. 64.

44. "Colombia's Overdose," *Harper's* (February 2000), p. 100. The paramilitaries committed an estimated 78 percent of Colombia's human rights atrocities. Serge F. Kovaleski, "Widespread Violence Threatens Colombia's Stability," *Washington Post,* March 1, 1998, p. A22; "Colombia in the Long Shadow of War," *The Economist,* July 17, 1999, p. 31.

45. "U.S. Issues Rights Report Criticizing Colombia," *Baltimore Sun,* February 26, 2000, p. 1A; "Colombia's President Vows to Crack Down on Death Squads," *Baltimore Sun,* July 25, 2000, p. 12A.

46. Richard Wagner, "Kolumbien's illusionsloser Kampf gegen das Kokain," *Frankfurter Allgemeine Zeitung,* May 30, 2000, p. 4.

47. "Victories, but No Waterloo," *The Economist,* July 15, 2004.

48. Cited by Tim Collie, "Noriega Played All Angles in Ascent," *Tampa Tribune,* December 25, 1989, p. 22A.

49. Ibid., pp. 22A, 25A.

50. The unprecedented sentencing of Noriega took place shortly after the U.S. Supreme Court upheld the federal government's right to kidnap a Mexican national who had participated in the torture murder of a U.S. narcotics agent. In doing so, the court ignored international law and the extradition treaty between the United States and Mexico. The governments of Mexico and Canada, with which the United States had a similar extradition treaty, protested that the Bush administration had violated the sovereignty of a neighboring nation.

# 14

# The People's Republic of China and Taiwan

In the mid-1990s, many of the countries of Asia were Third World nations, and several—such as Bangladesh, Cambodia, Myanmar (Burma), and Laos—were among the world's poorest. The two giant Asian nations, the People's Republic of China and India, each with a per capita GNP under $400 in 1990, also qualified as Third World nations. Other countries in Asia, however, all on the Pacific rim, had far higher GNPs and growth rates and were by no means Third World or underdeveloped nations. Japan immediately comes to mind, but other Asian countries were following Japan's footsteps in the 1970s and were rapidly becoming highly industrialized nations.

The twentieth century was an age of social and political experimentation and upheavals, and China, the world's most populous nation, had its share of both. The Chinese Communist government's efforts to transform and modernize China warrant an examination, not only because of the magnitude of the task but also because of the great lengths to which the Chinese Communists went to achieve a Marxist society. The endeavor to put Marxism into practice in this huge country, however, caused enormous political and economic upheavals. Only after the death of Mao Zedong in 1976 did China attain a significant measure of both political stability and economic growth.

India, the other Third World giant in Asia, maintained a democratic form of government and enjoyed a greater degree of political stability than China, but its economic performance was no better. India, too, engaged in social and economic experimentation, mixing elements of capitalism and socialism while avoiding radical shifts in policy. In their own ways, India and China struggled to come to terms with a massive population and massive poverty. Not until the 1980s were they able to register substantial economic gains, and since then China has decidedly outpaced India. By the end of the century, China had indeed achieved a remarkable level of economic growth and modernization.

# ■ MAO ZEDONG'S QUEST
# FOR A COMMUNIST UTOPIA

The enormity of China is the starting point of any inquiry into China's economic progress, for its size alone sets it apart. Never before in history has there been a nation of over a billion people. China has always been an agrarian nation with a mass of poor peasants. The Communist government of China stressed industrialization, agrarian growth, and improvement of the standard of living. At the same time, it devoted itself to building a revolutionary Communist society. The interplay of the economic and political objectives is the key to understanding revolutionary China and its efforts to achieve economic growth.

First, one must note the objective conditions in China and the country's past efforts to deal with those conditions. China's overriding problem in modern times (for at least the past two centuries) has been how to feed itself. The population continued to grow rapidly both before and after the Communists came to power in 1949. At that time, it was about 535 million; by 1970, it was 840 million; and in the early 1980s, it passed the 1 billion mark. Traditionally, about 90 percent of the people were peasants engaged in subsistence agriculture. Despite the country's great size, there was hardly enough arable land to support the people. Only about 20 percent of the land is arable, with the remainder either too mountainous or too arid. China's huge population, therefore, was heavily concentrated in the areas with arable land, mainly the coastal regions. But even in these areas there is a scarcity of land. And because of the unequal distribution of land, in the past the bulk of the peasants either owned too little land or none at all. This set of conditions—the plight of the impoverished peasants and their exploitation by the landowning class—gave rise to Mao Zedong's Communist movement, which was committed to putting an end to these conditions.

China had made little progress toward industrialization prior to Communist rule. The Nationalist regime in the 1930s attempted to industrialize, but this endeavor was cut short by the eight-year-long war with Japan. In 1949, the Communists inherited a country that had suffered the destruction of that war, as well as three subsequent years of civil war. The country had only very meager industrial development, was wracked with uncontrolled inflation and economic chaos, had an impoverished and illiterate peasantry, and its cities were swollen with jobless, desperate people. Moreover, China lacked many of the basic elements for modernization: capital, technology, and an educated working class.

Under the rule of Communist Party chairman Mao, politics—which is to say, Marxist revolution—had greater priority than did economic growth. Mao's often-quoted dictum "politics take command" meant that every activity in China was to be defined politically in Marxist terms. Thus, to study economic development in Mao's China is to study the Marxist politics of Mao and his comrades in the Chinese Communist Party (CCP).

Initially, upon coming to power in 1949, the Communists stressed economic rehabilitation and postponed their socialist objectives. In the first three years, they managed to establish economic and political order, control inflation, and restore production in the existing industries to their prewar level. Major industries were nationalized, foreign enterprises were confiscated, and private enterprise was eliminated gradually as state control of the economy was increased. The new regime also addressed the peasant question—an issue that could not wait—by instituting wholesale land reform. The redistribution of land was carried out swiftly and ruthlessly, resulting in the transfer of millions of acres to over 300 million peasants and the elimination of the "landlord class." Estimates of the loss of life vary greatly, but possibly several million Chinese met their deaths during this revolutionary upheaval.

By 1953, the Chinese government was ready to institute its First Five-Year Plan, which was modeled on that of the Soviet Union and guided by Soviet economic advisers. Economic assistance from the Soviet Union was of great importance to China—the technical aid more than the monetary loans, which were rather meager (although more than China obtained from anywhere else). As in the Soviet Union, the First Five-Year Plan stressed rapid development of heavy industry. It was implemented successfully, and as a result China's production of steel, electricity, and cement increased remarkably.

## ☐ Great Leap Forward

As the Second Five-Year Plan was about to be launched, Mao questioned the effect this method of economic modernization was having on the Chinese revolution; he feared it would result in the entrenchment—as in the Soviet Union—of a powerful bureaucracy, a new elite that would exploit the Chinese masses. In early 1958, Mao suddenly called a halt to the Second Five-Year Plan, thereby rejecting the Soviet model for development, and called instead for a "Great Leap Forward." This plan called for tapping the energies of the masses of people—China's greatest resource—to industrialize and collectivize at the same time. In the countryside, the agricultural collectives, which had been formed in the mid-1950s, were to be reorganized into large communes that were to embody the basic Marxist principle, "From each according to his abilities, to each according to his needs." Mao's approach was to mobilize the masses through the use of ideology to develop and sustain a revolutionary fervor. This frenzied pace could not be maintained, however, and the excess of zeal, lack of administrative ability, and poor planning soon produced an economic disaster. Matters were made worse by Soviet premier Nikita Khrushchev's withdrawal of all Soviet technicians from China in 1960, and by three consecutive years of crop failures (1959–1961). The Great Leap Forward was, in fact, a disastrous leap backward, and it cost China dearly—crippling the economy, causing untold hardship, and taking a huge toll in lives. It is impossible to know the number of Chinese who died as a result of this revolutionary experiment, and the violence and famine it caused, but it may have been as high as 10 million.[1]

From this point, we can clearly detect the contention between two conflicting strategies in Communist China. One we can label Maoist or radical, the other moderate. The radical approach was reflected in the manner in which Mao had built the Communist movement in China in the 1930s, in the Great Leap Forward, and later in the Great Cultural Revolution. This approach stressed the "mass line," meaning the power of the people and their active engagement in the revolution. It called for intense ideological training of the CCP cadre, the dedicated party activists who served as a model for the masses. The cult of Mao was also an important tool for politicizing the masses. It was not an end in itself but a means to an end: a thoroughly revolutionary society that was egalitarian and free of exploitation of the masses.

The moderate line deemphasized ideology and revolutionary zeal and instead stressed state planning, bureaucratic leadership, and development of the skills and expertise necessary for the advancement of China. Its main feature was pragmatism—a rational, problem-solving, do-what-works approach. This approach was, therefore, less political, ideological, and emotional than the Maoist line, and it gave higher priority to bureaucratic management and economic modernization than to ideology.

## ☐ *The Great Cultural Revolution*

After the Great Leap Forward fiasco, the moderates took charge of cleaning up the mess Mao had made. Gradually, during the first half of the 1960s, the economy recovered under the guiding hand of such moderate leaders as Liu Shaoqi (Liu Shao-ch'i) and Deng Xiaoping (Teng Hsiao-p'ing). But once again, Mao became disturbed about the trend toward bureaucratic elitism. Using his immense prestige as "the Great Helmsman," Mao bypassed the Chinese Communist Party structure and in July 1966 initiated a new political movement aimed at purging the CCP of its elitist leaders: the "Great Proletarian Cultural Revolution."

Mao was determined once and for all to eradicate bureaucratism in the Chinese revolution. He charged his opponents not only with elitism, meaning they were guilty of selfishly guarding and advancing their own personal power and privilege, but also with revisionism, meaning they were guilty of revising (distorting) Marxism-Leninism, just as Mao felt recent Soviet leaders had done. He claimed many party leaders were taking the "capitalist road" and thus destroying the Communist revolution. Mao enlisted the active support of the youth of China, who were dismissed from colleges and schools en masse, organized into the "Red Guards," and instructed to go out and attack all those who were guilty of selfish elitism. "Serve the people" was the slogan, and Mao's writings were the guidelines. Throughout China, the Red Guards pressured all people high and low—officials, soldiers, peasants, and workers—to reform themselves through arduous study of the thought of Mao Zedong as presented in capsule form in the "Little Red Book," and they severely rebuked and punished all those found wanting.

Mao's Cultural Revolution was a unique event—a revolution within an ongoing revolution, a people's revolt against the revolutionary party ordered by the head of that party. Mao called upon the masses to purge their leaders—even in his own Communist Party—to put the revolution back on track. This upheaval was an embodiment of Mao's theory of "permanent revolution"—that is, continuing class struggle and use of revolutionary violence to purge the enemies of the revolution and prevent backsliding toward capitalism.

Coercion, Mao contended, was necessary to rid people of wrong ideas, just as "dust never vanishes of itself without sweeping." Mao's own Revolutionary Committee was to do the sweeping. Even though his Cultural Revolution was proclaimed in the name of lofty ideals, to bring about a utopian, egalitarian society utterly free of class exploitation, it would produce unimaginable mayhem—terror, death, and destruction. Mao's Red Guards, pumped up by Mao's revolutionary charge, rampaged throughout the country as on a crusade—wreaking havoc, destroying property, and capturing, condemning, brutalizing, and sometimes killing those deemed to be less than ideologically pure. Their excessive fervor soon rendered the Cultural Revolution a terrifying witch-hunt that not only destroyed the political order in China but disrupted the economy and caused untold torture, suffering, and death for countless people—probably in excess of 1 million.[2] When the Red Guard radicals met resistance, clashes occurred. In time, opposing bands of Red Guards, each claiming to have the correct Maoist line, engaged in pitched battles fought with weapons secured from the police or army units. As the violence and disruption mounted, Mao had to call in China's military forces, the People's Liberation Army, to restore order.

Two other victims of Mao's Cultural Revolution were the economy and education. Unchecked political violence caused disruption of the economy: work stoppages, decreased production, shortages, and inflation. In the long run, however, education, science, and technology may have suffered the greatest damage. High schools and universities were shut down for about five years; teachers and professors were taken to the countryside for political reeducation (forced labor and study of Mao's writings); and books and laboratory equipment were destroyed. When schools reopened, academic standards were replaced with ideological standards—that is, students and teachers were evaluated not on the basis of measurable knowledge but on their dedication to Mao's doctrine of Communism. This was political correctness to the extreme. The disruption in Chinese higher education probably retarded China's economic development by more than a decade.

It took several years for the Cultural Revolution to wind down. It was never repudiated or terminated until after Mao's death in 1976, but, in fact, it was being quietly abandoned by the beginning of the 1970s. By then, Mao was aged and ill, and leadership passed into the hands of the very able Zhou Enlai. Zhou was actually a moderate, but he managed to dodge an attack by the Maoists as such, and now, more than ever, Mao trusted and relied on him. Gradually, Zhou reinstated moderates who had been expelled from the CCP and relied on them to put China back on the track toward economic development. It was Zhou who engineered the new foreign policy of rapprochement with the United States in the early 1970s.

But the tensions between radicals (Maoists) and moderates were mounting under the surface of calm maintained by Zhou and Mao. These tensions erupted in 1976, the eventful "Year of the Tiger," during which both Zhou and Mao died. Mao's designated successor, Hua Guofeng (Hua Kuo-feng), was able to quash an attempt by the radicals to gain control of the CCP and the government. Hua arrested the ringleaders, the so-called Gang of Four. One of the principal culprits was none other than Mao's wife, Jiang Qing (Chiang Ch'ing). For the next several years, Hua and resurrected moderate leader Deng Xiaoping conducted a political campaign of denunciation of the Gang of Four as a means of attacking the radicalism the Gang (and the departed Mao) had stood for. By the end of the 1970s, Deng was in full control of the party—although he did not hold any of its highest positions. He gently nudged Hua aside, and the Gang of Four was put on trial for its crimes. Cautiously, the new leadership undertook the de-Maoization of China, as even the once-adored and infallible Mao was denounced for his "mistakes" during the Cultural Revolution. Clearly, the moderates were back in the saddle again. It was their turn to reorganize Chinese society.

## ■ DENG XIAOPING'S MODERNIZATION DRIVE

Under Deng's leadership, the march toward economic development gained momentum. China normalized relations with the United States and Japan with the objectives of developing trade relations, attracting foreign capital, and purchasing technology. These and other programs, such as providing bonuses as material incentives for production and restoring a capitalistic market mechanism, stimulated economic growth and modernization. In their drive to close the technology gap, Chinese leaders welcomed foreign visitors—especially scientists, technicians, and industrialists—and began sending large numbers of Chinese students abroad, especially for the study of science and technology.

Deng instituted in 1979 a new agrarian program called the "responsibility system." Under this system, the peasants contracted for land, seeds,

Chinese leader Deng Xiaoping, chairman of the Chinese Communist Party Central Advisory Commission, December 14, 1985. *(Embassy of the People's Republic of China)*

and tools from the state; at harvest time, they met their contract obligations (paid their rent) and were allowed to keep as personal income all they had earned over and above what they had contracted for. They then sold their surplus production on the open market. The incentive for personal profit led to more efficient farming and served to increase overall agricultural production. An able farmer could rent a large amount of land and even hire other workers, and thus become an entrepreneur.

The new system, which worked rather well, struck observers as more like capitalism than Communism. It surely represented a radical departure from Mao's brand of Communism, with its emphasis on egalitarianism. But Deng, the dauntless pragmatist, remained determined to pursue whatever course would speed China's modernization and strengthen its economy. The new pragmatism was promoted by Deng's two slogans: "Practice is the sole criterion of truth" and "Seek truth from facts."[3] Deng also said, "It doesn't matter what color the cat is, as long as it catches mice." Soviet leaders, who once had criticized Mao for moving too far to the left, condemned Deng's programs as going too far to the right. A Soviet visitor to China is said to have remarked, "If this is Marxism, I must reread Marx."[4] The following commentary, which appeared in the authoritative *People's Daily* in December 1984, made it abundantly clear that the Chinese leaders had indeed adopted a new view of Marxism:

> [In addition to Marx] we must study some modern economic theories, as well as modern scientific and technological know-how. We can never

rigidly adhere to the individual words and sentences or specific theories [of Marx]. Marx died 101 years ago.

His works were written more than 100 years ago. Some of his ideas are no longer suited to today's situation, because Marx never experienced these times, nor did Engels or Lenin. And they never came across the problems we face today. So we cannot use Marxist and Leninist works to solve our present-day problems. . . . If we continue to use certain Marxist principles, our historic development will surely be hampered.[5]

Deng's regime put a new face on China. Economic liberalization transformed China from a drab proletarian society, in which individual expression was suppressed, into a lively new consumer society in which individuality was expressed much more freely. This transformation was even more dramatic than the one instituted by Mao's revolution. In Deng's China, private enterprise, profit seeking, capital investment, consumerism, and the pursuit of private wealth were no longer taboo but instead were encouraged. Enterprising Chinese became successful in business ventures and displayed their newfound wealth in conspicuous ways, purchasing large homes and automobiles and taking trips abroad. Although authorities were concerned about the jealousy this behavior caused, they nonetheless encouraged people to seek their fortunes in the belief that doing so was for the betterment of both the individual and the economic development of the nation. Deng went so far as to proclaim, as a new credo for the Chinese people, "to get rich is glorious," an utterly outlandish notion by Maoist standards but one welcomed by the new entrepreneurs.

Deng's economic reform program represented a bold attempt to restructure the economy of the world's largest nation, and it proved to be remarkably successful. By 1987, eight years after Deng's ascent to power, the nation's GNP grew by leaps and bounds; rural incomes had tripled and urban incomes had doubled; foreign trade had doubled, reaching $10 billion; and direct foreign investment in China had risen dramatically. Between 1980 and 1994, China sustained an average annual growth rate of nearly 8 percent.[6] The rapid rise in agricultural output in the first half of the 1980s resulted in self-sufficiency and even a modest surplus in food production. This feat, previously considered impossible for this nation of 1.1 billion people, was the result of both the new profit-motivated farming system and new population control measures enacted by the government.

The great, persistent problem of modern China remained overpopulation, but the Communist regime addressed this problem effectively. The regime instituted a stringent birth control program that rewarded families with no more than one child (with increased food rations and employment and education benefits, for example) and penalized families with more than one child (through decreased food rations and increased taxes). This policy and its related family-planning program, including coerced abortions, resulted in a significant reduction of the rate of population growth. It served to hold in check a population explosion that threatened to swallow up any increased economic output. One of its social consequences, however, was an increase in infanticide—that is, parents killing unwanted newborn children.

The economic modernization program, so successful in the early 1980s, began to falter by 1987, when it encountered new problems. Agricultural output crested and began to fall in the mid-1980s, as many farmers sought enrichment in other, more profitable economic enterprises now open to them. Moreover, the efforts to institute price reforms resulted in sharply rising inflation. Deng and his protégé, Premier Zhao Ziyang, the most vigorous of the economic reformers, regarded price reform as the key to the continued success of the economic reform program. Heretofore, prices of consumer goods had been rigidly controlled and kept artificially low by government subsidies. When the government began removing price controls on such basic commodities as food and fuel, prices soared. By 1988, the inflation rate reached about 30 percent. Only those whose income had increased significantly as a result of new business opportunities or those able to take advantage of Communist Party connections could afford the new prices. The vast majority of people whose incomes were fixed and relatively low—factory workers, intellectuals, lower- and middle-level government workers—were less fortunate.

Inflation also brought a government decision to slow the economic modernization program. Li Peng, newly appointed as premier in early 1988, emerged as the leading proponent of retrenchment. Under his influence, in September 1988, the government called for a two-year program of austerity, renewed centralized planning, reinstatement of state trading monopolies, and postponement of further price reform. The aim was to curb inflation, cool off the "overheated" economy, and maintain a "reasonable" economic growth rate.

## ■ THE TIANANMEN SQUARE MASSACRE AND ITS AFTERMATH

The program of economic liberalization represented a significant departure from Marxism, a rejection of the Stalinist-type economic system, and considerable ideological flexibility, but it was not attended by a program of political liberalization. Deng's regime, however, did embark on a program of cautious political reform, which gradually offered a greater degree of openness and accountability in reporting governmental affairs, permitted freer access to information and ideas, reduced censorship, and allowed greater freedom of personal expression. The reform plans specifically called for administrative reforms that decentralized decisionmaking and made individual political leaders more accountable for their decisions; legal reforms aimed at replacing arbitrary and personal power with the rule of law; and a larger role for public opinion in the governing of China through such means as opinion polling and encouragement of suggestions and criticism in letters to editors of newspapers.

These political reforms were attended by considerable rhetoric about "democratization." The reforms were never intended, however, to introduce a democratic political system characterized by free elections contested by rival political parties vying for power. Deng strongly rejected the notion that "bourgeois liberalism" was appropriate for China. Deng made it clear that there were limits to "democratization" and to dissent in the People's Republic.

Deng's regime, reformist though it was, had no intention of sharing power or allowing contested elections, but its rhetoric of democratization, as well as the greater political and personal freedoms it had already permitted, whetted the appetites of many Chinese for a greater measure of political liberalization. Since the early 1980s, hundreds of thousands of Chinese had gone abroad to study and had been exposed to institutions, ideas, and to social values that gave greater rein to individual rights and liberties. By the mid-1980s, however, the government began a crackdown on the new wave of Western-styled popular culture (such as rock music), condemning it as "spiritual pollution." The crackdown extended to the more vocal proponents of genuine democratic reform.

A growing demand for democratic change was suddenly made manifest by university students in large political demonstrations in December 1986 and January 1987. First in Shanghai and then in Beijing, students turned out by the hundreds of thousands to register their demand for political reforms. These demonstrations, by far the largest to date in the People's Republic, continued for almost two weeks before being broken up by the government, which showed considerable restraint and offered vague promises of addressing the students' concerns. In reprisals that followed, however, Deng underscored the Communist Party's position as the final arbiter of all political matters.

The movement for reform erupted again in the spring of 1989. In the interim, students and intellectuals chafed not only at growing repression but also at the increased economic hardship. They were also perturbed by the increasing evidence of widespread corruption, especially among high-ranking government officials and their families. Further, they were repulsed by a ruling Communist Party that had, in effect, abandoned Marxism and the ideals of Mao and offered nothing worthy of commitment in their place. For many disillusioned youths, state ideology had become irrelevant. Some looked back to Mao's rule with nostalgia, not because it had been democratic, but because it had at least inspired people with high ideals and a sense of purpose. Many felt the party had lost its moral authority to govern China. At the very least, the students who rallied in 1989 demanded accountability from government leaders, and an unfettered press, without which accountability could not be achieved.

The occasion that triggered the student demonstrations in late April 1989 was the death of party chief Hu Yaobang, the most outspoken advocate of political reform. Students from several Beijing universities defied government orders by marching on Tiananmen Square in the heart of Beijing—first to commemorate Hu, whom they heralded as a champion of the democratic cause, and then to call for political reforms. On their posters they demanded increased respect for human rights, the release of political prisoners, a new democratic constitution, greater freedom of speech and press, and the right to hold demonstrations.[7]

The student leaders exploited Western press coverage, deluding themselves by thinking that the government would not risk its international prestige by using force against unarmed demonstrators. By May 4, their numbers in Tiananmen Square had grown to over a hundred thousand, and the movement had spread to other cities. Government leaders considered it too dangerous to forcefully stop the demonstrations, partly because of the scheduled arrival of Soviet leader Mikhail Gorbachev on May 15. Gorbachev's visit had enormous diplomatic significance in its own right. Chinese leaders were eager to ratify the end of the Sino-Soviet feud, and they were determined not to allow the student protesters to interfere with this important diplomatic objective. Beijing could not afford to jeopardize good relations with the new Soviet leader by using brutal force against the students on the eve of, much less during, his visit. Two days before Gorbachev arrived, two thousand student protesters began a public hunger strike in Tiananmen Square, and the next day hundreds of thousands flocked to the square in support, ignoring the deadline the government had issued for clearing the area.[8]

No sooner had Gorbachev left Beijing than the government declared martial law. Over the next three weeks, the drama unfolding in Tiananmen Square gripped the nation and the worldwide viewing public. Student demonstrators had been emboldened by the fact that the government had not taken action to enforce the martial decree and that large numbers of workers in Beijing and other cities had openly embraced their movement. It was precisely this fact that caused the government to crack down on the demonstrators, for it could not afford to allow the antigovernment agitation to spread to the general public. The protesters took heart when the troops that assembled to suppress the movement seemed disinclined to use force against them. Emotions were fired up all the more by the erection of a "goddess of democracy" statue (resembling the Statue of Liberty in New York harbor) in Tiananmen Square as a symbol of their cause. Meanwhile, as the protesters became more defiant in their demands—no longer merely calling for dialogue but demanding the overthrow of the government— other army units were brought into position to crush the revolt. Finally, under the cover of darkness in the early hours of June 4, columns of tanks rumbled toward the square, and a terrible massacre began. The extent of the carnage may never be known, but estimates range from several hundred to three thousand deaths. The government's claim that no students were killed *on* Tiananmen Square was scoffed at around the world, but it may not be far from the truth, insofar as it was in the streets leading to the square, and not in the square itself, that the carnage took place.[9]

The June 4 crushing of the Tiananmen Square demonstration was not the end but only the beginning of the government's effort to suppress political opposition and reassert its authority. No sooner was the shooting over than the Chinese government employed a second tool of repression, the controlled media, to broadcast to the nation—and the world—its version of what had taken place and to block out any other version. First came the denial of a massacre and then the rationalization of the crackdown. The Chinese were told that the army had heroically defended the nation against an armed counterrevolution. Then came the reprisals, as dissidents were hunted down, arrested, pronounced guilty of treasonous acts, and, in some cases, executed. Thousands of others were imprisoned. Cowed by state power, Chinese citizens who had witnessed the events in (or near) Tiananmen Square denied having witnessed anything at all.

In the year that followed, Deng's government was steadfastly determined to stay the course by cracking down on "counterrevolutionary offenders," silencing dissent, intensifying ideological education, and warding off international criticism. The government's effort to renew ideological fervor was met with the sullen compliance of a demoralized society. Rather than accept the party leaders' campaign for ideological purity, many Chinese reverted to the style of mutual self-protection they had learned in earlier Maoist times. Of the thousands arrested after the massacre, about forty were executed and eighteen were given long prison sentences. When a U.S. State Department official inquired into possible violations of the dissenters' human rights, Beijing countered with charges that such inquiries constituted a violation of China's sovereignty and lectured foreign observers that those in jail were not "dissidents" but "offenders."[10]

Beijing sought to repair the damage caused abroad by Tiananmen and to induce foreign investors and buyers to continue to do business with China. The crackdown had cost China an estimated $2–$3 billion in investments and developmental assistance, but by the second anniversary of that event, Beijing had succeeded in wooing most major industrial democracies back into normal diplomatic and economic relations. A major reason for the return to business as usual was the pull of China's own economy, which in the first half of 1991 grew at a rate of 13.7 percent. Meanwhile, China gained international respectability through diplomatic moves such as supporting UN resolutions against Iraq during the Gulf War, signing the Nuclear Non-Proliferation Treaty, and playing an active role to bring an end to the decade-long civil war in Cambodia.

## ■ CHINA IN THE 1990S

A long-festering debate between reformers and hard-liners among the Chinese Communist leaders over economic policy came into the open in early 1992. Chief among the ideological hard-liners was Li Peng, who remained critical of the market system reforms Deng Xiaoping had instituted in the 1980s. Li Peng was clearly in ascendance among Chinese leaders in the immediate post-Tiananmen period, despite the widespread public view of him as "the most hated man in China." But Deng settled the issue decisively by calling unequivocally for speeding up the economic reforms. In January 1992, the eighty-seven-year-old Deng reemerged from retirement to make a trip to southern China to inspect the most advanced special economic zones and witness firsthand the spectacular progress of these commercial boomtowns, where foreign capital and technology was concentrated to build modern, world-class industrial plants producing for world markets. In Shenzen, near Hong Kong, Deng declared that henceforth "everything should serve economic construction."[11] Li Peng and the hard-liners in Beijing initially were stunned by Deng's strong pronouncements, but within a month, all members of the ruling Politburo jumped on Deng's bandwagon, publicly endorsing his campaign for accelerated economic liberalization. The *People's Daily* trumpeted Deng's command: "Seize the opportunity to speed up reform and opening up to the outside world to improve the economy."[12]

Deng's full-speed-ahead policy remained in force through the 1990s and produced spectacular results. In 1993, China's GNP grew by 13 percent, industrial output by 21 percent, and foreign trade by 18.2 percent; during that single year China received $27 billion in foreign capital—the largest sum for any nation—and 140,000 new foreign-funded businesses were created.[13] China was bolting swiftly toward capitalism as consumerism swept the country, a stock market was created, and old, inefficient state enterprises gave way to privately owned businesses. China was on a building binge as modern high-rise buildings sprouted in cities large and small and new high-speed railroads and highways were built. Meanwhile, China's foreign trade was soaring. By the end of the 1990s, China had a surplus of over $60 billion in its bilateral trade with the United States, surpassing Japan. Shanghai's modern transformation was especially spectacular. By 1993, it had over two thousand new projects, involving more than $3.5 billion in foreign investments, and more than 120 new multinational corporations had begun operations there.[14] While it is true that China's economic boom benefited primarily the major cities in eastern China and the new economic zones, it is also true that there was a significant improvement in most of the Chinese people's standard of living. By the end of the decade, its people were generally wealthier, freer, and better fed, dressed, and housed than at any time in the past. China's robust economy was able to withstand the financial crisis that caused havoc in Asian nations in the late

1990s and continued to grow at a rate of over 7 percent while annual trade surpluses continued to grow.

The economic surge served to drive out the legacy of Tienanmen and divert attention away from politics. But there were problems attendant with such rapid economic development. Beijing's leaders—especially the hard-liners—feared that unrestrained growth would lead to gross inequality in wealth, as well as corruption, social instability, and discontent among restless youth. The new economic forces also unleashed a flood of over 100 million rural migrants flocking to China's cities in search of economic opportunity. Only some of them were able to find work, usually in low-paying menial jobs, and most of them struggled to meet minimum needs while living in horribly crowded and unsanitary conditions. Pollution levels—including those from chemical fertilizers and pesticides—were so severe that by the late 1990s, several Chinese cities were rated as the most polluted in the world.

The party's legitimacy rested on its success in maintaining unprecedented economic progress and the sociopolitical stability necessary for sustaining that progress. Deng's regime regarded the army and economic reform as the keys to the Communist Party's maintaining power and political stability. Reform was to be limited to the economic arena. Dissenters who dared to call for radical democratic reform were arrested and given long prison terms. Brushing aside criticism of human rights violations, authorities continued such crackdowns periodically through the 1990s.

The government's anxiety about stability is also reflected in its paranoid reaction to the Falun Gong, a new popular movement that arose in the early 1990s and quickly grew to attract millions of followers. This movement combined elements of meditative religion and physical and spiritual training based on traditional martial-arts disciplines. It was thus not a political movement, but it did have a devoted and disciplined membership. Authorities in Beijing were alarmed by its rapid growth and viewed it as a potential source of instability, since its members seemed to have a higher allegiance to their leader than to the state. The authorities well remembered that the massive and destructive Taiping rebellion of the mid-nineteenth century began when charismatic leaders gained a widespread following. When some ten thousand Falun Gong members staged a defiant protest at the gates of the government leaders' compound in Beijing in April 1999, the government broke up the demonstration, outlawed the Falun Gong, and eventually arrested thousands of its members.[15]

As long as Deng lived, political stability held, but by the mid-1990s, he had reached the age of ninety and was becoming rather feeble. Deng retained authority even in infirmity as China's "paramount leader," but in 1996, he designated a successor, Jiang Zemin, who by then already held the offices of president and general secretary of the CCP. When Deng, who had ruled about as long as Mao had, died in March 1997, the transition to Jiang was a smooth one. Jiang, formerly an engineer, was determined to press forward with economic modernization while maintaining political order under strong Communist Party control.

In the 1990s, China's leaders were also confronted with several persistent foreign policy issues, especially the worsening of relations with the United States. Ever since Tiananmen Square, Washington had pressured China about its human rights record. The United States threatened to deny China most-favored-nation treatment (trade terms equal to those enjoyed by other nations), thus restricting continued virtually unlimited access to the huge U.S. market unless China took measures to safeguard human rights, particularly in regard to its treatment of political dissenters. Beijing contended that such demands constituted unwarranted encroachment on China's sovereignty. In 1993, President Bill Clinton chose to separate human rights and economic issues in order to grant most-favored-nation status to China, but international rebuke of China on human rights persisted. Beijing, however, rebuffed criticism on this and on such issues as its suppression of Tibet, its atmospheric testing of nuclear weapons, and its sale of missiles and nuclear technology to Pakistan. Trade relations with the United States remained contentious as China built up an enormous trade surplus at U.S. expense and came under attack for pirating intellectual property (computer software, videos, compact disks, and the like). Beijing was infuriated by the U.S. bombing of the Chinese embassy in Yugoslavia during the Kosovo war in 1999 and refused to accept Washington's explanation that it had been a mistake. Beijing also protested continued U.S. military support of Taiwan, including the sale of advanced jet fighters to Taiwan, and it strongly denounced U.S. plans to shelter Taiwan under a proposed missile defense system.

Early in the twenty-first century, the reign of the aging Jiang Zemin gave way to the reign of Hu Jintao. In November 2002, Hu became the secretary general of the Communist Party, the most significant position within the political system. In March 2003, he took control of the government bureaucracy when he became president of China. And in September 2004, he completed his consolidation of power by replacing the aging Jiang as the chairman of the Central Military Commission, in effect becoming the commander of the world's largest military force consisting of 2 million men and women.

The change was one of style, not substance. There would be little change but plenty of continuity. Hu offered no departure from Jiang's policies on the economy (integration with the world would continue), political dissent, and Taiwan.

## ■ TAIWAN—THE OTHER CHINA

After arriving on the island of Taiwan in 1949 with 2 million soldiers and civilian supporters, Nationalist ruler Jiang Jieshi (Chiang K'ai-shek) created the political myth that the Nationalist government (the Republic of China), now situated on the island of Taiwan, remained the only legitimate government of China. Although lauded for many years by the United States as the "democratic" alternative to the oppressive Communist regime on the mainland, the "free China" under Jiang was anything but free or democratic. When the Nationalist army wrested control of Taiwan from the Japanese after World War II, it was met with resistance by the native Taiwanese, which was brutally suppressed.[16] Jiang maintained a one-party dictatorship. The National Assembly became a rubber-stamp legislative body, made up entirely of Nationalist Party politicians who had been elected on the mainland in 1948, and it remained without Taiwanese representation until the 1980s. The Taiwanese majority of about 13 million people in the 1950s had no political voice. Until his last breath, Jiang remained ever vigilant against Communist subversion, and he ruthlessly suppressed all opposition, including a nascent Taiwanese independence movement. When he passed away in 1975, he was succeeded by his son, Jiang Jingguo (Chiang Ching-kuo), who continued his father's anti-Communist and undemocratic policies.

Taiwan suffered a major diplomatic setback in 1972, when the United States normalized relations with the People's Republic of China, and again in 1979, when Washington broke off official relations with the Nationalist government. Economic ties with the United States, Japan, and other industrial countries remained intact, however, and the people of Taiwan directed their attention to developing a strong export economy. In this they were far more successful.

Through the 1960s, 1970s, and 1980s, Taiwan was undergoing a remarkable economic transformation. The GNP of Taiwan rose from $8 billion in 1960 to $72.5 billion in 1986, and for most of the 1970s it maintained double-digit growth rates. Taiwan's annual volume of foreign trade increased from $2.2 billion to $100 billion between 1969 and 1988. By virtue of its burgeoning exports, by 1988 Taiwan had accumulated a foreign exchange reserve in excess of $70 billion, second in the world only to Japan. (See Chapter 16 for Japan's economic performance.)

Taiwan, together with South Korea, Singapore, and Hong Kong, the so-called four tigers, followed in the footsteps of Japan in achieving rapid industrialization and stunning GNP growth rates in this period. Among the four, the two most successful, South Korea and Taiwan, had several common characteristics that set them apart. Both countries were highly militarized, with each facing threats to its security—from Communist North Korea and from the Communist mainland, respectively. Like South Korea, Taiwan thrived on adversity. The maintenance of large military establishments and the burden of large military budgets seem to have had the effect of spurring economic development instead of being a drag on the economy. Moreover, the presence of a threat produced a sense of national urgency and purpose that was useful to these governments and government-supported industrialists as well.

Taiwan's economic success can also be attributed to other factors unique to the island, including the infrastructure the Japanese had built in Taiwan before 1945, the influx of highly educated Chinese from the mainland in 1949, a quarter century of U.S. economic aid, an open U.S. import policy for Taiwanese goods, the growth-oriented economic policies of the Nationalist government, and its industrious people. In the 1950s, a sweeping land reform was carried out and agricultural production grew steadily, paving the way for capital accumulation and investment in industrial development. By the 1960s, Taiwan's industries began shifting from production for domestic consumption to export-oriented production. Lured by Taiwan's cheap, high-quality labor, U.S. and Japanese companies made substantial investments, and Taiwanese industrialists and workers rapidly absorbed modern technology. In the late 1970s, Taiwan gravitated toward capital-intensive and knowledge-intensive industries, a shift that paid huge dividends in the 1980s. By the end of the 1980s, electronics had replaced textiles as the leading export, and Taiwan became one of the world's leaders in microcomputers and computer parts.

It was not until the 1980s that Taiwan's economic modernization engendered political modernization. Liberalization became possible by the passing of the old guard, the lowering of Cold War tensions, the challenge of a modernizing Communist China, the new prosperity in Taiwan, the spread of education, and the government's increased confidence in the nation's security. In 1986, a newly formed opposition party, the Democratic Progressive Party (DPP), whose platform called for full implementation of democracy, welfare, and self-determination for Taiwan, was permitted to run candidates in the National Assembly election—although the DPP had not yet been legalized—and it won a surprising 25 percent of the vote. In July 1987, the government lifted the martial law decree, which had been in effect for thirty-eight years, granted freedom of the press, and legalized opposition parties. It also dropped the ban on travel to Communist China, for the first time permitting its people to visit families on the mainland. Tens of thousands of residents quickly took advantage of this new opportunity.

President Jiang Jingguo died in January 1988, thus ending the sixty-year Jiang dynasty. His successor was his vice-president, Lee Teng-hui, who was not from mainland China but from Taiwan. Although Lee did not advocate independence for Taiwan, the fact that a native Taiwanese was now president encouraged those who did. Moreover, Lee, without a strong power base of his own, could hardly revert to the strong-man type of rule characteristic of the Jiang dynasty. Instead, he continued the political liberalization begun by Jiang Jingguo. The first signal event in Taiwan's democratization under Lee was the December 1989 National Assembly election, which was the first free, multiparty election in Chinese history. The result of this election, in which 78 percent of eligible voters cast ballots, was an assembly far more representative than the previous one. Another major step on the road to democracy was the first direct election of the president of the republic, held in April 1996. The incumbent Lee, the head of the ruling Nationalist Party, was reelected as president, but his party's share of the vote decreased while the opposition parties made substantial gains. The Nationalist Party's rule finally ended in March 2000, when the DPP candidate, Chen Shuibian, won the presidential election.

## ■ DIVIDED CHINA: TAIWAN AND THE PEOPLE'S REPUBLIC

Democratization in Taiwan not only carried the risk of the Nationalist Party being voted out of power, but it also raised serious questions about the very status of the Republic of China and its relations with the People's Republic of China. Taiwan's liberalization movement, especially the growing independence movement it unleashed, was of great concern to the People's Republic of China (PRC), which was vehemently opposed to the permanent separation of Taiwan from China. The PRC had consistently maintained that Taiwan was merely a renegade province of China that sooner or later must be reunited with the mainland. Prior to the deaths of Jiang Jieshi and Mao Zedong in the mid-1970s, relations between the PRC and Taiwan had been extremely hostile, but the 1980s saw the beginnings of a thaw in those relations. This was fostered on the one hand by Deng Xiaoping's policy of liberalization and openness on the mainland and on the other by the political liberalization taking place in Taiwan. Moreover, Deng eagerly sought Taiwanese investments as much as Taiwan's financiers sought profitable investments. Trade and contact between the two Chinas increased vastly after Taiwan lifted the ban on travel to China in 1987. By 1993, over 1.5 million Taiwanese had traveled to the mainland.

That year, the two contending regimes cautiously opened a formal diplomatic channel, the so-called cross-strait talks, for negotiating economic and social issues. Although both governments professed the goal of reunification, they remained far apart on the terms. Beijing offered assurances that upon reversion, Taiwan would become an autonomous region within the PRC, retaining its capitalist economy. The Taiwan government refused to accept such assurances and insisted that as a first step the PRC must renounce the use of military force to coerce reunification. This Beijing refused to do. Moreover, Taiwan argued that reunification would not be possible until genuine democratization was achieved in China.

The growth of the Taiwanese independence movement brought a new sense of urgency to these talks. In one sense, it tended to bring the two sides (the PRC and the Nationalist government) closer together, since both opposed Taiwanese independence. But Beijing expressed concern that President Lee, as a Taiwanese, might succumb to political pressure to endorse the independence movement. It remained wary of any action or assertion by Lee suggesting Taiwan's independent status, such as Taiwan's seeking membership in the United Nations.

Beijing was not content merely to register protests; it attempted to intimidate Taiwanese voters by threatening the use of force and engaging in military exercises near the coast of Taiwan. In April 1996, just prior to Taiwan's first presidential election, the PRC carried out large-scale military maneuvers—including missile tests with live ammunition—dangerously close to Taiwan's main port cities. It was not clear what effect this show of force had on Taiwan's voters, since President Lee was reelected by a comfortable margin. However, it did provoke a strong response from the United States, which warned Beijing against an attack on Taiwan.

The return of Hong Kong by the United Kingdom to China in July 1997 (see below) and the reversion of the tiny Portuguese colony of Macao in 1999 served to quicken Beijing's insistence on the return of Taiwan. Beijing offered Taiwan the Hong Kong reversion formula of "one-country, two systems" that would reunite Taiwan under the PRC but allow it to retain its capitalist economy and a degree of autonomy. Taiwan, however, flatly rejected this offer, arguing that its own situation was utterly different from Hong Kong's, for Taiwan was not a foreign-controlled colony and had a much larger population and much greater economic and military power than Hong Kong.

The feud between the two Chinese governments heated up in July 1999, when President Lee Tung-hui stated explicitly that negotiations between them must be conducted on a state-to-state basis: that is, two sovereign governments negotiating on equal terms. Beijing vehemently rejected the notion of two separate and equal Chinese governments and warned that any step by Taiwan toward separation would be met by force. This was taken in Washington as a threat of war, and an alarmed President Clinton warned against the use of force while strongly cautioning President Lee against abandoning the "one-China" position. At the same time, there was talk in Washington of increasing military assistance to Taiwan and providing Taiwan with an antimissile defensive shield. This, too, met with vociferous protest from Beijing.

The PRC-Taiwan tug-of-war continued unabated and tensions remained high when the next presidential election in Taiwan took place in March 2000. Chen Shui-bian, candidate of the DPP that had openly espoused Taiwanese independence, won the election. But as a candidate, then as the new president, Chen cautiously shied away from his party's independence agenda and chose a safer course: maintaining the status quo (that is, de facto independence.) As such, Chen's position remained diametrically opposed to the government in Beijing, where the new leader, Hu Jintao, held fast to the position of his predecessor, Jiang Zemin: if possible, "peaceful reunification" of Taiwan with the mainland, but "we shall by no means . . . forsake the use of force."[17]

# ■ HONG KONG

The former British Crown Colony of Hong Kong, which emerged after World War II as a budding mecca of Asian capitalism, also experienced phenomenal economic growth in the post–World War II era. Britain's "gunboat diplomacy" had pried Hong Kong away from China in the nineteenth century, and it remained in British control even after the Communists came to power in China. In its early years, the PRC was militarily too weak to attempt to recover Hong Kong by force, and Beijing eventually took a pragmatic, rather than a doctrinaire, view of the British presence there, deciding that it represented not a threat to China but an opportunity for maintaining profitable economic relations with the West.

The British governors of Hong Kong had presided over a docile populace (only 6 million in 1990) and a prospering economy. Hong Kong steadily developed as a major financial, trade, and insurance center, and in the 1980s it also became highly industrialized. The thriving business environment attracted huge investments from Western countries and Japan, further stimulating economic growth. Hong Kong's average annual rate of growth was 5.5 percent between 1980 and 1992, but it rose as high as 13.5 percent in 1987. Although Hong Kong had a large number of poor people, mainly recent arrivals from the PRC, its per capita GNP reached $15,360 in 1992. The central section of the city-state became resplendent with wealth, with gleaming skyscrapers soaring above Mercedes-Benz automobiles and free-spending shoppers crowding the streets below.

The main threat to Hong Kong's continued economic stability and prosperity was the fact that it was scheduled to revert to Chinese rule in 1997. As early as the 1970s, when that target date was still twenty years away, the British and Chinese governments began discussing the return of Hong Kong. International business interests became nervous about their investments, and to head off a flight of capital and financial chaos the British government was eager to secure an early agreement for an orderly transition. Similarly, it was in the PRC's interest to maintain the financial strength of Hong Kong, since the city-state played an important role in China's international trade and economic development plans.

In 1984, London and Beijing signed a joint declaration that provided a framework for the Chinese takeover, still thirteen years away. The agreement stipulated that Hong Kong would retain its capitalist system while maintaining "a high degree of autonomy" as a "special administrative region" of the People's Republic for fifty years after the reversion in 1997. With this formula, the Chinese and British sought to preserve political and economic stability through 1997 and beyond. The agreement also stipulated that the ethnic Chinese citizens of Hong Kong (98 percent of the population) would become citizens of China at the time of reversion but that they were free to leave the colony prior to that time.

The reversion agreement produced mixed results as the years ticked away. Economic growth did not decline appreciably, and, in fact, foreign and domestic investments increased dramatically. Even in 1996, with reversion to China only a year away, the Hong Kong government was pumping record amounts ($21 billion) into a series of new projects, including a new international airport, a high-speed rail line to link the airport to the inner city, new superhighways, vast new housing projects, a new harbor tunnel, and the world's longest suspension bridge.

But if investors remained confident about Hong Kong's future, many of its residents were less so. In the late 1980s, about fifty thousand people emigrated from Hong Kong annually (mainly to Canada, Australia, and the United States). This exodus of residents—largely wealthy, well-educated elites—reflected fear of Chinese rule.[18] The exodus caused consternation in Beijing, which sought to reassure the people in the colony and avert the hemorrhage of wealth and talent. The bloody suppression of the prodemocracy movement in Tiananmen Square in June 1989 and the subsequent political repression carried out by the Chinese government further damaged its credibility in Hong Kong and caused even greater emigration. Within five years, however, the annual rate of emigration had leveled off, and by this time about 12 percent of those who had emigrated had returned. Many Hong Kong residents sought to leave open the possibility of emigrating after the reversion by securing a British passport beforehand.

After Tiananmen, mutual distrust and suspicion lingered between the British and the Chinese. London took the position that Beijing—its promises notwithstanding—had already taken too many steps to curtail Hong Kong's autonomy. Shortly after arriving as the newly appointed governor of Hong Kong in July 1992, Christopher Patten abruptly announced a plan to substantially broaden the voting franchise for Legislative Council elections and thus to strengthen democracy and autonomy in the Crown Colony before its transfer to China. Beijing lost no time in venting its indignation, arguing that London had shown little interest in promoting democracy in the colony in the past and was now violating the spirit of the transfer agreement. When talks on this issue reached an impasse, the PRC declared in 1996 that Hong Kong's elected legislature would be abolished after reversion and replaced with an appointed one.

As the date neared for handing China the keys to Hong Kong, its economy was still growing (at a steady 5 percent annually), and plans for the transition were being worked out with improved cooperation. All involved—the Chinese, the British, and the residents of Hong Kong—seemed to recognize the importance of Hong Kong's future as the dynamic economic capital of southern China and Southeast Asia. Yet apprehension and uncertainty remained palpable, especially for its residents, because of the enormous gulf between Hong Kong's system—said to be the freest economic system in the world—and the politically controlled economy of the PRC.

The long-awaited date for the return of Hong Kong to China came on July 1, 1997. The colorful ceremony marking the event mixed nationalistic celebrations by China, nostalgia on the part of Britain witnessing the end of its long imperial presence in Asia, and uneasiness on the part of Hong Kong. For the most part, the transition from British Crown Colony to Special Administrative Region went smoothly, and Hong Kong continued to prosper.

The PRC then started the countdown to the reversion of the Portuguese colony of Macao at the end of 1999, and having achieved that, it turned expectantly to Taiwan.

## ■ RECOMMENDED READINGS

Copper, John. *A Quiet Revolution: Political Development in the Republic of China.* Lanham, Md.: University Press of America, 1988.

Evans, Richard. *Deng Xiaoping and the Making of Modern China.* London: Penguin Books, 1995.

Hinton, William. *Fanshen: A Documentary of Revolution in a Chinese Village.* New York: Monthly Review Press, 1966.
An enthusiastic report on Maoism at work in the countryside in the early years of the revolution.

Hsu, Immanuel C. Y. *China Without Mao: The Search for a New Order.* New York: Oxford University Press, 1982.

Kristoff, Nicholas, and Sherl Wudunn. *China Wakes.* New York: Random House, 1994.
One of the best recent accounts of China's economic surge by *New York Times* correspondents.

Meisner, Maurice. *Mao's China and After: A History of the People's Republic.* New York: Free Press, 1986.
Assesses Chinese politics on its own Marxian terms.

Nathan, Andrew J., and Bruce Gilley. *China's New Rulers: The Secret File.* New York: New York Review of Books, 2003.

Perkins, Dwight. *China: Asia's Next Economic Giant.* Seattle: University of Washington Press, 1986.

Schell, Orville. *In the People's Republic.* New York: Random House, 1977.
A lucid eyewitness account of the PRC shortly after Mao's death.

———. *Mandate of Heaven: The Legacy of Tienanmen and the Next Generation of Chinese Leaders.* New York: Simon and Schuster, 1994.
A superb analysis of China in the wake of Tiananmen and its remarkable economic boom in the early 1990s.

Wilson, Dick, ed. *Mao Tse-tung in the Scales of History.* New York: Cambridge University Press, 1977.
A composite view of Mao's leadership by various scholars; among the best books on Mao.

Zhang Liang, Perry Link, and Andrew J. Nathan. *The Tienanmen Papers: The Chinese Leadership's Decision to Use Force Against Their Own People—In Their Own Words.* New York: New York Review of Books, 2003.

# ■ NOTES

1. R. J. Rummel, *China's Bloody Century: Genocide and Mass Murder Since 1900* (New Brunswick, N.J.: Transactions Publishers, 1994), arrives at the estimate of 10,729,000 deaths caused by the Great Leap Forward and its aftermath by averaging the highest and lowest estimates available.

2. After the death of Mao in 1976, the CCP condemned his Cultural Revolution and its excessive violence and encouraged the Chinese people to testify to its cruelty, but the party remained reticent to reveal the number of lives the violence had claimed.

3. Immanuel C. Y. Hsu, *The Rise of Modern China* (New York: Oxford University Press, 1983), p. 804.

4. Quoted in John F. Burns, "Canton Booming on Marxist Free Enterprise," *New York Times,* November 11, 1985, p. A1.

5. Deng Xiaoping quoted in "China Calls Rigid Adherence to Marxism 'Stupid,'" *New York Times,* December 9, 1984. Based on an article that appeared as a front-page commentary in the December 7, 1984, edition of *People's Daily,* the official organ of the Chinese Communist Party.

6. World Bank, *World Development Report, 1996* (Washington, D.C.: World Bank, 1996).

7. John Schidlovsky, "Strike Gains Momentum in China," *Baltimore Sun,* April 25, 1989.

8. Scott Shane, "Gorbachev Praises China for Dialogue with Demonstrators," *Baltimore Sun,* May 18, 1989. The students hailed Gorbachev as a true champion of democratization and lampooned Deng, the dauntless author of the post-Mao reforms, as a stodgy old hard-liner. Gorbachev deftly managed neither to support nor discourage the students, and he gave faint praise to Chinese leaders for "opening a political dialogue with the demonstrators."

9. Orville Schell, *Mandate of Heaven* (New York: Simon and Schuster, 1994), p. 154. The Chinese government took the position that no unarmed students were killed in Tiananmen Square, that a total of three hundred people died in the clashes between the soldiers and the rebels that took place on the avenues approaching the square, and that most of the dead were soldiers.

10. Robert Benjamin, "China Reiterates Hard-Line Views of Human Rights," *Baltimore Sun,* December 21, 1990, p. 4A. China's foreign ministry spokesman stated: "We should not . . . interfere in the internal affairs of other countries under the pretext of human rights. China will never do this, and we will never allow any other country to do the same."

11. Quoted in Schell, *Mandate of Heaven,* p. 343.

12. Cited in the *Baltimore Sun,* March 13, 1992, p. 3.

13. Schell, *Mandate of Heaven,* p. 433.

14. Ibid., p. 388.

15. *The Economist,* July 31, 1999, p. 32.

16. In February 1947, an anti-Nationalist demonstration was suppressed by the Nationalist army with enormous violence, leaving between five thousand (the Nationalist figure) and twenty thousand (the Taiwanese figure) Taiwanese dead. For four decades, Jiang's martial law decree forbade anyone from speaking of this massacre on punishment of death.

17. Cited in Richard Halloran, "How Will Hu Change China's Foreign Policy?" *Baltimore Sun,* September 29, 2004, p. 17A.

18. "New Record Set in Exodus," *Free China Journal,* December 22, 1988.

# 15

## The Indian Subcontinent and Southeast Asia

The Himalayan Mountains separate the two Third World giants—China and India. India shares many of China's problems, not the least of which is a burgeoning population. About one-fifth of the world's population lives on the Indian subcontinent, which consists mainly of India, Pakistan, and Bangladesh. In the postwar era, India and the other heavily populated nations of this region struggled to hold population growth in check and to elevate the standard of living, but only recently have they met with moderate success. Although they shared many problems, these nations have not lived in peace with one another. Hostility between India and Pakistan has flared up several times, and both countries have confronted violent internal disorders. The maintenance of large armies to deal with these problems has drained the limited resources of each of these quarreling neighbors.

To speak of India is to speak of population and poverty. At the time of the partition in 1947, India's population was about 350 million, and it has grown steadily ever since at a rate of almost 3 percent a year. This meant an average annual increase of about 5 million people in the 1950s, 8 million in the 1960s, and 13 million in the 1970s. An electronic display in New Delhi reminded Indians that in mid-July 1992, the country's population stood at 868 million and was increasing by two thousand people per hour, forty-eight thousand per day, or 17.5 million per year.[1] By the year 2000, the population reached 1 billion, almost triple that of 1947. Moreover, about 40 percent of the Indian people were concentrated in the Ganges River Basin, where the population density was the highest in the world. Although in the mid-1980s India had eight cities with over 1 million inhabitants, over 80 percent of the people still lived in rural villages.

India's primary task was to feed its huge population. The twin aims of the Indian government, therefore, were population control and increased food production. Its birth control program, however, had minimal effect in rural areas. The largely illiterate villagers were suspicious of the purpose and methods of birth control, and they clung to the age-old ideas that a large family was a blessing and that it represented wealth and security. Moreover, one way Indians combated the high infant mortality rate was simply to have more children in the hope some would survive. But even where birth control had some effect, it did not produce a significant decrease in population growth. Offsetting the slight decrease in the birth rate was a declining death rate; thus, the pressure of overpopulation on India's economy remained undiminished.

Indian food production increased steadily following independence, but it remained barely adequate. In general, the rate of increase of output was slightly higher than the rate of population growth, but this was offset by occasional years of crop failure caused by droughts or flooding. Moreover, the increased food production was unevenly distributed. Indian agriculture consisted largely of subsistence farming and was one of the world's least efficient in terms of yield per acre. Among the reasons for this inefficiency were the small size of farms, the lack of farming machinery, a general lack of irrigation, a tradition-bound social system, and widespread malnutrition. The last of the reasons suggests a cruel cycle of cause and effect: malnutrition and disease contributed to low agricultural productivity, which in turn led to greater poverty and hunger.

In India, as in the other agrarian nations in this part of the world, a wide gulf existed between the wealthy landowners and the far more numerous poor peasants, many of whom were landless. This great discrepancy between well-to-do farmers and the rural poor was an age-old problem that was inherent in the traditional society and the farming system. The practice of dividing land among sons contributed to making the average family farm so small that it did not support the family; thus, the farmer was often forced to borrow money at high rates of interest to make ends meet. All too often, he was unable to repay the loan without selling what little land he had left. The result was a steady increase in the number of landless peasants and an increase in the size of the farms of the wealthy.

More recent developments—the so-called Green Revolution and agricultural mechanization—produced an increase in agricultural output in India and thus increased food supply. The Green Revolution refers to the introduction of newly developed plants—high-yield varieties of wheat and rice—and new farming techniques to grow the new types of grain.[2] In certain areas of India, wheat production doubled between 1964 and 1972, and the new rice strains had a similar effect when introduced in the late 1960s. The Green Revolution, however, turned out to be a mixed blessing. It benefited mainly the minority of India's farmers—the wealthy landowners who could afford the new seeds and the additional irrigation works, fertilizers, and labor required to grow the new high-yield grain. The majority of the rural population—small landholders, landless peasants, and dry-land farmers—lacked the capital or the means to borrow enough money to grow the new crops. Not only were they unable to reap the benefits of the increased food production, but they were actually hurt by it; the increased yield lowered the market price for grain crops, which meant a lower income for peasants who still used the traditional mode of farming. The Green Revolution thus tended to make the rich richer and the poor poorer.

The mechanization of farming, meaning primarily the increased use of tractors, had a similar effect. On the one hand, it contributed to a rise in food production; on the other hand, mechanization benefited only those who could afford the expensive new equipment. Furthermore, the use of farm tractors greatly reduced the need for farm laborers and, by eliminating many jobs, increased the ranks of the unemployed. More and more impoverished villagers of India were reduced to collecting firewood and animal droppings to sell as fuel. Even progress sometimes breeds poverty.

One of the consequences of the dislocation of the landless in the countryside was the overcrowding of Indian cities. Many of those who migrated to the cities to find work found life little better there than in the villages they had left. Cities such as Calcutta and Bombay (today's Mumbai) were teeming with hungry and homeless people, many of whom literally lived and died in the streets. In the mid-1980s in Calcutta—which had a population of about 11 million—around nine hundred thousand people were living in the streets with scant shelter.

## ■ INDIA'S ECONOMIC DEVELOPMENT

India's efforts to modernize its economy and increase industrial production met with moderate success in the first two decades after independence. India opted for a mixed economy, whereby major industries such as iron and steel, mining, transportation, and electricity were nationalized—that is, owned and operated by the government. The government instituted its First Five-Year Plan for economic development in 1951. The plan's relatively modest goals for increased industrial output were attained, and it was followed by a sequence of similar five-year plans. In 1961, at the conclusion of the second plan, Prime Minister Jawaharlal Nehru admitted that his country "would need many more five-year plans to progress from the cow dung stage to the age of atomic energy."[3] Although some impressive large-scale, modern industrial plants were built, most of India's industry remained small in scale and lacked modern machinery.

The overall growth rate of India's economy was steady but insufficient. Following independence in 1947, India maintained an average annual GNP growth rate of between 3 and 4 percent.[4] A large gap existed between the incomes of the educated elite, technicians, and skilled laborers in the modern sector and unskilled laborers and peasants in the traditional sector—not to mention the many unemployed or underemployed city dwellers.

India was handicapped by most of the problems of Third World countries: a lack of capital, difficulty in attracting foreign capital, illiteracy, and a lack of technology. To this list one might add India's unique social conservatism—the weight of tradition, especially a Hindu religious tradition around which much of Indian life was centered. The remnants of the ancient caste system militated against social mobility and the advancement of all members of society. Ethnic and linguistic diversity was also an obstacle to economic modernization. Still another factor retarding India's economic growth was the continual "brain drain" the country experienced. Many of India's best foreign-trained scientists and engineers chose not to return and remained in Western countries that provided career opportunities, modern technology, and creature comforts unattainable in their native land.

One important prerequisite for economic development is the existence of a market, either domestic or foreign. In India, the poverty of the masses meant a lack of purchasing power and thus the lack of a strong domestic market. India strived to increase its exports of raw materials and manufactured goods to pay for its large volume of imports—a substantial portion of which consisted of petroleum, foodstuffs, and industrial equipment. The impact of the oil crisis in the 1970s and global inflation and recession made it virtually impossible to maintain a favorable balance of trade. India was unable to match the increased cost of its imports with its substantially increased exports. Over the years, its trade deficit, its need of capital to finance continued industrialization, and its periodic food shortages forced India to rely heavily on foreign loans. In the 1950s and 1960s, India received huge shipments of food grains, mainly from the United States. After that time, however, India needed less food relief, and in fact it became a net exporter of food in the early 1980s. After U.S. developmental aid was terminated in 1971, the Soviet Union became India's primary source of foreign aid. India also received substantial amounts of developmental aid and assistance from other sources, such as the World Bank, the Asian Development Bank, and Japan.

Political stability is an important asset for developing nations, and India possessed a degree of stability—at least at the beginning. The nation retained a functioning parliamentary system, an institution inherited from the British. It also had prolonged rule by one dominant party—the Congress Party—and continuity of leadership in the persons of Jawaharlal Nehru, who ruled from independence (1947) until his death in 1964; his daughter, Indira Gandhi, who ruled (except for one brief interlude) from 1966 to 1984; and her son, Rajiv Gandhi, who ruled until 1989. But beyond the capital, stability was lacking, however.

After gaining independence, India's leaders were confronted with the monumental task of binding together in nationhood the numerous subgroups of diverse ethnic, religious, and linguistic identities. Ethnic tension was punctuated time and again by violent clashes between one or another of the ethnic groups and the Hindu majority. In the mid-1970s, the Indian political consensus, guided by Nehru and then by Gandhi, began to fray at the edges. The economy had suffered from the steep rise of oil prices in the early 1970s, dissent increased as railroad workers threatened to paralyze the vast railroad system, and popular agitation spilled into the streets. In June 1975, Gandhi responded with a twenty-one-month-long "National Emergency," accompanied by the suspension of the constitution, stringent press censorship, and the arrest of political opponents. The emergency ended when Gandhi called for elections that she then lost, Congress's first electoral defeat. The emergency cast a long shadow as it had weakened India's commitment to its constitutional principles. The chief beneficiaries were the Hindu far-right groups, which until then had carefully been kept out of politics. Among the Hindu jingoists arrested in 1975 were members of what became the rightist ruling political coalition of the late 1990s, including the prime minister.[5]

## ■ INDIA, PAKISTAN, AND BANGLADESH

India's foreign relations were not peaceful, despite the "live and let live" policy of neutralism proclaimed by Prime Minister Nehru in the 1950s. Nehru's efforts to exert the moral influence of India as a neutral peacemaker in the early Cold War years were noteworthy and gained him considerable international prestige, but they did little to help the country in its troubled relations with its neighbors. India's conflicts with Pakistan and China served to undermine its neutralist diplomacy and necessitated large military expenditures that drained its meager resources.

Indian-Pakistani relations were strained from the time of partition and became rapidly worse as the two countries feuded over disputed territory. Both countries claimed the remote mountainous state of Kashmir. In 1948 and 1949, Indian and Pakistani forces clashed over this issue, despite UN efforts to keep the peace. India managed to secure control of Kashmir and turned a deaf ear to Pakistan's continual demands for a plebiscite there. The Pakistani claim to sparsely populated Kashmir was based on the fact that the majority of its people were Muslim, which explains why Pakistan wished to settle the matter with a plebiscite. India's claim rested mainly on the expressed will of the local ruler of Kashmir to remain within India.

India was confronted by a more formidable foe in Communist China over still another territorial dispute in the Himalayas. Both China and India laid claim to the southern slopes of the Himalayan Mountains north of the Assam Plain, each staking its claim on different boundaries drawn by nineteenth-century British surveyors in this remote mountainous area. India took the position that its claim was nonnegotiable and turned down repeated diplomatic efforts by Beijing to settle the issue. In 1962, India's forces suffered a humiliating defeat by China in a brief border war.

While India was still recovering from this setback, and not long after the death of its highly revered ruler, Prime Minister Nehru, Pakistan decided to seek a military solution to the Kashmiri issue. Tensions had mounted as skirmishes along the disputed border occurred with increasing frequency. Pakistan's forces then crossed the cease-fire line in August 1965, and the conflict quickly escalated into a brief but fierce war. Both sides had been fortified with modern weapons purchased mainly from the United States. U.S.-built jet fighters battled each other—bearing Pakistani and Indian insignia. In the end, India rallied to defeat Pakistan.

At this point, Indian-Pakistani conflicts began to take on important global dimensions, because both sides had lined up the support of the superpowers. India rebuked the United States for increasing its military aid to Pakistan after the 1965 war and selling it modern weapons. Consequently, India increasingly turned to the Soviet Union, which was only too willing to provide support to a new client and extend its influence in the region. Pakistan, meanwhile, found another friend, the People's Republic of China (PRC). Ironically, the supporters of Pakistan—the United States and the PRC—were bitter Cold War foes during these years.

During the 1960s, Pakistan was worse off than India in terms of economic development, overpopulation, and poverty. Much of what was said about India's plight and the causes for its problems generally applied to Pakistan as well, but Pakistan was beset by additional problems stemming from its peculiar situation as a nation with two separate parts. West Pakistan, where the capital was located, was separated from East Pakistan by nearly 1,000 miles of Indian territory. The distance between the two parts was even greater culturally and politically. The people of East Pakistan are Bengalis who, except for their Muslim religion, had little in common with the West Pakistanis, who are made up of several ethnic groups—the largest of which is the Punjabi. Political and military power was concentrated in the West, despite the fact that the more densely populated East contained over half of the nation's population. According to the constitution, however, East Pakistan comprised only one of the nation's five provinces and thus had only 20 percent of the seats in the Pakistani parliament. Moreover, only about 35 percent of the national budget was earmarked for East Pakistan. The Bengalis also argued that East Pakistan was treated as a captive market for West Pakistani goods.

Bengali frustration mounted until it erupted in late 1970, when East Pakistan was hit first by a terrible natural catastrophe and then by a manmade disaster. In November of that year, a powerful cyclone was followed by an enormous tidal wave and widespread flooding, leaving approximately two hundred thousand people dead and 1 million homeless. The lack of effective government relief measures was further evidence for the Bengalis of their government's indifference toward their problems and thus fed the flames of Bengali separatism. While still suffering the prolonged effects of the flooding, East Pakistan fell victim to a disaster of an entirely different kind: an assault by the military forces of West Pakistan.

The military regime of General Yahya Khan had called for an election in December 1970 for a national assembly to draft a new constitution for Pakistan and thus end thirteen years of military rule. In the election, Sheikh Mujibur Rahman, the Bengali leader and head of the Awami League, a political party that stood for elevating the status of East Pakistan, won a large majority. General Khan and Zulfikar Ali Bhutto, head of the leading West Pakistan–based party, were shocked by the election results and conspired to block the scheduled convening of the National Assembly. Consequently, the Bengalis of East Pakistan began to stir, but their protest demonstrations were met with a military crackdown and the imposition of martial law. Sheikh Mujibur, who was solidly supported by the Bengali people, met with General Khan and Bhutto in an attempt to resolve the political crisis, but he refused to yield to their demand to stand aside. As a showdown approached in March 1971, General Khan unleashed a military attack on East Pakistan, striking first at the leaders of the Awami League and placing Mujibur under arrest. Thus began the bloody suppression of the Bengali people in which, ultimately, some 3 million people of East Pakistan met their deaths at the hands of a Pakistani army of seventy thousand troops. The indiscriminate brutality, in turn, led to resistance by the Bengalis, who now demanded independence. Meanwhile, roughly 10 million of the terrorized Bengali people began fleeing their ravaged homeland, crossing the borders into India.

The assault on East Pakistan was met by Bengali armed resistance, mainly in the form of guerrilla warfare, and the conflict soon escalated into a full-fledged civil war. In December 1971, India entered the fray and, after two weeks of intensive combat, forced Pakistan's surrender in the East. India had seized an opportunity to deliver a blow to its longtime foe by intervening on the side of the Bengalis, whose cause for independence the Indian government supported. The result, after nine months of bloody battle and casualties in the millions, was victory for India over Pakistan and the birth of a new nation, Bangladesh.

After the war, the United States felt obliged to stick by its ally, Pakistan, despite the latter's widely reported brutality; the United States, therefore, opposed the independence movement that created Bangladesh. During the war, Washington had denounced India for its aggression and terminated its economic aid. This, combined with PRC support of Pakistan, caused India to strengthen its ties with the Soviet Union, with which India signed a twenty-year pact of friendship in August 1971. In effect, the United States had lost ground to its Soviet adversary in a regional Cold War battle. The United States delayed recognizing the new state of Bangladesh until May 1972 and delayed for almost as long sending shipments of economic aid, which Bangladesh desperately needed. For its part, the PRC withheld recognition of the new nation until 1975 and continually vetoed Bangladesh's efforts to gain admission to the United Nations.

The impact of the 1971 war was even more profound on the nations directly involved. India's victory was more decisive than victories in previous wars with Pakistan, and its national security was greatly enhanced— at least for the time being—by the severity of Pakistan's loss, as well as by India's new ties with the Soviet Union. In India, Prime Minister Indira Gandhi's popularity was strengthened immensely by the victory, and this served her well in upcoming elections.

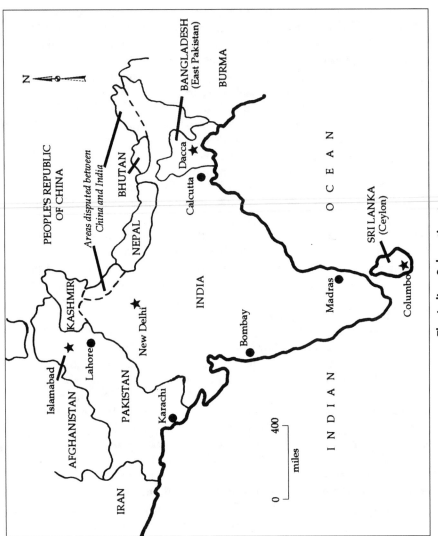

**The Indian Subcontinent**

For Pakistan, the 1971 war had a sobering effect. Now limited to what had been West Pakistan and with a population reduced by more than half, Pakistan turned to the tasks of rehabilitation and reorganization. Military government was ended when General Yahya Khan resigned and transferred power to Bhutto, whose Pakistan People's Party had come in second in the December 1970 election. One of Bhutto's first acts was to release Sheikh Mujibur from prison and arrange his return to Bangladesh, where he was to become president of the new country. Bhutto also saw the wisdom of reducing tensions with India, and for that purpose he agreed to meet with Indira Gandhi in 1972. Indian-Pakistani relations were substantially improved through the diplomacy of the two leaders, at least until May 1974, when India successfully tested what it called a "nuclear device." By demonstrating its nuclear capacity, India established even more conclusively its position as the dominant power in South Asia, but at the same time it aroused Pakistani fears.

Bangladesh, born of disaster, learned that independence produced no significant improvement in the lives of its people. After the war, India ordered the return of the 10 million Bengali refugees who found little to support them in their ravaged homeland. The catastrophic flood damage and war destruction had left the country devastated and unable to cope with the continuing wave of starvation and disease. Mujibur's government confronted not only a destitute people but also crime, corruption, and general disorder. The government declared a state of emergency in 1974, and in 1975 the once popular Mujibur was killed in a military coup. In the years that followed, political instability was prolonged by feuds between military factions contending for power.

After independence, Bangladesh became synonymous with poverty. It is one of the most densely populated nations in the world. No larger than the state of Georgia, it was the home of over 90 million people (118 million by 1994, with a per capita GNP of $220). There was simply too little land to support its swollen population. About 90 percent of the people lived in the countryside, and about half of them owned less than an acre of land—an amount insufficient to feed the average household of six. Thirty years later, it remained one of the poorest countries in the world. Since the mid-1990s, however, it was able to sustain an annual GDP growth rate of about 5 percent. Nevertheless, in 2004, half of its 135 million people still lived below the poverty line, its incidence of malnutrition remaining among the highest in the world.[6]

# ■ SOUTH ASIA SINCE 1980

## □ India

The 1980s brought to the Indian subcontinent a measure of economic growth and a modest improvement in the standard of living. In both India and Pakistan, one could witness the slow but steady growth of industry, increased urban construction, greater agricultural output, and the expansion of the middle class. Yet, because of continued population growth, both countries remained among the poorest in the world in terms of per capita GNP, which in 1994 was $320 for India and $430 for Pakistan. Both countries endeavored to control their population growth, which threatened their economic futures. Family-planning programs in past years had witnessed scant success. Activists were hoping for a feminist revolt against the grain of societies dominated by men.[7]

Another problem was the separatist movement of the Sikhs in the northern state of Punjab and the repressive measures Indira Gandhi used in response to that movement. The Sikhs, whose religion is a mixture of Hinduism and Islam, made up about 2 percent of India's population, but they constituted the majority in the state of Punjab. A brutal raid by government security forces on the Sikhs' Golden Temple in Amritsar in June 1984 left twelve hundred dead and as many taken prisoner. The Sikhs became unrelenting in their demand for an independent state—to be called Khalistan—and the Indian police were overzealous in their effort to ferret out Sikh militants, sometimes taking the law into their own hands by torturing and even murdering suspects. Thousands of Sikhs became political prisoners held with neither charges nor trials. An immediate consequence of these events was the assassination of Indira Gandhi by two of her Sikh bodyguards and the subsequent massacre of an estimated thousand Sikhs by Hindus.

Indian prime minister Rajiv Gandhi, a former pilot who succeeded his mother, Indira Gandhi, as prime minister in October 1984. *(Embassy of India)*

Indira Gandhi was succeeded by her son, Rajiv, who continued to deal with the Sikhs with a heavy hand. In May 1987, after four months of escalating violence during which over five hundred Sikhs were killed by security officers, he imposed direct federal rule over Punjab and ousted the elected state government of the Sikh moderates.

In November 1989, the Congress Party was narrowly defeated in the parliamentary election, and Rajiv Gandhi resigned as prime minister. His administration was followed by two caretaker governments that wrestled with India's faltering economy and divisive religious/ethnic disputes. While campaigning for reelection in May 1991, Rajiv Gandhi was assassinated, the victim of a terrorist bomb attack by members of the Tamil Liberation Tigers, who felt Gandhi had betrayed them in their war for independence against the Singhalese majority in the island nation of Sri Lanka. He died as his mother had, the victim of an ethnic movement seeking independence.

In the early 1990s, India had limited economic options. It was burdened with a foreign debt of $71 billion and dwindling foreign reserves. Moreover, India could no longer count on the Soviet Union for support, as the latter itself was disintegrating at that time (1991). India embarked on the road of abandoning its centrally planned economy to open the country to foreign investment and provide incentives for private business and technological development. It began to move away from the system of state economic planning established over three decades earlier by Jawaharlal Nehru.

The first step was to reverse India's balance-of-payments crisis by securing emergency loans from the International Monetary Fund (IMF) and the World Bank. In return, India slashed government spending, cut red tape, reduced import duties, invited foreign investment, and loosened interest rates to encourage private business and increase exports.

In December 1992, India suffered a renewal of religious violence. Fighting between Hindus and Muslims erupted in Ayodhya, where Hindu zealots tore down a Muslim mosque built in 1528 by the Mogul emperor Babur at the birthplace of the Hindu god Ram. This was the first time Hindus had razed a mosque since the 1947 partition. The violence spread to numerous Indian cities. Before order was restored, the casualty toll reached over 1,200 dead and 4,600 wounded in the worst Hindu-Muslim clashes within India since 1947. The destruction of the mosque and the ensuing attacks on Indian Muslims provoked anti-Indian protests in Pakistan and other Islamic nations.

In the late 1990s, Congress lost its political power to the Hindu nationalist Bharatiya Janata Party (BJP) under the leadership of Atal Bihari Vajpayee. The BJP stood for making India a Hindu state and curbing the rights of India's Muslims and other religious minorities. At its most extreme, its supporters expressed admiration for Hitler and insisted that India was a Hindu nation, that the Vedas—the sacred, primary texts of Hinduism—were the only source of Indian culture, and that the Indus Valley was the birthplace of its civilization more than five thousand years ago. Islam came to India by force, only recently at that, and Muslims—and other religious groups, including Christians—should be reconverted to the Vedas. The caste system, steeped in Hinduism, was the natural order of things.

The BJP program, if enacted, meant a break with the political tradition established by Congress Party rulers—Nehru and Gandhi—who held that India must remain a secular state tolerant of religious and ethnic diversity.[8]

Vajpayee eventually managed to establish a stable coalition that became the first non–Congress Party government to complete its term. Vajpayee had come to power advocating a tougher line against Pakistan and declaring openly that India possessed a nuclear weapons arsenal—something all previous Indian governments had refused to do.

In May 1998, India publicly acknowledged its nuclear arsenal when it set off five underground nuclear explosions. Pakistan responded with six of its own. For a while, it appeared that a nuclear war in South Asia was a distinct possibility. In the end, both sides backed off and Vajpayee, in fact, was able to mend fences with Pakistan after he stunned his nation in April 2003 by calling for a dialogue with Pakistan over Kashmir. He also established closer ties with Beijing, no mean feat, and with Washington.

Under Vajpayee, India joined the global economy. He broke down trade barriers, dismantled state monopolies, and sold off state assets to private investors. A rising middle class—estimated between 150 and 300 million, depending on the criteria used—found employment in information technology, business-processing outsourcing, and biotechnology. Despite the growth of per capita income—from $370 to $480 in four years—it remained one of the world's lowest.

The greatest blot on the Vajpayee tenure in office were the Gujarat riots of 2002, worse than the religious violence in Ayodhya a decade earlier. After a Muslim attack on Hindu activists on a train left fifty-nine dead, Hindu retaliation—replete with rapes of hundreds of women and girls, looting, and a flood of refugees estimated at a hundred thousand—claimed the lives of approximately two thousand Muslims.[9]

In the spring of 2004, Vajpayee, confident of winning reelection, suffered a surprising defeat. All the experts were caught off guard when the Congress Party returned to power. Its leader, Sonia Gandhi, the Italian-born widow of Rajiv Gandhi, however, rejected the post of prime minister after Hindu nationalists bitterly complained about a foreign-born premier. The party then turned to Manmohan Singh, a Sikh, who became the first prime minister from a religious minority. Singh, who as finance minister during 1991–1996 had begun the reform program, continued to open the economy to the outside world.

The election outcome was largely the result of the anger of those left behind, particularly the rural poor. Privatization had thrown many out of work, reduced the number of government jobs, and had been accompanied by rising prices. The BJP slogan, "Shining India," was popular with the monied classes at home and abroad, but neoliberal policies were not as popular in

India. Unchecked greed was responsible for stock market and banking scams, drug trafficking, and political corruption. There were nearly 35 million unemployed in 2002, and their numbers continued to rise. Even the educated had trouble finding jobs. The suicide rate was rapidly increasing; 40 percent of the population lived below the poverty line; 47 percent of children suffered from malnutrition; clean water was scarce; and the UN Human Development Index showed India slipping from 115th place in 1999 to 127th in 2001. Of the world's 800 million people living below the starvation line—defined as 1,960 calories a day—223 million lived in India.[10]

## ☐ *Pakistan*

Pakistan, too, witnessed swings of the political pendulum in the late 1980s and the 1990s. Until 1988, it remained under the rule of military strongman General Mohammed Zia ul-Haq, who disregarded critics who called for a return to civilian rule, citing the national emergency caused by the ongoing war in Afghanistan on Pakistan's northwestern border. The influx of hundreds of thousands of refugees from that war-ravaged country strained the economy and threatened internal security. Zia also pointed to the perceived threat of Indian aggression, which remained a Pakistani obsession.

Military rule ended abruptly in August 1988, however, when General Zia died in an airplane explosion—an apparent assassination—and parliamentary elections were held in November to return the country to civilian rule. The election produced a stunning victory for Benazir Bhutto as the new prime minister. The thirty-five-year-old Bhutto became the first female head of government of a Muslim nation. She was the daughter of Zulfikar Ali Bhutto, Pakistan's last civilian ruler, who had been deposed in 1974 and executed in 1979 by the same General Zia she now succeeded. After returning from extended exile early in 1988, the British-educated Bhutto had led a national movement against Zia.

Bhutto's grip on power was tenuous from the beginning because she had only a slight parliamentary plurality, and the opposition parties, the military, and the conservative clergy were watchful lest she make a slip. Her task was nothing less than ruling a nation beset with all the problems of Third World nations and at the same time satisfying its military leaders, who remained distrustful of her. Bhutto endeavored to steer a careful course between delivering promised increases in social spending and implementing an austerity program required by international lending agencies for desperately needed loans. During her first year in power, Bhutto's government played a key role in negotiating the terms by which the Soviet military withdrew from neighboring Afghanistan, while officially maintaining Pakistani support for Afghan rebels based in Pakistan.

Although Bhutto appeared on Pakistan's political scene like an angel of democracy and enjoyed popular support among younger Pakistanis, she was confronted by formidable political foes. Military leaders, suspicious of her popular appeal, were eager to find a pretext for her removal, lest she become too popular. Corruption and ethnic violence, although not new to Pakistan, proved cause enough to overthrow Bhutto in August 1990. She and her husband were charged with abuse of power and misconduct. The real force behind her demise was General Mirza Aslam Beg, who resented Bhutto's attempts to rein in the military.

The winner of the parliamentary elections held in October 1990 was Nawaz Sharif, who immediately set out to make good on his campaign pledge to establish an Islamic state in which the Koran became the supreme law and all aspects of life were subjected to its ultimate authority. Sharif's government, however, was ineffective in dealing with endemic corruption, recurrent violence (such as kidnapping for ransom), a mounting foreign debt, and worsening relations with India. Moreover, Pakistan suffered a major diplomatic and economic setback when the United States withdrew an annual $500 million in aid in protest of Pakistan's program to develop nuclear weapons.

Meanwhile, Benazir Bhutto was again waiting in the wings. When elections were held in 1993, Bhutto narrowly defeated Sharif in a bitter contest. As had been true during her previous stint as prime minister, Bhutto's government was insecure. Although she defended Pakistan's position on the two key foreign policy issues—the territorial dispute over Kashmir and Pakistan's development of nuclear weapons—her military and political adversaries faulted her for her lack of diplomatic toughness. Her position was made more difficult when opposition party leader Sharif declared publicly in August 1994 that Pakistan had produced nuclear weapons and even threatened their use against India in another war over Kashmir. In doing so, Sharif broke Pakistan's long-held silence regarding its nuclear capability and inflamed relations with India and with the United States, its erstwhile ally.

Bhutto's second term was beset with scandals and accusations. Corruption was so rampant that neither her vehement denials, her personal charisma, nor her family name were sufficient to save her from the wrath of her political opponents and the general public. She was forced to resign. Sharif, the militant Muslim, was returned to power in 1997 with a strong electoral victory, but his administration soon proved to be no less afflicted with corruption. When the supreme court began hearings on corruption charges against Sharif, he had mobs surround the court and then he sacked the chief justice. He used similar methods to silence the press and control the police. Meanwhile, much of the country was in chaos because of violent feuds among rival ethnic, religious, and political groups beyond the pale of law and order. Sharif neglected the nation's infrastructure, and with that came a steep decline in such basic services as health care, education, and public transport. Matters got worse as the economy slumped in mid-1998, partly as a result of punitive economic sanctions imposed on Pakistan for its nuclear weapons testing in May of that year.

To draw attention from his own corruption and the chaotic social situation, Sharif allowed Islamic militants to pick a fight with India high up in the Himalayas. In early 1999, Pakistani "freedom fighters" made an incursion across the "line of control" in Kashmir into the Indian side. The result was the most pointless of wars imaginable as Pakistani and Indian soldiers engaged in sporadic combat high in the Himalayas at an altitude of 19,000 feet, even in the dead of winter on the Siachen Glacier, a region so desolate it was known as the "third pole." Although Sharif insisted that the Pakistani guerrillas were volunteers and thus the government was not responsible for their actions, he was challenged by President Clinton to end this action unless he wanted to forgo a $100 million IMF loan. But to withdraw from this conflict meant enduring the wrath of enraged militants who insisted on fighting in Kashmir "until the last drop of blood." Sectarian violence between Shiites and Sunnis and other groups escalated as well.

Finally the army, which Sharif failed to control, had enough: in October 1999, it arrested him and thereby ended twenty-two years of ineffective and corrupt civilian rule. The army chief of staff, General Pervez Musharraf, who headed the coup, was roundly criticized worldwide for having sacked a democratically elected ruler. Many Pakistanis, however, expressed relief. Now it was once again the army's turn to attempt to make Pakistan governable.

# ■ SOUTHEAST ASIA

Southeast Asia, the region stretching from Burma in the west to the island countries of Indonesia and the Philippines in the east, was made up of nations that emerged from colonialism in the 1950s. Each faced the various problems common to Third World nations, particularly the lack of economic development. The struggle for independence had fostered nationalism, which, on the one hand, abetted the nation-building cause and, on the other, created contention among ethnic minorities as well as among the nations in the region. Moreover, the region was made insecure by the continuing Cold War struggle in Indochina, where the United States had committed half a million troops to stop the spread of Communism. In quest of greater security and particularly in response to the perceived threat of Communism, five of the region's non-Communist nations—Indonesia, Malaysia, Thailand, Singapore, and the Philippines—formed the Association of Southeast Asian Nations (known by its acronym, ASEAN) in 1967. ASEAN's founders proclaimed that its purpose was "to promote regional peace and security," as well as to foster regional economic cooperation.

ASEAN was a loosely organized group of nations whose leaders talked ardently of regional cohesion and cooperation. Nationalism remained an inhibiting force, however, as each of ASEAN's member states tended to be preoccupied with its own national interests and internal affairs. Antipathy toward Communist Vietnam was the glue that kept ASEAN together and gave it meaning in the 1970s. The U.S. withdrawal from Indochina in 1973 and the Communist victories in Vietnam and Cambodia in 1975 increased the members' fears of Communist expansion and served as the impetus for building stronger diplomatic ties among them and strengthening their respective economies and their armies, albeit without taking steps to establish a regional military alliance. The ASEAN members acted in concert in denouncing Vietnam for its invasion of Cambodia in 1979 and in turning down requests from the warring parties there—Vietnam and the Khmer Rouge—for economic assistance and better relations.

In the 1980s, ASEAN diplomatic solidarity served as a platform on which to seek greater regional economic coordination. With the exception of the Philippines, each of the ASEAN nations had registered steady economic growth in the 1960s and 1970s. The countries were making substantial progress toward industrializing their economies while shifting to an export-oriented pattern of economic growth. The mid-1980s brought an economic downturn caused largely by the contraction of the U.S. market, but it engendered not only corrective economic policies by ASEAN countries but new cooperative ventures among them. Increased cooperation, such as tariff reductions, contributed to remarkable new economic growth for the region, especially in Indonesia, Thailand, and Malaysia.

## □  Indonesia

After a long and difficult struggle for independence in the 1940s, Indonesia faced the daunting task of bringing its large, ethnically diverse population (the fifth-largest in the world), which is spread over thousands of islands, into a functioning national entity. Its many ethnic groups had little in common except that they had been under Dutch colonial rule for three centuries. Indonesia's revolutionary leader and new president, Achem Sukarno, continued to provide nationalistic and charismatic leadership in the first two decades after independence. After experimenting with parliamentary democracy for several years, in the 1950s Sukarno turned to "guided democracy," which was a barely disguised dictatorship. His regime failed to stimulate economic growth, but he sought to quiet the growing discontent by harping on the theme of nationalism. Meanwhile, many disenchanted Indonesians joined the rapidly growing Communist Party of Indonesia (PKI). Before long, Sukarno himself turned to the PKI for support of his faltering government.

It was then, in September 1965, that a military coup led by General Suharto brought the army into power. The army claimed that its action was actually a countercoup that crushed an attempted coup plotted by leftist army officers and the PKI. Suharto's determination to exterminate the PKI resulted in one of the greatest bloodbaths in modern times. Within a year, hundreds of thousands of Indonesians—Communists and suspected Communists—were slaughtered. In the process, the discredited Sukarno was pushed aside and later placed under house arrest. Suharto's military regime then ruled Indonesia for the next three decades.

Washington was curiously silent during the Indonesian military's rampage. Although some analysts speculate on U.S. complicity in the crushing of the Indonesian Communists, its role in the affair remains unclear. It is noteworthy that earlier in the same year the United States had launched its massive military intervention in nearby Vietnam to crush the Communist movement there. In any case, Washington welcomed the destruction of the largest Communist party in Asia outside China.

To legitimatize his rule, Suharto created a "government party," which leading military and administrative officers were required to join, and an election system in which his party always managed to handily defeat the two opposition parties allowed. Having settled into his own pattern of "guided democracy," Suharto decreed that Western-style liberal democracy was inappropriate for a nation with Indonesia's traditions, diverse makeup, and needs.

In his quest for national integration, Suharto readily resorted to armed force to suppress the Timorese independence movement on the island of East Timor. East Timor never had been part of Indonesia, but had been a Portuguese colony for over four hundred years and had been granted independence in 1974. In December 1975, as rival leftist revolutionary groups were fighting for power in East Timor, Suharto—with the apparent support of Washington—sent his army in to claim the territory as Indonesian. In the meantime, the administration of Gerald Ford had provided the Indonesian army with an array of weapons, with the congressional stipulation that they be used for "defensive" purposes only. In December 1975, Ford and his secretary of state, Henry Kissinger, met Suharto in Jakarta where, with a wink and a nod—referred to as the "big wink" in State Department circles—they gave him the green light for an invasion, which began the day after *Air Force One* left Indonesian air space.[11] For the next twenty-three years, every U.S. president—from Ford to Clinton—armed Indonesia's armed forces and consistently backed its brutal occupation of East Timor.

The invasion of East Timor touched off a long and bitter war. The resilience of the revolutionaries and the massive force applied by Suharto's army to defeat them resulted during the next two decades in a death toll of over two hundred thousand. Insofar as this was about one-third of the population of East Timor and most of the dead were noncombatants, the slaughter may well be considered genocide.

Suharto was more successful in achieving economic development, a major goal of the "New Order" he had proclaimed in 1966. With the help of his Western-educated bureaucrats, he embarked on an ambitious program of economic growth. He courted foreign investment, especially from oil companies, that greatly increased Indonesia's production of petroleum. Oil export earnings increased still more with the international increase in oil prices in the 1970s, and this windfall fueled continued economic development. By the early 1980s, oil accounted for 78 percent of the country's export earnings. Steady, though not spectacular, economic growth continued until oil prices tumbled in the mid-1980s. The government then introduced reforms that called for a reduction in government expenditures, diversification, less reliance on oil revenues, and even more foreign investment and joint ventures. These reforms were generally successful, and Indonesia's GNP continued to climb.

If Suharto's record as ruler of Indonesia were to be based on GNP alone, he would have to be given high marks, but the impressive economic figures masked a grim reality of the military dictatorship's unbridled corruption, unabashed nepotism, and gross inequities in the distribution of wealth. Under Suharto the flow of money went mainly to the island of "imperial Java," specifically Jakarta, the capital city, at the expense of the rest of the country. Indeed, hundreds of millions of dollars of the new wealth flowed into the hands of Suharto himself and his family members.[12] Still, even as the financial crisis that began in Thailand hit his country in late 1997, Suharto (now seventy-six years old) was confident that his hand-picked consultative assembly would elect him in March 1998 to his seventh five-year term as president. But by that time the economy was in a meltdown. Indonesia's currency, the *rupiah,* had lost 70 percent of its value against the dollar. According to the World Bank, no nation in recent history "has ever suffered such a dramatic reversal of fortune" in such a short time.[13] (In contrast, the decline of the Russian economy had taken place over several years.) Inflation reached 70 percent a year; widespread unemployment meant that an estimated two-thirds of the population were now living in poverty, unable to purchase the 2,000 calories of food necessary for a minimum diet. This led to looting and violence, particularly against ethnic Chinese scapegoats, who were blamed for the financial disaster.

Student protesters, demanding Suharto's ouster and democratic reforms, took to the streets day after day, clashing with police and army troops. As the crisis worsened, Suharto's own privileged military, which had benefited handsomely during his tenure, abandoned him to save its own skin. Suharto stepped down and turned the reins over to an old crony, B. J. Habibie.

Habibie introduced several political reforms aimed at mollifying the protesters and foreign critics and held parliamentary elections in June 1999, which brought to power Abdurahman Wahid, an elderly, moderate Muslim scholar. His first task was to take the U.S.-trained and equipped military out of politics. He placed Jakarta under the command of generals loyal to him and then, in February 2000, he dismissed the army chief (and defense minister) Wiranto, the man largely responsible for the "dirty war" of 1999 in East Timor.

Early in 1999, the government agreed to a referendum on independence to be held in East Timor under UN auspices in August of that year. But this did not prevent the Indonesian army commander in East Timor from ignoring the government's decision and declaring that in the event of independence "everything will be destroyed, so that East Timor will be worse off than it was 23 years ago."[14] Despite such threats and brutal assaults on civilians by heavily armed "militias," nearly 80 percent of the East Timorese voted for secession. The "militias," the instruments of the Indonesian army, then moved to deny the people their independence, going on a rampage that destroyed much of East Timor's infrastructure, killing an estimated three to seven thousand people, and deporting to West Timor another one hundred and fifty to two hundred thousand. They also killed several unarmed UN workers, the remainder fleeing to nearby Australia. Indonesia's National Human Rights Commission later placed the blame squarely on the shoulders of General Wiranto, who had done nothing to stop the massacres and thus was "morally responsible." A helpless United Nations was unable to stop the violence. Australia finally decided to act. It landed its forces on the island, expelled the military and its militias, and restored order. Then came the difficult task of rebuilding East Timor, the UN's newest, devastated member.

Wahid turned to another pressing problem, the growing restlessness in other regions, notably Aceh and Irian Jaya. He offered them federalism, that is, a share of local control, a concession hitherto unthinkable. The greatest challenge was Aceh, the westernmost outpost of the far-flung archipelago. It was here, in "Mecca's verandah," that the first contacts with Islam had been established in the eighth century: its people remained particularly religious and resistant to outside control. It had taken the Dutch more than a quarter of a century to conquer Aceh at the end of the nineteenth century, and even then it was never fully pacified. In 1945, its people were particularly enthusiastic for independence and thus their disappointment was much the greater when the heavy hand of Sukarno, and later Suharto, came down on them. Aceh's wealth from its lucrative oil industry did not go to its people, schools, and hospitals, but to Jakarta. In 1976, Aceh declared independence and the military reacted predictably, and in the 1990s the army tortured and murdered an estimated five thousand people there.

Irian Jaya, the western half of the island of New Guinea, on the eastern fringe of the archipelago, nurtured its own dreams of secession that dated back to 1961 (when it was still under Dutch rule). After the Netherlands handed the region over to Indonesia in 1969, Suharto suppressed its independence movement there. Irian Jaya holds substantial natural resources, among them the world's most lucrative copper and gold mines. The mines, however, employed a scant three hundred of the indigenous population; the other eleven thousand workers came from other parts of Indonesia and from abroad. Wahid was not alone in believing that, particularly after East Timor, the loss of another province would mark the beginning of the end of Indonesia. Wahid, who earlier had spoken of federalism, backtracked in December 2000, when the army launched a crackdown in Irian Jaya, killing and jailing demonstrators who had hoisted the separatist flag.

Decades of exploitation and misrule by Suharto greatly weakened the idea that the 200 million people of Indonesia had a common heritage, something they had believed in when they fought to rid themselves of Dutch rule. The centrifugal forces at the end of the twentieth century were severely testing the commitment to Indonesian nationhood.

## ☐  Thailand

Having escaped colonization, Thailand was spared the pains and devastation of a revolutionary war for independence in the postwar period. This, and the political stability provided by military regimes, accounts for Thailand's relatively earlier economic growth. Benefiting from increased agricultural production and foreign investment, Thailand built up an infrastructure for industrial development and diversification. The country sustained an average annual GNP growth rate of 7 percent for over two decades until a brief slowdown in the mid-1980s, after which it rebounded with a growth rate of about 11 percent for three years (1987–1989)—the highest in the world at the time.

But, as in Indonesia, the new prosperity was by no means enjoyed by all elements of society; indeed, the hard-suffering, underpaid working class saw precious little of the national earnings its labor helped to generate. Moreover, Thailand's political tradition of deference to authority and patron-client relationships was more conducive to military rule than to democracy. In the 1930s, the military had entrenched itself in power and only occasionally had given way to civilian rule, which usually proved unstable. Thus, when the military high command took control of the government in February 1991, it followed a traditional pattern. The leader of the 1991 coup and strongman of the new regime, General Suchinda Kraprayoon, arrested the prime minister, abolished the constitution, dissolved parliament, and established the National Peace Keeping Council, which had powers of martial law. But to reassure the Thai public and international investors, Suchinda appointed as prime minister a highly respected businessman and diplomat, Anand Panyarachun, and promised elections within a year. But in April 1992, Suchinda and his generals reclaimed ruling power. This time, however, their intervention touched off angry antimilitary demonstrations in the capital of Bangkok. Soon, over a hundred thousand protesters—mainly students—took to the streets demanding a return to civilian rule and constitutional revisions to block further military rule. As the demonstrations grew larger and more riotous, the highly revered Thai king, Bhumibol Adulyadej, who had occupied the throne since 1946, intervened, calling on leading parties to amend the constitution as the protesters demanded.

But General Suchinda refused to give in to the protesters and in May 1992, he unleashed a ruthless assault on the demonstrators. For three days, fifty thousand troops scattered the unarmed protesters, firing live ammunition and killing over a hundred. The bloody spectacle was seen on television screens around the world—except in Thailand, where the military controlled the media. Once again, King Bhumibol interceded to put an end to the massacre.[15] Business leaders condemned the army's resort to brute force, warning that such measures damaged Thailand's international image and drove away much-needed foreign investors.

Suchinda was forced to resign and was replaced by former prime minister Anand who, bolstered by the king's mandate and public support, set out to break the military's sixty-year control of power. He commissioned an investigation of the recent massacre and, on the basis of its findings, sacked four leading military officers. Meanwhile, the parliament enacted amendments to the constitution intended to ensure civilian rule in the name of democracy.

The military influence was curtailed but by no means eliminated, for it retained control of many levers of power, including the police and important state industries (e.g., telecommunications, airlines, shipping, and trucking). Yet the military learned that it could no longer dominate Thai politics without incurring strong public rebuke and that political stability was essential for sustaining the nation's prosperity. Gradually, in the 1990s a consensus emerged among political-party, military, bureaucratic, and business elites on the priority of keeping the nation on a more democratic course.

☐  *Malaysia*

With a per capita income of $3,000 in 1995, Malaysia had become one of the most economically successful Third World nations. The manufacturing share of the economy had grown from less than 10 percent in 1960 to 27 percent in the mid-1990s. Malaysia's economic development was all the more remarkable in light of its ethnic and geographic diversity. The main part of the nation is on the Malay Peninsula south of Thailand; the other two parts, Sabah and Sarawak, are on the island of Borneo, over a thousand miles to the east. Malaysia began in 1963 as a federation composed of those three parts and Singapore, and as such it had an ethnic Chinese majority. But in 1965, Singapore—with its predominantly Chinese population—seceded and became independent. The population of the federation, renamed Malaysia, then consisted of 50 percent Malay, 36 percent Chinese, and 9 percent Indian.

With the exception of a two-year interval (1970–1972) of military rule, Malaysia has maintained stable civilian rule under a peculiar parliamentary system designed to maintain the Malays in power and to keep the Chinese and other ethnic minorities satisfied with limited representation in parliament and thus a lesser role in the government. The country's paramount ruler, Tuanku Azlan Muhibbudin, established the Malay-dominated Alliance Party, which secured governing power by winning successive rigged elections. But in the 1969 election, the Alliance Party lost its majority. The resultant celebration by the mainly Chinese supporters of the opposition parties touched off four days of ethnic violence between Chinese and

Malays. The government proclaimed a state of emergency, brought in troops to restore order, disbanded parliament, and created a National Operations Council as the ruling body. The council then enacted the "New Economic Policy," which granted special rights and privileges to Malays, excluding Chinese and other ethnic groups. The government also enacted "sedition acts" prohibiting criticism of "sensitive issues," meaning the special rights granted to Malays.

During the 1970s, the economy—driven largely by petroleum and natural-gas exports—grew at a rate of nearly 8 percent annually. The new wealth offered advantages for many educated Malays and Chinese. It served to reduce ethnic tensions. At the same time, the new wealth did not trickle down to the lower class. Still, even they could benefit somewhat from such improvements as electrification, piped water, and paved roads.

Malaysia, however, like other export-oriented Southeast Asian nations, experienced an economic downturn in the mid-1980s. Prime Minister Mahathir Mohamad introduced new policies to revitalize the economy, including the privatization of public utilities and the expansion of state-owned heavy industries through increased foreign investment and joint ventures. He also initiated a "Look East" policy that stressed emulating the Japanese and Korean industrial models and attracting more investments and technology from those countries. The result was continued robust economic growth (8 percent annually) in the late 1980s. By the 1990s, manufactured goods accounted for half of the country's exports, and Malaysia became the world's largest exporter of semiconductors. The showpiece of Malaysia's economic success was its gleaming capital city, Kuala Lumpur, which boasted the world's tallest building.

But after a decade of continued economic growth, Malaysia, like the other rapidly developing ASEAN countries, was hit hard by an Asia-wide financial crisis in the late 1990s (see Chapter 17).

## ☐ Singapore

Singapore, located at the southern tip of the Malay Peninsula, is a city-state and a former British colony that won its independence in 1964. Unlike the other ASEAN nations, its population was overwhelmingly ethnic Chinese. Moreover, Singapore's economic takeoff came in the 1960s, about a decade earlier than that of the other ASEAN members. Under its authoritarian ruler, Lee Kuan Yew, Singapore became one of the most prosperous countries in Asia, with a per capita GNP of $22,500 in 1994. A combination of political stability, population growth control, high standards of education, a disciplined and skilled work force, efficient economic management, export-oriented planning, and a free-market system worked miracles for its 2.8 million people. Strategically situated at the center of the Southeast Asian sea-lanes, Singapore also became a conveyor belt for the shipment of goods from outside the region to neighboring ASEAN countries, as well as a major regional financial center.

Singapore's remarkable economic development was also largely a result of the stewardship of Prime Minister Lee Kuan Yew, whose authoritarian rule extended well beyond the bounds of conventional politics. Lee endeavored to make Singapore a spotless, crime-free, morally upright, and austere society; toward that end, he took it upon himself to dictate social and moral standards and to enforce them with strict laws and strong penalties. He decreed, for example, that men could not grow their hair long, and offenders were subject to arrest, fines, and even imprisonment. Possession of drugs, even small amounts, was punishable by death. Nor did Lee, who had exercised unlimited authority in Singapore since the late 1950s, allow dissent. He maintained that the curbs on individual freedom were not regimentation, but paternalistic guidance that made for a more disciplined and productive people whose work habits contributed to ever higher productivity and the betterment of society.

## ■ DICTATORSHIP AND REVOLUTION IN THE PHILIPPINES

While the ASEAN nations of Thailand, Malaysia, and Singapore registered impressive economic growth in the 1970s and 1980s, the Philippines fell behind. This multi-island nation, once a Spanish dominion (1571–1898) and then a U.S. colony (1898–1946), struggled to sustain economic growth and maintain a semblance of democratic institutions after gaining independence in 1946. Under a succession of dictators, the Philippines lost ground on both fronts, especially during the twenty-year rule of Ferdinand Marcos. When Marcos came to power in 1965, the country was developing at a pace with Taiwan, Singapore, and Thailand. When Marcos was driven from power in 1986, those nations had per capita incomes three to four times higher than that of the Philippines. By then, the country had a foreign debt of $27 billion and had been unable to make payment on the principal of that debt since 1983. The GNP had fallen by over 25 percent since 1982, unemployment had risen to over 20 percent, and inflation had reached 70 percent. Corruption was rampant.

At the center of mismanagement and corruption was Marcos himself. He had been elected president in 1965 as a social reformer, but he soon succumbed to the pattern of patron-client corruption common to Philippine political tradition, and he proved to be a master at it. Governing the Philippines became so lucrative for Marcos that he made certain he would stay in power despite a constitution that permitted only two four-year terms. As the end of his second term approached, Marcos declared martial law, citing a mounting Communist insurgency as the justification for canceling elections, suspending the constitution, and writing a new constitution that gave him a new term and broad powers. He also rounded up and jailed political opponents and critical journalists. Marcos and his wife, Imelda, became very wealthy by schemes such as demanding kickbacks from businessmen and pocketing foreign aid.

Marcos—who promoted himself as the nation's indispensable leader—claimed to be a lawyer who had never lost a case, a heroic military officer who had never lost a battle, a lover who had won the heart of the nation's beauty queen, a great athlete and marksman, a good father, a good Catholic, and an honest and modest man. The popularity of his wife, Imelda, the former Miss Philippines, was an added attraction to his cult of personality. Successive administrations in Washington turned a blind eye to what was taking place in Manila and instead honored Marcos as a stalwart opponent of Communism and a champion of democracy.[16] Washington remained tolerant as long as Marcos provided the political stability considered necessary to protect substantial U.S. financial investments in the Philippines and to retain the two mammoth U.S. military installations on the islands—Subic Bay Naval Station and Clark Air Base—considered vital to U.S. strategic interests in East Asia. Marcos skillfully traded assurances regarding the military bases for ever-larger economic and military aid packages from Washington.

In the early 1980s, however, Marcos's regime began to unravel. In 1981, he released his foremost political opponent, Benigno Aquino, from prison to allow him to go to the United States for heart surgery. Aquino, the likely winner of the 1973 presidential election (had it taken place) decided to end his exile in August 1983 to return home to lead a movement to unseat Marcos. Upon arriving at the Manila airport, he was shot to death before even setting foot on the tarmac. Responding to the outrage of the Filipinos, Marcos appointed a commission to investigate the murder. After lengthy deliberations, the commission reported that evidence pointed to a military conspiracy reaching all the way to Chief of Staff General Fabian Ver, a cousin of Marcos. The verdict of the eight-month trial that followed was predictable: Ver and the twenty-four other military defendants were acquitted. Meanwhile, a vigorous opposition movement developed that regarded the fallen Aquino as a martyr and his wife, Corazon, as a saint. While Marcos was losing credibility at home and abroad, the economy was deteriorating rapidly, largely because of the flight of capital triggered by Aquino's assassination. In the hinterlands, a Communist-led New People's Army stepped up its insurgency.

In response to mounting pressure, in November 1985 the undaunted dictator, who had won every election he had entered thus far, announced his decision to hold a presidential election in February 1986. Corazon Aquino had already stated she would run against Marcos should he allow an election. The stage was set for an election that had all the makings of a morality play. Although the sixty-eight-year-old Marcos was visibly ill, suffering from kidney disease, and was roundly attacked by the press, he remained confident of victory and appeared unfazed by the enormous throngs of people who rallied in support of his opponent. Aquino, who presented herself as Cory, a humble housewife, sought to redeem the legacy of her murdered husband and called for a return to democracy, decency, and justice. Moreover, she did not hesitate to charge that "Mr. Marcos is the No. 1 suspect in the murder of my husband."[17] As election day approached, it appeared Cory's "people power" would surely sweep her to victory—if the elections were fair. Big business and the middle class were abandoning Marcos, and the Roman Catholic Church openly supported Aquino. Many feared, however, that the cagey Marcos, who paid people to attend his political rallies, would find ways to rig the voting to ensure his reelection.

No clear winner emerged from the election, as each side claimed victory and charged the other with fraud. Despite indisputable evidence of election interference and fraudulent vote counting by the Marcos-appointed election commission, Marcos proceeded to plan for inauguration ceremonies.[18] Meanwhile, at the encouragement of Roman Catholic leader Jaime Cardinal Sin, hundreds of thousands of people went into the streets to express their support of Aquino and demand that Marcos step down. At this point, Marcos's defense minister and several high-ranking army officers decided to change sides. The climax came when the pro-Marcos troops, advancing toward the rebel encampments, were stopped by the human wall of Aquino supporters and Catholic nuns kneeling in prayer in front of stalled tanks. At that juncture, the Reagan administration, which had steadfastly supported Marcos, bowed to the manifest will of the majority of the Filipino people and arranged for the fallen dictator to be airlifted to Hawaii. Marcos and his wife fled the country with millions—possibly billions—of dollars they had stolen from the Filipino people. With the help of people power, the Church, and her new military allies, Cory Aquino proclaimed victory for a democratic revolution.

After the exultation over Aquino's triumph against dictatorship and corruption, the new and inexperienced president had to face the hard realities of governing the nation and restoring its shattered economy. Aquino moved swiftly to restore civil rights, free political prisoners, eliminate pro-Marcos elements from the government, and enact political reforms. Aquino, whose family owned large stretches of land, had promised land reform during her campaign, but afterward she showed little interest in it. The power of the old oligarchy and the old economic system remained intact. The Philippines were still saddled with a large foreign debt, the payment of which consumed about one-third of the country's export earnings. In 1988, the country was granted a $10 billion developmental grant from the combined sources of the IMF and several European and Asian nations, but to little avail. Affluence for the few and misery for the many remained the dominant trend. On the eve of Aquino's fourth anniversary in power in February 1990, people power was but a distant memory. She had lost support in virtually all segments of the population.

One of the major issues she confronted was the status of the two large U.S. military facilities, Subic Bay Naval Station and Clark Air Base. Nationalist groups saw these bases as an affront to Philippine sovereignty, a social blight, and potential targets in a nuclear war. Aquino promised not to abrogate the agreement on the bases, which was due to expire in September 1991, but she had placed clauses in the new Philippine constitution that forbade nuclear weapons on Philippine territory and required that any extension of the lease agreement beyond 1991 be approved by a two-thirds majority of the Philippine senate.[19] Meanwhile, Aquino accepted an interim agreement in October 1988, by which the United States boosted its annual military and economic aid to the Philippines to $481 million—more than twice the amount pledged in the previous (1983) agreement.

Two events in 1991 intervened to cause an unanticipated resolution of the issue of the military bases: the sudden end of the global Cold War and a powerful volcanic eruption. The former caused the United States to reconsider its Asian security needs, and the latter provided sufficient cause to vacate the two bases. In June, Mount Pinatubo, a volcano dormant for six hundred years, erupted, sending a towering plume into the air and blanketing the surrounding region—including the two bases—with a thick layer of powdery ash. With Clark Air Base buried under volcanic ash, U.S. authorities decided to abandon the base rather than spend the estimated $500 million to dig it out. Soon afterward, when the Philippine senate rejected a ten-year extension of the lease of Subic Bay Naval Station, the United States decided to pull up stakes there as well. The U.S. military presence in the Philippines, which had existed since the Spanish-American War of 1898 (except from 1942 to 1944), was at an end.

The combination of the disastrous volcanic eruption and the loss of the two foreign bases dealt a severe blow to the Philippine economy, which was already stagnant and debt-ridden. The volcano and the base closing cost over 680,000 people their jobs.

The country remained in need of fundamental political and social reform and was still confronted with insurrections from both the right and the left. It was little wonder that the weary but still personally popular Aquino decided against running for reelection in spring 1992. The burden of pulling the Philippines out of its morass of poverty, stagnation, and political corruption fell to General Fidel Ramos, winner of the presidential election.

## ■ RECOMMENDED READINGS

### □ South Asia

Ali, S. Mahmud. *The Fearful State: Power, People, and Internal War in South Asia.* London: Zed Books, 1993.
    A study of insurrection in South Asian separatist groups, such as the Sikhs and the Tamils.

Barnds, William J. *India, Pakistan and the Great Powers.* New York: Praeger, 1972.

Bhatia, Krishan. *The Ordeal of Nationhood: A Social Study of India Since Independence, 1947–1970.* New York: Atheneum, 1970.

Brecher, Michael. *Nehru: A Political Biography.* London: Oxford University Press, 1959.

Brown, W. Norman. *The United States and India, Pakistan and Bangladesh.* 3d ed. Cambridge, Mass.: Harvard University Press, 1972.

Dhar, P. N. *Indira Gandhi, the "Emergency," and Indian Democracy.* New Delhi: Oxford University Press, 2000.

A combination of memoir and history, highly critical of Indira Gandhi, by one of her close advisers at the time of the "Emergency."

Kangas, G. L. *Population Dilemma: India's Struggle for Survival.* London: Heinemann, 1985.

Margolis. Eric S. *War at the Top of the World.* New York: Routledge, 2000.

On the extension of the India-Pakistan conflict onto the glaciers of the Himalayas.

## ☐ Southeast Asia

Ali, Anuwar. *Malaysia's Industrialization: The Quest for Technology.* Singapore: Oxford University Press, 1992.

Crouch, Harold A. *The Army and Politics in Indonesia.* Ithaca, N.Y.: Cornell University Press, 1988.

Diamond, Larry, Juan Linz, and Seymour Martin Lipset, eds. *Democracy in Developing Countries: Asia.* Boulder, Colo.: Lynne Rienner Publishers, 1989.

Kulick, Elliot, and Dick Wilson. *Thailand's Turn: Profile of a New Dragon.* New York: St. Martin's Press, 1992.

Neher, Clark D. *Southeast Asia in the New International Era.* 2d ed. Boulder, Colo.: Westview Press, 1994.

Palmer, Ronald D., and Thomas J. Reckford. *Building ASEAN: 20 Years of Southeast Asian Cooperation.* New York: Praeger, 1987.

Taylor, John G. *Indonesia's Forgotten War: The Hidden History of East Timor.* London: Zed Books, 1991.

An exposé of Indonesia's ongoing effort to suppress with brutal violence the Timorese nationalist movement.

Wurfel, David. *Filipino Politics: Development and Decay.* Ithaca, N.Y.: Cornell University Press, 1988.

## ■ NOTES

1. "Population Commentary," *Baltimore Sun,* July 12, 1992, p. 2A.

2. The development of new plants producing more grain and less stem per plant was the result of years of scientific work financed by the Rockefeller and Ford Foundations. Under ideal conditions, the new rice plants produced twice as much grain per acre and reduced the growing period in half, so that two crops could be grown in one growing season.

3. Quoted in Stephen Warshaw and C. David Bromwell, with A. J. Tudisco, *India Emerges: A Concise History of India from Its Origins to the Present* (San Francisco: Diablo Press, 1974), p. 132.

4. World Bank, *World Development Report, 1984* (New York: Oxford University Press, 1984). India's average annual rate of growth of GNP between 1955 and

1970 was 4.0 percent; during the 1970s, it fell to 3.4 percent. The rate of growth of GNP per capita for these two periods was 1.8 percent and 1.3 percent, respectively.

5. P. N. Dhar, *Indira Gandhi, the "Emergency," and Indian Democracy* (New Delhi: Oxford University Press, 2000).

6. World Bank, "The World Bank in Bangladesh," September 2004.

7. Steve Coll, "Burgeoning Population Threatens India's Future," *Washington Post*, January 21, 1990, p. H7.

8. According to its constitution, India is a secular state, despite the fact that the vast majority, about 83 percent, are Hindu; 11 percent are Muslim.

9. Human Rights Watch figures. Human Rights Watch, in its April 2002 report, *"We Have No Orders to Save You" : State Participation and Complicity in Communal Violence in Gujarat,* accused the government of giving the Hindu killers the addresses of Muslim families and of police participation in the pogroms.

10. Pankaj Mishra, "India: The Neglected Majority Wins!" *New York Review of Books,* August 12, 2004, pp. 30–37.

11. Kissinger gave Suharto the same advice he gave the assassins of Latin America's Operation Condor: "It is important that whatever you do succeeds quickly" (a phrase reminiscent of Macbeth's contemplation of the murder of Duncan: "If it were done when 'tis done then 'twere well it were done quickly"). Jeffrey A. Winters, "U.S. Media and Their Ignorance Partly Blamable for E. Timor's Misery," *The Jakarta Post Online,* May 28, 2002. Also, John Pilger, "Journey to East Timor: Land of the Dead," *The Nation,* April 25, 1994.

12. "Indonesia to Probe Riches Amassed by Suharto Since '66," *Baltimore Sun,* June 2, 1998, p. 10A. Estimates of the personal riches he and his family amassed vary greatly, but one estimate puts it at about $40 billion.

13. Floyd Norris, "In Asia, Stocks Melt Faster Than in '29," *New York Times,* January 11, 1998, p. BU1; wire service reports, "Indonesia Falls Rapidly from Riches to Rags," *Baltimore Sun,* October 8, 1998, p. 2A.

14. Colonel Tono Suratnam, cited in Erhard Haubold, "Verraten und verkauft?" *Frankfurter Allgemeine Zeitung,* September 18, 1999, p. 12.

15. According to the British ambassador to Thailand, the king learned about the massacre from his daughter, who was in Paris where she saw it on the TV news. "Months of Grace," *The Economist,* June 20, 1992, p. 32. The king summoned the general and the leader of the opposition movement for an audience. As they knelt before him, he rebuked them and instructed them to restore order immediately—a scene also seen on television screens around the world and this time in Thailand as well.

16. When U.S. vice-president George H. W. Bush visited the Philippines in 1981 after nine years of martial law, he told Marcos, "We [the United States] love your adherence to democratic principles and to the democratic processes." Cited in William J. vanden Heuvel, "Postpone the Visit to Manila," *New York Times,* September 8, 1983, p. A23.

17. Cited in "A Test for Democracy," *Time,* February 3, 1986, p. 31.

18. Marcos was emboldened by U.S. president Ronald Reagan who, although noting concern about charges of election fraud, accepted Marcos's claim of victory and stated that his administration wanted "to help in any way we can . . . so that the two parties can come together." Cited in William Pfaff, "The Debris of Falling Dictatorships," *Baltimore Sun,* February 17, 1986, p. 9A.

19. The constitutional provision outlawing nuclear weapons on Philippine territory begged the question of enforcement, because the U.S. government's position was that it would neither confirm nor deny the presence of nuclear weapons on its ships or bases.

# PART 5

# TRANSITION TO A NEW ERA

During the 1980s, the Cold War took the world on a roller-coaster ride, escalating in the first half of the decade and descending rapidly at the end. In the United States, the Reagan administration stepped up its confrontation with the Soviet Union. All the while, the pace of the nuclear arms race was quickening.

The combination of the continued East-West conflict and the widening gulf between North and South produced a host of dilemmas for the world in the 1980s. Many Third World countries were politically unstable, and the superpowers continued to battle each other through proxies, as in Nicaragua and Afghanistan. The rise of militant Islam in Iran and other Islamic nations produced a powerful third ideological force in the Middle East. As the global standoff between East and West continued, other power centers emerged. Japan and the European Community sustained remarkable economic growth and became new economic forces to be reckoned with. Once the Cold War ended, international economic issues became more nettlesome.

At the end of the decade came a series of momentous events that, taken together, signified the disappearance of the forty-five-year post–World War II world order. The Soviet Union, under a dynamic new ruler, Mikhail Gorbachev, began a program of restructuring that not only resulted in the transformation of the Communist system, but also had an explosive effect on its East European satellites.

We begin with the emergence of Japan as an economic superpower and South Korea's remarkable economic development, the main topics of Chapter 16. One of the premier postwar success stories is the rise of Japan from the ashes of war to become the world's second-largest economic power in the 1980s. We discuss Japan's "economic miracle" and the friction that developed in its economic relations with the United States. Also presented in this chapter are South Korean industrialization and democratization, and the ongoing Cold War contention between South Korea and North Korea, where a Stalinist regime continued to hold power.

Chapter 17 examines major developments and issues in international economics, beginning with the progress of the European Union toward economic and political integration. Its success spurred economic regionalism in other parts of the world, namely the creation of the North American Free Trade Agreement and regional economic blocs in Latin America and Asia. The issues of protectionism, economic interdependence among nations, and globalization are also discussed, with particular emphasis on the impact of globalization on Third World nations. Also examined are the impact of the Organization of Petroleum Exporting Countries (the oil cartel), the problem of Third World debt, and the issue of climate change.

We turn in Chapter 18 to the incredible cascade of events in the Soviet Union at the end of the 1980s. Our focus first is on Mikhail Gorbachev, the architect of the Soviet empire's radical transformation. We examine the various aspects of his program of restructuring—*perestroika*—and his call for openness—*glasnost*—which touched off a wave of nationalistic unrest among the non-Russian Soviet republics and soon disrupted the unity of the Soviet Union. We then analyze the sudden fall of Gorbachev and the collapse of the Soviet Union. We next treat Boris Yeltsin's endeavors to steer the new Russian Federation toward capitalism and democracy while struggling to maintain political and social order—and to stay in power—and the politics of his successor, Vladimir Putin.

We then examine the breakup of the Soviet empire, beginning with the 1979 Soviet invasion of Afghanistan, its impact on the Cold War, and its aftermath: the withdrawal of Soviet troops leaving behind a shattered nation. We then turn to Poland, where in the early 1980s a dramatic showdown between Solidarity, the Polish labor movement, and the Communist government took place. Next we examine the upheaval in the Eastern European countries triggered by Gorbachev's call for sweeping reforms and his pledge of noninterference. For more than forty years, Poland and other Soviet satellites in Eastern Europe had been ruled by Communist regimes that answered to Moscow, but suddenly in 1989, when it became clear that Moscow would not intervene to prop up faltering governments, these regimes soon crumbled. We trace the parade of events leading to an end of Communist rule, first in Poland, then in the other satellites. Included in the account of the dismantling of European Communism is the dramatic story of the fall of Communism in East Germany and the reunification of Germany. The chapter closes with an examination of the breakup of Yugoslavia and the ongoing turmoil in the Balkans.

In Chapter 19, we turn to one of the gravest issues facing the world since 1945: the nuclear arms race. As both cause and effect of the Cold War, the arms race continued unabated for over forty years, but in the early 1980s, it became more menacing than ever. Each of the superpowers insisted on maintaining an arsenal sufficient to deter an attack by the other, and the deadly logic of deterrence compelled both sides to build ever more weapons and continually upgrade them. We briefly review earlier efforts at nuclear disarmament and then turn to the Strategic Arms Limitation Talks (SALT I and II) and the controversy over the Strategic Defense Initiative (SDI, or "Star Wars"). Next we take up the dramatic progress toward disarmament that came suddenly with the end of the Cold War, and together with the collapse of the Soviet Union greatly diminished the threat of nuclear war. The next major concern was nuclear proliferation, and that is the focus of attention in the last section in this chapter.

Beginning in the late 1970s, the world felt the impact of the revival of Islam and its political militancy. Although long one of the world's great religions, Islam is little known by Westerners; for that reason, we have seen fit to devote the first section of Chapter 20 to an exposition of the tenets of Islam and its political dimensions. It is necessary to see that in Islam, religion and politics are inseparable and that an Islamic state is not merely one in which the predominant religion is Islam, but one in which politics are rooted in that religion. The political power inherent in Islam became evident most dramatically in the Iranian revolution. In Iran, leaders of the Shiite branch of Islam led a revolt that overthrew the shah and brought a new order to the country. In Chapter 20, we also turn our attention to the Iran-Iraq War and the problem of Middle East terrorism. We conclude the chapter with an account of the Gulf War, ignited by Iraqi ruler Saddam Hussein's attack on Kuwait in August 1990.

In Chapter 21, we turn to the dramatic events of September 11, 2001, and its consequences: U.S. president George W. Bush's "global war on terror," his invasion of Afghanistan, and, inexplicably, of Iraq.

# 16

# Japan, Korea, and East Asian Economic Development

In the early 1940s, the United States and its allies were at war with Germany and Japan. Less than a half century later, those two countries again posed a challenge, this time an economic one. After World War II, the United States, the world's only economic superpower, assisted West Germany and Japan in their economic recovery and provided them security. By the 1980s, however, the European Community, in which West Germany was economically the strongest member, and Japan became major economic powers. We discuss Germany's postwar resurgence and the development of the European Community in the following chapter; here we examine the remarkable postwar economic development of Japan, the strains in its economic relations with the United States, and its economic slump in the 1990s. About a decade after Japan's "economic miracle" of the 1960s, four Asian nations followed Japan's path in rapid economic development. The so-called Four Tigers were South Korea, Taiwan, Hong Kong, and Singapore. Among the four, South Korea, which was most closely connected to Japan historically and economically, will also be treated in this chapter. In addition to South Korea's industrial progress, we will examine its struggle for democracy and its troubled relations with Communist North Korea.

## ■ JAPAN'S "ECONOMIC MIRACLE"

Between the late 1940s and the late 1970s, Japan underwent an incredible transformation. This nation, no larger than the state of California, gutted by bombs in World War II and lacking in virtually all the raw materials needed for modern industry, grew in the space of thirty years to become the second-largest economic power in the world.[1] Only the United States had a larger GNP. But Japan's industrial productivity—in terms of output per person—was already as efficient as that of the United States.

Japan's recovery was rapid, but it did not occur immediately. It was not until 1953 that Japan's economic output reached its prewar level. This resulted from U.S. assistance, Japan's own assets and hard work, and some good luck as well. The luck was the timely occurrence of the Korean War, which provided the Japanese with opportunity to sell their light industry goods to the UN forces in Korea and thereby earn capital to invest in the rebuilding of Japan's industries.

U.S. assistance came in various forms. In addition to a total of about $2 billion in direct economic aid (spread over a span of five years), the United States (1) persuaded its Western wartime allies to drop their demands for reparations from Japan, (2) pressured Japan to curb inflation and regain fiscal solvency, (3) provided modern technology by making U.S. patents available cheaply, (4) opened the U.S. market to Japanese goods, (5) persuaded other countries to resume trade with Japan, (6) tolerated Japan's protective tariffs for its industries, and (7) took up the burden of Japan's defense. This assistance was not mere kindness to a former enemy, but the strengthening of a new, strategically located Cold War ally. The Japanese appreciated the generous assistance and took full advantage of it. Without the diligent work of the Japanese themselves, however, the economic recovery would not have been possible.

Japan's economy began its skyrocket growth in the late 1950s, and it kept on zooming upward through the 1960s. The average annual growth rate of Japan's GNP in the 1960s was about 11 percent, far higher than other industrialized nations. The double-digit growth rate continued into the 1970s, until Japan's economic drive was thrown off track in 1974 by the global oil crisis. Detractors were quick to point out the fragility of Japan's economy because of its resource dependency, and some declared that Japan's miracle had ended. But the Japanese made adjustments, reducing their oil consumption and diversifying their energy sources, and were back on track by 1976. Until the late 1980s, Japan's average annual growth rate was about 4.5 percent, still the highest among the world's industrialized nations.

Japan surged past most European industrial leaders—Italy, France, and Britain—in the 1960s, and then in the early 1970s it surpassed West Germany, whose postwar economic recovery was also impressive. By 1980, Japan ranked first in production in a number of modern industries. It had long been first in shipbuilding; in fact, it has built more than one-half of the world's ships by tonnage since the early 1970s. It outpaced the Germans in camera production and the United States in the production of electronic equipment such as radios, televisions, sound systems, and video recorders. Japanese motorcycles left their rivals in the dust, and Japanese automobiles captured an increasing share of the world's markets, so that Japan became the world's leader in automobile production in 1980. In the 1970s, it had the most modern and efficient steel industry. By 1980, Japan was poised to mount a challenge to U.S. leadership in the new, all-important high-tech industries, especially in the computer and microelectronic fields.

Many in the West tended to belittle Japan's success and explain it away with self-serving excuses or outdated, if not entirely erroneous, notions— for example, Japan's cheap labor. Japan, they argued, was competitive because its people were willing to work for very low wages. This assertion had some truth to it in the 1950s and early 1960s, but by the early 1970s, Japan's wages had reached the level of most industrial nations. Another notion was that Japan's prosperity was a consequence of its free ride on defense because the United States guaranteed its security. Japan surely benefited from having a much lower level of defense spending than the United States.[2] However, other factors were more important in explaining Japan's economic growth.

## ■ THE BASES FOR JAPAN'S ECONOMIC GROWTH

Following are seven major categories of domestic factors for the economic success Japan had achieved by the mid-1970s.

1. *The government-business relationship in Japan was complementary and cooperative, rather than antagonistic.* The government, particularly the Ministry of International Trade and Industry (MITI), charted a course for the economy and coordinated its industrial growth. Government and industrial firms engaged in long-term planning, and both made use of consensus decisionmaking. The MITI bureaucracy, with its ties to political and business leaders, steered a steady course, thereby providing policy continuity. It guided industrial development not only by targeting specific industries for growth, but also by designating declining industries to be scaled down or dismantled. It also targeted foreign markets on which the Japanese would concentrate their attack. In sum, the Japanese government fostered a national consensus on the priority of economic growth and established industrial and trade policies.

2. *The labor-management system in Japan stressed mutual harmony between the workers and management, rather than confrontation.* Japan's "lifetime employment" system, with its built-in rewards for worker seniority, provided job security to the workers who in turn developed strong identity with and dedication to their firms. The companies, in their turn, were able to count on the services of a well-trained and loyal work force. Generally, management treated its work force as an investment. Worker morale and motivation were increased by various management programs, such as a generous bonus system, educational benefits, housing, insurance, and recreational facilities, resulting in greater worker loyalty and productivity. There were labor unions in Japan, but they were organized locally (as opposed to

national trade unions) and their relations with management tended to be cooperative rather than confrontational. Worker participation in management decisionmaking and in quality-control circles also contributed significantly to the mutual benefit of employer and employee.

3. *The Japanese educational system, which is controlled by the central government, maintained uniform, high standards and was extremely competitive.* In Japan, university entrance examinations determined a person's future, and only the cream of the crop were admitted to the best universities, whose graduates obtained the best jobs. Therefore, students at all levels studied intensely—incredibly so—in preparation for entrance examinations or, as they are called in Japan, "examination hell." The result was a highly educated society with well-developed work habits.

On the whole, the Japanese students received *more,* if not better, education than their counterparts in other countries. The Japanese school year was sixty days longer than in the United States, and Japanese schoolchildren typically studied many hours a day after school with tutors or in private schools. About 33 percent of Japanese high school graduates entered universities, compared to over 55 percent in the United States, but in Japan a higher percentage of students graduated from universities. The education system was centralized under the Ministry of Education, which stressed high standards, especially in math and science. This and the fact that Japanese universities turned out more engineers (even in absolute terms) than the United States help to explain Japan's technological progress.

4. *The Japanese aggressively sought new technology in quest of industrial rationalization and greater productivity.* The Japanese were swifter than their foreign competitors to modernize their steel plants with the most recent, efficient, and cost-saving technology. When the oxygen-burning type of steel furnace was developed in Austria in the early 1960s, the Japanese quickly purchased the patents and invested a vast amount of capital to rapidly convert their plants to the new technology. They also adopted the new continuous casting process at about the same time, and the result was that within a decade they had in operation the world's most efficient and cost-competitive steel plants. This explains why the Japanese were able to compete with U.S.-made steel in the United States, even though they had to import their iron ore and ship their finished steel across the Pacific Ocean. Japan swiftly gained the lead over the rest of the world in robotics and the automation of the production line. Data show that by the late 1980s Japan had twice as many industrial robots in operation than the rest of the world combined.[3]

5. *The high rate of personal savings by the Japanese and Japan's financial and banking practices were beneficial to capital formation for economic growth.* Japanese workers saved a remarkable 18 percent of their salaries, compared to about 6 percent for U.S. workers.[4] The banks then invested the surplus capital in industry and commerce. Although Japanese

firms were also financed by selling stock, a great portion of their capital came from banks, which, unlike stockholders, did not insist on quarterly profits. Instead, the banks financed long-term business enterprises, which at times operated in the red several years before they began to turn a profit. The ready availability of capital made possible continuous plant modernization.

6. *Japan developed superior mechanisms for marketing its products abroad.* Japanese comprehensive trading companies set up branch offices all around the world collecting data, conducting thorough market research, and in numerous other ways facilitated Japanese trade. They also worked with MITI to arrange the most advantageous trade agreements, secure long-term supply of vital raw materials, and direct Japanese investment abroad. Although Japan was vulnerable because of its lack of natural resources, it made itself much less so by becoming indispensable to resource-supplying nations, both as a reliable buyer and as a supplier of technology and capital. Other nations had nothing comparable to Japan's comprehensive trading companies for conducting a large volume of foreign trade.

7. *There were also certain intangible factors unique to Japan—or to East Asian countries—that contributed to economic growth.* The Japanese were served well by historically conditioned cultural traits, such as acceptance of authority, paternalism, a desire for harmony, loyalty to superiors, discipline, and a sense of duty and sincerity. Group consciousness prevailed over individualism. Without these traits, Japan's labor-management system would hardly have been possible. Additionally, there were certain historical circumstances that fortuitously benefited Japan, such as the timing of its industrial development during a period of global economic expansion. It may also be argued that Japan thrived on its own deprivation. Japan's dearth of raw materials, for example, necessitated hard work to attain, conserve, and use them efficiently. By necessity, the Japanese came to excel in industry and foreign commerce.

There were, no doubt, other factors involved in Japan's economic performance, such as industrial rationalization or efficient organization of the industrial workplace and the rapid growth of Japan's domestic market. Japan's relatively low level of defense spending also worked to Japan's economic advantage, but the importance of this factor is debatable. Chalmers Johnson, a noted authority on Japan, has pointed out that "the effect of low defense expenditures was negligible" because of Japan's high rate of capital formation, meaning it had money for both guns and butter.[5] Lower military spending may have been an enabling factor in the first decade after World War II (when the United States saw fit to protect the nation it had just demilitarized), but from the 1970s, Japan's military spending steadily increased, and eventually it had one of the world's largest military budgets.

A more important explanation for Japan's economic success was the preferential treatment Japan received from the United States throughout the

Cold War years. Japan was strategically important to the U.S. policy of containment, and for that reason the United States tolerated Japan's protectionist policies and threw its doors wide open to Japanese products. However, as Japan's industrial competitiveness improved and its trade surpluses increased sharply in the 1970s and 1980s, its trade partner across the Pacific became less tolerant. Then, another explanation (more an accusation) for Japan's economic miracle became commonplace: its unfair trading practices.

## ■ STRAINS IN U.S.-JAPANESE ECONOMIC RELATIONS

### □ 1980s: Japan's Economic Boom

Bilateral trade between the United States and Japan in the 1980s became the largest volume of overseas trade between any two nations in history. (Only U.S.-Canada trade, which is not overseas commerce, was larger.) Japan had a deficit in its commodity trade with the United States until 1964; that is, it exported less than it imported from the United States. From that point, it has been the reverse, with the U.S. deficit in the bilateral trade rising to $1 billion in 1972, $12 billion in 1978, $25 billion in 1984, and then soaring to an astronomical $56 billion in 1987.[6] No nation ever had such a huge trade imbalance with its trading partner. Table 16.1 compares the U.S. trade deficits with Japan and other trading partners in 1987.

**Table 16.1  U.S. Trade Deficits with Selected Areas, 1987 (in US$)**

| | |
|---|---|
| Total U.S. trade deficit | −153,035,000 |
| with Japan | −56,326,000 |
| with the Four Tigers of Asia | −34,117,000 |
| with the European Community | −20,613,000 |
| with OPEC | −12,895,000 |
| with Latin America | −11,507,000 |

In the late 1970s, people in the United States were caught by surprise by Japan's seemingly boundless economic growth and began to wonder about the contrast between Japan's economic success and the recession in their own country. Many of those disaffected by the latter, especially the unemployed, began to blame their problems on Japan. They saw a direct relationship between the growing volume of Japanese imports and rising U.S. unemployment.

In the 1980s, "Japan bashing" became one of Washington's favorite pastimes, even though economists and government officials recognized that declining U.S. industrial competitiveness was an important cause of the trade imbalance. Consumers found Japanese products, especially cars and electronic equipment, superior and less expensive than U.S.-made products. Japan did, however, engage in trade practices such as "dumping" (selling its products abroad at a loss or at lower prices than in Japan) and protecting its own market from foreign imports by high tariffs, import quotas, and various nontariff barriers. Politicians gained political points by calling for "get tough" trade policies and economic sanctions against Japan. If the Japanese did not lower their trade barriers, they argued, then the United States must erect barriers against the flood of Japanese products. In the 1980s, President Reagan, like his immediate predecessors in the White House, opposed taking this protectionist route, knowing that it could lead to a mutually damaging trade war; instead, he put pressure on Japan to open its markets to U.S. goods.

Generally, Washington joined Tokyo in accentuating the positive aspects in U.S.-Japanese relations, which the U.S. ambassador to Japan, Mike Mansfield, liked to call "the most important bilateral relationship in the world, bar none."[7] But despite the talk of partnership and cooperation, Washington maintained pressure on Tokyo, which grudgingly and gradually gave in to some of its persistent demands. On the one hand, Tokyo agreed "voluntarily" to various trade limitations and quotas on its exports to the United States; on the other hand, Washington endeavored to pry open Japan's doors to U.S. products by removing Japan's trade barriers. In the 1960s, Japan agreed to quotas on its textiles exports to the United States, in the 1970s to limitations on steel exports, and in 1981 to a voluntary ceiling on U.S.-bound automobiles. Japan also began building automobile plants in the United States, partly to reduce the volume of Japanese automobile imports and partly to quiet the argument that Japanese cars robbed U.S. workers of their jobs. Moreover, since the late 1960s, Tokyo had, in fact, gradually reduced its own tariffs and quotas to make foreign goods more competitive in Japan, and by the early 1980s, it had agreed to a schedule of tariff reductions.

Japan, however, persisted in the continued protection of its farmers from foreign suppliers of such foodstuffs as beef, oranges, and especially rice. After years of hard bargaining, the two sides managed only to achieve interim agreements gradually elevating its quotas on beef and oranges. But Tokyo continued to hold out on rice, even if it meant that the Japanese would continue to pay seven times the world price for their precious home-grown staple. Still, Tokyo could respond to U.S. charges by pointing out that Japan was already by far the world's largest importer of U.S. agricultural commodities.

Washington became convinced that Japan kept U.S. goods out of its market through nontariff barriers such as restrictive licensing, excessive inspection of imports and burdensome customs-clearing procedures, rigid safety standards, a uniquely cumbersome distribution system, and nettlesome purchasing regulations. It particularly targeted Japan's *keiretsu,* the informal but powerful corporate network that controlled the distribution system and excluded foreign suppliers. These were complicated matters involving peculiarities of the Japanese business system as well as cultural patterns, and in any case they would be difficult to change or adjust.

The Reagan administration hoped that a weak dollar (which lowered the prices of goods produced in the United States) would make U.S. goods more attractive in Japan. The weak dollar, however, also lowered he cost of Japanese investments in the United States. This, as well as high interest rates in the United States, attracted Japanese investors. As a result, the Japanese, who had accumulated a tremendous amount of capital from selling goods in the United States (and elsewhere), recycled these profits and went on a buying spree, purchasing U.S. banks, businesses, and real estate. Most conspicuous were the highly visible real estate acquisitions of Japanese investors in Hawaii, California, and New York City. U.S. senator Ernest F. Hollings, an advocate of retaliatory sanctions against Japan, noted that the effect of Reagan's monetary approach was to transform the United States "into a coast-to-coast yard sale, with our assets available to foreigners at cut-rate, foreclosure-sale prices."[8]

By 1982, Japan had won a crucial battle in the "high-tech wars" when it gained an edge on U.S. competitors in the production and sales of microchips (particularly the 64K RAM chips—which were at the time the cutting edge).[9] In the early 1980s, Japan found a booming market in the United States for VCRs (video cassette recorders), a product that, ironically, had been invented in the United States but abandoned as commercially impractical. The Japanese also won increased shares of the U.S. market for other industrial products such as precision tools, musical instruments, and power tools. Meanwhile, Japan surpassed the United States in nonmilitary technological research and development expenditures, and its research programs either gained the lead or challenged the U.S. lead in a number of new and important fields, particularly in robotics, magnetic levitation, fiber optics, and superconductivity.

Japan pulled ahead of the United States in several other ways during the decade. In the mid-1980s, the United States swiftly fell from the status of the leading creditor nation in the world to the largest debtor. Japan just as swiftly became the world's leading creditor. Japan's assault on the money market in the United States in the late 1980s was breathtaking. By the end of the decade, eight of the ten largest banks in the world were Japanese; six of the twelve largest California banks were Japanese-owned; 20 percent of U.S. government bonds were placed by Japanese financial firms; the top four security companies in the world were Japanese, with the largest, Nomura, being ten times larger than Merrill Lynch, the largest in the United States; and the Tokyo Stock Exchange surpassed the New York Stock Exchange in capital value, while the Osaka Exchange surpassed the London Stock Exchange.[10]

The dramatic elevation of Japan's economic status raised new questions about the relative wealth of the United States and Japan. Older Japanese, clinging to outdated images, still worried about Japan's "poverty," such as its paucity of natural resources, and still stood in awe of the prosperity of the United States with all its land and resources. But younger Japanese and many in the United States as well held that Japan had indeed become a rich nation and that the United States with its double deficits (trade deficit and budget deficit) and declining productivity had become weaker.[11]

## ☐ The 1990s: Japan's Long Economic Downturn

Two major developments at the outset of the 1990s greatly affected Japan's relations with other nations: (1) the end of the Cold War and the collapse of Communism in Eastern Europe and in the Soviet Union, and (2) the Gulf War in 1991. With the demise of the Soviet Union, economic rather than military competition promised to become the order of the day. The Cold War had tied Japan and West Germany to the United States for over four decades, and when it ended these ties loosened—if only ever so slightly. With the Cold War over, Japan could no longer rely on U.S. favors, and Washington began to take a harder line against Japan on trade issues. In the minds of many in the United States, especially among the critics of Japan's trade policies, Japan had replaced the Soviet Union as the main adversary.

The Gulf War of 1991 also affected Japan's relations with the United States and other nations. Japan's constitution barred it from sending military forces to the gulf, but this did not shield it from criticism in the United States and in Europe, where many were unhappy by Japan's unwillingness to engage in a war fought to protect its main source of oil. After months of parliamentary debate, the Japanese government finally pledged $13 billion toward the cost of the war, and it offered a token contribution to the post–Gulf War peacekeeping effort by sending a fleet of minesweepers for duty in the gulf. The gulf problem touched off a heated debate in Japan over the issue of permitting its Self Defense Forces (SDF) to participate in UN peacekeeping operations. Within a year the Japanese Diet passed legislation allowing its SDF to take part in such operations. This new interpretation of the constitution prepared the way for Japan to play a leading role in the UN operation in Cambodia aimed at ending the decade-long civil war there.[12]

U.S. criticism of Japan persisted in the early 1990s, when polls showed Japan's popularity in the United States plummeting.[13] Contributing to the growing acrimony were U.S. media coverage of the fiftieth anniversary of Pearl Harbor in December 1991, President Bush's twice-postponed and—as it turned out—ineffective visit to Japan in February 1992, several tactless (actually racist) remarks by Japanese political leaders critical of the U.S. work ethic, and the publication of several books in the United States strongly critical of Japan. A novel (and later movie) by Michael Crichton, *Rising Sun,* painting a strongly unfavorable portrait of a Japan covertly seeking to destroy the U.S. economy, became a best-seller. Moreover, a new "revisionist" view of U.S.-Japanese economic relations was finding favor in the United States. Writers such as Karel Van Wolferen, Lester Thurow, James Fallows, and Clyde Prestowitz argued that the Japanese political economy was fundamentally different from the Western market economies and operated in ways that gave it distinct advantages in international economic competition. Japanese international business activity, they argued, was driven primarily by national considerations, as if in a war with the rest of the world. It was not enough for Japanese businesses merely to make a profit; they sought, instead, to control the market. Predictably, the revisionists called for strong counter-measures against Japan. Such sentiments reinforced the impression that inter-national trade was becoming national cutthroat competition.

However, the acrimony in U.S.-Japanese relations over trade in the early 1990s suddenly vanished as Japan fell into an economic recession. What the Japanese first regarded as a "downturn" became a full-blown recession by late 1992; the economic bubble—the overheated economy—had burst. The real estate and stock markets that had soared to dizzying heights declined sharply, leaving Japan's financial institutions with a mas-sive debt problem, which is to say billions of dollars worth of "bad" (that is, uncollectible) loans. The annual growth rate of the gross domestic prod-uct (GDP) fell suddenly from over 5 percent to about 2 percent, where it remained for most of the decade; industrial production and plant spending declined, as did savings and interest rates; businesses tightened their belts and reduced their payrolls; and unemployment rose to over 3 percent, which was unusually high in Japan.

As serious as the prolonged recession was for the Japanese, it had sur-prisingly little effect on Japan's trade imbalance with the United States. In fact, Japan's bilateral trade surplus crept further upward. As Japanese cut back on the purchase of goods—foreign as well as domestic—the U.S. appetite for Japanese goods remained strong. As Japan's doldrums continued, the U.S. economy began a period of sustained growth from the early 1990s. This rever-sal, which now had Japan headed downward and the United States upward, had the effect of silencing the shrill voices of trade-war rivalry of the previous decade. Japan virtually disappeared from the pages of U.S. newspapers.

Economic-recovery stimulus packages, consisting mainly of increases in government spending for public works and tax cuts, failed to jump-start the Japanese economy. Consequently, the economy remained stagnant. Toward the end of the 1990s, things got worse before they got better. In 1998, when most of Asia was struggling with a financial crisis, Japan had its worst year. Its GDP shrank again by 2 percent, the largest decline yet. Businesses had declining profits, bankruptcies hit an all-time high, and unemployment rose to a postwar high of 4.4 percent.

Just how bad was Japan's decade-long recession? By one estimate, businesses and households suffered a combined capital loss of $7.2 trillion between 1992 and 1996.[14] The government shelled out some $802 billion in economic stimulus packages between 1992 and November 1998. As bad as it was, however, Japan's economy was not in a meltdown, as some alarmists outside the country seemed to think. Its economy was quite different from those of other Asian nations in recession such as Indonesia, Thailand, or South Korea, for it had a huge current account surplus and foreign currency reserves, far larger industrial capacity, and world-class technology. Throughout the recession, the value of the yen against foreign currency held fairly steady; there was only a marginal decline in living standards; and Japan remained the world's largest provider of overseas developmental aid.

Moreover, the recession was not all bad for Japan. It forced Japan to realize the fragility of its prosperity and the weaknesses in the system that caused the crash. It was necessary to rethink the economic system, especially the cozy relations among politicians, bankers, and industrialists. Reforms were instituted to make the economy more transparent, that is, free of hidden business deals. The cost-reduction measures taken by manufacturers promised greater competitiveness. The restructuring of the Japanese economy had a stabilizing or maturing effect and resulted in a leveling of the growth rate to the new lower, but more sustainable and steady level.

## ■ THE FOUR TIGERS OF ASIA

By the 1980s, besides Japan, four other prospering nations had emerged along the Asian shores of the Pacific Ocean: South Korea (the Republic of Korea), Taiwan (the Republic of China), Hong Kong, and Singapore. These nations, sometimes referred to as the Four Tigers of Asia, followed in Japan's footsteps in the 1970s and 1980s to produce their own economic miracles. Their economic performance, especially their vigorous export-oriented industrial development, together with that of Japan gave rise in the 1980s to such notions as the coming "Asian century" and to the concept of the "Pacific Rim" as the arena of the world's fastest economic growth and largest international trade flow. The Four Tigers became the source of a flood of imports into the United States and a major source of its mounting trade deficit. The U.S. trade gap with the four countries grew from $3.6 billion in 1980 to over $35 billion in 1987.

The Four Tigers all shared with Japan certain common features that accounted for their remarkable economic performance (Table 16.2). They shared a Chinese historical and cultural heritage, particularly an ingrained Confucian value system. It appears that this philosophy—long ridiculed by the West (and by westernized Asians) as antiquated and a barrier to modern progress—was a major source of traits and attitudes such as discipline, loyalty, respect for authority, paternalism, desire for harmony, sincerity, a strong sense of duty, and respect for education—that accounted for the high productivity of Asian workers and the efficiency of Asian management. The

**Table 16.2  Growth Rates of the Four Tigers (by percentage)**

|  | 1977–1981 | 1982–1986 | 1987 | 1988 |
|---|---|---|---|---|
| South Korea | 7.3 | 8.5 | 12.2 | 10.3 |
| Taiwan | 9.0 | 6.9 | 12.3 | 7.4 |
| Hong Kong | 10.8 | 5.9 | 13.5 | 7.1 |
| Singapore | 7.1 | 4.4 | 8.8 | 9.1 |

*Sources*: Bank of Japan, *Comparative International Statistics,* 1988; International Monetary Fund, *International Financial Statistics,* 1988, Tokyo; and *Wall Street Journal,* Washington, D.C., November 1, 1988, p. A24.

Confucian legacy became a vital ingredient for making capitalism work in East Asia.

Other factors were no doubt involved in the economic success of the Four Tigers, including the model of Japan and the investments and technology flowing from abroad. Another major cause of the economic boom in these countries was their ready supply of relatively cheap labor. Moreover, each of these countries had authoritarian governments that curbed democratic development but made economic development their highest priority and marshalled the power of the state toward that end. Their rulers centralized power and economic planning, enforced political stability (except for South Korea, as noted later), and effectively mobilized human resources. They also emphasized public education, the development of technology, and birth control.[15] Like Japan, all four nations, as newly industrializing countries, stressed export-oriented industrial development and took advantage of the global free-trade system established by the industrialized nations of the West after World War II.

South Korea and Taiwan, the two most successful of the Four Tigers, had several things in common that contributed to their economic growth and eventual democratization. As noted in Chapter 14, both countries seem to have thrived on adversity. Both were "divided nations" that shared the experience of having been separated from a larger whole back in the 1940s as a result of Cold War struggles, and both faced continuing serious threats to their security by Communist opponents—North Korea and the People's Republic of China, respectively. The persistent threat fostered a sense of urgency and national purpose that facilitated the mobilization of people and resources to strengthen the military and the economic base. In both cases, these Cold War exigencies fostered authoritarian government, but after a couple of decades of strong economic growth and modernization, a prosperous middle class emerged and began to assert itself, demanding political liberalization.

☐  *South Korea*

South Korea catapulted from the level of a miserably poor Third World nation in the 1950s to the status of a rapidly industrializing nation by the early 1990s. Both North and South Korea had suffered from the division of the Korean nation after World War II because most of the minerals and electric power were located in the North and most of the agricultural land was in the South. At that time, Korea, as a whole, had a better economic infrastructure—particularly in terms of transportation and communications—than most Third World countries, owing to construction done by the Japanese before World War II. Nonetheless, Korea was an impoverished nation, and the devastation it suffered in the Korean War made matters still worse. North Korea, with Soviet-style political regimentation, attained economic recovery sooner than the South, which was less stable politically.

Only gradually in the 1950s did production increase and living standards improve in South Korea, and from the mid-1960s, the nation began its economic takeoff. Its annual rate of economic growth rose to over 14 percent in the early 1970s and, after a brief slowdown in the early 1980s, it climbed again to the rate of 12 percent in 1986 and 1987. In 1964, the per capita GNP of South Korea was a mere $103, but by 1994, it had soared to $8,260.

South Korea's economic resurgence occurred mainly during the nineteen-year rule of General Park Chung Hee. Park, who came to power as a result of a coup in 1961, made economic growth his highest priority. He planned a strategy for a government-led industrialization drive led by large state-supported industrial firms, financed by generous developmental loans from the United States and Japan. Park, having been trained in the Japanese army, was familiar with Japanese organizational methods, and he assiduously employed the Japanese model for economic development. By the 1970s, Korea was rapidly becoming an industrialized nation.

Park was assassinated in 1979, and soon afterward South Korea found itself with another military government with General Chun Doo Hwan at the helm. Korean students protested vehemently against the continuation of the dictatorship. In response to student demonstrations, General Chun expanded martial law, closed universities, dissolved the national assembly, banned all political parties, and for good measure threw their leaders into prison. Then came the crackdown in the city of Kwangju in May 1980, where perhaps as many as three thousand civilian protesters were gunned down by security forces. The event transpired with the implicit approval of the Carter administration, which knew the military's heavy hand was about to come down. The goal of the United States was to prevent South Korea from becoming another Iran, where demonstrations had brought down another U.S.-supported dictator (see Chapter 20).[16]

Through the 1980s there was no letup in student agitation. All the while, as the police and army cracked down on the students, South Korea's economic modernization continued on its rapid course. Korean industries were churning out quality goods competitive in the world marketplace.

*Halting steps toward Korean democracy.* The showcase of South Korea's emergence as a modern nation were the summer Olympic Games in Seoul in September 1988. In anticipation of the event, there was great concern over the possible disruption of the games either by acts of terrorism by North Korea or by violent student demonstrations. After President Chun rejected the pleas of opposition parties for reform of election laws—to allow the direct election of the president—he faced still larger and more volatile demonstrations, spearheaded by university students now joined by many of the country's new middle class. Finally, to head off a bloody confrontation that could result in the cancellation of the Olympics, Chun backed down. In June 1987, he appointed his military academy classmate, Roh Tae Woo, as his successor, and Roh announced a general election to be held in December in which he would run as candidate for president. In that election, the first free presidential election in South Korean history, Roh won a narrow victory, but only because the two popular opposition candidates, Kim Dae Jung and Kim Young Sam, had split the opposition vote.

A political lull prevailed in summer and fall of 1988, while South Korea basked in the international limelight of the Olympics. But the political rancor resumed soon afterward. In the national assembly Roh's political opponents demanded that his predecessor, General Chun, be put on trial for corruption. And in the streets students cried for Chun's head for having been responsible for the Kwangju massacre and protested the continued presence of U.S. forces in Korea. As President Roh achieved some startling breakthroughs on the diplomatic front—establishing diplomatic and economic relations with both the Soviet Union and China—he encountered new problems on the home front in the early 1990s: a series of political scandals and an economic downturn.

The presidential election of December 1992 established a precedent when two civilian candidates—Kim Dae Jung and Kim Young Sam—competed for the office. The winner was Kim Young Sam who, as president, took bold steps to reform South Korean politics, including purging corrupt politicians from the legislature, curbing the power of the internal security agency, and arresting military officers charged with corruption. He also sought to pacify the student protesters by pledging a full-scale investigation of the 1980 Kwangju massacre and compensation for its victims. The students, however, kept the pressure on; fifty thousand marched in May 1993, demanding that former presidents Chun and Roh be punished for the bloody massacre and for corruption. In November 1995, Roh was arrested after he had admitted receiving huge contributions from business tycoons and operating a $653 million slush fund. High-ranking military officers and industrial leaders of the most powerful business groups (Hyundai, Samsung, and others) were also implicated. Kim Young Sam brought indictments against Chun and Roh for their role in the Kwangju massacre and, in a sensational trial, Chun was found guilty and sentenced to death (subsequently commuted to a lengthy prison term) for his role in the 1979 military coup and the 1980 Kwangju massacre, and Roh was sentenced to a twenty-two-month prison term for accepting half a million dollars in bribes. South Korea was under way in freeing itself from its own military.

It was finally the other Kim's turn. Kim Dae Jung, long the country's leading dissident and democracy's most fervent advocate, won the presidency in December 1998. (Kim had previously been kidnapped by the Korean CIA, imprisoned on sedition charges, and sentenced to death; he was exonerated and freed by his predecessor.) Kim pledged to rid the country of corrupt, authoritarian rule and to revive its economy. South Korea had been hard hit by the economic depression that had swept across Asia in 1997. In that year the value of Korean currency against the dollar fell 54 percent, the GDP fell by 5.8 percent, several of its largest companies went bankrupt, and some of its banks were unable to collect on loans and became insolvent.

The first step to recovery was a huge bailout of $57 billion put together by the IMF, the World Bank, and eight donor nations. Kim then took the difficult steps, including regulating the financial industry, holding down inflation, legalizing foreign investment, and liquidating weak businesses. These policies were a bitter pill for business, labor, and consumers, but Kim's government persisted. Within two years the reforms succeeded in reviving the economy, more so than in any of the other East Asian nations. In 1999, for example, South Korea achieved its largest surge in industrial production in twenty years.

*Divided Korea: North versus South.* For decades after the Korean War, Korea remained the site of the Cold War's most intense confrontation, as South Korea and North Korea sought reunification on their own terms and armed themselves against attacks by the other. In the North, Kim Il Sung consolidated his power over a Stalinist regime, which by the early 1960s had achieved an impressive economic and military recovery. In the 1960s, Kim occasionally sent commandos across the demilitarized zone (DMZ) and in 1968, he went so far as to send agents in an—unsuccessful—attempt to assassinate President Park.

North Korean policy toward the South was marked by a bewildering fluctuation between threats and provocation and appeals for talks. Examples of the former were the digging of tunnels under the two-and-a-half-mile-wide DMZ wide enough to infiltrate large numbers of North Korean troops into the South; attacking U.S. border guards and killing two of them with hatchets at Panmunjom in 1978; an attempted assassination of President Chun on a state visit to Burma in 1983 in a bomb attack that killed seventeen South Korean officials, including four cabinet members; and, in 1987, the bombing of a South Korean airliner in flight from Africa to Seoul, killing all 115 people on board. Such reckless provocations brought talk of war in the South and assurances of support from Washington. One of North Korea's long-standing major objectives was the removal of U.S. troops from South Korea. These forces, about forty thousand strong through the 1980s, were armed with tactical nuclear weapons, which Washington made clear it would use in the event of a North Korean attack on the South.[17]

After Mikhail Gorbachev came to power in the Soviet Union in March 1985, the international climate improved drastically as he sought to end the Cold War. With it came the opportunities for a resolution of the Korean conflict. The Soviet Union and the People's Republic of China became interested in lowering tensions and were less willing to support the pesky Communist regime in Pyongyang, North Korea's capital. Moreover, they sought to do business with the prosperous South. South Korean president Roh met with Gorbachev in June 1990 and secured an agreement establishing diplomatic and trade relations between their countries. He also won Gorbachev's support for South Korea's admission to the United Nations.[18] Roh then increased diplomatic pressure on Kim to join negotiations for the peaceful reunification of Korea. Later in 1990, direct talks between the two Koreas produced some surprising results when they signed a nonaggression pact and an agreement banning nuclear weapons from the Korean peninsula.

The latter agreement was especially remarkable, since North Korea's clandestine nuclear bomb project had become a major bone of contention. Washington and Seoul insisted that Pyongyang submit to inspections by the International Atomic Energy Agency (IAEA), but Kim steadfastly denied that he was building a bomb and refused to comply.

Throughout, North Korea's diplomatic isolation and economic stagnation worsened, and the economic disparity between it and the South—already vast—increased further.[19] In April 1992, Kim's government finally agreed to open its nuclear facilities to IAEA inspection, which reported that although North Korea had built a large plutonium reprocessing plant, it had probably not produced enough nuclear material to make an atomic bomb. Pyongyang, however, refused to allow inspectors to see all of its nuclear facilities and was thus able to perpetuate uncertainty in Seoul and Washington. Not until 1994, after the United States had threatened North Korea with UN economic sanctions, was the issue of Pyongyang's plutonium program resolved, but even then the wily North Korean regime continued to hedge and win major concessions from its foes. (For details, see Chapter 19.)

In July 1994, Kim Il Sung, the eighty-two-year-old dictator, the world's longest-surviving ruler, finally died. His fifty-two-year-old son, Kim Jong Il, succeeded him. Kim Jong Il, like his father, was the object of the state-promoted cult, which dubbed him the "Dear Leader."

North Korea's worsening economy caused it to become more pragmatic. In July and August 1995, North Korea was inundated by a deluge of floods of biblical proportion. Torrents of water destroyed reservoirs, farms, farm animals, roads, bridges, schools, and more than a million metric tons of food reserves. UN officials declared the food situation the worst in the world. Rations were set at 450 calories a day, but not everyone had access to even that meager amount.[20] North Korea was reduced to accepting a donation of 150,000 tons of rice from South Korea (but it took pains not to reveal to its people the source of the handout). In the spring of 1996, the United States, South Korea, and Japan provided an additional $15 million in food. Swallowing its pride, Pyongyang accepted these badly needed food shipments, even from its erstwhile capitalist enemies.

North Korea's economic blight was not merely the result of bad weather. For years its failing economy had been propped up by economic assistance and preferential trade arrangements with the Soviet Union, but Gorbachev slashed that support in the mid-1980s, and it ended altogether at the end of the decade when the Soviet Union collapsed. As a result, the North Korean economy took a nose dive, shrinking by one-half in the 1990s.

Still, Pyongyang was not ready to abandon its belligerence toward South Korea. Of greater concern to South Korea and Japan, and the United States as well, was North Korea's missile program. In August 1999, it tested a medium-range missile that flew—inadvertently—over Japan. In answer to protests from both Tokyo and Washington, Pyongyang insisted that it had not been a military missile but a satellite-launching rocket.

From the day he took office as president of South Korea in February 1998, Kim Dae Jung had pledged to conduct a "sunshine policy" toward North Korea, a policy of engagement aimed at seeking better relations and ultimately the peaceful reunification of Korea. He persisted in that policy undeterred by provocations by the North. Year after year the South sent ever larger amounts of food relief, fertilizer, and other aid to the North, where the famine was worsening. To negotiate and administer the food aid program, South Korean officials and businessmen traveled into North Korea, something that had been impossible before. Contacts between North Korean, U.S., Japanese, and officials of other nationalities involved in famine relief also increased. In February 1998, the North suddenly responded to Kim Dae Jung's "sunshine policy" with a surprising peace overture of its own, calling for the promotion of "co-existence, co-prosperity, common interests, mutual collaboration, and unity between fellow countrymen."[21]

The diplomatic ice between the United States and North Korea was broken when Pyongyang agreed to receive a visit from a special envoy from the United States in May 1999, and agreed to send a high-ranking diplomat for talks in Washington.

Another breakthrough came with a historic summit meeting of the rulers of North and South Korea in Pyongyang in June 2000. After almost a half century of Cold War enmity that had continued more than a decade after the Cold War had ended, the democratically elected South Korean president Kim Dae Jung and the reclusive dictator Kim Jong Il of North Korea met face-to-face and mutually declared their commitment to bury the hatchet. At their meeting, the two discussed the whole range of issues that separated them and, while not resolving those issues at once, signed an agreement to work toward the eventual reunification of Korea. The agreement also called for the reunion of thousands of families that had been divided by the closed border since the Korean War, promoting South Korean investment in the North, and holding another summit in Seoul. The meeting proved to be more than diplomatic theater, for it was followed by a series of confidence-building gestures by both sides, such as conducting the first exchange of visits by separated families, the first meeting of the respective defense ministers, the preparation to open highways and railroads across the heavily armed border, and the mutual cessation of propaganda attacks against each other. In July 2004, North Korean loudspeakers at the DMZ, which had broadcast propaganda into the South, fell silent, but not before one final statement that called upon Koreans, "from one blood and using one language," to put an end to "the tragedy of national division."[22] In August 2004, in another sign of the times, North and South Korean athletes marched under one flag at the opening ceremony at the Olympic Games in Athens.

The historic summit in Pyongyang and the new openness of North Korea paved the way for renewing negotiations among that regime, Japan, and the United States, including a diplomatic visit to Pyongyang by U.S. secretary of state Madeline Albright. The summit was hailed as a great diplomatic success, and helped Kim Dae Jung garner the Nobel Peace Prize, but both sides acknowledged that it was but a first step and that the road to reunification would be a long and difficult one.

The changing of the guard in Washington in 2001, however, produced a 180-degree turn in U.S.–North Korean relations. The new president, George W. Bush, wanted no part of the "sunshine policy," nor President Clinton's negotiations with Kim Jong Il. He declared, instead, "I loathe Kim Jong Il." He then revived Reagan's so-called Star Wars program, this time aimed at defending the United States against missiles from North Korea. After the events of September 11, 2001, he lumped North Korea, together with Iraq and Iran, into his "axis of evil." Finally, he asserted the right to wage a preventive war against North Korea, just as he was about to actually do against Iraq.

Bush pulled the rug out from under Kim Dae Jung and his "sunshine policy." A war was the last thing the South Korean government wanted, since Seoul was highly vulnerable and within range of North Korea's massive array of howitzers and rocket launchers a scant thirty miles away across the DMZ.

Kim once again played his nuclear card by making a stunning announcement in October 2002 that not only was North Korea restarting its plutonium-processing program but had launched a uranium production program as well.

Bush, with his hands full in Afghanistan and Iraq, had no answer, except to shrug off the significance of this sensational disclosure. Moreover, Bush steadfastly rejected Kim's call for bilateral talks with Washington and insisted instead on multilateral talks with six nations (U.S., North Korea, South Korea, China, Japan, and Russia), which he felt certain Kim would reject. The standoff continued.

## ■ RECOMMENDED READINGS

### ☐ *Japan*

Christopher, Robert. *The Japanese Mind*. New York: Fawcett, 1983.
   One of the most readable of the many books on Japan's "economic miracle."
Dower, John. *Embracing Defeat: Japan in the Wake of World War II*. New York: W. W. Norton, 1999.
   A definitive study by a first-rate scholar of modern Japanese history.
Johnson, Chalmers. *MITI and the Japanese Economic Miracle: The Growth of Industrial Policy, 1925–1975*. Stanford, Calif.: Stanford University Press, 1982.
   A superb analysis of the role of government in Japan's economic growth.
Lincoln, Edward. *Japan's New Global Role*. Washington, D.C.: Brookings Institution, 1993.
   A critical analysis by a noted expert on the Japanese economy.
Nakamura, Takafusa. *The Postwar Japanese Economy: Its Development and Structure*. Tokyo: University of Tokyo Press, 1981.
Reischauer, Edwin O. *The Japanese Today: Change and Continuity*. Cambridge, Mass.: Harvard University Press, 1986.
   A masterful survey of many facets of modern Japan by one of the foremost Japanists in the United States.
Vogel, Ezra. *Japan as Number 1: Lessons for America*. Cambridge, Mass.: Harvard University Press, 1979.
   Not only offers an explanation for Japan's economic success, but also suggests ways in which the United States can learn from the Japanese.

### ☐ *U.S.-Japan Relations*

Buckley, Roger. *U.S.-Japan Alliance Diplomacy: 1945–1990*. London: Cambridge University Press, 1991.
   Provides an evenhanded historical survey of the recently troubled U.S.-Japanese relationship.
Forsberg, Aaron. *America and the Japanese Miracle: The Cold War Context of Japan's Postwar Economic Revival, 1950–1960*. Durham: University of North Carolina Press, 2000.
   Stresses the U.S. role and the importance of the Cold War in Japan's postwar economic recovery.
Green, Michael J., and Patrick M. Cronin, eds. *The U.S.-Japan Alliance: Past, Present and Future*. New York: Council on Foreign Relations, 1999.
Johnson, Chalmers. *Blowback: Costs and Consequences of American Empire*. New York: Henry Holt and Co., 2001.
   In this expansive and provocative study, the author offers a sharply critical analysis of both U.S. and Japanese economic policies.
Kearns, David T., and David A. Nadler. *Prophets in the Dark: How Xerox Reinvented Itself and Beat Back the Japanese*. New York: Harper Business, 1992.

By former Xerox CEO David T. Kearns and his business consultant, who took back market shares from the Japanese.

Kuttner, Robert. *The End of Laissez-Faire: National Purpose and Global Economy After the Cold War.* New York: Knopf, 1991.
Argues that since Japan and the European Union have close government-business cooperation, strategic economic planning, and managed trade, the United States must also develop a national strategy.

LaFebre, Walter. *The Clash: A History of U.S.-Japanese Relations Throughout History.* New York: W. W. Norton, 1997.
An excellent survey by a seasoned diplomatic historian.

McCraw, Thomas K., ed. *America Versus Japan.* Boston: Harvard Business School Press, 1986.
Topical essays offering a comparative analysis of economic policies and an excellent overview and conclusion by the editor.

Prestowitz, Clyde V. *Trading Places: How We Are Giving Our Future to Japan and How to Reclaim It.* 2d ed. New York: Basic Books, 1989.
A revisionist interpretation of the twin causes of Japan's rise to economic power: Japan's strategic, long-range program and the U.S. "flight from reality."

Thurow, Lester. *Head to Head: The Coming Economic Battle Among Japan, Europe and America.* New York: William Morrow, 1992.
A revisionist treatment of the nature of the Japanese economy and the consequences of European economic integration.

## ☐ Korea and East Asia

Amsden, Alice. *Asia's Next Giant: South Korea and Late Industrialization.* New York: Oxford University Press, 1989.
Examines South Korea's economic surge in the 1960s, 1970s, and 1980s.

Cumings, Bruce. *Korea's Place in the Sun: A Modern History.* New York: W. W. Norton, 1997.
A comprehensive and critical survey of modern Korean history focusing on the postwar period.

Keon, Michael. *Korean Phoenix: A Nation from the Ashes.* Englewood Cliffs, N.J.: Prentice-Hall, 1977.

Oberdorfer, Don. *The Two Koreas: A Contemporary History.* Rev. ed. New York: Basic Books, 2001.

Vogel, Ezra. *The Four Dragons: The Spread of Industrialization in East Asia.* Cambridge, Mass.: Harvard University Press, 1991.
Explains the common causal factors for economic growth in the Four Tigers.

## ■ NOTES

1. The size of the GNP of the Soviet Union was not known for certain, but it was generally believed in the West that Japan's GNP was as large and probably larger by 1980. Its per capita GNP was certainly much larger.

2. From the 1950s, Japan steadily increased its defense spending; by the 1980s it was about 6 percent of the annual budget, or 1 percent of its GNP, compared to U.S. defense expenditures of approximately 6 to 8 percent of its GNP.

3. Robot Institute of America, *Japan 1989: An International Comparison* (Tokyo: Keizai Koho Center, 1988), p. 27.

4. This remarkably high rate of savings was accounted for in part by the government taxation laws and the relatively low pensions for Japanese workers, but other factors included the huge lump-sum biannual bonuses Japanese workers received and traditional habits of saving for future security. Similar saving habits were found in other Confucian-influenced Asian countries such as South Korea and Taiwan.

5. Chalmers Johnson, *MITI and the Japanese Miracle: The Growth of Industrial Policy, 1925–1975* (Stanford, Calif.: Stanford University Press, 1982), p. 15. Johnson points out that for a nation with a very low rate of investment, such as China, a large defense expenditure does retard economic growth, but for nations where investment rates were high, such as South Korea and Taiwan, "their very high defense expenditures have had little or no impact on their economic performance."

6. Japan also built up a large surplus—$20 billion in 1987—with its trade with the European Community, where the demand for protection against Japanese imports was even stronger than in the United States. Japan also had large trade surpluses with most Asian nations.

7. John E. Woodruff, "Veteran Envoy Mansfield to Retire from Tokyo Post," *Baltimore Sun,* November 15, 1988.

8. Ernest F. Hollings, "We're Winning the Cold War While Losing the Trade War," *Baltimore Sun,* December 17, 1989, p. 4N.

9. See Clyde V. Prestowitz, *Trading Places: How We Are Giving Our Future to Japan and How to Reclaim It,* 2d ed. (New York: Basic Books, 1989), chapter 2. By August 1982, the Japanese had captured 65 percent of the world market for microchips. In 1980, when the United States was still trying to get its 64K chip out of the lab, the Japanese had already produced prototypes of the 256K chip.

10. Richard W. Wright and Gunter A. Pauli, *The Second Wave: Japan's Global Assault on Financial Services* (New York: St. Martin's Press, 1987).

11. Prestowitz, *Trading Places,* pp. 98–113, expresses this view in an alarming way. Also see Ellen L. Frost, *For Richer, For Poorer: The New U.S.-Japan Relationship* (New York: Council on Foreign Relations, 1987).

12. The bulk of the UN peacekeeping forces in Cambodia were Japan's SDF personnel, serving in a noncombat role. This marked the first time since World War II that Japanese military forces had been deployed abroad. Moreover, the director of the UN operation was Japanese, and the bulk of its financial support came from Japan.

13. Edwin Reischauer Center for East Asian Studies, *The United States and Japan in 1992: A Quest for New Roles* (Washington, D.C.: Johns Hopkins University Press, 1992), pp. 51–58. A *Washington Post*–ABC News poll on February 14, 1992, reported that U.S. respondents who felt that anti-Japanese feelings were increasing rose from 33 percent in November 1991 to 65 percent in February 1992.

14. Shigeyoshi Kimura, "Japan Blames Inaction for Economy," Associated Press, December 12, 1998, *AOL News Profiles.*

15. The World Health Organization rated Taiwan's birth control program first among developing nations in 1989. Singapore rated second, South Korea third, and Hong Kong fifth. The PRC was fourth. "ROC Rated Top for Birth Curbs by World Group," *Free China Journal,* December 21, 1989.

16. The South Korean government admitted to only 240 deaths. See Chalmers Johnson, *Blowback: The Costs and Consequences of American Empire* (New York: Henry Holt, 2000), pp. 112–116. Johnson bases his account on the work of U.S. journalist Tim Shorrock.

17. David Rees, *A Short History of Modern Korea* (New York: Hippocrene Books, 1988), p. 168. In 1975, U.S. secretary of defense James Schlesinger stated explicitly that in the event of a North Korean attack, the United States would not

become involved in "endless ancillary military operations" but would "go for the heart" of its opponent.

18. North Korea had consistently opposed the entry of either of the two Koreas into the United Nations and had been able to count on a Soviet veto, but now it had to acquiesce. In September 1991, both Koreas were admitted.

19. "Placing Bets on a New Korea," *The Economist,* December 21, 1991, pp. 27–28. In 1990, South Korea had over five times higher per capita income and twenty times more foreign trade than the North; the North spent more than 20 percent of its meager GNP on its military, whereas the South spent only 4 percent of its burgeoning GNP on its military.

20. Walter Russell Mead, "More Method Than Madness in North Korea," *New York Times Magazine,* September 15, 1996, p. 50.

21. "North Korea Makes Overture to South," *Baltimore Sun,* February 26, 1998, p. 14A.

22. Anthony Faiola, "As Tensions Subside Between Two Koreas, U.S. Strives to Adjust," *Washington Post,* July 25, 2004, p. A16.

# 17

## The Globalization
## of the Economy

The modern age—that is, since the days of European exploration—witnessed the expansion of trade across the globe. By the beginning of the twentieth century, a global, interconnected economy was a long-established fact. The central question was always over the organization of international trade.

Should commerce be regulated according to the principles of mercantilism, that is, for the benefit of the state? This school of thought coincided with the rise of the European nation-states and their absolute monarchs who sought to control trade to fill their royal treasuries. Mercantilism called for a favorable balance of trade as exemplified by the flow of gold and silver to capital cities such as Lisbon, Paris, and London.

Or should commerce be relatively free to serve primarily the interests of individual enterprise, as the school of Adam Smith (*The Wealth of Nations,* 1776) had proposed? This school of thought gave rise to the argument that the economic activity of individuals and nations should be engaged in unfettered competition, or "free" trade, with the promise that it is beneficial for all involved. Gradually, the European world (i.e., Europe and its extensions overseas, such as the United States, Australia, etc.) in fits and starts, moved toward this free-trade paradigm.

The debate between the proponents of free trade and mercantilism, however, was never resolved. Free trade was never absolutely free; it always had its national restrictions as countries repeatedly sought protection behind economic barriers—mainly tariffs—to keep out competitors who all too often were demonized as exploiters.

Nowhere was this more evident than the U.S. response to the stock market crash of 1929. To protect the nation's economy, Congress passed the Smoot-Hawley tariff (1930), which raised tariffs by 50 percent, and it was this rather than the dramatic collapse of the overvalued stock market that brought about the Great Depression of the 1930s. The trading partners of the United States responded in kind, and a trade war resulted with grave consequences all around. Germany's devastated economy, for example, was a major factor in bringing Adolf Hitler to power in 1933.

Before World War II came to an end, the Western Allies took steps to ensure that history would not repeat itself. They expected an economic downturn after the war, but they resolved to deal with it without resorting to national solutions. In July 1944, at Bretton Woods, New Hampshire, the representatives of forty-four Allied nations met for the purpose of facilitating the resumption of international trade after the war. They established the International Monetary Fund (IMF) for the purpose of the restoration of the system of multinational international payments that had broken down during the Great Depression. Eventually, by the end of the twentieth century, nearly all nations had joined the IMF.[1]

The fund consists of a pool of money contributed by the member states, of which the United States is the largest contributor. For that reason, the United States is in a position to determine how the fund's money is spent. When a debtor nation proves unable to meet its international obligation, the IMF takes on the role of a financial St. Bernard and steps in to eliminate the specter of "nonperforming" loans and the subsequent breakdown of the international system of payments. The IMF lends money and lines up the banks that will lend money. It is the lender of last resort, particularly for the poorest nations. But the IMF also insists that the recipients remain in compliance with the lending terms. The fund here performs two functions. It lends money to shore up the international system of obligations and trade, and at the same time it holds a most powerful weapon over the heads of many governments: the threat of withholding additional funds necessary to keep impoverished nations afloat.

In time, this second aspect created much resentment in the Third World, for the IMF appeared to be more interested in bailing out the private lending institutions than in helping the desperate recipients. The IMF was not alone in dealing with Third World nations, but it was the most visible and thus served as a lightning rod for the ire of people and politicians who felt they were victimized by the developed, capitalist First World. The defenders of the IMF replied that the institution provided, first of all, much-needed capital, and second, it merely demanded a proper, although painful, treatment to restore the patient to health. The result of this arrangement was a love-hate relationship between desperate nations that needed assistance and a Western, capitalist agency that provided aid and as part of the bargain insisted on interfering in the internal affairs of nations. For the IMF, it was all too often but a short step from the welcome mat to becoming the target of political violence.

The other institution that came out of the Bretton Woods conference is the World Bank. It began its operations in 1946 for the purpose of providing the finances for specific projects throughout the world. Its original working capital came from its members' contributions, but the bulk of its capital comes from borrowing in the world's money markets. It operates as any bank; it has to borrow money (frequently at high rates), and it lends money at a markup.

Shortly after World War II, the victors created yet another international organization, the General Agreement of Tariffs and Trade (GATT), initially a club of twenty-three members.[2] Through eight rounds of lengthy negotiations (the last one, the Uruguay Round, took place between 1986 and 1994), GATT was remarkably successful in managing to reduce the average tariff on the world's industrial goods from 40 to 5 percent of their market value. It marked the first multilateral agreement to reduce trade barriers since Napoleonic times.

GATT was created as a temporary expedient but lasted for nearly half a century. In 1995, it voted itself out of existence to be replaced by the World Trade Organization (WTO), a body designed to take the case of trade liberalization even further. The WTO was established as a permanent institution with much greater powers to arbitrate trade disputes. Its rules demanded that countries found in the wrong must change their behavior or face sanctions. When China applied to join the WTO, the argument in favor of admission was that as a member it would have to reduce its extraordinarily high tariffs, which ran as high as 100 percent on certain commodities.

## ■ THE EUROPEAN UNION

The best example of free trade in practice is the European Union. It is the outgrowth of the European Coal and Steel Community, founded in 1952, designed to facilitate international trade in these commodities, the building blocs of postwar reconstruction. Its members were France, West Germany, Italy, Belgium, the Netherlands, and Luxembourg. In 1957, by the Treaty of Rome, the same nations created the European Community (EC)—also known as the Common Market—the purpose of which was to eliminate eventually trade barriers on all commodities.

The founding fathers of the EC were two Frenchmen, the foreign minister Robert Schuman and the economist Jean Monnet. They sought more than efficient trade; they hoped that an interdependent Western Europe would lead to nothing less than a change in the psychological makeup of its citizens, to change Europe, which had just undergone the most devastating war in history, to a force for peace. Schuman's emphasis was on preventing war, more than on economics. When Schuman presented his historic proclamation of May 9, 1950—five years to the day after the end of World War II—he underscored that the Coal and Steel Community's purpose first and foremost was to establish a lasting peace, particularly between Germany and France.

Schuman's proclamation became the day of birth of what eventually became the European Union. For more than half a century it not only kept the peace in Western Europe among former bitter enemies, but also created a genuine peace of mutual understanding. Perhaps it should not have been surprising, therefore, that in September 2003—upon the fortieth anniversary of Schuman's death—the Roman Catholic bishop of Metz submitted to the Vatican a stack of documents to support a request for the beatification of Schuman. For Schuman to enter the pantheon of Catholic saints, however, the Church would have to show that Schuman had worked a miracle. The mitigation of centuries-old national hatred would qualify as a miracle.

In March 1985, the European Council, whose members included the heads of the governments of the twelve member states at the time,[3] announced its intention of establishing a single integrated market by the end of 1992, which would fulfill the goal set in 1957. In its 1985 white paper, *Completing the Internal Market,* the council called for the removal of national rules and regulations in areas such as banking, transport, and border controls in favor of supranational regulations. It was a mammoth task encompassing 279 areas, from the rights of labor and women to banking and insurance, agricultural subsidies, border controls, immigration, pollution, health standards, transportation, and communication. It even called for the creation of a common currency to put an end to the eleven different currencies then in use.[4]

Within a few years after its creation in 1957, the European Community—or Common Market as it was then known—broke down many of the formidable trade barriers between the nations of Western Europe. Many remained in place, however. Moreover, some nations at times turned to "national solutions" to solve their economic problems. But in the early 1980s, several factors came together: the French and Spanish socialists, who in the past had favored governmental regulations and control of the economy, acknowledged the superiority of the market over a planned economy. They began to extol the virtues of competition tied to deregulation of the economy. The EC of 1992 was the logical result of this trend of deregulation.

The first nation to take the road to 1992 was France, which at the time was no longer ruled by the nationalist Charles de Gaulle, but by the "European" François Mitterrand. In January 1984, Mitterrand became the president of the Council of Ministers of the EC, and in this capacity he became a convert to European unity. His term as president of the council, a French diplomat noted, became his "road to Damascus."[5] Helmut Kohl, the chancellor of West Germany, felt that the strong German economy could only benefit from the removal of national economic barriers. Margaret Thatcher, the prime minister of Britain, long an apostle of laissez-faire capitalism, had no reason to object to a free market. The main goal was to strengthen the competitiveness of Western Europe against the other great players—the United States, which in 1989 created its own free-trade zone with Canada, and particularly Japan, the primary target. The Europeans resented Japan's aggressive economic expansion and its continued protection of its own domestic market. In European eyes, competition with Japan had turned into economic war.

The driving force behind European economic unification was the business elite; it was not a popular mass movement. Many, in fact, viewed the full integration process with misgivings. West Germans, for example, feared the influx of immigrants from southern Europe. In the 1960s, West German industry had recruited a large number of workers from Turkey, Yugoslavia, and Greece, many of whom had not returned home. The EC had its own north-south division. Northern workers feared competition from immigrants from southern countries such as Portugal, Spain, and Greece, where the standard of living was less than half that in the north. Labor also feared that the removal of barriers could mean relocation of businesses to countries with lower wages and few social benefits.

At the end of the 1980s, the EC's competitors, such as the United States and Japan, increasingly took notice of the emerging structure. The EC sought to allay fears abroad that it was creating a "Fortress Europe" by stressing its commitment to international trade. After all, total exports of its member nations (including exports to each other) amounted to 20 percent of international trade, compared to the United States with 15 percent, and Japan with 9 percent. To forestall the impact of future protectionism, U.S.

U.S. president Bill Clinton received by Jacques Delors, president of the EU's European Commission, Brussels, January 1994. *(European Commission)*

and Japanese companies invested heavily in EC countries. Toyota invested $1 billion in an automobile factory in Great Britain; AT&T bought into Ital-tel in Italy to circumvent the rules of origin. For the Japanese the central problem was access. Should the walls go up, Japan's global companies hoped to qualify as insiders by building industrial plants within EC nations. For this reason, their direct investments in EC countries increased from $1 billion in 1984 to about $9 billion in 1989.

After 1987, the EC cracked down on "dumping" by Asian firms, par-ticularly against Japanese companies, but also enterprises in other countries of East Asia. It drew up "rules of origin" and "local-content regulations" to determine the national origin of goods. They were meant to prevent the establishment of Asian "screwdriver plants" in Europe.

The Europeans remained divided over the issue of Japanese invest-ment. Margaret Thatcher's government particularly welcomed Japanese investment to shore up the economy of Britain, where in 1989 one hundred Japanese-owned factories employed over twenty-five thousand workers. But many European industrialists feared that unrestricted Japanese invest-ments could lead to Japan's domination of entire sectors of the European economy.

During the late 1980s, the four leading members of the EC—West Ger-many, France, Italy, and the United Kingdom—ranked third through sixth in the world in GNP. West Germany alone, with one-half the population of Japan and one-quarter that of the United States, had become the world's leading exporting nation in 1988, surpassing the United States for the first time and extending its lead in 1989. West Germany's 1989 commodity trade surplus of $61 billion equaled that of Japan and exceeded it in 1990.[6]

## ■ THE 1980S: THREE ECONOMIC SUPERPOWERS

As recently as the 1960s, the United States had accounted for 33 percent of the world's GNP, but by 1989 its share had slipped to 20 percent. By then, the U.S. current account deficit had reached $125 billion, while Japan's surplus had risen to $72 billion, Taiwan's to $70 billion, and Ger-many's to $53 billion. Japan and West Germany had begun to take on the role of the world's bankers. Through the 1980s, Japan and the Asian newly industrializing countries on the one hand, and West Germany and the EC on the other, were gaining momentum, while the United States was struggling. Its massive domestic debt was a symptom that the nation was living beyond its means, consuming too much and unable to pay its bills.

During the 1980s, Japan ran up annual trade surpluses with the United States in the neighborhood of $50 billion, and such a large trade imbalance was bound to cause friction. Many of the economic problems that plagued the United States were of its own making: a high defense budget (around

$300 billion annually), the quest for short-term gain at the expense of investment and planning for the long haul (which frequently led to shoddy craftsmanship and with it the loss of market share, in automobiles in particular), and the opening of its markets to many competitors.

The oil crises of the 1970s hit the U.S. automobile industry particularly hard as it produced a host of gas-guzzling behemoths when the world demanded smaller, more fuel-efficient cars. Germany and especially Japan benefited handsomely because they produced the smaller cars and efficient diesel automobiles now much in demand. Japan also profited from the production of other sought-after, relatively inexpensive consumer goods of high quality—cameras, television sets, stereo equipment, and video tape recorders.

The open U.S. market also served Japan well. It was in part the product of the Cold War. The foreign policy in Washington, particularly at the Pentagon and the State Department, continued to favor a strong Japan allied with the United States, while the Commerce and Treasury Departments fretted over the trade imbalance and the outflow of the nation's wealth.

For international trade to work smoothly, there must be an even flow of goods. An imbalance inevitably leads to friction. A case in point was the imbalance of trade between the United States and East Asia. During the early 1980s, U.S. trade with Communist China was still negligible, but during the next twenty years, China's trade surplus continued to grow rapidly and even overtook that of Japan's. The Chinese trade surplus with the United States in 2003 was a record $124 billion. Other nations, too, ran up large surpluses in their trade with the United States.

The U.S. economy continued to be the locomotive pulling the economies of the world by purchasing vast amounts of goods from abroad. As a

**Table 17.1 Comparative Data on the EC, the United States, and Japan, 1987**

|  | Population | Per Capita GNP (US$) |
| --- | --- | --- |
| European Community | 322,871,000 | 10,730 |
| West Germany | 61,200,000 | 14,400 |
| United States | 243,800,000 | 18,530 |
| Japan | 122,100,000 | 15,760 |

**Table 17.2 U.S. Trade Deficit, 2003 (in US$ billions)**

| With China | 124 | (record) |
| --- | --- | --- |
| With Canada | 54 | (record) |
| With Mexico | 40 | (record) |
| With Japan | 66 | (lowest since 1998) |

*Source*: "Record U.S. Trade Deficit in 2003," CBSNews.com, February 13, 2004.

result, the U.S. trade deficit rose dramatically: in 1998, it stood at a record $164 billion; in 1999, it jumped to $271 billion; in 2003, it reached the staggering figure of $489 billion.[7]

In the 1980s, when "Japan-bashing" became fashionable in the United States, many blamed the declining U.S. economic performance on Japanese trade barriers. These barriers tended to be informal, "nontariff" constraints that made it frustratingly difficult for U.S. businesses to crack the lucrative Japanese market of more than 120 million buyers with deep pockets. The EC, too, complained about the restricted access to the Japanese market. Europeans showed even less compunction to charge the Japanese with unfair trading practices. In 1989, the leading West German news weekly, *Der Spiegel*, launched a broadside of articles in which it charged that the Japanese were not interested in trade but in ambushing their competitors, not merely to gain a share of the market but to dominate certain sectors completely—and all this by unfair means, such as dumping, stealing technology, and excluding foreign competitors from their shores. The Japanese Ministry of International Trade and Industry, *Der Spiegel* charged, not only organized trade, it was the headquarters of an economic war machine on a mission to dominate the world.[8]

During the early 1990s, a rift began to emerge in the United States between those who pushed for ever greater integration of the world's economies and those who argued for measures against what they perceived as unfair competition. But interdependence was too deeply entrenched and the proponents of the second argument were fighting an uphill battle. Several examples illustrate the extent of interdependence. General Motors no longer saw itself as a U.S., but an international corporation. The U.S. Chrysler Corporation held 50 percent ownership in a joint venture with Mitsubishi Motors to produce cars in the United States and 15 percent interest in Mitsubishi of Japan, which produced cars in Japan for Japanese and foreign markets. General Motors, Ford, and several British corporations entered into similar joint ventures with Japanese car producers. In the late 1990s, Chrysler merged with the venerable German automobile manufacturer Daimler-Benz, the head of the new conglomerate being in Germany. Many "U.S.-made" or "British-made" cars had a large percentage of Japanese parts, produced in Japan. Honda, the Japanese car builder, shipped some of its cars manufactured in Ohio by U.S. workers to Japan.

Interdependence notwithstanding, international capitalism frequently resembled a zero-sum game, one of winners and losers. It sometimes produced a nationalist backlash against foreigners. In the United States, during the 1980s, resentment built up first against the Arabs with their oil money and then against the sharp rise in Japanese investments, particularly after the latter had gone on a highly publicized buying binge, purchasing hotels in Hawaii, studios in Hollywood, and Rockefeller Center in New York City. Foreign investment in the United States was hardly a new phenomenon, however. Foreign capital, mainly from Britain, had contributed substantially to the industrialization of the United States in the latter half of the nineteenth century. During World War I, it was the United States that became the world's leading foreign investor. In the 1980s, the United States again benefited from foreign capital that helped keep the U.S. government and banks solvent and revitalize U.S. industries.

The last GATT round of negotiations aimed at eliminating trade barriers stumbled in the early 1990s on the rock of French resistance to opening European markets to U.S. grains and vegetable oils. Only after explicit threats of strong U.S. retaliation did the year-long talks produce a solution acceptable to Washington. The Japanese sat nervously on the sidelines watching with great interest, because if the GATT agreement held, Japan might have to open its market to foreign rice. Japanese political leaders continued to assuage their rural constituents with the pledge of allowing not "a single grain of foreign rice" into the country, but in 1993, Tokyo finally agreed to a gradual and limited importation of foreign rice.

# ■ REGIONAL TRADING BLOCS

## ☐ *The Deepening and Widening of the European Union*

In Europe, the member states of the EC continued to pursue the goal of full economic integration. In December 1991, in line with the white paper of 1985, representatives of the twelve EC nations worked out a treaty in the Dutch city of Maastricht committing the EC to a "deepening" process, among them the creation of an economic and monetary union with a single currency and a common central bank. In addition, border controls were to come down, and foreigners were to be cleared at whatever border (or airport) they arrived. Maastricht also called for standard environmental, labor, and social laws such as the minimum wage, vacation days, and maternity leave. All citizens would be free to work and live anywhere they chose and even be able to vote in local elections.

The Maastricht Treaty, before it could go into force, had to be ratified. In nine of the nations, the governments quickly did so. But in Denmark, Ireland, and France it would be the voters, by way of a referendum, who would decide. In June 1992, the voters of Denmark, the third-smallest member of the EC, rejected Maastricht by the narrow majority of just over 50 percent. The French voters ratified the treaty, but by a scant majority of the vote; Irish voters ratified it by a comfortable margin.

The Danish vote underscored a general uneasiness with the Maastricht plan. The deepening process, the handiwork of the business and governing elites, clashed with the skepticism of the general public, who felt that their politicians had gone too far and too fast along the road to political, social, and economic integration by insisting to an unprecedented degree on the subservience of national sovereignty to a supranational community. The Danes were not necessarily against a unified Europe, but against granting bureaucrats in Brussels authority to decide, for example, on the maximum speed of a Danish moped.[9] There was also the danger of the EC being dominated by a resurgent Germany, and on this the Danes were not alone in their fear. The plans for 1992 had been drawn up before German reunification, something no one had predicted, at a time when Germany was first among equals, but equal nevertheless, and not as dominant as it became during the early 1990s. Earlier, the French had used the metaphor of the French rider controlling the German horse. With unification, however, the horse threw its rider and galloped off to the east to reclaim its former sphere of influence.[10]

The Maastricht Treaty finally went into effect in November 1993 (after the voters of Denmark approved a modified version of the treaty in a second referendum in May 1993). At this juncture, the European Community took a new name that reflected its commitment to integration; henceforth, it would be known as the European Union, or EU.

Despite the ratification of the Maastricht Treaty, a measure of pessimism over the deepening process remained. How deep should integration become? Britain's leaders, in particular, were having second thoughts about further EU integration. And the enlargement of the EU (to fifteen members in 1995, and twenty-five in 2004) made the intergovernmental process more unwieldy. Since the implementation of the ambitious Maastricht Treaty, public expressions of "euro-pessimism" had become widespread. Many, particularly in Germany and Britain, wanted no part of a single monetary system—"esperanto money," as it was called derisively—preferring instead their national currencies. But for the politicians there was no alternative to further integration. The deepening of the EU—that is, the granting of additional powers to the European Parliament at the expense of the national legislatures—would slow down, but it would continue nonetheless. A case in point was the acceptance of the EU's currency. With the exception of Britain, Sweden, and the ever-skeptical Danes, the EU committed itself to the embrace of the "euro" on January 1, 2002. The bank notes featured open doors and windows and bridges, symbolic of the EU's mission of the integration of a Europe that in recent history had witnessed unprecedented bloodshed.

Even before the Maastricht Treaty's ratification, the EU took steps to widen its membership. The first to seek admission was Austria in July 1989—months before the Berlin Wall, the symbol of Europe's division, came down. Austria's 1955 treaty with its former occupying powers had prevented it from joining any sort of association with Germany—economic or military. The Western powers (the United States, Britain, and France) had no objection to Austria's membership in the EU. It was primarily the

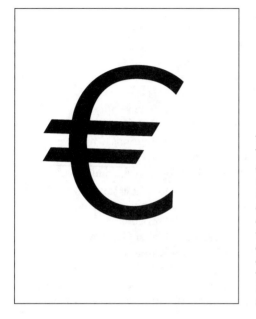

The symbol for the euro. The symbol was chosen after extensive public opinion research across the European Union. A cross section of EU citizens between the ages of eighteen and seventy-five gave their evaluations of eight different symbols. This one was chosen for its stability, combination of modern look and classic lines, and because it projects a strong image.

Soviet Union that did not want to see another German *Anschluss,* or annexation, of Austria, creating another *Grossdeutschland,* or Greater Germany. Earlier, however, Mikhail Gorbachev had spoken of a culturally and economically unified Europe, "our common home." He, too, raised no objections to Austrian membership in the EU.

Sweden asked for membership in July 1991, and Finland and Norway followed suit in March 1992. Finland had close trade and defense arrangements with the Soviet Union based on the treaty of 1948. But Finland suffered from an unemployment rate of 20 percent—the highest since World War II—and it saw the EU as a potential life raft. Membership in the EU would also give Finland the window of opportunity to formally become a part of Western Europe. Again, Moscow did not object.

In June 1994, Austrian voters said "yes" to membership in the EU by a wide margin. In Scandinavia, however, the votes were much closer. There, the farmers opposed the opening of their markets to imports from the south. Voters in Sweden and Finland ratified entry into the EU by narrow margins; in Norway, however, the voters (as they had done twenty years earlier) narrowly rejected EU membership, preferring to go it alone. Norway was self-sufficient in agricultural products and energy (by virtue of North Sea oil), and its fishers did not relish the thought of fishing vessels from Portugal and Spain gaining entry into their coastal waters.

When the three new members officially joined the EU on January 1, 1995, its population increased from 349 million to 370 million, and its GNP increased by 7 percent. The EU's economy was now 10 percent larger than that of the United States. And still more applicants—mostly in Eastern Europe—were waiting in the wings. The projected expansion raised questions even among previous champions of the EU. For one, the EU operated on the principle of unanimity, something much more difficult to achieve in a greatly expanded organization. Then there was the question of whether the new applicants could meet the stringent entrance requirements on environmental standards, low unemployment, low state operating deficits, a viable private economy, and solid democratic institutions. Moreover, financial assistance to these nations would strain the budgets of EU governments that were in the process of curtailing social programs for their own citizens.

Former champions of the EU were beginning to ask whether it should not concentrate on integration, i.e., the "deepening" of the union, before focusing on the uncertain consequences of "broadening." Among them were Helmut Schmidt, the former chancellor of West Germany, and Jacques Delors, the former president of the European Commission. Delors feared that with the expansion into Eastern Europe, the EU would become nothing more than a free-trade zone at the expense of the common social and political ideals, particularly as spelled out in the Maastricht agreement. The skeptics, however, lost the battle. In May 2004, the EU accepted ten additional members—Poland, the Czech Republic, Slovakia, Lithuania, Latvia, Estonia, Hungary, Malta, and the Greek part of Cyprus. Candidates for future membership include Bulgaria, Croatia, Romania, and Turkey. Turkey had sought membership for decades, but its application was always put on hold, in part because of the EU's demand that its members must be genuinely democratic. Moreover, many Europeans raised the question whether Turkey, with its Muslim population and located primarily in Asia Minor, was a suitable candidate to join a *European* union.

The new members brought the EU's population to 456 million (as compared to 290 million in the United States). Because of the relative poverty of the new members, the EU's per capita GDP dropped from $33,000 to $25,000 (as compared to nearly $38,000 in the United States).

After "broadening" its membership in May 2004, the EU returned to the complex task of "deepening" the integration of its members. In October 2004, the head of the twenty-five member states signed the European Constitution, scheduled to be ratified within two years. The first such transnational entity in history, it became in effect an attempt to create the "United States of Europe." Many Europeans, particularly the young "Generation E," already saw themselves as Europeans first and only second as citizens of their countries.

The constitution was steeped in the tradition of the Enlightenment and social democracy. It granted a host of civil liberties that closely represented the guarantees found in the Bill of Rights of the U.S. Constitution. Yet there were differences since the Europeans defined rights differently. The European

Constitution specifically stresses the need for "peace, justice and solidarity throughout the world." The right-to-life clause is a rejection of the death penalty. In the United States, the future of Social Security and social assistance is widely debated, but the Europeans see it as an inalienable "right," as is universal health care, which is yet a distant dream across the Atlantic.

## ☐ NAFTA: The North American Free Trade Agreement

During the early 1980s, the United States, to improve its global competitive position, took the lead in negotiating with Canada and Mexico a North American Free Trade Agreement (NAFTA). Its aim was to eventually establish a free-trade zone encompassing more than 400 million consumers.

The roots of NAFTA may be traced back to the mid-1980s, when Mexico decided to join the global economy and began to open its economy to foreign goods and investors. The movement toward that end began after Mexico had accrued a staggering foreign debt of over $100 billion. At that point its creditors, such as U.S. banks, urged the privatization of Mexico's state enterprises, some of which were sold off to the creditors. In 1986, Mexico joined GATT and, as a result, protective tariffs as high as 100 percent dropped to 20 percent or less. Foreign investments in Mexico began to increase. Between 1986 and 1991, U.S. investments increased from $5 billion to $11.6 billion and U.S. exports to Mexico rose from $12 billion to $33.2 billion. NAFTA was meant to eliminate by 2008 all tariffs among Mexico, the United States, and Canada (which already had a free-trade agreement with the United States, effective January 1, 1989). Among the goals of NAFTA were protecting the rights of North American investors in Mexico, opening Mexico to foreign capital, locking it into the global economy, and foreclosing radical options in the future.

In June 1990, Presidents George H. W. Bush of the United States and Carlos Salinas de Gortari of Mexico first proposed NAFTA, hailing it as a "powerful engine for economic development, creating new jobs and opening new markets." From the outset, an intense debate ensued over NAFTA's pros and cons. The business elites in all three countries, as well as all five living former U.S. presidents and all former secretaries of state, favored the agreement. Three hundred of the best-known U.S. economists signed a letter of support. In corporate boardrooms across Mexico, the United States, and Canada, support for NAFTA was nearly unanimous. To obtain congressional ratification of the agreement,[11] President Clinton needed to persuade the U.S. public of its benefits. He repeatedly promised that NAFTA would produce hundreds of thousands of new jobs in the United States—and high-skilled, well-paying ones at that.

There were those, however, who had misgivings about NAFTA. The rebellion in the state of Chiapas in Mexico began on the very day—January 1, 1994—that NAFTA went into effect, in part because the agreement made it possible for foreigners to purchase even more Mexican lands. Canadian and U.S. workers expressed concern that competing with lower-paid Mexican workers could lower their standards of living. Between 1989 and 1993, even before NAFTA, the free-trade agreement with Mexico had cost already more than 360,000 U.S. manufacturing jobs. The American Federation of Labor–Congress of Industrial Organizations (AFL-CIO) estimated that the United States would lose five hundred thousand manufacturing jobs to Mexico, where the average wage was one-seventh of that in the United States. An AFL-CIO official correctly predicted:

> What is unstated . . . is that you are adding 50 million low-wage Mexican workers, many of them skilled, to the United States labor force. They are not located across the Pacific, but in a country that is attached to ours, as if it were another state.[12]

The concerns of U.S. workers were not alleviated when, in October 1993, President Clinton asked large corporations to pledge that they would not outsource jobs to Mexico and found he had no takers. This came at a time when the Mexican state of Yucatan advertised that workers there could be hired for less than $1 an hour (including fringe benefits), an annual savings of $15,000 per worker.

NAFTA went into effect on January 1, 1994, at a time when the Mexican economy already suffered from the effects of a deep recession and when the government of President Ernesto Zedillo introduced drastic measures to pay off Mexico's obligations. The Mexicans had to swallow a very bitter pill. Zedillo raised taxes; clamped down on wages to make Mexican goods more competitive in the world economy (labor unions meekly accepted an 8 percent cut in real wages); raised interest rates to retain the capital of foreign investors; cut back on state-subsidized prices for basic items such as food, bus transportation, and gasoline; cut spending on social programs (such as pensions); and sold off state-owned enterprises—often at bargain prices to cronies of politicians. These measures went a long way to address the concerns of international investors. When Zedillo raised taxes in March 1995, Wall Street received the news enthusiastically, the U.S. stock market rose, and the peso gained 18 percent in value. These steps also produced a deeper recession in Mexico during which 1 million workers lost their jobs. Unemployment, fiscal austerity, and the decline of the value of the peso drove down the purchasing power of many Mexicans by as much as 50 percent. The middle class, which had hoped for a better day, was particularly hard hit.

NAFTA also drove down the wages of workers in the *maquiladoras,* the assembly plants established by foreign companies across the Mexican border. The *maquiladoras* were "restructured"—that is, wages were lowered and workers were dismissed—to become more competitive in the global economy. Mexican farmers, too, felt the impact of NAFTA when they suddenly found themselves facing competition from the efficient farmers in the United States and Canada who sent large volumes of processed meat, powdered milk, corn, and other commodities across the border.

NAFTA was an experiment that had never been tried before. It marked the first time that fully developed economies had agreed to eliminate all barriers with a low-wage, developing country that had a minimum wage of $4.20 a day, and in this regard it was very different from the EU.

NAFTA benefited primarily investors who were granted a set of new rights and privileges that promoted the relocation of factories. NAFTA was first and foremost *not* a free-trade agreement, but a free-investment agreement. It worked to the advantage of employers who, in a global deregulated free market, could move from country to country and purchase labor as a commodity at the lowest possible price.

After ten years of NAFTA, workers had little to cheer about. Investment in Mexico had quintupled from 1994 to 2001, but the influx of money had not translated into jobs. Moreover, the wages of Mexican manufacturing workers had dropped 13.5 percent. The Mexican government's minimum daily wage of $4.20 had not changed since 1994. In the United States, NAFTA was a contributing factor to the loss of nearly 880,000 jobs. Half a million U.S. workers entered government retraining programs to prepare them for lower-paying jobs.[13]

## ☐ Economic Regionalism in South America: MERCOSUR

In 1991, four nations in the southern part of South America—Argentina, Brazil, Uruguay, and Paraguay—established a trade bloc known as MERCOSUR, the Southern Cone Common Market. After Chile and Bolivia joined as associate members in 1996, MERCOSUR represented 210 million people, 60 percent of Latin America's aggregate GDP, and 40 percent of its total trade. Among its objectives were the elimination of tariffs among its members and the creation of a common external tariff for nonmembers. In December 1994, it began negotiations with NAFTA in the hope of creating a free-trade zone encompassing the thirty-four nations of the Western Hemisphere.

The creation of MERCOSUR, led by Brazil and Argentina, represented a marked improvement in the relations between those two countries, ending their traditional rivalry. It also advanced the cause of democracy in the region by calling for the suspension of commercial benefits to any member nation that deviated from democratic principles.

## ☐ ASEAN: Economic Regionalism in East Asia

ASEAN, the Association of Southeast Asian Nations, was formed in 1967 by Indonesia, Malaysia, the Philippines, Singapore, and Thailand, primarily for political and security purposes. Brunei joined in 1968 and, after the Indochina wars were over, Vietnam, Cambodia, Laos, and Burma were admitted. The diplomatic solidarity created by ASEAN in the 1970s served as a platform on which to build greater regional economic coordination. ASEAN sought agreements on regional tariff reduction and other forms of economic cooperation, such as joint industrial ventures and increased intra-ASEAN investment. With the exception of the Philippines, each of the original ASEAN nations had registered steady economic growth in the 1970s and early 1980s by shifting to the manufacture of export-oriented goods.

Japan established a strong economic bond with the fast-growing economies from South Korea through Taiwan to the Southeast Asian countries. Japan's dominant position in the region is sometimes referred to as the "yen bloc," but this did not represent a formal association such as a free-trade zone. There existed between Japan and the other "Asian tigers" a mutually beneficial relationship whereby Japan was their major source of investment, developmental aid, and technology, and they provided markets and natural resources for Japan, cheap labor for Japanese overseas industrial plants, and healthy returns on other investments. Western nations, especially the United States, found this bond a barrier to their own penetration of Asian markets.

In 1996, a number of nations bordering the Pacific Ocean formed the Asian Pacific Economic Cooperation (APEC). The representatives of the diverse member nations—including the United States, Canada, Japan, China, Mexico, Peru, and even Russia—met annually to discuss such economic issues as lowering tariffs. APEC represented two-thirds of the world's population, 60 percent of its output, and over 40 percent of world trade.

## ■ GLOBALIZATION: REMEDY OR CURSE?

In the mid-1990s, the term "globalization" became a buzzword to describe the growing integration of the international economy. For its proponents it was a call for free trade to facilitate the flow of goods and services extending to all parts of the world. Globalization was the new reality, it was argued; one had better get on board or be left behind. U.S. President Clinton was particularly fond of the globalization concept and became its leading champion. It became a gospel to be preached and practiced throughout the world as a cure-all. If all nations removed barriers to free trade it would result in economic growth, make more goods available at cheaper prices, and thus ultimately benefit everyone—consumers as well as businesses, poor nations as well as rich ones. "A rising tide," the promoters of globalization argued, "lifts all boats."

Globalization came to embrace a set of recommendations for economic reform, including deregulation (reduction of government controls of the economy), privatization (putting more state-owned property and operations under private ownership and management), austerity (reduction of government budgets), and trade liberalization (lowering of tariffs and other barriers to free trade). This formula, often referred to as the "Washington Consensus," was adopted by the IMF and the World Bank as the basis for their financial-assistance operations. It meant that nations applying for assistance had to meet stringent conditions and were required to undertake a stipulated set of painful reforms. In these nations, politicians and the public at large often complained, but they were assured that the pain was only temporary. That was certainly the message to the various Asian nations suffering from a serious economic crisis that began in mid-1997. It was touched off by international currency traders, who speculated on the value of one currency against another. Investors lost confidence in overvalued currencies—of Thailand, South Korea, Indonesia, Malaysia—which, in the course of currency speculation, lost much of their value. The 50 percent drop in the value of the Thai *bhat*, for example, meant that Thailand exported much cheaper goods for which it received less and less and imported more expensive goods. Thailand's economy declined by 12 percent in 1998. The slump was even more severe for Indonesia, where economic output declined by 19 percent.

The IMF, the World Bank, and various industrialized nations came quickly to the rescue of these countries with massive loans totaling over $100 billion to shore up the currencies. This was not merely a matter of generosity, for the loans were intended to keep the financial disaster from spreading beyond Asia. With the bailout came the famous IMF "discipline," calling for the recipient nations to undergo economic liberalization. The IMF's view was that these Asian economies had suffered from overvalued currencies, heavily indebted banks, excessive government control, and "crony capitalism" (close ties among politicians, big business, and bankers). Thus, a strong dose of deregulation, privatization, and market liberalization was called for. Led by South Korea, the failing Asian countries gradually pulled themselves out of recession.

As in other parts of the world, the IMF prescription for Asia ran into resentment. The IMF's solution conflicted with the Asian growth model borrowed mainly from Japan. Critics of the IMF maintained that imposing the U.S. model of capitalism—replete with unrestricted speculation by traders on the other side of the globe as far away as New York and Frankfurt—was part of the problem. Particularly harsh was the criticism of the leader of Malaysia, Mahatir, one of the most strident voices against globalization. He and others called for the retention of certain features of the "Asian" capitalist system, particularly its paternalistic concern for workers, restrictions on imported goods, and government direction of the economy.

The impact of globalization in Latin America was more negative than positive. In the case of Mexico, the demands for deregulation and privatization called for an economy entirely free of government involvement. The globalists (also known as neoliberals) sought a balanced budget, and to achieve it they slashed government spending by cutting out "expendable" items, which consisted all too often of social programs such as health care, education, and welfare. In the last two decades of the twentieth century many Latin American countries employed this approach to stimulate economic growth, but at the same time their poverty was not reduced. In Latin America and the Caribbean, the percentage of those who lived on an income of $1 a day remained constant in the years between 1987 and 1998.[14]

The persistence of poverty was not unique to Latin America. The World Bank spoke of it as "a global problem of huge proportions." It acknowledged that between 1990 and 1998, the number of people who lived below the international poverty line of less than $2 per day had risen from 2.1 billion to 2.8 billion—nearly half of the world's population—and that 1.2 billion existed on less than $1 per day.[15] In Africa, the most impoverished continent, many countries had an incredible 80 to 90 percent of the population living on less than $2 a day. And in the three most heavily populated Asian countries the percentage of people living on $2 a day or less were India (86 percent), Indonesia (66 percent), and China (53 percent.) The report also pointed out that the wealth of the world's richest two hunded *individuals* was greater than the combined income of the poorest 2 billion people. These shocking facts made it abundantly clear that a serious maldistribution of wealth existed, and that two decades of aggressive globalization had not solved the problem but, instead, had contributed to it.

One of the strongest opponents of globalization was organized labor. Unions protested against it on two fronts: on the one hand, it lamented the loss of jobs for workers in their own country (after large firms relocated abroad to take advantage of cheap labor), and on the other, they decried the exploitation of workers abroad and their lack of union rights. Labor leaders charged that globalization was most destructive in countries where independent unions did not exist and organizing was suppressed. Labor also sought a seat at board meetings where decisions were made affecting the lives of millions of workers.

Among the most persistent opponents of globalization and its drive for ever greater expansion were the environmentalists. Their focus was on pollution, a historic by-product of industrialization. In developing countries, in particular, factories polluted the water and air with little or no restriction. A good example was China, which after two decades of rapid industrialization had seven of the world's ten most polluted cities. Environmentalists also faulted industrialists for their voracious consumption of the earth's raw materials and their pollution of the land, water, and air. They insisted that business leaders make a commitment to environmentally sustainable growth.

In the past, environmentalists and union workers were generally on opposite sides, the former seeking to limit industrial growth and the latter seeking to preserve their jobs. Now they were being drawn a bit closer in a loose "blue-green" coalition of blue-collar workers and green activists.

The wrath of various antiglobalization groups—among them environmentalists, organized labor, human rights activists, and the "G-77" (representing the world's poorest nations)[16]—became manifest in huge protest demonstrations in November 1999 in Seattle on the occasion of a WTO conference. The protesters disrupted the conference and grabbed the headlines in their attempts to attract a global audience and publicize their cause.

At the end of the century, economists and First World politicians were split along the following lines. There were those who continued to believe in the missionary work of the World Bank and the IMF, namely that economic growth will eventually solve the problems of widespread human misery and the inequality of wealth distribution. And there were those who argued that unequal distribution of wealth was a major factor in causing poverty and that World Bank and IMF programs only compounded the problem. During the debate the once-solid World Bank–IMF consensus began to break down. Joseph Stiglitz, the World Bank's chief economist, who had been brought on board to write its annual *World Development Report* and previously had served as an economic adviser to President Clinton, broke ranks when he criticized the "Washington Consensus" and its austerity programs, deregulation, and privatization as the standard panacea for the developing world. The market alone, he insisted, would not abolish poverty. He used the 1977 East Asian economic crisis as an example, saying that it was the consequence of reckless decisions by private investors pressured by World Bank bureaucrats.

> The older men who staff the fund [IMF] . . . act as if they are shouldering Rudyard Kipling's white man's burden. IMF experts believe they are brighter, more educated, and less politically motivated than the economists of the countries they visit. In fact, the economic leaders of those countries are brighter or better-educated.[17]

The irony here is that Stiglitz and several of his co-workers at the World Bank moved toward the ideological camp of the protesters in the streets.

Another example of the reevaluation of the effects of globalism was the bestowing of the 1998 Nobel Prize for Economics, which traditionally had gone to the champions of the free market, to the Indian economist Amartya Sen, an expert on social welfare. The Nobel Prize committee explained that Sen "had restored an ethical dimension to the discussion of vital economic problems" by pointing out how little of the resources were allocated to the poorest members of society. Sen argued that poverty, not food shortages, caused famines. During the famine of 1974 in Bangladesh, for example, workers simply did not have the money to purchase the available food to feed their families.[18]

One of the great challenges for the twenty-first century was the question of how to distribute as equitably as possible the astonishing volume of wealth the world's economies produced.

## ■ THE ORGANIZATION OF
## PETROLEUM EXPORTING COUNTRIES

Adam Smith had argued that the free market worked best when regulated by the benevolent "invisible hand" of the market. The self-regulating market, however, has not always worked as anticipated. The oil shocks of the 1970s are a case in point. In the fall of 1973, the world suddenly woke up to find that the supply of petroleum products did not meet the demand. Since 1945, oil had become increasingly important as an energy source vital to industry, transportation, and heating. The unprecedented oil shortages of the 1970s had an immediate and long-term destabilizing effect on economies all over the world, on developing as well as industrialized nations. The sharp rise in the price of oil had many ramifications in business, industry, and international trade, such as reduced industrial production and higher retail prices of food, industrial goods, and transportation.

The Organization of Petroleum Exporting Countries (OPEC)—the association responsible for the shortages—argued that there was only a finite amount of fossil fuel—particularly petroleum—and that it was being consumed much too fast. Politicians across the globe hastened to legislate remedies such as energy conservation, diversification of energy sources, and reducing dependence on foreign oil. A second shortage in 1979 was not as shocking or severe as the first, but it too fed the feelings of uncertainty and insecurity.

The oil shortages had been artificially created by OPEC, led by Saudi Arabia and the shah of Iran, and by the Western oil companies. In the 1970s, the thirteen members of OPEC included all of the oil-exporting states of the Middle East—Saudi Arabia, Iran, Iraq, the United Arab Emirates, Qatar, and Kuwait. The rest were the African states of Algeria, Libya, Nigeria, and Gabon; the two South American nations of Venezuela and Ecuador; and Indonesia. Equally important were the oil-exporting nations that did not belong to OPEC: the Soviet Union (among the world's leading exporters of oil in the 1970s and 1980s), Mexico, Great Britain, the United States, and Canada.

When OPEC conspired to limit the supply of oil, the result was a fifteen-fold increase—from $2 a barrel to about $30, at one point even to $40—in the price of crude oil by the end of the decade. During the 1970s, OPEC managed to dictate the price of oil by virtue of the fact that in 1979 it controlled 63.4 percent of the world's market.

OPEC dominance, however, began to weaken during the early 1980s, when a global oil glut was in the making and the bottom of the oil market began to drop out. The surplus was the result of conservation, a worldwide economic recession (which lessened the demand for all fuels), the discovery of new deposits (on the North Slope of Alaska and in the North Sea, as well as the Mexican contribution), a worldwide increase in production once prices rose, and the cold, hard fact that even during the shortages at the pump there had always been a surplus of oil. By 1984, OPEC's share of oil on the global market dropped to 42.8 percent; by 1985, it fell to 30 percent. In 1985, as its market share continued to decline, OPEC members, desperate for oil revenues, began to break ranks by surreptitiously selling more than their allotted quotas. The most important task before OPEC in the mid-1980s, therefore, was to reestablish discipline among its members and thus to regain the means to set the price for crude oil. But this proved to be a difficult task.

The 1980s brought renewed competition for the petrodollar, a return to the laws of the marketplace, and with it an end to the artificial oil shortages. The laws of supply and demand damaged not only OPEC, but also the prospects of several nations that had banked on a prosperity based on the sale of a scarce commodity to a world addicted to the consumption of petroleum products. As an overabundance of supply drove down the price of oil, countries such as Mexico, Venezuela, and Nigeria suffered a large decrease in oil earnings and became saddled with large foreign debts.

For years, Mexico (although not a member of OPEC) sought to follow OPEC's pricing levels, but in the summer of 1985, it began to establish its own pricing policy in direct confrontation with OPEC. It lowered the price of a barrel of crude oil to about $24. The Soviet Union followed Mexico's lead, thus placing additional pressures on OPEC. OPEC, in its turn, tried to cut back on production to reestablish an artificial scarcity, but with little impact on prices. OPEC output declined to about 14.5 million barrels per day, the group's lowest level of production in twenty years. Saudi Arabia, the linchpin of OPEC, in order to maintain the level of the price of oil, dropped its production to 2.3 million barrels a day (almost half of its quota allotted by OPEC), its lowest level since 1967. At the meetings of OPEC oil ministers in the summer of 1985, the debates centered on a "Hobson's choice," whether to cut prices or production. In the end, OPEC wound up doing both. No event underscored OPEC's dilemma as sharply as Ecuador's defection in September 1992, when it became the first member to leave the organization. For Ecuador, membership in OPEC, with its quotas for its members, had become pointless. Without OPEC restraints, Ecuador's oil industry hoped to double its output.

In June 1998, the price for a barrel of oil dropped to rock bottom, to $10, the result of a number of factors such as overproduction and a steep decline in demand caused by the Asian financial crisis of the year before. OPEC's income in 1998 of $80 billion—in real terms—was its lowest ever. To recover its losses, OPEC, supported by such nonmembers as Norway, Russia, and Mexico, cut production at a time of renewed rising demand and thus managed to drive up the price of a barrel of oil to $38 by the fall of 2000. Still, in real terms, the price for a barrel of oil was less than half of what it had been during the 1970s.

In 2004, a number of factors, notably China's rapidly increasing demand for oil, pushed the price past the benchmark of $50 dollars a barrel for oil. That price, however, was still at 62 percent—in constant dollars—of the cost during 1979–1980. The spike in oil prices, however, was not the result of a speculative bubble—that is, buyers of oil futures driving up the price—but a reflection that the world's oil production and reserves had reached a plateau that promised to keep prices high.[19]

## ■ INSURMOUNTABLE DEBTS

During the 1980s, Third World debts mounted higher and higher, mainly a consequence of the sudden increase of available money in the form of "petrodollars"—money invested in Western banks by oil-rich nations. By the mid-1980s, the combined debt of Africa and Latin America rose to more than $500 billion—Mexico and Brazil owing around $100 billion each. A default by any one of the major nations of these regions threatened to trigger an economic crisis with worldwide repercussions. Default threatened bank failures and the slowdown of international trade, perhaps even a global recession, one certain to produce extraordinary political fallout, particularly in the regions the hardest hit, namely the Third World.

Third World countries at times raised the specter of default, but they were at pains to avoid such a drastic measure. They sought, instead, to meet their obligations. When, in early 1987, Brazil announced a halt in its foreign debt payments, its government was careful to spell out that this was a temporary emergency measure and eventually hoped to find a solution. Similarly, in March 1987, after Ecuador was hit with a devastating earthquake that cut its main oil pipeline from the interior to the coast, it temporarily suspended its foreign debt payments. Third World leaders well understood that a declaration of bankruptcy was no solution. It would cut their nations adrift, incapable of borrowing additional funds, and even facing economic retaliation.

The staggering Latin American debt gave the Communist Fidel Castro of Cuba the opportunity to take center stage as the region's elder statesman. In 1985, Castro spoke several times of the need to create a "debtors' cartel" to resolve Latin America's debt obligations. Oddly, Castro, the revolutionary, urged a resolution of the crisis, with the help of the U.S. government and the Western capitalist banks, for the purpose of avoiding the repercussions of widespread unrest. Castro wanted the cancellation and the mitigation of debts to prevent revolution. He pointed to the example of the Soviet Union, which repeatedly had written off its assistance to Cuba.[20]

In the summer of 1985, Peru's newly elected president, Alan García, declared that his nation would limit its foreign debt payments to 10 percent of its export earnings. This was the first time a debtor nation had tried to link payments to the ability to export. When, in early 1987, Brazil and Ecuador suspended their payments, they took as their model Peru's argument. Such a solution was an attractive alternative to the impossible payments and domestic austerity measures the IMF demanded.

Donor nations were forced to begin to grapple with the prospect that some debts could not be recovered. A number of nations (such as Canada, Finland, Germany, the Netherlands, Norway, Sweden, and Great Britain) converted loans to grants. France decided to write off its $2.4 billion in loans to the thirty-five poorest African countries, and Belgium canceled debts of $200 million to thirteen African countries. The amount of money involved, however, was relatively small and affected only government-to-government loans.[21] Private banks, however, were in no mood to write off the massive—and unrecoverable—loans to Third World nations.

The end of the Cold War made possible a reevaluation of what had gone wrong with international monetary lending practices, why some countries were showing little if any economic growth and were therefore unable to repay their debts. In 1991, the internal World Bank study "Managing Development: The Governance Dimension" concluded that dishonest and inefficient governments were at the core of the problem. Britain's Ministry of Overseas Development came to a similar conclusion and as a result began to shift substantial amounts of money to train efficient local officials in Commonwealth nations such as Zambia, Ghana, and India in an effort to eliminate widespread corruption, a by-product of the Cold War when officials were permitted to skim off aid in exchange for loyalty to the donor. The ministry also increased its funding of private organizations in an attempt to bypass corrupt government officials. It gave as an example the British Red Cross's contributions to health care on the local level. The World Bank called nongovernmental organizations "eyes and ears," capable of providing a system of checks and balances of corrupt governments and of monitoring the effective uses of aid.[22]

Debtor nations, therefore, took steps necessary to meet their obligations. Yet these measures demanded putting one's economic house in order. In essence, it meant the raising of taxes, which could be achieved by various means: the elimination of subsidies on food, sales taxes on fuel, a limitation on imports (particularly luxury items), and the devaluation of money. Such steps, however, promised inevitable political repercussions, for they entailed the lowering of the standard of living for large segments of the population. Resentment was particularly great when the price of meeting international obligations was an increase in the cost of food. Public outbursts and riots in the streets shook governments that sought to administer such bitter medicine. Sudan, Tunisia, the Dominican Republic, Jamaica, Bolivia, and Argentina all experienced the politically dangerous consequences of such actions. It was little wonder that Egyptian president Hosni Mubarak referred to the IMF as the "International Misery Fund."

The Third World was caught between two unpalatable choices: (1) default and with it the potential of economic ruination, which in turn threatened to produce political unrest; or (2) compliance and political unrest. Either way, the Third World was not a place to look to for political stability, which can exist only hand-in-hand with economic progress.

The mid-1980s witnessed another phenomenon that compounded the debtors' plight, the flight of Third World capital. A case in point was Mexico, where a high rate of inflation had undermined the value of money in Mexican banks. Depositors, therefore, sought safer havens—Western Europe and the United States—where the rate of inflation had been brought under control. Since the mid-1980s, the Third World changed from a net importer of capital to a net exporter, a trend that only served to widen the gap between the rich and the poor nations, the North and the South.

The reassessment of reckless lending practices to poor nations scarcely able to repay the loans brought the bankers back to the fiscal conservatism of the earlier days of the World Bank when its second president, Eugene Robert Black (1949–1962) insisted that in the struggle against Communist influence, investments would have their greatest impact only if they made "the greatest possible contribution, raising living standards and opening opportunities for further investment." Black was not interested in providing money for questionable projects simply to bring a leader of a Third World nation into the Western ideological camp. He insisted above all that money must be lent for projects that created income, which then could be used to repay the loans. Black's fiscal conservatism made possible the lending of billions of dollars by the World Bank without a default, a basic lesson the lending spree of the 1980s forced international lending institutions to relearn.[23]

Throughout the 1990s many developing nations sank much deeper into debt, and the mounting debt continued to be a drag on their economic development (see Table 17.3). Between 1970 and 1980, their debt grew more than tenfold, from $59 million to $603 billion; by 1990, it had more than doubled, and in the period 1990–1997, it grew at an average annual rate of over $100 billion to reach the figure of $2.1 trillion. Moreover, in the years between 1985 and 1999, the Third World's share of the world GNP declined steadily: in 1985 it was 31 percent; in 1989, 28 percent; and in 1999, 21 percent.[24]

Zambia was a case in point of a poor nation trying to repay its external debt. The IMF and World Bank political and financial leaders in donor nations worked out a program for Zambian debt relief under the international Heavily Indebted Poor Countries (HIPC) initiative. Under this plan the IMF and World Bank would restructure a nation's debt, providing an additional infusion of money, but only on strict conditions. The IMF and World Bank insisted on "structural adjustments," which meant that the Zambian government drastically cut its expenditures.

Under the HIPC initiative, Zambia was required to increase its debt payments from $70 million a year to $200 million. The additional outflow of $130 million meant the curtailment of vital social services. The World Bank then praised Zambia's "reformed" health care system as a model for the rest of Africa. The "reforms," however, consisted of slashing state subsidies, which did eliminate long lines in the hospitals but only because people who could not afford admission were dying at home. The reforms also meant the reduction of government payrolls and the privatization of state

**Table 17.3  Foreign Debt Increase of Selected Nations, 1990–1998
(in US$ billions)**

| Country | 1990 | 1998 | Percent of 1998 GNP |
|---|---|---|---|
| Algeria | 27 | 30 | 66 |
| Argentina | 62 | 144 | 52 |
| Brazil | 119 | 232 | 29 |
| China | 55 | 154 | 15 |
| Indonesia | 69 | 150 | 169 |
| Malaysia | 14 | 44 | 69 |
| Mexico | 104 | 159 | 39 |
| Nigeria | 33 | 30 | 74 |
| Philippines | 30 | 47 | 66 |
| Poland | 49 | 47 | 28 |
| Romania | 1 | 9 | 23 |
| Russia | 59 | 183 | 62 |
| South Korea | 34 | 139 | 43 |
| Turkey | 49 | 102 | 49 |
| Thailand | 28 | 86 | 79 |

*Source*: World Bank, *World Development Report, 2000/2001*, pp. 314–315.

enterprises. The result was increased unemployment. Children, particularly girls, were withdrawn from school and put to work to augment their families' income; primary-school enrollment dropped from 96 percent to 77 percent. The reforms also indirectly contributed to malnutrition, an increase in preventable disease, and a decrease in life expectancy; in Zambia, 20 percent of the children died before they reached the age of five.[25] It must be added that the economic and social disaster was not the making of the IMF and World Bank alone. Zambia's dilemma was compounded by such problems as government corruption, political instability, and human rights abuses.

By the end of the century, debtor nations found lenders somewhat more responsive to their pleas for greater debt relief, and on more lenient terms. A few nations took the first halting steps. In June 1999, Japan wrote off $3.3 billion of its $8.2 billion in loans to some of the world's most impoverished countries. Several months later, at a global summit in Cologne, Germany, world leaders pledged to forgive some of the debts of at least twenty nations.

## ■ GLOBAL ENVIRONMENTALISM

Toward the end of the twentieth century, industrialized nations became concerned with the issue of climate change caused by global warming. Records showed that the earth's temperatures had been steadily rising. The twentieth century was the warmest on record, its last decade setting new records. The chief cause was the emission of carbon dioxide, mainly from the exhaust pipes of the ever-increasing number of motor vehicles and other "greenhouse gases" that were polluting the atmosphere and trapping the planet's heat. A number of scientists forecast a temperature increase of 6 degrees Fahrenheit by 2100, and speculated that the effects of such change could be catastrophic, leading to widespread droughts and desertification, more frequent devastating storms, and the rise of the oceans by as much as 3 feet, submerging heavily populated and cultivated lands.

In 1988, the United States, the world's largest polluter, responsible for one-quarter of global carbon dioxide emissions, proposed an international panel to investigate scientific evidence of climate change. The Netherlands, Germany, the United Kingdom, and Japan took the next step by setting targets for reducing carbon dioxide emissions, something the United States opposed. The first agreement to cut back on emissions came out of the international conference on climate change in Kyoto, Japan, in October 1997, with 150 nations represented.

The Kyoto Protocol called for the reduction of emissions by at least 5 percent below 1990 levels by 2010, with demonstrable progress to be achieved by 2005. Developing countries received exemptions from the mandatory emissions cuts. Over European objections, the Kyoto Protocol also included the U.S.-sponsored plan for international trading of emission quotas. This scheme allowed U.S. factories to obtain the right to continue emitting pollutants by "buying the rights" from countries that did not fully use their quotas. Europeans and environmentalists objected to this as a giant loophole allowing the United States to escape its obligations. French president Jacques Chirac scolded the United States for ducking its responsibility, adding that "no country can elude its share of the collective effort."[26]

Meanwhile, environmentalists wrung their hands and lamented the meager progress toward slowing global warming. But the news soon got worse. The newly elected U.S. president, George W. Bush, bluntly announced in April 2001 his administration's flat rejection of the Kyoto Protocol, claiming that its provisions would be harmful to the U.S. economy. The world's number-one polluter just picked up his marbles and left the game, and left all the other global players aghast. Nonetheless, the Kyoto treaty finally went officially into effect when in November 2004, Russia ratified it, the 127th nation to do so. With the world's insatiable appetite for machines driven by internal-combustion engines undiminished, however, and with the world's leading polluter on the sidelines, there was little hope that global warming could be halted in the short term.

■ **RECOMMENDED READINGS**

Dinan, Desmond, ed. *Encyclopedia of the European Union.* Updated ed. Boulder, Colo.: Lynne Rienner Publishers, 2000.
    A comprehensive reference work on the European Union.

Frank, Thomas. *One Market Under God: Extreme Capitalism, Market Populism, and the End of Economic Democracy.* New York: Doubleday, 2000.
A critical view of the negative consequences of globalization.

Galeano, Eduardo. *Upside Down: A Primer for the Looking-Glass World.* New York: Henry Holt, 2000.
By a Guatemalan writer whose book *Open Veins of Latin America* (1971) sent shock waves across Latin America. He was denounced, arrested, banned, and eventually exiled. *Upside Down* tells the story of globalization from the perspective of the South.

Garten, Jeffrey E. *A Cold Peace: America, Japan, Germany, and the Struggle for Supremacy.* New York: Oxford University Press, 1992.
Examines the potential for economic cooperation and conflict among the three nations as the world economy grew ever more interdependent.

Grubb, Michael, et al. *The Kyoto Protocol: A Guide and Assessment.* London: The Royal Institute of International Affairs, 1999.

Harrison, Paul. *Inside the Third World: The Anatomy of Poverty.* 2d ed. New York: Penguin, 1981.
A useful introduction by an English journalist to the realities of the Third World.

Kuttner, Robert. *The End of Laissez-Faire: National Purpose and Global Economy After the Cold War.* New York: Knopf, 1991.
Argues that since Japan and the EU have close government-business cooperation, strategic economic planning, and managed trade, the United States must also develop a national strategy.

Reich, Robert B. *The Work of Nations: Preparing Ourselves for 21st Century Capitalism.* New York: Knopf, 1991.
A provocative postulation of the seamless global economy in which the national competition and the nationality of business no longer have importance.

Reid, T. R. *The United States of Europe: The New Superpower and the End of American Supremacy.* New York: Penguin, 2004.

Sampson, Anthony. *The Sovereign State of ITT.* 2d ed. New York: Fawcett, 1974.
The history of an international corporation and its reach throughout the globe.

Sen, Amartya. *Inequality Reexamined.* Cambridge, Mass.: Harvard University Press, 1995.
One of a number of books by the recipient of the 1998 Nobel Prize for Economics. For decades, Sen has concentrated on the downside of globalization, on its impact on those left behind.

Stiglitz, Joseph E.. *Globalization and Its Discontents.* New York: Norton, 2002.
By a former high-ranking economist at the World Bank, a critique of how the major institutions of globalization failed many of the developing nations.

Stiglitz, Joseph E., and Shahid Yusuf, eds. *Rethinking the East Asian Miracle.* New York: Oxford University Press, 2000.
A collection of articles on the pitfalls of globalization.

Yergin, Daniel. *The Prize: The Epic Quest for Oil, Money, and Power.* New York: Simon and Schuster, 1990.
The definitive account of the geostrategic quest to control the world's supply of oil.

## ☐ OPEC

Blair, John M. *The Control of Oil.* New York: Pantheon Books, 1976.
An analysis of the large oil companies' control of supply and market.

Emerson, Steven. *The American House of Saud: The Secret Petrodollar Connection.*
Danbury, Conn.: Franklin Watts, 1985.
    An account of the link between the U.S. oil companies and Saudi Arabia.
Lacey, Robert. *The Kingdom: Arabia and the House of Sa'ud.* New York: Avon, 1983.

## ■ NOTES

1. The sole exceptions were Cuba and North Korea.

2. By the time of its dissolution in 1995, GATT membership stood at 125 nations.

3. The twelve members of the European Council and their years of admission, listed in order of size of GNP in the early 1990s: West Germany (1958), France (1958), Italy (1958), Great Britain (1973), Spain (1986), Netherlands (1958), Belgium (1958), Denmark (1973), Greece (1981), Portugal (1986), Ireland (1973), and Luxembourg (1958).

4. Belgium and Luxemburg had a common currency. A citizen of an EC country on a journey to all member nations might lose 47 percent of his money changing it into local currencies. Stanley Hoffmann, "The European Community and 1992," *Foreign Affairs* (fall 1989), p. 28.

5. Andrew Moravcsik, "Negotiating the Single Act: National Interests and Conventional Statecraft in the European Community," Cambridge, Mass., Harvard University, Center for European Studies, Working Paper Series 21, n.d., pp. 14–15.

6. The figures are those issued in December 1989 by the Organization for Economic Cooperation and Development (OECD); Hobert Rowen, "Bonn Next in Line as Power Center," *Washington Post,* January 7, 1990, pp. H1, H8.

7. U.S. Commerce Department, Associated Press, "Trade Deficit Surges to All-Time High in 1999," *New York Times,* February 18, 2000; Associated Press, "September Trade Deficit Hits New High," *Baltimore Sun,* November 22, 2000, pp. C1–C3. "Record U.S. Trade Deficit in 2003," www.CBSNews.com, February 13, 2003.

8. "Der Krieg findet längst statt" ("The War Began Long Ago"), *Der Spiegel,* December 6, 13, and 20, 1989.

9. *Berliner Zeitung,* June 5, 1992, in "Pressestimmen zum dänischen EG-Referendum," *Deutschland Nachrichten,* June 5, 1992, p. 3.

10. Conor Cruise O'Brien, "Pursuing a Chimera: Nationalism at Odds with the Idea of a Federal Europe," *Times Literary Supplement,* March 13, 1992, pp. 3–4.

11. NAFTA was not a treaty (which the Senate would have to ratify by a two-thirds vote) but a "trade agreement," which needed a majority vote from both houses of Congress.

12. Cited by Clyde N. Farnsworth, "What an Earlier Trade Pact Did up North," and Louis Uchitelle, "NAFTA and Jobs: In a Numbers War, No One Can Count," *New York Times,* November 14, 1993, p. 1E.

13. David Bacon, "NAFTA's Legacy—Profits and Poverty," *San Francisco Chronicle,* January 14, 2004; James Cox, "10 years ago, NAFTA was born," *USA Today,* December 30, 2003.

14. World Bank, *World Development Report 2000/2001: Attacking Poverty* (New York: Oxford University Press, 2000), p. 23.

15. Ibid., pp. vi, 3–6, 23, 280–282; Joseph E. Stiglitz, *Globalization and Its Discontents* (New York: Norton, 2002), p. 259.

16. G-77 is in contrast to another group, the G-7, representing seven of the leading capitalist nations. (With Russia's addition, it became the G-8.)

17. Stiglitz and Summers cited in Doug Henwood, "Stiglitz and the Limits of Reform," *The Nation,* October 2, 2000, pp. 20, 22. The man who fired Stiglitz and Kanbur was another former chief economist at the World Bank (1991–1993) and subsequently U.S. treasury secretary, Lawrence Summers. As treasury secretary, Summers thought that Africa was "vastly underpolluted" and that "the economic logic behind dumping of a load of toxic waste in the lowest wage country was impeccable."

18. Wire reports, "Expert on Welfare Who Studied Famine Wins Economic Nobel," *Baltimore Sun,* October 14, 1998, p. 14. See also Amartya Sen, *Poverty and Famines: An Essay on Entitlement and Deprivation* (New York: Oxford University Press, 1981.)

19. Matt Piotrowski, "Oil Sets New Records: 'This Is Not a Speculative Bubble,'" *Oil Daily,* Energy Intelligence Group, October 11, 2004.

20. Joseph B. Treaster, "Cuban Meeting Stokes Emotions on Latin Debt," *New York Times,* August 1, 1985, p. D1.

21. *Sub-Saharan Africa: From Crisis to Sustainable Growth: A Long-Term Perspective Study* (Washington, D.C.: World Bank, 1989), pp. 176–179.

22. Barbara Crosette, "Givers of Foreign Aid Shifting Their Methods," *New York Times,* February 23, 1992, p. 2E.

23. "Eugene R. Black Dies at 93; Ex-President of World Bank," *New York Times,* February 21, 1992, p. A19.

24. Tahir Beg, "Globalization, Development and Debt-Management: A Third World Perspective," http://www.balanced-development.org.

25. World Bank, *World Bank Development Report, 2000/2001,* p. 315; Oxfam International press release, September 18, 2000, "HIPC Leaves Poor Countries Heavily in Debt: New Analysis," http://www.oxfaminternational.org; Mark Lynas, "Letters from Zambia," *The Nation,* February 14, 2000.

26. Matt Daily, "U.S. Offers to Break Deadlock in Climate Talks," Reuters, November 20, 2000, *AOL News Profiles.*

# 18

The Soviet Union: From Perestroika
to Retreat from Empire

After Leonid Brezhnev came to power in the Soviet Union in 1964, he showed little taste for reform. Innovations in the economic sector that his predecessor, Nikita Khrushchev, had introduced were quickly shelved. Under Brezhnev, the Soviet Union entered a seventeen-year-long "era of stagnation" that only a change in leadership could reverse. In 1979, the Soviet Union's ministries ceased publishing statistics in order not to reveal the fact that the country was falling further behind the West in productivity, health care, and the standard of living. In March 1985, the Communist Party elected as general secretary Mikhail Gorbachev, who immediately took a number of highly publicized steps to transform the Soviet Union.

Gorbachev advocated a new openness, *glasnost,* giving Soviet citizens and officials alike the freedom to discuss not only the strengths but also the weaknesses of society. This approach was reflected in *Pravda,* the newspaper of the Communist Party, which began to cover disasters such as the nuclear accident at Chernobyl, floods, and collisions between ships in the Black Sea, corruption, cover-ups, shoddy workmanship, police abuse, Stalin's impact on society, and so on. Motion pictures never before shown to the public played to sell-out crowds. The Gorbachev revolution was on its way.

## ■ GORBACHEV'S "NEW THINKING"

When the Communist Party turned to Mikhail Gorbachev, the Soviet public and the West knew little about him, although in December 1984 he had made a successful appearance on the world stage during his visit to London where he had behaved unlike previous Soviet visitors. Khrushchev's visit in 1955 had turned sour when he reminded his hosts ominously of his country's potentially devastating nuclear arsenal. Gorbachev spoke, instead, of the need to disarm and reminded the British of their wartime alliance with the Soviet Union and their losses at Coventry. Instead of the customary visit to Karl Marx's grave at Highgate Cemetery, Gorbachev visited Westminster Abbey. Margaret Thatcher, Britain's conservative prime minister, concluded: "I like him. We can do business with him."

Gorbachev soon caused another stir with his speech in February 1985, in which he declared that the Soviet Union was in need of a radical transformation. "Paper shuffling, an addiction to fruitless meetings, windbaggery and formalism" would no longer do.[1] He proved to be a careful reformer who understood that politics is the art of the possible. In his first speech as general secretary of the party, he placated the right wing with his reaffirmation of the old values. As time went by, however, he showed that he intended to reorganize the system. The Soviet Union, he declared, must undergo a radical *perestroika,* or restructuring. To that end, "new thinking" was required.

Among Gorbachev's targets were the centrally planned industrial system and the collective farms Stalin had introduced beginning in the late 1920s. He ended the long and debilitating conflict between the state and organized religion, ended the isolation of his country's intellectuals, invited those who had been expelled from the Soviet Union to return to their native soil, sent an unprecedented number of Soviet citizens abroad, permitted the sale of Western publications, forced the Soviet Union's conservative historians to come to grips with their history, and broke the party's monopoly on political power. He also redefined the Soviet Union's position vis-à-vis China, Eastern Europe, the West, and the Third World and took the Soviet army out of Afghanistan. In sum, Gorbachev turned the science of "Kremlinology" on its head; he did what had been thought no leader in the Kremlin could or would even try to do.

Gorbachev called for an open and honest discussion, "to call things by their name." To this end, he had to give society, not just the party, a voice. Glasnost, from the Russian for "voice," therefore, became the first order of business. The most severe test of glasnost came in April 1986 when an atomic reactor in Chernobyl, in the north of the Ukrainian Republic, suffered a meltdown and an explosion, spewing radioactive matter into the Belorussian Republic, Scandinavia, down into Germany, and as far south as Italy. Soviet technology was contaminating what Gorbachev earlier had called "our common European home." The recognition of mistakes, he said, was the "best medicine against arrogance and complacency." But for the first nineteen days after Chernobyl, no acknowledgment of the disaster came out of Moscow. When Gorbachev finally spoke on national television, he admitted that a nuclear plant had burned out of control.

Gorbachev used Chernobyl to weaken the conservative wing of the party, the chief obstacle to perestroika. Gorbachev repeatedly used political, natural, and man-made disasters—on the surface, setbacks—to his advantage.

Artists and writers quickly tested the limits of glasnost. The consequence was a veritable flood of works that had been created years before "for the drawer," waiting to see the light of day. Among them were Anatoli Rybakov's *Children of the Arbat,* a novel set in 1933–1934 at the beginning of Stalin's terror, and films such as *Our Armored Train,* a critical analysis of the legacy of the Stalin era.

The acid test of glasnost would be how the Kremlin treated the writings of the exiled Alexander Solzhenitsyn, whose novel *One Day in the Life of Ivan Denisovich* had been the literary sensation of 1962. Khrushchev had used this exposé of the prison system to further discredit Stalin. In his later writings, however, Solzhenitsyn, in his three-volume *Gulag Archipelago,* laid the blame for the prison system squarely at the feet of the revered Lenin—whose stature in the Soviet Union was no less than that of a saint. Gorbachev and his Politburo initially opposed the publication of *Gulag Archipelago* since it undermined "the foundation on which our present life rests." But public pressure, expressed in thousands of letters and telegrams, had an unprecedented impact on Soviet cultural history. In June 1989, Gorbachev told his Politburo that the decision whether to publish Solzhenitsyn should be made by editors, not the party. After an absence of twenty-five years, Solzhenitsyn was reintroduced to Soviet readers.[2]

Historians generally wanted no part of Gorbachev's "new thinking." Early 1988, however, saw the purge of the editorial boards of the leading historical journals. The lead article in the February 1988 issue of *Voprosy istorii* (Problems of History) announced that the time had come to discuss events hitherto taboo, including Stalin's purges of the party, the "tragedy" of collectivization in Kazakhstan, and the nationality problem. The journals participated in the political rehabilitation of Khrushchev and victims of Stalin's purges and went so far as to publish Leon Trotsky's essay, "The Stalin School of Falsification of History." In the huge Lenin Library in Moscow, "new" books were made available to readers—books that had been published decades earlier and then suppressed.[3]

Most intellectuals, freed from the constraints of the past, expressed distinctly liberal, Western values. They supported Memorial, an organization in remembrance of those who had fallen victim to Stalin's purges. But glasnost also gave writers of an anti-Western, antiliberal persuasion a voice and showed that the nativist tradition still ran deep. Their organization, Pamiat (Remembrance), recalled history differently from Memorial. The Russian National-Patriotic Memory Front, Pamiat's formal name, did not consider the Stalinist legacy to be the nation's source of difficulty; instead, it blamed Zionists. In Pamiat's view, Stalin had played the role of the good tsar, terrible but righteous, who had punished the wicked and brought the nation to its military and industrial power.

☐ *Industry*

When Gorbachev first began to speak of perestroika, he intended a rapid process of reform. It became clear, however, that the process of reconstruction would be extraordinarily difficult, compounded by the fact that many workers and managers of factories and collective farms looked upon the Gorbachev revolution with skepticism, even resentment. They had learned to fulfill the plan on paper and saw few reasons to embrace a new approach that threatened to punish those who failed. In the mid-1960s, Premier Alexei Kosygin had sought to reorganize the economy so that factories would have to sink or swim on their own. In 1965, "accountability" became the watchword of the Kosygin-led reforms. The conservatives, however, who had their hands on the political levers, soon brought this experiment to a halt.

The majority of the population expected the state to solve their problems; this was an attitude that had seeped into their blood. When Gorbachev suggested that government subsidies—on bread, milk, apartments, education, health care, transportation, and so on—come to an end and spoke of closing down inefficient factories and raising prices, he hit a raw nerve. His comments produced a resistance to an economic perestroika that promised not only higher prices but also unemployment. The relative security of the past began to give way to an uncertain future.

### □ Farming

In his speech on November 3, 1987, at the seventieth anniversary of the October Revolution, Gorbachev—under pressure from conservatives—still

Soviet leader Mikhail Gorbachev and U.S. president Ronald Reagan in Geneva for their first summit meeting, November 19, 1985. (AP/Wide World Photos)

defended the necessity of Stalin's collectivization. In October 1988, however, in a televised address, he proposed radical changes. Farmers, he
insisted, must once again become "masters of their land." Five months
later, in March 1989, Gorbachev took his case to the party's decisionmaking body, the Central Committee, where he summarized the failure of
Soviet agriculture. Between 1946 and 1953, Stalin had bled the farmers by
setting low farm prices. Khrushchev and Brezhnev subsequently had spent
huge sums to improve the productivity and eliminate waste on the collective and the state farms, but to little avail. The time had come to abandon
decisionmaking at the top and to learn from experimentation, and from the
United States, China, India, and the Green Revolution.[4]

Gorbachev did not manage, however, to abolish the collective farms.
His conservative opponents in the Politburo were strong enough to prevent
such a drastic measure. But on April 9, 1989, the government did pass a law
permitting private individuals and collectives to lease land, buildings, min-
eral deposits, small factories, and machines from the state "for up to 50
years and more." TASS, the Soviet news agency, underlined that the law
was intended to promote the establishment of family farms.

## ☐  The Role of the Party

When Gorbachev established a new legislature, the Congress of People's
Deputies, which held its first session in May 1989, not only were the majority of the delegates freely elected but many were non-Communists. Moreover, the delegates had to compete for office. The weakness of the party
became glaringly apparent when numerous party candidates failed to receive
a majority of votes, although they ran unopposed.

Gorbachev, however, did not yet go so far as to support the abolition of
Article 6 of the 1977 Constitution, which granted the Communist Party a
monopoly of political power. He still lacked the votes in the party's Central
Committee to do so. The sentiment to scrap Article 6 ran deep, however.
During his January 1990 visit to Vilnius, Lithuania, where the republic's
Communist Party had already legalized a multiparty system and elections,
Gorbachev stated that "we should not be afraid [of a multiparty system], the
way the devil fears incense."[5] In early February 1990, during an extraordinary session of the party's Central Committee, after three days of debates,
the party did the unthinkable when it legalized opposition parties. Lenin's
legacy, the Communist Party as the sole driving force in the Soviet Union,
became the casualty of the "February Revolution" of 1990.

## ☐  The Nationality Question

Gorbachev's emphasis on glasnost set into motion a discussion of the
Soviet Union's nationality question. The Russians made up 145 million of

the total population of 282 million people; of the other Slavs, 51 million were Ukrainians, and 10 million were Belorussians. Over the centuries, however, Ukrainians and Belorussians had developed their own national consciousness, and many among them sought independence from Moscow.

The Communist revolution of 1917 had taken place in an empire that consisted of well over a hundred nationalities. Many had only one thing in common: they had been conquered by the dominant Russians. According to the official interpretation, the revolution had forged a new social consciousness among the varied ethnic groups that now voluntarily resided in the new Soviet state. The fact that none had requested to secede from the Soviet Union—as permitted under the constitution—was taken as proof that the new Communist consciousness had obliterated national antagonisms, that the Soviet citizens made up one happy family.

Glasnost blew the official theory apart. Discussions revealed deep-rooted grievances among national minorities, and they were directed not necessarily against the dominant Russian majority but against each other.

The discussions produced two approaches. For one, the fourteen non-Russian republics demanded substantial economic and political autonomy. This demand envisioned strong republics with a strong center, something on the order of the Swiss model—a nation of four nationalities with four official languages. Gorbachev favored this approach, as it would keep the nation together and fit into the framework of his plan for "democratization."

Another solution called for the dismemberment of the empire. It would mean a 180-degree reversal of Russian history. It was no coincidence that the Russian monarchs who had been granted the appellation "Great"—Ivan III, Peter I, and Catherine II—had earned it by virtue of expanding their empire's borders.

The most serious challenge came from the Baltic states—Lithuania, Latvia, and Estonia—where so-called popular fronts began to test the limits of Gorbachev's "democratization." First, they demanded economic autonomy, stating they were merely supporting perestroika—that is, the decentralization of the top-heavy economy. Then they insisted on—and gained—the right to fly their old flags, openly practice their religions, and rewrite their histories. They spoke of fielding their own teams for future Olympic Games and declared their Communist parties to be independent of the party in Moscow. Then came the inevitable talk of secession.

The reason for the radicalism in the Baltic states can be found in their recent history. They had been part of the Russian empire for over two hundred years, but after the 1917 revolution they had managed to establish their independence—which, however, lasted only until 1940. On the eve of World War II, Hitler and Stalin agreed on a nonaggression pact and for good measure decided, on the basis of a secret protocol, to divide Eastern Europe. After the Baltic states fell to the Soviet Union, Stalin deported or murdered hundreds of thousands of suspected nationalists. As glasnost produced a critical reassessment of the Stalin era, the infamous Hitler-Stalin pact could not be ignored. After much soul-searching and hesitation, official Soviet historians finally admitted that, yes, there had been a secret protocol in violation of international law.

In December 1989, the Communist Party of Lithuania voted to establish its independence from Moscow. The mass movement Sajudis demanded (1) "freedom and independence" and the repeal of the Hitler-Stalin pact, (2) removal of the "occupant Soviet Army," (3) compensation for "the genocide of Lithuanian citizens and their exile" and for environmental destruction, and (4) the establishment of friendly relations between Lithuania and the Soviet Union on the basis of the 1920 peace treaty.

In January 1990, Gorbachev took a highly publicized trip to Lithuania in an attempt to convince the people there of the dangers of secessionism. He pleaded, cajoled, and issued thinly veiled threats, all to no avail. As his limousine departed for the airport, the crowd jeered him. In Moscow, the spokesman for the Foreign Office, Gennady Gerasimov, remarked that the divorce between Lithuania and Russia must follow an orderly course. Lithuanians quickly replied that there had been no marriage, only an abduction and rape, and that there was nothing to negotiate. On March 11, 1990, the newly and freely elected parliament of Lithuania unilaterally declared its independence.

Not all nationalist grievances were directed against the Russians. As Lithuanians demonstrated against the Russians, the Polish minority in Lithuania demonstrated for incorporation into Poland. Nearly every Soviet republic had territorial claims against a neighbor. As the Georgians sought to free themselves from Moscow, Muslim Abkhazians in western Georgia demonstrated against the heavy hand of the dominant Christian Georgians.

The bloodiest clash among Soviet nationalities was between the Christian Armenians and the Shiite Muslim, Turkic-speakers of Azerbaidzhan. When Gorbachev gave the Armenians a voice, they immediately demanded the return of a piece of their historical territory, Nagorno-Karabakh, which Stalin had placed under Azeri administration in 1923.

Armenian national consciousness is deeply affected by the 1915 massacre at the hands of the Turks, in which 1.5 million Armenians died.[6] The Turks then drove the Armenians from their historic territory in what today is eastern Turkey. As a result, the symbol of Armenian nationalism, biblical Mount Ararat, is in Turkey, just across the border from Armenia's capital, Yerevan.

Tensions rose in February 1988, when up to a hundred thousand people demonstrated in Yerevan over a period of several days against Azerbaidzhan but also against Moscow and Communism. At the end of the month, Azeris staged a pogrom in Sumgait, a city just north of Baku, the capital of Azerbaijan, where thirty-two Armenians were murdered.

In June 1988, the Communist Party of Armenia voted to reconquer Nagorno-Karabakh, and the Communist Party of Azerbaidzhan voted to defend it. For the first time, Communist parties of the Soviet Union split along national lines and went to war against each other. Only Moscow's intervention minimized further bloodshed, but the fear and hatred remained. When, in December 1988, an earthquake destroyed much of eastern Armenia, killing tens of thousands, Azeris rejoiced over the misery of their neighbors.

On January 13, 1990, Azeri-Armenian violence erupted anew—this time in Baku, where Azeris murdered at least sixty Armenians in a replay of the Sumgait pogrom. Gorbachev decreed a state of emergency in the region; when it had no effect, he sent the Soviet army and troops of the Interior Ministry into Baku. In a televised address, he explained that he had no choice because "neither side listened to the voice of reason."[7]

* * *

The Gorbachev revolution was the product of historical processes. The social conditions that had produced support for Lenin and Stalin had undergone significant changes since 1917. The number of Soviet citizens, for example, who had a high school education or better had increased since 1964 from 25 million to 125 million in the mid-1980s.[8] When de-Stalinization began with Khrushchev's 1956 speech, more than half of the nation's population still lived in the countryside; that figure was down to about one-quarter by the late 1980s. Gorbachev inherited a nation with a sizable and largely urbanized middle class. Gorbachev's generation (he was born in 1931) came to political maturity during Khrushchev's "thaw" and his attacks on Stalin. Perestroika became a battle between reformers and the dead weight of history, the legacy of centralization and intolerance bestowed on the nation by generations of tsars and commissars.

In December 1988, the West German newsweekly *Der Spiegel* named Gorbachev its "Man of the Year: Man of the Hour"—the first time it had bestowed such recognition on anyone. It compared him to the westernizer Peter the Great, the Protestant reformer Martin Luther, and the emancipator Abraham Lincoln. In January 1990, *Time* named him the "Man of the Decade." But the applause was for a tightrope walker who had not yet reached the other side.

## ■ THE END OF THE SOVIET UNION

Gorbachev's perestroika alienated both those on the right, who thought he was irrevocably disrupting Soviet society, and those on the left, who felt the reforms were not going far enough, that too much of the old power structure remained intact. By autumn 1990, the left and the right both wanted Gorbachev out.

After years of hesitation, Gorbachev and his economic advisers eventually concluded that the freeing of prices (determined by supply and demand) and the right to make a private profit were not merely necessary evils but positive economic forces. In other words, the Soviet Union would legalize capitalism. By autumn 1990, Gorbachev was about to accept a radical proposal by Stanislav Shatalin, an economist long opposed to the Soviet centralized economy. The Shatalin Plan called for a sudden transition—during a period of a scant five hundred days—from centralization to what was still called a "market" economy, a pseudonym for capitalism. But Shatalin was unable to answer questions regarding the economic, social, and political consequences of his bold proposal.

At this juncture, Gorbachev moved to the right. He feared the so-called democratic opposition on the left, led by Boris Yeltsin, who sought to topple him and dismantle the Soviet Union. In July 1990, Yeltsin staged his dramatic exit from the party. Gorbachev began to surround himself with conservatives who had become uncomfortable with perestroika.

As the conservatives sought to prevent the dissolution of the Soviet Union, Gorbachev moved back to the left. In April 1991, he and Yeltsin worked out the "9-plus-1" formula, which called for a decentralized Soviet Union. The republics would be able to exercise virtually unlimited power on the local level, while the Soviet government would continue to handle matters such as currency, diplomacy, and the military.

In June 1991, Yeltsin won a historic victory at the polls when he was elected president of the Russian republic, becoming Russia's first popularly elected head of state. Gorbachev continued to move to the left when he commissioned the economist, Grigorii Yavlinskii, with the help of economics professors from Harvard and the Massachusetts Institute of Technology, to launch the capitalist experiment.

These developments triggered a military coup by desperate party members who saw their power slipping away. On August 19, 1991, as Gorbachev vacationed in the Crimea, the leaders of Soviet military and paramilitary organizations—Defense Minister Dmitrii Yazov, the chief of the secret police (the KGB) Vladimir Kriuchkov, and Minister of the Interior Boris Pugo—sent tanks into the streets of Moscow and declared a state of emergency. Their front men were Gorbachev's recent appointees, Gennadii Yanaev and Valentin Pavlov. They declared that Gorbachev had taken ill and Vice-President Yanaev was assuming the position of president. At a live news conference later that same day, Yanaev stated that "his good friend Gorbachev" would some day return to political life in another capacity. Virtually no one believed his account, particularly as neither Gorbachev nor his physician was present to attest to Gorbachev's illness. A subversive camera operator, instead, focused on the trembling hands of Yanaev.

Since the days of Lenin, Communist ideology had always stressed unity of action. During the attempted coup, however, there was none. The conspirators had acted in desperation and haste, without planning or coordination.[9] They never managed to enlist a unified military or KGB. Some commanders were deeply unhappy with the state of affairs to which perestroika had brought them, but even they were unwilling to use force against fellow citizens. Other commanders openly opposed the coup. A similar division was apparent in the press and television, the diplomatic corps, the KGB, and the party. The coup collapsed with scarcely a shot fired. The conspirators had but one hope: that Soviet society would tacitly accept the transfer of power. In 1964, when the party changed leadership, the KGB was surprised to find out that not a single demonstration or voice of support was heard on behalf of Khrushchev. This time it was different. President Yeltsin, standing on top of a renegade tank in front of the "White House," the parliament building, denounced the coup and demanded the return of Gorbachev. The conspirators had gone after Gorbachev, the head of both the party and the Soviet government, without taking into account the fact that political power had already become diffused throughout the Soviet Union. Yeltsin's election as president of Russia in June 1991 had already created a situation of "dual power": Yeltsin and Gorbachev were in effect coequals. Had Yeltsin been arrested and had Gorbachev accepted the transfer of power (as he was pressured for three days to do), the coup might have succeeded.

Yeltsin held the party—and indirectly Gorbachev, the party's general secretary—responsible for the coup and suspended the party indefinitely. The conspirators had hoped to preserve the Soviet Union; instead, they hastened its demise. The 9-plus-1 formula no longer served a purpose. Yeltsin and the radicals dissolved the Soviet Union. By the end of 1991, the red flag with its golden hammer and sickle, the symbol of the Bolshevik seizure of power in 1917, came down from the buildings of the Kremlin and was replaced with the old flag of imperial Russia.

## ☐ The Former Soviet Republics

Yeltsin and the presidents of the now independent republics inherited a disintegrating economy. By 1990, the Soviet Union was already in a depression as severe as that the West had experienced in the 1930s. In the midst of this depression, Yeltsin committed Russia to the full embrace of capitalism. The movement toward a market economy, however, further disrupted the network of resource allocation, and factories had to fend for themselves to obtain the necessary supplies. Suppliers asked for hard—that is, Western—currency, which factories simply did not have. Ethnic tensions added to the economic chaos. Armenians no longer provided parts to machine tool factories in Moscow, and Russians refused to deliver steel to the huge truck factories of independence-minded Tatarstan on the Volga River. The result was increased idleness in factories, empty stores, and a continued decline in the standard of living.

The collapse of the Communist regimes in Eastern Europe brought an end to COMECON, the Kremlin-imposed system of economic integration. It meant, for instance, that the former Soviet Union, which had obtained about half of its medicines from COMECON trading partners, saw a drastic decline in its already perilous health care. Hungarians were still willing to sell buses to Russia, but now only for hard currency.

To cushion the shock of higher prices, Yeltsin's government printed ever more money. The result was a rate of inflation of 2,000 percent and a government budget deficit of 25 percent in 1992. Wages declined relative to the newly freed prices to the point where during winter 1991–1992, 90 percent of Russians lived below the official subsistence level.[10]

Yeltsin and his economic advisers were committed to a "grand bargain," the entrance into the global market economy and membership in the International Monetary Fund (IMF). It was predicated on obtaining aid from the capitalist nations, which were basking in the glow of their ideological victory over the Soviet Union. Unfortunately, the money markets had dried up. U.S. president Ronald Reagan's push for military superiority had produced a binge of borrowing. A worldwide economic recession and the collapse of the Japanese stock market—a decline of approximately 60 percent of its value since 1986—ended the era of cheap capital. The German government provided more assistance to the former Soviet Union than did any other nation, but it, too, had little money to spare because of the heavy cost of German reunification. A cynical Russian political analyst quipped that "as long as we pretend that we are carrying through reforms . . . the West will pretend to help us."[11]

The former Soviet republics turned to the IMF for assistance. In turn, the IMF demanded from the recipients a balanced budget, the repayment of debts, a convertible currency to permit foreign investors to take their profits out of the country, the freeing of prices (notably of energy), letting unprofitable businesses fail, and protecting the sanctity of foreign investments. Once the price of oil—previously sold to the Soviet Union's consumers at $3 a barrel—was raised to the world market's price of $19, Western investments and technology arrived. But it also made driving a car very expensive, undermined the farmers' ability to raise food cheaply, and shut down factories unable to pay the drastically higher price for energy.

The transition to capitalism produced a class of private entrepreneurs (who only recently had been called capitalist exploiters), as well as an impoverished, humiliated, and increasingly embittered mass of people who could not understand how their great nation had reached this juncture in its history. When the Communist Party went on trial in fall 1992, the Russian people were more concerned with their economic lot. A political commentator remarked that even to dream of such a trial in the past could have led to arrest—but now no one cared.[12]

## □ The Fragmentation of the Soviet Union

After the dissolution of the Soviet Union, the nationality problems remained. Armenia had the most homogeneous population, as approximately 90 percent of its citizens were Armenians. But in Latvia, 34 percent were Russian, as were 38 percent in Kazakhstan and 13 percent in Ukraine; in Moldova, 14 percent were Ukrainian and 13 percent Russian.[13]

Georgia witnessed the most serious political problems of any of the former Soviet republics. In May 1991, the anti-Communist Georgian nationalist, Zviad Gamsakhurdia, became the first democratically elected president of a republic of the Soviet Union; he was also the first dissident to come to power. In the past he had expressed admiration for Western political ideals. Within months, however, Gamsakhurdia began to arrest political opponents, whom he denounced—in language reminiscent of his countryman Joseph Stalin—as spies, bandits, and criminals, "enemies of the people" all. In a fit of chauvinism and paranoia, he sought to ban interracial marriages by which, he charged, the Russians sought "to dilute the Georgian race."[14] In September 1991, he declared a state of emergency. The ensuing civil war between Gamsakhurdia loyalists and the renegade National Guard reached its climax at the end of the year. Two weeks of heavy fighting destroyed the center of the capital, Tbilisi, and forced Gamsakhurdia to flee. The victorious faction then turned to Eduard Shevardnadze, Gorbachev's former foreign minister, to bring stability to Georgia.

Yeltsin had frequently criticized Gorbachev for refusing to grant the Baltic states independence. When the Soviet empire broke up, however, he began to face secessionist tendencies in Russia. The Muslim Chechen-Ingush (in November 1991) along the Georgian border and the Tatars (in March 1992) along the Volga River declared their independence.

An even more ominous development began to appear: the call for "ethnic cleansing." Russians demanded the expulsion of Jews and Azeris from Moscow, Chechen-Ingush were driven out of Volgograd, and in Stavropol attempts were made to force out Armenian families. In the Kuban, north of the Caucasus Mountains, Russian Cossacks appeared in their traditional dress, insisting upon the ouster of Turkic-speaking Meskhetians.[15]

## ■ THE YELTSIN PRESIDENCY

One of the by-products of the Yeltsin economic program was the transfer of state property to individuals with connections to the government. The oil and gas industry, once the Soviet Union's chief source of Western currency, fell into private hands. Politicians began to milk state-owned properties, and managers paid themselves generous salaries. The situation was corrupt even by Soviet standards.[16] Those left behind found the former Soviet safety net contained increasingly larger holes as state subsidies were eliminated. Inflation wiped out the savings of millions. The capitalist experiment did not turn out as many had hoped. The cynics remarked that "we thought the Communists were lying to us about [the glory of] socialism and [the evils] of capitalism, but it turns out they were lying only about socialism."[17]

The consequence of the economic disaster triggered a rebellion by Russia's parliament. By early spring 1993, Yeltsin began to talk of dissolving the parliament and holding new elections. Parliament countered with an attempt to impeach Yeltsin. The issue was settled with violence.

On September 22, 1993, Yeltsin—already accustomed to ruling by fiat—issued Decree No. 1,400, ordering the dissolution of parliament. Parliament refused to go quietly, and its building—the so-called White House—soon became a defiant armed camp surrounded by concertina wire. In early October, ten thousand proparliament demonstrators overwhelmed the police and then they marched to the state television complex (which was heavily biased in favor of Yeltsin) in an attempt to seize it. Yeltsin declared a state of emergency, and troops loyal to Yeltsin soon joined the fray, eventually shelling the White House—the same building that had served as a symbol of democracy and resistance to the Communists in August 1991. Russia's short-lived democratic experiment was over.

In the end, Yeltsin disbanded the parliament, suspended the Constitutional Court, and banned the opposition press and television. A total of 144 Russians lay dead, and the top half of the once gleaming White House was charred by tank artillery fire. Throughout, the Western powers refused to condemn Yeltsin and continued to refer to him as a "democrat," declaring that the radicals had forced his hand. The new constitution promulgated later in 1993 gave Yeltsin the power to rule virtually without the legislature.

## ☐  The First Chechen War

Then came the war in Chechnya. It began at the end of 1994, when Yeltsin decided he could no longer tolerate claims of independence by Chechnya, one of Russia's eighty-nine territorial subdivisions. Yeltsin, the chief architect of the dissolution of the Soviet Union, now stood fast against a breakup of the Russian Federation.

Chechnya is located along the northern slopes of the Caucasus Mountains. The Muslim Chechens had been brought under Russian control in the mid-nineteenth century, but it took another quarter century for the imperial Russian army to finally subdue them. During World War II, as the German army pushed into the Caucasus, a number of Chechens—acting on the time-honored principle that "the enemy of my enemy is my friend"—collaborated with the Germans. The Chechens paid a heavy price for it. Stalin meted out collective punishment and in 1943–1944 deported the Chechens (along with other ethnic groups in that region) to Central Asia and Siberia. In his "Secret Speech" of 1956, Nikita Khrushchev listed the deportation of the Chechens as one of many crimes Stalin had committed, and in 1957 he permitted the Chechens' return to their ancestral home. But the Chechens never forgot what the Soviet state had done to them; at the first opportunity they declared their independence.

For three years, Yeltsin had ignored Chechen claims to independence. But then Dzhokhar Dudayev, the leader of the Chechen rebels, reminded the Russians that the northern Caucasus is one of the great fault lines where the Christian and Muslim worlds meet. He predicted that all Muslims in the Caucasus would rebel, Siberia would also secede, and the Russian Far East would align itself with East Asia, adding "Russian racism in the Caucasus will not go unpunished."[18]

Yeltsin decided to act. Instead of quickly reasserting control, however, Russian troops walked into deadly ambushes set by Chechen rebels, particularly in Grozny, the capital city. The heavy-handed Russian response reduced the city to ruins; by the end of 1996, an estimated forty-five thousand people had died in Chechnya, and almost 2 million had become refugees.[19] Television images from Grozny reminded Russians of the devastation of World War II.

When the Chechen resistance proved to be much tougher than anticipated, Yeltsin sent his security adviser, Alexander Lebed, to negotiate a solution. The best Lebed was able to obtain in August 1996 was a five-year cease-fire during which both sides would negotiate the political future of Chechnya.

Lebed's accomplishment played to mixed reviews. Many Russians wanted to see an end to a war; others, however, accused him of betraying the fatherland for having granted the Chechens independence. It took Yeltsin more than five weeks to give his support to the agreement. The situation was not helped when at that very moment Aslan Maskhadov, the Chechen chief of staff who had signed the agreement with Lebed, flatly declared, "No Chechen has ever signed any kind of document saying that Chechnya is part of Russia and there will never be such a Chechen."[20]

☐ *The Election of 1996*

Early in 1996, few gave Boris Yeltsin much chance of winning the presidential election. Opinion polls showed that initially a scant 10 percent of voters planned to cast their ballots for him. The unpopular war in Chechnya, a drastic increase in the crime rate, Yeltsin's poor health, and money and political power in the hands of the *nouveaux riches,* commonly known as the "mafia," all took their toll. The Communist Party candidate, Gennadi Zyuganov, appeared the likely winner.

But in April 1996, Yeltsin overtook Zyuganov in the polls and in the end won the election by a comfortable margin. Voters—even those who suffered hardships because of the new economic order—ultimately proved reluctant to place their future in the hands of a Communist who unabashedly praised Stalin and promised a return to economic policies that had been tried and had failed. Zyuganov offered no new ideas; he did not even bother to change the name of his party.

In the ten weeks before the election in June, Yeltsin unabashedly used the power of the incumbent to its fullest measure. He issued decrees that doubled the minimum pension—effective immediately—and compensated those who had lost their savings because of the hyperinflation of the past years. He singled out students, teachers, war veterans, single mothers, small businesses, and the agro-industrial, military, and aviation complexes and one region after another for special treatment and subsidies—from the heart of Russia to the farthest reaches of Siberia.

A woman who worked for a coal mine in Vorkuta asked for and received from Yeltsin a car, an event carried on national television. Yeltsin's aides blatantly handed out cash. Yelstin's largesse cost the hard-strapped Russian treasury the astonishing sum of $11 billion. The IMF—which had a stake in keeping the capitalist reforms of Yeltsin on track—underwrote his spending spree with a new $10.2 billion loan.[21]

Yeltsin and his advisers had showed no intention of accepting a defeat. In March 1996, when Yeltsin's prospects for a victory were still dim, he leaned toward a so-called forceful option by which, under the pretext of a bomb threat, he would dissolve parliament and cancel the election. In the meantime, he followed the "softer option": television controlled by the government (running footage of Communist atrocities) and money spent to curry favor with the voters. As one of Yeltsin's advisers bluntly declared, "If Yeltsin loses, he will not give power to the Communists. He has said that more than once."[22] Either way, Zyuganov would not win.

Throughout, the Clinton administration turned a blind eye to the political and economic conditions in Russia, arguing that they were part of the growing pains of the transition from a planned to a market economy. By the end of the decade, approximately one-half of the population was living below the official poverty line of $30 to $35 a month and perhaps another 25–30 percent were close to it. The political scientist Stephen Cohen concluded that "in modern peacetime, never have so many fallen so far."[23]

## ■ THE PUTIN PRESIDENCY

In 1999, Yeltsin dismissed one prime minister after another until he found in August 1999 a man to his liking, the obscure Vladimir Putin, a product of the KGB, the Soviet Union's political police. Under Yeltsin, Putin had risen to head the KGB's successor, the Federal Security Service, and also served as the chair of the government's commission to combat terrorism. Yeltsin, physically ailing and with little popular support, understood that he would have to leave office after his second term ended in the summer of 2000. He was also looking for a way to avoid a criminal investigation. One of his earlier prime ministers, Evgeny Primakov, had refused to grant him and his corrupt clan immunity from prosecution. Putin, however, had no such qualms. Thus, on New Year's Eve 1999, came the stunning announcement that Putin had replaced Yeltsin and had become the acting president until the election in March 2000. Yeltsin obliquely apologized for past "mistakes" for which, however, he would not be punished.

After the first Chechen war, the Chechen rebels behaved as if they governed an independent—although scarcely functioning—state that had become a training base for Muslim terrorists. The economic activities consisted of trading in slaves, drug smuggling, operating stolen-car rings, counterfeiting, and taking hostages, ranging from a general of the Russian Interior Ministry to foreign aid workers.

Putin came to power two days after a radical fringe group of Chechens launched an attack on neighboring Dagestan to establish the "independent Islamic state of Dagestan" in hopes of sparking an Islamic anti-Russian uprising. Putin responded to the challenge. Five days later the Russian fighter jets came, an omen of things to come.

Three weeks later a series of explosions shook Moscow. There was no question in the minds of most Russians that the bombings had been the work of Chechen terrorists.[24] Although it remained unclear who was responsible for the bloody deeds, Putin had his justification to go to war, not only to avenge the recent bombings but also Russia's defeat in the first Chechen war.

This time, the Russian military did not simply walk into Grozny in the expectation of a quick victory. It prepared, instead, a massive assault. The war left tens of thousands of Chechens dead, mostly civilians. Little was left standing of Grozny or other rebel strongholds. The world stood by idly, wringing its hands but not daring to challenge a power in decline—economically, militarily, and morally—but one that still possessed approximately seven thousand strategic nuclear warheads. After the Russian army took Grozny, the rebels retreated into the mountains, vowing to continue the fight. In the end, the conflict became more than merely a war of secession: it took on ethnic and religious connotations, with Russians against Chechens and Christians against Muslims.

Putin had no discernible foreign policy except to argue repeatedly that Russia must once again play the role of a great power. With that in mind, he emphasized the need for a strong state and patriotism and urged that the economy had to rest on an "ideological" basis—with the state playing a major role. The stress was on executive power and discipline, not democracy. He offered his people, instead, a "dictatorship of the law," adding later "as I choose to rewrite it."[25]

Putin never solved the Chechen issue. In October 2002, forty-one Chechen terrorists, including several "black widows," women who had lost relatives to the Russian terror, seized seven hundred hostages in a Moscow theater. The rescue attempt went terribly awry when 129 hostages perished (as well as the terrorists who were summarily executed). In the months to come, Chechens bombed a train in southern Russia, the Grozny headquarters of the government the Kremlin had installed, and a subway station in Moscow. At the end of the summer of 2004, "black widows" brought down two Russian airliners, and then in September 2004 came the shocking spectacle of Chechens seizing a school in Beslan in the south of Russia. Putin, who had always refused to negotiate with renegade Chechens, sent the army to carry out what turned out to be another ill-fated rescue attempt. Among the 335 dead, most were children. Immediately thereafter, Putin issued a decree ending popular elections of regional governors to establish a "single chain of command" to strengthen the "unity of the country and prevent further crises."

Under Yeltsin the news media had been left alone. Putin, however, quickly declared war on the independent voices in Russia. When Andrei Babitsky, a reporter for Radio Free Europe/Radio Liberty, reported honestly on the brutality of the second Chechen war, Putin arranged Babitsky's kidnapping. Babitsky was "on the side of the enemy," Putin charged; what he did was "much more dangerous than firing a machine gun."[26] It was largely because of an international outcry that Babitsky was eventually released. Putin then turned against Media-Most, a company that published a daily newspaper and owned a radio station and NTV, the only Russian television network not controlled by the government. In June 2000, the company's owner, Vladimir Gusinsky, was arrested and briefly jailed because exposure of corruption in the Kremlin had hit too close to home and the fact that Gusinky's television station had satirized Putin. Public criticism of Putin came to an end after the October 2003 arrest—on charges of tax evasion—of Mikhail Khodorkovsky, the chief executive of the YukosSibneft oil company and one of the world's richest men, with an estimated personal fortune of $8 billion. The arrest of Khodorkovsky—who had used his wealth to challenge Putin, the real reason for his arrest—achieved its purpose. Other tycoons quickly took pains to show their loyalty to Putin.

One of Putin's priorities was the rebuilding of the military. He was photographed flying an Su-27 fighter jet into Grozny and on board the ill-fated submarine *Kursk*. His point was clear: Russia must once again be respected as a military power. But in August 2000, seismologists in Norway noted two powerful blasts in the Barents Sea. The *Kursk,* Russia's state-of-the-art, nuclear-powered, missile-launching submarine, commissioned only five years earlier, had been ripped apart by its own torpedoes. Putin reacted slowly to the catastrophe. Surviving sailors continued to hammer on the hull until they ran out of oxygen. The disaster, the slow response, and the inability of Russian divers to open the hatch put into sharp detail the sorry state of Russia's once-vaunted military forces. At first, Putin refused to accept foreign assistance (particulary from NATO), but in the end he had to swallow his national pride and ask for help from Britain and Norway.

## ☐ The Non-Russian Successor States

A number of Soviet republics—notably Estonia, Latvia, and Lithuania—managed to establish functioning democracies. But in most instances, the road to democracy proved to be difficult. The Caucasus and Central Asia were plagued by ethnic strife and wars for political supremacy. When elections were held, they were often tampered with. The president of Uzbekistan, Islam Karimov, for instance, was reelected in September 1996 with an approval rate of 99.6 percent—in a country that had neither freedom of speech nor freedom of the press.

Belarus was another case where things did not go according to plan. In July 1994, its voters elected a conservative, Alexander Lukashenko, a Communist functionary who had no taste for change. Instead, he called for a return to the not-too-distant past. He saw privatization as stealing from the state and insisted on the retention of collective farming and state control of factories. Among his heroes were Felix Dzherzhinski, the legendary founder of the Soviet secret police.[27]

Belarus, Lukashenko stated, should be ruled by "one strong man." He fired the editor of the country's largest newspaper and demanded that citizens seeking to travel abroad register with the proper authorities. He called demonstrators "enemies of the people" and blamed a strike by subway workers in the capital of Minsk on the U.S. State Department. In October 2004, in a rigged referendum, he gained the right to amend the constitution to run for a third presidential term.

In 2003, there were manipulated elections in Azerbaidzhan, Armenia, and Georgia. In November 2003, the Georgian president Eduard Shevardnadze, who had come to power as a champion of democracy in 1991, rigged the parliamentary election. After twelve years in power, Shevardnadze had overstayed his welcome; corruption and the violation of the rule of law had taken their toll. He faced large demonstrations, aided by outside forces such as Serbian activists who had brought down their dictator, Slobodan Milosevic, and the United States. In the end, neither the army nor police backed Shevardnadze. In January 2004, Georgia's bloodless "rose revolution" brought to power Mikhail Saakashvili, a thirty-five-year-old U.S.-trained lawyer, as Georgians gave democracy another try.

# ■ THE RETREAT FROM EMPIRE

A cursory glance at the Soviet Union's position in the world in the early 1980s revealed a powerful presence in Europe and Asia. At the same time, however, a restless population in Eastern Europe showed no signs of coming to terms with their status subordinate to Moscow's interests. Along its other borders, the Soviet Union had its hands full. A hostile Communist China tied down more than one-third of the Soviet army at the Sino-Soviet border. The Ayatollah Khomeini's Islamic government in Iran did not hide its distaste for the secular, atheistic government in Moscow, and Afghanistan, governed by a socialist regime since the early 1970s, remained torn asunder by a bloody civil war that threatened to topple the Kremlin's clients in the Afghan capital of Kabul.

## ☐ The Afghan Crisis

In December 1979, by an act that stunned the world, the Soviet Union sent eighty thousand troops into Afghanistan. For the first time since the end of World War II, the Soviet Union had sent troops into a territory beyond its sphere of influence.

Since 1973, the political orientation in Afghanistan had been toward the left, yet it was generally considered a neutral nation, a part of the Third World outside the spheres of any of the great powers. Until 1973, both the United States and the Soviet Union had jockeyed inconclusively for influence in Afghanistan, one of the poorest nations on earth, with an annual per capita GNP in 1979 of $170.[28]

## ☐ The U.S. Reaction

The Soviet invasion came at an unfavorable time for the United States. For one, the country's recent Vietnam experience, its first defeat in war, did not sit well with many. Second, 1979 had seen the second oil shortage of the decade. Third, the traumatic hostage crisis had just begun in Iran, where the takeover of the U.S. embassy in Tehran pointed to the limitations of U.S. power. One setback after another produced frustration and belligerence.

The U.S. response to the invasion of Afghanistan was swift. President Jimmy Carter, if only for political reasons at home, had to act. On the eve of the 1980 presidential election, Carter could ill afford to be blamed for the "loss of Afghanistan." A country of extraordinary poverty and of little significance in the international balance of power suddenly took on an importance unmatched in its modern history.

There was scarcely a debate in the United States of the motives behind the invasion. The CIA explained that the Soviet Union faced an "extremely painful" decline in oil supplies and the invasion of Afghanistan was intended to move the Soviet Army closer to the lucrative oil fields of the Persian Gulf. "Moscow is already making the point," said CIA director Stansfield Turner, "that Middle Eastern oil is not the exclusive preserve of the West." (The CIA later retracted its statement when it declared that the Soviet Union was not likely to suffer from oil shortages in the near future.)[29] A Soviet thrust through Afghanistan directed at the oil refineries of the gulf, however, made little sense. Why take a five-hundred-mile detour through rugged terrain and at the same time tip off your enemy?

Carter's options were limited. A direct military challenge to the USSR was out of the question; he had to find different ways to express U.S. displeasure. He refused to permit U.S. athletes to participate in the Soviet showcase, the 1980 Summer Olympic Games in Moscow, unless the Soviets withdrew from Afghanistan. The Soviets were stung by the boycott, for they had envisioned the Olympic Games as a stepping-stone toward legitimacy and final acceptance as one of the world's two great powers. They ignored Carter's ultimatum and held the Olympic Games without the United States and other Western nations. Carter also halted U.S. grain sales to the Soviet Union. The glut on the world market in agricultural commodities, however, meant that the Soviets shifted their orders to more reliable sources. Lastly, Carter began to look for clients willing to help him contain the Soviet Union in Asia. Communist China and the United States were drawn a bit closer, and both began in secret to provide weapons for Afghans fighting the Soviets, with Saudi Arabia underwriting much of the cost. As the United States expanded its military assistance to Pakistan, situated along Afghanistan's eastern frontier, the Soviets continued to beef up their forces, which soon numbered over a hundred thousand.

The invasion of Afghanistan finished off the détente of the 1970s. Neither Brezhnev nor his Politburo understood the West's definition of détente, which linked improved relations with Soviet behavior. The Soviets could not expect a thaw in the Cold War and at the same time intervene in the internal affairs of another nation. The Soviets replied that détente would not prevent the Kremlin from playing the role of a great power: détente and throwing one's weight around in the Third World—as the United States had done in Vietnam—were not antithetical.

## □ Soviet Objectives in Afghanistan

The reason the Soviet Union intervened in the internal affairs of Afghanistan was to bring order to a chaotic political situation in a neighboring socialist country. In the simple arithmetic of the Cold War, a setback for the forces of one side meant a victory for the other. The argument was generally the consequence of a sense of loss of prestige and image rather than rational analyses of the needs of national security. It rested on what conclusions others might draw from one's own misfortune.

Political instability has long been endemic in Afghanistan; coups and countercoups often followed in rapid succession. In 1973, the leftist Prince Mohammed Daoud exiled his cousin, King Zahir Shah. In April 1978, Daoud himself was ousted and killed in a coup by the Marxist People's Democratic Party under the leadership of Nur Mohammed Taraki, who established closer ties with the Soviet Union. Taraki in turn was ousted and murdered in a third leftist coup carried out by Hafizullah Amin, who was in power in Kabul at the time of the Soviet invasion. All this bloodletting took place within Afghanistan's Marxist Party.

It is here that one can find another clue to the Soviet Union's decision to invade Afghanistan. Taraki and Amin had a falling out, with Taraki looking to Moscow for support and Amin looking to Washington. Amin met a number of times with then U.S. ambassador Adolph Dubs. What transpired between these two men was not clear, but the Soviets feared the worst. To them, Amin was at the threshold of following in the footsteps of Anwar Sadat, the Egyptian head of state, who in 1972 had ousted the twenty thousand Soviet advisers in Egypt and then invited in the U.S. military. That more than anything else, the fear of an Afghan diplomatic revolution—from Moscow to Washington—prompted the Soviet invasion.

The Kremlin's concerns were not unfounded. Washington had shown interest in Afghanistan even before the Soviet invasion. CIA director Robert Gates confirmed in his memoirs that the United States had begun to assist Afghan rebels six months earlier. In 1998, President Carter's national security adviser, Zbigniew Brzezinski, acknowledged that Carter, on July 3, 1979, signed the first directive granting assistance to the rebels in the hope that this provocation would lead to a Soviet invasion.[30] The Carter administration did not have to wait long.

In March 1979, when Taraki initially asked for Soviet intervention to fight the Afghan rebels, Brezhnev and his prime minister, Andrei Kosygin, were resolutely opposed to such a drastic step. Brezhnev told Taraki: "We must not do this. It would only play into the hands of enemies—both yours and ours." But after Taraki's murder at the hands of Amin, the Kremlin, against its better judgment, sent the Soviet army into Afghanistan to restore order.[31] Soviet commandos killed Amin and replaced him with his rival, Babrak Karmal. The Kremlin then announced that it had acted upon invitation from the government of Afghanistan.

In the name of freedom, Islam, and anti-Communism, the *mujahidin,* or freedom fighters—as they called themselves—rose against a succession of Marxist governments in Kabul, which found themselves increasingly isolated. Resistance has long been a central feature of Afghan politics, with local rulers in outlying regions jealously guarding their authority and freedom of action. This time they had other grievances, the social and economic transformation of their tradition-bound society, untouched even by colonial rule. Resentment of reform—such as the establishment of coeducational schools (which touched off the rebellion in western Afghanistan in March 1979), the elimination of the veil and bridal dowries, particularly when carried out with brutality and in direct opposition to popular will—ran deep.

The Kremlin also feared the spread of radical Islam into Central Asia, where most of the Soviet Union's 50 million Muslims lived. As the Soviet army crossed into Afghanistan, it mobilized recruits from Central Asia, a step in line with the standard procedure of using the most readily available reserves. But this policy soon ran into trouble when Muslim soldiers showed little inclination to fight their ethnic and religious counterparts. Some deserted, others even went over to the rebels. Within three months, the Soviet army began to bring in politically more reliable Slavic troops.

Unlike guerrilla movements in other parts in the world, the Afghan rebels had no program of social, political, and economic reform. There was no literacy campaign (in 1979, primary-school enrollment stood at 30 percent, mostly in the cities; the adult literacy rate was 15 percent), no declaration of the rights of women, no medical programs (life expectancy at birth was thirty-six years; in the industrial nations of the West it was twice that), and no political experiments such as elected village councils. Gerard Chaliand, a French specialist on Third World guerrilla movements, concluded: "The current Afghan resistance movement looks [more] like a traditional revolt [against the capital] . . . than like modern guerrilla warfare. Among contemporary guerrilla movements, only the Kenyan Mau Mau [of the early 1950s] are less sophisticated in their strategy and organization."[32] The Afghan *mujahidin* represented the preservation of a traditional society to the exclusion of the industrial revolution and all it entailed. In a strange twist of fate, the United States, the standard-bearer for the industrial revolution and parliamentary democracy, became the main arms supplier for the Afghan rebels who drew their inspiration from seventh-century Arabia.

Not only did the United States support Afghanistan's Islamic fundamentalists, but also foreign *jihadists* who began to flock to Afghanistan, recruited largely through the efforts of Saudi Arabia. The United States looked with favor upon their participation in the war and, in fact, sought ways to increase it, despite warnings—ignored by the CIA and State Department—of their anti-U.S. sentiments.[33]

## ☐ The Soviet Exodus from Afghanistan

Shortly after Gorbachev came to power in March 1985, he sought to extricate the Soviet army from Afghanistan. He sought to establish a dialogue with the resistance, but the Afghan rebels were not interested in sitting down with either the Soviets or their clients.

The Gorbachev attempt to end the Cold War, however, demanded the retreat from Afghanistan. At first Gorbachev was unwilling to accept a defeat along the southern flank of the Soviet Union, and for that reason he escalated the war. But the rebels were too well equipped. Their effective, U.S.-made Stinger ground-to-air missiles, for example, brought down numerous Soviet aircraft (including passenger airplanes). When Gorbachev finally accepted the withdrawal, he stated that the invasion had not been merely another mistake on the part of the Brezhnev administration, but also a sin.

But the Soviet retreat would not be unilateral. Gorbachev insisted—and Reagan agreed—that Afghanistan must not be allied with the West. On February 15, 1989, the last Soviet troops marched out of Afghanistan, leaving a client government led by President Najibullah in power in Kabul.

Earlier, Gorbachev had declared several times that the days of Soviet interference in the internal affairs of other Communist countries was over. The retreat from Afghanistan in February 1989 marked the end of the Brezhnev Doctrine. The withdrawal also offered the Afghans a respite, however brief, from nearly a decade of violence. The war had claimed the lives of approximately 1 million Afghans (out of a population of 15 million). Between 5 and 6 million had become refugees in Pakistan and Iran; another 2 million had been displaced within Afghanistan. The estimated physical damage—to agriculture, industry, power stations, schools, hospitals—was $20 billion.[34]

## ☐  The Aftermath: Civil War

Old habits were hard to break as Washington and Moscow continued to prop up their clients. Weapons and ammunition continued to pour into Afghanistan. The government in Kabul managed to survive the Soviet army's withdrawal—if only for the time being—because of the extraordinary fragmentation of the Afghan resistance.

In December 1991, however, Moscow stopped supplying arms to Najibullah and Washington ended its arms deliveries to the *mujahidin,* who, however, were still able to obtain weapons from Iran, Pakistan, and Saudi Arabia. Najibullah was on his own, and when in January 1992, he proved unable to suppress a local army mutiny, his generals sensed his vulnerability and began to switch sides. By April 1992, Najibullah negotiated the transfer of political power to the *mujahidin* and then took refuge in a UN compound in Kabul.

As the *mujahidin* closed in on Kabul, Najibullah, prophetically, told reporters:

> We have a common task—Afghanistan, the U.S.A., and the civilized world to launch a joint struggle against fundamentalism [that, if it] comes to Afghanistan, will continue for many years. Afghanistan will turn into a center of world smuggling for narcotic drugs. Afghanistan will be turned into a center for terrorism.[35]

No one in the West listened to Najibullah, however.

Kabul fell to the Islamic fundamentalist Shiite, Gulbuddin Hekmatyar, who had been the chief recipient of U.S. aid. In April 1992, a coalition led by the ethic Tadzhik, Ahmad Shah Masoud, entered Kabul from the north and expelled Hekmatyar. Hekmatyar, now supported by Shiite Iran, continued to fight from entrenched positions in the hills south of Kabul. In August 1992, he launched a deadly artillery barrage in which over twelve hundred residents lost their lives. Kabul suffered greater death and destruction in the single year after the fall of Najibullah than during the previous fourteen years of revolution, foreign invasion, and civil war. Continued bombardments over the next three years turned the city of 1 million inhabitants to rubble, killing as many as ten thousand and sending over half the population to flight.

Between January and September 1992, a succession of corrupt and brutal Islamic governments vied for control of Kabul. But then the country witnessed the emergence of yet another—the most extreme—Muslim movement, the Taliban. The Taliban ("student" in Pushtun) was created in August 1994 by former Islamic seminary students (many from across the border in Pakistan). Led by its supreme leader, the one-eyed Mullah Mohammed Omar, the Taliban had become disgusted with the corruption and factional fighting and demanded an Afghan government subject to the laws of the Koran. It quickly gained popular support and began to rule wide stretches of the country, where it applied stern measures against transgressors against the laws of Islam. It closed girls' schools, confined women to their homes, punished thieves by cutting off their hands, and carried out public executions.

In September 1996, the Taliban—already in control of more than half of Afghanistan—began its final push toward Kabul. Upon taking the city, its first act was to seize Najibullah in the UN compound, beat him, then shoot him and finally hang him and his brother from a traffic post as a warning to any and all who opposed it.

The Taliban's second act was to forbid women to work in offices, hospitals, and so on, and demand that they wear *burqas,* a garment that covers the wearer from head to toe. It also ordered government officials to grow beards, closed Kabul's sole television station (because Islam equates the reproduction of images of humans with idolatry), and banned Western music.

The Taliban now controlled more than three-quarters of Afghanistan, but the fighting was not over. The history of Afghanistan—a struggle between the center and the provinces—continued. When Taliban moved into the Panjshir valley, ninety miles north of Kabul, Uzbek and Tadzhik forces blocked their way.

## ■ POLAND AND SOLIDARITY

In December 1970, the Polish Communist Party elected Edward Gierek to lead an increasingly radicalized country. Gierek's tenure coincided with

Willy Brandt's *Ostpolitik,* which was marked by an easing of tensions between East and West. With détente came a considerable increase in East-West trade, underwritten by Western bankers who made available increasingly larger amounts of "petrodollars"—money deposited by the oil-rich nations. Gierek, unlike his frugal predecessor, Wladyslaw Gomulka, began to borrow heavily. In 1973, Poland owed $2.5 billion to the West; by 1982, the debt had risen to $27 billion. With the influx of Western capital and goods—machinery, grain, and consumer items—the standard of living rose, but the day of financial reckoning had to come.

That day came in July 1980, when the Gierek government, in order to pay off Poland's large foreign debt, decreed an increase in food prices. The announcement at first led to—illegal—strikes and demonstrations and then to the emergence of Solidarity.

In the past, the government had bought off striking workers with economic concessions. This time, however, the workers refused to take the bait. Instead, workers at the mammoth Lenin Shipyard in Gdansk insisted on concessions from the government that were nothing short of revolutionary. They

Polish solidarity leader Lech Walesa, surrounded by supporters, Warsaw, Poland, November 11, 1980.
*(AP/Wide World Photos)*

General Wojciech Jaruzelski, prime minister, defense minister, and first secretary of the Polish Communist Party, addressing the UN General Assembly, September 27, 1985.
*(AP/Wide World Photos)*

demanded that a settlement would have to be with the country's workers as a whole, rather than merely with the shipyard workers. This demand gave rise to Solidarity, a union at one point representing 10 million in a country of 35 million people. Lech Walesa, the head of Solidarity, became one of the most powerful men in Poland.

Solidarity, with the support of the vast majority of the population as well as the Roman Catholic Church, was able to wring concession after concession from the government. During the next sixteen months, the attention of the world was riveted on Poland, where the impossible was taking place. According to Marxist ideology, Polish workers were striking against themselves, for, in theory at least, they were the owners of the "means of production," the factories. Strikes by workers against their places of employment were, therefore, both illogical and illegal. Yet this right to strike was the first and most important concession Solidarity wrenched from the state. Solidarity here established its independence from the state and thus became the only union in Eastern Europe not controlled by the government.

Solidarity then demanded additional concessions. It broke the government's monopoly of the information media. It received the right to put out a daily, uncensored newspaper and access to radio and television. It then wrested from the state the materials necessary to erect monuments in honor of workers the state had shot to death in the riots of 1956 and 1970. Finally, Solidarity managed to obtain free local parliamentary elections with a secret ballot.

The Polish Communist Party was paralyzed in the face of Solidarity's demands. It was also deeply split. Some members openly supported Solidarity; others even quit the party to join Solidarity. The party began to look for a savior, a Napoleon Bonaparte, to bring the revolution under control. It turned to a man of considerable moral authority, General Wojciech Jaruzelski, who in 1970 and 1976 as minister of defense had refused to use force against workers, declaring that "Polish troops will not fire on Polish workers."[36] In rapid succession, the party promoted him to prime minster in 1980, and then first secretary of the party in October 1981.

Jaruzelski well understood the precariousness of his position. He now held the three paramount positions in Poland and yet was unable to govern effectively. Lech Walesa, the head of Solidarity, who held no government position, was his coequal.

Powerful forces were lining up against each other. Party hard-liners always resented the concessions granted to Solidarity; Solidarity hard-liners felt there could be no coexistence with the party. One of them, Jacek Kuron, long a bitter critic of the party, put it succinctly: the regime either "must die, or it must destroy Solidarity. There is no other solution."[37]

On December 12, 1981, a radicalized Solidarity decided to call for a popular referendum—one it was sure to win—on the fate of the Communist Party. The government and TASS, the Soviet news agency, warned against an attempt by Solidarity to seize political power.

Brezhnev and his party hesitated. They knew that the cost of intervention would be high; it could well result in war between the two most important members of the Warsaw Pact, particularly at a time when the Soviet army was already bogged down in Afghanistan. When in November 1980, the Soviet army attempted to mobilize troops along the Polish border in order to intimidate Solidarity, it proved to be a disaster when reservists could not be found; others failed to answer the call, and so many deserted and went home that the authorities gave up trying to punish them.[38]

The day after Solidarity's call for the referendum, the government arrested its leadership and declared martial law—effectively outlawing Solidarity and reestablishing the primacy of the party.

The commonly held view in the West was that the Soviet Union bore direct responsibility for Jaruzelski's actions. But there was no clear proof of this. No doubt, Jaruzelski did what the Soviet Union had demanded all along, the restoration of order. But he also knew that either he would do it or the Kremlin would do it for him.

The extraordinary gains of the previous sixteen months were now largely erased. Jaruzelski's security forces acted with remarkable efficiency in restoring order, which astonished most observers, including Solidarity itself. Jaruzelski and the party, however, did not manage to win the hearts and minds of the nation. This chapter of Polish history was far from closed.

## ■ ANNUS MIRABILIS

In Europe, 1989 became known as *annus mirabilis,* the "year of miracles." When the year began, all of Moscow's satellite Communist parties appeared firmly in control. By year's end, however, the ring of Communist states along the Soviet Union's western borders, which Stalin had created in 1945, was no more.

The events of 1989 underscored the fact that the governments of Eastern Europe had little popular support. In the past, whenever a Communist party had shown signs of being overwhelmed by its own people, Moscow had always intervened—in East Germany in June 1953, in Hungary in 1956, and in Czechoslovakia in 1968. Intervention and threats had maintained a deceptive calm.

Early in his reign, Gorbachev announced that the Brezhnev Doctrine was dead, that no nation had the right to impose its will on another people. He restated this position several times, including in his address to the United Nations in December 1988. The Communist parties in Eastern Europe now stood alone, and they had to face their people without Moscow's support.

Economic factors played a large role in the events of 1989. The economies of Eastern Europe had done tolerably well in the first decade or so when the Communist parties had organized large factories. The test was whether the Communist system could sustain productivity, absorb new technology, and produce a wider range of sophisticated products. When it could not, the result was that in 1989, every East European country was much poorer compared to the West than it had been in the 1970s. In 1987, per capita gross national product for Poland and Hungary, for example, was 14 percent of that of either West Germany or Sweden.[39] Moreover, the Iron Curtain had long ceased to be a barrier to the flow of information. Many East Germans regularly watched West German television—via cable, no less. That and the steady flow of visitors from the West gave the East Europeans a clear picture of how far they had fallen behind.

## □ Poland

The dam began to crack first in Poland. After Jaruzelski had declared martial law, he found out that he could not rule Poland without Solidarity, particularly as the economy continued to deteriorate. In January 1989, Jaruzelski resumed talks with Solidarity, leading to its relegalization in April and to elections in June. The Communist Party proposed that Solidarity's representation in parliament be limited to 35 percent of the seats. Solidarity balked at this offer. The deadlock was broken only after the government agreed to create an upper house, or senate, that would be elected democratically.

The free and competitive elections sealed the fate of the party. The senate elections gave Solidarity 99 of the 100 contested seats and became what Poles termed "the only known crucifixion in which the victim has nailed himself to the cross."[40] After Solidarity's smashing victory in the senate elections, the Peasant Party, which over the past forty years had been little more than a front for the Communists, suddenly bolted and joined the opposition. Solidarity and the Peasant Party now controlled a majority of the seats and became the government. In August 1989, they elected Tadeusz Mazowiecki as prime minister, the first non-Communist leader in Eastern Europe since shortly after World War II.

Mazowiecki flew to Moscow to assure Gorbachev that his non-Communist government did not plan to leave the Warsaw Pact, as the Hungarian Communists had attempted in 1956. Moreover, Solidarity would not make the mistake it had made in 1981; it refrained from language suggesting the abolition of the Communist Party, which, in any case, was on its way to becoming irrelevant. Gorbachev replied that he had no intention of invoking the Brezhnev Doctrine; instead, he welcomed the events in Warsaw.

The Mazowiecki government now had to manage an economy deeply in debt and run aground on the shoals of central planning. On New Year's Day 1990, it abolished numerous subsidies to which Poland's citizens had long become accustomed. Immediately, the price of bread rose by 38 percent and that of coal, which many used for heating, went up 600 percent. A drastic increase in gasoline and automobile insurance prices forced some

Poles to turn in their license plates.[41] The primary advocates of such "shock therapy" were the Western banks and governments and the IMF, all of which insisted that Poland must put its fiscal house in order to be eligible for aid.

Poland's plan for dismantling its centralized economy was the boldest in Eastern Europe. By the summer of 1991, however, the government began to roll back some of its free-market policies to stave off a popular rebellion. It intervened to check the rising rate of unemployment by preventing state-owned factories from going bankrupt and introduced protective import tariffs on certain goods. Economists who had envisioned a "big bang" transformation to capitalism began to speak of an evolution taking place over ten years. Poland's problems were but a microcosm of those facing all East European economies seeking a break with the centrally planned economies of the past.

## ☐ East Germany

In the summer of 1989, Hungarian soldiers went to work to dismantle the fortifications along the Austro-Hungarian border, the first example of the physical demolition of the Iron Curtain. The Communist Hungarian government already had granted its citizens the right to a passport and with it the freedom of travel and emigration. Moreover, Hungary made no effort to keep East Germans from taking the same road to the West. Hungary, officially still a Communist country, became a hemorrhaging wound that threatened to bleed Communist East Germany, which for the first time since 1961—when the Berlin Wall was built—was losing tens of thousands of its citizens. In September 1989, twelve thousand East Germans crossed into Austria in the span of three days. Other East Germans left through Czechoslovakia and Poland. East Germany's Warsaw Pact allies had become the road by which East Germans abandoned what they considered a sinking ship.

East Germany's rigid Communist Party chief, Erich Honecker, declared that he would ride out the storm. But in May 1989, after the party had rigged the results of local elections, the voices of protest grew louder. Church leaders, in particular, grew increasingly critical of the regime; they were joined by civic groups such as the New Forum. Then came the summer's exodus. But more important, the summer saw repeated demonstrations in many cities, notably in Leipzig, where increasingly larger crowds demanded change and insisted "we're staying here." Honecker promised "another Beijing" (in reference to the massacre of protesters there in June 1989) and ordered the security police, the despised and dreaded Stasi, to use "any means" to put down the "counterrevolution."

The showdown came in Leipzig on the night of October 9, 1989, one month after Hungary had become an unimpeded escape road and the day after Gorbachev's visit to East Berlin to commemorate the fortieth anniversary of

Between November 9 and 12, 1989, more than 1 million East Germans walked or drove into West Berlin, where they received a joyous reception. *(German Information Service)*

the East German state. Gorbachev made clear that he had not come to support Honecker but to say good-bye to him. He reminded the East German Politburo that a leadership that isolates itself from its people loses the right to exist. During the demonstration on October 9, the party backed down and did not use force. Nine days later, the Politburo forced Honecker to step down in favor of his protégé, Egon Krenz.

Krenz's first trip as head of the party was a visit to Moscow, where he took pains to describe himself as a disciple of Gorbachev's "new thinking." Mass protests, Krenz now insisted, were a healthy sign of change. The demonstrators wanted "better socialism and the renovation of society."

The demonstrations continued, nevertheless. On November 6, 1989, five hundred thousand people demonstrated in Leipzig on a cold, rainy night. There were also rallies in Dresden, Erfurt, Schwerin, Halle, Cottbus, and Karl-Marx-Stadt. The Dresden march was sanctioned by authorities and led by the mayor and the reformist local party chief. The march was the first officially approved antigovernment demonstration in that city. What only a short time ago would have been sensational concessions by the government were no longer enough. On November 9 came the historic announcement that East Germans wishing to emigrate to the West could do so by applying for passports. Moreover, East Germans who wanted to visit West Berlin would be able to pass through the checkpoints along the Berlin Wall. The Berlin Wall was crumbling.

The logic of revolution, however, demands that halfway measures are not enough. Dissidents now demanded the abolition of Article I of the constitution, which granted the party its political monopoly. The party caved in and scuttled Article I on December 1, 1989. This cleared the way for free elections.

## ☐ German Reunification

The demise of the Berlin Wall put the unification of Germany on the agenda. Washington, Moscow, and the nations of Europe were bracing themselves for the inevitable.

After the creation of the West German government in May 1949 and that of East Germany in October 1949, the division of Germany had taken on an aura of permanence. Officially, however, the West German government rejected the notion of a divided Germany that, moreover, had been divided not just into two but into three parts; there was still the issue of Silesia, Pommerania, and East Prussia—under Polish and Soviet "administration" since 1945.

When West German chancellor Helmut Kohl began to speak of unification in November 1989, Moscow declared that just because East Germans had been granted unrestricted access to West Germany, this did not mean the automatic unification of the two Germanies. Kohl's statements also received a cool reception in the West. The wartime allies and most Europeans did not relish the re-creation of a strong and unified Germany in the heart of the continent. Such an eventuality dredged up unpleasant memories of Germany's past.

The unification of Germany in October 1990 and the decision to move the capital from Bonn to Berlin was taken by the West German government without much consultation with its allies. In the end, Germany did calm the fears of its neighbors, particularly Poland, when it officially accepted the borders the victors of World War II had drawn up and, concomitantly, the loss of East Prussia and the lands beyond the Oder and Neisse Rivers.

With the decline of the Soviet empire, the economy of a united Germany became the most powerful in Europe. Immediately after the failed coup in Moscow in August 1991, it was Germany that took the lead in recognizing the independence of the Baltic states. In Yugoslavia, Germany broke ranks with the European Community (EC) and the United States when it recognized the breakaway republics of Slovenia and Croatia and convinced its reluctant EC partners to do the same. During the Gulf War, Germany sent troops abroad for the first time since 1945, an air squadron to Turkey. In the summer of 1992, the German navy showed its flag in the Adriatic Sea off the coast of Yugoslavia to help the United Nations enforce its embargo against Serbia, an action the government did not even deem worth discussing in the parliament.

Germany also took the lead in providing economic assistance to Eastern Europe. It was in part designed to prevent the dreaded consequences of a collapse of the East European economies—a flood of refugees westward. West Germany was already grappling with the unpopular fact that approximately 10 percent of its population consisted of foreigners. As residents—whether as workers or refugees—they were entitled to services from a government whose resources were stretched to the limit. The result was an antiforeign backlash; in 1992, there were two thousand assaults—including a number of fatalities—against Turks, black Africans, and Jews. The attackers were generally young males who unabashedly proclaimed themselves neo-Nazis. By the end of 1992, the euphoria and promise of German reunification had given way to bitterness, violence, and economic stagnation.

After unification, nearly all physical traces of the Berlin Wall were immediately erased. But the psychological gulf between the Easterners and the Westerners remained. The Easterners had lived since 1933 under two consecutive dictatorships, first the Nazis and then the Communists. Their past experience was different from those in the West. Many recoiled from the open democratic political discourse. Unification also meant the East German economic enterprises were thrown into a marketplace in which they had little chance of surviving. Economic recovery in East Germany came slowly, despite the infusion of massive sums—raised by drastic, unpopular tax increases.

☐ *Hungary*

At the time that Solidarity in Poland conducted its noisy challenge to the Communist Party, events in Hungary, though quieter, also contributed to the transformation of Eastern Europe.

Janos Kadar had come to power in 1956 after the Soviet army crushed the Hungarian rebellion. By the late 1960s, Kadar and his party began a cautious program of domestic innovation that, by East European standards, was remarkable. While gradually moving away from the Soviet model, Kadar remained at pains to assure the Soviets that he would not threaten to break up their East European empire.

Kadar's innovations were made possible by the détente of the late 1960s, which made possible experiments in small-scale capitalism. The result was a mixed economy. The "commanding heights" of the economy—heavy industry, transportation, banking—remained in the hands of the state. At the same time, however, small private enterprises—such as small shops, restaurants, bars, food stands, artisan shops, garages employing no more than three persons—were permitted. Western journalists called it "goulash Communism." Hungarians spoke of "Communism with a capitalist facelift."

From a rigid Marxist point of view, the Hungarian innovations were acts of heresy. But at no time did Karl Marx waste his time discussing the malfeasance of the man who owned a barbershop or the peasant woman

**Eastern Europe (1995)**

selling flowers at a street corner. When Marx wrote his *Das Capital,* he denounced, instead, what the poet William Blake had called the "dark Satanic mills" of the early industrial revolution.

On June 8, 1985, Hungarian voters cast their ballots for representatives to parliament and local councils, in which at least two candidates ran for nearly all seats. This was the first election under a 1983 law that demanded a choice for the voters, something unique in a Soviet-bloc country.

In May 1988, the reform wing of the Communist Party nudged Kadar aside as party leader. It paved the way for the political, posthumous rehabilitation of Kadar's victims. For the first time since 1956, it became possible in Hungary to mention the names of Imre Nagy, Hungary's party chief at the time of the 1956 revolution, and Pal Maleter, the general who had fought the Soviet army. They had been among those Kadar had executed and dumped face-down, with their hands still tied behind their backs, in an unmarked mass grave. Their names had disappeared from the official histories but not from the collective memory of the nation. Their rehabilitation culminated in the solemn June 1989 reinternment of Nagy and his associates, a ceremony broadcast live on national television.

In September 1989, the Communist Party renamed itself the Socialist Party, and parliament rewrote the constitution to permit multiparty elections the following spring. On October 23, 1989, the thirty-third anniversary of the beginning of the 1956 uprising, parliament declared Hungary no longer a "People's Republic." It became the Republic of Hungary and the red star on top of the parliament building came down. Two rounds of elections, in March and April 1990, shattered whatever illusions the Socialist Party still had of clinging to power. The voters gave the Hungarian Democratic Forum, a populist, nationalist umbrella organization with a right-of-center orientation, a plurality of the seats in parliament and its leader, Jozsef Antall, set out to create a coalition with the other conservative parties. The Socialist Party won but 8 percent of the parliamentary seats. The Communist experiment in Hungary was over.

□ *Czechoslovakia*

The fourth Communist domino to fall in 1989 was Czechoslovakia. The revolutionary vanguard against the old Communist regime initially consisted of intellectuals and students. In the center of the opposition stood Charta 77, a loose union of 1,600 individuals who in 1977 had signed a petition demanding civil rights. Their leaders were Jiri Hajek, the country's foreign minister during the Prague Spring, and the dissident writer Vaclav Havel. Since June 1989, a petition demanding the release of all political prisoners, freedom of expression and assembly, and an independent news media had circulated throughout the nation, and forty thousand citizens had signed it. Czechoslovakia's "velvet revolution" was under way.

As long as the demonstrating crowds remained relatively small—two thousand in January 1989 and still only ten thousand at the beginning of November 1989—the police were able to maintain a semblance of order by arrests and occasional beatings. The workers who enjoyed a relatively high standard of living were slow to join. When they did join the demonstrators on St. Wenceslas Square in Prague, the end had arrived for the Communist regime. It folded like a house of cards at the end of November 1989.

Nearly the entire nation stood in opposition to the Communist Party. Not even a bloodbath could save it. Once the party agreed to abandon its ruling monopoly on November 29, 1989, events moved quickly. The opposition established a provisional government until the voters were able to choose the country's first freely elected government since 1948. Havel, who earlier in the year had been arrested and jailed for antistate activities, became the new prime minister. Alexander Dubcek, one of the architects of the Prague Spring, became the country's new president.

At a Warsaw Pact meeting in December 1989, the five participants in the 1968 invasion of Czechoslovakia—the Soviet Union, East Germany, Poland, Hungary, and Bulgaria—formally declared that the invasion had been "illegal" and pledged in the future strict noninterference in each other's internal affairs. The declaration marked the formal repudiation of the Brezhnev Doctrine. The Soviet government issued a separate statement admitting that the reasons for intervention had been "unfounded" and that its decision to do so had been "erroneous."[42]

Havel, in a pointed reminder that Czechoslovakia was a part of Central and not Eastern Europe, went on his first official state visit to Berlin and then to Warsaw. "It's not good-bye to Moscow," a foreign ministry official explained, "but it's a new orientation toward West and Central Europe."[43]

In the summer of 1992, militant Slovaks in the eastern part of the country decided to secede from their Czech cousins. Czechoslovakia had come into existence in 1918 as a federation of Czechs and Slovaks under the leadership of the Czech Tomas Masaryk. From the outset, Slovaks resented Czech domination, particularly the fact that they never received the autonomy the Czechs had promised. Remarkably, there was little sentiment among Czechs to preserve the union with their ungrateful cousins. The breakup became official on New Year's Day 1993.

## ☐ Bulgaria

Next in line was Bulgaria, the most loyal member of the Warsaw Pact. The seventy-eight-year-old boss of the Communist Party, Todor Zhivkov, in power since 1954, at first showed no signs of stepping down. But his long rule had bred widespread opposition. He had been responsible for reviving the ancient quarrel between Bulgarians and Turks in 1984 when he forced the 1-million-strong Muslim Turkish minority to adopt Slavic names. In

May 1989, he pressured 310,000 Turks to emigrate. Not only did he damage Bulgaria's international standing, but the exodus also wrought havoc with the nation's economy. When Zhivkov promoted his son to the Central Committee's Department of Culture in 1989, even his old allies deserted him. In the end, the Politburo demanded his resignation.

The charges against Zhivkov consisted of corruption and nepotism. But the ouster of Zhivkov was too little and too late. Increasingly larger and more defiant crowds focused on the party's monopoly on power.

On January 15, 1990, the Communist Party caved in to popular pressure and agreed to give up its leading political role and hold free elections. In September 1992, after an eighteen-month trial, the now eighty-one-year-old Zhivkov was found guilty of the embezzlement of nearly $1 million and sentenced to seven years in prison (commuted to house arrest due to ill health and old age). Zhivkov here became the first former Soviet-bloc leader to be judged by a post-Communist court.

## ☐ Romania

The last and least likely of the Communist dictators to be toppled in 1989 was Nicolae Ceauşescu, who had come to power in 1965. Ceauşescu carved out a foreign policy independent of Moscow without, however, leaving the Warsaw Pact. He reserved Romania's right not to join in the pact's annual war exercises, continued to recognize Israel after the 1967 Six Day War, and refused to participate in the invasion of Czechoslovakia in 1968. In 1984, he did not follow the Moscow-led boycott of the Olympic Games in Los Angeles, where the Romanian team received a standing ovation at the opening ceremonies. The West rewarded maverick Romania with most-favored-nation treatment, and U.S. presidents Richard Nixon and Jimmy Carter paid highly publicized visits to Bucharest, where they spared no words in heaping praise on the Romanian dictator. The West ignored the fact that the Ceauşescu regime was by far the most repressive in the Warsaw Pact.

Ceauşescu decided what few dictators even dared to contemplate. Romania would pay off its $10 billion foreign debt, never mind the social consequences. The result was a sharp drop in the standard of living. Large amounts of food were exported, the workweek was increased to six days, the price of gasoline was raised, apartments were kept at about 50 degrees Fahrenheit in the winter, electricity was rationed, and hospitals lacked supplies. The 24 million people of Romania, an agrarian land, were reduced to a meager diet. Pigs' feet, commonly known as "patriots," remained in abundance; they were the only parts of the pig that stayed behind when the rest was exported.

Ceauşescu's style was a combination of that of Stalin and the fascist Benito Mussolini of Italy. He dropped the label "comrade" and began to call himself "Conducator," or leader. Ceauşescu ruled not through his party but, similar to Stalin, through the secret police, the Securitate. The party existed merely to legitimize Ceauşescu's rule. The most prominent feature of Romanian television was the glorification of Ceauşescu and his wife, Elena, the nation's second-most-powerful figure. Their son, Nicu, was groomed to follow in his father's footsteps. Forty other relatives were on the government payroll.

In June 1989, Ceauşescu sent a congratulatory message to Deng Xiaoping for crushing the Chinese student demonstrations. He promised to respond likewise should dissidents take to his streets. A party official explained the Ceauşescu method of governance: "All the systems of the world are based on reward and punishment. Ceauşescu works only with punishment. It is a reward that there is no punishment."[44]

After the foreign debt was largely repaid, economic conditions in Romania did not change. Ceauşescu continued to bleed his people by initiating a massive building program, a monument to his megalomania. Fifteen thousand workers began work on the thirteen-story, thousand-room House of the Republic of white marble, on the Avenue of Socialist Victory. To make room for this palace, nearly forty thousand people were moved and many historic buildings were destroyed—among them the sixteenth-century Monastery of Michael the Brave, the ruler who in 1600 had unified Wallachia, Moldavia, and Transylvania into modern Romania. Ceauşescu personally supervised the project, visiting it two or three times a week. His other projects included the razing of entire towns in Transylvania, many inhabited by ethnic Germans and Hungarians whose ancestors had built them over seven centuries.

The city of Timişoara, in Transylvania, lit the spark that brought down the seemingly impregnable Ceauşescu dictatorship. In early December 1989, the government decided to deport from Timişoara a little-known Hungarian Protestant priest, Laszlo Tokes. The decision touched off demonstrations, forcing the government to reconsider. The concession was a victory of sorts for the people in the streets and produced an even greater demonstration on December 16. Economic considerations also played a part. In October, additional food had been rationed—this in a city that contained large food-processing factories and bakeries. Workers who knew nothing of Tokes but who handled the food destined for export joined the ranks of the demonstrators.

The fall of the other East European Communist parties had taken place without a single fatality; Romania was destined to be different. Ceauşescu took a page from the Chinese book by sending the Securitate into Timişoara. The Conductor, the "hero of the nation, the brilliant son of the people," began murdering his own people.[45] The uprising might have been contained by the police, had it not continued the practice of refusing to return the bodies of those killed, who were then dumped into a mass grave on the outskirts of the city. "Give us our dead," the demonstrators demanded.

In a speech in Bucharest, Ceauşescu vowed to win the war against the "terrorists and hooligans." That speech—before what appeared to be a traditionally docile crowd assembled by the authorities—became a disaster, as it turned into an anti-Ceauşescu demonstration. Ceauşescu never finished it and fled the presidential palace. At that point, he also lost control of the army. He had never trusted the military, and for good reason. After initially firing into the crowd, soldiers turned their guns on the police. Ceauşescu and his wife fled, only to be captured.

The Ceauşescus were put before a military tribunal and charged with genocide, the murder of sixty thousand Romanian citizens, theft, and the creation of Swiss bank accounts. Elena Ceauşescu termed the last accusation a "provocation." The unrepentant Conducator denied all charges and still claimed to be the leader of Romania. A firing squad ended the discussion on Christmas Day 1989. Romanian television showed a tape of the trial and the elegantly dressed corpses of the Ceauşescus.

The new provisional government was headed by Ion Iliescu, Gorbachev's classmate in Moscow in the 1950s and party boss in Timişoara in the late 1960s, who had become popular with many party members for speaking out against Ceauşescu's economic measures.

On the surface, the new government followed the precedents established in other East European countries. It declared that Romania was no longer a socialist state, stocked the stores with food, reduced the workweek to five days, cut the price of electricity by more than half, permitted each farm family an acre of land for private cultivation, abolished the death penalty after the Ceauşescus' execution, dissolved the Securitate, and promised free elections in April 1990. The government also arrested Ceauşescu's closest associates, including the entire Politburo and ranking officers of the Securitate, promising punishment for "all evildoers from the old regime."

What had taken place in Romania, however, was neither a political nor a social revolution. The Ceauşescus were executed by their own henchmen, among them Iliescu, who now tried to save their own necks. Their aim was to eliminate the dictator but not the dictatorship. The "red aristocrats," as the party leaders were known, then made sure to stress the myth of a political revolution.[46]

The conspirators produced the trappings of parliamentary democracy yet continued Ceauşescuism without Ceauşescu. Their task was facilitated by the fact that Romania never had known a modern party system, a responsible political intelligentsia, or an autonomous church. Romania's political culture was steeped in intrigue, conspiracy, and subservience to authority.

Six months after the death of Ceauşescu, the Marxist Iliescu found solace in fascism. He announced the formation of a national guard reminiscent of the fascist Iron Guard of World War II, and proceeded to arrest opposition leaders, insisting all along that he was defending democracy.[47]

By the beginning of the twenty-first century, Romania remained at best a society in transition to democracy. It was plagued with widespread economic and political corruption. It sought to join the European Union (EU), but that organization always insisted that its members follow the rules of democracy.

Then there was the brutal economic collapse. Forty percent of the population lived on less than $35 per month, that is, around the international poverty line of $1 per day. The Craiova giant heavy machine and tool complex, for instance, which once had employed seven thousand workers, ten years later employed but eight hundred.[48]

The presidential election of 2000 pitted the discredited Ion Iliescu against Corneliu Vadim Tudor, once Ceauşescu's court poet, the head of the ultranationalist Greater Romania Party. Tudor declared that Romania can be governed only at "the point of a machine gun" and promised to end corruption "with a Kalashnikov." He continued to call Ceauşescu a "great patriot" and filled his publications with racist articles and cartoons railing against "dirty Jews," "fascist Hungarians," and "criminal Gypsies." Iliescu handily defeated Tudor, who had become an embarrassment to many voters who had to choose between the lesser of two evils. With Tudor, Romania had no choice of joining the EU; with Iliescu its chances improved a little. Still, when the EU added ten new members in 2004, Romania was not among them.

☐ *Albania*

The Communist state of Albania, the creation of Enver Hoxha in 1944, became the next casualty. Hoxha's regime, a fusion of the worst features of Stalinism and Maoism, was even more oppressive than that of Ceauşescu. Poverty-stricken and isolated, Albania was the world's only official atheist state. Defendants were often executed without trials or simply disappeared; their relatives were punished for good measure. After Hoxha's death in April 1985, Ramiz Alia continued his policies. After 1989, however, Alia introduced reforms to an increasingly restless population. He rescinded, for example, the "crime" of religious propaganda and granted free elections, which ended Communist rule in March 1992.

# ■ YUGOSLAVIA

Before its breakup, Yugoslavia was a nation of eight ethnic regions—Slovenia, Croatia, Bosnia-Herzegovina, Macedonia, Montenegro, Kosovo, Vojvodina, and Serbia. After World War II, the Croat Joseph Tito established a federation in which no one people would dominate another, particularly the numerically and historically dominant Serbs. Tito understood the potential danger that ethnic strife posed for Yugoslavia—literally "South Slavia"—an artificial nation formed in 1918 after the collapse of Ottoman Turkish control. To appease the nationalities, the 1974 constitution granted the ethnic regions a measure of autonomy. The Serbian nationality, because of its great size, remained first among equals but an equal nevertheless. After Tito's death in 1980, the new Communist Party leader, the Serb Slobodan Milosevic, however, stripped the Albanian majority in Kosovo Province of its autonomy. Milosevic here gave notice that he sought a Greater Serbia dominating the other nationalities. On June 28, 1989, he added fuel to the fire when he led a Serb demonstration of 1 million people into Kosovo to commemorate the 600th anniversary of the Battle of Kosovo Field in which the Muslim Turks (with the help of Muslim Albanians) had defeated the Christian Orthodox Serbs. The time had come to restore Serbia to its former greatness.[49]

Although most Yugoslavs were of Slavic origin, there were serious divisions among them. Slovenes and Croats in the west had fallen under the influence of Roman Catholicism, while the Slavs farther to the east, such as Serbs and Macedonians, belonged to the Eastern Orthodox Church. The country, moreover, contained a sizable Muslim population—the Albanians and Bosnians—the legacy of centuries of Turkish control. To complicate matters, the diverse population was interspersed. Yugoslavia was thus a fusion of Western and Eastern Christianity and Islam.

Assertive Serbian nationalism produced a fearful reaction from other nationalities. Taking their cue from the independence movements in the Soviet Union, they began to demand their independence. The first to do so, in June 1991, was Slovenia—with a population of 2 million—in Yugoslavia's northwestern corner. At the same time, the larger (4.8 million people) and more powerful Republic of Croatia also seceded. Bosnia followed suit in 1992. These events triggered a bloody conflict—the first on the European continent since 1945—when the Serbian-dominated Yugoslav army invaded Croatia.

At this point, the United Nations intervened. It brokered a cease-fire that took effect in January 1992. Blue-helmeted UN troops—14,400 from thirty-one nations—became the first such deployment on the European continent. But the troops did not have a combat role; they merely served to keep the belligerents apart. Germany became the first nation officially to recognize Slovenia and Croatia in January 1992, and the other members of the European Community followed suit. The United States continued to hold out hope that a united Yugoslavia could somehow remain a viable option. But in April 1992, the administration of George H. W. Bush came into line with the EC when it simultaneously recognized Slovenia, Croatia, and Bosnia.

☐ *Bosnia*

The ethnic makeup of Bosnia was the most complex of all the regions—92 percent of its people were of Slavic origin, but 44 percent were Muslim, 31 percent were Serbian and Orthodox, and 17 percent were Catholic Croats.[50] Milosevic, stymied in Croatia, then turned against Bosnia, ostensibly to protect the threatened Serb minority. He provided weapons for Serbian militia forces in Bosnia who proceeded to lay siege to Bosnia's capital, Sarajevo. The siege lasted more than a thousand days, one of the longest in history.

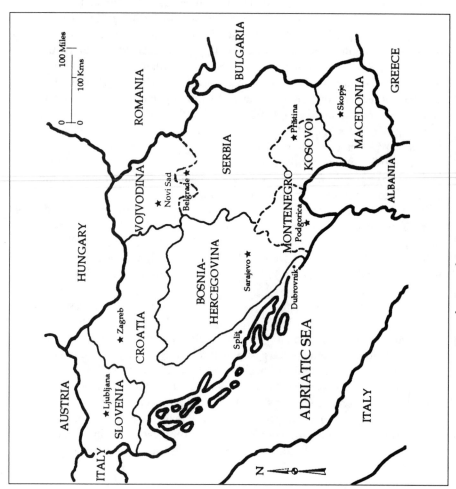

**Yugoslavia and Its Successor States**

The conflict in Bosnia became a war of extraordinary brutality. Serbs established concentration camps and undertook the "ethnic cleansing" of parts of Bosnia—replete with rape, torture, massacres, and forcible deportation of civilians in freight cars. These actions were reminiscent of crimes last committed in Europe by Stalin and Hitler. Serbian perpetrators were well aware that they faced potential charges as war criminals, and for that reason often wore masks. The violence in Yugoslavia produced approximately 2.5 million refugees by 1992, the first on such a scale in Europe since 1945.

By 1992, what had once been Yugoslavia was reduced to five separate entities: a rump state of Yugoslavia (Serbia and the once autonomous provinces of Kosovo and Vojvodina and the Republic of Montenegro), Slovenia, Croatia, Bosnia, and Macedonia. The Serbian chauvinist Milosevic had become the destroyer of Yugoslavia, its peoples, cities and villages, economy, and currency (inflation ran at 25,000 percent per year, which rendered the Yugoslav *dinar* worthless.) As recently as 1989, many Europeans had exulted in the spiritual rebirth of the continent. Yet in 1992, the EC, the United Nations, and the United States were stymied by a defiant, virulent Serbian chauvinism.

The Muslims in Bosnia were able to obtain little help from the outside world because of a UN weapons embargo. The Bosnian Serbs, in contrast, were able to obtain large quantities of arms from their kinsmen in Serbia. Led by their president, Radovan Karadzic, and the commander of their forces, General Ratko Mladic, the Serbs of Bosnia proclaimed the creation of an ostensibly independent Serbian Republic.

The homicidal Mladic saw himself as the vindicator of Serbian history. To him, there was hardly a difference between the past and the present; the violence of the 1990s was part of the continuum of Serbian history. Serbs were again fighting to save Europe from an Islamic tide.[51]

It became increasingly difficult for the United Nations and NATO to stand by idly as the evidence of atrocities began to mount. In February 1994, as Serbs made gains in eastern Bosnia, the UN declared several regions there as "safe areas" and threatened NATO air strikes to maintain them. But when NATO carried out its first air strikes against Serb forces near Gorazde in April 1994, the Serbs responded with their own attacks on the "safe areas." In 1995, they seized 270 UN peacekeepers and shackled them to potential bombing targets. French general Bernard Janvier, whose troops made up more than one-half of the hostages, arranged with Mladic their release, but the price was a halt to air attacks on the Serbs. The deal left the UN powerless, and the forty thousand Bosnian Muslims in Srebrenica—officially still under UN protection—were now defenseless.[52]

By the early summer of 1992, the U.S. government had gathered evidence that the Serbs were conducting widespread massacres of Muslims. It knew conclusively that in the northern town of Brcko, Serbs had herded three thousand Muslim men into an abandoned warehouse, and tortured and murdered them. U.S. satellites had recorded a part of the slaughter. The United States had even intercepted telephone conversations in which Mladic spoke of his intentions to cleanse Gorazde and Zepa.[53] In July 1995, Serbs carried out yet another massacre, this one in Srebrenica, of six to eight thousand Muslim men and boys. According to eyewitnesses, Mladic was present at the killings. This time, Madeleine Albright, the U.S. ambassador to the United Nations, revealed photographs of fresh graves taken from U.S. spy planes.

In May 1993, the UN Security Council established an "International Criminal Tribunal for the Former Yugoslavia," the first such court since the Nuremberg and Tokyo trials after World War II. In May 1996, a young Croat, Drazen Erdemovic, who had fought for the Serbs, became the first person to plead guilty to war crimes—confessing he had murdered scores of unarmed Muslim men at Srebrenica. His defense was that, fearing for his life, he had only followed orders.[54]

At the end of the summer of 1995, the tide turned against the Serbs when Croatian forces wrested southeastern Croatia from them, sending more than 170,000 Serbs fleeing in fear. In October 1995, the three warring sides—by now thoroughly exhausted—agreed to a cease-fire and to hold talks in the United States.

Bosnian Muslims hoped a settlement of the conflict would not recognize the partition of Bosnia and the consequences of "ethnic cleansing." "Bosnia is the place to draw the line against ultranationalism on the march," a Bosnian journalist pleaded; "appeasement of Serbian conquests and ethnic partition of Bosnia would encourage such forces."[55] But to no avail. The Dayton agreement of November 1995 divided Bosnia between a Serbian-controlled Serbian Republic and the Bosnian Federation (of Croats and Muslims) by a ratio of forty-nine to fifty-one, respectively. In effect, the split rewarded Serb aggression. A small NATO force was left behind to monitor a precarious cease-fire.

Officially, Bosnia remained a single country but one divided into two republics. As of June 1996, 1,319,250 Bosnian refugees had made their way to European nations that did not want them. They were unable to return to their former domiciles, which—as likely as not—had been "ethnically cleansed."[56]

There were still scores to be settled. Muslims in Bosnia remained bitter that the world had done little to protect them, and Serbs in Croatia, who had been put to flight, dreamed of retribution.

☐  Kosovo

After the partition of Bosnia, the focus shifted to the Yugoslav province of Kosovo. Its population, 90 percent Albanian, was ruled by the Serb minority there and by Milosevic in Belgrade. Early in 1999, violence between an Albanian Kosovo Liberation Army (UCK) and the Serbian authorities began to escalate. By March 1999, the number of dead was estimated between fifteen hundred and two thousand.

This time, the Clinton administration—prodded primarily by its secretary of state, Madeleine Albright—decided to act. The United States would not idly stand by as it had in the recent Balkan wars. Moreover, Third World leaders had criticized the West for doing nothing while the Hutus had gone about their business of exterminating Tutsis in Rwanda. This time the West took action.

Clinton knew that he would not be able to act through the United Nations, as President Bush had done in the Gulf War, because Russia was certain to cast its veto. Russia has historic ties to Serbia: Russians and Serbs are Slavic peoples, they tend to be of the Orthodox faith, and in the not-too-distant past Russia had come to the assistance of Serbia against the Turks, Austrians, and Germans. Moreover, the Russian government looked with disfavor at some of the recent activity on the part of the United States, specifically NATO's eastward expansion.

It took Washington a bit to persuade its NATO allies to join the fray in Kosovo, but in the end they came on board. They agreed with Clinton and Albright that the Western alliance could no longer ignore another case of genocide, this one in Europe.

Clinton demanded that Milosevic withdraw his army from Kosovo. When Milosevic refused, NATO began an air war of seventy-eight days' duration—from March 24 until June 9, 1999. NATO here went into combat for the first time, even though the war had nothing to do with a threat against one of its members; at best, it was a war for the defense of the self-esteem of its member nations.

The immediate consequence of the war was precisely what the West had feared, the brutal ethnic cleansing of Albanians—accompanied with rape, mass executions, and arson. A stream of 850,000 refugees headed to the Albanian and Macedonian borders.

The air war involved the deployment of 1,100 airplanes flying 38,000 sorties, the largest concentration of air power in history. Serb forces in Kosovo were subjected to a hail of thousands of "smart" bombs and cruise missiles. NATO, however, did not suffer a single combat fatality in the first war ever won solely by air power. It was dubbed as the first "telecommunication war" waged by remote control, the first "virtual war" with pilots watching on their computer screens as the bombs headed for their targets.

NATO repeatedly insisted that it was not waging a war against the Serbian people, only against the government of Milosevic. "Collateral damage" among Serb civilians was relatively small, particularly when one considers the scale of the sustained air attacks—about five hundred dead caused by approximately one hundred sorties gone astray.[57]

Officially, NATO did not go to war to create a separate state of Kosovo or create a "Greater Albania," as most Albanians and the UCK wished. The status of Kosovo remained unresolved, its territory occupied by NATO forces from five nations: the United States, Germany, France, Italy, and Britain. The German general who headed NATO's deployment of occupation troops thought that NATO might have to remain in Kosovo for "at least ten years" to set up or rebuild viable institutions—a government, universities, schools, roads, factories, and so on.

Meanwhile, sporadic violence tested the diplomatic skills of the occupying forces. Towns were divided, both sides vowing to make them eventually theirs. It was now the turn of the Albanians, particularly the UCK, to exact their revenge. In the eight months after the war, 250,000 Kosovo Serbs were driven from their homes. The fighting had ended, but peace remained a distant mirage.

Milosevic finally agreed to withdraw from Kosovo. After three wars in the span of less than a decade and an international economic boycott, the economy of what was left of Yugoslavia was in shambles. When Milosevic agreed to hold a presidential election in September 2000, the winner, to his surprise, was the candidate of the Socialist Party, Vojislav Kostunica. At first Milosevic refused to acknowledge Kostunica's victory, but when street demonstrations became uncontrollable, he finally stepped down.

Kostunica, however, was no more inclined than Milosevic to accept the loss of Kosovo. And Albanians were still trying to drive Serbs out of lands they considered theirs. In December 2000, the two sides were trading mortar rounds across the three-mile buffer between Kosovo and Serbia. Kostunica warned that a declaration of independence by ethnic Albanians in Kosovo would touch off yet another Balkan war.

Of the three men primarily responsible for the violence, only one was apprehended. In 2001, after he had lost the election, Milosevic became the first head of state since World War II to face charges of war crimes and genocide. At the International Criminal Court for the former Yugoslavia, Milosevic, acting as his own lawyer, managed to drag out the procedures for years; at the end of 2004, he still had not called the 1,631 witnesses for the defense. The Bosnian Serb leaders, Karadzic and Mladic, indicted in 1995, continued to live quite openly in Belgrade as long as Milosevic remained in power. After that they went into hiding.

## ■ RECOMMENDED READINGS

Brown, Archie. *The Gorbachev Factor.* New York: Oxford University Press, 1996.
    A positive assessment of Gorbachev's role in the perestroika of the Soviet Union.
Cohen, Stephen F. *Failed Crusade: America and the Tragedy of Post-Communist Russia.* New York: W. W. Norton, 2000.

A critical assessment of the U.S. role urging the Yeltsin government to accept capitalism and to dismantle Soviet institutions.

Goldman, Marshall I. *Gorbachev's Challenge: Economic Reform in the Age of High Technology*. New York: W. W. Norton, 1987.
A discussion of the magnitude of Gorbachev's economic problems.

Gorbachev, Mikhail. *The August Coup: The Truth and the Lessons*. New York: HarperCollins, 1991.

——. *Perestroika: New Thinking for Our Country and the World*. New York: Harper and Row, 1987.

Hollander, Paul. *Political Will and Personal Belief: The Decline and Fall of Soviet Communism*. New Haven, Conn.: Yale University Press, 2000.
Focuses on the lack of faith in Communism as an all-encompassing ideology.

Karny, Yoav. *Highlanders: A Journey in Quest of Memory*. New York: Farrar, Straus and Giroux, 2000.
By an Israeli journalist who discusses the complexities of the Caucasus.

Matlock, Jack F., Jr. *Autopsy of an Empire: The American Ambassador's Account of the Collapse of the Soviet Union*. New York: Random House, 1995.

Medvedev, Zhores A. *Gorbachev*. New York: W. W. Norton, 1986.
By a dissident Soviet historian.

Putin, Vladimir. *First Person: An Astonishing Frank Self-Portrait: Interviews with Nataliya Geborkyan, Natalya Timakova, and Andrei Kolesnikov*. London: Hutchinson, 2000.
Putin's black-and-white view of the world.

Reddaway, Peter, and Dmitri Glinski. *The Tragedy of Russia's Reforms: Market Bolshevism Against Democracy*. Washington, D.C.: United States Institute of Peace, 2000.
Detailed, scathing analysis of the events in Russia, 1985–2000.

Schmidt-Häuer, Christian. *Gorbachev: The Path to Power*. Boston: Salem House, 1986.
A Moscow-based West German journalist's account of how the party elected Gorbachev as its chief.

Smith, Graham, ed. *The Nationalities Question in the Soviet Union*. London: Longman, 1990.
Various authors analyze the historical development and claims of twenty nationalities of the former Soviet Union.

## ☐ Afghanistan

Bradsher, Henry S. *Afghanistan and the Soviet Union*. 2d ed. Durham, N.C.: Duke University Press, 1985.
A detailed account of the events leading up to the Russian invasion.

Chaliand, Gerard. *Report from Afghanistan*. New York: Penguin, 1982.
A useful introduction to the history, geography, and politics of Afghanistan.

Garthoff, Raymond L. *Detente and Confrontation: American-Soviet Relations from Nixon to Reagan*. Washington, D.C.: Brookings Institution, 1985.
Argues that the Soviets feared that Amin would expel their advisers and bring in U.S. personnel.

## ☐ Eastern Europe

Ascherson, Neal. *The Polish August: The Self-Limiting Revolution*. New York: Viking Press, 1982.

A survey of the political climate in Poland that set the stage for the rise of Solidarity.

Ash, Timothy Garton. *The Polish Revolution: Solidarity.* New York: Charles Scribner's Sons, 1984.

Discusses the rise and fall of Solidarity.

————. *The Magic Lantern: The Revolution of '89 Witnessed in Warsaw, Budapest, Berlin and Prague.* New York: Vintage, 1993.

An eyewitness account by a British journalist whose specialty is Eastern Europe.

Behr, Edward. *Kiss the Hand You Cannot Bite: The Rise and Fall of the Ceauşescu.* New York: Villard Books, 1991.

Political biography that focuses on the deep social and cultural roots of the dictatorship.

Brumberg, Abraham, ed. *Poland: Genesis of a Revolution.* New York: Random House, 1983.

A collection of essays by Polish activists.

Carre d'Encausse, Helene. *Decline of an Empire: The Soviet Socialist Republics in Revolt.* New York: Harper and Row, 1978.

An introduction to the ethnic complexity of the Soviet empire.

Djilas, Aleksa. *The Contested Country: Yugoslav Unity and Communist Revolution, 1919–1953.* Cambridge, Mass.: Harvard University Press, 1993.

An analysis of why Tito's concept of a unified Yugoslavia eventually failed.

Gati, Charles. *The Bloc That Failed: Soviet–East European Relations in Transition.* Bloomington: Indiana University Press, 1990.

Brief history of the Soviet bloc in Eastern Europe, with the emphasis on the impact of Gorbachev's reforms.

Glenny, Misha. *The Balkans: Nationalism, War and the Great Powers, 1804–1999.* New York: Viking, 2000.

By a BBC correspondent who covered the disintegration of Yugoslavia.

Stokes, Gail. *From Stalinism to Pluralism: A Documentary History of Eastern Europe Since 1945.* New York: Oxford University Press, 1996.

Sullivan, Stacy. *Be Not Afraid, For You Have Sons in America: How a Brooklyn Roofer Helped Lure the U.S. into the Kosovo War.* New York: St. Martin's Press, 2004.

# ■ NOTES

1. "On a Course of Unity and Solidarity," *Pravda,* February 21, 1985; *Current Digest of the Soviet Press,* March 20, 1985, p. 7.

2. David Remnick, "Solzhenitsyn—A New Day in the Life," *Washington Post,* January 7, 1990, p. B3.

3. B. Minonov, "'Otkryvaia dver' v 'spetskhran,'" *Pravda,* September 10, 1988, p. 6.

4. "On the Agricultural Policies of the Communist Party of the Soviet Union Under Present Conditions," *Pravda,* March 16, 1989.

5. Cited in Ester B. Fein, "Gorbachev Hints He Would Accept Multiparty Rule," *New York Times,* January 14, 1990, p. 1.

6. The exact number is unknown. In fact, the Turkish government bitterly resents any mention of a massacre, denying it ever took place; it merely admitted to Turkish-Armenian violence in which both sides suffered fatalities.

7. Esther Schrader, "Baku Refugees Celebrate Deaths of Azerbaijanis," *Baltimore Sun,* January 23, 1990, p. 4A.

8. Jerry F. Hough, "Gorbachev's Politics," *Foreign Affairs* (winter 1989-1990), p. 30.

9. See the interrogations of the conspirators in V. A. Zatova and T. K. Speranskaia, eds., *Avgust-91* (Moscow: Politizdat, 1991), pp. 253–271.

10. Leslie Gelb, "The Russian Sinkhole," *New York Times,* March 30, 1992, p. A17; Steven Greenhouse, "Point Man for the Rescue of the Century," *New York Times,* April 26, 1992, section 3, pp. 1, 6.

11. Nina Plekina, "Posle Miunkhina, v chetverg," *Novoe vremia,* no. 30 (1992), p. 24.

12. Aleksandr Pumpianskii, "Sud na partiei, kotoraia byla pravitel'stvo," *Novoe vremia,* no. 42 (1992), p. 5.

13. *Baltimore Sun,* April 28, 1991, p. 11A; based on *Europa World Yearbook,* 1989 Soviet Census, and *World Almanac.*

14. Joe Murray in an interview with Gamsakhurdia, "Outside the Stronghold," *Baltimore Sun,* October 30, 1991, p. 9A.

15. Galina Kovalskaia, "Kavkaztsam v Stavropole doroga zakazana," *Novoe vremia,* no. 28 (1992), pp. 8–9.

16. Zhores A. Medvedev, "Property Rights," *In These Times,* April 19, 1993, p. 29; Stephen F. Cohen, "American Policy and Russia's Future," *The Nation,* April 12, 1993, p. 480.

17. Cited by Stephen F. Cohen, *Failed Crusade: America and the Tragedy of Post-Communist Russia* (New York: W. W. Norton, 2000), p. 115.

18. Cited in Michael Specter, "From Mother Russia with Brute Force," *New York Times,* January 21, 1996, p. 6E.

19. The estimated fatalities vary widely. Among the highest, eighty thousand, is that of Michael Specter, "The Wars of Aleksandr Ivanovich Lebed," *New York Times Magazine,* October 13, 1996, p. 44.

20. "Chechnya Will Never Be Part of Russia, Top Rebel Leader Says," *Baltimore Sun,* October 7, 1996, p. 7A.

21. David Remnick, "The War for the Kremlin," *New Yorker,* July 22, 1996, p. 49. Daniel Treisman, "Why Yeltsin Won," *Foreign Affairs* (September-October 1996), pp. 64–77.

22. Comment by Sergei Karaganov to Remnick, "The War for the Kremlin," p. 50. In October 2000, Yeltsin, in his third book of memoirs, confirmed this scenario.

23. Cohen, *Failed Crusade,* p. 49. According to World Bank figures, about one-third lived in poverty; *World Development Report 2000/2001: Attacking Poverty* (New York: Oxford University Press, 2000), p. 281.

24. Igor Nadezhdin, "Volna terrora, vozmozhno, tol'ko nachinaetsia," *Russkaia Germania,* September 20–26, 1999, p. 2.

25. Andrew Meier and Yuri Zarakhovich, "Putin Tightens His Grip," *Time,* May 29, 2000, p. 24.

26. Cited by Amy Knight, "Hit First and Hit Hard," *Times Literary Supplement,* June 9, 2000.

27. Galina Koval'skaia, "Fenomen Lukashenko: Belorussia, ty tozhe odyrela?" *Novoe vremia,* no. 26 (1994), pp. 10–11.

28. The last year for which the World Bank had figures for Afghanistan was 1979. Its income put it among the "low-income developing countries . . . with incomes below about a dollar per person per day."

29. Associated Press, "Soviets Facing Oil Crunch, CIA Director Says," *Baltimore Evening Sun,* April 22, 1980, p. A5. In September 1981, the CIA announced that the Soviet Union's energy prospects looked "highly favorable for the rest of the century." Bernard Gwertzman, "Soviet Is Able to Raise Production of Oil and Gas, U.S. Agency Says," *New York Times,* September 3, 1981, pp. A1, D14.

30. Raymond L. Garthoff, *Detente and Revolution: American-Soviet Relations from Nixon to Reagan* (Washington, D.C.: Brookings Institution, 1985), pp. 887–965; Chalmers Johnson, "Abolish the CIA!" *London Review of Books,* October 21, 2005, p. 25.

31. Michael Dobbs, "Secret Memos Trace Kremlin's March to War," *Washington Post,* November 15, 1992, pp. A1, A32. Also the memoirs of KGB colonel Alexander Morozov, the deputy of intelligence operations in Kabul during 1975–1979, "Kabul'skii rezident," *Novoe vremia,* nos. 38–41 (1991); and "KGB i afganskie lidery," *Novoe vremia,* no. 20 (1992), pp. 30–31.

32. Gerard Chaliand, *Report from Afghanistan* (New York: Penguin, 1982), p. 49.

33. Steven Coll, *Ghost Wars: The Secret History of the CIA, Afghanistan, and bin Laden from the Soviet Invasion to September 10, 2001* (New York: Penguin, 2004), pp. 155–156.

34. "Spravka 'NV,'" *Novoe vremia,* no. 17 (1992), p. 26.

35. Coll, *Ghost Wars,* p. 234.

36. Cited in "Another Bloody Sunday," *Baltimore Sun,* December 18, 1981, p. A22.

37. Michael Dobbs, K. S. Karol, and Dessa Trevisan, *Poland, Solidarity, Walesa* (New York: McGraw-Hill, 1981), p. 70.

38. Andrew Cockburn, *The Threat: Inside the Soviet Military Machine* 2d rev. ed. (New York: Random House, 1984), pp. 111–114, 178–180; Michael T. Kaufman, "Bloc Was Prepared to Crush Solidarity, a Defector Says," *New York Times,* April 17, 1987, p. A9.

39. World Bank, *World Development Report, 1989* (Washington, D.C.: World Bank, 1989), p. 165.

40. "A Survey of Eastern Europe," *The Economist,* August 12, 1989, p. 10.

41. Craig Whitney, "East Europe Joins the Market and Gets a Preview of the Pain," *New York Times,* January 7, 1990, p. E3.

42. For the statements, see *New York Times,* December 5, 1989, p. A15.

43. Diana Jean Schemo, "Soviet Troops to Leave Czech Soil," *Baltimore Sun,* January 6, 1990, p. 2A.

44. Cited in William Pfaff, "Change in a Vulnerable Land," *Baltimore Sun,* December 22, 1989, p. 17A.

45. The death toll in Timişoara ran into several hundreds, not the 4,500 initially reported. Mary Battiata, "State's Violence Sparked Rebellion," *Washington Post,* December 31, 1989, p. A1.

46. Edward Behr, *Kiss the Hand You Cannot Bite: The Rise and Fall of the Ceauşescus* (New York: Villard Books, 1991), chapter 13, pp. 251–268. Behr cites a Romanian proverb: "A change of rulers is the joy of fools." Antonia Rados, *Die Verschwoerung der Securitate: Rumaeniens verratene Revolution* (Hamburg: Hoffmann und Campe, 1990); Bartholomaeus Grill, "Revolution der Funktionaere," *Die Zeit,* January 11, 1991, p. 30.

47. William Pfaff, "Romania Moves Forward to the Past," *Baltimore Sun,* June 21, 1990, p. 11A; Associated Press, "Iliescu Inaugurated with Pledge to Defend Democracy," *Baltimore Sun,* June 21, 1990, p. 4A.

48. New York Times News Service, "Romanian Voters Look Both Left and Right," *Baltimore Sun,* November 26, 2000, p. 29A.

49. June 28 is St. Vitus Day. It was on that day in 1914 that Gavrilo Princip, a member of the Serb nationalist group, the Black Hand, assassinated the heir to the Austrian throne, Francis Ferdinand, touching off World War I.

50. Helsinki Commission on Security and Cooperation in Europe, *The Referendum on Independence in Bosnia-Herzegovina, February 29–March 1, 1992* (Washington, D.C.: U.S. Government Printing Office, 1992), p. 3.

51. Robert Block, "The Madness of General Mladic," *New York Review,* October 5, 1995, pp. 7–9.

52. Newsday, "French General's Deal Ensured Massacre in Bosnia," *Baltimore Sun,* May 30, 1996, p. 18A.

53. Charles Lane and Thom Shanker, "Bosnia: What the CIA Didn't Tell Us," *New York Review of Books,* May 9, 1996, pp. 10–15.

54. Commission on Security and Cooperation in Europe, "Prosecuting War Crimes in the Former Yugoslavia: An Update," *CSCE Digest* (May 1996), pp. 13, 21–27.

55. Kemal Kurspahic, former editor-in-chief of the Sarajevo daily, *Oslobodjenje,* ". . . And Don't Divide Bosnia," *Washington Post,* September 8, 1995, p. A25.

56. Figures by the United Nations High Commissioner for Refugees, "Doors Slam," *The Economist,* September 28, 1996, p. 64.

57. Constanze Stelzenmueller, "Tote sind Tote," *Die Zeit,* March 23, 2000, p. 16.

# 19

---

# The Nuclear Arms Race

The Cold War of the 1950s and early 1960s produced an unchecked nuclear arms race. Throughout, the United States took the lead despite the campaign rhetoric of bomber and missile gaps favoring the Soviet Union. Presidential candidate John F. Kennedy's charge against the Eisenhower administration that it had been asleep at the helm and had permitted the Soviets to forge ahead in the missile race was laid to rest shortly after Kennedy's election, when the Pentagon announced in 1961 a U.S. second-strike capability more powerful than a potential Soviet first strike. This cold, cruel fact of the arms race, and the Soviet humiliation during the Cuban missile crisis the following year, put two items on the Kremlin's agenda: the closing of the gap favoring the United States and subsequent negotiations with Washington that acknowledged nuclear parity between the great powers.

The immediate consequence of the Cuban missile crisis, however, was a gradual improvement in East-West relations, for both sides had faced the moment of truth when they looked down the nuclear gun barrel. Détente of the late 1960s and the early 1970s produced a number of treaties between the Soviet Union and the United States designed to limit the nuclear arms race. The first was the partial nuclear test ban treaty of 1963, which prohibited nuclear testing in the atmosphere, in outer space, and on the high seas. The United States and the Soviet Union then took their nuclear weapons tests underground, thus limiting environmental contamination. More than a hundred nations signed the treaty. Notable exceptions were France, already a nuclear power, and Communist China, soon to become one when it exploded an atomic bomb in 1964. (Both signed the treaty in 1992.)

Other agreements soon followed. They included the Outer Space Treaty (1967), which banned nuclear weapons in space and earth orbit; the Nuclear Non-Proliferation Treaty (1968), by which the Soviet Union, the United States, Great Britain, and eighty-three other nations pledged to prevent the spread of nuclear weapons and technology; the Seabed Pact (1971), which prohibited nuclear arms on the ocean floors beyond a nation's twelve-mile limit; and the Biological Warfare Treaty (1972), which outlawed the development, production, and stockpiling of biological weapons.

## ■ THE SALT TREATIES

Nonetheless, the superpowers continued to add to their nuclear arsenals by developing and testing new weapons and adding warheads. Toward the end of the decade, the governments of the United States and the Soviet Union, seeing the need for renewed efforts to control the open-ended arms race, initiated the Strategic Arms Limitation Treaty (SALT) negotiations. Their purpose was to limit—and eventually abolish—a costly and potentially deadly nuclear arms race. When the talks began during the late 1960s, both sides had more than enough to destroy the other side many times over. The SALT talks were meant to bring an element of control and rationality to the arms race.

President Richard Nixon and Communist Party chief Leonid Brezhnev signed the first SALT agreement in Moscow in May 1972. Its aim was a modest one, a limit on the deployment of "strategic weapons." Strategic weapons consist of nuclear warheads launched from one's territory and from submarines against the enemy's territory. They include the intercontinental bomber forces, intercontinental ballistic missiles (ICBMs), and submarine-launched ballistic missiles (SLBMs). SALT I, however, did not put a dent in anyone's nuclear arsenal. It merely put a ceiling on the destructive power each side possessed. But it marked the beginning of a process of mutual consultation on a pressing question. The negotiators expressed the hope that later treaties would address the more difficult problem of reducing nuclear arsenals.

SALT I froze the existing number of land-based missiles, the ICBMs, leaving the Soviet Union with an advantage in ICBMs: 1,398 to 1,052. The Nixon administration, to appease its domestic critics, argued that the agreement had prevented the buildup of the Soviet arsenal of SS-9s.[1] Moreover, the treaty offered the United States several advantages. It ignored the questions of intercontinental bombers (in which the United States always enjoyed a marked superiority), intermediate-range missiles in Europe (which became a major issue during the arms-reduction talks of the early 1980s), and the French and British arsenals. The Soviets also accepted, if only for the time being, a U.S. advantage in the number of strategic warheads, a category in which the United States led by a ratio of two to one.

But the treaty did not address the question of limiting MIRVed missiles, a U.S. invention, where the United States held a large, if only temporary, lead. A MIRVed missile, short for "multiple independently-targeted reentry vehicle," has the capability of carrying several warheads, each with the ability of finding a different target. The missile—the expensive component—carries a number of warheads—the less expensive components. During the SALT I negotiations, the United States had refused to discuss the Soviet proposal of banning MIRVed missiles; it saw no reason to give away its most sophisticated nuclear weapon. U.S. negotiators soon had reasons to regret their decision, however.

SALT I was not expected to halt the arms race. For one, the treaty did not prevent the improvement in the quality of weapons, which continued to become increasingly more sophisticated. The emphasis on limiting launchers (bombers, missiles, submarines) was beginning to make less and less sense, since launchers, particularly missiles, were beginning to carry more and more warheads. And it is the warheads that do the damage. By the mid-1970s, the Soviet Union had begun to deploy its own MIRVed missiles. By then, MIRVed missile technology had begun to work to the Soviet Union's advantage because the Soviet missiles were larger and more powerful than U.S. ICBMs and thus capable of carrying up to thirty warheads. The U.S. Minuteman III missile, in contrast, carried but three. SALT II, which the negotiators hammered out by 1979, attempted, therefore, to limit not only launchers but also the number of warheads, by placing a ceiling on missiles that could be MIRVed.

In June 1979, after years of difficult negotiations, Brezhnev and President Jimmy Carter met in Vienna to sign SALT II. The treaty placed a ceiling of 2,400 missile launchers for each side, of which only 1,320 could be fitted with MIRVs. It also limited the number of warheads in an ICBM to ten. SALT II thus put a cap on the Soviet Union's strategic strength, its land-based ICBMs. But it also left the Soviet Union with a five-to-two advantage in ICBM-launched warheads. U.S. advocates of the treaty argued that the gap in this category would have been much wider had it not been for the treaty. The treaty also left Washington with a decided advantage in other categories, particularly in SLBMs.

The signing ceremony proved to be the last act of détente. By that time a climate of mutual suspicion had already set in. U.S. critics of negotiations with the Soviet Union were becoming increasingly vocal. They argued that the Soviet Union could not have it both ways. It could not have normal relations with the West and at the same time support revolutionary movements in Africa and Asia. Détente, they insisted, must be tied to improved Soviet behavior, especially abroad. The international climate worsened when, in November 1979, the Iranian hostage crisis began, for which some even blamed the Soviet Union, followed in December by the Soviet intervention in Afghanistan.

Even more important than Soviet behavior abroad was the charge that détente and the SALT treaties had made it possible for the Soviet Union to pass the United States in the arms race. The most vocal critic of détente by

1980 was the Republican presidential hopeful, Ronald Reagan, who declared that the SALT treaties had opened a "window of vulnerability" and that only one side, the Soviet Union, was engaged in the arms race. The United States, he declared, had in effect disarmed unilaterally. As a political argument, Reagan got considerable mileage out of it. But, in fact, during the 1970s, the United States had doubled its strategic arsenal. By the time of the presidential election year of 1980, the Soviet Union had closed the wide gap, but the United States continued to lead. It was never a race with one contestant.

Détente thus became a casualty of the renewed Cold War. Détente had already been in trouble, but the events of 1979 finished it off. The U.S. Senate never ratified SALT II, in part because critics such as Reagan had hammered home the point that it was advantageous to the Soviet Union. Once Reagan became president, however, he gave tacit recognition to the fact that the treaty had after all put a limit on the Soviet Union's strategic strength, a fact the Joint Chiefs of Staff had acknowledged when they urged the treaty's ratification, calling it "a modest but useful step."[2] Reagan agreed to abide by the unratified terms of SALT II for the next five years.

## ■ THE CORRELATION OF FORCES

A discussion of the number and types of nuclear weapons generally focused on numbers. It became clear, however, that one could not readily prove that one or the other side was "ahead." What criteria did one use to determine who was ahead? What did one count? How did the weapons compare? What were the needs of the two sides? The geographic considerations? The nature of the threat each faced?

The Soviet Union largely relied on powerful, land-based ICBMs, equipped with up to ten warheads. U.S. missiles were smaller and contained smaller, but more accurate warheads. Which type was preferable? Which was more deadly? The Soviet Union, because its missiles were less accurate, relied on the larger missiles and thus enjoyed an advantage in the category known as "payload," also known as "megatonnage." (One megaton is equal to 1 million tons of TNT.) As missiles became increasingly more accurate, both sides reduced their megatonnage. The United States, because of its more precise missiles, did not need to build large warheads. Thus, if one focused on payload, then the Soviet Union was ahead in the arms race; but if one took into account missile accuracy, then the advantage went to the United States.

During the first half of the 1980s, there was no progress toward nuclear disarmament; instead, both sides produced more and more improved nuclear weapons at a furious pace. In December 1981, the Soviet Union

---

# GLOSSARY

**ABM** Anti-Ballistic Missile; a defensive missile to destroy incoming enemy missiles

**ASAT** Anti-Satellite Missile; a missile to neutralize satellites in earth orbit; a central component of Star Wars

**CSCE** Conference on Security and Cooperation in Europe

**ICBM** Intercontinental Ballistic Missile

**INF** Intermediate-Range Nuclear Forces; see "theater weapons" below

**IRBM** Intermediate-Range Ballistic Missile (such as the Pershing II and the SS-20)

**MIRV** Multiple Independently-targeted Reentry Vehicle; a missile carrying several smaller missiles, each capable of reaching a different target

**NMD** National Missile Defense; U.S. program for an antimissile defense system; a scaled-down version of SDI

**payload** destructive power of a warhead, measured in megatonnage (1 megaton equals 1 million tons of TNT; a kiloton is the equivalent of 1,000 tons of TNT); a bomb with an explosive force of about 12 kilotons destroyed Hiroshima, where at least 70,000 died; in the 1970s, U.S. strategic warheads carried an average payload of more than 4 megatons, or more than 300 times the Hiroshima bomb; the warheads of the Soviet Union were even larger

**SALT** Strategic Arms Limitations Treaty; the emphasis is on strategic and limitations

**SDI** Strategic Defense Initiative; the official name of Star Wars

**SLBM** Submarine-Launched Ballistic Missile

**START** Strategic Arms Reduction Treaty; the emphasis is on reduction rather than limitation

**strategic weapons** weapons capable of delivering warheads over long distances (usually over 3,000 miles); they include intercontinental missiles, bombers, and submarine-launched missiles

**tactical weapons** short-range nuclear battlefield weapons (such as artillery shells)

**theater weapons** intermediate-range weapons for use in a specific global region, or theater (such as Europe or the Far East); also known as **INF**

**warhead** a nuclear bomb

walked out of arms-reduction talks in Geneva when it failed to halt the deployment of U.S. intermediate-range missiles, the Pershing II, and cruise missiles. The talks were not resumed until March 1985. During the intervening forty months, both sides added approximately a warhead a day to their strategic arsenals—and this did not take into account intermediate-range nuclear weapons, which both sides continued to deploy. In all, during the first half of the 1980s, each side added more than two thousand strategic warheads to its already bloated arsenal.

The configuration of strategic forces, approximately equal in numbers, was not identical, however. The Soviet Union put most of its eggs into one basket: 65 percent of its nuclear warheads were in land-based missiles; 27 percent in submarines; and a scant 8 percent (an amount sufficient to destroy the United States, however) in intercontinental bombers.

In contrast, the United States had a more balanced strategic arsenal, a "triad" of three components. The strongest leg was the submarine-based nuclear deterrent, with 51 percent of its warheads in submarines; 30 percent in the air force's intercontinental bomber force; and only 19 percent in land-based missiles. As such, the United States had the more sensible balance. Should the Soviets knock out one of the triad's legs, U.S. retaliatory power still would have been more than enough to provide a credible second-strike deterrent. And unlike those of the Soviets, most U.S. warheads were not in stationary missiles on land, whose location was all too well known to spy satellites in orbit, but were instead constantly in motion in the oceans of the world.

All of this caused a problem in determining an equitable formula in the attempt to limit the arms race. The Soviet Union, with its massive land-based force, was not about to sit down to negotiate solely a reduction in its strength, its land-based missiles.[3] But this is also where the Soviet Union was most vulnerable. Its missiles in the ground were inviting targets. These missiles, powerful and deadly once launched, were nevertheless slow to fire, for they were propelled by a liquid fuel. U.S. missiles, in contrast, could be fired virtually at will, for they contained a solid-fuel propellant. For this reason, the Soviet Union moved toward the deployment of a smaller, mobile, solid-fuel intercontinental ballistic missile. Such a mobile ICBM promised to add new elements to the arms race—an increasing difficulty in verification and the ability to effect a quick response.

By the end of 1985, the strategic balance of terror stood approximately as shown in Table 19.1. Various studies over the previous three decades had concluded that between two and three hundred warheads could destroy the Soviet Union. An equal number could mean the ruination of the United States. The strategic arsenal both sides had was thus of a fantastic dimension. "Overkill," the ability to destroy the enemy several times over, however, became institutionalized—and thus rationalized. There was a logic behind it all if one sought security in sheer numbers—in which case, neither side could ever have enough. In the mid-1980s, the United States possessed the capability of destroying the Soviet Union fifty times with its strategic arsenal alone. It was little wonder that U.S. strategic planners ran out of targets. The surfeit of atomic warheads made possible the luxury of targeting grain elevators in Ukraine and open fields Soviet bombers could conceivably use on their return trips from the United States.[4] And the Soviet Union's ability to destroy the United States was no different. The pointlessness of continuously adding to one's nuclear arsenal led Henry Kissinger to ask in 1974: "What in the name of God is strategic superiority? . . . What do you do with it?"[5]

\* \* \*

The Europeans, and the Soviets in particular, with their record of suffering and defeat, had a better understanding than most in the United States that history is all too often tragedy. The destruction wreaked by World War II, a conventional war fought with primitive weapons by today's standards, was still a recent memory. Berlin, Stalingrad, and many other cities still contained the ruins, now displayed as memorials and museum pieces, of that war. The persistence of attempts to negotiate if only a limitation to the arms race was mute tribute to the uncomfortable fact that a nuclear war could not have winners. The ruins of the Soviet Union and Germany in 1945 did not reveal which country had won the war and which had lost.

**Table 19.1 U.S. and Soviet Strategic Arsenal, 1985**

| Weapon Carrier | Number of Warheads | Percentage of Strategic Arsenal |
|---|---|---|
| *United States* | | |
| 1,025 ICBMs | 2,125 | 19% |
| 36 submarines with 640 missiles | 5,728 | 51 |
| 263 B-52 bombers, 98 of which carry 12 cruise missiles each | 3,072 | 27 |
| 61 FB-111 bombers | 366 | 3 |
| Total | 11,291 | 100 |
| | | |
| *Soviet Union* | | |
| 1,398 ICBMs | 6,420 | 65 |
| 62 submarines with 924 missiles | 2,688 | 27 |
| 173 bombers, 25 of which carry 10 cruise missiles each | 792 | 8 |
| Total | 9,900 | 100 |

*Source*: *New York Times*, October 4, 1985. All figures are estimates of classified information. They were compiled from Pentagon publications, the International Institute for Strategic Studies, the Arms Control Association, and the Center for Defense Information.

# ■ INTERMEDIATE-RANGE WEAPONS

The late 1970s saw the end of détente. The reasons for the deterioration of relations between the Soviet Union and the West were many. One factor, however, was the lack of understanding by the Soviets of the U.S. definition of détente. Détente, in the U.S. mind, was always linked to a change in Soviet behavior. To the Soviets, however, it meant Western acceptance of the Soviet Union as a major power, an equal of the United States—and with it an acceptance of the global role that a great power traditionally plays. After all, they argued, the Soviet Union and the United States had normalized their relations at a time when the United States was engaged in a war against "international Communism" in Vietnam. From the U.S. viewpoint, however, Soviet good behavior, particularly in Afghanistan, was a precondition to maintaining détente. The Soviet Union countered by arguing that, for them, détente had been more important than Vietnam—but for the United States, Afghanistan was more important than détente.[6] With détente at an end, the arms race began to take ominous turns. The introduction of an increasingly more sophisticated generation of intermediate-range nuclear weapons added to the complexity of the debate on how to limit these weapons.

The strategic arsenal, originally the sole line of deterrent, was joined by shorter-range theater weapons. From the early 1960s, both sides accumulated an extraordinarily destructive arsenal of these intermediate-range nuclear arms. Military strategists saw Europe as the most likely theater where such weapons might be employed. There, the Soviets put into place their most sophisticated medium-range missiles—the mobile SS-20s—capable of reaching, and devastating, all of Europe.

The SS-20 was a significant improvement over the older, single-warhead, liquid-fuel SS-4s and SS-5s. It had a range of over three thousand miles, was mobile, contained three independently targeted warheads, and was a solid-fuel missile that could be fired with a minimum of delay. This new addition to the Kremlin's military might produced a psychological shock among Western military strategists. The SS-20 did not change the nuclear balance of terror, but it did give the appearance of a Soviet escalation of the arms race, a perception that was largely correct.

The United States responded, predictably, with its own enhanced intermediate-range weapons in Europe, the Tomahawk cruise missile and the Pershing II. The slow-moving cruise missile hugged the ground on its approach and was therefore difficult to detect. With a range of two thousand miles, it was capable of reaching the Soviet Union from West European soil. The Pershing II was a fast-flying missile with a range of over eleven hundred miles. Its mobility, range, accuracy, and speed made it one of the premier weapons in the U.S. arsenal. It was a potential first-strike weapon suitable for the elimination or "decapitation" of the Soviet command structures. The distinction between "strategic" and "theater" missiles became increasingly blurred. What was the difference, for example, between a Minuteman missile fired from Wyoming (thirty minutes' flying time to a Soviet target) and a Pershing II missile fired from West Germany (six minutes' flying time)?

For the Soviet Union, this round in the arms race was filled with contradictions and irony, something all participants in this dangerous game experienced. The United States was first to witness this strange twist of logic. The atomic bomb had given the United States the "ultimate weapon," only to subject the country to the prospect of nuclear annihilation within ten short years. Similarly, the SS-20 briefly gave the Kremlin an advantage in case of a nuclear exchange in Europe—provided the contest could be limited to Europe, a most unlikely prospect. When the United States countered with the deployment of increasingly more dangerous weapons, the Soviet Union became less secure.

To be effective, U.S. intermediate-range missiles had to be stationed on European soil. Presidents Carter and Reagan had their work cut out in selling their deployment to their NATO allies. The Europeans understood all too well that both the Soviet and the U.S. arsenals threatened to turn Europe into a nuclear shooting gallery—particularly after President Reagan said, "I could see where you could have the exchange of tactical weapons in the field [in Europe] without it bringing either one of the major powers to pushing the button."[7] The upshot was a split in the NATO alliance. Still, the United States was able to convince its European allies to accept 464 cruise and 108 Pershing II missiles.[8]

This round of escalation produced a series of discussions at Geneva beginning in the spring of 1981. Each sought to eliminate the other side's missiles and at the same time hold on to what it had. It was a prescription for a deadlock. Negotiators, instead of seeking compromises, played to larger audiences, notably the people back home and the nervous Europeans. Propaganda and accusations of bad faith became the order of the day.

The two chief negotiators, Yuli Kvitsinsky for the Soviet Union and Paul Nitze for the United States, did manage at one point to agree on a compromise formula, their so-called walk-in-the-woods proposal. It called for a rough balance between the Soviet Union's seventy-five SS-20s (each carrying three warheads) and the United States' seventy-five Tomahawk cruise launchers (each with four warheads). By this agreement, the Soviets would have had to curtail, but not scrap, the deployment of their SS-20s, while the United States would have had to forgo the deployment of its deadly Pershing IIs. Hard-liners in Moscow and Washington quickly denounced this attempt at a compromise. In December 1981, the Soviets left the conference table when the United States proceeded to deploy on schedule the first cruise and Pershing II missiles in Great Britain and West Germany, respectively. The deadlock lasted three and a half years, while missile deployment accelerated.

In April 1985, about one month after the Soviet and U.S. negotiators had resumed their talks in Geneva, the new Soviet leader, Mikhail Gorbachev, announced a freeze on further deployment of SS-20s until November 1985, provided the United States halted the deployment of its missiles. Yet there was nothing in Gorbachev's proposal suggesting a reduction of the Soviet arsenal—whose deployment was largely completed. The Soviet gesture was too little and too late. Instead of facing seventy-five slow-moving cruise missiles, as proposed in the "walk in the woods," the Soviets now faced fifty-four of the deadly Pershing IIs and forty-eight cruise missiles, with the prospect of more to come. And Western Europe faced 250 of the Soviet Union's 414 SS-20s.

## ■ STAR WARS: THE STRATEGIC DEFENSE INITIATIVE

In March 1983, the arms race took another twist when President Reagan went public with a military research program long on the drawing board. It was a missile defense system officially called the Strategic Defense Initiative (SDI), but commonly known as "Star Wars." Its purpose was to develop the means to offer U.S. land-based missiles a measure of protection in case of a nuclear war with the Soviet Union, particularly in the event that the Soviet Union struck first with its powerful and accurate land-based missiles, notably the SS-18s. With this pronouncement, Reagan officially committed the United States to the creation of a brand new, futuristic defense against Soviet ICBMs. The research program was now no longer a scientific quest for a hypothetical defensive weapon. Instead, the government of the United States committed its resources to finding a technological breakthrough to neutralize hostile projectiles.

Thus far, the prevention of nuclear war had been based on deterrence, a balance of terror, that is, on the assumption that neither side wanted to commit suicide. It was a strategy known as Mutually Assured Destruction, or MAD. And in fact, this balance of terror kept the peace. The Soviet Union and the United States became hostages of the nuclear arsenals pointed at them.

In the late 1960s, the Soviets had entertained the idea of a defensive shield of their own, which, however, was unacceptable to the United States. U.S. officials pointed out that it would only lead to similar measures by the United States, which would, moreover, increase its number of warheads. The result would be an escalation of the arms race, one that promised no security for anyone. The United States prevailed upon the Soviet Union to abandon its missile defense program. The resultant accord, the Anti-Ballistic Missile (ABM) treaty between the United States and the Soviet Union (1972), permitted both sides to create two limited defensive systems each, which neither bothered to develop fully. The agreement put an end to the prospect of a new element in the nuclear arms race—the building of antimissile defenses only to witness the adversary drastically increase its nuclear arsenal to overwhelm the defenses.

The ABM treaty became part and parcel of the SALT I agreement, without which SALT I would have been impossible. The United States was not about to sign an agreement with the Soviet Union by which it limited its missile strength and at the same time sit by idly as the Soviets took unilateral steps to put in place a defensive shield designed to neutralize the U.S. strategic arsenal. Once the Soviets understood this, the door was opened for the ratification of SALT I and the limited ABM treaty. The simple, brutal deterrent of Mutually Assured Destruction remained intact.

In March 1983, eleven years after the superpowers had agreed to limit their nuclear firepower and their antinuclear defenses, Reagan announced plans to build a highly complex defensive system over the next twenty-five years. Reagan had never been comfortable with arms agreements that accepted Soviet parity with the United States. That and his unlimited faith in U.S. ingenuity and technical skills led him to opt for a program that, he argued, would not cause an escalation of the arms race.

Reagan's proposal challenged the policy of Mutually Assured Destruction. It was immoral, he insisted, to rely on a military strategy predicated on the potential annihilation of the nation. He proposed instead the development of high-technology barriers to make nuclear war impossible. In fact, he went so far as to suggest that once U.S. scientists had solved the riddle of how to intercept incoming Soviet rockets, the U.S. government would hand over the secret to the Soviets. Nuclear war would then become impossible and peace would prevail. The ultimate goal, President Reagan said, was "to eliminate the weapons themselves."[9]

Star Wars played to mixed reviews. Its theoretical underpinnings could not be faulted readily. But there were several serious problems in implementing a defense of such staggering complexity. First, to be effective it would have to be nearly perfect. Since 2 percent of the Soviet Union's strategic arsenal could destroy the United States, a 90 percent efficiency in the Star Wars defense system—which according to some scientists was the best that could be gained—would not be nearly enough to protect the United States. Mutually Assured Destruction, therefore, would continue to prevail and the rubble would still bounce, for even 10 percent of a strategic arsenal of ten thousand warheads would destroy the United States several times over.

Star Wars, even if only 90 percent efficient, threatened, however, to bring about the unilateral U.S. neutralization of a sizable portion of the Kremlin's arsenal, something it was not likely to accept. Star Wars promised only to contribute to another spiral of the arms race, for the Soviets threatened to produce an ever-increasing number of warheads. In short, the Soviets were being given the alternative of accepting U.S. nuclear superiority or of deploying enough weapons capable of overwhelming the Star Wars defense.

Second, there was the staggering cost. Reagan requested a budget of $30 billion ($3.7 billion for fiscal 1986) for research and development during the first five years. There was some doubt whether the U.S. government, already running a record deficit of over $200 billion a year, could afford the program.

Third, there was the very complexity of the system. Star Wars called for a new generation of sensors for the surveillance, tracking, and destruction of enemy missiles. The sensors would have to work flawlessly in the face of thousands of incoming warheads and decoys. The program also envisioned the deployment of energy weapons consisting primarily of powerful lasers based either on the ground (and deflected by huge mirrors in orbit) or in orbit. The most crucial part of the entire program, "systems concepts and battle management," called for an error-free computer system that instantaneously linked the system's diverse elements.[10]

Fourth, ways had to be found to protect the system from destruction by hostile elements. Mirrors and spy satellites in orbit would be inviting targets that could be neutralized easily. They would have to be defended somehow.

Last, the Soviet scientists were sure to work overtime to find ways over, under, around, and through any missile defense thought up by their U.S. counterparts.

In light of these obstacles, it was little wonder that Pentagon officials told Congress, which had to finance all of this, that this was a long-range program of at least twenty-five years' duration. There was talk, however, of an "interim deployment" to protect land-based missiles. This put first things first; civilians would have to wait. Former defense secretary Harold Brown admitted that "technology does not offer even a reasonable prospect of a population defense."[11]

Domestic critics of Star Wars feared that it would only militarize space, add little to anyone's security, and bankrupt the government. The deployment of a space-based defense promised to produce an open-ended contest in space. *Pravda* repeatedly announced that the Soviet Union would not accept Star Wars, which the Soviets considered as an attempt to disarm them. They would join the race into space. Reagan's secretary of defense, Caspar Weinberger, when asked how he would view a unilateral deployment of a Soviet version of Star Wars, replied that such an act "would be one of the most frightening prospects I could imagine."[12]

## ■ GORBACHEV'S PEACE OFFENSIVE

In April 1985, one month after Mikhail Gorbachev came to power, he launched his most significant "peace offensive" of the Cold War. Gorbachev was determined to bring about not only a domestic perestroika but one in foreign relations as well. "We will rob you of your enemy," he told the West. His proposal to freeze the deployment of Soviet SS-20 intermediate-range missiles was but his first move.

Soon the world witnessed a number of summit meetings between Gorbachev and Reagan, who had previously resolutely refused to sit down with his Soviet counterparts. Brezhnev, Andropov, and Chernenko were clearly dying men; moreover, Reagan felt there had been nothing to talk about with the leaders of what he had called early in his presidency the "evil empire." The first meeting between Reagan and Gorbachev was a get-acquainted session in November 1985, in neutral Geneva. Several factors played a role in Reagan's turnabout. He had been criticized at home as being the first president since 1945 who had not met with Soviet leaders. He also realized he was dealing with a new type of Soviet leader. The Reagan-Gorbachev summits led to a series of negotiations that in the end produced the first reduction of nuclear armaments on both sides.

The first order of business was the recent escalation of the nuclear race in the heart of Europe: the deployment of intermediate-range nuclear forces (INF) such as the U.S. Pershing II and cruise missiles and the Soviet SS-20. Gorbachev surprised the Reagan administration when he suddenly dusted off an old Western proposal, the zero-option: if the Soviet Union did not deploy its missiles, the United States would not counter with the deployment of its own rockets. Gorbachev would undo Brezhnev's error; he would take Soviet INF forces out of Europe if the United States were to do the same. Moscow called Washington's bluff; if Reagan rejected Gorbachev's proposal of eliminating all INFs, the U.S. position would be exposed as another example of Cold War propaganda.

Reagan responded positively. The consequence—after a year of difficult negotiation—was the INF treaty of May 1988, which eliminated an entire category of nuclear rockets, those with a range between 310 and 3,400 miles. The superpowers then proceeded to dismantle the costly weapons—1,752 Soviet and 867 U.S. rockets[13]—under the watchful eyes of on-site inspectors from the other side.

Reagan was then able to turn to one of his favorite programs, namely START, the Strategic Arms Reduction Talks. Early in his presidency, he had argued correctly that SALT had accomplished little. It had merely kept the nuclear arms race within certain parameters, making it possible, nevertheless, for both sides to increase their strategic arsenals. At the time of the signing of the INF treaty, the U.S. arsenal still contained 13,134 strategic warheads, while the Soviets' contained 10,664.[14] The time had come to reduce them. Reagan found a responsive partner in Gorbachev. Earlier, in October 1985, Gorbachev had already proposed a 50 percent reduction of strategic nuclear forces, which would lessen the Soviet threat against U.S. land-based missiles. In October 1987, at their meeting in Reykjavik, Iceland, Gorbachev went so far as to offer Reagan the elimination of all strategic

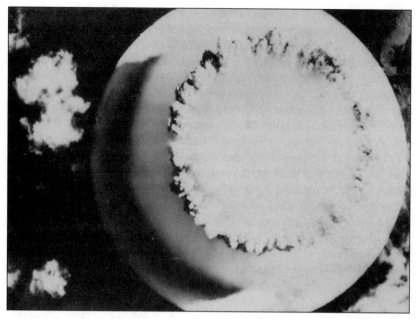

Radioactive substances released in the U.S. nuclear bomb test, boiling skyward—taken from a plane directly above the blast, July 12, 1948. *(National Archives)*

nuclear weapons. A surprised Reagan was on the verge of accepting before his advisers interfered. They feared that a world free of nuclear weapons would leave Western Europe at the mercy of the superior Soviet conventional forces.

Gorbachev was not finished with his surprises, however. On December 7, 1988, he launched another volley in his peace offensive. He announced—unilaterally and without precondition—the reduction in the Soviet armed forces by 10 percent (500,000 soldiers), 800 airplanes, 8,500 pieces of artillery, and 5,000 tanks within two years. Included in the offer was the promise to dissolve six of the fifteen divisions in East Germany, Hungary, and Czechoslovakia by 1991. But most important, Gorbachev included the withdrawal of assault troops and mobile bridges for crossing rivers. Gorbachev's speech marked a 180-degree turn in Soviet military doctrine as it had existed since the early 1960s. The East German party chief Erich Honecker recognized immediately what he called the "immense historical significance" of the Soviet troop withdrawal.[15] Gorbachev's speech also shocked many in the U.S. defense community; some saw it as another Pearl Harbor, a propaganda offensive designed to disarm the West.

The Western critics of Gorbachev's speech of December 7, 1988, were in part correct. The first casualty of that speech was the U.S. program of "modernizing" the short-range Lance rocket, a tactical nuclear weapon. The Lance II, a new rocket with a range of just under the 310-mile limit as stipulated by the INF treaty, made possible the circumvention of the spirit, if not the letter, of the INF treaty. Lance II would give the United States a back door to an INF arsenal.

West German politics torpedoed the U.S. "modernization" program. Many in West Germany, especially the powerful Social Democratic Party in opposition, insisted that the shorter-range rockets, too, must go. "The shorter the rockets, the deader the Germans" became the West German watchword. In February 1989, Egon Bahr, the national security expert of the West German Social Democratic Party, explained to Brent Scowcroft, U.S. president George Bush's national security adviser, that the United States had no chance of deploying the Lance II. If the conservative government in Bonn capitulated to U.S. pressure and accepted them, his party would win the next election and take them out.[16] West German foreign minister Hans-Dietrich Genscher, who was born in Halle, East Germany, and whose relatives still lived there, declared: "I have sworn an oath to avert harm from the German people and that includes East Germany."[17]

East German scientists joined the debate. Even in case of conventional war, they argued, Europe would still be contaminated with nuclear fallout. The continent contained 220 civilian reactors that, if damaged, would turn into radioactive weapons. Because of the type of fuel they used, they would emit greater doses of radiation than atomic weapons. The large concentrations of chemical plants—such as along the Rhine River in Western Europe and in cities such as Halle and Leipzig in East Germany—would spill their deadly poison on humans, plants, and animals. Even a conventional war would turn Europe into an "atomic, chemical and genetically contaminated desert." It would lead to the "destruction of what the aggressor would seek to conquer."[18]

Gorbachev stood in stark contrast to the cautious Bush, who only late in 1989 began to accept the idea that he, too, could play a role in affecting the course of history. Gorbachev had been the engine of change, Bush a mere spectator. The demise of the Communist parties in Eastern Europe produced a situation in January 1990 whereby Czechoslovakia, Hungary, and Poland insisted that the Soviet army leave their territories by the end of 1991. An Eastern Europe without Soviet forces became a question of when, not if. It was at this point that Bush took the initiative and proposed the reduction of U.S. and Soviet forces to a level of 195,000 each in Central Europe. "New thinking" finally came to Washington. Even the most hawkish officials in the Pentagon had to admit that in the fourteen months since Gorbachev's speech of December 7, 1988, the Soviet Union had dismantled its capability to invade Western Europe. Bush's speech was welcome news in Warsaw, Budapest, Prague, and Moscow because it facilitated the Soviet army's withdrawal from its forward position in Eastern Europe. The military confrontation in the heart of Europe was coming to an end.

After the last Russian combat troops stationed in Poland pulled out in October 1992, President Lech Walesa declared: "Polish sovereignty has finally been confirmed." Problems of logistics and the lack of adequate housing at home for the Russian troops and their dependents produced a longer timetable for the withdrawal from the newly independent Baltic states and East Germany. The departure from there was finally completed by 1993 and 1994, respectively.

## ■ THE START TREATIES

The START negotiations, begun in 1982, initially proceeded at a snail's pace for eight years, during which the intricacies of attaining balanced reductions in Soviet and U.S. arsenals were debated in twelve rounds of formal negotiations, thirteen foreign ministers' meetings, and six summit conferences. Finally, in May 1990, at a Bush-Gorbachev summit meeting in Washington, the two leaders announced the framework of a treaty they pledged to have ready for signing by year's end. As it turned out, it would take another fourteen months to complete the treaty.

Ironically, the signing of the treaty in Moscow in late July 1991 was attended with little fanfare—certainly not what had been expected for the signing of one of the most important nuclear disarmament treaties, one that had reversed the forty-five-year-old strategic nuclear arms race. START seemed anticlimactic because it had been so long in coming and its main features had long since been known. Moreover, the deteriorating situation in the Soviet Union and the fading of the Soviet military threat made the treaty seem less significant. START, however, broke new ground by calling for a reduction rather than merely a limit on the growth of strategic weapons. The U.S. arsenal would be cut from 12,646 warheads to 8,556 and the Soviet Union's from 11,012 to 6,163 by 1999. To the distinct advantage of the United States, START reduced the Soviets' heavy ICBMs by 50 percent, yet allowed the United States to retain a three-to-one advantage in submarine-launched nuclear missiles. The treaty, however, did not place limitations on nuclear weapons modernization. Thus, it left the development of weapons systems such as the U.S. B-2 bomber and the Trident submarine, not to mention the Star Wars, unhampered.

By the end of 1991, the Soviet Union had ceased to exist, and Washington now had to deal with Boris Yeltsin, the president of the new Russian Federation, and with the heads of the other fourteen successor states of the former Soviet Union. Yeltsin proclaimed his commitment to stand by the START treaty and the disarmament pledges made by Gorbachev. In addition to Russia, however, three of the new sovereign republics—Belarus, Ukraine, and Kazakhstan—now had nuclear weapons. All three announced their intention of getting rid of them. Confident that Russian security was not threatened by the United States and greatly in need of slashing military costs and attaining Western economic assistance, Yeltsin declared his intentions of scrapping still more nuclear weapons.

At the first U.S.-Russian (as opposed to U.S.-Soviet) summit, in Washington in February 1992, Yeltsin joined Bush in signing a "Declaration of Friendship" and agreed to begin new negotiations for further nuclear disarmament. Four months of negotiations produced another startling agreement, one that promised far deeper cuts in strategic nuclear forces than the yet-to-be-ratified START treaty had called for. Yeltsin, given to grandstanding, came with offers Bush could hardly refuse, and the result was a spectacular agreement, the basis for a second treaty, START II, which called for the reduction of strategic nuclear weapons on each side to 3,000–3,500 by the year 2003. This was just over one-half of what START I allowed and amounted to a reduction of 73 percent of the existing strategic nuclear warheads. The most extraordinary feature of the Bush-Yeltsin agreement was its call for banning all MIRVed land-based missiles, leaving each side with only five hundred single-warhead, land-based strategic weapons. This represented a Russian abandonment of its long-held advantage in heavy land-based missiles, which Washington had regarded as Moscow's first-strike capacity. In announcing this concession, Yeltsin stated that Russia now needed only a "minimum-security level" of nuclear forces and said that it was abandoning the concept of nuclear parity, which had caused Russia "to have half its population living below the poverty line."[19] In return for this concession, Bush agreed to a ceiling on submarine-launched missiles of 1,744, a 70 percent reduction.

But which delivery systems were to be destroyed? At the very end of 1992, a compromise was reached. Russia agreed to the conversion of U.S. strategic bombers (including the new B-2, or Stealth bomber) to conventional use, rather than destroying them. The United States, in its turn, agreed that Russia, as a cost-cutting measure, could keep 90 of its SS-18 silos for conversion to use by single-warhead SS-25 missiles as well as 105 of its 170 MIRVed (six warheads) SS-19s, provided they were refitted with single warheads. Similarly, the United States would convert its Minuteman III missile to carry but a single warhead. The compromise became possible only after each side accepted unprecedented verification procedures. Bush and Yeltsin then signed START II in Moscow in January 1993. It pledged the two powers to return by 2003 to approximately where they had been in the early 1970s, before the MIRVing of their missiles. As such, it was a tacit admission of the mindlessness of the nuclear arms race.

Table 19.2 provides comparative data on the size of the arms reductions called for in the START treaties.

Implementation of these agreements proved to be a difficult matter.[20] Ratification of START I was delayed mainly by complications caused by the breakup of the Soviet Union. Both Washington and Moscow wanted to

**Table 19.2  1991 Strategic Warhead Levels and Reduction Proposals**

| | Land-based (ICBMs) | Sea-based (SLBMs) | Air-launched (bombers) | Totals |
|---|---|---|---|---|
| U.S. | 2,450 | 5,760 | 4,436 | 12,646 |
| USSR | 6,612 | 2,804 | 1,596 | 11,012 |
| | | | | 23,658 |
| START I, to be implemented by 1999; a reduction of 38% from the 1991 levels | | | | |
| U.S. | 1,400 | 3,456 | 3,700 | 8,556 |
| USSR | 3,153 | 1,744 | 1,266 | 6,163 |
| | | | | 14,719 |
| START II, to be implemented by 2003; a reduction of 73% from the 1991 levels | | | | |
| U.S. | 500 | 1,728 | 1,272 | 3,500 |
| Russia | 500 | 1,744 | 752 | 2,996 |
| | | | | 6,496 |

be certain that all four former Soviet republics with strategic weapons abided by the treaty. In May 1992, the four successor states to the Soviet Union—Russia, Belarus, Ukraine, and Kazakhstan—signed a protocol making them parties to START I. They agreed to place their strategic weapons under Russian control, to remove them in accordance with the terms of START I, and then to sign the Non-Proliferation Treaty (NPT) as non-nuclear nations. Satisfied with these arrangements, the U.S. Senate finally ratified the START I treaty in October 1992, and one month later the Russian parliament did so as well.

Ukraine, in contrast to earlier professed intentions of becoming a nuclear-free nation, had second thoughts about giving up its nuclear weapons without something in return, namely substantial financial assistance for its struggling economy. In November 1994, Ukrainian president Leonid Kuchma was finally able to convince his parliament to ratify the NPT. He argued that the nation could not afford nuclear arms and would gain nothing by holding on to them. The ratification of START II was now on the agenda.

The Ukrainian wish to be paid to disarm pointed to an additional, unforeseen problem regarding the removal and destruction of the thousands of missiles: the high cost involved. Russia and the other three republics could ill afford the cost of dismantling so many missiles. In order to facilitate the process, Washington pledged some $800 million to that end.

But it was only a down payment. The cost of nuclear disarmament figured to be much higher. Moreover, there was still the cost of the environmental cleanup. One estimate of the cost to clean up the nuclear weapons environmental mess in the United States alone was $300 billion.[21] Once these costs were factored in, nuclear weapons did not turn out after all to be the financial bargain its defenders had claimed. Eventually, the piper would also have to be paid in the former Soviet Union, where environmental pollution and safety hazards at many of its nuclear weapons sites had reached crisis proportions.

The U.S. Senate ratified START II in January 1996; in Russia, however, the treaty ran into opposition. President Boris Yeltsin sought ratification, but the volatile domestic political situation forced the treaty onto the back burner until after the presidential election in June 1996. Russian nationalists and Communists stressed that START II sold out national interests. The ultranationalist Vladimir Zhirinovsky, leader of the Liberal Democratic Party—the second-largest in the Duma (parliament)—glossed over the fact that the treaty called for parity between the United States and Russia and charged that the reduction of nuclear weapons "makes Russia a secondary state." His party would not ratify an agreement that would "humiliate, insult or limit Russia as a great nation."[22]

It was not until shortly after Vladimir Putin's election as president in March 2000 that he succeeded in getting the parliament to ratify START II. Putin also managed to obtain the parliamentary ratification of the Comprehensive Nuclear Test Ban Treaty, leaving it up to the U.S. Senate to do likewise.

## ☐ The Expansion of NATO

When Gorbachev agreed to withdraw Soviet troops from Eastern Europe, he insisted that the region must remain a neutral buffer between the NATO powers and the Soviet Union. NATO was not to expand into a military vacuum once occupied by the Warsaw Pact. But then came the sudden end of the Soviet Union, after which Poland, Hungary, and the Czech Republic asked for membership in NATO as insurance against renewed Russian military ambitions. The United States then took the lead in preparing the eastward extension of NATO.

NATO tried to present the expansion as benign, meant largely to shore up democracy in Eastern Europe and somehow "strengthen European security." But the Russians well remembered the numerous invasions of their land from the west—through Germany and Poland. In June 1996, at a Berlin meeting of the foreign ministers of the sixteen NATO nations, Russian foreign minister Yevgeny Primakov warned that NATO expansion was "unacceptable."

Gorbachev joined the debate by pointing out that the agreement regulating the Soviet withdrawal from East Germany had demanded that East German troops must not be integrated into the unified German army. The "borders" of NATO must not expand. Such a move could only have one meaning—namely, the isolation of Russia from Europe, resulting in "highly unpredictable consequences."[23]

The expansion of NATO in 1999—into Poland, the Czech Republic, and Hungary—put on hold the ratification of START II by the Russian parliament and marked another humiliation of a Russia impotent in the face of expansion by its victorious Cold War adversary. NATO's ambitious move came at a time when much of Russia's military-industrial complex had been dismantled, its nuclear and conventional forces had been reduced, and its emphasis had shifted to defense.

NATO could not resist filling the military vacuum in Eastern Europe. NATO was also touted as a means of shoring up democracy in Eastern Europe. The European Union, however, with its insistence that its members be democracies (never a criterion for NATO membership), was a better vehicle to that end. In March 2004, NATO accepted for membership seven additional East European nations—Estonia, Latvia, Lithuania, Slovenia, Slovakia, Romania, and Bulgaria—that produced additional resentment in Moscow.

President George W. Bush and Putin struck up a good personal relationship. That and Putin's acceptance of the expansion of NATO—there was little he could do about it—led to agreements to discuss further cuts in nuclear armaments. In 2002, U.S. and Russian nuclear warhead deployment was adjusted as shown in Table 19.3.

## ■ NATIONAL MISSILE DEFENSE

With the end of the Cold War, Star Wars appeared to be dead. U.S. presidents George W. Bush and Bill Clinton, however, continued to fund the research project at about $3 to 4 billion per year. But then a coalition of political conservatives, corporate interests representing the aerospace industry, and the Pentagon sought to deploy a more modest version of it, dubbed the National Missile Defense (NMD) system. The cost of NMD, projected at about $60 billion, was not cheap, yet it was a far cry from the estimated price tag for SDI, up to $1 trillion. Its aim was also more modest; it was designed to intercept a few dozen warheads launched by "rogue" states, as North Korea, Iran, and Iraq were dubbed by Washington. As Clinton's term

**Table 19.3  U.S.-Soviet Deployment of Warheads**

|  | U.S. Forces | | Russian Forces | |
|---|---|---|---|---|
|  | 2002 | 2012 | 2002 | 2012 |
| ICBMs | 1,700 | 500 | 3,364 | 230[a] |
| SLBMs | 2,784 | 1,440 | 1,868 | 616 |
| Bombers | 1,660 | 280 | 582 | 240 |
| Total | 6,144 | 1,968 | 5,814 | 1,086 |

*Source: The Economist,* May 16, 2002.
*Note*: a. Depending on number of warheads per missile.

of office came to an end, he left the decision of whether to go forward with the controversial weapons system to his successor.

There were a number of problems with the system, however. First, tests showed that it was unable to carry out its functions. Second, there was the cost, which was sure to rise over time. Third, as in the case of SDI, the interceptor missiles could be fooled by inexpensive decoys. Fourth, it would violate the 1972 Anti-Ballistic Missile treaty with the Soviet Union, without which nuclear arms reduction treaties would be put into jeopardy. The Russians warned that they would not reduce their arsenal while the United States further "disarmed" them via the NMD system. China, too, declared that it would not accept a U.S. system capable of intercepting "tens of warheads" in light of the fact that it possessed a nuclear deterrent of only eighteen to twenty single-warhead ballistic missiles.

None of that had an impact on President George W. Bush. Shortly upon coming to power, he declared that the United States would deploy the system, the main purpose of which would be to guard against North Korean missiles. But Bush's NMD, however, ran into the same problems Star Wars, its more ambitious predecessor, had faced. Tests showed that it, too, was unable to carry out its functions.

## ■ NUCLEAR PROLIFERATION

Of the types of weapons of mass destruction, nuclear weapons remain by far the most dangerous. Chemical and biological weapons instill a particular horror because of their nature. The very idea of these weapons arouses revulsion. When U.S. president George W. Bush went to war against Saddam Hussein, ostensibly to eliminate his chemical and biological arsenal, the now-famous weapons-of-mass-destruction (WMDs), he struck a responsive chord among his fellow citizens, this despite the fact that conventional weapons have by far produced much greater "mass destruction."

Chemical weapons are not well suited for the battlefield. In World War II, Germans did use poison gas, but they did so against defenseless prisoners in gas chambers, not enemy soldiers. Saddam Hussein also used it against defenseless civilians—75 percent of them women and children—in Halabja in March 1988, but he had less success against Irani troops.

On the field of battle, conditions have to be just right. When the Germans launched their devastating poison gas attack at Ypres in April 1915, killing five thousand French soldiers, it was the fifth such attack during World War I, but the first to succeed. The Germans had to wait six weeks for the wind to be just right. Not only did it have to blow in the right direction, it could not be over seven miles an hour, otherwise it would quickly disperse the poison's effectiveness. For the Western Allies, chemical weapons caused fewer than 1 percent of all battlefield deaths. World War I showed that protective clothing can be very effective in negating the impact of chemical weapons. Biological weapons are even more difficult to employ effectively against enemy forces.[24]

Atomic bombs remain the most potent weapons. There is no defense against a missile armed with a nuclear warhead. It was the proliferation of such delivery systems and bombs that became the most pressing issue during the 1990s.

As the superpowers rushed to eliminate thousands of nuclear weapons, other countries were working surreptitiously to develop such weapons of their own. Suddenly, in the early 1990s, nuclear proliferation began to replace superpower confrontation as the leading potential threat to international peace and security.

The 1968 Non-Proliferation Treaty required signatory nations without nuclear weapons not to produce or receive them and to open their nuclear power facilities to inspection by the UN's International Atomic Energy Agency (IAEA). Signatory nations with nuclear weapons were treaty-bound not to make such weapons available to nonnuclear nations and to negotiate in good faith toward nuclear disarmament. Only in 1992 did China and France sign the NPT, bringing all five declared nuclear powers under its regime. By that time, 149 nations had signed the treaty. There were several holdouts, however—notably India, Pakistan, Israel, Argentina, Brazil, and Algeria, all of which had nuclear weapons programs in various stages of development. These nations were thus beyond the pale of IAEA inspectors. Other nations that had signed the NPT, such as Iraq, North Korea, South Africa, Iran, and Libya, had nonetheless managed to acquire nuclear materials and had begun nuclear weapons programs.

Several nations took steps to halt their nuclear weapons production and permit external inspection. South Africa, which had begun its nuclear weapons project in secret in the 1970s, closed its nuclear plants in 1990, signed the NPT, and opened its nuclear facilities to IAEA inspectors, thus becoming the only nation to abandon its nuclear weapons program voluntarily. In March 1993, South Africa admitted that by 1989 it had built six nuclear bombs, which, however, it had destroyed prior to the signing of the NPT. Brazil and Argentina both built large uranium-enrichment facilities in the 1980s and thus had the potential for making nuclear weapons. In December 1990, they too accepted inspection of their nuclear materials and facilities and permitted full IAEA monitoring.[25]

The danger of nuclear proliferation increased with the collapse of the Soviet Union and the prospect that its critical nuclear material, technology, and technicians might become available to the highest bidder. In 1991, the Soviet Union had over forty thousand nuclear weapons; about seven hundred thousand people worked at its nuclear weapons plants, over two thousand of whom had access to the key technical information; and since the 1940s it had produced some 100–150 tons of weapons-grade plutonium and

500–700 tons of enriched uranium, only a pound of which is needed for a Hiroshima-size bomb. The problem was how to keep nuclear fuel and technology out of unauthorized hands or the hands of rulers with past records of, or propensity for, military aggression.

While Israel never confirmed that it had nuclear weapons—estimated at well over one hundred warheads, the product of an effort that began in the early 1960s—it made sure that no Arab country acquired them. In 1982, Israeli fighter planes destroyed a nuclear reactor Iraq had purchased from France, the centerpiece of Saddam Hussein's nuclear weapons program. When the United States invaded Iraq in 2003, ostensibly to rid the country of "weapons of mass destruction," which included atomic weapons, it found that he had not rebuilt what the Israelis had destroyed twenty-two years earlier.

## ☐ Pakistan's Role

In December 2003, the United States and Libya ended their twenty-year-long confrontation, which began during the Reagan administration and then reached crisis proportion when Libyan agents destroyed a U.S. airliner over Lockerbie, Scotland, killing all 259 on board as well as 11 on the ground. The settlement of the dispute was the product of a decade of negotiations. Libya's diplomatic isolation and a UN-led economic boycott forced the hand of Muammar Qaddafi. He handed over the agents who had planted the Lockerbie bomb and agreed to pay reparations to the families of the victims. Finally, he agreed to open his country to inspections on the part of the IAEA.

The inspections revealed a primitive nuclear bomb program, courtesy of Abdul Qadeer Khan—the chief of the Khan Research Laboratories, the father of the Pakistani bomb, a national hero—who had provided assistance to several nations, notably Iran and North Korea. The head of the IAEA spoke of "a veritable Wal-Mart" of the nuclear trade. Khan did it mostly for money, but in the case of North Korea, he traded nuclear know-how for missile technology. These were not private transactions. None of this could have been arranged without the assistance of Pakistan's military, which provided the cargo airplanes.

Pakistan's role in nuclear proliferation had long been suspected in the West. Still, there was little that President Bush could do when he heard the stunning news. He had enlisted Pakistan in his war against the Taliban and al Qaeda in Afghanistan and was still looking for Osama bin Laden in Pakistan's rugged northwest frontier. He did not challenge, therefore, the explanation of Pakistan's military dictator, General Pervez Musharraf, who claimed that his military, too, had been shocked by the deeds of a lone wolf. Musharraf was more annoyed by the duplicity of his Libyan "Muslim brothers." Without a word of public rebuke, Musharraf then pardoned Khan.[26]

For the paltry sum—estimated between $60 and $100—Libya had obtained enriched uranium, plutonium, centrifuges to enrich uranium, and warhead designs. One U.S. official called it "the complete package." It was all useless, however, for Libya did not know how to use it.

## □ The Case of North Korea

One of the most severe challenges to the NPT system was North Korea's nuclear weapons program. In the 1980s, North Korea had built nuclear reactors and a plutonium-processing plant capable of turning spent nuclear fuel into weapons-grade plutonium. Not known to the West was whether such plutonium had already been produced and, if so, how much. All the while, North Korea's dictator, Kim Il Sung, remained tight-lipped, denying possession of a bomb or the intention of building one, yet skillfully creating uncertainty and playing on the fears of others. There was indeed much to fear. A nuclear-armed North Korea could threaten South Korea, which had forsworn nuclear weapons (but which, however, was under U.S. nuclear protection), and Japan. Moreover, the prospect of North Korean nuclear bombs, missiles, or technology exported to other nations posed a danger to the global nonproliferation efforts.

In 1994, the issue of the possible North Korean bomb became an international crisis. North Korea, which had signed the NPT in 1985, suddenly barred all further monitoring by IAEA inspectors in September 1993. But on the promise of opening high-level talks with the United States, it agreed in January 1994 to allow the international inspectors to continue their work. Yet two months later, when the inspectors returned to North Korea, they were prevented from entering the key plutonium-processing plant and from testing samples.

Tensions escalated rapidly. The Clinton administration sounded the call for UN sanctions and began talks with China and others to rally support for such a move. North Korea's response that sanctions would be regarded as an act of war, provoked talk of war in Washington. A visit by former U.S. president Jimmy Carter to Pyongyang in June 1994 served to cool things off. Carter secured from Kim Il Sung a pledge not to expel IAEA inspectors as long as good-faith negotiations continued between the United States and North Korea. Clinton then declared that talks would resume only if North Korea would "freeze" its plutonium weapons program and accept international safeguards. Kim agreed and a new round of high-level talks began in Geneva. But these talks had barely opened when Kim Il Sung, the eighty-two-year-old Stalinist who had ruled North Korea since 1945, died. The negotiations were suspended while the North Korean government regrouped under its new ruler, Kim Jong Il, son of the long-lived dictator.

In August 1994, the negotiations in Geneva resumed. They soon produced an outline of an agreement whereby North Korea pledged to freeze its plutonium production and the United States would replace North Korea's graphite rod nuclear reactors with light-water reactors, which have far less potential for producing plutonium. The new reactors were to be produced jointly by the United States, Japan, and South Korea at an estimated cost of $4 billion. Moreover, the same three nations would provide North Korea with fuel oil to meet its energy needs until the new reactors were in operation. The agreement, which in effect rewarded North Korea handsomely for ceasing its violations of the NPT, was finally signed in October 1994.

The agreement, however, was silent on the question of processing uranium as a fuel for nuclear weapons. Beginning with 1998, Kim Jong Il began to circumvent the spirit, although not the letter of the agreement, when he acquired from Pakistan the means to build several uranium bombs. After September 11, 2001, President Bush pronounced his "axis of evil" by lumping together Iraq, Iran, and North Korea as terrorist nations without making much of a distinction between them. Kim Jong Il's uranium bomb here became his ace in the hole. In an act of defiance, in October 2002 he volunteered that North Korea had joined the nuclear club. Bush, already stretched thin in Afghanistan and Iraq (see Chapter 21), had no answer. Kim wanted bilateral talks with the United States with the purpose of obtaining a nonaggression treaty, i.e., a U.S. pledge not to attack North Korea, thus officially ending the Korean War. Bush, however, resolutely refused to sit down with a man he loathed. Instead, he insisted on multilateral negotiations—including South Korea, China, Japan, and Russia—and threatened Kim with preventive war. Bush's secretary of defense, Donald Rumsfeld, had declared that the United States had the military means to fight a two-front war, against Iraq and North Korea, two nations that the Bush administration asserted had weapons of mass destruction. Events in Iraq, however, belied Rumsfeld's confident claim. There was little left for Bush but to change course and pretend that North Korea hardly posed a problem. Meanwhile, North Korea proceeded with its uranium and plutonium weapons projects.

## ☐ The Cases of India and Pakistan

India, which had developed and tested a "nuclear device" as early as 1974, but never admitted to possessing a nuclear bomb, refused to sign the NPT. Pakistan, seeking a deterrent to India's bomb, finally succeeded in the mid-1990s, with some assistance from China, in developing its own nuclear bomb, but it did not announce its achievement. It, too, declined to sign the NPT. For three and a half decades after China tested its nuclear weapon in 1964, there were only five declared members of the club of nuclear weapons nations.

This all changed in May 1998, when in rapid succession India and Pakistan conducted successful tests of their nuclear weapons. Shortly after coming to power, India's nationalists displayed their nuclear muscle by exploding five thermonuclear bombs in underground tests in the space of three days. India's prime minister, Atal Bihari Vajpayee, explained that the tests were purely defensive in character. The events caused jubilation in India, but caused strong rebuke around the world. All five members of the nuclear club and many other nations called upon India to halt its nuclear program. India declared a moratorium on further testing, which it avowed would hold even if Pakistan conducted its own nuclear tests. The major powers warned Pakistan against attempting to match India with tests of its own nuclear weapons, but Pakistan was in no mood to listen. Within two weeks Pakistan answered with six nuclear bomb tests. It was the Pakistanis' turn to rejoice. Pakistan, too, spoke of national defense needs.

With India and Pakistan brandishing nuclear weapons, there was good reason to fear that the low-intensity warfare still going on in Kashmir might trigger a South Asian nuclear war. The animosity between India and Pakistan was deep-seated and intense, and now the nuclear face-off heightened tensions and created a sense of urgency. Both nations had missiles systems capable of delivering the weapons. The UN Security Council quickly adopted a resolution calling for restraint and urging India and Pakistan to halt their nuclear weapons programs. Later in 1998, India and Pakistan backed away from their confrontation and met in high-level negotiations to discuss confidence-building measures for averting the risk of nuclear war, but failed to reach a specific agreement on halting a nuclear arms race.

## ☐ The Case of Iran

Iran had begun a nuclear weapons program in the early 1970s, during the days of the shah. In 1970, it had joined the NPT, permitting surprise inspections. The Islamic revolution of 1979 briefly suspended the program. In 1984, Khomeini's government resumed the program that it managed to hide for eighteen years. At the outset of the twenty-first century, Iran, with the assistance of the Soviet Union (and later the Russian Federation), North Korea, and Pakistan, was well on its way to becoming a nuclear power. After September 11, 2001, Bush declared Iran—with which the United States had had no diplomatic or economic relations since 1979[27]—as part of his "axis of evil" and repeatedly threatened war. Iran, witnessing the consequences of the U.S. invasion of neighboring Iraq, became increasingly determined to complete the project. In the face of potential attacks on the part of the United States and economic sanctions on the part of the UN and the European Union, Iran remained defiant. In October 2004, Hasan Rowhani, Iran's chief nuclear negotiator, declared that "no other country can stop us exploring technology, which is the legal right of Iran."[28]

## ■ THE QUEST FOR A COMPREHENSIVE NUCLEAR TEST BAN

The partial nuclear test ban treaty of 1963 had done little to halt the spread of nuclear weapons. The treaty had committed the signatories to cease testing in the atmosphere, on the high seas, and in outer space; it thus simply drove nuclear testing underground. By the 1990s, three of the five declared nuclear powers—the United States, Britain, and Russia—were bound by the treaty. The other two—China and France—however, continued to test their weapons in the atmosphere. (Tests are crucial in giving a nation its first reliable nuclear weapons or the ability to reconfigure them.) To curtail nuclear proliferation, a comprehensive international treaty was needed that would end all tests by both declared and undeclared nuclear powers. To that end, in 1996 the United Nations worked out a Comprehensive Test Ban Treaty at a UN Conference on Disarmament in Geneva. India, however, one of the participating members at the conference, repeatedly resisted such an agreement. India presented two arguments against the treaty: it preserved the division between nuclear haves and have-nots, and it did not commit the haves to get rid of their weapons altogether.

When the vote came before the UN General Assembly in September 1996, India voted against the treaty (along with Libya and Bhutan, whose foreign policy India controlled). After 2,045 nuclear explosions since the first one in the New Mexico desert fifty-one years earlier, a permanent nuclear ban became a possibility. Still, for the treaty to become international law, the legislatures of all forty-four countries possessing nuclear reactors had to ratify it.[29] The vote of 158 to 3 did mean, however, that all future nuclear testing would fly in the face of world opinion.

The treaty could not go into effect, however, unless 44 designated—major—nations ratified it. By September 2004, 116 nations had ratified it, including Russia, which did so in April 2000. The U.S. Senate, however, had rejected it in October 1999.

As Table 19.4 below indicates, as of September 1996, the various nuclear powers had conducted 2,045 tests of nuclear weapons. To these figures must be added the recent tests by India and Pakistan.

In 1998, the Brookings Institution, a moderate think tank in Washington, offered a balance sheet of the cost of a half century of nuclear armaments for the United States. It did not question the worth of the expenditures, but sought instead to establish a base for "an honest and fully informed debate." When the United States initially decided to deploy nuclear weapons, it was thought that these weapons were relatively cheap, that they provided "more bang for a buck." The Brookings Institution disabused this assumption. The various stages leading to nuclear deployment—research, development, deployment itself, command and control, defense, and dismantlement—had cost the United States since 1940 a staggering $5.8

**Table 19.4 Known Nuclear Tests, 1945–1996**

|  | U.S. | USSR | France | Britain | China | India |
|---|---|---|---|---|---|---|
| Atmospheric | 215 | 219 | 50 | 21 | 23 | 0 |
| Underground | 815 | 496 | 159 | 24 | 22 | 1 |
| Total | 1,030 | 715 | 209 | 45 | 45 | 1 |

*Sources*: UN; Physicians for Social Responsibility; Barbara Crosette, "U.N. Endorses a Treaty to Halt All Nuclear Testing," *New York Times*, September 11, 1996, p. A3.

trillion dollars, an average of $21,646 per citizen. The development and manufacturing of the bombs was relatively cheap, as they used up only 7 percent of the total spent. But the infrastructure—missiles and bombers, submarines, personnel, and so on—made up 86 percent of the cost.

The deployment of these weapons had taken on a life of its own. In 1964, Secretary of Defense Robert McNamara stated that a force of 400 megatons (the equivalent of 400 million tons of TNT) was enough for the MAD (Mutually Assured Destruction) deterrent. Yet at the time, the United States already possessed 17,000 megatons, or more than forty times the amount deemed necessary, and had plans to add to its nuclear arsenal.[30] And it continued developing new weapons and had plans for more.

## ■ RECOMMENDED READINGS

Bottome, Edgar M. *The Balance of Terror: A Guide to the Arms Race*. 2d rev. ed. Boston: Beacon Press, 1986.

Broad, William J. *Teller's War: The Top-Secret Story Behind the Star Wars Deception*. New York: Simon and Schuster, 1992.
How Edward Teller, the "father" of the U.S. hydrogen bomb, managed to sell SDI to the Reagan administration.

Bundy, McGeorge. *Danger and Survival: Choices About the Bomb in the First Fifty Years*. New York: Random House, 1988.
John Kennedy's national security adviser describes how successive U.S. governments worked out a "tradition of non-use."

Cockburn, Andrew. *The Threat: Inside the Soviet Military Machine*. New York: Random House, 1983.
A sober assessment of Soviet capabilities and weaknesses.

Cox, Arthur Macy. *Russian Roulette: The Superpower Game*. New York: Times Books, 1982.

FitzGerald, Frances. *Way Out There in the Blue: Reagan, Star Wars and the End of the Cold War*. New York: Simon and Schuster, 2000.
A critical analysis of a program which, after $60 billion, had little to show for it.

Freedman, Lawrence. *The Evolution of Nuclear Strategy*. New York: St. Martin's Press, 1981.

Garthoff, Raymond L. *Deterrence and the Revolution in Soviet Military Doctrine*. Washington, D.C.: Brookings Institution, 1990.
Explains the Soviet emphasis on war prevention instead of deterrence.

Gervasi, Tom. *The Myth of Soviet Military Supremacy.* New York: Harper and Row, 1986.
Challenges the claims that the Soviet Union had overtaken the West in the arms race in the 1980s.

Holloway, David. *Stalin and the Bomb: The Soviet Union and Atomic Energy, 1936–1956.* New Haven, Conn.: Yale University Press, 1994.

Matlock, Jack F. *Reagan and Gorbachev: How the Cold War Ended.* New York: Random House, 2004.
By Reagan's ambassador to the Soviet Union.

Mazarr, Michael J. *North Korea and the Bomb: A Case Study in Non-Proliferation.* New York: St. Martin's Press, 1997.
A thorough study by an expert, focusing on the 1994 nuclear weapons issue between North Korea and the United States.

McDougall, Walter A. *The Heavens and the Earth: A Political History of the Space Age.* New York: Basic Books, 1984.

Newhouse, John. *Cold Dawn: The Story of SALT.* New York: Holt, Rinehart and Winston, 1973.

Office of Technology Assessment. *SDI: Technology, Survivability and Software.* Princeton, N.J.: Princeton University Press, 1988.
Reprint of a study conducted for the House Armed Services and Senate Foreign Relations Committees that concluded that SDI would fail in case of war.

Rhodes, Richard. *Dark Sun: The Making of the Hydrogen Bomb.* New York: Simon and Schuster, 1995.
A definitive study of the first two decades of the nuclear arms race.

Schell, Jonathan. *The Fate of the Earth.* New York: Knopf, 1982.
The best-seller on the potential consequences of nuclear war.

Sigal, Leon. *Disarming Strangers: Nuclear Diplomacy with North Korea.* Princeton, N.J.: Princeton University Press, 1999.
A study of North Korea's nuclear weapons project, arguing that the crisis in 1994 came dangerously close to war.

Smith, Gerard. *Doubletalk: The Story of SALT I.* Garden City, N.Y.: Doubleday, 1980.
By the chief U.S. arms negotiator at the talks.

*Soviet Military Power.* Washington, D.C.: U.S. Government Printing Office, six editions, 1981–1987.
The Pentagon's exaggerated assessment of the Soviet threat.

Spector, Leonard S. *Nuclear Ambitions: The Spread of Nuclear Weapons, 1989–1990.* Boulder, Colo.: Westview Press, 1990.
The fifth in a series by this recognized expert provides a detailed country-by-country analysis.

Talbott, Strobe. *Deadly Gambits: The Reagan Administration and the Stalemate in Nuclear Arms Control.* New York: Knopf, 1984.
This book and the following book by the same author, a former correspondent for *Time*, are among the most detailed and lucid accounts of recent arms negotiations.

———. *Endgame: The Inside Story of SALT II.* New York: Harper and Row, 1979.

Union of Concerned Scientists. *The Fallacy of Star Wars.* New York: Vintage, 1984.

Zuckerman, Solly. *Nuclear Illusion and Reality.* New York: Random House, 1982.
A critical view of the nuclear arms race by a former scientific adviser to the British Ministry of Defence: neither side can gain nuclear advantage.

# ■ NOTES

1. SS (surface-to-surface) is the U.S. designation of Soviet missiles. As soon as a Soviet missile was tested, the Pentagon assigned it a number.

2. George McGovern, "SALT II: A Political Autopsy," *Politics Today* (March-April 1980), p. 64.

3. This was the basis of Ronald Reagan's "window of vulnerability." It went something like this: the Soviet Union's land-based arsenal, which during the late 1970s had become increasingly more accurate, was capable of overwhelming the U.S. land-based missiles in their silos and thereby threatened the very existence of the United States. This argument ignored the fact that either of the other two legs of the U.S. "triad," the submarines and the bomber force, was more than enough to keep the Soviets honest. Reagan promised that, if elected president, he would close this window. In 1984, he declared that he had closed the window—without, however, having done anything to protect U.S. land-based missiles.

4. Thomas Powers, "Nuclear Winter and Nuclear Strategy," *Atlantic Monthly* (November 1984), p. 60.

5. Kissinger cited in Lawrence Freedman, *The Evolution of Nuclear Strategy* (New York: St. Martin's Press, 1981), p. 363.

6. Georgy Arbatov, director of the Institute of U.S. and Canadian Studies of the Academy of Sciences of the Soviet Union, in Arthur Macy Cox (with a Soviet commentary by Georgy Arbatov), *Russian Roulette: The Superpower Game* (New York: Times Books, 1982), pp. 177–178, 182.

7. Leonid Brezhnev and Ronald Reagan, "Brezhnev and Reagan on Atom War," transcripts of statements, *New York Times,* October 21, 1981, p. 5.

8. Great Britain accepted 160 cruise missiles; West Germany, 108 Pershing II and 96 cruise missiles; Italy, 112 cruise missiles; Belgium and Holland, 48 cruise missiles each. Norway, Denmark, Greece, and Turkey rejected U.S. missiles. Turkey, by virtue of the agreement between the Soviet Union and the United States in the wake of the Cuban missile crisis of 1962, was prohibited from stationing U.S. missiles. The Greek government of Andreas Papandreou carved out a neutralist position despite the fact that Greece was a member of NATO. Papandreou considered Turkey, a fellow member of NATO, to be a greater threat to Greece than the Warsaw Pact to the north. In Norway and Denmark, pacifist sentiment prevented the acceptance of U.S. weapons.

9. Ronald Reagan, quoted in "President's Speech on Military Spending and a New Defense," *New York Times,* March 24, 1983, p. A20.

10. Star Wars "system concepts and battle management" was one of five components of Star Wars research; Wayne Biddle, "Request for Space Weapons Reflects Early Goals," *New York Times,* February 4, 1985, p. A10. With a computer-driven system, the fate of the world would be in the hands (or the chips and software) of computers. "Perhaps we should run R2-D2 for president in the 1990s," Senator Paul Tsongas (D-Mass.) commented at a congressional hearing. "At least he'd be on line all the time. Has anyone told the President that he's out of the decision-making process?" George Keyworth, President Reagan's science adviser, replied, "I certainly haven't." Philip M. Boffey, "'Star Wars' and Mankind: Consequences for Future," *New York Times,* March 8, 1985, p. A14. In January 1987, the Office of Technology Assessment, on behalf of the House Armed Services and Senate Foreign Relations Committees, conducted workshops on potential Soviet responses to SDI and on the feasibility of producing SDI software, to determine whether the controversial program would in fact work. Its report concluded that the software would have to be written "without the benefit of data or experience from battle use," that

is, it could not be properly tested. It would have to rely on theoretical "peacetime testing," which, however, would offer "no guarantee that the system would not fail catastrophically . . . as a result of a software error . . . in the system's first battle." Office of Technology Assessment, *SDI: Technology, Survivability and Software* (Princeton, N.J.: Princeton University Press, 1988), p. 249.

11. Harold Brown, December 1983, quoted in Boffey, "Star Wars," p. A14.

12. Caspar Weinberger quote, ibid., p. A14.

13. The Soviet SS-20 rockets carried three warheads each; thus the Soviet Union gave up more than three times as many warheads as the United States.

14. Arms Control Association, from data supplied by the U.S. Defense Department, the Joint Chiefs of Staff, and the Arms Control and Disarmament Agency, *New York Times,* May 26, 1988, p. A12.

15. "Wir werden euch des Feindes berauben," *Der Spiegel,* December 12, 1988, p. 22.

16. Christian Schmidt-Häuer, "Die Armee gerät unter Beschuss," *Die Zeit,* November 11, 1988, p. 8.

17. "Unsere Antwort wird Nein sein," *Der Spiegel,* May 1, 1989, p. 21.

18. Wolfgang Schwarz of the Institute for International Politics and Economy in East Berlin, in a report to the East German Council of Ministers, "DDR-Wissenschaftler warnt vor Atomverseuchung Europas," *Frankfurter Rundschau,* June 21, 1989, p. 2.

19. John F. Cushman, Jr., "Senate Endorses Pact to Reduce Strategic Arms," *New York Times,* October 2, 1992, pp. A1, A6.

20. Jack Mendelsohn, "Big Deal at the Summit," *Baltimore Sun,* June 21, 1992, p. 3G. Yeltsin's offer was not cleared with nor necessarily supported by his government in Moscow. Some deputies in Moscow expressed shock at the extent of the cuts Yeltsin had proposed.

21. George Petrovich, "Counting the Costs of the Arms Race," *Foreign Policy* (winter 1991–1992), p. 87.

22. Cited in David Hoffman, "Russian Says Arms Treaty Vote Should Follow Election," *Washington Post,* February 1, 1996, p. A17.

23. Mikhail Gorbachev, "'Geroi' razrusheniia Sovetskogo Soiuza izvestny . . . ," *Novoe vremia,* nos. 2–3 (1995), p. 27.

24. William K. Blewett, "Chemical and Biological Threats: The Nature and Risk," *HPAC Engineering* (September 2004), pp. 2–4; William Blewett, "75 Years of Chemical Warfare," *Baltimore Sun,* April 20, 1990.

25. Leonard S. Spector, "Repentant Nuclear Proliferants," *Foreign Policy* (fall 1992), pp. 26–27.

26. Seymour M. Hersh, "The Deal: Why Is Washington Going Easy on Pakistan's Nuclear Black Marketers?" *New Yorker,* March 8, 2004, pp. 32–37.

27. Exceptions were the illegal transactions by the Reagan administration, which sold missiles to the mullahs in Tehran and made business deals on the part of U.S. corporations in circumvention of U.S. law.

28. Associated Press, "Iran Threatens to End Nuclear Talks with Europeans," *Baltimore Sun,* October 28, 2004, p. 14A.

29. "A Nice Red Afterglow," *The Economist,* March 14, 1992, p. 43.

30. Walter Pincus, "U.S. Has Spent $5.8 Trillion on Nuclear Arms Since 1940, Study Says," *Washington Post,* July 1, 1998, p. A2.

# 20

# Political Islam and the Middle East

The Cold War was largely a bipolar struggle between Western liberalism and the Soviet variant of Communism, with much of the world simply trying to stay out of harm's way. In the late 1970s, however, a new political force emerged: militant Islam. This political movement sought to resurrect the world of Islam, to free it from the debilitating and overbearing influence of such outside forces as Communism, secularism, and above all the pervading Western presence. Militant Islam left its mark throughout Islamic societies in a region that stretches, with few interruptions, from the Atlantic shores of Africa to the easternmost tip of the Indonesian archipelago in Asia, encompassing nearly a billion people in the 1980s.

## ■ ISLAM: THEORY AND PRACTICE

Islam is the third of the world's great religions to come out of the Middle East. It represents to Muslims the third and last of the "true revelations" by a divinity whom the Jews call Jehovah, the Christians call God, and the Muslims call Allah.

This final revelation came in the seventh century of the Christian era when Allah spoke to His Prophet Mohammed of Mecca, Islam's holiest city, located in what today is Saudi Arabia. Mohammed had been born into a society of idol worshipers, Jews, and Christians, and he fell under the influence of Arabia's two dominant monotheistic faiths, Judaism and Christianity. In fact, these were the starting point of Mohammed's teachings. He was always at pains to acknowledge that God had revealed himself to his prophets of another age—Abraham, Moses, and Jesus Christ among them. In fact, Islam recognized that Jews and Christians were "people of the book," that is, God's revelation in the Old and New Testaments.[1] Mohammed, however, also insisted that Christians and Jews had gone astray and had ignored God's commandments and corrupted the original scriptures.

Mohammed held the view that uncorrupted Judaism and Christianity were early manifestations of Islam, literally "submission" to God. Abraham, according to Mohammed, had been the first Muslim. But since Jews and Christians had strayed from God's word, God then revealed Himself to the last in the long line of prophets, Mohammed. The links between Islam and Christianity were such that some seventh-century Christian theologians believed that Islam was a heterodox Christian doctrine, similar to Nestorianism, a deviation that attributed to Jesus two natures—divine and human— a heresy that had been suppressed but continued to have adherents in the Middle East.[2]

Islam in this fashion became an offshoot of Judaism. Its linear relationship to the earlier faiths resembles Christianity's link to Judaism. For this reason there remain numerous significant similarities among the three faiths. At one time, Muslims, including Mohammed, faced Jerusalem while in prayer. All three religions stress justice and compassion. Islam has a heaven and a hell; God spoke to Mohammed through the Archangel Gabriel; Islam has its Day of Resurrection and Judgment, "and the hour is known to no one but God." Believers who are created "from an essence of clay . . . shall surely die hereafter, and be restored to life on the Day of Resurrection," a "day sure to come."[3]

Arabs and Jews both claim Abraham as their ancestor. The Jews descended from Abraham's second son, Isaac, born of his wife Sarah; the Arabs descended from the first son, Ishmael, born of Hagar, Sarah's Egyptian maid. The Bible prophesied that great nations would descend from the two sons of Abraham. The biblical account, however, also stresses that God renewed with Isaac the covenant he had made with Abraham, while the Muslim account makes no distinction between the sons of Abraham. Islamic scholars have argued that it is inconceivable that God would favor one son over the other. In Islamic teachings, the conflict between Jews and Muslims, therefore, becomes a family divided against itself. Since both Muslims and Jews trace their religious ancestry to Abraham, it was not surprising that both sought to control the West Bank city of Hebron, which contains the tombs of Abraham and his family (notably his wife Sarah and his son Isaac). Some Jews consider Hebron their second-holiest city.

The revelations to Mohammed were codified in the Koran (literally "recitation" of the word of God), the holy, infallible book of the Muslims, which contains God's commands to the faithful. The Koran is God's word, last in time and the completion and correction of all that had been written before.

A deviation from established religions is no trifling matter; it is nothing less than an attempt to replace established faiths with one that claims to be the only true revelation from God. The consequences of such an attempt have been religious conflicts, which in the case of Islam began in Mohammed's day and have lasted centuries down to our time. Neither Judaism nor

Christianity has ever recognized the validity of Islam. Western scholars have often used the label "Mohammedanism" to describe Islam, a term insulting to Muslims because it suggests that it is an invention of one man rather than God's final word. And Islam, in its turn, has denied the Holy Trinity, and thus the divinity of Jesus Christ, which amounts to a demand for "the unconditional surrender of the essence of Christianity."[4] Islam does, however, recognize Jesus as one of a long line of God's prophets.

Islam means "submission" to Allah, and a Muslim is someone who has submitted to the will of God. It is a religion that encompasses the totality of one's existence. It is a complete way of life, both secular and religious. There can be no separation between one's spiritual and secular existence. In an Islamic nation, therefore, a believer cannot make a distinction between secular and religious law. All laws must be based on the Koran; they cannot be otherwise. And the rulers and their governments must reign according to the word of Allah. Islam is, after all, a religion of laws.

There is an elemental simplicity to the fundamental laws, the "five pillars" of Islam. They include, first and foremost, the affirmation that consists of one of the shortest credos of any religion in the world: "There is no god but God and Mohammed is the Prophet of God." All that a convert to Islam has to do is to state this credo in the company of believers. No other rite or ceremony is required. (The very simplicity inherent in the act of conversion explains in part why Islam was the fastest-growing religion in Africa at the end of the twentieth century.) Second, a Muslim is obliged to pay an alms tax (the *zakat*) of around 5 percent. Islam emphasizes the importance of charity: "Whatever alms you give . . . are known to Allah . . . and whatever alms you give shall be paid back to you in full."[5] In an Islamic state, the alms tax also has become a source of revenue for the government. Third, a Muslim must say five daily prayers facing toward Mecca. The *muezzin* (crier) calls the faithful to prayer from the minaret (a slender tower) of a mosque (or temple) at various times during the day: at sunset, during the night, at dawn, at noon, and in the afternoon. Fourth, Islam demands abstention from food, drink, and sexual intercourse from dawn to sunset during the lunar month of Ramadan, which commemorates Allah's first revelation of the Koran to Mohammed. Fasting here becomes a spiritual act of renunciation and self-denial. Last, a Muslim must attempt to make at least one pilgrimage, or *haj,* to the holy city of Mecca.

In the seventh century, following the death of Mohammed, Islam spread quickly throughout the Middle East and North Africa. With Islam came the establishment of one of the world's great civilizations, centering on the cities of Damascus and Baghdad. Yet, ultimately, this golden age of Islam gave way to a European ascendancy, which may be dated to the crusades of the Middle Ages. In more recent times, Western powers (notably Great Britain, France, and Italy) managed to establish their presence in the Muslim lands of the Middle East, only to find their grip weakening after World

War II. Islam today seeks to free the Muslim countries from the centuries-old overbearing influence of the Christian West and to reassert the sovereignty and dignity denied them in the past. Militant Islam is, therefore, a potent political and revolutionary weapon.

## ☐ The Shiites and the Sunnis

The most visible and radical advocates of resurgent, militant Islam are the Shiites, the smaller of the two main branches of Islam. The other wing, the Sunnis, represents what is generally called the mainstream of Islam and, in fact, it makes up approximately 90 percent of all Muslims. Shiites are little known in Africa among the Arabs in the north or among the blacks in sub-Saharan Africa. The same is true of southern Asia, in countries such as Indonesia, Malaysia, Bangladesh, India, Turkey, and Pakistan. The keepers of the holy places in Mecca and Medina, the Saudi royal family, and their subjects are mostly Sunnis. In Iran, however, nearly all Muslims belong to the Shiite branch; in fact, Shiism became a state religion there. The majority of the Muslims of Iraq and of the former Soviet Republic of Azerbaijan are Shiites. Shiites may also be found in large numbers in all the other states of the Persian Gulf, Syria, Lebanon, Yemen, and in Central Asia.

The split in Islam came two decades after the Prophet's death in A.D. 632. A line of *khalifa,* or caliphs, took Mohammed's place as his deputies and successors. The first four caliphs, the Rightly Guided, were selected from the ranks of Mohammed's associates, and after that the line became hereditary. From the very outset there were strains in the Muslim community over the question of succession. As the caliphs became more tyrannical, they increasingly appeared as usurpers. There were those who insisted that Ali, the husband of Mohammed's daughter Fatima, was the true successor. The assassination of the reigning caliph in 656 set off a civil war between the party of Ali (in Arabic, *shia* means party or sect), who also was assassinated, and the main branch (*sunna* in Arabic means practice or custom). The struggle lasted until the Battle of Kerbala in 681, when the Sunnis established their domination and the Shiite resistance went underground. The struggle was both political and religious in nature. Its political content lay in the fact that the Shiites became the champions of the oppressed and the opponents of privilege and power. The Shiites found their inspiration in the actions of Mohammed in Mecca, where the Prophet first made his mark as the advocate of the downtrodden. As such, the Shiites in Iran, for example, have always been in conflict with the throne in their attempts to re-create a social and political order in line with the teachings of the Koran. Politics and religion, in the Shiites' eyes, cannot be separated. When in 1963, the shah of Iran offered his uncompromising critic, the Ayatollah Ruhollah Khomeini, his freedom on condition he leave politics to the politicians, Khomeini replied: "All of Islam is politics."[6] Khomeini was the shah's most vocal opponent, who charged the monarch with having sold his country into bondage on behalf of U.S. interests. In 1964, Khomeini was arrested for having publicly refused to recognize the government, its courts, and laws. Ten days after his release in 1964, Khomeini delivered the first of his political sermons. Later that year he was rearrested and then exiled.[7] Obedience to civil authority has never been a hallmark of Shiite behavior. Shiites, in their challenges to entrenched political power, have time and again elevated political disobedience to a religious duty.

Sunnis and Shiites both accept the Prophet's promise of the return of one of his descendants who will "fill the world with justice and equity."[8] For the Shiites, however, the spirit of messianism is central to their creed. They look to an *imam*, a divinely appointed descendant of Mohammed, whose purpose is the spiritual—as well as political and at times insurrectional—guidance of the faithful. The Sunnis, the party of custom and practice, have always stood for the continuity of the social, political, and religious order. They have emphasized consensus and obedience to civil and religious authority. The Sunnis, in contrast to the Shiites, have looked for inspiration to Mohammed's work in Medina, where he created the first Muslim state and ruled as a military commander, judge, and teacher to whom Allah's word was revealed.

Radicalism in the name of Islam, however, is not a Shiite monopoly. The Shiites have a lower boiling point when it comes to dealing with corruption and oppression. The militant Muslims in Iran, Iraq, Lebanon, and Saudi Arabia were generally Shiites; the Islamic radicals in Algeria, Hamas in Gaza, the Taliban in Afghanistan, and members of al Qaeda were Sunnis. What militant Islam—whether Shiite or Sunni—sought to achieve was the elimination of foreign influences that humiliated and degraded their societies. The militants in Algeria fought a military dictatorship still heavily dominated by French culture, those in Iran combated Western (at first largely British and later U.S.) influence, and the Soviet Muslims (whether Shiite Azeris or Sunni Chechens or Uzbeks) sought to free themselves of Moscow's rule and dreamed of a restoration of their once glorious civilizations.

■ **THE REVOLUTION IN IRAN**

☐ *The Shah and the United States*

From the end of World War II until the late 1970s, Iran stood in sharp contrast to its neighbors. Shah Mohammed Reza Pahlavi and his country appeared to be a rock of stability in the turbulent Middle East, a bulwark against political radicalism, Islamic fundamentalism, and Soviet expansionism. It was little wonder that, even after the shah's internal position had been shaken by violent protests, U.S. president Jimmy Carter could still praise him for his stabilizing influence in the Middle East. Surely, there was no solid reason to believe that the shah, still apparently a vigorous man in middle age, would not continue to rule Iran as he had in the past. Moreover, he was preparing his young son to succeed him on the Peacock Throne.

But Iran turned out to be another case of U.S. involvement in a foreign land of which few people in authority in Washington had an adequate understanding. The outward stability of the nation only masked the volatile undercurrents, which had deep historic roots. The shah had ruled for a long time, ever since 1941, but his reign had often been unstable, an uncomfortable fact that too many U.S. policymakers often conveniently overlooked. The militant clergy were a nuisance, they reasoned, but they certainly appeared to be no threat to the shah.

Successful resistance to Iran's shahs by the militant Shiite clergy over the centuries was a constant thread running through Iranian history. This was particularly the case with those shahs who made deals with foreigners, granting them favorable concessions at the expense of the nation. In 1872, for example, Nasir ed-Den Shah granted Paul Julius de Reuter, a British subject, such comprehensive monopolies that the shah, in effect, had sold him the country. De Reuter received monopolies in the construction of railroads, canals, and irrigation works, the harvesting of forests, the use of all uncultivated lands, and the operation of banks, public works, and mines. The British leader Lord Curzon called this "the most complete and extraordinary surrender of the entire industrial resources of a kingdom into foreign hands that has ever been dreamed of, much less accomplished."[9] In 1892, the shah faced an angry mob that had stormed his palace demanding the repeal of a monopoly granted to a British firm in the production, sale, and export of tobacco. This exercise of political power in the streets was sufficient to bring about the repeal of these concessions. But the shah's troubles persisted, and in 1896, he was assassinated. Nasir ed-Den Shah's reign points to a recurring pattern of Iranian politics: royal complicity with foreign powers, the power of the mobs in the streets, and the inability of most shahs to maintain their power. During the past 360 years, only four shahs died natural deaths while still in possession of the throne. The rest were either dethroned or assassinated. Iran is not a likely place to look for political equilibrium.

After Nasir en-Den Shah's assassination, the practice of selling favors to foreigners—British, French, and Russian—continued. In 1906, the Iranian parliament, the *majlis*, took away this privilege from the shah. But despite the prohibition, the practice continued, contributing to a legacy of bitterness and resentment directed toward the ruling Qajar dynasty (1779–1925) that ultimately led to its demise. In its place, a usurper pronounced the creation of his own ruling house. He was Colonel Reza Khan, who subsequently crowned himself Reza Shah Pahlavi.

Years later, Reza Khan's son, Mohammed Reza (1941–1979), attempted to identify his ruling house, the Pahlavi dynasty, with the glories of Persia's past. In 1971, he staged an elaborate ceremony in Persepolis, the ancient city of Cyrus the Great. Guests from far and wide attended the gala celebration. The shah then proceeded to date the calendar from the reign of Cyrus, symbolizing over 2,500 years of historic continuity.[10] He became the Shahansha (the King of Kings), the Light of the Aryans, who ruled by divine right, a man who claimed to have experienced religious visions.[11]

This spectacle impressed the world, but many Iranians, particularly the clergy, saw the shah in a different light. The Shiite clergy demanded submission to their will, that is, the will of Allah. They considered the shah merely a usurper—only the second in the short line of the Pahlavi dynasty—who had been educated in the West and who had sent his own son to study there.

Reza Shah did not act appreciably differently from the previous monarchs when it came to dealing with foreign powers. In 1933, he granted new favorable concessions to the Anglo-Iranian Oil Company, an enterprise that was largely controlled by the British. His close association with the British continued until World War II, when he shifted toward Nazi Germany at a time when it threatened to take the Soviet Union's oil fields north of the Caucasus along the western shores of the Caspian Sea, notably around the city of Baku. A successful German drive in that direction would have linked German-occupied territory with Iran. The upshot was the joint occupation of Iran by the Soviets (who took control of the northern part) and the British (who occupied the southern regions). The shah was then sent packing when the British and Soviets forced him to abdicate in favor of his young son, who turned out to be the second and last of the Pahlavi dynasty.

The greatest source of wealth for the Pahlavi dynasty was the country's oil. By 1950, Iran was one of the largest producers of oil in the Middle East. By that time Iran's own share of the oil profits had increased, but many nationalists, including many of the clergy, were not satisfied. For one thing, the Arab-American Oil Company, a U.S. concern operating in Saudi Arabia, had offered the Saudis more favorable terms. More important, the lion's share of the profits from Iran's natural resources still went to the foreign investors, who were mostly British.

The result was that in 1951, parliament, under the direction of Prime Minister Mohammed Mossadegh, challenged the shah and voted for the nationalization of the oil industry. The British, predictably, declared such an act illegal. U.S. President Truman sought to negotiate the dispute, eventually siding with the British, but refusing to become involved in Iraq's internal affairs. The new Eisenhower administration, however, had no such qualms; its secretary of state, John Foster Dulles, and his brother, Allen, the chief of the CIA, decided to act. Truman had thought that Mossadegh was a barrier against the aspirations of the Communist (*Tudeh*) Party; the Dulles brothers thought that Mossadegh was contributing to an eventual Communist takeover.

Mossadegh's challenge to the West struck a responsive chord in Iranian society. As tensions rose higher, the CIA and British intelligence were plotting to oust Mossadegh. Washington also put economic pressure on Iran by cutting off aid and refusing to buy Iranian oil. The use of an economic weapon only inflamed the militants in Tehran, the Iranian capital. In August 1953, street riots forced the shah to flee to Rome. There he apparently came to the conclusion that his reign had ended.

The CIA moved quickly and decisively. With the help of elements in the Iranian army and others opposed to Mossadegh, the United States and Britain managed to return the shah after only three days in exile. Demonstrations in the streets had ousted the shah; counterdemonstrations in these same streets created a political climate permitting the shah to return.

The shah now owed his throne to a foreign power, something he always resented. But his ties with the United States continued to grow. Oil production and export to the West continually increased, and in the process the shah became one of the United States' best overseas customers. He then took steps to modernize Iranian society by launching his conservative "white revolution." Such a transformation, however, came at a price. Modernization created a gulf between a new privileged class, which benefited from the shah's close link with the West, and much of the rest of the country. The influx of Western technicians, engineers, military advisers, and sales representatives disturbed many Iranians. The distribution of the country's enormous wealth and the attendant Westernization and modernization led to a distortion of traditional Iranian social patterns. Too many were left out, and it was inevitable that the shah's actions would breed resentment. Traditional Iranian self-sufficiency became a thing of the past. By the 1970s, Iran became greatly dependent on foreign imports; it even bought food from abroad. And since Iran based much of its wealth on a one-product economy (80 percent of its export earnings came from the sale of oil), its dependency on the West appeared to be total.

Much of the money the shah spent abroad went for the purchase of modern military equipment, most of it U.S.-made. Between 1972 and 1978, he ordered $19.5 billion in U.S. arms. The greater the oil revenues, the more weapons he bought. After 1973, about one-third of the government's spending went for armaments. This proved to be a boon for U.S. arms manufacturers, for by the end of the 1970s, one-third of all U.S. arms sales went to Iran.

The U.S. government, particularly the Nixon administration, applauded such a course: Iran, armed to the teeth, would preserve stability in the Middle East, particularly in the Gulf, the waterway through which passed much of the oil on which the industrial powers depended. It was here that the "Nixon Doctrine" appeared to work best. Nixon had first formulated his doctrine toward the end of the war in Vietnam. According to the Nixon Doctrine, the United States would arm and support a client who would do the actual fighting in support of U.S. interests. In South Vietnam the doctrine collapsed like a house of cards in 1975, when its army took to its heels. In Iran the doctrine seemed to be working to perfection.

In the early 1970s, it was not clear how Iran would pay for the massive military equipment the shah demanded. But good fortune intervened. October 1973 saw the fourth Arab-Israeli conflict, the Yom Kippur War, which led to an oil embargo by the Arab members of the Organization of Petroleum Exporting Countries (OPEC) and a doubling of oil prices. The shah took the lead in demanding this increase in the price of oil. The Nixon administration, however, saw a silver lining in all of this. The United States was now able to supply Iran with military equipment without raiding the U.S. treasury. Henry Kissinger, Nixon's secretary of state, explained in his memoirs: "The vacuum left by British withdrawal [from Iran during the early 1950s], now menaced by Soviet intrusion and radical momentum, would be filled by a power friendly to us . . . And all of this was achievable without any American resources, since the Shah was willing to pay for the equipment out of his oil revenues."[12]

But this scenario began to fall apart in a most unexpected way when militant Islam drove the shah, whom it denounced as a servant of the "Great satan" (the United States), from power.

## ☐ The Return of Khomeini

The best-known practitioner of militant Islam was the Ayatollah Ruhollah Khomeini. He identified Western civilization as Islam's enemy; an Islamic society, therefore, must be purged of it. The shah, with the trappings of Western civilization all around him, was little different from the tens of thousands of Western technicians he had invited to Iran. In the eyes of the *mullahs,* the Muslim clergy, the shah stood in direct violation of the history and religion of Islam.

Khomeini's denunciations of the shah at first had little effect. They were regarded merely as the ravings and rantings of an old man in exile. But as dissatisfaction with the shah's rule increased, Khomeini's sermons on cassette tapes, smuggled into Iran, began to have an effect. By January 1979, it became apparent that the shah could only maintain his throne if the notoriously brutal SAVAK (the secret police established in 1957 with the help of the CIA) and the army were willing to suppress all manifestations of discontent, with much loss of life. Civil war loomed on the horizon. The shah, unsure of the loyalty of the army and unable to obtain a clear-cut U.S. commitment from the Carter administration, decided to leave the country. Corruption, favoritism, police brutality, poverty and luxury existing side by side, the lack of justice, the influence of foreigners—all contributed to the fall of the shah.

The events of the late 1970s showed that the shah had merely maintained an illusion of power. In February 1979, the Ayatollah Khomeini returned in triumph from exile in Paris, where he had been the most visible symbol of righteous Islamic resistance to a ruler who had betrayed both his religion and his people. Iran, under the leadership of the Muslim clergy, could now be expected to experience a spiritual and national rejuvenation. There was little doubt that the support for Khomeini's regime was massive in those heady days when the shah was put to flight.

But the shah had not officially abdicated. When he left in January 1979, he emphasized that he and his family were going abroad for an unspecified period. In effect, he promised to return.[13] It was clear that the United States preferred the shah over the anti-U.S. militants who now governed Tehran. The militants, for their part, feared a repetition of the events of 1953, when the CIA had returned the shah to power from his brief exile in Rome. Radicals, bitterly hostile to a U.S. government on which they blamed all of Iran's ills, were able to stir up deep emotions. Anti-U.S. street demonstrations became daily affairs, and two weeks after Khomeini's return from exile, the first attack by militants on the U.S. embassy took place. The organizers of the attack claimed—correctly—that the embassy housed the CIA. Khomeini forces at this time dispersed the attackers.

Shah Mohammed Reza Pahlavi, monarch of Iran, with U.S. secretary of defense James Schlesinger, Washington, D.C., July 26, 1973. *(AP/Wide World Photos)*

Ayatollah Ruhollah Khomeini, Shiite leader of the Iranian revolution, 1979. *(Embassy of Iran)*

The Khomeini government, instead of concentrating on the consolidation of power, sharpened its differences between his revolution and the United States when it repealed the 1947 law authorizing a U.S. military mission in Iran. Tensions were already high when, in October 1979, the shah arrived in New York for medical reasons. To the militants, this marked the first step of what to them was a U.S. attempt to bring the shah back to power. They never believed the shah was in need of treatment.

On November 4, a group of radical students decided to take matters into their own hands. They climbed over the walls of the U.S. embassy compound in Tehran, seized its diplomatic personnel, demanding that the United States extradite the shah to Iran to stand trial. Only then would they release their fifty-two hostages who were kept blindfolded in the embassy. There was no evidence that Khomeini had ordered them to engage in an act that clearly violated international law. Still, it suited his political position since it drove political sentiments in Iran further to a radical extreme. The huge crowds who gathered daily in the square in front of the embassy in support of the students limited Khomeini's options.

The hostage crisis came at a time when memories of helicopters lifting off the rooftop of the U.S. embassy in Saigon were still fresh in the U.S. public's eye. And, eight weeks after the onset of the hostage crisis, the United States was hit with another jolt when the Soviet Union sent eighty thousand troops into Afghanistan—a country bordering Iran—to bail out a bankrupt Communist government. The hostage crisis and the Soviet army's invasion of Afghanistan had a dramatic impact on U.S. public opinion. The United States had lost a sphere of influence in Iran, and the Soviets had sent troops outside their postwar sphere for the first time. The U.S. loss and what appeared to be the Soviet Union's gain gave President Carter a foreign policy headache that ultimately played a major role in his defeat in the presidential election of 1980.

The hostages eventually came home, but only after the 1980 election and after 444 days of captivity. President Carter had punished the Soviets with a grain embargo and a U.S. refusal to attend the 1980 summer Olympic Games in Moscow. But Carter's actions were too little and too late. He could not shake the damaging public perception that he was indecisive and a "wimp." Voters decided to give the tough-talking Republican Ronald Reagan the chance to handle the nation's foreign policy.[14]

At home, the Khomeini government set out to transform Iran according to the strictures set down in the Koran. The Islamic revolution transferred sovereignty from the shah to the clergy. The secular parties, however, had a different vision of the future of the Iranian Republic. The upshot was a bloody conflict between the Shiite clergy and its opponents. The challenge to the revolution came mainly from the numerous splinter groups on the left—Marxists, Maoists, socialists—who feared the replacement of one dictatorship by another. When the bloodletting was over, the Islamic revolution had consolidated its power. Waves of revolutionary terror had brought about the execution of approximately ten thousand Iranians, and another half million, many of them of the professional classes, went into exile. The revolution in Iran swept aside all remnants of the Pahlavi dynasty and many of the Western influences it had introduced, and denied the United States a client in the Middle East.

Khomeini's revolution brought a redistribution of land and gave the nation a new constitution based on Islamic laws. In addition, it threatened to spread beyond the confines of Iran. Large Shiite communities in Lebanon, Iraq, the Gulf states, and Saudi Arabia began to look to Iran for guidance. Khomeini's revolutionary message in support of the downtrodden masses and his virulent opposition to the West added a new and dangerous element to the Middle East. The shah, until the very end, had always felt that Communism posed the greatest danger to his throne. But with the Iranian revolution, the conflict in the Middle East ceased to be primarily a contest between Western democracy and Communism. Militant Islam, in direct challenge to the Soviet Union and the West, became another force to be reckoned with.

Revolutionary movements have a tendency to run their course. The fervor that makes a revolution possible cannot be sustained indefinitely. As long as Khomeini was alive and was able to inspire his followers, the revolution appeared secure. After his death in June 1989, however, many Iranians were ready for change. After 1979, Shiite-led Iran was isolated diplomatically, economically, spiritually, and intellectually from the rest of the world. It was branded a "terrorist state," and some of its officials were sought to stand trial abroad for criminal complicity in terrorist acts. The clergy exercised great power in the application of religious laws, regulating private affairs and imposing strict press censorship. (The newspaper editor Abdullah Nouri, for example, was declared a heretic and sentenced to a five-year prison term after he had enraged the religious hierarchy by questioning their absolute power.) It was a country in which the majority of the young people—and in particular women, who were now second-class citizens—faced an uncertain future.

The presidential election of 1997 brought to power the reformist candidate Mohammed Khatami who, however, had to deal with a parliament—the *majlis*—still controlled by conservatives, the keepers of the revolutionary flame, who held 190 of the 270 seats. On the eve of the parliamentary elections in February 2000, it became obvious that Iran was about to undergo a political change. President Khatami's sister-in-law, who was also the granddaughter of the Ayatollah Khomeini, declared that her grandfather would have approved the reform program.[15] The only question was the size of the reformers' victory. With an estimated record 87 percent of Iran's 38 million eligible voters casting their ballots, the reformers won large majorities not only in the capital but in the conservative provinces. Among the big losers was the sixty-six-year-old Ali Akbar Rafsanjani, once a comrade-in-arms of Khomeini, who had twice been elected leader of the *majlis.*

Khatami's task was to steer a reformist course between his supporters and the old guard without provoking civil strife. The new *majlis,* consisting largely of reformers with little previous governing experience, faced debates over subjects such as the extent of press freedom, the legalization of satellite dishes, and other manifestations of foreign cultures that were prohibited but widely embraced by the public.

## ■ THE IRAN-IRAQ WAR

With Iran in the throes of a revolution, the government of Saddam Hussein of Iraq availed itself in September 1980 of the opportunity to invade Iran. Hussein had three objectives. He sought (1) to destroy Khomeini's revolution, which he feared might spread to his subjects, most of whom, although Arabs, were Shiites; (2) to secure disputed territory at the confluence of the Tigris and Euphrates Rivers, the Shatt el-Arab; and (3) to emerge as the paramount leader in the Arab world.

Hussein's plan called for securing the Shatt el-Arab, capturing Iran's oil ports on the other side of the river, and crippling Iranian forces in a drive eastward into Iran. He calculated that Iran was unprepared for war because of extensive losses to the officer corps and to its pilots due to purges and desertions during the revolution. Iran, however, still had many loyal middle-grade officers and pilots, and it rallied its people quickly to a conflict that it saw as the resumption of the ancient wars between Persians and Arabs.

Because Iraqi forces moved too cautiously, Iran gained time to rapidly build up its Revolutionary Guard (its regular forces) from seven thousand to two hundred thousand men and to create a new militia of more than three hundred and fifty thousand men to fight a "holy war." Iran was thus able to offset Iraq's initial advantage of a better-trained and better-equipped army. With the two sides evenly matched, neither side was able to score a decisive victory. The war became a stalemate after Iran's counteroffensive in 1982 regained lost territory and captured almost sixty thousand Iraqi troops on the battlefield.

The United States and the Soviet Union, as well as the European powers, declared their neutrality in the conflict. But as the war dragged on, over forty nations supplied weapons to one side or the other, and several nations, including the United States, sold weapons to both sides. Israel and the United States both sold weapons covertly to Iran to keep the war going. Israel's defense minister, Yitzhak Rabin, stated frankly, "We don't want a resolution of this war."[16] Iran was supported also by Libya and Syria. Iraq received financial support from Saudi Arabia and the other oil-exporting Arab states on the Gulf, all of which feared Iran's ideological revolution.

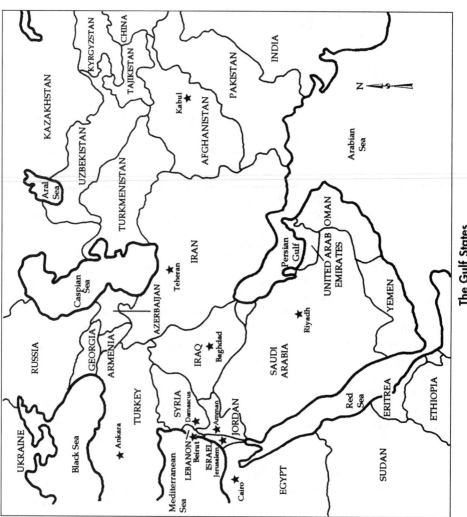

**The Gulf States**

Both sides understood the importance of oil in financing the war, and each targeted the other's oil-producing and shipping facilities in the Gulf. The United States, however, was determined to keep the Gulf open as the passageway through which much of the Western world's and Japan's oil flowed. It accepted, in December 1986, a request of the Kuwaiti government to protect its oil tanker fleet. Kuwaiti tankers were then "reflagged"; that is, they were placed under the U.S. flag and escorted by U.S. naval vessels.

The war also saw the first extensive use of chemical weapons—by both sides—since World War I. In March 1988, Iraq launched a chemical weapons attack on its own city of Halabja, which was populated by Kurds, a non-Arab Islamic people hostile to Hussein's regime. The lethal chemicals killed as many as five thousand of the city's residents. Iraq's use of chemical weapons brought strong worldwide rebuke, for it underscored the new potential danger the world faced, "the poor man's atomic bomb," as some in the Third World called it.

The long war of attrition left its mark on both sides. In the summer of 1987, Hussein accepted a UN Security Council resolution calling for an armistice. Khomeini held out for another year, demanding that Hussein must first step down and Iraq pay $150 billion in reparations. But after suffering a series of military setbacks and a decline in oil profits, Khomeini reversed himself, announcing in July 1988 that he must take "the bitter drink of poison" and accept the UN peace formula.[17]

There was no winner of the absurd eight-and-half-year-long war. Each side suffered almost a million casualties and enormous economic losses. Iraq emerged from the war with the stronger military forces. But Iran was not defeated, and its Islamic revolution remained very much intact.

## ■ TERRORISM IN LEBANON AND LIBYA

Inspired by Islamic fundamentalism and frustrated by setbacks at the hands of Israel, Arab and pro-Iranian extremists resorted to desperate, sometimes suicidal, acts of violence against Israeli troops in Lebanon. They considered terrorism as a moral act, whatever the cost to themselves, their enemy, or for that matter, innocent parties. In some instances, they acted to redress specific grievances or to gain specific ends, such as the return of prisoners taken by Israel. Israeli defense forces responded in kind with bombing raids and kidnappings.

The United States, by its military intervention on behalf of the Phalangist government of Lebanon in 1983 and its naval bombardment of Muslim strongholds in the mountains, made itself the target of terrorism. In retaliation, terrorists took Westerners in Lebanon as hostages. In March 1984, William Buckley, a CIA agent, was kidnapped in Beirut by the Islamic Jihad, a pro-Iranian Shiite group, and was later killed by them. In the following two years, at least twenty others—college teachers, journalists, businessmen, and priests from the United States, Britain, France, and several other countries—were taken hostage by the Islamic Jihad and other revolutionary groups in Lebanon. Lacking knowledge of the specific identity of the kidnappers or the location of the hostages, Western governments were unable to rescue them. In January 1986, Terry Waite, an envoy of the Church of England, went to Beirut in an effort to negotiate the release of foreign hostages, only to be kidnapped himself by the Islamic Jihad. Although most of the hostages were eventually released, at least ten were killed.[18]

Exasperated by the continuing wave of terrorism and determined to stop it, the Reagan administration vowed to retaliate. It found a likely target for retaliation in Muammar Qaddafi, dictator of Libya. Qaddafi, a strident Arab extremist, had already raised President Reagan's ire for his support of the Palestine Liberation Organization and for his brash threats against the United States for trespassing in what he proclaimed to be Libya's territorial waters, the Gulf of Sidra. Moreover, Qaddafi had maintained terrorist training camps in Libya and had provided financial support for Lebanese extremist groups suspected of terrorism.[19] In April 1986, a terrorist bomb ripped through a discotheque in West Berlin, killing two people, among them a U.S. soldier, and leaving 204 injured. Reagan blamed Qaddafi and ordered a punitive air attack on the Libyan cities of Tripoli and Benghazi. One bomb landed yards away from Qaddafi's residence, leaving him unharmed but, Qaddafi claimed, killing his adopted infant daughter. The U.S. attack, which was not supported by its European allies, was little more than an act of frustration and vengeance and was of questionable value as a deterrent to terrorism, which, in any case, continued unabated.

Two years later, in December 1988, one of the most savage of terrorist attacks occurred when a U.S. jetliner, Pan Am flight 103, exploded in flight over Lockerbie, Scotland, killing all 258 people aboard and dozens on the ground. After three years of masterful detective work, investigators were able to identify two suspects, agents in the Libyan secret service. In the interim, Qaddafi sought improved relations with the West by renouncing and apparently refraining from terrorism. He refused, however, to hand over the suspects to be tried, no doubt fearing that in a trial the two defendants might point the finger at him. After Qaddafi ignored an April 1992 UN Security Council resolution demanding the extradition of his agents, the United Nations imposed economic sanctions and an international ban on air traffic and arms sales to Libya.[20]

# ■ THE GULF WAR

## □ A War of Nerves

On August 2, 1990, Saddam Hussein launched a full-scale invasion of neighboring Kuwait and quickly conquered this small, virtually defenseless, oil-rich nation. The ruler of Kuwait, the Emir Sheikh Jabir al-Sabah, his cabinet, and his family fled to Saudi Arabia. International reaction was swift. Four days later, the UN Security Council voted unanimously to impose a worldwide trade embargo and three weeks later approved the use of armed force to execute it. U.S. President George H. W. Bush responded to a request from Saudi Arabia for protection by ordering Operation Desert Shield, a massive airlift of U.S. ground troops, aircraft, and naval vessels, to guard that country and its oil fields from further Iraqi aggression. Meanwhile, Arab League nations held an emergency meeting at which twelve of its twenty-one members, including Egypt and Syria, voted to send troops to protect Saudi Arabia.

In speeches full of bravado, Hussein promised a "holy war" against whatever "aggressive invaders" dared attack his forces in Kuwait. In the weeks prior to the invasion, he had accused Kuwait of cheating on its OPEC-approved quota of oil production; of dumping large quantities of oil on the market to keep prices low, thus depriving Iraq of badly needed revenue; of stealing oil from the Ramaila oil field, which straddled the Iraqi-Kuwaiti border; and of refusing to cancel the billion-dollar loans it had granted Iraq during its long war against Iran. Hussein ordered his massed troops into action three days after Kuwait rejected his demands for some $14 billion compensation for lost oil revenue and for the cession of two Kuwaiti islands to Iraq. Hussein then revived old Iraqi claims to the entire territory of Kuwait and proclaimed it Iraq's nineteenth province. He ordered the foreign embassies in Kuwait closed and took many of their diplomatic personnel hostage, removing them to military sites in Iraq.

Hussein found little international support. His "naked aggression," as Bush called it, was a quest for oil, the consequence of Iraq's fiscal bankruptcy brought on by the long and inconclusive war with Iran. Critics also focused attacks on Hussein personally, on his unsavory past, his political beginnings as an assassin, his summary execution of political opponents, and his use of poison gas in his earlier war against Iran and his own Kurdish population. They charged him with violations of international law for annexing Kuwait, committing acts of brutality against its people, and taking diplomats hostage.

President Bush equated Hussein with Adolf Hitler and made his removal from power a political objective. He took the lead in building an international military coalition and ambitiously spoke of creating a "new world order." He projected a vision of a new era in which the United Nations—led by the United States—maintained international peace and order. Bush also came to see the Gulf crisis as a means of restoring the honor of the U.S. military and of purging the United States of its "Vietnam syndrome."

Bush's outrage against Hussein masked concerns about the failure of his policies toward Iraq prior to the attack on Kuwait. In September 1990, Baghdad released a transcript of U.S. ambassador April Glaspie's final talk with Hussein, on July 25, one week before he attacked Kuwait. In the transcript, which the U.S. State Department confirmed as 80 percent accurate, she was quoted as saying: "I know you need funds. We understand that and . . . you should have the opportunity to rebuild your country. But we have no opinion on the Arab-Arab conflicts, like your border disagreement with Kuwait."[21] The ambassador not only had failed to read Hussein's aggressive intentions, but also had failed to object clearly to his explicit threats against Kuwait.

Revelations after the Gulf War also indicated that the Bush administration had been far less than candid about its pre-August 1990 relations with Hussein. It had consistently pursued a policy of providing substantial economic, military, and intelligence support to Hussein, a policy begun by the Reagan administration early in the 1980s when Iraq was at war with Iran. In 1983, Reagan had sent a special envoy, Donald Rumsfeld, for the purpose of reestablishing diplomatic relations—which had been broken off in 1967—and offering economic and military assistance.[22] Washington here ignored Hussein's record of human rights violations, took Iraq off the State Department's list of terrorist nations, offered Hussein intelligence secrets, and suppressed warnings regarding Iraq's atomic bomb project.

Bush rejected economic sanctions to get Hussein out of Kuwait. At his urging, the UN Security Council, on November 29, 1990, passed by a twelve-to-two vote Resolution 678 authorizing the use of military force if Iraq did not leave Kuwait by January 15, 1991. It now became a forty-eight-day countdown during which allied forces readied for a war already

Saddam Hussein, former president of Iraq. *(Iraqi Office, Embassy of Algeria)*

sanctioned by the United Nations. By mid-January 1991, a thirty-one-member coalition massed in the Gulf region, led by more than 503,000 U.S., 35,000 Egyptian, 25,000 British, 22,000 Saudi, 19,000 Syrian, and 5,500 French fighting forces; in all nearly three-quarters of a million troops. Hussein responded that if war occurred, it would be a horrible "mother of all wars" with "columns of dead bodies that may have a beginning but which would have no end."[23]

## ☐   A Most Unusual War

The Gulf War, code-named Desert Storm, was fought almost exclusively from the air. Iraqi pilots chose not to engage attacking allied aircraft in battle and instead flew their planes on a one-way trip to Iran, apparently for safekeeping. As a result, the allies were able to strike at Iraqi targets at will. In the first fourteen hours they flew more than two thousand unimpeded sorties, and the round-the-clock bombing of Baghdad and other parts of Iraq continued day after day. Television coverage of the war provided viewers with an impressive display of the new, seemingly pinpoint-accurate high-tech weaponry deployed against defenseless Iraqi targets.

Iraq answered the air attacks with Scud missile attacks against Israel. On the first day of the war, it fired eight missiles, two hitting Tel Aviv, and three exploding near Haifa. Although no one was killed by the Scud attacks, they caused great fear and anger in Israel. Especially frightful was the prospect that the next Scuds might be armed with chemical weapons. Hussein hoped that this diversionary attack would draw a military response from Israel, which might cause Arab nations to withdraw from the coalition. Washington was able to restrain Israel with promises of destroying Iraqi Scud missile sites and providing Israel protection with U.S. Patriot antimissile missiles.

The air war produced only a small number of allied casualties, but the anticipated, potentially bloody ground war against Hussein's armies had yet to be fought. When it finally came, the ground war lasted only one hundred hours because the coalition forces, carrying out a well-laid battle plan under the command of U.S. Army General Norman Schwarzkopf, met far less resistance than expected in liberating Kuwait and entering Iraq. Iraq's vaunted Republican Guard forces retreated from the battle, leaving the weaker, poorly trained, poorly fed, and exhausted regular troops to absorb the brunt of the invasion.

In compliance with UN Resolution 660, which called for a cease-fire and Iraqi withdrawal to the pre-invasion lines, Hussein withdrew from Kuwait. Nevertheless, the retreating, demoralized army was massacred on the "highway of death," a stretch of road running sixty miles from Kuwait to Basra. U.S. airplanes trapped the long retreating convoy by disabling the vehicles at the front. One U.S. pilot likened it to "shooting fish in a barrel." Tens of thousands of Iraqis perished.[24]

At the United Nations on March 3, Iraqi foreign minister Tariq Aziz stated that Hussein accepted the UN terms for a cease-fire, including the requirement that it make reparation payments for damage to Kuwait, but not before opening oil pipeline valves in Kuwait to create in the Gulf the largest oil spill in history and torching some seven hundred Kuwaiti oil wells, creating an environmental catastrophe.

Despite the decisiveness of the allied military victory, the war's outcome was ambiguous. Before and during the war, Bush spoke not only of liberating Kuwait but also of removing Hussein from power, of trying him as a war criminal, and of completely destroying Iraq's military forces, including its weapons of mass destruction. Only the first of these objectives was achieved. Removing Hussein would have meant a march into Baghdad. As Bush later explained in his memoirs:

> Trying to eliminate Saddam . . . would have incurred incalculable human and political costs. . . . We would have been forced to occupy Baghdad and, in effect, rule Iraq. . . . There was no viable "exit strategy" we could see. . . . Had we gone the invasion route, the United States could conceivably still be an occupying power in a bitterly hostile land.[25]

Another unusual feature of the war was that the militarily powerful United States did not have to carry the entire cost of the war. For the first time, a superpower sought contributions from other nations to pay for a military operation it had already undertaken. Several Gulf nations and wealthy nonparticipants (Germany and Japan) ended up paying nearly the entire bill. The UN victory was obtained at low price in allied lives. The coalition lost fewer than 300 on the battlefield, the U.S. alone losing 148 troops, two-thirds of them from "friendly fire."

## □ The Aftermath

The single undisputable accomplishment of the Gulf War was the liberation of Kuwait, but this was no victory for democracy. Two weeks after the war, the ruling emir, his family and government, and the wealthy Kuwaiti elite returned from their seven-month exile to reclaim their devastated homeland, now darkened by the smoke from the oil wells on fire. But there would be no significant postwar political change in Kuwait. When the emir formed a new cabinet in April 1991, it included no members of political opposition groups; it was, as before, composed almost entirely of members of the ruling Sabah family. His government was mainly concerned about rehabilitation and security. Initial estimates for reconstruction costs ranged as high as $110 billion, with the most serious problem being the sabotaged oil wells, which took nine months to cap.

Rebellion against Hussein's government broke out spontaneously during the war in southern Iraq, where the Shiites, who made up 55 percent of the nation's population, briefly took control of the bombed-out city of Basra, and in northern Iraq, where the Kurds fought to take control of the region where they were the majority. During the war, Bush had openly encouraged rebellion by the Shiites and Kurds, only to betray them later when he stated that he would not support or protect them. Hussein quickly moved his forces against them. He flew his helicopters unimpeded, as no foreign forces came to the rescue of the Kurds and Shiites. Hussein's troops crushed the insurrection in the south by the end of March, killing perhaps as many as thirty thousand Shiites and driving more than 1 million into Iran.

## ☐ The Kurds

The Kurds in the north suffered a similar fate. Kurdish leaders claimed that the "whole of Kurdistan [in Iraq] had been liberated," but they spoke too soon. In the following week, Iraqi forces using helicopter gunships drove Kurdish forces out of their strongholds. Ultimately, Hussein's troops killed about fifty thousand Kurds and turned more than 1 million of them into refugees. Bush followed the lead of British prime minister John Major in sending food and supplies and implementing a plan to create a "safe haven" for the refugees in northern Iraq, to be policed by U.S., British, French, and Dutch troops. In June, the United Nations assumed responsibility for humanitarian aid and protection of the Kurds.

The defeat of the Kurds was but another chapter in the long and tragic history of an ancient people whose Indo-European language and distinct culture set them apart from their neighbors. In 1990, there were approximately 10 million Kurds in eastern Turkey, 5 million in western Iran, 4 million in northern Iraq (about 20 percent of the population), and 1 million in northeastern Syria. These nations were always able to agree on one thing: that there must be no independent Kurdistan. Since 1961, Kurds fought the authorities in Baghdad and Tehran whenever the opportunity availed itself, only to be defeated repeatedly by one or the other and sometimes both. In the 1970s, the United States supported the Kurds, only to drop them after the shah and Hussein worked out an agreement to bring the Kurds to heel. In 1971, when the Kurds asked for continued U.S. aid, Secretary of State Henry Kissinger ignored the request, explaining that "covert action should not be confused with missionary work."[26] Turkey wanted no part of a successful rebellion of Kurds in Iraq. In the past, Turkish Kurds had been prevented from speaking their language in public and their very existence was denied by their government. Turkish politicians and newspaper publishers were sentenced to long prison terms for even mentioning the Kurds. Predictably, Bush obliged Turkey, a NATO ally and participant in the Gulf War, by delivering the Kurds into the arms of Hussein.

The Sunni Arabs of Iraq, who live mainly in the central region, fared only somewhat better than the Shiites and Kurds, for they, too, suffered from deprivation and disease. One study calculated that as many as seventy thousand Iraqis died during the war as a result of allied bombing of electric power plants and transport facilities, which affected water purification, sewage treatment plants, and the distribution of food and medicine.[27]

\* \* \*

The UN-brokered cease-fire was accompanied by severe economic sanctions. Under its terms, Iraq agreed to destroy its chemical, biological, and nuclear weapons and production facilities.

For the next seven years UN weapons inspectors endeavored to gain Iraq's compliance with the 1991 cease-fire weapons inspections regimen. Some weapons-producing facilities were opened to them and some of these were dismantled, but Hussein continued to thwart full inspection. The issue of inspections was brought to a head in December 1998, when Hussein ordered all U.S. members of the inspection teams out of Iraq. As a result, still another test-of-wills crisis was played out, with President Clinton launching a series of bombing attacks in an unsuccessful attempt to force the defiant Hussein into compliance. In October 1998, a frustrated U.S. Congress went so far as to pass the "Iraq Liberation Act," calling for the overthrow of Hussein by "the Iraqi opposition." President Clinton, however, upon signing it, made no mention of a U.S. invasion.[28]

## ■ RECOMMENDED READINGS

### ☐ Islam

Dawood, N. J., trans. *The Meaning of the Glorious Koran.* New York: Penguin, 1956.
    A translation of the Koran for Western readers, as well as a valuable introduction to the early history of Islam, by Mohammed Marmaduke Pickthall, an English convert to the faith.
Guillaume, Alfred. *Islam.* 2d rev. ed. New York: Penguin, 1956.
    The classic analysis of the theological basis of Islam by one of the West's recognized scholars in the field.
Jansen, G. H. *Militant Islam.* New York: Harper and Row, 1979.
    Explains to Western readers the philosophic foundations of Islam and the reasons for its militant form in Iran.
Kedourie, Elie. *Islam in the Modern World.* New York: Holt, Rinehart and Winston, 1980.
    Focuses on the link between Islam and Arab politics.

### ☐ Iran and Its Revolution

Bakhash, Shaul. *The Reign of the Ayatollahs: Iran and the Islamic Revolution.* New York: Basic Books, 1984.

A scholarly account of Khomeini's revolution.

Kapuscinski, Ryszard. *Shah of Shahs.* San Diego: Harcourt, Brace, Jovanovich, 1985.
By a veteran Polish journalist, an eyewitness to the Iranian upheaval.

Rubin, Barry. *Paved with Good Intentions: The American Experience and Iran.* New York: Oxford University Press, 1980.
An analysis of what went wrong with the U.S. scenario for Iran.

Said, Edward W. *Covering Islam: How the Media and the Experts Determine How We See the Rest of the World.* New York: Pantheon Books, 1981.
A critical analysis, by a U.S. citizen of Palestinian descent, of how the U.S. press handled the Iranian hostage crisis.

Salinger, Pierre. *America Held Hostage: The Secret Negotiations.* Garden City, N.Y.: Doubleday, 1981.
By a U.S. journalist who was directly involved in settling the crisis.

Sick, Gary. *All Fall Down.* New York: Random House, 1985.
A member of President Carter's National Security Council presents a firsthand account of the hostage deliberations.

☐ **Iraq and the Gulf War**

Arnett, Peter. *Live from the Battlefield: From Vietnam to Baghdad: 35 Years in the World's War Zones.* New York: Touchstone, 1994.
By a New Zealand correspondent who was a voice of CNN in Baghdad during the war.

Bush, George, and Brent Scowcroft. *A World Transformed.* New York: Knopf, 1998.
The memoirs of the U.S. president and his national security adviser.

Gordon, Michael R., and Bernard E. Trainor. *The General's War: The Inside Story of the Conflict in the Gulf.* Boston: Little, Brown, and Co., 1994.

Schwarzkopf, H. Norman. *It Doesn't Take a Hero.* New York: Bantam, 1992.
The memoirs of the commander of U.S. forces in the Gulf War.

■ **NOTES**

1. Western scholars have gone so far as to argue that Mohammed did not believe he was "founding a new religion" as much as bringing to "fullness . . . divine revelation . . . granted to earlier prophets." Richard Fletcher, *The Cross and the Crescent: Christianity and Islam from Muhammed to the Reformation* (New York: Viking, 2004); cited in William Dalrymple, "The Truth About Muslims," *New York Review of Books,* November 4, 2004, p. 32.

2. Dalrymple, "The Truth About Muslims," p. 32.

3. N. J. Dawood, trans., *The Koran,* 4th rev. ed. (New York: Penguin, 1974), p. 220, Surah 23:14–16; p. 375, Surah 4:87.

4. Alfred Guillaume, *Islam,* 2d rev. ed. (New York: Penguin, 1956), p. 38.

5. Dawood, *The Koran,* pp. 362–364, Surah 2:261–265, 270–277.

6. Khomeini in June 1963, when visited in prison by the chief of SAVAK, cited in Bernard Lewis, "How Khomeini Made It," *New York Review of Books,* January 17, 1985, p. 10.

7. His exile lasted for fourteen years. In one of his speeches Khomeini denounced a law that his country's parliament had passed in October 1964, by which U.S. citizens in Iran had been granted extraterritoriality, the right to be tried according to U.S.,

instead of Iranian law. Khomeini called the law "a document for the enslavement of Iran" that "acknowledged that Iran is a colony; it has given America a document attesting that the nation of Muslims is barbarous." Lewis, "How Khomeini Made It," p. 10.

8. The basis of the Shiite creed, in Bernard Lewis, "The Shi'a," *New York Review of Books,* August 15, 1985, p. 8; Shiites point to Allah's will "to favour those who were oppressed and to make them leaders of mankind, to bestow on them a noble heritage and to give them power in the land." Dawood, *The Koran,* p. 75, Surah 28:5.

9. Robert Graham, *Iran: The Illusion of Power* (New York: St. Martin's Press, 1979), p. 33.

10. Ibid., p. 61. In March 1976, a dutiful parliament created the "monarchy calendar" (dating from the coronation of Cyrus the Great, 2,535 years prior), replacing the Islamic calendar based on the date of the *hegira* (flight) of Mohammed from Mecca to Medina in A.D. 622.

11. "Aryans" here is in reference to the Farsi- (Persian-) speaking peoples of Iran, originally from northern India. It was an attempt to identify the shah with the nation's earliest history.

12. Henry Kissinger, *The White House Years* (Boston: Little, Brown, and Co., 1979), p. 1264.

13. After the shah's death in 1980, his son became the claimant to the throne, and many Iranian exiles pinned their hopes on him.

14. It came as a surprise to the U.S. public, therefore, when in November 1986, it was revealed that Reagan, who for six years had bitterly denounced any and all terrorists and had vowed never to deal with any of them, was found to have paid ransom to terrorists in Lebanon who were holding U.S. hostages and then going so far as to ship weapons to the government of the Ayatollah Khomeini, at that time engaged in a long and bloody war with Iraq.

15. Susan Sachs, "Iran Election Presents Referendum on Reform," *New York Times,* February 18, 2000.

16. Quoted in Mansour Farhang, "Iran-Iraq Conflict: An Unending War Between Two Despots," *The Nation,* September 20, 1986.

17. Graham E. Fuller, "War and Revolution in Iran," *Current History* (February 1989), p. 81.

18. Seventy hostages were finally released between August 1991 and June 1992; some had been in captivity over ten years.

19. In October 1989, Qaddafi admitted to having bankrolled terrorist groups but added: "When we discovered that these groups were causing more harm than benefit to the Arab cause, we halted our aid to them completely and withdrew our support." "Kadafi Admits Backing Terrorists, Says He Erred," *Baltimore Sun,* October 26, 1989.

20. Britain and the United States took the lead in pressing for extradition. They were joined by France, which demanded Libyan cooperation in an investigation of four Libyan suspects in the explosion of a French airliner over Niger in 1989, killing 404.

21. Cited in Jim Hoagland, "Transcript Shows Muted U.S. Response to Threat by Saddam in Late July," *Washington Post,* September 13, 1990, p. A33. In March 1991, before the Senate Foreign Relations Committee, Glaspie refuted the Iraqi version of her conversation with Hussein; the State Department, however, refused to make public its transcript of the meeting or its correspondence with Glaspie.

22. In April 1984, the Reagan administration gave the Bell Helicopter Corporation the green light to sell helicopters to the Iraqi ministry of defense, provided

that they "can not be in any way configured for military use." The National Security Archive, http://www2.gwu.edu/~nsarchive.

23. Cited in Robert Ruby, "Security Council OKs Military Force," *Baltimore Sun,* August 26, 1990, p. 1A.

24. Joyce Chediac, "The Massacre of Withdrawing Soldiers on 'The Highway of Death.'" From her report at the New York Commission hearing, May 11, 1991, http:// www.deoxy.org/wc/wc-death.

25. George Bush and Brent Scowcroft, *A World Transformed* (New York: Knopf, 1998.)

26. Quoted in Raymond Bonner, "Always Remember," *New Yorker,* September 28, 1992, p. 48. At the end of World War I, U.S. president Woodrow Wilson proclaimed in his Fourteen Points that the ethnic minorities of Ottoman Turkey should have "absolutely unmolested opportunity of autonomous development." The Treaty of Sèvres (1920), intended to deal with the consequences of the breakup of the Ottoman Empire, called for an independent Kurdish state, but the Turkish government of Kemal Ataturk refused to accept it.

27. "70,000 Postwar Civilian Deaths in Iraq Laid to Bomb Damage," *Baltimore Sun,* January 9, 1992, p. 2A.

28. Presidential press release, October 31, 1998.

# 21

## September 11 and Its Consequences

On September 11, 2001, nineteen young Arabs, fifteen of them from Saudi Arabia, under the leadership of the Egyptian Mohammed Atta, hijacked four U.S. domestic airliners. Two of them slammed into the twin towers of the World Trade Center in New York City, bringing the skyscrapers down in minutes. Another airliner plowed into the Pentagon across the Potomac River from the White House. A passenger revolt caused the crash of the fourth airplane in a field near Shanksville, Pennsylvania. In all, almost three thousand individuals perished, nearly all of them civilians.

Within hours, the U.S. government identified the hijackers as members of al Qaeda, a shadowy organization under Osama bin Laden, a citizen of Saudi Arabia, living in exile in Afghanistan under Taliban protection. Bin Laden had waged war against the United States for nearly a decade. He had been responsible for the February 1993 attempt to topple one of the towers, a bomb attack in which six U.S. citizens died, and the simultaneous suicide bombings of U.S. embassies in Nairobi, Kenya, and Dar-es-Salaam, Tanzania, in August 1998 that killed 224 and injured over 5,400. The victims were mostly East Africans, many of them Muslims, as well as twelve U.S. citizens.

After the attacks on the embassies, U.S. president Bill Clinton and his staff quickly identified al Qaeda as the perpetrators and then lashed out with cruise missiles against targets in Afghanistan in the hope of killing bin Laden. The U.S. government at the time, however, in the words of the congressional *9/11 Report,* "knew little about the organization,"[1] which was one of the reasons why the strikes failed. Moreover, Clinton was at that time embroiled in the Monica Lewinsky scandal, which severely restricted his freedom of action; besides, there was little outcry on the part of the public to take more drastic action. Then came a suicide attack against the USS *Cole* in October 2000 in the harbor of Aden, Yemen, which claimed the lives of seventeen U.S. sailors, and less than a year later, the September 11 attacks.

In his first speech after the September 11 attacks, U.S. president George W. Bush vowed to find the perpetrators and bring them to justice, to take them "dead or alive." He declared that it was an act of war and that the United States was now engaged in a global "war on terrorism." He called on not only the people of the United States, but on all nations, to join the fight to defeat terrorism, adding that "you are either with us or against us."

It was difficult to understand what had driven nineteen young, educated Arabs to commit mass murder and at the same time sacrifice their lives. Attempts to comprehend their motives, however, did not last long. Four weeks after September 11, Bush launched a counterattack in Afghanistan and henceforward the focus shifted to that war, the alleged threat emanating from Iraq, and then the war in Iraq itself.

As for the reasons for the terrorist attacks on the United States, Bush could offer nothing better than that "they hate us for our freedoms." As such, Bush came down squarely on the side of those who saw the Islamic militants as individuals driven by resentment, hate, irrationality, and a flawed religion. When Osama bin Laden appeared on a videotape at the end of October 2004, he disputed "Bush's claims that we hate freedom." "We fight you because we are free," he went on to say, "and we want freedom for our nation."[2]

Israeli intelligence tried for years to come up with a typical profile of suicide terrorists, only to conclude that they could not establish one. Not surprisingly, then, every statement about suicide terrorists will be speculative. Moreover, there is a taboo against trying to understand their motives because it dignifies the suicide.[3] Some of the terrorists have personal problems, while others are deeply affected by the deaths of relatives or friends at the hands of the enemy. The majority—55 percent—of Palestinian suicide bombers, for example, saw their fathers humiliated or beaten by Israelis. They often mention a specific event for which they sought revenge. Once life becomes unbearable, suicide becomes an option. Psychologists have long known that those who experienced inhumanity were likely to respond with inhumanity.

When a conflict becomes cloaked in religious arguments—absolute and dogmatic—killing and dying become easier. The struggle for Palestine, for example, initially a secular conflict between socialist Zionists and the secular Palestine Liberation Organization (also in part socialist), became a holy war for both sides that made it easier for true believers to kill and die for.

Terrorists may be driven not only by alienation and humiliation but also for the struggle for land that frequently leads directly to ethnic cleansing accompanied by murder, and the redemption of history, a quest for a return to a Golden Age that becomes ever more glorious when compared with the current situation.[4]

Militant Islam is in conflict with the legacy of Western imperialism, with the "filth of disbelief" and "moral bankruptcy" it had brought to the

September 11, 2001: Smoke
and debris erupt from the South
Tower of the World Trade Center
as it collapses after terrorists
crashed two passenger airliners
into the twin towers.
*(AP Wide World Photos)*

House of Islam. As a graduate student in urban planning in northern Germany, Mohammed Atta dedicated his master's thesis to Allah and to the preservation of the ancient, vast market, the *souk,* in Aleppo—perhaps the world's oldest continuously inhabited city—a living symbol of the Arab world. Yet despite the Syrian government's best efforts to preserve the *souk,* it was dying, under siege by Western influences such as fast-food restaurants and concrete tourist hotels. In Cairo and Aleppo, Atta fell under the influence of the Muslim Brotherhood. Living among the prostitutes and heroin dealers in the red-light district of Hamburg, an alienated Atta came to accept the noble obligation of martyrdom.[5]

Bush was in part correct when he asserted that Islamic terrorists hated what U.S. society represented. Al Qaeda's war against the West, however, was not against the Bill of Rights but what the West "represented" within the House of Islam. Islamic militants singled out as "anti-Islam" the Western support of apostate and corrupt, tyrannical governments in the Arab world. Moreover, they decided the support for Israel, U.S. troops on the Arabian peninsula, the support for Russia, India, and China, among others, in their suppression of Muslims (in Chechnya, Kashmir, Central Asia, etc.), and the pressure on Arab suppliers of oil (notably Saudi Arabia) to keep prices low.[6]

Terrorism is an example of "asymmetric" warfare. It is a common phenomenon, the choice of last resort by the weak against the powerful—from

Vietnam, Algeria, Chechnya, Iraq, Sri Lanka, on and on. In the 1965 motion picture *The Battle of Algiers,* a terrorist in the dock is asked: "Isn't it cowardly to use your women's baskets to carry bombs that have killed so many innocent people?" To which he replies: "And you? Is it less cowardly to drop napalm on defenseless villages, killing thousands more? With planes, it would have been easier for us. Let us have your bombers and you can have our women's baskets."[7]

Islam does not permit suicide. A Muslim's life belongs to Allah and only he has the right to take it. But it does encourage martyrdom. A Hamas official explained the difference between suicide and martyrdom: "If a martyr wants to kill himself because he is sick of being alive, that's suicide. But if he wants to sacrifice his soul in order to defeat the enemy and for God's sake—well, then he's a martyr."[8]

The hijackers came from established, well-to-do families who had grown up in the shadow of the culture, wealth, power, and constant overbearing presence of the West. Their resentment of the West eventually turned into the conviction that the West sought to destroy Islam. The militants insisted that little had changed since the days when the Crusaders first arrived at the end of the eleventh century. After the 1991 Gulf War, bin Laden denounced the U.S. occupation of "the most sacred lands of Islam: the Arab Peninsula . . . stealing its resources, dictating to its leaders, humiliating its people. . . . It is using its rule in the Peninsula as a weapon to fight the neighboring peoples of Islam."[9] Ayman al-Zawahiri, bin Laden's chief lieutenant, stated that history must not repeat itself: "We will not accept the tragedy of Al Andalus [i.e., the 1492 traumatic expulsion of Arabs after seven hundred years from Andalusia, today's Spain] will be repeated in Palestine."[10]

Osama bin Laden's aim was to rearrange the unequal relationship between the West and the Islamic world. Five weeks after the deadly bombings of Madrid railway stations in March 2004 that claimed the lives of 191 people (and injured another 1,800), bin Laden offered the Europeans reconciliation that "will start with the departure of the last soldier from our country."[11] In late October 2004, he made the same offer to the United States. Predictably, his offers were rejected.

After World War II, as the Arab states gained their independence from France and Britain, Arabs looked to a new beginning, a renaissance that would restore the Arab world to its previous grandeur. In most Arab nations, socialist movements came to power with the promise of such a revival. In fact, the Ba'ath Party, which seized power in Syria and Iraq, took its name from the Arabic for "rebirth." But the rebirth was not to be. Arab governments—whether socialist or monarchist—became corrupt, propped up by either oil money, a secret police, or armies equipped by infidel nations such as the United States and the Soviet Union. This was true across the board, from Morocco in North Africa to the very heart of the Arab world—to Syria, Lebanon, Iraq, and Saudi Arabia.

The disenchantment, particularly among young Arabs, was heightened by the fact that they had limited professional opportunities at home. Some went abroad, some sought solace in religion, some joined the terrorists. The problem was especially acute in Saudi Arabia. Between 1980 and 1998, it had the highest population growth rate in the world, at the phenomenal annual rate of 4.4 percent. By 2002, its population had swollen from 6 to 22 million, 43 percent of them fourteen years of age or younger. The number of princes, seen by many in the Arab world as hypocrites who feigned piety while serving foreign interests, rose from about two thousand to seven thousand. At the same time, oil revenues declined from $227 billion in 1981 to $31 billion in 1986. Saudi Arabia's per capita income peaked at $19,000 in 1981, only to drop to $7,300 in 1997 (in constant U.S. dollars). Moreover, the universities produced far more graduates than the economy needed. It was not surprising that Saudia Arabia became a hotbed for Islamic militancy. It is after all the only modern Muslim state created by *jihad,* i.e., by Wahhabi warriors who espoused a particularly strict interpretation of Islam. It was also one of but a handful of Muslim countries that had escaped European imperialism, Afghanistan being another. The Saudi royal family's dilemma was that having come to power with the assistance of the Wahhabi clergy, it now spent lavish sums in the vain hope of tempering its anti-Western militancy.[12]

Militant Islam's quest to purify society and return it to its former glory has a long history. In the recent past, it was the Muslim Brotherhood that played the leading role in the revival of Islam. Founded in Egypt in 1928, the Brotherhood was the response to the calamity of the destruction of the caliphate, which had ruled the House of Islam since after Mohammed's death. Moreover, the Arab world had been parceled out among the powers of Europe. The Brotherhood rejected nationalism, communism, socialism, and liberalism and dreamed, instead, of the creation of an Islamic system that provided divine instruction for politics, laws, and daily behavior. The Brotherhood's founder, Hassan al-Banna, railed against the West's corruption of Islam with "their half-naked women . . . their liquors, their theaters, their dance halls." The Brotherhood's credo was "Good is our objective, the Koran is our constitution, the prophet is our leader, the struggle is our way; and death for the sake of God is the highest of our aspirations."[13] By the late 1940s, the Westernized Egyptian government and the Brotherhood were in a deadly embrace; after the Brotherhood assassinated the prime minister in 1949, the police shot Banna to death.

The mentor of present-day Arab radicals was the Egyptian Sayyid Qutb. In his magnum opus, *Milestones* (1964), Qutb popularized the view that the Arab world—its governments and people—lived in the state of *jihaliya,* a darkness that had existed before Mohammed's revelations. The state of apostasy, the rebellion against Allah, must—and will—give way to a true Muslim state after the purification of "the filthy marsh of the world."

Qutb developed his views in part as the consequence of a two-year stint among the *kuffar*, the unbelievers, at the Colorado State College of Education. A student of U.S. literature and popular culture, Qutb became repulsed by certain aspects of U.S. culture, such as dances in church recreation halls—organized by ministers no less—and by a people who attended the numerous churches in Greeley, Colorado, yet appeared uninterested in spiritual matters.[14]

The quest to return to the prophet's teachings led to a vicious war between the militants and the socialist/militarist government of Egypt. President Gamal Abdel Nasser arrested members of the Brotherhood and in August 1966 had Qutb hanged. Upon hearing his death sentence, Qutb replied: "Thank God. I performed jihad for fifteen years until I earned this martydom."[15] In October 1981, the Brotherhood, after infiltrating the Egyptian army, assassinated the "pharaoh" Anwar Sadat for his peace treaty with Israel.

Sadat's successor, Hosni Mubarak, introduced a permanent state of emergency. Tens of thousands of Islamicists and other political dissidents filled the prisons where they were subjected to systematic torture. The Brotherhood responded with assassinations that ended only after another crackdown, which was the result of the murder in 1997 of sixty-two people in Luxor—mostly foreign tourists—at the hands of the Brotherhood. By that time, however, Arab Islamic militancy—born in the mosques and coffeehouses and nurtured in the prisons of Egypt—had already begun its migration to the far corners of the earth.

In the 1980s, the attention of the Islamicists was diverted to Afghanistan. After the Soviet invasion, Ayman al-Zawahiri, a member of one of the most prominent Egyptian families, deeply affected by Qutb's world view, became one of the first Arabs to arrive in Afghanistan. There he linked up with the charismatic Osama bin Laden, the scion of one of the most prominent—and wealthy—Saudi families. Their organizations, al Qaeda and Egyptian Islamic Jihad, formally merged into one, Qaeda al-Jihad. Zawahiri was vital for bin Laden because of his organizational abilities—he had helped to form an underground cell at the age of fifteen—and experience in secret work. It was Zawahiri who plotted the attacks on U.S. targets, including that of September 11. An Egyptian lawyer for the Brotherhood explained that in the early 1980s, bin Laden already "had an Islamic frame of reference, but he didn't have anything against the Arab regimes."[16] Under Zawahiri's influence, that would change.

In Afghanistan, bin Laden spent much of his time between Saudi Arabia and Peshawar, Pakistan, raising money for the anti-Soviet cause. Bin Laden imported bulldozers for civilian and military projects, and in April 1987, he became engaged in a battle against Soviet troops, including their special forces. It was here that he earned the public reputation as a *jihadist* warrior. There is no evidence that he worked directly with the CIA, but

U.S. officials looked favorably on the recruitment of Arabs (and their money). In fact, the CIA sought ways to increase their participation in the war, despite rumors of anti-U.S. attitudes among the Arabs.

In Afghanistan, the United States won a historic victory over the Soviet Union. The CIA's victory had been orchestrated by Milt Bearden, the station chief at the U.S. embassy in Islamabad, Pakistan. At night he kept the lights on in his office to give the impression to the KGB across the way that he never slept. After the last Soviet soldier left Afghanistan in 1989, Bearden cabled Washington "WE WON," turned out the lights, and joined the celebration at the embassy.[17] But it would be a costly victory. The CIA left behind in Afghanistan a network of jihadists—stronger and wealthier than ever—who now put into their gun sights on the U.S. presence in the Islamic world.

The Arab-Israeli conflict was a contributing factor to the rise of Arab resentment against the West, particularly the United States for its role in backing Israel, even though the United States professed to be but an honest broker in the conflict, something virtually no Arab believed. Arabs always saw Palestinians as hostages to Western imperialism. At the beginning of the conflict, the United States had refrained from becoming involved, but gradually it began to side with Israel. In the Yom Kippur War of 1973, for example, the Nixon administration openly sided with Israel, and in 1983, Reagan sent the marines into Lebanon, ostensibly in the capacity of neutral peacekeepers, only to have the guns from the battleship *Missouri* shell Arab targets. In his videotape of October 2004, bin Laden stated that it had been this event, the destruction of "towers in Lebanon," that made him determined to give the United States a taste of its own medicine.

Al Qaeda began its work shortly after the Gulf War of 1991, when bin Laden began to criticize sharply the Saudi royal family for granting the United States a permanent military base in Saudi Arabia. Eventually, bin Laden crossed the line in his criticism and he was ordered to leave. He went first to Sudan, at that time a haven for terrorists. In 1996, after he had written an open letter to Saudi king Faud, once again denouncing the U.S. presence on the soil of the Prophet, he left for Afghanistan where the Taliban had just come to power.

Al Qaeda's first attempt to challenge the West came during the Serbian-Bosnian conflict, when militant Arabs began to arrive in Bosnia to fight the Orthodox Christian Serbs. They brought with them the military expertise acquired in Afghanistan, as well as money they laundered with the help of cultural and benevolence societies set up in places such as London, Milan, Chicago, Hamburg, and Saudi Arabia. The engagement in Bosnia proved to be a failure, however. Bosnians resented the Arabs for their viciousness, and the Dayton peace accord called for their eviction.

Al Qaeda then turned its attention on U.S. interests in the Middle East. Richard Clarke, the White House expert on terrorism under Clinton and

Bush, warned that al Qaeda "dreamed" of a "Christian government attacking a weaker Muslim region," allowing it "to rally jihadists from many countries to come to the aid of the religious brethren."[18] Bush, paying no attention to voices urging him to proceed with caution, subsequently obliged bin Laden with the invasion of Iraq. Upon being told that U.S. troops in Iraq would entice jihadists to engage them there, he famously responded on July 1, 2003, saying "bring 'em on." Bush did not have to wait long. Jihadists from across the Middle East began to descend on Iraq. A CIA intelligence official concluded that "if Osama bin Laden believed in Christmas, this is what he'd want under his Christmas tree." In October 2003, only seven months after the U.S. invasion of Iraq, the London-based International Institute for Strategic Studies concluded that al Qaeda, despite having suffered considerable losses in Afghanistan, was now "fully reconstituted," with an estimated strength of eighteen thousand members and with a "new and effective modus operandi" operating in as many as ninety countries.[19] In fact, al Qaeda–sponsored acts of terrorism had spread not merely into the heart of Iraq but also to countries such as Spain, Morocco, Indonesia, Tunisia, Pakistan, Kenya, Turkey, and Saudi Arabia.

## ■ ACT I: THE HUNT FOR OSAMA BIN LADEN

The attacks of September 11 called for an immediate and forceful response.[20] The recently elected president, George W. Bush, rallied a stunned and angry nation. He would go after Osama bin Laden, he announced, and get his man "dead or alive." (In fact, a CIA agent requested a box with dry ice in anticipation of bringing home the supreme war trophy, the head of bin Laden.) Bush would take the pursuit of bin Laden to the four corners of the earth. He dismissed Clinton's response to al Qaeda, the "launching a cruise missile into some guy's . . . tent," as a "joke."[21] This time the United States would do it right. Moreover, global support for the United States was nearly universal. For the first time in its existence, NATO treated September 11 as an attack on one of its members.

As U.S. forces rapidly mobilized, Bush demanded that the Taliban hand over bin Laden. When the head of the Taliban, Mohammed Omar, refused, Bush—on October 7, 2001—took the fight into Afghanistan. First came the bombs, dropped by state-of-the-art airplanes from nearby carriers and B-2 bombers from as far away as Missouri. Bush then sent a highly mobile, efficient contingent of special forces equipped with the latest computers, CIA agents, air force personnel, soldiers, and sailors supported by NATO forces. They were assisted by the Northern Alliance—primarily Tadzhiks and Uzbeks—who had held out against the Pushtun Taliban during the past five years.

It was an uneven contest—one between the richest and strongest nation with powerful allies on its side, against the poorest. By early December

Osama bin Laden, spiritual
and operational chief of al
Qaeda, was the inspirational
leader of the September 11
terror attacks. (F.B.I.)

2001, the Taliban and al Qaeda were beaten, their surviving forces stream-
ing toward the Pakistani frontier from where the Taliban had originally
come.

Bush's secretary of defense, Donald Rumsfeld, held a series of press
conferences where he basked in the adulation of a grateful nation. Yet it
was at this point that things began to go sour. No doubt, the enemy had
been mauled, but the United States, its NATO allies, and the mercenaries of
the Northern Alliance did not finish the job.[22] Mohammed Omar, the head
of the Taliban regime, and bin Laden disappeared into the rugged terrain
along the northern Afghan-Pakistani border, surviving to fight another day.
When the allies began their assault on the caves in the mountains of Tora
Bora, they did not have a sufficient number of U.S. and NATO "boots on
the ground." The United States, even with its NATO allies, had about a
quarter of the number the Soviet Union had deployed in Afghanistan a
decade earlier when it failed to secure its power over the country.

Osama bin Laden was not captured because General Tommy Franks, the
U.S. commander in Afghanistan, initially relied on Afghans to do the job.
They were either not up to the task or, worse, collaborated with the fleeing
al Qaeda fighters, something Franks—already hard at work planning the
invasion of Iraq from his command center in Tampa, Florida—grasped too
late. Still, Bush proclaimed victory. Bin Laden, he explained on March 14,
2002, had "met his match," he had been "marginalized," or "may even be

dead." He went on to say that "I truly am not that concerned about him."[23] After that, administration references to the still-at-large bin Laden became fewer and fewer.

Even before September 11, Bush had not been all that concerned about al Qaeda, although the outgoing Clinton administration—notably national security adviser Sandy Berger and terrorist expert Richard A. Clarke—had warned Bush's national security team that they would spend more time on terrorism than on anything else. Clarke stayed on as terrorist expert, but he lost his cabinet-level status and now reported to Condoleezza Rice, Bush's national security adviser. Bush appointed his vice-president, Dick Cheney, to chair a task force on terrorism that, alas, never met. His attorney general, John Ashcroft, on July 5, 2001, rejected a request from the acting head of the FBI, Thomas Pickard, for another $59 million to combat al Qaeda, and went on to tell him that he did not want to hear about al Qaeda anymore.[24]

Even after Bush received from the CIA the now-famous Presidential Daily Brief ("Bin Laden Determined to Strike in US") of August 6, 2001, warning of an al Qaeda attack using airplanes against government buildings, he continued his vacation in Texas working to clear the underbrush on his ranch. All this, despite the fact that, beginning in late March 2001, the "system was blinking red." In the summer, Clarke cancelled all vacation leave for his staff in a desperate attempt to stave off an attack. As a member of the Clinton staff, he had participated in the successful disruption of the "millennium plot" against the Los Angeles international airport by "shaking the trees"—pursuing every lead, working with various U.S. as well as foreign authorities, notably in Canada and Jordan.[25] This time, however, the White House, despite the warnings, showed little concern.

Early in the war in Afghanistan, General Franks told the Pakistani president Pervez Musharraf that "we won't stop until we get" bin Laden.[26] Yet in 2002, with Osama bin Laden still at large, inexplicably, Franks was ordered to shift his resources to another theater of war, Iraq, leaving behind a scant four thousand U.S. troops, augmented by five thousand NATO soldiers (subsequently increased by October 2004 to twenty thousand and ten thousand respectively.)[27] In his memoirs, Franks spoke of a "historic victory" in Afghanistan, this despite the unpleasant fact that the perpetrators of September 11 remained at large.

In all likelihood, the Taliban and al Qaeda escaped to Waziristan, across from Tora Bora, in the northwest frontier of Pakistan. The Waziris, ethnic Pushtuns who claim to be descendants of King Saul, have fought successfully since 600 B.C. against any and all invaders—Alexander the Great, Genghis Khan, and Great Britain included—to keep their realm "pure and clean." When the Pakistani army—at the urging of the Bush administration—entered Waziristan in March 2004, it ran into a wall of silence and came away empty-handed, despite the FBI's $50 million bounty on the head of bin Laden.

During the Soviet invasion of Afghanistan, Waziristan had fallen under the thrall of radical Islam, becoming the home of at least ninety *madrasas*—religious schools—preaching a radical strain of Islam for which the Taliban were known. Before the invasion, the Waziris had considered themselves primarily Pushtuns; afterward, they increasingly began to see themselves as Muslims and Pushtuns. In October 2003, an exclusively Islamist government took power in Waziristan, a region that by this time had become an exporter of heroin, which, by Islamic law, was *haram* (forbidden). But if heroin killed a single non-Muslim, it was defensible.[28]

## ■ ACT II: "MISSION ACCOMPLISHED"

Immediately after the September 11 attack, Bush and his cabinet began to focus on Iraq. When told by Richard A. Clarke, his terrorist expert, that there was no link between Osama bin Laden and Saddam Hussein, Bush sought a second opinion and when that failed to materialize, he manufactured one. Bush was ably aided and abetted by his foreign policy and military advisers, a group collectively known as the neoconservatives, or "neocons" for short. They called themselves the Vulcans, from the Roman god of fire. Its leading members were Vice-President Dick Cheney, Secretary of Defense Donald Rumsfeld, Deputy Secretary of Defense Paul Wolfowitz, and National Security Adviser Condaleezza Rice. Many of them had gotten their start in the 1970s as members of the Committee on the Present Danger and the CIA's B Team under Bush Sr., both of which persistently had exaggerated the Soviet threat.

The neocons had a Cold War frame of reference, and for them defeat in Vietnam was a central event. Nevertheless, they were optimistic about U.S. power and believed a powerful military was essential to guarding and expanding U.S. interests. They dismissed arguments about overextension of U.S. forces and were skeptical about the need to consult with either allies or the United Nations. They rejected the realpolitik of Richard Nixon and Henry Kissinger, who had pursued détente and had negotiated with both the Soviet Union and Communist China. The neocons embraced a highly ideological and idealistic view of U.S. power being capable of bringing progress and morality to a world wracked by evil forces. To that end, they believed in preemptive war. They also believed in the moral superiority of the United States, still the "city on the hill," the shining—Christian—beacon for other nations. Once U.S. forces went into Iraq, the neocons were certain, they would be received with open arms.

In the early 1990s, the neocons, led by Dick Cheney, secretary of defense at the time, issued a document, "Defense Planning Guidance," that called for the permanent expansion of U.S. power abroad. After they returned to power in January 2001 as part of the Bush administration, it took them but two months to draw up plans for war against Iraq without, however, knowing how to implement them. September 11 gave them the opportunity to put these plans into effect.[29]

As the neocons prepared for war, they faced the task of convincing the U.S. public—and the world—that the "global war on terror" demanded regime change in Baghdad because, for one, Hussein was in league with bin Laden and that, second, Hussein possessed a vast arsenal of chemical, biological, and nuclear weapons—"weapons of mass destruction" (WMD). The neocons never tired of stressing that in the 1980s, Hussein had possessed such weapons and had, in fact, used poison gas against Iranian troops and then against the Kurds in Iraq. The neocons reckoned that working hand-in-glove with al Qaeda, Hussein was about to make these weapons available to terrorists. The smoking gun, the neocons insisted, must not appear in the form of a mushroom cloud.

This argument shunted aside the fact that bin Laden and Hussein were adversaries. When bin Laden spoke of apostate Arab governments, he also had Hussein in mind, something Hussein well understood. When in 1991 the United States went to war against Hussein for the first time, bin Laden sought—unsuccessfully—Saudi backing to unleash a jihad against Hussein.[30] It was no secret to Hussein that the greatest domestic threat he faced was militant Islam, whether of the domestic Shiite or al Qaeda Sunni variety. In 2004, the *9/11 Report* destroyed one of the rationales for the war when it pointed out that Hussein had not responded to a bin Laden request to establish anti-U.S. terrorist camps in Iraq. The report did mention, however, several nations that had provided assistance—either officially or unofficially—to al Qaeda: Pakistan, Saudi Arabia, the United Arab Emirates, and Afghanistan. Iraq, however, was not on that list.

To prepare public opinion for an invasion of Iraq, the neocons turned to Ahmed Chalabi, a U.S.-educated Iraqi whose family, one of Iraq's wealthiest, had been dispossessed by the Ba'athist revolution of 1958. In the early 1990s, he joined a conservative think tank, the American Enterprise Institute, created the Iraqi National Congress (INC), and began to lobby for a U.S. invasion to return him to Iraq. Chalabi's INC was the primary force behind a 1998 U.S. congressional resolution calling for "regime change" in Baghdad. Chalabi charmed high-level officials in Washington to the degree that between 1992 and 2004, three administrations funneled at least $100 million to his INC. The CIA and State Department considered him a charlatan;[31] he had, however, more powerful champions in Rumsfeld, Wolfowitz, and Cheney. Much of the information used by the Bush administration to sell the war against Iraq came from Chalabi's disinformation channeled through the Pentagon. When told, for example, that U.S. officials thought that Hussein might have mobile chemical and biological laboratories, it was Chalabi who provided the information that Hussein did in fact have them and that he could provide their addresses. He also circulated stories of al Qaeda terrorist camps in Iraq and stated that it would take but a thousand U.S. troops to topple Hussein. There would be no fight; instead, the troops would be received with flowers and sweets.

The commander of the U.S. Marine Corps, Anthony Zinni, called Chalabi's plan a "pie-in-the-sky fairy tale." Bush had been told of the State Department's and CIA's doubts about Chalabi, but sided with the neocons nevertheless. In short, as a former CIA official explained, "Chalabi was scamming the U.S. because the U.S. wanted to be scammed."[32] In March 2003, Chalabi had his war and when his Free Iraqi Fighters arrived in Baghdad, they joined the looting in progress, except that they focused on villas, SUVs, and the like. When the time came to establish an interim government, the UN opposed Chalabi's candidacy. The Bush administration subsequently dropped Chalabi, who by now had done his duty, after it discovered that he had sold intelligence to Iran.

At first, Bush sought United Nations approval for an invasion, but all he was able to obtain was a resolution authorizing the return of the UN weapons inspectors, who Hussein had kicked out in 1998. The United Nations commissioned Hans Blix, a Swedish diplomat, to scour Iraq for WMD. But after Blix was unable to come up with evidence of WMD and sought to continue the search, Bush pulled the rug out from under him.

During his State of the Union address in January 2003, Bush gave a hair-raising appraisal of the threat emanating from Iraq. He accused the Iraqi dictator of having enough biological and chemical weapons (500 tons of sarin, mustard, and nerve gases) "to kill several million people" as well as enough botulinum toxin "to subject [an additional] millions of people to death."

To bolster his case for war, Bush sent his secretary of state, Colin Powell, before the UN—and the world—to present "incontrovertible" proof of the existence of these weapons. Powell, who initially had refused to read the report,[33] nevertheless came on board. He soldiered on and in the process converted many a doubter. He offered evidence, such as photographs and specific addresses where the weapons were produced and stored, and even held up a small vial, the contents of which could kill thousands. Chalabi could not have done a better job. Yet nearly everything Powell said that day was incorrect. His speech was a combination of half-truths and misconceptions.

The neocons piled "evidence" on top of "evidence"—much of it incorrect—to prove their case. They argued, for example, that a man no less than Hussein's son-in-law, Hussein Kamal, who had defected to Jordan, had confirmed in August 1995 the existence of WMD. In his speech before the UN, Powell invoked Kamal's name. Only after Kamal's testimony found its way to the Internet did it become evident that he had made no such claim. He had told the CIA, instead, that Hussein had destroyed his WMD in 1991. The dogmatic certainty that Hussein had WMD trumped the evidence that he did not. As a result, the Bush administration went to war against a figment of its own imagination.[34]

In the months before and after the invasion of Iraq, neither Blix, nor the CIA, nor the Pentagon found evidence of WMD or a Hussein–bin Laden connection. In October 2003, David Kay, the Pentagon's chief weapons inspector in Iraq, after scouring the country with 1,500 agents on behalf of the Pentagon's Iraq Survey Group, issued an interim report that no WMD had been found. A year later, the massive final report by the same group, produced by Kay's successor, Charles Duelfer, confirmed the earlier findings: there were no Iraqi WMD.

The U.S. news media did its share in bolstering the administration's case when it time and again—albeit with exceptions—uncritically restated whatever the White House and Pentagon churned out: Hussein "will acquire nuclear weapons fairly soon" (Cheney, August 2002); "we know with absolute certainty" that Hussein was building nuclear weapons (Cheney, September 2002); Hussein posed "a threat of unique urgency" (Bush, October 2002); "no terrorist state poses a greater or more immediate threat" than Hussein and his "sleeper cells armed with biological weapons" (Rumsfeld, September 2002); Hussein was "a threat because he is dealing with al Qaeda" (Bush, November 2002); "I really do believe that we will be greeted as liberators" (Cheney, March 2003). In December 2001, the prestigious *New York Times* spoke of sources with direct knowledge of twenty secret chemical and biological sites.[35]

When the UN—led by France, Germany, Russia, and China—insisted that containment of Hussein continue, instead of resorting to force—Bush decided to go it alone. Of all the major nations, only one, Great Britain—whose government, too, had hyped the imminent threat from Iraq—offered meaningful assistance when it sent ten thousand troops. British prime minister Tony Blair thought that by supporting Bush he would be able to assert a measure of influence in Washington. Blair wanted Bush to engage in the Palestinian-Israeli conflict as an honest broker. He did not, however, tell Bush that British support depended on that issue being addressed. In the end, Blair had nothing to show for his efforts except a disillusioned electorate, which increasingly saw him as Bush's "poodle."

Then came the invasion of Iraq. No one doubted that the United States would be able to make short shrift of Hussein's army, which had been mauled in 1991 and had not been rebuilt. Hussein had approximately one-third the troops, artillery, and armor left from 1991. His inventory contained Soviet T-55 tanks nearly fifty years old. Moreover, he had virtually no air force.

When the Vietnam War ended for the United States in 1973, its armed forces were in shambles. Nearly sixty thousand of its troops had died in Vietnam and hundreds of thousands were maimed. In Vietnam, the U.S. military had been plagued by a host of problems: low morale, draft evasion and avoidance, widespread drug use, soldiers turning against their officers—all a consequence of a drawn-out, bloody, and ultimately aimless conflict. To avoid a repetition of the Vietnam debacle, military strategists understood the next war would have to be fought differently. For nearly two decades, staff officers searched for solutions that came in the form of the Powell Doctrine, named after Colin Powell, at that time the chairman of the Joint Chiefs of Staff: in the next war, U.S. leaders must define their objectives clearly—including an "exit strategy"—and the military must marshal all its resources to achieve victory here and now.

In the 1991 Gulf War, the Powell Doctrine worked to perfection. The UN-sanctioned coalition consisted of more than 530,000 U.S. troops—accompanied by a vast array of air power—and another 160,000 allied soldiers. After the initial aerial bombardment, the ground war lasted a hundred hours. The United States lost 148 troops in combat, two-thirds by "friendly fire"; its allies lost another 150. Moreover, the United States had an "exit strategy." Hussein would be driven out of Kuwait and after that the UN would keep an eye on his attempts to rebuilt the Iraqi armed forces, particularly its arsenal of WMD.

In 2002, Colin Powell, this time acting in his capacity as secretary of state, warned the administration that if it intended to occupy Iraq, it must not go in "light." It must not repeat the mistakes of Vietnam. The army chief of staff, Eric Shinseki, and the former commander of the U.S. Marine Corps, Anthony Zinni, too, spoke of the need for up to four hundred thousand troops, not the seventy-five thousand the civilian leadership at the Pentagon (notably Rumsfeld and Wolfowitz) had in mind. (The hundred and fifty thousand troops ultimately deployed were the result of a compromise between the military and the civilians in the Pentagon.[36]) The academician Wolfowitz publicly ridiculed Shinseki, whose estimates, Wolfowitz declared, were "wildly off the mark." Wolfowitz went on to say that "it's hard to conceive that it would take more forces to provide stability . . . than it would take to conduct the war itself. . . . Hard to imagine." It marked the first public dressing down of a four-star general since the Harry Truman–Douglas MacArthur clash more than fifty years earlier. Zinni fared even worse, being called a traitor in meetings in the Pentagon.

Many of the problems the United States subsequently faced in Iraq stemmed from the fact they it did not have sufficient "boots on the ground." The comparison with the 1991 Gulf War is instructive. A coalition of 690,000 troops was given but one task, to drive Hussein out of Kuwait. In 2002, a force less than of one-quarter that size was deployed to defeat the Iraqi army, to dismantle it, occupy a resentful nation of 25 million people the size of Texas, and administer and rebuild it.

Powell also warned that the United States was responsible for the destruction of Iraqi society, invoking the "Pottery Barn rule"—if you break it, you own it. Powell's admonition was dictated not only by common sense, but also by international law: the occupier is responsible for the well-being of the citizens he controls, something, that could not be done by going in "light." The first casualty of this war, as always, was truth; the second was the Powell Doctrine.

Events quickly proved Powell, Shinseki, and Zinni correct. Hussein's army did not stand and fight; instead, it melted away to fight another day. Determined to sweep away the symbols of the old order, U.S. troops pulled down statues and portraits of Hussein, and U.S. "ambassador" Paul Bremer went so far as to disband the four-hundred-thousand-men-strong Iraqi army, dissolve the police, dismiss Ba'athist bureaucrats, and begin to privatize the state sector of the Iraqi economy. In one fell swoop, Bremer not only had thrown hundreds of thousands of Iraqis out of work, but also had torn apart the complex fabric of Iraqi society that the Ba'ath Party had stitched together over thirty-five years.

As the United States dismantled the old order, Iraqis were no longer under any sort of constraint, and they began to loot stores, museums, hospitals, all of the government ministries, and army depots. They carted off whatever was not nailed down, including vast stores of weapons and explosives. U.S. forces made no effort to stop the looting. At first, plundering was confined to east Baghdad, as U.S. tanks on Tigris bridges prevented it from spreading. When the tanks were withdrawn after two days, west Baghdad was looted too.[37] Rumsfeld dismissed reporters' concerns by declaring that "free people are free to make mistakes and commit crimes and do bad things"—a comment revealing of the administration's view of their responsibility in postwar Iraq.

Bush stated that the United States would withdraw as soon its objectives—however nebulous—were accomplished. But his actions belied his promises. For one, the United States began to build fourteen permanent military bases to shore up future Iraqi governments. Second, Bremer was busy handing out contracts to U.S. companies poised to establish their control of a revamped economy now plunged into the global market. Every economic sector, with the exception of oil, was now up for grabs by foreigners who had the right to take any and all profits out of the country.

On May 1, 2002, three weeks after the fall of Baghdad, President Bush, donning an aviator's suit, was dropped off on the aircraft carrier USS *Lincoln* where, standing under a banner proclaiming "MISSION ACCOMPLISHED," he declared that "major combat" had ended. The number of U.S. dead at that point stood at 138.

## ■ ACT III: DENOUEMENT

Policymakers in Washington expressed the hope that the political and economic reconstruction of Iraq would follow the lines of the postwar occupations of Germany and Japan. The problem with that scenario, however, was that in those countries the people well understood why they were under foreign occupation. The neocons sold the invasion of Iraq as an act of liberation, and many Iraqis, particularly the Kurds in the north and the Shiite Muslims in the south, did see it as such. But Iraqis of all religious and political stripes shortly became unhappy with the botched nature of reconstruction and with what appeared to be a permanent U.S. and British presence in Iraq. Iraqis, with their keen sense of history, well remembered the recent occupations of their country—at the hands of the Ottoman Turks and the British during the first half of the twentieth century—and saw the invasion as the first step leading to recolonization. Resistance to the occupation began to build when the Iraqis came to the conclusion that they were once again at the mercy of foreigners who pursued their own interests and who understood neither their language, customs, nor religion.

In Germany and Japan there had been no resistance to occupation. The people there focused, instead, on clearing the rubble and on rebuilding their cities and factories. Equally important, the Western Allies during World War II did not dismantle the efficient bureaucracies of these nations. In Japan, in particular, the government in power during the war scarcely skipped a beat as it continued to run the country under the occupation. Whatever denazification and demilitarization took place, it was done on an individual basis, not as a wholesale purge.

Bush's first envoy to Iraq, General Jay Garner, was a pragmatist who saw the country as "our coaling station in the Middle East," on the model of Cuba and the Philippines. Garner thought the United States should fix the economic infrastructure, hold quick elections, and leave economic shock therapy to the International Monetary Fund. Garner lasted but three weeks. The neocons wanted more than a coaling station. They pursued a mission to radically transform Iraq's economy from the ground up. Iraq was to become the poster child for free markets. On May 12, 2003, Bush replaced Garner with Paul Bremer.

Iraq now belonged to the true believers, who initiated the most drastic economic shock therapy anywhere. Iraq was now open for business by foreigners who were invited to participate in the privatization of the two hundred state-owned enterprises. They also received the right to own 100 percent of Iraqi assets and take all profits out of the country. *The Economist* called Iraq "a capitalist's dream." U.S. businessmen drooled over an economic climate that would permit a well-stocked 7-Eleven store knocking out thirty Iraqi family-owned stores. Yet all this was illegal. UN Resolution 1483 (May 2003) recognized the United States as the occupier who, however, was limited by the Geneva Conventions of 1907 and 1949: the occupier must abide by the nation's laws and had no right to the nation's assets and thus could not sell them. In October 2003, Iraqi politicians who were willing to work with Bremer began to challenge him on that score.

The solution was to establish a government in Iraq that would sanction the neocons' economic experiment. To that end, in late June 2004, the United

States transferred power to an Iraqi government headed by the interim president, Iyad Allawi, yet another exile with an unsavory past. Allawi immediately gave himself the power to invoke martial law, threatened to postpone the national elections scheduled for January 2005, reintroduced the death penalty (which the United States had abolished), and shut down the offices of the Qatar news organization of *Al-Jazeera,* accusing it of inciting violence. Peter Galbraith, the former U.S. ambassador to Croatia, wrote that Allawi's exile organization, the Iraqi National Accord "stood for an Iraq more or less like the one Saddam Hussein ran but without Saddism and without the worst abuses." Before Allawi's appointment, an opinion poll commissioned by the United States showed that 61 percent of Iraqis were strongly opposed to Allawi, a revelation, however, that mattered little to the Bush administration.[38]

Because of escalating violence, U.S. corporations were slow to respond to Bremer's invitation to set up shop in Iraq. Security costs alone were estimated at eating up a quarter of the reconstruction budget. The escalating resistance was largely in response to the economic shock therapy. In 2003, the U.S. Congress appropriated nearly $20 billion for reconstruction, yet whatever money was spent went to Western corporations at the exclusion of Iraq's state-owned enterprises, which were now operating at 50 percent capacity. The ubiquitous concrete barriers (aka "blast barriers" or "Bremer walls"), for example, were available from Iraqi contractors for $100 each; instead, they were imported at $1,000 each. Iraqi workers, out of a job, joined the ranks of the unemployed—and the resistance. Estimates of the number of unemployed in the summer of 2004 ranged between 50 and 70 percent.[39]

One of the problems facing reconstruction was that few of the individuals recruited had the expertise in either running Iraq or rebuilding its economy. Many of them were chosen on the basis of political loyalty to Bush's Republican Party. That was one of the reasons why only approximately 5 percent of the allocated reconstruction money had been spent by the summer of 2004.

The resistance began to target foreign business interests—U.S., South Korean, Japanese, Italian, Turkish, and others—by kidnapping, ransoming, and killing hostages. By November 2004, more than 170 foreigners had been kidnapped, more than three dozen of them were murdered or "disappeared." Iraq, the neocons' dream laboratory, became the most dangerous place to do business, a mirror image of what had been envisioned.[40]

The resistance came from many quarters, including an indeterminate number of foreigners, the most important of whom was Abu Musa Zarqawi, a Jordanian who appeared to have been personally responsible for the decapitation of two U.S. contractors in September 2004 and who, the U.S. military claimed, led the foreign contingent in the city of Fallujah. Zarqawi, who had his own organization that had caused bloodshed throughout

Europe and the Middle East, was both a rival and ally of al Qaeda. As with so many of the Islamic militants, he had cut his teeth in Afghanistan, where he made contact with al Qaeda and where he began to construct a distinct network, Monotheism and Jihad.[41] Zarqawi was particularly effective in the conservative Sunni city of Fallujah, where he called for resistance against the United States as well as a sectarian war against the heretic Shiites.

Shiite clergy were among the early critics of the occupation. The most vociferous of them was Moqtada al Sadr, a young ayatollah who had inherited the mantle of his revered father who had been assassinated in 1999, presumably by Hussein's agents. The Shiite sector of Baghdad, home to more than 2 million impoverished residents, formerly known as "Saddam City," became "Sadr City" (renamed in honor of the father). In March 2004, Bremer padlocked the offices of Sadr's weekly newspaper after it had charged that "Bremer Follows the Steps of Saddam."[42] Bremer put an end to this experiment in press freedom and promised to establish "law and order" by issuing a warrant for the arrest of the "outlaw" Sadr for his alleged complicity in the—unresolved—April 2003 murder of a rival Shiite cleric, Abdel-Majid Khoei, the son of a grand ayatollah, whom the CIA had brought back from exile.

Sadr's resistance movement, the Mahdi Army—named after the legendary lost imam of Shiism whose second coming the faithful await—was a classic example of "blowback." Its members were the young, the unemployed, the disillusioned. "Sadr took Bremer's economic casualties," a Canadian journalist explained, "dressed them in black and gave them rusty Kalashnikovs."[43] In April 2004, at a time when U.S. forces were first engaged in Fallujah, the Mahdi Army ambushed U.S. patrols in Sadr City. The battle was on.

The U.S. military command considered Sadr a more important target than Fallujah because of his stature and uncompromising militancy. The pitched battles between the Mahdi Army and U.S. troops ended in a stalemate after a final round of fighting in the Shiite holy city of Najaf, the burial place of the founder of the Shiite branch, Mohammed's son-in-law Ali. The United States won the engagements without, however, being able to finish off Sadr and his militia. The most influential ayatollah in Iraq, Ali al Sistani, brokered a truce under the terms of which the United States withdrew from Najaf and the militia agreed to give up their weapons. Sadr, who had long called for elections, decided to conserve his forces and wait for the promised national elections at the end of January 2005.

The troubles in Fallujah, the "city of mosques," a conservative Sunni religious center of approximately three hundred thousand inhabitants, thirty-five miles west of Baghdad, began at the end of April 2003, after U.S. troops commandeered a local school to use as a military base. During the confrontation that followed, U.S. troops killed thirteen residents, several of them children. The resistance in Fallujah began as an act of revenge for the killings.

A year later came the disturbing images on television and the Internet of four U.S. "contractors" working for the Pentagon, who had been trapped in Fallujah, killed, and their dismembered bodies hanged from one of the city's bridges. U.S. forces sought to retake the city with the help of a U.S.-trained militia—the "Fallujah Brigade"—only to see its members go over to the other side. Fallujah became a symbol of a national and religious resistance and a haven for jihadists, many of them foreigners—from Saudi Arabia, Jordan, Egypt, and Syria—under the apparent command of Zarqawi.

It was a situation that the Bush administration and the Allawi government were unable to resolve for more than six months. In November 2004, however, immediately after the U.S. presidential election, ten thousand U.S. marines, augmented by five thousand Iraqi soldiers, finally took Fallujah after a bloody, week-long battle that produced a flood of civilian refugees and left many dead and much of the city in ruins. Once again, the United States proclaimed victory, but there was still the question of how many of the resistance had escaped being captured or had been killed by U.S. forces. The resistance had held off the marines and their superior firepower for as long as possible, only to vanish at the end. Zarqawi was nowhere to be found. Moreover, as the battle for Fallujah raged, renewed outbreaks of violence took place in cities across Iraq, including Baghdad and the country's third-largest city, Mosul.

In late April 2004, came the shocking revelation—by photographs posted on the Internet—that U.S. troops had been engaged in systematic torture of Iraqis at the prison of Abu Ghraib, just west of Baghdad. That state of affairs had already been reported by Amnesty International and the International Red Cross, but dismissed by U.S. officials. Early in 2002, Rumsfeld characterized such complaints by the international agencies as "isolated pockets of international hyperventilation."[44] This time, however, the graphic photographs could not be readily dismissed. Ironically, the Abu Ghraib prison had first gained notoriety for torture, rapes, and executions under Hussein. The Pentagon and the White House feigned shock at such behavior and immediately placed the onus on a "few" low-ranking "bad apples." It soon became evident, however—on the basis of documents leaked from the White House—that the decision to use methods that might well be considered torture had been made at the highest levels in the Bush administration.

In earlier engagements elsewhere throughout the world, the United States had long been engaged in torture, but it had generally done so surreptitiously through intermediaries, such as South Vietnamese forces and the Latin American military who had learned their lessons at the School of the Americas in Fort Benning, Georgia. Post–September 11 torture began in Afghanistan when the Bush administration lumped the Taliban and al Qaeda together in a new category of "enemy combatants," not enemy soldiers, and thus not subject to the provisions of the 1949 Geneva Convention that insisted that the torture of any and all prisoners "shall remain prohibited at any time and in any place whatsoever."

Torture accompanied the defeat of the Taliban in Afghanistan, particularly in Mazar-e-Sharif—the home of Hazari, Tadzhik, and Uzbeks—a city with a bloody past. In May 1997, Persian-speaking Shiite Hazaris murdered two thousand Pushtun Sunni Taliban. Fifteen months later, in August 1998, the Taliban conquered Mazar-e-Sharif after going house to house to conduct the most vicious bloodbath since the Soviet invasion, killing an estimated three to four thousand Hazaris. The cycle of violence continued in November 2001, when the Northern Alliance—this time with U.S. assistance—vented its fury once more against the Taliban.

Beginning in February 2002, the Bush administration took several steps legitimizing torture when White House counsel Alberto Gonzales offered a novel reinterpretion of the Geneva Conventions that, in any case, he argued, had become "irrelevant." He went on to declare that the president was not bound by any law—U.S. or international—when acting as commander in chief of the armed forces, and that inflicting pain on prisoners was permitted as a "necessity," "in self-defense," or the result of "superior orders." In the Pentagon, Donald Rumsfeld signed off on several similar directives.

After the Bush administration withdrew the Geneva protection from the Taliban and al Qaeda, torture migrated to the Guantanamo Naval Station to which the Taliban and al Qaeda prisoners had been taken, and from there to Iraq. U.S. difficulties in Iraq became acute in the summer of 2003, when the insurgency grew in strength. Desperate to gain information about the ubiquitous insurgents, U.S. soldiers began to arrest civilians at the site of attacks, often raiding homes, wrecking furniture, and dragging people out. Eventually the number of detainees reached fifty thousand, guarded by understaffed, ill-prepared National Guard troops. Even though few had information to give, few of the detainees were released.

At the end of August 2003, torture became institutionalized in Iraq when Major General Geoffrey Miller, commander of the detention camp at Guantanamo, arrived in Baghdad. Miller demanded "actionable intelligence" any way possible—by beatings, sexual humiliation, "water-boarding" (near drowning of detainees), and the use of dogs. All this was sanctioned by the commander of U.S. forces in Iraq, General Ricardo Sanchez. The system was self-defeating, however, since it merely created more hostility. In June 2004, at Friday prayers in Baghdad, an imam charged that the only freedom the United States had brought to Iraq was the freedom to abuse Iraqis: "They express the freedom of rape, the freedom of nudity and the freedom of humiliation."[45]

At Guantanamo, just as the "enemy combatants" were about to be tried by novel "military commissions," the federal courts intervened. These "commissions" marked the first time that a U.S. government, which had ratified the Geneva Convention of 1949, had denied enemy soldiers prisoner-of-war status. It had been granted even to the Viet Cong, farmers by day and fighters at night. In November 2004, U.S. District Judge James Robertson declared that the "commissions" were neither lawful nor proper. Defendants were entitled to hear the charges against them and to challenge their imprisonment in U.S. federal court.[46]

Another problem the United States faced in Iraq was the country's ethnic complexity. When ambassador Paul Bremer began to draw up the first transitional laws, he stated that ethnicity had no place in the new Iraq, that the country's citizens were all Iraqis. It was a tall order. The Kurds, for instance, did not see themselves as Iraqis; 75 percent of Kurdistan's adult population had signed a petition demanding independence. Kurds flew their own flag, paid no Iraqi taxes, controlled their own borders, and had their own army. Neither Allawi nor the United States had the power—or inclination—to change the situation in Kurdistan. To complicate matters, the Shiites—60 percent of the population—wanted an Islamic state; the Sunnis saw the Shiites as heretics and believed that—based on tradition and history—it was their right to govern the country. The potential for ethnic and religious violence was particularly great in the northern oil center Kirkuk, a city of 850,000 people, roughly evenly divided among Kurds (35 percent), Sunni Arabs (35 percent), and Turkomen (26 percent), the latter of which were ethnic Turks hostile to both Kurds and Arabs. Each of them had their own versions of historic claims to the city and its oil.[47]

None of the neocons had expected that by the end of November 2004, the number of U.S. military and civilian dead would reach nearly fourteen hundred with approximately eight thousand seriously wounded. U.S. forces were stretched to the breaking point and regular and National Guard units had their tours of duty extended. The cost in dollars, initially estimated at $30 billion, had reached $200 billion. The economic costs of the Iraq war contributed to the weakening of the U.S. economy. President Clinton's budget surplus was now a distant memory wiped out by September 11, homeland security, the wars in Afghanistan and Iraq, and tax cuts, the first in history, anywhere, in time of war.

As for the Iraqi casualties, the Pentagon claimed that it did not keep track of the number of dead and wounded. In late October 2004, the Public School of Health at Johns Hopkins University estimated that the number of dead may have reached 100,000. *Al Jazeera* put the number at over 36,000; www.iraqbodycount.net estimates put it between 14,000 and 16,000.

When the United States went to war against the Taliban, the world, including many Muslims and even Arabs, believed that its cause was just. Iraq, however, quickly drained the reservoir of goodwill. Clerics at Cairo's Al Azhar University, an esteemed center of Muslim thought, who had condemned the attacks of September 11, now preached that every Muslim had an obligation to defend Iraq.[48]

# ■ AFGHANISTAN

With the overthrow of the Taliban government in Afghanistan imminent, the UN, in December 2001, convened a council in Bonn, Germany, to choose an interim head of state for that country. There, the United States engineered the selection of Hamid Karzai, a royalist who had gone into exile after the Soviet invasion and who then established close ties to the CIA and the U.S. oil giant, Unical. When the United States returned Karzai to Kabul, he came as a president who had no army of his own and no authority beyond the capital. The deal worked out in Bonn, however, also returned to Kabul members of the Northern Alliance, whose rapacious rule in the recent past had made possible the Taliban's seizure of power in the first place.

In October 2004, Karzai defeated a large field of challengers in the first presidential election in Afghan history. By this time, Karzai could boast that schools had been reopened and the beginning of the physical reconstruction of the country was under way. Economic indicators were up: the annual per capita GDP since the days of the Taliban had doubled from $123 to $246 and daily wages had risen from $2.70 to $6.25. Primary-school enrollment, a more significant measure of progress, had increased from 1 million to 3.5 million.[49] But much of this progress was limited to the capital city of Kabul.

Moreover, much of the new wealth came from the production of opium; banned by the Taliban and virtually nonexistent in 2001, opium production was estimated at 3,600 metric tons in 2004. Among the chief beneficiaries were the warlords and their militias, who retained their prewar strength of about ninety thousand. The U.S. military tried to create an Afghan army of seventy thousand men, subject to Karzai's rule, but by early October 2004, it had recruited and trained only about one-fifth that number. It was a force insufficient to protect foreign-aid personnel and election workers, more than sixty of whom had been killed by the Taliban, whose strength had increased by 50 percent since 2003.[50]

Nor could Karzai rely on his army to protect him; his safety was assured by U.S. "contractors" paid by the Pentagon. And when the United States shifted its attention to Iraq, the regional warlords began to reassert themselves. As they did so, the economy of a desperately poor Afghanistan resorted to producing and marketing the sole export commodity it had, opium—the raw material for heroin. In November 2004, the UN issued a warning that opium cultivation was up nearly two-thirds from the previous year; only bad weather and disease prevented a record harvest. Despite these setbacks, Afghanistan provided 87 percent of the world's heroin, up from 76 percent in 2003.[51] The United States was not in the best position to wage a "war on drugs," the kind of which it had conducted in the past—unsuccessfully—at home and abroad. The opium trade threatened to turn Afghanistan into a failed narco-state on the Colombian model.

The invasion of Afghanistan brought back from Iranian exile the vicious Gulbuddin Hekmatyar and his militia. During the war against the Soviet Union, Hekmatyar had been the chief recipient of money and arms from the United States and Pakistan, but upon his return in 2002, he made common cause with his former enemies, the Taliban and al Qaeda. In April 2004, in the west, the Uzbek warlord Abdul Rashid Dostum, another former recipient of U.S. assistance, reasserted his authority, a further reminder of Karzai's fragile position.[52] And Mohammed Omar, still in control of the Taliban, was smuggling seditious "night letters" into Kabul urging Afghans to resist the infidel foreigners.

A sign of the times was the withdrawal in July 2004 of the international agency, Médecins Sans Frontières (Doctors Without Borders). Its dissatisfaction with the Taliban, the U.S. military, and the Afghan government, which had failed to go after the murderers of six of its workers (thirty in all since the beginning of 2004), led to the pullout after twenty-four years of continuous operation in Afghanistan through all sorts of travail—since the early days of the Soviet invasion.[53]

\* \* \*

In Iraq, conflicts between U.S.-led troops and insurgents continued into 2005. As the world became subjected to a steady stream of images from Iraq, the United States became increasingly more isolated. At a NATO summit in Turkey in June 2004, which Bush attended, the delegates were not convinced of his conversion to multilateralism, and offered him virtually no additional assistance in either Iraq or Afghanistan.[54] A number of nations that had initially offered assistance (notably Spain and Poland) ended their involvement. In September 2004, even Kofi Annan, the UN's secretary-general, stated his opposition to the war—albeit a year and a half after it had begun—declaring it to be "illegal" because the United States had not obtained authorization from the UN Security Council.

When, in November 2003, Bush expressed the hope that Egypt would "show the way toward democracy in the Middle East," Hosni Mubarak, the president of Egypt, wanted no part of such talk. The following month, he conducted the most extensive crackdown on the Muslim Brotherhood in ten years. Mubarak had reason to do so, for the war in Iraq had bred resentment and had contributed to heightened animosity toward the United States, leading to an escalation of Brotherhood recruitment, training, and deployment of jihadists to Iraq. Mubarak had always feared the consequences of an invasion of Iraq, predicting that it would lead to more terror and the spawning of "100 bin Ladens." Mubarak was not alone. The secretary-general of the Arab League warned that it would "open the gates of hell."

The United States faced a contradiction in the Middle East. Free and honest elections, in a region where Osama bin Laden was far more highly regarded than George W. Bush, would bring Islamic parties to power. A graduate student at the American University in Cairo explained the U.S. paradox thus: "The nightmare for the West is that they advocate democracy and then they find that these countries elect Islamic governments. Islamists have gained a lot of legitimacy through their social work, even in their jobs as engineers or doctors. They have a certain status."[55]

In November 2004, despite the chaos in Iraq, Bush was reelected when he convinced enough of the electorate that only he could defend the United States from global terror. That, plus the lackluster campaign of his Democratic opponent and the voting strength of evangelical Christians who opposed gay marriage and abortion and continued to believe in large numbers that Hussein had something to do with September 11, gave him four additional years to sort out the problems in Iraq to which he had so greatly contributed.

## ■ RECOMMENDED READINGS

### ☐ *Militant Islam*

Armstrong, Karen. *The Battle for God*. New York: Ballantine Books, 2000.
　　A discussion of the force of fundamentalism in Judaism, Christianity, and Islam since 1492.
Davis, Joyce M. *Innocence, Vengeance and Despair in the Middle East*. New York: Palgrave Macmillan, 2003.
　　A U.S. journalist's explanation of the reasons for Middle Eastern violence.
Kepel, Gilles. *The War for Muslim Minds: Islam and the West*. New York: Belknap, 2004.
Stern, Jessica. *Terror in the Name of God: Why Religious Militants Kill*. New York: Ecco Press, 2003.
　　Based on interviews of zealots—Muslims, Jews, and Christians.

### ☐ *"Global War on Terror"*

Michael Scheuer, *Imperial Hubris*. New York: Potomac Books, 2004.
　　By the operative in charge of the CIA's bin Laden unit, 1996–1999.
Blix, Hans. *Disarming Iraq*. New York: Pantheon, 2004.
　　By the head of UNMOVIC, the UN's weapons inspection team.
Brzezinski, Zbigniew. *The Choice: Global Domination or Global Leadership*. New York: Basic Books, 2004.
　　By President Carter's former national security adviser, who argues for leadership instead of the neocons' preference for domination.
Clancy, Tom, with Tony Zinni and Tony Koltz. *Battle Ready*. New York: G. P. Putnam's Sons, 2004.
　　A biography of the former commander of the U.S. Marines.
Clarke, Richard A. *Against All Enemies: Inside America's War on Terror*. New York: Free Press, 2004.
　　The memoirs of Bush's former antiterrorist chief, by the highest-ranking official in both the Clinton and George W. Bush administrations in charge of dealing with al Qaeda. Bush, Clarke writes, ignored warnings about al Qaeda and

when 9/11 came, he focused immediately on Iraq, telling Clarke to find a link between 9/11 and Hussein.

Coll, Steven. *Ghost Wars: The Secret History of the CIA, Afghanistan, and bin Laden: From the Soviet Invasion to September 10, 2001*. New York: Penguin, 2004.

Definitive account of the CIA involvement before and after the Soviet Union's withdrawal from Afghanistan in February 1989.

Hersh, Seymour M. *Chain of Command: The Road from 9/11 to Abu Ghraib*. New York: HarperCollins, 2004.

By an investigative journalist who was among the first to break the Abu Ghraib story.

Johnson, Chalmers. *The Sorrows of Empire: Militarism, Secrecy, and the End of the Republic*. New York: Metropolitan, 2004.

A discussion of the negative consequences of empire.

Mann, James. *The Rise of the Vulcans: The History of Bush's War Cabinet*. New York: Viking, 2004.

A former correspondent of the *Los Angeles Times* discusses the rise of the neocons.

*The 9/11 Commission Report: Final Report of the National Commission on Terrorist Attacks upon the United States*. New York: W. W. Norton, 2004.

The scholarly, lucid, bipartisan national best-seller.

Woodward, Bob. *Bush at War*. New York: Simon and Schuster, 2002.

By a *Washington Post* correspondent who had nearly unlimited access to Bush and his cabinet during the war in Afghanistan.

———. *Plan of Attack*. New York: Simon and Schuster, 2004.

Discusses the road to war and its early stages in Iraq.

# ■ NOTES

1. *The 9/11 Commission Report: Final Report of the National Commission on Terrorist Attacks upon the United States* (New York: W. W. Norton, 2004), p. 118.

2. Reuter transcript, "Bin Laden Speaks to American People," *Washington Post,* October 30, 2004, p. A16.

3. When a British member of Parliament and the wife of Tony Blair, Britain's prime minister, attempted to do so, the Israeli embassy complained and the government apologized. Jacqueline Rose, "Deadly Embrace," *London Review of Books,* November 4, 2004, pp. 21–24.

4. Avishai Margalit, "The Suicide Bombers," *New York Review of Books,* January 16, 2003; Jessica Stern, *Terror in the Name of God: Why Religious Militants Kill* (New York: Ecco Press, 2003).

5. Jonathan Rabin, "My Holy War," *New Yorker*, February 4, 2002; Steven Coll, *Ghost Wars: The Secret History of the CIA, Afghanistan, and bin Laden: From the Soviet Invasion to September 10, 2001* (New York: Penguin, 2004), pp. 470–474.

6. Michael Scheuer *Imperial Hubris* (New York: Potomac Books, 2004); Baruch Kimmerling, "Sacred Rage," *The Nation,* December 15, 2003, pp. 23–30; Stern, *Terror in the Name of God.*

7. *The Battle of Algiers,* written and directed by Gillo Pontecorvo (Rialto Pictures Release and Janus Films, 1965).

8. Abdel Aziz al-Rantissi cited in Rose, "Deadly Embrace," p. 24.

9. Cited in Coll, *Ghost Wars,* p. 380.

10. Lawrence Wright, "The Terror Web," *The New Yorker,* August 2, 2004, p. 47.

11. Ibid., pp. 40–53.

12. David B. Ottaway and Robert G. Kaiser, "Marriage of Convenience: The U.S.-Saudi Alliance," *Washington Post,* February 12, 2002, p. A10; Max Rodenbeck, "Unloved in Arabia," *New York Review of Books,* October 21, 2004, pp. 22–25.

13. Cited in David Remnick, "Letter from Cairo: Going Nowhere," *New Yorker,* July 12 and 19, 2004.

14. Lawrence Wright, "The Man Behind bin Laden," *New Yorker,* September 16, 2002; Karen Armstrong, *The Battle for God* (New York: Ballantine Books, 2000), pp. 239–244; Rabin, "My Holy War."

15. Wright, "The Man Behind bin Laden."

16. Montasser al-Zayat cited in Wright, "The Man Behind bin Laden."

17. Coll, *Ghost Wars,* pp. 87, 155–157, 162–163, 185.

18. Richard Clarke, *Against All Enemies,* chapter 6, "Al Qaeda Revealed," pp. 133–154.

19. Peter Bergen, "Backdraft," *Mother Jones* (July-August 2004), pp. 40–45.

20. Bush's first order of business, upon being told of the attack, was to continue listening for another seven minutes to grade-school children in Florida reading a book about a pet goat. The second, was to meet with his staffers for fifteen minutes on how to spin the story. "The focus" during these fifteen minutes, the *9/11 Report* explained, "was on the President's statement to the nation." *The 9/11 Commission Report,* p. 39.

21. And, of course, pikes to mount the prize. Bob Woodward, *Bush at War* (New York: Simon and Schuster, 2002), pp. 38, 141, 143.

22. When Mohammed Fahim, the Tadzhik commander of the Northern Alliance, demanded a $7 million dollar bribe, U.S. commander Tommy Franks, standing on principle, walked out of the meeting. But that was Fahim's opening bid and there was no need for Franks to leave the bazaar. And, in fact, one of Franks's aides then negotiated a deal for $5 million. Tommy Franks, *American Soldier* (New York: Regan Books, 2004), pp. 312–313.

23. Barton Gellman and Thomas E. Ricks, "U.S. Concludes Bin Laden Escaped at Tora Bora Fight," *Washington Post,* April 17, 2002.

24. Lisa Meyers, NBC News, "Did Ashcroft Brush Off Terror Warnings?" June 22, 2004; Dan Eggen and Walter Pincus, "Ashcroft's Efforts on Terrorism Criticized," *Washington Post,* April 14, 2004.

25. *The 9/11 Commission Report,* pp. 174–182, 254–277.

26. Franks, *American Soldier,* p. 309.

27. Michael E. O'Hanlon and Adriana Lins de Albuquerque, *Afghanistan Index: Tracking Variables of Reconstruction & Security in Post-Taliban Afghanistan* (Washington, D.C.: Brookings Institution, updated October 8, 2004).

28. Eliza Griswold, "Where the Taliban Roam," *Harper's* (September 2003), pp. 57–65; Eliza Griswold, "In the Hiding Zone," *New Yorker,* July 26, 2004, pp. 34–42.

29. James Mann, *The Rise of the Vulcans: The History of Bush's War Cabinet* (New York: Viking, 2004), pp. 208–215, and chapter 15, "The Vulcan Agenda," pp. 234–247; Woodward, *Bush at War,* p. 49.

30. Coll, *Ghost Wars,* p. 380.

31. In the 1990s, Chalabi and members of his family were found guilty of embezzlement of vast sums of money in Switzerland, Lebanon, and Jordan, where he was sentenced to twenty-two years of hard labor, only to flee to London. In the summer of 2004, the Allawi government charged him with circulating counterfeit money and his nephew with the murder of a finance ministry official.

32. Jane Mayer, "The Manipulator," *New Yorker,* June 7, 2004, pp. 59–66.

33. During the first of five rehearsal sessions, Powell tossed the papers in the air, saying, "I'm not reading this. This is bullshit." The initial draft, which ignored much of what the CIA had told the White House and the Pentagon, was the handiwork of Cheney's office. In the end, Powell read a modified report. Bruce B. Auster, Mark Mazetti, and Edward T. Pound, "Truth and Consequences: New Questions About U.S. Intelligence Regarding Iraq's Weapons of Mass Terror," *U.S. News and World Report,* June 9, 2003.

34. The *New York Times* journalist Thomas Friedman, who had originally beaten the drums for war, told the Israeli newspaper *Ha'aretz* that the invasion had been the handiwork of twenty-five individuals who worked within "a five-block radius" of Friedman's office. "If you had exiled them to a desert island a year and a half ago," Friedman went on to say, "the Iraq war would not have happened." Cited by Danny Postel, "Look Who's Feuding," *The American Prospect* (July 2004), p. 22.

35. Michael Massing, "Iraq: Now They Tell Us," *New York Review of Books,* February 26, 2004. It was only in May 2004 that the *New York Times* acknowledged its errors.

36. The seventy-five-thousand-troop level fit Rumsfeld's preference for small, mobile armies; interview of James Fallows, PBS, *Frontline,* February 26, 2004.

37. Alexander Cockburn, "Because We Could," *The Nation,* November 8, 2004, p. 46.

38. Allawi, who had helped Hussein to consolidate his power, subsequently became a member of the intelligence service working as an enforcer, and finally working for the CIA. A former CIA case officer described Allawi as someone who fancied himself as a man of ideas, but whose "strongest virtue is that he's a thug." Seymour M. Hersh, "Plan B," *New Yorker,* June 28, 2004, pp. 54–67. Also, Peter W. Galbraith, "Iraq: The Bungled Transition," *New York Review of Books,* September 23, 2004, p. 70.

39. A study conducted by the College of Economics, Baghdad University, put it as high as 70 percent; Ahmed Janabi, "Iraqi Unemployed Reaches 70 percent," *Al Jazeera,* August 1, 2004.

40. Naomi Klein, "Baghdad Year Zero: Pillaging Iraq in Pursuit of a Neocon Utopia," *Harper's* (September 2004), pp. 43–53.

41. Craig Whitlock, "Grisly Path to Power in Iraq's Insurgency," *Washington Post,* September 27, 2004, pp. A1, A15.

42. Pamela Constable, "Paper Closed by U.S. Is Back in Business," *Washington Post,* July 25, 2004, p. A15.

43. Klein, "Baghdad Year Zero," p. 51.

44. Seymour M. Hersh, "Chain of Command," *New Yorker,* May 17, 2004, p. 41; and Seymour M. Hersh, *Chain of Command: The Road from 9/11 to Abu Ghraib* (New York: HarperCollins, 2004).

45. Cited in Mark Danner, "Abu Ghraib: The Hidden Story," *New York Review of Books,* October 7, 2004, p. 44.

46. Carol D. Leonnig and John Mintz, "Judge Says Detainees Trials Are Unlawful," *Washington Post,* November 9, 2004, pp. A1, A10.

47. Galbraith, "Iraq: The Bungled Transition," pp. 72–73; David Ignatius, "Kirkuk as Car Bomb," *Washington Post,* July 20, 2004, p. A17.

48. Peter Bergen, "Backdraft," *Mother Jones* (July-August 2004), pp. 40–45.

49. O'Hanlon and Lins de Albuquerque, *Afghanistan Index.*

50. Ibid.

51. Associated Press, "Heroin Production Rises Sharply in Afghanistan," *Baltimore Sun,* November 19, 2004, p. A18.

52. Douglas Birch, "Afghan Governor Escapes After Warlord Seizes City," *Baltimore Sun,* April 9, 2004, p. 13A; Kim Baker (of the *Chicago Tribune*), "Rebels Take Over Afghan Town," *Baltimore Sun,* June 19, 2004, p. 10A.

53. From the report of the British government's Foreign Affairs Select Committee, July 2004, "Report: Afghanistan Could Implode," http://www.CNN.com, July 29, 2004.

54. Jackson Diehl, "NATO's 'Myth' in Afghanistan," *Washington Post,* July 5, 2004, p. A17.

55. Remnick, "Letter from Cairo: Going Nowhere."

# 22

## Epilogue:
## The End of the Postwar Age

If historical processes are a combination of continuity and change, it was inevitable that half a century after World War II, the world would be different from that the Big Three had faced in their moment of triumph in 1945. The new order the victors created in 1945 had considerable staying power, but it was bound to end one day. Since the French Revolution of 1789, none of the international configurations of power survived much longer than a biblical generation of forty years.[1] Since 1945, the world has seen a number of major trends that, taken together, have put us at the beginning of a new, uncertain era. Among the major changes in the world since 1945 are the following.

### □ 1. The Fall of Communism

The most surprising and sudden development since 1945 took place in Eastern Europe, where all the Communist parties gave up their once seemingly immutable hold on power in the short span of two years, between 1989 and 1991. Soviet socialism's most visible accomplishment had been the creation of a powerful security apparatus designed to deal with threats from without and within. East European Communist leaders, however, neglected what Communist ideology always had considered significant, the substructure upon which the socialist house rested, namely the economic base. Gorbachev's perestroika eventually came to the conclusion that a new base was needed if the Soviet Union was to keep pace with the economies of the West. Once that position was reached, Communism as an ideology, as defined by Lenin and particularly Stalin, became a thing of the past.

### □ 2. The End of the Cold War

Equally astonishing was the end of the Cold War and its most dangerous feature, the military confrontation, when the Soviet army withdrew from

Eastern Europe. The Warsaw Pact ceased to exist, making possible NATO's expansion into Eastern Europe. The nuclear arms reduction agreements ended a dangerous contest by the superpowers paralyzed into immobility. The agreements, however, came at a late hour, as the genie of nuclear proliferation already had made its way out of the bottle. After the Soviet Union broke the U.S.-British monopoly in 1949, France, the People's Republic of China, India, Pakistan, and Israel joined the ranks of nuclear powers, and a number of aspirants began to appear, among them North Korea and Iran.

## ☐  3. The Triumph of Capitalism

The demise of Communism and the ideological message of U.S. president Ronald Reagan contributed to a return to a form of capitalism unchecked and deeply ideological in its content. Perestroika, designed to save Soviet socialism, opened instead the floodgate of criticism of Communism and produced a wild swing to a type of primitive capitalism the Western world had modified a hundred years earlier because of its destructive and cruel nature. The primordial aspects of capitalism were making their way also into the arena of international trade, where the pretense of open and mutually beneficial trade at times began to give way to fierce competition, a zero-sum contest, and the continuation of war by other means, in which there were invariably winners and losers. The unlimited "right" of one individual or nation to amass great wealth guaranteed the others' "right" to have little. By the early 1990s, the 1944 Bretton Woods ideals of free trade were severely tested by nationalist tendencies. This characteristic of international trade lay at the heart of the friction among the economic powers—the United States, the European Union, and Japan.

## ☐  4. The Age of High Technology

After the 1970s, the world witnessed a new stage in the industrial revolution, a shift away from "smokestack" industries. The production of steel, once the yardstick by which industrial progress had been measured, lost its importance to knowledge-intensive industries such as computers and their offshoots—robots, digital communication, and the like. A fundamental flaw in the Soviet economy, for instance, had been the continued emphasis on the production of basic materials such as steel and oil in which it led the world in production. During the heyday of the smokestack industries, catching up with other industrialized nations was a difficult process, yet a relatively easy one compared to the hurdles underdeveloped countries faced at the end of the twentieth century. The gulf between the haves and the have-nots grew increasingly wider.

## ☐ 5. The Relative Decline of the Economic Power of the United States

The decades following 1945 witnessed a gradual yet steady erosion of U.S. economic power relative to other parts of the world—East Asia (notably Japan) and Western Europe. The relative decline was the result of a number of factors. For one, the United States had spent vast sums of money on its national security without taking the necessary steps to ensure the viability of its economic base. It continued to lead the world in technological break-throughs, particularly as they applied to weapons research and develop-ment, but gave up its dominant position in the production of consumer goods. With the demise of the Soviet Union, the United States stood as the sole remaining superpower, its economy and military still dominant, but facing yet another challenge: a revitalized China.

## ☐ 6. The Reemergence of Germany

As the two superpowers declined, their old antagonists of World War II began to reassert themselves. Germany did so particularly after its reunifi-cation in 1990. The Gulf War witnessed the stationing of German troops abroad for the first time (in Turkey), and during the Yugoslav crisis German warships began to make their appearance in the Adriatic Sea and German airplanes over Kosovo. In the 1950s, the first West German chancellor, Konrad Adenauer, devoted himself to the integration of his nation into the West European community. But in the early 1990s, Germany began to play once again its traditional role in Eastern Europe, taking the lead in the eco-nomic penetration of that region and in the recognition of breakaway republics of the Soviet Union and Yugoslavia.

## ☐ 7. The Reemergence of Japan

Japan's reassertion was more muted. After its disastrous defeat in World War II, it abandoned militarism in favor of pacifism and was content to remain under the U.S. defensive and diplomatic umbrella as long as possi-ble while pursuing economic growth. But shortly after the end of the Allied Occupation in the 1950s, the United States already began to urge Japan to take a more active role as an ally in the Cold War. Once the Cold War ended, it was the United States that encouraged Japan to play a greater part in international affairs, particularly since Japan had the financial means to assist in underwriting U.S. and UN initiatives. Japan was cajoled into fund-ing a portion of the Gulf War (after all, it was heavily dependent on oil from the region), and it played a leading role in the UN peacekeeping oper-ation in Cambodia, where Japanese soldiers set foot on the Asian mainland for the first time since 1945. At the turn of the century, however, Japan's role in East Asia was largely limited to economic activity due to resistance from nations it had controlled before and during World War II, notably Korea and a resurgent People's Republic of China. Moreover, Japanese (and German) military involvement abroad put to a severe test the clauses in their constitutions that permitted only acts of defense.

## □ 8. The Rise of East Asia

Beginning with Japan's "economic miracle" of the 1960s, East Asia emerged as an arena of dynamic economic growth and new prosperity. First, the Four Tigers (South Korea, Taiwan, Hong Kong, and Singapore) imitated Japan, registering in the early 1980s the world's highest economic growth rates. Then, by the early 1990s, this economic success was emulated by Southeast Asian countries (Thailand, Malaysia, and Indonesia) to attain honors as the world's fastest-growing economies. Then came the astonishing growth of the People's Republic of China after it converted to a market economy in the 1980s. The success stories in East Asia, like that of Japan, represented a blend of a Western-derived capitalist system and elements of traditional Asian culture, an amalgam featuring state-directed economic modernization and capital formation, high rates of personal savings and capital investment, abundant and cheap labor consisting of disciplined workers, emphasis on new high-tech industries, and export-driven industrial growth. The economic competitiveness of many Asian nations posed a challenge to a smug industrialized West and to a struggling Third World.

## □ 9. The Fragmentation of the World

The bipolar camps had been the result of the Cold War, and once that confrontation had come to an end, there was no further need to rally around one camp's flag or the other. Even at the height of the Cold War, a number of nations had refused to be drawn into it. De Gaulle of France, for example, feared too close an embrace on the part of the United States, and Nehru of India wanted no part of either bloc. Communist Yugoslavia's break with Stalin underscored the fact that "international Communist solidarity" existed primarily in theory only. Other Communist nations (China, Vietnam, Romania, Albania, and Cuba) tended to guard their independence against both Washington and Moscow. This fragmentation only increased after the end of the Cold War. The Soviet Union's East European bloc was no more, and the United States could no longer take its allies for granted.

## □ 10. Globalism Versus Nationalism

During the late 1980s, two conflicting currents came into collision. On the one hand, the "global village" was becoming smaller and many of its citizens began to see themselves as members of one large family facing common problems and a common future; on the other hand, the world was becoming increasingly fragmented and parochial as nationalities asserted their claims to independence and made war on one another. Rapid communication and economic change were among the forces behind the trend toward internationalization. This in turn gave rise to economic integration, to what some called the "borderless economy," to regional groupings and trade blocs such as the European Union and others formed in Asia and North America, and to regular summit meetings of the "Group of Eight," the heads of state of the leading market-economy nations.

Hitler and the horrors of World War II had discredited talk of blood that tied individuals to their collective tribe, but his defeat had only driven such talk underground, waiting for its recrudescence. Eventually, ethnic consciousness gradually began to make a resounding comeback. This was evident in the Soviet Union, for example, after glasnost removed the restraints on its nationalities. With it came the call for separatism and "ethnic cleansing." Russians demanded the expulsion of Jews, and Estonians demanded the expulsion of Russians. Elsewhere, the Irish wanted Britain out of Northern Ireland, and Quebec wanted out of Canada, the Biafrans out of Nigeria, the Basques out of Spain, the Uighurs and Tibetans out of China, the Sikhs out of India, and the Kurds out of Turkey, Iran, and Iraq. Bulgaria expelled members of its Turkish minority; Arabs sought to drive Israelis into the sea, and Israelis demanded the expulsion of Palestinian Arabs; the nationalities of Yugoslavia decided they could not live in a Greater Serbia; and the misery in the Horn of Africa was in part the result of attempts to re-create a Greater Ethiopia and a Greater Somalia out of the same territory. Every East European nation had its "irredentists"[2] who claimed land at the expense of a neighbor. The Maastricht Treaty, the "deepening" of the EU, came at a time when much of the world was threatening to break up into ethnic fragments.

## ☐ 11. The End of Colonialism

The first significant development after World War II was the demand for the rapid dissolution of European colonial control in much of the world. What Europe had accomplished between the time of the first Crusade in the late eleventh century and the turn of the twentieth century was largely undone in less than three decades. The colonial powers had been able to contain the anticolonial movements until the dam finally burst after World War II. At first blush, independence promised a happier future, free of foreign domination. In sub-Saharan Africa, in particular, the hope was that the continent now would develop its economic and human potential. Instead, the colonial powers left behind artificially drawn borders and governments that clung to power at all cost by canceling elections and murdering their political opponents. Ethnic groups across the breadth of Africa repeatedly went to war against one another, leaving behind a devastated continent where the standard of living was lower in 1990 than it had been in 1960.

☐    *12. Superpower Competition in the Third World*

In retrospect, it became clear that neither Cold War protagonist intended to begin a war in Europe. The contest then moved to another venue, into the Third World, generally the former colonies. There, the superpowers competed for the hearts and minds of tyrants, their ideological beliefs (or generally the lack thereof) notwithstanding. The Soviet Union supported Nasser of Egypt, Sukarno of Indonesia, and Hussein of Iraq (none of whom had qualms about jailing local Communists). It also supported India against Communist China and the Sandinistas against the Nicaraguan Communist Party. The United States propped up a host of military dictators in Latin America, Africa, and Southeast Asia as well as in southern Europe. It even supported Marxist insurgents and governments in Somalia, Yugoslavia, Angola, and China against Moscow, the ostensible center of international Marxism. In the process, the superpowers strengthened dictators around the globe, many of whom remained in power for decades. Gorbachev's "new thinking" led the Soviet Union to abandon its client states, such as Cuba, and the United States no longer had the need to prop up its own associates, such as El Salvador. The Cold War ended, but its legacy remained—devastated countries and military factions armed to the teeth. In many nations (Afghanistan, Somalia, Angola, Cambodia) the bloodletting continued. The sale of weapons also continued, this time for commercial reasons rather than those of state. Russia and the United States, as well as a host of smaller nations, continued to do what they had done efficiently, namely produce weapons, and their economic woes dictated they sell them abroad. By the 1980s, they were joined in this by a new arms merchant—the People's Republic of China.

☐    *13. The Emergence of Militant Islam*

The late 1970s saw the appearance of a third global ideology challenging those of the superpowers—that of militant Islam as embodied in the sermons of Iran's Ayatollah Khomeini. It was the first significant ideological movement on a global scale since 1945. It was in part an appeal to the poverty-stricken masses of the Muslim world's more than 1 billion believers, most of whom lived in the Third World. It attacked the Western influence within Iranian society (as well as those of the Arab-speaking world, notably Lebanon, Kuwait, Iraq, Sudan, and Saudi Arabia), which it denounced as a corruption of the Koran and the consequence of Western influence. Militant Islam also sought to restore the Muslim world to its former power and glory and to eliminate its dependency on outside forces that long had humiliated it.

The most dramatic manifestation of militant Islam was the emergence of al Qaeda under the leadership of Osama bin Laden. What had begun as a civil war within Arab Islamic societies—militants challenging corrupt Westernized dictators (notably in Egypt, Saudi Arabia, Iraq, Afghanistan, and Algeria)—morphed into direct attacks against the visible symbols of Western power and influence in (and outside) the Muslim world.

## ☐ 14. A Fragile Ecological Balance

By the early 1970s, the world became aware that the blessings of the industrial revolution had a darker side—a record growth in population and the ecological degradation of the globe. The world's population increased from approximately 2.4 billion in 1945 to 6 billion in 1999 and was accompanied by an even more explosive growth in polluting industry. U.S. factories had polluted Lake Erie (but not irrevocably); Soviet irrigation had ruined Lake Aral (perhaps irreversibly); German, French, and Swiss industry had poisoned the Rhine River; and the air and water in large cities, especially in China (Shanghai, Beijing, and many others) and in the Third World (Mexico City, Cairo, Lagos, São Paolo, and others) had become scarcely suited for human habitation. Toxic wastes from nuclear weapons and power plants in many countries threatened serious ecological damage.

## ☐ 15. The Haves and the Have-Nots

The greatest challenges for the world's leaders at the dawn of the twenty-first century were not of a technological nature. Neil Armstrong already had set foot on the moon, computers were able to conduct complex calculations in nanoseconds, and machines were able to perform what once had been backbreaking work. The potentially explosive problems were of a human nature. Many individuals faced a superfluous existence. They were the members of a dispensable underclass of greater (and growing) numbers, primarily in the Third World. Mostly young and poverty-stricken, they witnessed a world capable of producing great wealth denied to them. This situation had the potential of producing great political turmoil. It was not something a magical "free market" or a "new world order" could resolve.

Year Zero came for Japan and Western Europe in 1945 when they began anew by putting the pieces back together again. For Eastern Europe, Year Zero came only in 1989; for the states of the former Soviet Union it did not come until 1991. China with its billion people started over after Mao's death in 1976. Year Zero came in 1960 to the societies of sub-Saharan Africa, who eventually had to realize that they had gone back in time; they were still grasping for the takeoff point, another Year Zero that would take them to a happier future. The Shiite Muslims regard the Iranian revolution of 1979 as Year Zero. For the Arab world, Year Zero has yet to arrive.

## ■ RECOMMENDED READING

Schell, Jonathan. *The Unfinished Twentieth Century.* New York: Verso, 2000.
A survey of the twentieth century's slaughter, from World War I to Stalin's reign of terror, the Holocaust during World War II, and the use of atomic weapons. Schell focuses on three crucial Augusts—in 1914, when World War I began and initiated mass extermination made possible by the industrial revolution; 1945, when atomic weapons were first used; and 1991, when the Soviet Union's political and social experiment came to an end.

## ■ NOTES

1. The French revolutionary system ended with Napoleon's defeat in 1815, and the "restored" conservative order lasted only until 1848. The wars for the unification of Germany and Italy rearranged the map of Europe by 1871, only to be destroyed by World War I (1914–1918). The international system that came out of World War I lasted until the outset of World War II (1939–1945).

2. From the Latin *terra irredenta,* "land unredeemed," the land of our forefathers that must be returned; first used by Italian nationalists during the nineteenth century, as *Italia irredenta.*

# ■ Index

# ■ About the Book

*The World Since 1945* traces the major political, economic, and ideological patterns that have evolved in the global arena from the end of World War II to the present day.

The sixth edition of this widely acclaimed textbook—thoroughly updated throughout—provides not only the background that students need in order to understand current international relations, but also new material on politics around the world. Among the current topics covered in this edition are the expansion of the European Union, the impasse in Palestinian-Israeli relations, the rightward movement in Russian politics, and the impact of the expanding Chinese economy on trade relations, military power, and the environment. A new chapter is devoted to the global consequences of the September 11 terrorist attacks.

Beautifully written and student friendly, *The World Since 1945* has made its place as the text of choice in scores of world history and introductory IR courses.

**Wayne C. McWilliams** and **Harry Piotrowski** are emeritus professors in the Department of History at Towson University.